The Lord shall come to recompense
unto every man according to his work,
and measure to every man according to the measure
which he has measured to his fellow man.
Wherefore the voice of the Lord is unto the ends
of the earth, that all that will hear may hear:
Prepare ye, prepare ye for that
which is to come, for the Lord is nigh;
And the anger of the Lord is kindled,
and his sword is bathed in heaven,
and it shall fall upon the inhabitants of the earth.
And the arm of the Lord shall be revealed;
and the day cometh that they
who will not hear the voice of the Lord,
neither the voice of his servants,
neither give heed to the words
of the prophets and apostles,
shall be cut off from among the people.
—D&C 1:10-14

For the hour is nigh and the day soon at hand
when the earth is ripe;
and all the proud and they that do wickedly
shall be as stubble;
and I will burn them up, saith the Lord of Hosts,
that wickedness shall not be upon the earth. . . .
For I will reveal myself from heaven
with power and great glory, with all the hosts thereof,
and dwell in righteousness with men on earth
a thousand years, and the wicked shall not stand.
—D&C 29:9, 11

Wherefore, prepare ye, prepare ye, O my people;
sanctify yourselves. . . . Yea, let the cry go forth
among all people: Awake and arise
and go forth to meet the Bridegroom;
behold and lo, the Bridegroom cometh;
go ye out to meet him. Prepare yourselves
for the great day of the Lord. Watch, therefore,
for ye know neither the day nor the hour.
—D&C 133:4, 10-11

The Millennial Messiah
The Second Coming of the Son of Man

Bruce R. McConkie

Deseret Book Company
Salt Lake City, Utah

Library of Congress Cataloging-in-Publication Data (Revised)

McConkie, Bruce R.
  The millennial Messiah.

  Includes index.
    1. Second Advent. 2. Mormon Church—Doctrinal and controversial works. I. Title.
BT886.M42   236′.3   81-19599
ISBN 0-87747-896-1   AACR2

Printed in the United States of America

20   19   18   17   16   15   14   13   12   11   10

THE MESSIANIC TRILOGY

The forerunners of this work are *The Promised Messiah: The First Coming of Christ*, which deals with the Messianic prophecies, and *The Mortal Messiah: From Bethlehem to Calvary*, a life of Christ published in four books as follows:

ABBREVIATIONS

Scriptural references are abbreviated in a standard and self-identifying way. Other books are cited by author and title except for the following:

Commentary   Bruce R. McConkie, *Doctrinal New Testament Commentary,* vol. 3. Bookcraft, 1965.

JST   Joseph Smith Translation (Inspired Version) of the Bible.

Mormon Doctrine   Bruce R. McConkie, *Mormon Doctrine,* 2nd ed. Bookcraft, 1966.

Teachings   Joseph Fielding Smith, comp., *Teachings of the Prophet Joseph Smith.* 1938.

CONTENTS

PREFACE

Our Blessed Lord, who came once as the *Promised Messiah,* shall soon come again in all the glory of his Father's kingdom.

The King of Israel, who dwelt among men as the *Mortal Messiah*, shall soon rule and reign over his chosen Israel and over all others who abide the day of his coming.

God's own Son shall soon come as the *Millennial Messiah.* It is of that millennial coming—*The Second Coming of the Son of Man*—that this work testifies.

There is not a more important course to pursue, for any of us who now live on earth, than to prepare for the Second Coming. The gospel has been restored and the great latter-day kingdom established in order to prepare a people for that dreadful yet glorious day.

There is also probably no doctrine and no event that is less understood than our Lord's personal return to live and be once more with men. Many strange and peculiar and false opinions are afloat. The Second Coming is totally unknown among non-Christians, totally misunderstood among Christians generally, and even some of the very elect need more enlightenment than they now have relative to what lies ahead.

In this work we attempt to set forth what the scriptures themselves, as properly interpreted, have to say about the great and coming day. We speak of the events precedent, the events concurrent, and the events subsequent. We speak of what must occur between his first and second advents, of the plagues and wars attending his return, and of the peace and glories that shall prevail during his millennial reign.

In the spirit of gratitude and appreciation I record here the name of Velma Harvey, a most able and efficient secretary. She has made many thoughtful suggestions, given much wise counsel, and handled a host of matters requiring care and insight.

The Millennial Messiah

The Second Coming
of the Son of Man

Chapter 1

THE SUPPER
OF THE LORD

Come: Learn of the Second Coming

Come feast on the good word of God; come learn of the Second Coming of the Son of Man!

Come feast on the word of Christ that he has given to prepare us for the great and dreadful day that even now is at the door—the day when every corruptible thing will be consumed as the elements melt with fervent heat, the day when the righteous shall be caught up to meet their Lord in the air.

Come and partake of "the supper of the Lord" that is now prepared at his "house" and "unto which all nations" are invited.

It is "a feast of fat things, of wine on the lees well refined." (D&C 58:8-11.) Heaped high on the table is that meat of which man may eat and never hunger more and that water of which he may drink and never thirst again.

Let all men forsake the tables of carnality and of false doctrine, where the scoffers of the world, "walking after their own lusts," are eating and drinking with gluttonous abandon as men did in the days of Noah. Let them no longer say: "Where is the promise of his coming?" (2 Pet. 3:3-4.) And let them no longer suppose that the promised hope of a millennial era of peace is something that must be brought to pass by the good deeds of men, rather than by the shaking of the heavens and with power from on high.

But be it known—whatever the ungodly may suppose, whatever views the spiritually untutored may espouse, whatever foods

1

may be eaten at the evil tables of the world—that here at the Lord's table is found living bread; here is the fountain from which streams of living water flow.

By his own voice the Lord has commanded his latter-day servants: "Prepare ye the way of the Lord, prepare ye the supper of the Lamb, make ready for the Bridegroom."

The marvelous work of restoration, reserved for the last days, has now commenced among the children of men; and to all who believe the restored gospel the Voice commands: "Pray unto the Lord, call upon his holy name, make known his wonderful works among the people."

The Church of Jesus Christ of Latter-day Saints, which is the kingdom of God on earth—the kingdom designed to prepare men to sit down with Abraham, Isaac, and Jacob, and all the holy prophets in the eternal kingdom—has been set up among men; and to all the citizens of the kingdom, the Voice commands: "Call upon the Lord, that his kingdom may go forth upon the earth, that the inhabitants thereof may receive it, and be prepared for the days to come, in the which the Son of Man shall come down in heaven, clothed in the brightness of his glory, to meet the kingdom of God which is set up on the earth." (D&C 65:3-5.)

And so it is that the servants of the Lord have prepared the supper. The banquet tables are heaped high with heavenly manna. The food and drink consists of "none other things than that which the prophets and apostles have written," and "that which is taught them by the Comforter through the prayer of faith." (D&C 52:9.)

We have invited "the rich and the learned, the wise and the noble," to come and bask in the light of the Lord and find nourishment for their souls. They have declined the invitation and continue to gorge themselves with the delicacies of Babylon. And so now, in the providences of Him who gives bread in the wilderness and who rains manna from heaven upon his people, cometh the day of his power. Now "shall the poor, the lame, and the blind, and the deaf, come in unto the marriage of the Lamb, and partake of the supper of the Lord, prepared for the great day to come." (D&C 58:10-11.)

2

As we begin to eat at the Lord's tables, we are both humbled and exhilarated by the glory and wonder of it all. Many prophets and righteous men saw this day, in dreams when the moon ruled the night and in visions when the sun ruled the day. Many of the ancient saints—saints from all the dispensations of the past—longed for the day of triumph and glory that was promised to the saints of latter days. Many would fain have changed places with us, that their eyes might see what we behold and their hands be put to the plough with which we labor in the fields of the Lord. Ours is the glorious privilege to lay the foundations of Zion with the full assurance that we, or our children, or their descendants after them, will live to see the face of Him who shall come to dwell with his saints and to reign among the righteous.

At the tables prepared in the Lord's house, we shall speak of the coming of the Son of Man, of the return of God's Almighty Son to take vengeance upon the wicked and to usher in the year of his redeemed. We shall talk of the signs of the times; of those things which the apostles and prophets say must precede his glorious advent; of the circumstances that shall attend his return; and of the paradisiacal glory that shall cover the earth when the wicked are destroyed and all things become new.

We shall also record in this work in plain words, often using the very words of holy writ, what has been revealed relative to the coming of the millennial King. Our words will take on life and breath as we interweave with them parables and similitudes and add the inspired imagery that unveils hidden and mysterious things.

We shall write living words, words that flow from the pen of prophecy, dipped in the ink of inspiration. Our message shall be one of joy and rejoicing for those who treasure up revealed truth, who desire righteousness, who seek the face of the Lord. It will be one of weeping and mourning for those who "know not God, and that obey not the gospel of our Lord Jesus Christ." (2 Thes. 1:8.)

We shall now turn the key, open the door, and enter the holy realm where the knowledge of God is poured out without measure upon the faithful. We shall seek the face of him who shall suddenly

3

come to his temple; it is our desire to know all things relative to the Second Coming of the Son of Man. "Prepare to meet thy God, O Israel." (Amos 4:12.)

Come: Believe in the Millennial Messiah

Our words are written to those who believe, those who have the testimony of Jesus burning in their souls, those who look forward with joy to that day when "the saints of the most High shall take the kingdom, and possess the kingdom for ever." (Dan. 7:18.) The feast that the Lord's servants have prepared in the last days is the fulness of the everlasting gospel. Only those who have oil in their lamps and who have taken the Holy Spirit for their guide will be seated at the banquet tables.

To set a proper tone and have a right spirit at our banquet—we are feasting in the house of the Lord, on the good word of God, as guided by the Comforter!—and to maintain that high spirituality which must shine forth from any work that speaks of our Lord's return to reign personally on earth, we shall make a brief introductory statement by way of testimony and of doctrine. This is our witness:

We know when Christ will come in the clouds of glory, attended by angelic hosts, to be with men on earth again—not the day or the hour, or even the month or the year, but we do know the generation.

We know where he will appear and the places on which the soles of his feet will once again walk. These are identifiable roads and known mountains whose descriptions and names are given in the prophetic word.

We know, if not all, at least the major things that must transpire before he comes again, those events that will attend his triumphal return, and those events that will result because his personal presence once more graces his earthly vineyard.

We shall name the time, identify the places, and set forth the attendant circumstances in due course. It is the privilege of the saints of the Most High to read the signs of the times, to stand in holy places, to escape (partially at least) the plagues and pestilences of the last days, and to abide the day of his coming. Those who treasure up his word are promised that they will not be deceived with respect to all these things.

We know that Christ is the Firstborn of the Father; that long eternities before the foundations of this earth were laid, he became like unto God; and that by him and through him and of him the worlds—worlds without number, all the worlds in all immensity—are and were created. He, under the Father, is the Creator, Upholder, and Preserver of all things.

We know that he was and is the God of our fathers, the God of the ancients, the God of Abraham, Isaac, and Jacob; that he is the Great Jehovah, the Eternal One, the Lord Omnipotent, who revealed himself and his gospel to Adam and the holy prophets; and that he is the same yesterday, today, and forever.

We know that he is the God of Israel who chose the house of Jacob as his own peculiar people; that he is the Promised Messiah of whom all the prophets testified; and that he is a God of miracles who delights to bless and honor those who love and serve him in righteousness and truth all their days.

We know that he came as the Seed of David and the Son of the Highest; that Mary was his mother and God was his Father; and that he was born, after the manner of the flesh, inheriting from his mother the power of mortality and from his Father the power of immortality.

We rejoice in his mortal ministry and know that when he dwelt as a man on earth he fulfilled all that was written of him for that day. In him the Messianic prophecies were all fulfilled, the law of Moses was both fulfilled and replaced, and the glorious gospel was again restored and preached to the world. Our knowledge of how and in what manner the Messianic word was honored and accomplished in time's meridian will guide us in learning how the prophetic word pertaining to his Second Coming will find a full consummation.

We know he worked out the infinite and eternal atonement, which was the crowning act of a glorious and perfect ministry; that he was crucified, died, and rose again the third day; and that he has ascended into heaven, there to reign with almighty power on the right hand of the Father whose son he is.

5

We know that when he comes again, he will take vengeance on the wicked and ungodly and usher in the year of his redeemed. He will establish Zion and build up the New Jerusalem, and he will reign on the throne of David, in peace and with equity and justice over all the earth, for the space of a thousand years. And his chosen Israel shall then walk in the light of his love—as the beloved and chosen people that they are—for the whole Millennium.

We know that when he comes the vineyard shall be burned; the wicked shall be as stubble, for they that come shall burn them up; and every corruptible thing, both of men and of beasts and of fowls, shall be consumed.

We know that all those who have overcome the world by the word of his power, who have kept the faith, who have been true and faithful in all things, shall live and reign with him on earth a thousand years.

We seek also to worship the Father, in the name of the Son, by the power of the Holy Spirit, and hope to be with them all on this earth when it becomes a celestial heaven, when the meek, who are the God-fearing and the righteous, inherit it forever and ever.

Having this testimony and knowing these doctrines, relying with a perfect surety on all of the promises made to the faithful, and rejoicing in such measure of the Holy Spirit as has been poured out upon us—in this setting, we the saints sit down at the supper of the Lamb and feast upon that of which only the God-fearing and the righteous can eat and drink.

Come: See Him Ascend into Heaven

To those living in his day and dispensation, Jesus asked: "What and if ye shall see the Son of man ascend up where he was before?" (John 6:62.) To all those who live in our day and dispensation, we ask: What and if you "shall see the Son of Man coming in the clouds of heaven, with power and great glory"? (JS-M 1:36.) And these two questions—his pertaining to his ascension to eternal glory, and ours as to his return in that glory which is his—are inseparably interwoven into one. There can be no Second Coming of the Son of Man unless there was a first coming, and he cannot descend from heaven above unless he first ascended to

6

those heights beyond the skies. Indeed, the foundation we are laying for our study of his return, and all that is incident thereto, must include a sure knowledge of these four eternal verities:

1. That there is a God in heaven who is infinite and eternal; that he is a Holy Man, having a body of flesh and bones; and that he sent his Only Begotten Son to redeem fallen man and put into full operation all of the terms and conditions of the gospel of God.

2. That the Lord Jesus, born of Mary in Bethlehem of Judea, was the Son of God in the literal and full sense of the word, and that he inherited from God his Father the power of immortality and from Mary his mother the power of mortality.

3. That this same Jesus, having worked out the infinite and eternal atonement in Gethsemane and on the cross, and having laid down his life to bring to pass the immortality and eternal life of man—this same Jesus rose from the dead in glorious immortality, having a resurrected body of flesh and bones like that of his Father.

4. That he ascended into heaven to sit down on the right hand of the Majesty on high, there to reign with almighty power until the day and hour appointed by the Father for his return to live and reign on earth a thousand years.

Of all these eternal verities we, with the ancients, bear witness. As to the doctrine of his ascension, we say with Peter: He "is gone into heaven, and is on the right hand of God; angels and authorities and powers being made subject unto him." (1 Pet. 3:22.) With Paul we say: "God was manifest in the flesh, justified in the Spirit, seen of angels, preached unto the Gentiles, believed on in the world, received up into glory." (1 Tim. 3:16.) Also: "Jesus the Son of God," our "great high priest," hath "passed into the heavens" (Heb. 4:14) where he is "holy, harmless, undefiled, separate from sinners, and made higher than the heavens" (Heb. 7:26). Again with Paul we testify that "God . . . hath in these last days spoken unto us by his Son, whom he hath appointed heir of all things, by whom also he made the worlds; Who being the brightness of his glory, and the express image of his person, and upholding all things by the word of his power, when he had by himself purged our sins, sat down on the right hand of the Majesty on high." (Heb. 1:1-3.) We also testify, yet again in Paul's words,

7

that "when he ascended up on high, he led captivity captive, and gave gifts unto men," meaning that when he "ascended up far above all heavens," he freed men from the captivity of sin and of the grave and gave them, as gifts, apostles, prophets, and true ministers. (Eph. 4:8-16.)

Knowing that the Lord Jesus was destined to ascend to his Father, there to reign until the day of his Second Coming, we are ready to view the events of that day of ascension. It is Thursday, May 18, A.D. 30, just forty days after he rose from the grave. The inhabitants of Jerusalem are ripening in iniquity. Having shed the blood of their King, they now seek to slay his apostles and friends. Some forty years hence, when their cup of iniquity is full, they shall be slain and scattered in such a blood bath as has seldom been known among men. Jerusalem will then die by the sword of Titus, and her temple will become a dung heap, every stone being wrenched from its foundation.

But now the new dispensation of Christians are walking in the marvelous light that quickens their souls. Many are yet glorying in the appearances of the resurrected saints to them. It is the day when Jesus is to be "taken up." And he has come to "the apostles whom he had chosen: To whom also he shewed himself alive after his passion by many infallible proofs, being seen of them forty days, and speaking of the things pertaining to the kingdom of God: And, being assembled together with them, commanded them that they should not depart from Jerusalem, but wait for the promise of the Father, which, saith he, ye have heard of me. For John truly baptized with water; but ye shall be baptized with the Holy Ghost not many days hence." (Acts 1:2-5.)

Luke in his Gospel tells us that on this occasion, after giving the promise that they would "be endued with power from on high," "he led them out as far as to Bethany, and he lifted up his hands, and blessed them. And it came to pass, while he blessed them, he was parted from them, and carried up into heaven." (Luke 24:49-51.) Mark says simply that "he was received up into heaven, and sat on the right hand of God." (Mark 16:19.)

But it is in the book of Acts, also written by Luke, that the details are given that set the stage for the Second Coming. Our inspired author identifies the place as "the mount called Olivet," records the conversation about the restoration of the kingdom to Israel, and then says: "And when he had spoken these things, while they beheld, he was taken up; and a cloud received him out of their sight. And while they looked stedfastly toward heaven as he went up, behold, two men stood by them in white apparel; Which also said, Ye men of Galilee, why stand ye gazing up into heaven? this same Jesus, which is taken up from you into heaven, shall so come in like manner as ye have seen him go into heaven." (Acts 1:6-12.)

What then is the promise of his coming? It is that the same Holy Being who burst the bands of death and gained the victory over the grave shall come again. He shall return, as he went up; he shall return to the Mount of Olives, having the same body of flesh and bones that was seen and felt and handled by the disciples of old. He shall again eat and drink with the faithful as of old. And as a few spiritually enlightened souls in ancient days awaited the coming of the Consolation of Israel, so a few believing souls today await his triumphant return.

What a glorious day that will be! For all of us, when we dwelt as spirits in the Eternal Presence, the most transcendent of all the events of preexistence—that which was of greatest concern and most worth unto us—was the selection of God's Beloved and Chosen One to be the Savior and Redeemer, to be born into the world as the Son of God, to come, thus, with power to work out the atoning sacrifice, which brings immortality to all men and eternal life to those who believe and obey.

For Adam and Eve and their children—those spirit children of the Father, at long last housed in tabernacles of clay—the great concern, which weighed so heavily upon them, was to pattern the earthly kingdom after the heavenly one whence they came. It was to set in order the system that would enable the hosts of heaven to come here, gain mortal bodies, and work out their salvation with fear and trembling before the Lord. It was to learn for themselves, and to teach their children after them, what all men must do as mortals to be born again into the kingdom of heaven so as to merit eternal life in the presence of Him who is Eternal.

9

For the wicked and rebellious who lived in the days of Noah, when all flesh was corrupt before the Lord, there was nothing of greater import than to cease from gluttony and sin and return unto the Lord, lest he send in the floods upon them, sweep their bodies to a watery grave, and send their spirits to that prison whence there was no escape until they were visited by the Chosen One and had the privilege of hearing again the truths of his everlasting gospel.

For Abraham—in Ur with his idol-worshipping father; in Egypt reasoning on astronomy in Pharaoh's court; in Palestine caring for his cattle on a thousand hills—that which was of greatest concern and worth to him was to enter that order of celestial marriage which would give him an eternal posterity, both in the world and out of the world, a posterity as numerous as the sand upon the seashore or the stars in the heavens.

For Moses and the house of Jacob, then enslaved by Pharaoh, that which concerned them above all else was to travel between the watery walls of the Red Sea, through a forty-year habitat in the wilderness and then into a land flowing with milk and honey where they would build the City of Zion.

For Jewish Israel—and all men—the great and burning questions were: Is this Jesus the one of whom Moses and the prophets spoke? Is he our Deliverer and Messiah, or does he do these works by the power of Beelzebub? Is he the Son of God, as he says, or look we for another?

And for the saints of God today—indeed, for all of earth's inhabitants, for every living soul in this day of preparation—the burning questions are: Will he come again, and if so, when? What will attend and precede the great and dreadful day of the Lord? Who will prepare the way? Will a people be prepared on earth to receive him, and if so, who? And who will abide the day of his coming and who shall stand when he appeareth?

It is to these and like matters that we shall now turn our attention.

Chapter 2

ETERNITY AND THE SEVEN AGES

Come: View His Return in Perspective

The Second Coming of the Son of Man is not an isolated comet blazing its way through the sidereal heavens without reference to the cosmos of which it is a part. It is not a single star whose rays pierce the darkness of heaven's dome, nor is it some shining sun that stands apart from the other luminaries of the skies, nor is it even the center of the universe around which all else revolves. But it is one bright and shining sun in a celestial galaxy composed of many suns, all moving in their orbits, all giving light and life according to the divine plan. It is one clear and brilliant star around which lesser stars revolve and which itself rolls forth in endless orbit around yet greater and more central rulers of the skies. It is part of an infinite universe, part of the eternal scheme of things, part of those great events which are all tied together into one eternal system. And in order to understand the Second Coming, we must view it in perspective, in its relation to other eternal verities, in its connection to all things. We shall approach our problem by naming the seven ages of eternity and noting the transcendent events transpiring or destined to transpire in each of them.

1. *Our Creation and Life as Spirits.*

It is the dawn of the first day. The great Elohim—he who dwells on high, whose throne is in the heavens above, whose kingdoms are governed from Kolob—that glorious and perfected being who is our Father in heaven has a Son, a spirit Son, a Son who is

11

the Firstborn. The Father of us all takes of the self-existing spirit element and creates spirit children, or in other words, he organizes spirits or souls from the intelligence that exists; and such spirit beings become "the intelligences that were organized before the world was." (Abr. 3:22.) They are the sons and daughters of God; creation has commenced; the eternal family of the Eternal God has its beginning.

As eternity rolls everlastingly onward, endless billions of spirit children are born. They become conscious entities in a sphere governed by laws, laws ordained by the Father to enable them to advance and progress and become like him. These laws are called the gospel of God. With their spirit birth they are endowed with agency; they may obey or disobey—the choice is theirs.

All are taught the gospel. In due course they develop talents of all kinds. Some acquire spirituality; others are rebellious and defiant. The noble and great among them are foreordained to be prophets and seers in the coming mortality. Christ, the Firstborn, is chosen to be born into mortality as the Son of God so that he can work out the infinite and eternal atonement. Lucifer and one-third of the spirits destined to come to this earth rebel; there is war in heaven; and the rebels are cast out, denied bodies, damned everlastingly.

Such was our creation and life as the spirit children of the Holy Man whose name, in the Adamic language, is Man of Holiness. Such was the establishment of the plan of salvation and the choosing of a Savior who would come to earth as the Only Begotten in the flesh to make salvation possible.

How glorious is creation! How wondrous the eternal plan of the Father! If there had been no creation, we would not be, and all things would vanish away into a primordial nothingness, having neither sense nor insensibility. If there were no plan of progression and advancement, none of the spirit children of the Father would be able to attain the exalted state he possesses and receive the eternal life he gives to all the obedient. Can we extol too highly the fact of creation and the ordaining of the great and eternal plan of salvation?

12

2. *The Temporal Creation and Our Life as Mortals.*

It is the age of the creation and peopling of planet earth. It is the day when those who have kept their first estate shall go down to receive the schooling and probation of mortality. It is the day when mighty Michael shall fall that mortal man may be. It is the age that shall set the stage and prepare the way for the redemption of man, for his immortality, for eternal life itself.

We are present in a grand council convened in the midst of eternity; we hear the voices of the Gods of Heaven speak. One who is like unto God, who was beloved and chosen from the beginning, says to the noble and great spirits who are his friends and with whom he serves: 'We will go down to yonder place; there is space there; and we will take of these materials and make an earth whereon we and all our fellows may dwell.'

We see the powers of heaven manifest as a new earth rolls forth in its ordained orbit. The temporal elements are organized and divided from the firmament of heaven; light and darkness divide the day from the night; dry land appears; seeds bring forth after their kind; and fowl and fish and animals are created and commanded to multiply, each in his sphere and after his own kind. The events of each creative day roll before our eyes, and on the sixth day man—a Son of God, his spirit housed in a tabernacle of clay—begins his life on earth.

Then we see the fall of man. Adam and Eve choose to step down from their immortal state to one of mortality; they forsake the paradisiacal glory of Eden for a world of wickedness and sorrow; and death—temporal death and spiritual death—enter the world. The first man and the first woman can now have children; they can begin the process of providing bodies for the eternal spirit children of the Eternal Father.

The effect of the fall passes upon the earth and all forms of life on its face. All things become mortal; death reigns supreme in every department of creation; and the probationary nature of man's second estate is in full operation. Thorns, thistles, briers, and noxious weeds afflict man. He is subject to disease, sorrow, and death. Plagues, pestilence, famines, and ills of every sort pour in upon him. And the great command comes forth that he must work; he must earn and eat his bread in the sweat of his face.

We see a gracious God reveal his gospel truths. The need for a Redeemer to ransom man from the temporal and spiritual death brought into the world by the fall of Adam is clearly set forth. If man will believe and obey, he will be redeemed and return to the presence of the Father. But Lucifer, the common enemy of all mankind, comes among the children of men; he teaches false doctrines and entices man to walk in carnal paths.

Thus we see the commencement of the long history of God's dealings with his earthly children. Prophets and seers teach and testify of that salvation which is in Christ. False prophets and Satanic powers spread hate and evil and war everywhere. The war begun in heaven is being fought anew on earth. And so it is that man gains experience that could come in no other way; thus he is privileged to pass through an existence that prepares him for eternal glory; thus it is possible for him to gain immortality and eternal life.

If there had been no temporal creation, this earth would not exist as an abiding place for man and all forms of life. If Adam had not fallen, there would have been no mortality either for man or for any form of life. Rather, "All things which were created must have remained in the same state in which they were after they were created; and they must have remained forever, and had no end." (2 Ne. 2:22.) And if there were no mortality, there could have been no immortality, no eternal life. Birth and death are as essential to the plan of holiness of the Father as is the very wonder of resurrection. Can we glory too much in the wonder of temporal creation, in the marvel of the peopling of our planet with mortal men, and in the heaven-sent revelation, to all who will receive it, of the plan of salvation?

3. *Redemption and the Age of the Atoning One.*

It is the meridian of time, the high point in the history of humankind, the day when a God will die to redeem those who otherwise would be doomed to eternal death. The Son of Righteousness is about to take upon himself the form of a man, to suffer as a servant, to lay down his life for the sheep, and to rise triumphant from the tomb. The Lord Omnipotent, the Eternal God, the Son of that

14

living God who is our Father, is coming to perform the most transcendent act that ever has occurred or ever will occur among the children of the Father. He will work out the infinite and eternal atonement. It is the age of incarnation and the age of redemption.

Again we are present in spirit and see and hear the wonders of his life and the works that he wrought. We, with Nephi, see a virgin most beautiful and fair above all the daughters of Eve. She dwells in Nazareth of Galilee. An angelic ministrant attests that the God of all gods has chosen her to be the mother of his Son after the manner of the flesh. And therein we are told is the condescension of God.

We are present in a humble peasant home in Nazareth when Gabriel, next in the heavenly hierarchy to Michael himself, comes down and delivers the divine word. Mary, for such is her blessed name, shall conceive by the power of the Holy Ghost, and the Fruit of her Womb shall be the Lamb of God, the Son of the Highest. He will thus inherit from her the power of mortality and from his Eternal Father the power of immortality. Being thus endowed, he will have power to lay down his life and to take it again as required of the Atoning One.

It is sometime in 4 B.C. (or earlier). Herod the Great reigns with Roman power as king of the Jews. He will die a demeaning and loathsome death—as befits one whose life has reeked with cruelties, blood, and a stream of murders—a few weeks after a lunar eclipse that is astronomically calculated to occur in early March of 4 B.C. But now, by decree of imperial Augustus, the evil Caesar of the moment, the world of Rome is to be counted so that capitation taxes may be imposed. And hated Herod, seeking to humor the prejudices of the people of Palestine, has decreed that this enrollment shall take place in their ancestral homelands. Hence Joseph and Mary, each a descendant of David, must go from Nazareth in the north to the Judean city of Bethlehem where David once reigned. There they will be numbered according to the decree of Rome.

We see the caravan of which they are a part, weary from long travel, arrive at the caravanserai where they desire to camp for the night. Their travel has been slow because Mary is big with child.

When they arrive all the inns or rooms surrounding the open court-yard where animals are tethered are full. Joseph and Mary and their party must bed down with the animals or go elsewhere. It is late. There is little time to cook a meager meal over an open fire and prepare for the needed rest that a well-earned sleep will bring. They stop and arrange to camp with the animals.

In all this there is a divine providence. Where must the Aton-ing One be born? Not in that glorious temple, the spiritual center of the world, whose very stones are covered with gold; not in the pal-ace of the high priest, who once each year enters the holy of holies to make an atonement for the sins of the people; not in the courts of Caesar in the capital of the world, nor even in Herod's palace in Jerusalem, as might befit the king of the Jews; not in any place of worldly power, renown, or wealth. Rather, the Almighty must descend below all things; he must breathe his first breath in Bethle-hem; he must lie in a manger among the beasts as he begins his mortal life. The prophetic word must be fulfilled. He whose go-ings forth have been from of old, from everlasting, must be born in Bethlehem of Judea according to the Messianic word.

And lo, he is born! A God becomes a man! It is what we call the incarnation. The Incarnate One dwells on earth. That body created in Mary's womb houses the Lord Jehovah. The Atoning One has come to work out the infinite and eternal atonement.

We see it all. He grows to a majestic maturity. When the hour of his ministry is come, he is baptized of John in Jordan; he goes forth speaking wondrous words and working mighty miracles; and after more than three years of crying in the wilderness of wicked-ness, he bows before the Father in Gethsemane to do that for which he came into the world—to suffer both body and spirit, bleeding from every pore, as he takes upon himself the sins of all men on conditions of repentance. We see him there, in agony beyond compare, an angel strengthening him, as the greatest miracle of the ages is wrought—the miracle of redemption.

And finally on the cross, climaxing and completing what com-menced in Gethsemane, we see him suffer until the cry goes forth, "It is finished." His work is done; he voluntarily gives up the ghost. The ransom is paid; the redemption is a reality; the atonement is accomplished. The work and glory of God—to bring to pass the immortality and eternal life of man—is now made glorious in the voluntary sacrifice of his Son. Let heaven and earth acclaim the deed, than which there has been no greater.

What need we say more? The miracle of incarnation! The mystery of redemption! The purposes of God prevail. Can we do aught but sing praises to Him who has done these things for us that we might live? Is there any language known to man that will portray the wonder and glory of it all?

4. *The Age of Immortality.*

It is very early in the morning of Sunday, April 9, A.D. 30. It is 784 A.U.C. in the calculations of the imperial Romans; and it is the seventeenth day of the Jewish month of Nisan. It is the day of the first resurrection of the first mortal, the day when the bands of death shall be broken, when the Victorious One shall take up the body with the riven side and use again the hands and feet wherein are the jagged gashes made by Roman nails.

Somewhere in Jerusalem a Jewish father is adjusting the Mezuzah on his doorpost and reminding himself that the Lord his God is one Lord, and his name one. He is also telling himself that the death, three days before, of the Prophet of Nazareth of Galilee removed from their midst an impostor whose miracles were wrought by the power of Beelzebub.

In a Galilean village—yes, in Nazareth itself—another Jew is reciting the Shema and telling his children they are to love the Lord their God with all their heart, might, mind, and strength. He is unmindful that scarcely forty-eight hours have elapsed since his friends and relatives in Jerusalem, urged on by the priestly spokesmen of their nation, had chanted, before Pilate and with reference to the very Lord of whom the Shema speaks, "Crucify him, crucify him." But his spirit is one with theirs, and he also recalls that Sabbath day three years ago when he and others drove the Son of Joseph from their synagogue because he claimed—oh, blasphemous thing!—that the Messianic prophecies were fulfilled in him.

A devout Jew in Bethany, a neighbor of Simon the leper and an acquaintance of Lazarus whom Jesus called back to mortal life, is at this very moment at that point in the Hallel where it is said:

"Save now, I beseech thee, O Lord. . . . Blessed be he that cometh in the name of the Lord." (Ps. 118:25-26.) But as he chants these words of praise to the God of Israel, his soul is filled with hate toward that Nazarene who accepted from the multitude, just one week ago, the blasphemous acclaim: "Hosanna to the Son of David: Blessed is he that cometh in the name of the Lord; Hosanna in the highest." (Matt. 21:9.) And in the same spirit of hate and murder, he recalls in his mind that scene at the nearby tomb of Lazarus, where his body, dead and decaying for four days, had come forth live and vibrant, filled with power and vigor. And the devout Jew is glad that he and others had reported this devil-born miracle to the chief priests and had conspired with them to slay Lazarus lest the ignorant multitude believe that this Galilean, whose voice had power over death, was indeed their Messiah.

Like scenes are unfolding on every side through all Jewry. The priests and Levites and Rabbis and elders and lawyers and leaders, together with the multitudes who heed their counsel, are all rejoicing in the death of this false prophet—was he not Beelzebub incarnate?—this false Messiah, this blasphemer who made himself God. They have returned from Golgotha to their homes and synagogues and street corners to thank God that they are not as these alien Gentiles around them, and to remind Jehovah that they keep the Sabbath, fast twice a week between the Paschal week and Pentecost, and between the Feast of Tabernacles and that of the Dedication of the Temple, and that they can read his law in the pure Hebrew of their fathers. Once more they can devote themselves to calculating their tithes on mint and anise and cummin, as the weightier matters of the law go unheeded. Thank God, they say, for the law of Moses and the traditions of their fathers to which they can now give full attention without the caustic denunciations of this Jesus Ben Joseph who lies in the Arimathean's tomb.

The Roman soldiers are still quenching a drunken thirst. Pilate, hardened in soul and resolute in demeanor, has cast off his fears. He is pleased that no deputation carried word of Jesus' claim to kingship to that half-mad wretch Tiberias. Now that this strange Galilean is dead, the Roman Procurator can occupy himself with more important matters. Herod Antipas, insulted because Jesus would not even speak to him, has visions by day and dreams by night of a gory head on a charger as Salome's lust-inspiring body dances in the background. He too rejoices in the death of one who defied him, one who reminded him of that stern and unrequiting man from the deserts of Hebron who had called him an adulterer and accused him of incest.

It is also a day when a select and favored few, the elect of God, are preparing themselves spiritually to become living witnesses that the age of immortality has arrived. Among them we see Peter and John and their apostolic fellows; among them we find those valiant souls who serve as seventies; among them also are choice disciples in all the villages and cities of Palestine. Could the deaf who hear, the blind who see, the lame who walk, the lepers who are cleansed, the dead who live—all because He willed it to be so—could any of them do other than believe him when he said he would rise again?

Favored among them all, early this Easter morning, we see Mary Magdalene; Mary, the mother of Joses; Salome, the sister of the Blessed Virgin and the mother of James and John; Joanna, the wife of Chuza, who is Herod's steward; and other women. We suppose the beloved sisters from Bethany, Mary and Martha, are among them, though we have no reason to believe the Virgin Mother herself was there. They are bringing spices and costly ointments to anoint and embalm the body of their Lord.

They arrive at the tomb, and lo, it is as though the earth stopped spinning on her axis; it is as though the sun ceased to shine and the stars hurled themselves from the firmament of heaven; it is as though time stood still and space ceased to be—for He is not there! He is risen! One that was dead lives. A cold corpse has escaped corruption. The linen strips wrapped around him by Joseph and Nicodemus and the napkin that covered his head lie as though wound still around his body. But he is risen; he is not here; he lives. Why seek they the living among the dead? Christ the Lord is risen this day. Alleluia!

Angelic voices testify that he who came to Jerusalem to die upon the cross of Calvary has risen on the third day as he promised. Then he himself appears to many. They walk and talk and commune and eat with him as though he were yet mortal. They feel the nail marks in his hands and feet and thrust their hands into his riven side as thousands of Nephites shall thereafter do. They eat and drink with him after he has risen from the dead. They are becoming witnesses, special witnesses, living witnesses, that he is the firstfruits of them that sleep.

First he spends a few sacred and precious moments with Mary Magdalene in the garden; then he appears to all of the women and they hold him by the feet. Next he appears to Simon; then he walks and talks with Luke and Cleopas on the Emmaus road; then he stands before a large group of disciples in an upper room. They see him with their eyes, feel him with their hands, and watch as he eats a piece of broiled fish and of honeycomb. All this happens the very day of his resurrection.

A week later a like visual witness is borne over again to the disciples and also to Thomas, who was not present on the first Easter evening. Still later, at the sea of Tiberias, the Risen Lord and six of the Twelve eat together. Then on a mountain in Galilee comes the grand appearance. More than five hundred brethren are present and many things transpire. Still later he appears to James, the son of Joseph and Mary, and finally to the eleven apostles at the time of his ascension. And not only does he appear, but many graves also are opened and saints long dead arise and appear to many in the Holy City. Each risen saint becomes a living witness that he who is Lord of all has himself first risen. It is the dawn of the age of immortality.

Christ is risen and all shall rise. The power of his resurrection passes upon all mankind. Immortality is as real as mortality, and indeed it applies not only to man but to all created things. It is no more difficult to believe in resurrection than in creation; one is not a greater mystery than the other. And so, as we see the eternal verities in perspective, shall we not praise the Lord for immortality and all that appertains to it, even as we praise him for life and being and for the atonement that makes all things operative?

5. *The Age of Triumph, Glory, and Millennial Splendor.*

This is the age whose dawning rays are now breaking through the mists and darkness that cover a weary and wicked world. It is the age of which we shall write in this work. It is the day sought by all the prophets and saints from the time of Adam to the present moment. It is the day when the earth shall rest and the saints find peace. And it shall be ushered in by the Second Coming of the Son of Man, to "sanctify the earth, and complete the salvation of man, and judge all things." (D&C 77:12.)

As we go forward in our study, we shall see apostasy, war, pestilence, and plagues; nations shall be drunken with their own blood; and the blood of the saints shall cry unto the Lord for vengeance. We shall see the fulfillment of every jot and tittle that has been promised.

We shall see a marvelous work and a wonder come forth; the gospel shall be restored; Israel shall gather; temples shall rise in many nations; the elect shall be gathered out of Babylon into the marvelous light of Christ; and all of the signs of the times shall be fulfilled.

Then, at the time appointed by the Father, the Son of Man will come in the clouds of heaven. It is an unknown day in the beginning of the seventh thousand years of the earth's temporal continuance. War, such as has not been known from the beginning of time, is in progress. All nations are assembled at Armageddon.

All things are in commotion. Never has there been such a day as this. The newspapers of the world, as well as radio and television, speak only of war and calamity and the dread that hangs like a millstone around every neck. False ministers speak seductive words into hired microphones, giving their twisted views of the signs of the times. Their private interpretations of the prophetic word are at odds with world events. The priests and preachers of every doctrine are confused and uncertain. Has God forsaken the world, or is it true, as millions now acclaim, that there is no God?

Cabinets are in session planning death and destruction. Kings and presidents make unholy alliances as they conspire to spread death and carnage in the assembled armies. A general is calling for atomic bombs on the plain of Esdraelon. All hell rages as the unseen demons join hands with men to spread sin and sickness, death and desolation, and every evil thing in all parts of the earth.

And the signs in heaven above are like nothing man has ever

21

seen. Blood is everywhere; fire and vapors of smoke fill the atmospheric heavens. No man has seen a rainbow this year. And that great sign in the eastern sky—does it portend an invasion from outer space? Or is a collision with another planet imminent?

And above all are the vexing words of those Mormon Elders! They are everywhere preaching their strange doctrine, saying that the coming of the Lord is near, and that unless men repent and believe the gospel they will be destroyed by the brightness of his coming.

In this setting, as these and ten thousand like things are in progress, suddenly, quickly, as from the midst of eternity, He comes! Fire burns before him; tempests spread destruction; the earth trembles and reels to and fro as a drunken man. Every corruptible thing is consumed. He sets his foot on the Mount called Olivet; it cleaves in twain. The Lord has returned and the great millennium is here! The year of his redeemed has arrived!

Now we see the salvation of our God. Israel is gathered; the waste places of Zion are built up. The law goes forth from Zion and the word of the Lord from Jerusalem. Those men who remain have beaten their swords into plowshares and their spears into pruning hooks. It is the day of the Prince of Peace; the Lord himself reigns gloriously among his people. It is the age of triumph, glory, and millennial splendor.

6. *The Day of Celestial Exaltation and Eternal Rewards.*

After the Millennium plus a little season—perhaps itself another thousand years—during which men turn again to wickedness, then cometh the end, not of the world, which occurred at the Second Coming, but the end of earth. Then the final battle against Gog and Magog, the battle of the Great God, will be fought. Michael will lead the armies of heaven and Lucifer the legions of hell. Again there will be a new heaven and a new earth, but this time it will be a celestial earth. This earth will then be an eternal heaven, and the meek, who are the God-fearing and the righteous, shall inherit it forever and ever.

In their state of glorious exaltation, earth's inhabitants will then be as their God. They will have eternal life, which consists of life in the family unit and the possession of the fulness of the power

22

of the Almighty. This is the final day toward which all things point.

7. *The Seventh Age—Eternity Begins Anew.*

When the elect are exalted, when the family unit continues in the highest heaven of the celestial kingdom, when the saints have spirit children in the resurrection, then the cycle begins again. It is, as it were, the age of the Sabbath, an eternal Sabbath in which there is rest from the toil and sorrow that went before.

Exalted parents are to their children as our Eternal Parents are to us. Eternal increase, a continuation of the seeds forever and ever, eternal lives—these comprise the eternal family of those who gain eternal life. For them new earths are created, and thus the on-rolling purposes of the Gods of Heaven go forward from eternity to eternity.

And thus we place the Second Coming of the Son of Man in its proper eternal perspective. Our foundation is laid. Let us feast at the table of the Lord and drink deeply of the sweet wine served at his banquet.

Chapter 3

THE TIME
OF HIS COMING

Let Us Pray: "Thy Kingdom Come"

Jesus our Lord—and blessed be his name—shall soon come down from heaven in all the glory of his Father's kingdom to be with men again on earth!

Weeping over doomed Jerusalem, testifying to the Jews that their temple and their city would be left unto them desolate, he said: "Ye shall not see me henceforth and know that I am he of whom it is written by the prophets, until ye shall say: Blessed is he who cometh in the name of the Lord, in the clouds of heaven, and all the holy angels with him."

Of this prophetic utterance the scripture says: "Then understood his disciples that he should come again on the earth, after that he was glorified and crowned on the right hand of God." (JS-M 1:1.)

How glorious is this word of truth! He shall come again. All glory to his holy name. He shall come to complete the salvation of men and give glory and dominion to his saints. Let saints and angels sing. Let those on both sides of the veil look forward with anxious expectation for that great and gracious day. "Thy kingdom come. Thy will be done in earth, as it is in heaven." (Matt. 6:10.)

In every devout and believing heart the burning questions are: When will he come? Will it be in my day, or the day of my children, or in some distant age? And will I be worthy to abide the day and to stand with him in glory when he appeareth? And so we find the disciples, alone with him on the Mount of Olives, pondering his pronouncement about the Second Coming. They ask: "What is the sign of thy coming, and of the end of the world?" (JS-M 1:4.) His answer is the majestic Olivet Discourse, each portion of which we shall study hereafter in its proper place and setting.

It is our privilege and our duty to learn the signs of his coming and to seek his face. Each of us would do well to take the prophetic pledge: "I will wait upon the Lord, that hideth his face from the house of Jacob, and I will look for him." (Isa. 8:17.) Indeed, "he that feareth me shall be looking forth for the great day of the Lord to come," he says, "even for the signs of the coming of the Son of Man. . . . And, behold, I will come. . . . And he that watches not for me shall be cut off." (D&C 45:39-44.) To his saints the command is: "Prepare for the revelation which is to come, when . . . all flesh shall see me together. . . . And seek the face of the Lord always." (D&C 101:23, 38.)

Those who seek his face and who long for his coming shall be rewarded with everlasting glory in that day. "For behold, the Lord God hath sent forth the angel crying through the midst of heaven, saying: Prepare ye the way of the Lord, and make his paths straight, for the hour of his coming is nigh." (D&C 133:17.) Their preparation consists in believing and obeying all the laws and ordinances of the gospel.

And for their blessing and use, the Lord revealed this prayer: "Hearken, and lo, a voice as of one sent down from on high, who is mighty and powerful, whose going forth is unto the ends of the earth, yea, whose voice is unto men—Prepare ye the way of the Lord, make his paths straight. . . . Pray unto the Lord, call upon his holy name, make known his wonderful works among the people. Call upon the Lord, that his kingdom may go forth upon the earth, that the inhabitants thereof may receive it, and be prepared for the days to come, in the which the Son of Man shall come down in heaven, clothed in the brightness of his glory, to meet the kingdom of God which is set up on the earth. Wherefore, may the kingdom of God go forth, that the kingdom of heaven may come, that thou, O God, mayest be glorified in heaven so on earth, that thine enemies may be subdued; for thine is the honor, power and glory, forever and ever. Amen." (D&C 65:1, 4-6.)

In seeking all these things, not only is it our privilege to learn from holy writ, but if we are true and faithful in all things we can also see and feel the very things that came to those whose words we have canonized. Thus the Prophet Joseph Smith teaches and testifies: "Search the revelations of God; study the prophecies, and rejoice that God grants unto the world Seers and Prophets. They are they who saw the mysteries of godliness; they saw the flood before it came; they saw angels ascending and descending upon a ladder that reached from earth to heaven; they saw the stone cut out of the mountain, which filled the whole earth; they saw the Son of God come from the regions of bliss and dwell with men on earth; they saw the deliverer come out of Zion, and turn away ungodliness from Jacob; they saw the glory of the Lord when he showed the transfiguration of the earth on the mount; they saw every mountain laid low and every valley exalted when the Lord was taking vengeance upon the wicked; they saw truth spring out of the earth, and righteousness look down from heaven in the last days, before the Lord came the second time to gather his elect; they saw the end of wickedness on earth, and the Sabbath of creation crowned with peace; they saw the end of the glorious thousand years, when Satan was loosed for a little season; they saw the day of judgment when all men received according to their works, and they saw the heaven and the earth flee away to make room for the city of God, when the righteous receive an inheritance in eternity. And, fellow sojourners upon earth, *it is your privilege to purify yourselves and come up to the same glory, and see for yourselves, and know for yourselves.* Ask, and it shall be given you; seek and ye shall find; knock, and it shall be opened unto you." (*Teachings*, pp. 12-13. Italics added.)

When Will the Son of Man Come?

The time for the Second Coming of Christ is as fixed and certain as was the hour of his birth. It will not vary as much as a single second from the divine decree. He will come at the appointed time. The Millennium will not be ushered in prematurely because men turn to righteousness, nor will it be delayed because iniquity abounds. Nephi was able to state with absolute certainty that the God of Israel would come "in six hundred years from the time my father left Jerusalem." (1 Ne. 19:8.) To a later Nephi the Divine Voice acclaimed: "The time is at hand, and on this night shall the sign be given, and on the morrow come I into the world." (3 Ne. 1:13.)

So shall it be with his return in glory. He knows the set time and so does his Father. Perhaps a latter-day prophet will hear the Divine Voice on the day the veil parts and the heavens roll together as a scroll. But there is this difference between his two comings: The fixed and known time of his triumphal return has not been and will not be revealed until the set hour and the fixed time and the very day arrives. "Jesus Christ never did reveal to any man the precise time that He would come," the Prophet Joseph Smith said. "Go and read the Scriptures, and you cannot find anything that specifies the exact hour He would come; and all that say so are false teachers." (*Teachings*, p. 341.)

The scriptures say he will come as a thief—unexpectedly, without warning, when least expected. This has two meanings, one for the wicked and ungodly and another for the faithful saints. Those who neither believe nor understand will be pursuing their own evil ways—eating as gluttons, drinking as drunkards, and reveling in all the abominations of the world. They will esteem the words of the living apostles and the modern prophets as of no great worth and as the mouthings of religious fanatics. To them the promise of a Second Coming and a millennial era seems but an eschatological echo from unenlightened days long past. And even those who have been born again, who are alive to the things of the Spirit, and who understand the prophetic word—even they shall not know the precise time of his return.

Thus we read that he said to all men, both the righteous and the wicked, that "of that day, and hour, no one knoweth; no, not the angels of God in heaven, but my Father only. . . . And what I say unto one, I say unto all men; watch, therefore, for you know not at what hour your Lord doth come. But know this, if the good man of the house had known in what watch the thief would come, he

27

would have watched, and would not have suffered his house to have been broken up, but would have been ready. Therefore be ye also ready, for in such an hour as ye think not, the Son of Man cometh." (JS-M 1:40, 46-48; Matt. 25:13.) These words were spoken on the Mount of Olives to his ancient disciples; to his modern friends he says of himself: "The Son of Man . . . has taken his power on the right hand of his glory, and now reigneth in the heavens, and will reign till he descends on the earth to put all enemies under his feet, which time is nigh at hand—I, the Lord God, have spoken it; but the hour and the day no man knoweth, neither the angels in heaven, nor shall they know until he comes." (D&C 49:6-7.)

Thus, also, we read that he said to his chosen ones, who had received the ordinances of his holy house, "Behold, I come as a thief. Blessed is he that watcheth, and keepeth his garments, lest he walk naked, and they see his shame." (Rev. 16:15.) These are the saints of the Most High, the ones of whom he said, "And whoso treasureth up my word, shall not be deceived" (JS-M 1:37); even though they can read the signs of the times, they shall not know the precise time of his coming. As Daniel expressed it, "None of the wicked shall understand; but the wise shall understand" (Dan. 12:10), and yet even they, along with the angels of heaven, shall not know the very day and the hour until it arrives.

This brings us to that glorious illustration, devised by Paul, which contrasts the knowledge of the saints and that of worldly people relative to "the coming of the Lord." The ancient apostle says: "The Lord himself shall descend from heaven with a shout, with the voice of the archangel, and with the trump of God." What glories shall attend the day none can tell! "But of the times and the seasons, brethren, ye have no need that I write you," he continues. These words of Paul are for the saints who have treasured up his word; they are for the wise who understand. "For yourselves"—ye favored and blessed ones—"know perfectly that the day of the Lord so cometh as a thief in the night." This is axiomatic; it is assumed in all discussions as to the time of his coming, and no informed person raises questions on this point. "For when they"—those without understanding and who cannot read the signs of the

a proposition regarded as a self evident truth.

28

times—"shall say, Peace and safety"—that is, when they shall say, 'We can bring peace on earth through our treaties; we can control our destinies; why should the Lord come to destroy the wicked and usher in the Millennium?'—"then sudden destruction cometh upon them, as travail upon a woman with child; and they shall not escape."

Such is his illustration. The Second Coming is as a woman about to give birth to a child. She and her husband, the midwife at her side, and all who are informed know the birth is near, but they do not know the day and the hour. Even when the pains commence they cannot know what minute the expected one shall arrive. The approximate time, "the times and the seasons," yes—but the precise time, no. "But ye, brethren," Paul continues, "are not in darkness, that that day should overtake you as a thief. Ye are all the children of light, and the children of the day: we are not of the night, nor of darkness."

Then comes the exhortation. Always and everlastingly the prophetic authors use the doctrine of the Second Coming to invite the wicked to repent and to exhort the righteous to keep the commandments. Paul is no exception. "Therefore let us not sleep, as do others; but let us watch and be sober," he says. "For they that sleep sleep in the night; and they that be drunken are drunken in the night. But let us, who are of the day, be sober, putting on the breastplate of faith and love; and for an helmet, the hope of salvation. For God hath not appointed us to wrath, but to obtain salvation by our Lord Jesus Christ." (1 Thes. 4:15-16; 5:1-9.)

In confirmation of Paul's account, the Lord's latter-day word to us is: "The coming of the Lord draweth nigh, and it overtaketh the world as a thief in the night—Therefore, gird up your loins, that you may be the children of light, and that day shall not overtake you as a thief." (D&C 106:4-5.)

In the light of these principles, we are able to understand this statement of the Prophet Joseph Smith: "It is not the design of the Almighty to come upon the earth and crush it and grind it to powder, but he will reveal it to His servants the prophets." (*Teachings*, p. 286.) The Prophet then identifies some events and signs destined to precede the Second Coming, all of which we shall hereafter consider. For our present purposes, it suffices to know that the children of light shall know, not the day or the hour, but the approximate time of our Lord's return.

This approximate time can certainly be narrowed down to a generation. After teaching that desolations would befall the Jews of his day "as a thief in the night," Jesus said: "And it shall come to pass, that this generation of Jews shall not pass away until every desolation which I have told you concerning them shall come to pass." (D&C 45:19-21.) In speaking of the signs of the times in the last days, he said: "Verily, I say unto you, this generation, in which these things shall be shown forth, shall not pass away until all I have told you shall be fulfilled." (JS-M 1:34.) It is on this basis that those who wait for the Second Coming of the Consolation of Israel seek to learn the signs of the times.

The Generation of His Return

Many scriptures attest that "the great and dreadful day of the Lord is near, even at the doors." (D&C 110:16.) In our revelations the Lord says, "The time is soon at hand that I shall come in a cloud with power and great glory" (D&C 34:7), and that "the great day of the Lord is nigh at hand. . . . For in mine own due time will I come upon the earth in judgment" (D&C 43:17, 29). Speaking of his coming, the Lord says in one revelation that it shall be "not many days hence" (D&C 88:87), and in another, that the wars to precede it are "not yet, but by and by" (D&C 63:35). These and like sayings fall into perspective when we hear him say: "These are the things that ye must look for; and, speaking after the manner of the Lord, they are now nigh at hand, and in a time to come, even in the day of the coming of the Son of Man." (D&C 63:53.) We conclude that in the eternal perspective the coming of the Lord is nigh, but that from man's viewpoint many years may yet pass away before that awesome and dreadful day. And we must remind ourselves that he will not come until all that is promised has come to pass.

Time, as measured "after the manner of the Lord," is that which prevails on Kolob. One revolution of that planet is "a day unto the Lord, after his manner of reckoning," such "being one thousand years according to the time appointed" for our earth. (Abr. 3:4.) This earth was created and destined to pass through "seven thousand years of . . . continuance, or . . . temporal existence," with the millennial era becoming its Sabbath of rest. "We are to understand," as it is set forth in the revealed word, "that as God made the world in six days, and on the seventh day he finished his work, and sanctified it, and also formed man out of the dust of the earth, even so, in the beginning of the seventh thousand years will the Lord God sanctify the earth, and complete the salvation of man, and judge all things, and shall redeem all things." Certain named events are then specified to precede his coming. They are "the preparing and finishing of his work, in the beginning of the seventh thousand years—the preparing of the way before the time of his coming." (D&C 77:6, 12.) That is to say, the Lord Jesus Christ is going to come "in the beginning of the seventh thousand years." We, of course, cannot tell with certainty how many years passed from the fall of Adam to the birth of Jesus, nor whether the number of years counted by our present calendar has been tabulated without error. But no one will doubt that we are in the Saturday night of time and that on Sunday morning the Lord will come.

Peter had the Lord's time in mind when he wrote that "there shall come in the last days scoffers," mockers who do not believe the scriptural accounts stating that God created the earth in six days and rested on the seventh. They will say: "Where is the promise of his coming?" They will reject the Second Coming with its millennial era of peace, with its new heaven and new earth wherein death and sorrow cease, because, as they falsely reason: "Since the fathers fell asleep, all things continue as they were from the beginning of the creation." They will say such things as: 'How can there be a millennial era during which men will live to the age of a tree, when everyone knows we are the end product of evolution and that death has always existed on earth?' But Peter says that they "willingly are ignorant" of God's true dealings with reference to the creation, with reference to the flood of Noah, and with reference to the coming day of judgment, a day when "the elements shall melt with fervent heat" and all things shall become new.

To the saints, among whom are we, he says: "But, beloved, be not ignorant of this one thing, that one day is with the Lord as a thousand years, and a thousand years as one day. The Lord is not slack concerning his promise. . . . But the day of the Lord will come as a thief in the night; in the which the heavens shall pass away with a great noise." (2 Pet. 3:3-13.)

Thus, also, we read in latter-day revelation: "Now it is called today until the coming of the Son of Man. . . . For after today cometh the burning—this is speaking after the manner of the Lord." (D&C 64:23-24.)

With reference to that day of which we write, Joseph Smith said: "I was once praying very earnestly to know the time of the coming of the Son of Man, when I heard a voice repeat the following: Joseph, my son, if thou livest until thou art eighty-five years old, thou shalt see the face of the Son of Man; therefore let this suffice, and trouble me no more on this matter. I was left thus, without being able to decide whether this coming referred to the beginning of the millennium or to some previous appearing, or whether I should die and thus see his face. I believe the coming of the Son of Man will not be any sooner than that time." (D&C 130:14-17.) A few days after making this statement the Prophet referred to it in a sermon and said: "I prophesy in the name of the Lord God, and let it be written—the Son of Man will not come in the clouds of heaven till I am eighty-five years old."

It was in this same sermon that he said: "Were I going to prophesy, I would say the end [of the world] would not come in 1844, 5, or 6, or in forty years. There are those of the rising generation who shall not taste death till Christ comes." The rising generation includes all those yet to be born to parents then living. Manifestly many of these are now among us and will be living after the year A.D. 2000 has come and gone.

In this sermon also the Prophet said: "The coming of the Son of Man never will be—never can be till the judgments spoken of for this hour are poured out: which judgments are commenced." (*Teachings*, p. 286.) At this point he alluded to Paul's statements that the saints are the children of light and not of darkness and that the coming day should not overtake them as a thief in the night.

And it is on these points—that he will not come until the signs of the times are fulfilled and that the children of light will recognize the signs—that we shall take our stand as we go forward in our studies.

To all of this we must append this verity: When the day arrives, he will come quickly. The time for repentance and preparation will be passed; the day of judgment will be upon us. His presence "shall kindle a burning like the burning of a fire. . . . And it shall burn and devour his thorns and his briers in one day." (Isa. 10:16-17.)

Hear, then, this counsel, O ye saints: "Be patient in tribulation until I come; and, behold, I come quickly, and my reward is with me, and they who have sought me early shall find rest to their souls." (D&C 54:10.) Also: "Stand ye in holy places, and be not moved, until the day of the Lord come; for behold, it cometh quickly, saith the Lord." (D&C 87:8.)

He Comes in Each Watch of the Night

Few things provide the saints with a more anxious desire to walk uprightly and keep the commandments than does the doctrine of the Second Coming. All those who love the Lord and who seek his face cry out for a place in his kingdom. They know that every corruptible thing will be consumed when he comes, and their hope is to abide the day and then to be with him forever.

Hence, the day when he shall return always has been and always will be a matter of uncertainty. Thus, no matter when they live, all his saints are placed in a position of anxious expectation. All are to await his return as though it were destined for their day. Written in words of fire, they have ever before them the command: Watch and be ready.

As succeeding events occur in the world, there is no question his faithful saints gain a clearer knowledge of when to expect his glorious return. Some of the saints in the meridian of time seem to have thought he would return in their day. Surely many of the Latter-day Saints in the dawning days of this dispensation expected him to come in their lifetimes. We today, as we see the unfolding of his work in all the world, are in the best position of any people up to now to envision correctly the approximate time of his coming. Our children should surpass us in understanding.

Thus it is that his program calls for all the saints, from the day he ascended from Olivet until he comes again to that same holy place, to live as though they would be present to welcome him back! If such be their course, because the Great Judge is no respecter of persons, they will be rewarded as though he had come in their day. And this brings us to one of the great discourses of his mortal ministry, a sermon in which he says he will come again and again, in every watch of the night, as it were.

"Let your loins be girded about and have your lights burning," he says, "That ye yourselves may be like unto men who wait for their Lord, when he will return from the wedding; that, when he cometh and knocketh, they may open unto him immediately. Verily I say unto you, Blessed are those servants"—he is speaking of his saints, of those who have entered into a covenant to serve him and keep his commandments—"whom the Lord when he cometh shall find watching; for he shall gird himself, and make them sit down to meat, and will come forth and serve them." His reward is with him. The faithful who abide the day shall be exalted. They shall be even as he is, and they shall serve each other.

But because all his saints shall not live at the fixed time of his millennial return, he says: "For, behold, he cometh in the first watch of the night, and he shall also come in the second watch, and again he shall come in the third watch." How equitable and just is our God! He shall come to all—not alone to his saints in the final days of the world, but to all his saints who have lived from the first Adam to the last of Adam's race—and all who are waiting in righteousness shall abide the day.

"And verily I say unto you, He hath already come, as it is written of him." He then ministered among them. "And again when he shall come in the second watch, or come in the third watch, blessed are those servants when he cometh, that he shall find so doing; For the Lord of those servants shall gird himself, and make them to sit down to meat, and will come forth and serve them."

Such is the divine plan of the divine being. And in this sense every faithful person lives until the Second Coming of the Son of Man.

"And now, verily I say these things unto you," he continues, "that ye may know this, that the coming of the Lord is as a thief in the night. And it is like unto a man who is an householder, who, if he watcheth not his goods, the thief cometh in an hour of which he is not aware, and taketh his goods, and divideth them among his fellows."

These expressions evoked an immediate and obvious response: "And they said among themselves, If the good man of the house had known what hour the thief would come, he would have watched, and not have suffered his house to be broken through and the loss of his goods."

To this Jesus agreed. "And he said unto them, Verily I say unto you, be ye therefore ready also; for the Son of man cometh at an hour when ye think not." (JST, Luke 12:38-47.)

Let all his people watch and be ready, for he shall surely come in their day, let them live whensoever a divine providence hath decreed.

Chapter 4

APOSTASY AND INIQUITY PRECEDE HIS COMING

Gospel Light in Ages Past

In the not far distant future there will be a day of millennial rest, ushered in by the glorious coming of him who is the Son of Man of Holiness. He who came once shall come again. "But before that day the heavens shall be darkened." That is, revelation shall cease, the visions of eternity shall be closed to view, and the voice of God shall no longer be heard. The pure light of heaven shall no longer shine in the hearts of men. "And a veil of darkness shall cover the earth." (Moses 7:61.) Men will no longer penetrate the gloom of ignorance and unbelief, and see and know for themselves the truths of salvation.

After our Lord's first coming and before his dreadful return, there is to be a day of absolute, total, and complete apostasy from the truth. Men are to be left to themselves, wanderers in darkness, without hope and without God in the world. This we shall set forth shortly. But before we can even begin to catch a vision of the enormity of the evil and ignorance that will shroud the earth, we must be reminded of the eternal plan of the Father for all his spirit children. The contrast between the heavenly light of the everlasting gospel and the darkness that covers the earth will be as between the sun at midday and the darkness prevailing at midnight.

The great God, who is the Father of us all, is the Creator of all

36

things. He made the sidereal heavens; the milky way is his; and worlds without number have rolled into existence at his word. Galaxies without end are governed by his will. Endless are the earths inhabited by his spirit children. And as pertaining to them all, he says: "This is my work and my glory—to bring to pass the immortality and eternal life of man." (Moses 1:39.)

Eternal life is the name of the kind of life he lives. Those who so obtain become like him and are as he is. They live in the family unit and bear spirit children of their own; they have all power, all might, and all dominion. They know all things. He ordained and established the plan of salvation to enable them to advance and progress and become like him. It includes, first, an eternity of preparation as spirit beings in a premortal life. Then comes a mortal probation, on one of the earths provided, during which the faithful must remain in communication with their Father. They must receive revelation, see visions, enjoy the gifts of the Spirit, and know God, if they are to be saved. The plan of salvation is the same on all worlds and in all ages.

Here on planet earth the gospel of God, which is the plan of salvation, was revealed first to Adam. It then remained on earth, in whole or in part, without interruption for more than four thousand years. Whole nations and kingdoms fell away from the truth, but there was no period of universal apostasy during the whole so-called pre-Christian era. From age to age, prophets and apostles and preachers of righteousness taught the gospel and performed the ordinances of salvation.

Whenever and wherever men had faith, they saw the face of God, entertained angels, and performed miracles; they healed the sick, raised the dead, and wrought righteousness. Enoch and his whole city so perfected their lives that they were taken up into heaven. A whole generation of Nephites walked so perfectly in the light that every living soul among them was saved. In the meridian of time, Jesus marked the course and charted the way. The apostles after him built up the kingdom as they were guided by the Spirit.

And thus for more than four thousand years there were men who had received revelation, believed the gospel, and walked uprightly before the Lord. He in turn had poured out his Spirit upon them so that they "subdued kingdoms, wrought righteousness, obtained promises, stopped the mouths of lions, quenched the violence of fire, escaped the edge of the sword, out of weakness were made strong, waxed valiant in fight, turned to flight the armies of the aliens." (Heb. 11:33-34.) They had power "to break mountains, to divide the seas, to dry up waters, to turn them out of their course; to put at defiance the armies of nations, to divide the earth, to break every band, to stand in the presence of God; to do all things according to his will, according to his command, subdue principalities and powers; and this by the will of the Son of God which was from before the foundation of the world." (JST, Gen. 14:30-31.)

In the Lord's view, and from his eternal perspective, the course and way of life here set forth is the norm. It is the way men should live. It is the way many—perhaps most—do live on the endless earths that roll through the immensity of space. It is a perfectly normal thing for faithful and righteous people on all earths to raise the dead, to be caught up to the third heaven, to see and hear unspeakable things. It is the way all men will live during the Millennium, when, as we suppose, more people will dwell on earth (perhaps many times more) than have dwelt here during all of the preceding six thousand years.

It is true that there have been apostate nations and peoples from the beginning. But never, never during more than four millennia, was there a day when the Lord was without some legal administrators to preach and teach his word. The day of universal apostasy was reserved for that period between the first and second ministries of the Messiah. It is no wonder that the apostles and prophets use such plain and harsh words to describe the day of apostasy which will usher in our Lord's return. It is an awful thing for millions—nay, billions—of people to be in rebellion and to have turned their souls over to Satan.

Apostasy is to forsake the gospel, and the gospel is the everlasting covenant of salvation that God makes with his people. The fulness of the everlasting gospel is the new and everlasting covenant—a covenant revealed anew from age to age, a covenant that is everlastingly the same, for its terms and conditions are eternal; they never vary. And so Isaiah, speaking of the last days and the Second Coming, says: "The earth mourneth and fadeth away, the world languisheth and fadeth away, the haughty people of the earth do languish." The vineyard is being prepared for the fire.

"The earth also is defiled under the inhabitants thereof." Why? Because of wickedness. What is the nature of the sin? Isaiah answers: "Because they have transgressed the laws, changed the ordinance, broken the everlasting covenant." His answer is complete. Men have forsaken the whole gospel system—its laws, ordinances, and saving truths. A covenant that is everlasting no longer continues; it has been broken by men! They have forsaken their God. For such a course they must pay the penalty. "Therefore hath the curse devoured the earth, and they that dwell therein are desolate"—or, better, 'they that dwell therein are found guilty'—"therefore the inhabitants of the earth are burned, and few men left." (Isa. 24:4-6.) The burning occurs at the Second Coming. In our modern revelations, the Lord says that in that day the wicked "shall be cut off from among the people: For they have strayed from mine ordinances, and have broken mine everlasting covenant." (D&C 1:14-15.)

Darkness Covers the Earth

"I clothe the heavens with blackness" (Isa. 50:3), and there is no more revelation.

"Behold, the darkness shall cover the earth, and gross darkness the people" (Isa. 60:2), so that none in that day shall know the truth.

"I will cause the sun to go down at noon, and I will darken the earth in the clear day." (Amos 8:9.) Men will no longer be enlightened from on high.

Thus saith our God. Such is his promise, spoken prophetically of our day. And here, given in modern times, is his announcement that as he spake, so has it come to pass: "Verily, verily, I say unto you, darkness covereth the earth, and gross darkness the minds of the people, and all flesh has become corrupt before my face." (D&C 112:23.)

It is an evil day, a damnable day. There is no salvation in the teachings or philosophies of men. The Judeo-Christian ethic cannot free men from their sins, and the sects of Christendom have all gone astray. Even those who have a form of godliness are quick to deny the power thereof. The gifts of the Spirit no longer pierce the mists of darkness which cover the earth. It is a day of apostasy, a day when men are ripening in iniquity, a day when the tares are being bound in bundles and made ready for the burning.

These are the days foretold in holy writ. "Behold, the days come, saith the Lord God, that I will send a famine in the land, not a famine of bread, nor a thirst for water, but of hearing the words of the Lord." How dire are these days, days in which men have sunk so low spiritually that they worship, as they suppose, a God who is unknown and unknowable and incomprehensible. But how could it be otherwise when there is no revelation! "And they shall wander from sea to sea, and from the north even to the east, they shall run to and fro to seek the word of the Lord, and shall not find it. In that day shall the fair virgins and young men faint for thirst." (Amos 8:11-13.)

The universal apostasy is one of the signs of the times. It was destined to be before his Second Coming. Paul wrote an epistle to the saints in Thessalonica telling them that as children of light they should know the times and seasons of our Lord's return. Apparently some of them gained the impression he would come in their day. In a second epistle the apostle testified again of the promised return of the Blessed One in flaming fire, and then added words of caution relative to the appointed time.

"Now we beseech you, brethren, by the coming of our Lord Jesus Christ, and by our gathering together unto him," he writes in words of soberness, "That ye be not soon shaken in mind, or be troubled by letter, except ye receive it from us; neither by spirit, nor by word, as that the day of Christ is at hand." 'Do not be deceived by any sermons or epistles which lead you to believe that Christ will come in your day.'

"Let no man deceive you by any means; for there shall come a falling away first, and that man of sin be revealed, the son of perdition." Two conditions are here set forth. Christ shall not come until there is a falling away from the faith once delivered to the saints, until there is a universal apostasy; and further, he will not come until the operations of Lucifer—the man of sin, the son of perdition—are manifest in the world to an extent and degree beyond anything before known.

Of the evil and iniquity destined to cover the earth before the Second Coming, the apostle Paul said: "The mystery of iniquity doth already work"—it has even now commenced—"and he [Lucifer] it is who now worketh, and Christ suffereth him to work"—it is part of the plan that men be tempted of the devil—"until the time is fulfilled that he shall be taken out of the way." That is, Satan shall go to and fro upon the earth, raging in the hearts of men, until he is bound in the millennial day. "And then," when the Millennium comes, "shall that wicked one be revealed, whom the Lord shall consume with the spirit of his mouth, and shall destroy with the brightness of his coming. Yea, the Lord, even Jesus, whose coming is not until after there cometh a falling away, by the working of Satan with all power, and signs and lying wonders." (JST, 2 Thes. 2:1-9.)

Light is of God, darkness of the devil. Gospel truths lead to salvation, false doctrines to damnation. The man Satan—a spirit man, a man of sin, the evil person of whom the scripture asks: "Is this the man that made the earth to tremble, that did shake kingdoms; That made the world as a wilderness, and destroyed the cities thereof; that opened not the house of his prisoners?" (Isa. 14:16-17)—the man Satan brings the apostasy to pass. He and his works have been manifest in all ages. And the worst lies ahead.

Our day of dreadful apostasy and woeful wickedness was known to ancient prophets without number. Nephi, for one, said that "in the last days . . . all the nations of the Gentiles and also the Jews," who dwell "upon all the lands of the earth, . . . will be drunken with iniquity and all manner of abominations." Addressing himself to earth's latter-day inhabitants he cried: "Behold, all ye that doeth iniquity, stay yourselves and wonder, for ye shall cry out, and cry; yea, ye shall be drunken but not with wine, ye shall stagger but not with strong drink. For behold, the Lord hath poured out upon you the spirit of deep sleep."

Drunken with blood and iniquity and evil! Staggering under the weight of false doctrines, false ordinances, and false worship! Spiritually dead—dead as pertaining to the things of righteousness! How awful is the day, and why is it thus? Nephi answers: "Behold, ye have closed your eyes, and ye have rejected the prophets." Without prophets, without apostles, without revelation, the mind and will of the Lord are not known among men. Nephi then tells why these are not present among men: "Your rulers, and the seers hath [the Lord] covered because of your iniquity." (2 Ne. 27:1-5.) "Where there is no vision, the people perish." (Prov. 29:18.)

"Iniquity Shall Abound"

When darkness covers the earth and apostasy is everywhere, then sin and evil rear their ugly heads over all the earth and are everywhere to be found. And the darker the apostate night, the more evil and damning are the sins. The acts of men grow out of their beliefs. When men believe the gospel and are blessed with true religion, their personal conduct conforms to the divine standard; but when they forsake the truth and sink into apostasy, sin takes over in their lives. Thus Jesus, in speaking of the day in which there would be a falling away from his gospel, said: "Iniquity shall abound." (JS-M 1:30.) It could not be otherwise in such an age. Sin and every evil thing always abound when there is apostasy. Their presence today is one of the signs of the times. Without God and true religion in their lives, men sink into unbelievable depths of degradation.

In the golden era of Nephite history when "the people were all converted unto the Lord, upon all the face of the land," "there was no contention in the land, because of the love of God which did dwell in the hearts of the people. And there were no envyings, nor strifes, nor tumults, nor whoredoms, nor lyings, nor murders, nor any manner of lasciviousness; and surely there could not be a happier people among all the people who had been created by the hand of God. There were no robbers, nor murderers, neither were there Lamanites, nor any manner of -ites; but they were in one, the children of Christ, and heirs to the kingdom of God. And how blessed were they!" (4 Ne. 1:2, 15-18.) The existence of all of these evils today is the conclusive and irrefutable proof that apostasy prevails.

On the other hand, and in a passage of superlative insight, Paul tells us what happens in the lives of men when they forsake the truth. He refers to some who once "knew God" but did not remain true to the faith. They "changed the truth of God into a lie," he says. That is, they forsook the gospel, they apostatized, and darkness supplanted the light that once was theirs.

"Wherefore God also gave them up to uncleanness through the lusts of their own hearts, to dishonour their own bodies between themselves." Because they turned away from him, "God gave them up unto vile affections"—think now of homosexuals, and lesbians, and all those in the last days who revel in unclean, unholy, and unnatural sexual perversions—"for even their women did change the natural use into that which is against nature: And likewise also the men, leaving the natural use of the woman, burned in their lust one toward another; men with men working that which is unseemly, and receiving in themselves that recompence of their error which was meet."

Be it known that the sexual perversions sweeping the United States and other nations in this day are not of God. Those who pursue them are evil, degenerate, and depraved. It matters not what these advocates of lewdness and license may believe or say. These things are of the devil and lead to hell.

Speaking of them, Paul continues: "And even as they did not like to retain God in their knowledge, God gave them over to a reprobate mind, to do those things which are not convenient; Being filled with all unrighteousness, fornication, wickedness, covetousness, maliciousness; full of envy, murder, debate, deceit, malignity; whisperers, Backbiters, haters of God, despiteful, proud, boasters, inventors of evil things, disobedient to parents, Without understanding, covenantbreakers, without natural affection, implacable, unmerciful: Who knowing the judgment of God, that they which commit such things are worthy of death, not only do the same, but have pleasure in them that do them." (Rom. 1:21-32.)

Paul also spoke prophetically of our day: "Now the Spirit speaketh expressly," he said, as the message was borne in upon him with power and clarity, "that in the latter times some shall depart from the faith, giving heed to seducing spirits, and doctrines of devils." Doctrines of devils! Harsh language this! Where will such be taught? Is it amiss for us to say plainly that Satan's churches teach Satan's doctrines? And are not his doctrines those which lead men, not to the heavenly kingdom where the righteous dwell, but to that realm where the enemy of all righteousness reigns?

And what of those who give heed to these seducing spirits who whisper their false doctrines into ears attuned to evil? The preaching of those so attuned will consist of "speaking lies in hypocrisy." Knowing full well that their words are false, they will yet send them forth because they are pleasing to the carnal mind. "Having their conscience seared with a hot iron," they will justify their own evil deeds. And to show forth a form of godliness, as it were, they will be "forbidding to marry, and commanding to abstain from meats," and many such like things. (1 Tim. 4:1-3.)

"This know also, that in the last days perilous times shall come," our apostolic authority continues. "For men shall be lovers of their own selves, covetous, boasters, proud, blasphemers, disobedient to parents, unthankful, unholy, without natural affection, trucebreakers, false accusers, incontinent, fierce, despisers of those that are good, traitors, heady, highminded, lovers of pleasures more than lovers of God; having a form of godliness; but denying the power thereof."

The perilous times foretold are here. Every alert person, every day of his life, can identify men of every kind named in the holy word. All these evil persons, taking pleasure in their own unholy deeds, are found in all nations. And there are times when their Gadianton bands are so powerful that whole nations persecute the saints, wage war, and revel in the most abominable practices. Think, for instance, of the utter depravity that caused evil men, having gained political control of a nation, to use their power to murder millions of Jews during World War II.

With reference to the whole assemblage of evil men whom he has named, Paul's counsel is: "From such turn away." Then, in a tone of sadness, he adds: "For of this sort are they which creep into houses, and lead captive silly women laden with sins, led away with divers lusts." It is one of the signs of the times that women shall rebel against the established order of right and decency, and that their course will demean and destroy the sanctity of the home and the blessings of a godly family. And all such, wise as they are in their own conceits, are "ever learning, and never able to come to the knowledge of the truth." (2 Tim. 3:1-7.)

"This generation is as corrupt as the generation of the Jews that crucified Christ," the Prophet Joseph Smith said in 1843, "and if He were here to-day, and should preach the same doctrine He did then, they would put Him to death." (*Teachings*, p. 328.) Social and world conditions are worse now than they were in 1843, and they will continue their downward rush until that great and dreadful day arrives in which a just God will come in flaming fire to take vengeance upon the wicked.

This is indeed a vile and hellish day in which carnality reigns, a day in which men are ripening in iniquity preparatory to the day of burning. In it there is but one ray of hope. The light of the gospel shines in the darkness, and all who will come to that light have power to rid themselves of the curses of carnality and to live as becometh saints.

True it is that sinners cannot be saved in their sins, but He who came to cleanse men from their sins will yet receive all who repent and come unto him. According to the holy word, "the works of the flesh" are "adultery, fornication, uncleanness, lasciviousness, idolatry, witchcraft, hatred, variance, emulations, wrath, strife, seditions, heresies, envyings, murders, drunkenness, revellings, and such like." These works cover the earth today. With reference to them, the scripture says: "They which do such things shall not inherit the kingdom of God." (Gal. 5:19-21.)

But men can repent and be saved. "Know ye not that the unrighteous shall not inherit the kingdom of God?" Paul asks. "Be not deceived," he says, for "neither fornicators, nor idolaters, nor adulterers, nor effeminate, nor abusers of themselves with man-kind, nor thieves, nor covetous, nor drunkards, nor revilers, nor extortioners, shall inherit the kingdom of God."

But—and herein lies man's hope!—our ancient friend then says: "And such were some of you"—some of you saints were once partakers of all these evils—"but ye are washed, but ye are sanctified, but ye are justified in the name of the Lord Jesus, and by the Spirit of our God." (1 Cor. 6:9-11.)

Men need not perish, not even in this dire day.

Chapter 5

FALSE WORSHIP ABOUNDS BEFORE HIS COMING

False Christs Precede His Coming

False Christs preceded the destruction of Jerusalem and the temple, both of which occurred in A.D. 70, and they shall be manifest again before the Second Coming. They are, in fact, now here, and their presence is one of the least understood of all the signs of the times.

Jesus told the meridian apostles, as they sat with him on the Mount of Olives, that before the destruction of the temple, which was then but forty years away, "many shall come in my name, saying—I am Christ—and shall deceive many." Then of the period between that destruction and his Second Coming, he said: "If any man shall say unto you, Lo, here is Christ, or there, believe him not; For in those days there shall also arise false Christs, and false prophets, and shall show great signs and wonders, insomuch, that, if possible, they shall deceive the very elect, who are the elect according to the covenant. Behold, I speak these things unto you for the elect's sake." (JS-M 1:6, 21-23.)

False Christs! False Redeemers, false Saviors! Will there actually be men who will claim to fulfill the Messianic prophecies and who will step forth to offer their blood for the sins of the world? Is it possible that some will say, "I am the way, the truth, and the life; come unto me and be ye saved"? Or that others will profess to return in glory bearing the wounds with which the true Christ was wounded in the house of his friends?

47

True, there may be those deranged persons who suppose they are God, or Christ, or the Holy Ghost, or almost anything. None but the lunatic fringe among men, however, will give them a second serious thought. The promise of false Christs who will deceive, if it were possible, even the very elect, who will lead astray those who have made eternal covenant with the Lord, is a far more subtle and insidious evil.

A false Christ is not a person. It is a false system of worship, a false church, a false cult that says: "Lo, here is salvation; here is the doctrine of Christ. Come and believe thus and so, and ye shall be saved." It is any concept or philosophy that says that redemption, salvation, sanctification, justification, and all of the promised rewards can be gained in any way except that set forth by the apostles and prophets.

We hear the voice of false Christs when we hear the Athanasian Creed proclaim that "whosoever will be saved" must believe that the Father, Son, and Holy Ghost are incomprehensible and uncreated, that they form a Trinity of equals, who are not three Gods but one God, and not one God but three Gods, and that unless we so believe we "cannot be saved," and "shall perish everlastingly." (*Book of Common Prayer*, The Church of England, pp. 68-71.)

We hear the voice of a false Christ when we read such things as these: "There is but one living and true God everlasting, without body, parts, or passions." (*Book of Common Prayer*, Article I.)

"Holy Scripture [meaning the Bible] containeth all things necessary to salvation: so that whatsoever is not read therein, nor may be proved thereby, is not to be required of any man, that it should be believed as an article of Faith, or be thought requisite or necessary to salvation." (Article VI.)

"We are accounted righteous before God, only for the merits of our Lord and Saviour Jesus Christ by Faith, and not for our own works or deservings: Wherefore, that we are justified by Faith only is a most wholesome Doctrine, and very full of comfort." (Article XI.)

"Predestination to Life is the everlasting purpose of God,

whereby (before the foundations of the world were laid) he hath constantly decreed by his counsel secret to us, to deliver from curse and damnation those whom he hath chosen in Christ out of mankind, and to bring them by Christ to everlasting salvation, as vessels made to honour. Wherefore, they which be endued with so excellent a benefit of God be called according to God's purpose by his Spirit working in due season: they through Grace obey the calling: they be justified freely: they be made the sons of God by adoption: they be made like the image of his only-begotten Son Jesus Christ: they walk religiously in good works, and at length, by God's mercy, they attain to everlasting felicity.

"As the godly consideration of Predestination, and our Election in Christ, is full of sweet, pleasant, and unspeakable comfort to godly persons, and such as feel in themselves the workings of the Spirit of Christ, mortifying the works of the flesh, and their earthly members, and drawing up their mind to high and heavenly things, as well because it doth greatly establish and confirm their faith of eternal Salvation to be enjoyed through Christ, as because it doth fervently kindle their love towards God: So, for curious and carnal persons, lacking the Spirit of Christ, to have continually before their eyes the sentence of God's Predestination, is a most dangerous downfall, whereby the Devil doth thrust them either into desperation, or into wretchlessness of most unclean living, no less perilous than desperation." (Article XVII.)

"The Baptism of young Children [infant baptism] is in any wise to be retained in the Church, as most agreeable with the institution of Christ." (Article XXVII.)

We hear the voice of a false Christ when we hear the divines of the day preach that salvation comes by the grace of God, not of works lest any man should boast, but simply by believing in and confessing the Lord Jesus with one's lips; or that signs and gifts and miracles are done away; or that ministers have power to represent the Lord and preach his gospel because they have a feeling in their heart that such is the course they should pursue.

We hear the voice of one false Christ, echoing from the camps of communism, expounding the devil-devised declaration that religion is the opiate of the people. We hear another such voice when races alien to Israel acclaim that the one God has no need for a Son to mediate between himself and fallen man.

We see the works of false Christs when women and homosexuals are ordained to the priesthood, as it is supposed; or when elaborate rituals pervert and twist and add to the sacrament of the Lord's supper; or when sins are forgiven through the doing of penance and the paying of money, as it is supposed.

Indeed, false Christs are everywhere. Joseph Smith named the Methodists, Presbyterians, and Baptists as among "the sects" who were crying "Lo, here!" and "Lo, there!" in that glorious spring of 1820. (JS-H 1:5.) The apostle John referred to false Christs as antichrists. He identified them as apostates, as those who "went out from us," as those who deny "that Jesus is the Christ," or who deny "the Father and the Son," and as those "who confess not that Jesus Christ is come in the flesh." (1 Jn. 2:18-23; 2 Jn. 1:7.)

The Church of the Devil Reigns on Earth

To say there will be false Christs in the last days means there will also be false prophets, false ministers, and false churches. We shall now show that false and evil and abominable churches do and shall exist before the coming of him who offers to all men membership in his one true Church.

We have heard Paul's prophecy announcing there would be a universal apostasy before "the coming of our Lord Jesus Christ." In it our apostolic colleague, speaking of the man of sin—of that evil spirit who acclaims himself as the God of this world—speaking of Lucifer, Paul says: He it is "who opposeth and exalteth himself above all that is called God, or that is worshipped; so that he as God sitteth in the temple of God, shewing himself that he is God." (2 Thes. 2:4.)

When Satan enters the Church of God, replaces Deity in the hearts of men, and commands them to worship him; when men forsake the doctrines of Christ and believe what they hear from false Christs; when they become carnal, sensual, and devilish by nature, and set their hearts upon the things of this world—to whose church do they give allegiance, Christ's or Satan's?

When miracles and gifts and revelations cease; when men teach with their learning and deny the Holy Ghost who giveth utterance; when the love of God and the peace of heaven are replaced with a spirit of lewdness and indecency—whose church is involved, the church of the Lord or the church of the devil?

To gain an understanding of how and why the presence of false churches is one of the signs of the times, let us turn now, with an open heart and mind, to that which is written by the prophets. Our best source material by far comes from the Book of Mormon, whose major pronouncements on the matter we shall consider in their proper settings.

Few men have equaled Nephi in seership and prophetic utterance. He saw in vision the birth, baptism, and ministry of the Holy One. He saw the call of the Twelve, the crucifixion of Christ, and the multitudes of the earth joining to fight against the apostles of the Lamb. He saw apostasy and wickedness sweep through the Gentile nations in the day that darkness covered the earth and gross darkness the minds of the people.

As he viewed this day of darkness, this evil day after the apostolic era, he said: "I saw among the nations of the Gentiles the foundation of a great church." An angel with whom he was then conversing said: "Behold the foundation of a church which is most abominable above all other churches." Note it well: There are degrees of abomination; there are levels of iniquity; one church sinks deeper into the cesspool of sin than any other. The angel then described it as the church "which slayeth the saints of God, yea, and tortureth them and bindeth them down, and yoketh them with a yoke of iron, and bringeth them down into captivity." This is the kind of inspired utterance that is fulfilled over and over again by the same or an equivalent organization. As it happened in the first centuries of the Christian era, so, we may be assured, it has happened and will happen again in our dispensation. The day of persecution and martyrdom has not passed.

"And it came to pass that I beheld this great and abominable church," Nephi said, "and I saw the devil that he was the founder of it." The man of sin is sitting in the temple of God, demanding worship, and proving thereby that he is God. "And I also saw gold, and silver, and silks, and scarlets, and fine-twined linen, and all manner of precious clothing; and I saw many harlots," Nephi continued.

Then from the angel came this word: "Behold the gold, and the silver, and the silks, and the scarlets, and the fine-twined linen, and the precious clothing, and the harlots, are the desires of this great and abominable church. And also for the praise of the world do they destroy the saints of God, and bring them down into captivity." (1 Ne. 13:1-9.)

John the Revelator saw the same vision that was given to Nephi. To John, an angel—perhaps the same one who conversed with Nephi—called the great and abominable church "the great whore that sitteth upon many waters." John saw her sitting "upon a scarlet coloured beast, full of names of blasphemy. . . . And the woman," he said, "was arrayed in purple and scarlet colour, and decked with gold and precious stones and pearls, having a golden cup in her hand full of abominations and filthiness of her fornication: And upon her forehead was a name written, MYSTERY, BABYLON THE GREAT, THE MOTHER OF HARLOTS AND ABOMINATIONS OF THE EARTH. And I saw the woman drunken with the blood of the saints, and with the blood of the martyrs of Jesus." (Rev. 17:1-6.)

This is the church of the devil that came into being after New Testament times. It was founded by Satan, and its interests lay in wealth and worldliness and carnality. This is the church into whose hands the scriptures came. These scriptures, so the angel said to Nephi, came "from the Jews in purity unto the Gentiles." As they were first written, they "contained the plainness of the gospel of the Lord."

But the word of God, recorded in purity and plainness, is as deadly poison to an apostate church. It is far better for such an organization to have them in a partial, twisted, and perverted form. Indeed, it is imperative, from their standpoint, that the scriptures be altered to conform to their practices.

And so, with reference to the scriptures, the angel said to Nephi: "After they go forth by the hand of the twelve apostles of the Lamb, from the Jews unto the Gentiles, thou seest the formation of a great and abominable church, which is most abominable above all other churches; for behold, they have taken away from the gospel of the Lamb many parts which are plain and most precious; and also many covenants of the Lord have they taken away."

Why have they done this terrible thing? The angel yet speaks: "And all this have they done that they might pervert the right ways of the Lord, that they might blind the eyes and harden the hearts of the children of men."

And then, repeating himself for emphasis, for there must be no question about the iniquity of that great church which is not the Lord's church, the angel said: "Wherefore, thou seest that after the book hath gone forth through the hands of the great and abominable church, that there are many plain and precious things taken away from the book, which is the book of the Lamb of God." (1 Ne. 13:24-28.)

The sad picture thus far portrayed is then softened somewhat by the angelic promise of a restoration of the gospel in the latter days; and the "abominable church" is further identified as "the mother of harlots," which accords with what John wrote, and which can only mean that other apostate churches spring from her. (1 Ne. 13:29-42.)

To introduce the promised gospel restoration, Nephi's angelic visitant alludes to the eventual fall of the Babylonish church. He calls it "that great and abominable church, which was founded by the devil and his children, that he might lead away the souls of men down to hell," and says that they whose church it is shall fall into the very pit "which hath been digged for them."

Then comes the glorious word that the Lord "will work a great and marvelous work among the children of men." Revelation, visions, gifts, miracles, all that the ancient saints enjoyed shall commence anew. Those who believe and obey the heavenly word shall gain "peace and life eternal," while the disobedient and rebellious shall be "brought down into captivity, . . . according to the captivity of the devil."

This brings us in point of time to the dispensation of the fulness of times. In this setting Nephi is to see the church of the devil again—to see it in a new perspective and from a different vantage point. He will see that it has matured and grown, that it has come of age, and that it has a power and an influence over nations and kingdoms that exceed anything of the past. "Look, and behold that great and abominable church, which is the mother of abominations, whose founder is the devil." Such is the angelic invitation.

As Nephi looks, the angel says: "Behold there are save two churches only"—at long last the gospel has been restored; universal apostasy is giving way before the light of heaven; there is a true church on earth as well as a false one; "the one is the church of the Lamb of God, and the other is the church of the devil." There is only light and darkness; there is no dusky twilight zone. Either men walk in the light or they cannot be saved. Anything less than salvation is not salvation. It may be better to walk in the twilight or to glimpse the first few rays of a distant dawn than to be enveloped in total darkness, but salvation itself is only for those who step forth into the blazing light of the noonday sun. "Wherefore, whoso belongeth not to the church of the Lamb of God," the angelic prophet proclaims, "belongeth to that great church, which is the mother of abominations; and she is the whore of all the earth."

Nephi tells us what he saw on earth in our day, in the day of restoration, in the day when the gospel was again found among men. "I looked and beheld the whore of all the earth," he says, "and she sat upon many waters." Her influence was everywhere. No land or people were rid of her power; the islands and continents, sitting as they do in the waters of the world, came under her dominion. Then, horrible and woeful as the reality is, Nephi saw that "she had dominion over all the earth, among all nations, kindreds, tongues, and people."

What is the church of the devil in our day, and where is the seat of her power? If we accept the angelic word, if we believe as Nephi believed, and if, the Lord willing, we see what Nephi saw, then we shall accept without question the reality around us. The church of the devil is every evil and worldly organization on earth. It is all of the systems, both Christian and non-Christian, that have perverted the pure and perfect gospel; it is all of the governments and powers that run counter to the divine will; it is the societies

54

and political parties and labor unions that sow strife and reap contention. It is communism; it is Islam; it is Buddhism; it is modern Christianity in all its parts. It is Germany under Hitler, Russia under Stalin, and Italy under Mussolini. It is the man of sin speaking in churches, orating in legislative halls, and commanding the armies of men. And its headquarters are everywhere—in Rome and Moscow, in Paris and London, in Teheran and Washington—everywhere that evil forces, either of church or state or society, can be influenced. The immanent and all-pervading presence of evil in high places is one of the signs of the times.

"And it came to pass that I beheld the church of the Lamb of God"—The Church of Jesus Christ of Latter-day Saints—"and its numbers were few," Nephi continues, "because of the wickedness and abominations of the whore who sat upon many waters; nevertheless, I beheld that the church of the Lamb, who were the saints of God, were also upon all the face of the earth." This pertains to a day yet future. The saints of the Most High are not yet, as a people and with organized congregations, established upon all the face of the earth. When the day comes that they are, they still will not compare in power with the forces of evil. Even then, as Nephi foresaw, "their dominions upon the face of the earth were small, because of the wickedness of the great whore whom I saw."

What follows in Nephi's account lies in the future. It will occur after the saints are established in all nations. Of that coming day Nephi says: "I beheld that the great mother of abominations did gather together multitudes upon the face of all the earth, among all the nations of the Gentiles, to fight against the Lamb of God." Our persecutions and difficulties have scarcely begun. We saw mobbings and murders and martyrdom as the foundations of the work were laid in the United States. These same things, with greater intensity, shall yet fall upon the faithful in all nations.

But as the hour of judgment nears, the Lord will preserve and glorify his people. "And it came to pass that I, Nephi, beheld the power of the Lamb of God, that it descended upon the saints of the church of the Lamb, and upon the covenant people of the Lord, who were scattered upon all the face of the earth; and they were armed with righteousness and with the power of God in great glory." The salvation of the saints, both temporally and spiritually, now and always is grounded upon obedience to the holy covenants they have made.

"And it came to pass that I beheld that the wrath of God was poured out upon the great and abominable church, insomuch that there were wars and rumors of wars among all the nations and kindreds of the earth." Such has been already to some extent, and hereafter will be to a greater degree.

"And as there began to be wars and rumors of wars among all the nations which belonged to the mother of abominations"—note this well: all nations are owned, as it were, by the evil and carnal powers of the world—as Nephi saw these things, the angel said: "Behold, the wrath of God is upon the mother of harlots; and behold, thou seest all these things—And when the day cometh that the wrath of God is poured out upon the mother of harlots, which is the great and abominable church of all the earth, whose founder is the devil, then, at that day, the work of the Father shall commence, in preparing the way for the fulfilling of his covenants, which he hath made to his people who are of the house of Israel." (1 Ne. 14:1-17.) Then shall the kingdom be restored to Israel in all its millennial glory, Zion shall be built up in perfection, and the Lord himself shall reign gloriously over those who are his.

Chapter 6

FALSE CHURCHES PRECEDE HIS COMING

"They Are All Wrong"

Let us now walk with Joseph Smith into a grove of trees in Western New York in the spring of 1820. He is troubled in mind and spirit; a great religious revival is sweeping the frontier areas around Palmyra, and he desires to know which church is true. As we walk we hear a faint echo of an apostolic sermon in the distance. It seems to say: "Is Christ divided?" (1 Cor. 1:13), and we, with the Lord's future seer, wonder: how can churches whose beliefs and practices conflict all be true?

We are there when the heavens open. There is a pillar of light. Two Personages, "whose brightness and glory defy all description," stand above the seeking seer-to-be. The Father testifies of his Beloved Son and commands, *"Hear Him!"* Joseph asks which of all the sects is right and which he should join. The word that comes back from the Son of God causes the very pillars of Christendom to totter and sway. Joseph is to "join none of them," for they are "all wrong." Some words are spoken about creeds that are an abomination in the Lord's sight and about professors of religion who are corrupt and whose hearts are far removed from divine standards. (JS-H 1:16-19.) Thus is ushered in the dispensation of the fulness of times; it comes in a day when all churches are false; it is a day in which Satan has power over his own dominions.

Being thus enlightened, and being thus fully aware of how the Lord views all churches, we turn to the Book of Mormon account.

57

We hear Nephi's words. He is speaking of our day. "The Gentiles are lifted up in the pride of their eyes, and have stumbled," he says, and "they have built up many churches"—not one true church, but many false churches—in which "they put down the power and miracles of God, and preach up unto themselves their own wisdom and their own learning, that they may get gain and grind upon the face of the poor." It is as though he saw the divinity schools of the day where the scriptures are dissected in Greek and Hebrew and where their true and plain meanings are spiritualized away; for how, as they suppose in the schools, can a man preach unless he has been trained for the ministry?

"And there are many churches built up which cause envyings, and strifes, and malice. And there are also secret combinations, even as in times of old, according to the combinations of the devil, for he is the founder of all these things; yea, the founder of murder, and works of darkness; yea, and he leadeth them by the neck with a flaxen cord, until he bindeth them with his strong cords forever." (2 Ne. 26:20-22.)

Nephi then tells of the coming forth of the Book of Mormon and of the restoration of the gospel. "It shall come to pass in that day," he says, "that the churches which are built up, and not unto the Lord, when the one shall say unto the other: Behold, I, I am the Lord's; and the others shall say: I, I am the Lord's; and thus shall every one say that hath built up churches, and not unto the Lord—And they shall contend one with another; and their priests shall contend one with another, and they shall teach with their learning, and deny the Holy Ghost, which giveth utterance." It is as though he saw the religious revivalism that led Joseph Smith to ask which of all the churches was right and which he should join.

"And they deny the power of God, the Holy One of Israel; and they say unto the people: Hearken unto us, and hear ye our precept; for behold there is no God today, for the Lord and the Redeemer hath done his work, and he hath given his power unto men; Behold, hearken ye unto my precept; if they shall say there is a miracle wrought by the hand of the Lord, believe it not; for this day he is not a God of miracles; he hath done his work."

After naming other "false and vain and foolish doctrines"

taught in our day, the inspired account says: "Because of pride, and because of false teachers, and false doctrine, their churches have become corrupted, and their churches are lifted up; because of pride they are puffed up. They rob the poor because of their fine sanctuaries; they rob the poor because of their fine clothing; and they persecute the meek and the poor in heart, because in their pride they are puffed up. They wear stiff necks and high heads; yea, and because of pride, and wickedness, and abominations, and whoredoms, they have all gone astray." These words, as with so many in the Nephite scriptures, are so clear and plain and have such obvious application to conditions known to every observant person in our day that they would only be weakened by further exposition.

Having spoken thus of the false churches of our day; having shown that they love the things of this world more than the things of God; having condemned the ministers who teach for doctrine the commandments of men, who have replaced the pure truths from heaven with the philosophies of men mingled with scripture—having so spoken, Nephi raises a warning voice. It is addressed to the members of "the only true and living church upon the face of the whole earth," with many of whose members the Lord is not "well pleased." (D&C 1:30.)

"They have all gone astray," he says of those who live in the last days, and then adds, "save it be a few, who are the humble followers of Christ." He is speaking of the day, be it remembered, in which the gospel in its everlasting fulness has been restored for the last time. And of the true saints he says: "Nevertheless, they are led, that in many instances they do err because they are taught by the precepts of men." (2 Ne. 28:3-14.)

Even in the true Church in the last days there will be some who do not believe the whole body of revealed truth; some who do not give full allegiance to the Cause of truth and righteousness; some who are members in name only and who continue to live after the manner of the world. This also is one of the signs of the times. It shall be as it was among some of old whom Paul rebuked: "When ye come together in the church," he wrote to the Corinthians, "there be divisions among you." Contention, debate, and false views have no place in the Church and kingdom of our Lord. The doctrines are his, not ours, and our concern should be to gain the mind of Christ and to think what he thinks on every point. But the fact is that there are divisions in the Church, for the very reason Paul now gives: "There must be also heresies among you, that they which are approved may be made manifest among you." (1 Cor. 11:18-19.)

Heresies among the Saints! Sadly it is so. Are there not those among us who believe the theories of men rather than the revealed word relative to the creation of the earth and organic evolution? Do we not still have teachers who say that God is progressing in knowledge and learning new truths; that there will be a second chance for salvation for those who reject the gospel here but accept it in the spirit world; that there will be progression from one kingdom of glory to another in the world to come? And are there not those among us who refuse to follow the Brethren on moral issues, lest their agency and political rights be infringed, as they suppose? Truly, there are heresies among us.

"They Teach for Doctrines the Commandments of Men"

Apostasy and false churches go hand in hand; they aid and abet each other. When men forsake the gospel they find a form of godliness in churches of their own creation, and these churches teach doctrines that sustain men in their apostasy. Moroni, in a great outburst of righteous indignation, speaks of the abominations in the lives of those who worship at the altars of the world. He names the day as the one in which the Book of Mormon shall come forth and be proclaimed to the world.

"It shall come in a day when the power of God shall be denied," he says, "and churches become defiled and be lifted up in the pride of their hearts; yea, even in a day when leaders of churches and teachers shall rise in the pride of their hearts, even to the envying of them who belong to their churches."

To this we add: It shall come forth and go to the world in a day when there are churches for homosexuals, churches that accept adulterers, churches containing murderers, and even churches for those who worship Satan. It shall come in a day when there shall be churches for sinners who imagine their sins are remitted, without any act on their part, simply because Christ died for sinners.

But back to Moroni. "It shall come in a day when there shall be great pollutions upon the face of the earth; there shall be murders, and robbing, and lying, and deceivings, and whoredoms, and all manner of abominations; when there shall be many who will say, Do this, or do that, and it mattereth not, for the Lord will uphold such at the last day. But wo unto such for they are in the gall of bitterness and in the bonds of iniquity." Such is the state of the world when men worship at the altars of the world.

"Yea, it shall come in a day when there shall be churches built up that shall say: Come unto me, and for your money you shall be forgiven of your sins." Viewing our day in vision, our ancient friend then says: "O ye wicked and perverse and stiffnecked people, why have ye built up churches unto yourselves to get gain? Why have ye transfigured the holy word of God, that ye might bring damnation upon your souls? Behold, look ye unto the revelations of God; for behold, the time cometh at that day when all these things must be fulfilled."

These harsh words do not say and do not mean that in the last days all men on earth will choose evil rather than good when the choice is placed before them. There are many who feel instinctively that their creeds are wrong and their doctrines false. There are those who seek truth and desire righteousness. As the inspired word has it: "There are many yet on the earth among all sects, parties, and denominations, who are blinded by the subtle craftiness of men, whereby they lie in wait to deceive, and who are only kept from the truth because they know not where to find it." (D&C 123:12.)

But again let Moroni speak. "Jesus Christ hath shown you unto me, and I know your doing," he says of those who live in this day when the word of the Lord is again coming forth. "And I know that ye do walk in the pride of your hearts; and there are none save a few only who do not lift themselves up in the pride of their hearts, unto the wearing of very fine apparel, unto envying, and strifes, and malice, and persecutions, and all manner of iniquities; and your churches, yea, even every one, have become polluted because of the pride of your hearts. For behold, ye do love money, and your substance, and your fine apparel, and the adorning of your churches, more than ye love the poor and the needy, the sick and the afflicted."

Do men today need prophetic warnings as did those in olden times? Let them hear Moroni's words, spoken as it were with the trump of God. "O ye pollutions, ye hypocrites, ye teachers, who sell yourselves for that which will canker, why have ye polluted the holy church of God?" he cries. How far removed are the rite-laden churches of Christendom from the pure and guileless worship of the primitive saints. How soft and compromising are the ear-tickling sermons of our day as compared to the divine invective of Paul and Peter and Jesus. How sad it is to see worshippers who think only of themselves and who care not a farthing for the widows and the orphans.

To those in the churches of our day Moroni calls: "Why are ye ashamed to take upon you the name of Christ? Why do ye not think that greater is the value of an endless happiness than that misery which never dies—because of the praise of the world? Why do ye adorn yourselves with that which hath no life, and yet suffer the hungry, and the needy, and the naked, and the sick and the afflicted to pass by you, and notice them not?

"Yea, why do ye build up your secret abominations to get gain, and cause that widows should mourn before the Lord, and also orphans to mourn before the Lord, and also the blood of their fathers and their husbands to cry unto the Lord from the ground, for vengeance upon your heads?

"Behold, the sword of vengeance hangeth over you; and the time soon cometh that he avengeth the blood of the saints upon you, for he will not suffer their cries any longer." (Morm. 8:26-41.)

Such is the divine word relative to the great and abominable church, to her harlot daughters, to the many churches in the last days, and to the part they all play in the falling away that precedes the Second Coming. Before recording the final fate—both of that great church which is not the Lord's church, and of all churches founded and nurtured and led by the devil and his children—we must weave into the great tapestry we are making a few words about secret combinations.

Secret Combinations Abound in the Last Days

In some detail and at extended length Ezekiel prophesies of the great premillennial warfare between Israel and those nations prophetically identified as Gog and Magog. He tells of the death and desolation spread by the assembled armies; that all men on earth shall shake at the presence of the returning Lord; and of the destruction of the wicked by divine power. With all these matters we shall deal in depth in their proper settings. For our present purposes we need only record that the Lord will then rain upon Gog "and upon his bands, and upon the many people that are with him, an overflowing rain, and great hailstones, fire, and brimstone," and that he "will send a fire on Magog." (Ezek. 38-39.) This is the promised day of burning when every corruptible thing shall be consumed.

In latter-day revelation the Lord confirms this prophetic word that death and destruction are destined to fall upon men at the day of his coming. He includes some of the specific things named by Ezekiel. Of the decreed consummation of the wars then in progress, the divine word says: "And the great and abominable church, which is the whore of all the earth, shall be cast down by devouring fire, according as it is spoken by the mouth of Ezekiel the prophet, who spoke of these things, which have not come to pass but surely must, as I live, for abominations shall not reign." (D&C 29:21.)

In Ezekiel's account, great nations with their armies of mighty men and their trains of munitions come to do battle. They have their planes and ships and tanks and atomic bombs and are waging such warfare as has never been known before. Then comes the devouring fire from heaven that destroys the armies of Gog and Magog, which armies are identified as the great and abominable church. That is to say, the church of the devil is more than an ecclesiastical organization that teaches false doctrines so as to lead men carefully down to hell. It is more than priests and ministers and places of worship. It is also the political powers that hold in their hands the destinies of nations. It is the churches and their religious doctrines, and it is also the governments and their political philosophies. It is the political doctrines in which men believe and for which they die to satisfy their innate needs to worship. And this brings us to a consideration of the secret combinations that are to be in the last days.

Our Book of Mormon authors speak a great deal about the secret combinations that arose among the Jaredites and among the Nephites and that were destined to arise among the Gentile nations in the last days. They tell us that these secret combinations brought to pass the destruction of the Jaredites and the Nephites and will bring similar destruction on any latter-day nations that permit them to gain an ascendancy. Writing of nations in the last days, Moroni says: "Whatsoever nation shall uphold such secret combinations, to get power and gain, until they shall spread over the nation, behold, they shall be destroyed; for the Lord will not suffer that the blood of his saints, which shall be shed by them, shall always cry unto him from the ground for vengeance upon them and yet he avenge them not." (Ether 8:22.)

What are these secret combinations which have such powers that whole civilizations are destroyed by them? They wear many guises and appear in many forms. They were the Gadianton robbers among the Nephites, and the perpetrators of the Spanish inquisition in the dark ages. Among us they include some secret and oath-bound societies and such Mafia-like groups as engage in organized crime. They include some political parties, some revolutionists who rise up against their governments, and those evil and anarchist groups which steal and kidnap and murder in the name of this or that political objective. They are always groups that seek money and power and freedom from the penalties that should attend their crimes.

Secret combinations are tools of Lucifer to accomplish his purpose and to destroy the works of God. The devil "stirreth up the children of men unto secret combinations of murder and all manner of secret works of darkness." (2 Ne. 9:9.) They keep men from accepting the gospel; they destroy the freedoms and true worship of the saints; and they spread wickedness and abominations everywhere. With reference to the Jaredites, the scripture says: "They did reject all the words of the prophets, because of their secret society and wicked abominations." (Ether 11:22.) Among the Nephites, the Gadianton robbers sought to destroy the rights and privileges of the true church, the way of worship of the saints, "and their freedom and their liberty." (3 Ne. 2:12.)

Shortly before the wicked were destroyed at the time of the crucifixion, the Gadianton robbers obtained "the sole management of the government" among the Nephites, "insomuch that they did trample under their feet and smite and rend and turn their backs upon the poor and the meek, and the humble followers of God." (Hel. 6:39.) Their minions filled "the judgment-seats"; they usurped "the power and authority of the land," laid "aside the commandments of God," flouted justice, condemned "the righteous because of their righteousness," and let "the guilty and the wicked go unpunished because of their money." They sought to "get gain and glory of the world," that they might "more easily commit adultery, and steal, and kill, and do according to their own wills." (Hel. 7:4-5.)

These Nephite descriptions of the secret combinations of their day give us an understanding of what their prophets meant when they spoke of like evil organizations in the last days. Speaking of the coming forth of the Book of Mormon, Moroni, for instance, said: "It shall come in a day when the blood of saints shall cry unto the Lord, because of secret combinations and the works of darkness." (Morm. 8:27.)

Moroni also said that these secret combinations caused the destruction of the Jaredite and Nephite nations and will cause our destruction if we permit them to control our government. Speaking directly to us he said: "It is wisdom in God that these things should be shown unto you, that thereby ye may repent of your sins, and suffer not that these murderous combinations shall get above you, which are built up to get power and gain—and the work, yea, even the work of destruction come upon you, yea, even the sword of the justice of the Eternal God shall fall upon you, to your overthrow and destruction if ye shall suffer these things to be." Any nation that permits a secret combination to gain control of its government shall be destroyed; such is the everlasting decree of a just God.

"Wherefore, the Lord commandeth you," Moroni continues, that "when ye shall see these things come among you that ye shall awake to a sense of your awful situation, because of this secret combination which shall be among you." Moroni here speaks of one particular secret combination and prophesies that it will be among us in our day. Either it will prevail over us or, alternatively, "Wo be unto it, because of the blood of them who have been slain; for their cry from the dust for vengeance upon it, and also upon those who built it up."

Next Moroni turns the key so that all who have ears to hear can understand what the secret combination is and can identify those who build it up. "For it cometh to pass," he says, "that whoso buildeth it up seeketh to overthrow the freedom of all lands, nations, and countries." This is a worldwide conspiracy. It is now entrenched in many nations, and it seeks dominion over all nations. It is Godless, atheistic, and operates by compulsion. It is communism. "And it bringeth to pass the destruction of all people, for it is built up by the devil, who is the father of all lies; even that same liar who beguiled our first parents, yea, even that same liar who hath caused man to commit murder from the beginning; who hath hardened the hearts of men that they have murdered the prophets, and stoned them, and cast them out from the beginning."

The issue is thus squarely put. Good and evil are arrayed in battle line. Good, in all its beauty and fulness, is found only where the gospel flourishes. Evil is everywhere; worldliness fills the world; and false churches and false political philosophies—combined as one in the great and abominable church—hold dominion over the nations. "Wherefore, I, Moroni, am commanded to write these things that evil may be done away, and that the time may come that Satan may have no power upon the hearts of the children of men, but that they may be persuaded to do good continually, that they may come unto the fountain of all righteousness and be saved." (Ether 8:18-26.)

We have read of the predicted fall of the armies of the great and abominable church as they come from Gog and Magog to make war against Israel. Truly, as Nephi said: "That great and abominable church"—in all its parts, be they ecclesiastical or political—

"the whore of all the earth, must tumble to the earth, and great must be the fall thereof. For the kingdom of the devil must shake, and they which belong to it must needs be stirred up unto repentance, or the devil will grasp them with his everlasting chains, and they be stirred up to anger, and perish." (2 Ne. 28:18-19.)

"And the righteous need not fear, for they are those who shall not be confounded," Nephi also says. "But it is the kingdom of the devil, which shall be built up among the children of men, which kingdom is established among them which are in the flesh—For the time speedily shall come that all churches which are built up to get gain, and all those who are built up to get power over the flesh, and those who are built up to become popular in the eyes of the world, and those who seek the lusts of the flesh and the things of the world, and to do all manner of iniquity; yea, in fine, all those who belong to the kingdom of the devil are they who need fear, and tremble, and quake; they are those who must be brought low in the dust; they are those who must be consumed as stubble." (1 Ne. 22:22-23.)

Chapter 7

FALSE PROPHETS PRECEDE HIS COMING

True Prophets Reveal True Doctrines

Our attention now turns to what the inspired word has to say about the false teachers, false ministers, and false prophets who shall spew forth their damning doctrines in the days of desolation and sorrow that precede the Second Coming of the true Teacher, the chief Minister, and the presiding Prophet. Their presence is one of the signs of the times, and they shall prophesy and teach so near the truth "that, if possible, they shall deceive the very elect." (JS-M 1:22.)

Lest we be deceived, we must know the differences between true and false prophets. "Beware of false prophets," Jesus said (Matt. 7:15), and we cannot recognize a false prophet unless we know what a true one is.

Our whole system of revealed religion calls for us to believe in true prophets, to cleave unto their counsels, and to conform to the word of the Lord that falls from their lips. Prophets and seers, how great they are! They stand in the place and stead of the Lord Jesus in administering salvation to fallen man. Their vision is endless and their understanding reaches to heaven. What, then, is the nature and mission of a true prophet?

A prophet is a living witness of the divine Sonship of the Lord Jesus Christ. He is one who knows by personal revelation that Jesus is the Lord who worked out the infinite and eternal atonement by which salvation comes. This "testimony of Jesus is the

68

spirit of prophecy" (Rev. 19:10), and one so gifted and so endowed has power, if need be, to "prophesy of all things" (Mosiah 5:3).

A prophet is a legal administrator who has been called of God to represent him in teaching the doctrines of salvation to men on earth. He is one who is empowered to perform the ordinances of salvation so they will be binding on earth and sealed everlastingly in the heavens. He is a teacher of eternal truth; he expounds the plan of salvation. He is a witness of the Lord; he testifies of Christ. He is a minister; he does everything for mortal men that is needed to save and exalt them in the highest heaven. When called to the ministry, he holds the priesthood and is endowed with power from on high. It is his privilege to receive revelation, to see visions, to entertain angels, and to see the face of God.

True prophets are always found in the true Church, and false prophets, as we shall see, are always found in false churches. In setting forth the chief identifying characteristics of the Lord's Church, Paul said: "God hath set some in the church, first apostles, secondarily prophets, thirdly teachers, after that miracles, then gifts of healings, helps, governments, diversities of tongues." (1 Cor. 12:28.) Indeed, the saints and the Church "are built upon the foundation of the apostles and prophets, Jesus Christ himself being the chief corner stone." (Eph. 2:19-20.)

Where there are apostles and prophets, there is the Church and kingdom of God on earth; and where these are not, the true Church and the divine kingdom are not present. How can a church be the Lord's Church unless it receives revelation from him? Who can head up the Lord's work on earth if there are no prophets? Who can preach and teach true doctrines without prophetic insight? Who can perform the ordinances of salvation with binding certainty and sealing surety unless they are legal administrators endowed with power from on high?

And so it is written that Christ "gave some, apostles; and some, prophets; and some, evangelists; and some, pastors and teachers"—all given as "gifts unto men." For what purpose? They are given "for the perfecting of the saints, for the work of the ministry, for the edifying of the body of Christ."

How long are they to remain in the Church? "Till we all come in the unity of the faith"; until that millennial day when every living soul is converted to the truth; until righteous men are prepared to receive their own instructions direct from the Lord.

What blessings come to men because there are apostles and prophets? These are many. The chief are that obedient persons have power to press forward in righteousness, to gain "the knowledge of the Son of God," to perfect their souls, and to become joint-heirs with Christ, than which there are no greater blessings. Further, those who give heed to true prophets and who take apostolic counsel are not "tossed to and fro, and carried about with every wind of doctrine." They know the truth and are not deceived by false prophets and teachers. Those who "lie in wait to deceive" have no power over them. They are not moved "by the sleight of men, and [the] cunning craftiness" of evil and designing persons. (Eph. 4:11-14.)

In this probationary estate we must choose between good and evil, virtue and vice, light and darkness. We must pursue an upward or a downward course; we must get nearer to the Lord or nearer to the devil. God's voice and his counsel come from the light of Christ and by way of his prophets; the devil's enticements are whispered into the minds of men from an evil source and are taught by false prophets who represent him whose word they teach. All men follow either true or false prophets. Those who do not give heed to the divinely sent representatives of the Lord, by virtue of that fact alone, follow those who are not of God.

False Prophets Teach False Doctrines

What are false prophets? They are teachers and preachers who profess to speak for the Lord when, in fact, they have received no such appointment. They are ministers of religion who have not been called of God as was Aaron. They may suppose—often sincerely and with pious devoutness—that it is their right to tell others what they must do to be saved when, in fact, they have received no such commission from on high.

They are teachers of religion who do not receive revelation and have not gained from the Holy Ghost the true testimony of Jesus.

70

They are ministers of religion who do not hold either the Aaronic or Melchizedek priesthoods, and try as they may it is beyond their power to bind on earth and have their acts sealed eternally in the heavens.

False prophets are false teachers; they teach false doctrine; they neither know nor teach the doctrines of salvation. Rather, they have followed cunningly devised fables that they suppose make up the gospel of Christ, and they preach them as such. They are the ministers who proclaim a false way of salvation, the expounders of doctrines that are not of God, and the proclaimers of every man-made system of religion on earth. They are the political leaders among the communists and the doctrinaires who lead men to accept freedom-destroying systems. They are the philosophers and sages who seek to explain God, existence, right and wrong, agency, immortality, and other religious concepts without reference to revelation. They are all of the political and religious leaders who proclaim philosophies and doctrines that lead men away from God and the salvation he offers to men.

The issue where false prophets are concerned is not one of their attempting to foretell the future and failing. True prophets do on occasions prophesy of that which is to be because they have the testimony of Jesus, which is the spirit of prophecy. But the great commission of prophets is to bear witness of Christ, to teach the doctrines of salvation that he has revealed to them and their associates, and to perform with power and authority those ordinances that he has ordained. When men who are not called and appointed and empowered to do these things nonetheless assume the prerogative of so doing, they are false prophets.

In the Book of Mormon we have an account of the course pursued by a particularly vocal and evil false prophet. His teachings illustrate what many with a like bent are wont to acclaim. The curse and untimely death that fell upon him are symbols of the fate of all who raise their voices against the Divine Voice. It was about 74 B.C. when this antichrist, whose name was Korihor, arose among the Nephites. He taught that there should be no Christ whose atonement would remit their sins; that the Messianic prophecies were the foolish traditions of their fathers, because no man

71

could foretell the future; that men prospered according to their own genius, and conquered according to their own strength, and that whatever they did was no crime. He said there was no life after death, and many, as a consequence, were led to commit whoredoms and to wallow in wickedness.

In a confrontation with Alma, in the typical way of an adulterous and evil priest, Korihor demanded to see a sign. After he was struck dumb by the power of God, he wrote these words: "The devil hath deceived me; for he appeared unto me in the form of an angel, and said unto me: Go and reclaim this people, for they have all gone astray after an unknown God. And he said unto me: There is no God; yea, and he taught me that which I should say. And I have taught his words; and I taught them because they were pleasing unto the carnal mind; and I taught them, even until I had much success, insomuch that I verily believed that they were true; and for this cause I withstood the truth, even until I have brought this great curse upon me." (Alma 30:53.)

Lucifer does not come personally to every false prophet, as he did to Korihor, any more than the Lord comes personally to every true prophet, as he did to Joseph Smith. Such an appearance— either of God on the one hand or of Satan on the other—is, however, the end result of full devotion to the respective causes involved. In each instance an earthly representative, by obedience to the laws that are ordained, may see the face of the master he serves. But in every case the will of the evil one is manifest to his false prophets, just as the will of the Righteous One is manifest to his true prophets. All prophets are spokesmen: true prophets speak for God, and their words lead to life and salvation; false prophets speak for the devil, and their words lead to death and damnation.

False Prophets Minister on Every Hand

There is only one true doctrine: it is the doctrine of Christ; it is the gospel of salvation by conformity to which men may gain peace in this life and eternal life in the world to come. But there are many false doctrines—doctrines of every hue and color, of every size and dimension, of every shape and kind, all of which lead men on the downward course. True prophets speak with one voice, false prophets with as many voices as there are prophets. Most of the false prophets of our day fall into one or more of the following categories:

1. *False prophets serve false Christs and belong to false churches.*

We live in "a crooked and perverse generation" (D&C 34:6); the sects of the day are "the congregations of the wicked" (D&C 60:8), and their ministers are false teachers, meaning false prophets. We have already seen that false Christs are false systems of religion, which proclaim a Christ of this sort or that, and which suppose that salvation comes through their way of worship. Jesus' warning is against "false Christs, and false prophets." He said: "If they"—meaning false prophets—"shall say unto you: Behold, he"—a supposed Christ or system of salvation—"is in the desert; go not forth: Behold, he is in the secret chambers; believe it not." (JS-M 1:22, 25.)

If there are false Christs, there are false witnesses of these Christs. If there are false churches, there are false ministers. It is, "as with the people, so with the priest." (Isa. 24:2.) If true ministers preach in the congregations of the saints, false ministers hold forth in the congregations of the wicked. "Beware of false prophets." (Matt. 7:15.)

2. *False prophets worship false gods and teach others so to do.*

Eternal life comes to those who worship "the only true God, and Jesus Christ," whom he hath sent. (John 17:3.) There is no salvation in worshipping a false god. "Shall a man make gods unto himself, and they are no gods?" Jeremiah asked with reference to the great day of apostasy. (Jer. 16:20.) Isaiah spoke of men worshipping idols, which would be utterly abolished at the Second Coming. (Isa. 2:8-22.) In that graphic imagery which came so naturally to him, John said men in our day would "worship the beast." (Rev. 14:8-11.) And the Lord said of those in our day: "They seek not the Lord to establish his righteousness, but every man walketh in his own way, and after the image of his own God, whose image is in the likeness of the world, and whose substance is that of an idol." (D&C 1:16.)

If men worship a three-in-one spirit essence that fills the immensity of space and is everywhere and nowhere in particular present, are they worshipping a true or a false God? If men are invited to worship false gods in false churches, what must we think of the preachers who issue the invitations and who expound upon the nature of the Deity there adored?

3. *False prophets serve Satan, whose prophets and ministers they are.*

Paul tells us that the great apostasy before the Second Coming would result from "the working of Satan with all power and signs and lying wonders, and with all deceivableness of unrighteousness in them that perish; because they received not the love of the truth, that they might be saved. And for this cause God shall send them"—or, better, allow them to have—"strong delusion, that they should believe a lie: That they all might be damned who believed not the truth, but had pleasure in unrighteousness." (2 Thes. 2:9-12.)

Now, who is to bring this horrible thing to pass? The scripture ascribes it to Satan. But does he do it as a single soul, or does he have an organized corps of workers? The scriptures also teach that the Lord will proclaim his word in every ear, but he does it through his servants. So it is with Satan. He has his servants, and they do his bidding.

If there is a church of the devil, will not Satan also have his ministers to govern its affairs? If the devil sows tares in the fields of the Lord, will he not do it by the mouths of the servants of sin who follow him? How aptly does Moroni say: "A bitter fountain cannot bring forth good water; neither can a good fountain bring forth bitter water; wherefore, a man being a servant of the devil cannot follow Christ; and if he follow Christ he cannot be a servant of the devil." (Moro. 7:11.)

4. *False prophets are all corrupt.*

In that glorious theophany manifest in the spring of 1820, when God once more unveiled his face, the Beloved Son told young Joseph Smith that all the sects were wrong and all their creeds an abomination in his sight. Then came the divine word relative to those who governed the churches and taught the creeds.

The Son of God said "that those professors were all corrupt."
(JS-H 1:19.)

Corrupt ministers! Ministers no longer in that state of uprightness, correctness, and truth that becometh the servants of the
Lord; ministers who were changed into a bad and some into even a
depraved state. How aptly is it written in the holy book that "there
should be mockers in the last time, who should walk after their
own ungodly lusts"; that "these be they who separate themselves,
sensual, having not the Spirit"; and that "these are murmurers,
complainers, walking after their own lusts; and their mouth
speaketh great swelling words"—how great their sermons are!—
"having men's persons in admiration because of advantage."
(Jude 1:16-19.)

Speaking of such, Peter has left us some of the most severe and
harsh language found in holy writ. He says they "walk after the
flesh in the lust of uncleanness, and despise government. Pre-
sumptuous are they, selfwilled, they are not afraid to speak evil of
dignities." He says they "shall utterly perish in their own corruption; and shall receive the reward of unrighteousness. . . . Spots
they are and blemishes, sporting themselves with their own deceivings while they feast with you; having eyes full of adultery,
and that cannot cease from sin; beguiling unstable souls: an heart
they have exercised with covetous practices; cursed children:
which have forsaken the right way, and are gone astray."

How well the Spirit guides him in his choice of words. He continues: "When they speak great swelling words of vanity, they
allure through the lusts of the flesh, through much wantonness."
That is, men can obey their counsel and still live after the manner
of the world. "While they promise them liberty, they themselves
are the servants of corruption: for of whom a man is overcome, of
the same is he brought in bondage." (2 Pet. 2:10-19.)

5. *False prophets teach false doctrines.*

In the vision that opened our dispensation, we also hear the
Divine Voice say with reference to the corrupt professors that
"they draw near to me with their lips, but their hearts are far from
me; they teach for doctrines the commandments of men." (JS-H

1:19; Isa. 29:13.) Truly this is the day of which Isaiah spoke: "The priest and the prophet have erred, . . . they are out of the way, . . . they err in vision, they stumble in judgment." And then with reference to the spiritual food they offer their congregations, he acclaimed: "All tables are full of vomit and filthiness, so that there is no place clean." (Isa. 28:7-8.)

The scriptures abound in statements relative to the evil teachings of the corrupt professors of religion in the last days. Paul said: "The time will come when they [the people of the world] will not endure sound doctrine; but after their own lusts shall they heap to themselves teachers, having itching ears; and they shall turn away their ears from the truth, and shall be turned unto fables." (2 Tim. 4:3-4.)

And these words of Peter apply: "There were false prophets also among the people, even as there shall be false teachers among you, who privily shall bring in damnable heresies [that is, heresies of perdition], even denying the Lord that bought them, and bring upon themselves swift destruction. And many shall follow their pernicious ways; by reason of whom the way of truth shall be evil spoken of. And through covetousness shall they with feigned words make merchandise of you." (2 Pet. 2:1-3.)

But nowhere do we find plainer preachments about false prophets than in the writings of Nephi. He says of our day: "There shall be many which shall say: Eat, drink, and be merry, for tomorrow we die; and it shall be well with us. And there shall also be many which say: Eat, drink, and be merry; nevertheless, fear God—he will justify in committing a little sin; yea, lie a little, take the advantage of one because of his words, dig a pit for thy neighbor; there is no harm in this; and do all these things, for tomorrow we die; and if it so be that we are guilty, God will beat us with a few stripes, and at last we shall be saved in the kingdom of God. Yea, and there shall be many which shall teach after this manner, false and vain and foolish doctrines, and shall be puffed up in their hearts, and shall seek deep to hide their counsels from the Lord; and their works shall be in the dark." (2 Ne. 28:7-9.)

If there is a great and abominable church, surely its ministers will teach abominable doctrines. If the Lord sends his servants to preach saving truths, should it come as any surprise to find ministers of Satan teaching damning lies? What a terrible thing it is to teach false doctrines that lead men carefully down to hell! Should we be shocked to hear Nephi acclaim: "And all those who preach false doctrines, . . . wo, wo, wo be unto them, saith the Lord God Almighty, for they shall be thrust down to hell!" (2 Ne. 28:15.)

6. *The teachings of false prophets deny God and the Godhead.*

Just as some shall gain eternal life by worshipping the true and living God, so shall others inherit eternal damnation by worshipping false gods. The greatest truths known to man are that God is a personal being in whose image we are made, that he is our Father, and that we have power to become as he is. The greatest heresy found in Christendom is that God is a spirit, an essence that fills immensity, an uncreated force or power having neither body, parts, nor passions.

The heart and core and center of revealed religion is that the Son of God atoned for the sins of the world, that he abolished death so that all shall rise in the resurrection, and that he made salvation available on conditions of obedience. The second greatest heresy in Christendom is that men are saved by grace alone without works, merely by confessing the Lord Jesus with their lips.

The greatest gift men can receive in this life is the gift of the Holy Ghost and the resultant revelation and gifts of the Spirit that thereby come into their lives. And the third greatest heresy in Christendom is the teaching that God is dead, that he has done his work in times past, and that there are not gifts and signs and miracles today.

True prophets teach the true doctrines; false prophets teach heresies.

7. *The teachings of false prophets destroy the family unit and deny the purposes of God.*

Our whole purpose in life, the very reason for our mortal probation, is to enable us to create for ourselves eternal family units patterned after the family of God our Father. Those who so obtain will have eternal life, and it is the very glory of God to lead his children to this high state.

Where among all the ministers of the world are there any who teach such a plan of salvation as this? And if they do not teach the true plan of salvation, what system and plan do they proclaim?

8. *False prophets malign Joseph Smith, fight against the Book of Mormon, and deny the restoration of the gospel.*

Peter said of false prophets: "These, as natural brute beasts, . . . speak evil of the things that they understand not." (2 Pet. 2:12.) Where is this seen better than in the reaction of ministers of religion to the Lord's great latter-day work? Of the coming forth of new revelation, they say: "We have received the word of God, and we need no more of the word of God, for we have enough!" (2 Ne. 28:29.) Of the coming forth of the Book of Mormon, their cry is: "A Bible! A Bible! We have got a Bible, and there cannot be any more Bible." (2 Ne. 29:3.) And their cries of "Delusion, false prophets, Mormon fraud," only fulfill the Lord's promise to Joseph Smith, that "fools shall have thee in derision, and hell shall rage against thee." (D&C 122:1.) Truly, Satan and his ministers sow tares in the fields of the Lord. (D&C 86:3.)

9. *False prophets teach with their learning rather than by the power of the Holy Ghost.*

In the true Church, all faithful people enjoy the gift of the Holy Ghost. The Holy Ghost is a revelator. His appointment is to testify of Christ, to bring all things of God to our remembrance, and to guide men into all truth. "By the power of the Holy Ghost ye may know the truth of all things." (Moro. 10:5.) In the true Church, prophets and preachers speak by the power of the Holy Ghost. So strict is this law that they are told: "If ye receive not the Spirit ye shall not teach." (D&C 42:14.)

It follows that in false churches, where the gifts of the Spirit are not found, men "teach with their learning, and deny the Holy Ghost, which giveth utterance." (2 Ne. 28:4.) In such churches they "preach up unto themselves their own wisdom and their own learning, that they may get gain and grind upon the face of the poor." (2 Ne. 26:20.) Where ministers of religion preach by the power of the Holy Ghost, there is the true Church; where they do not, there the true Church is not.

10. *False prophets teach for hire and divine for money.*

"Thus saith the Lord concerning the prophets that make my

78

people err, . . . The priests thereof teach for hire, and the prophets thereof divine for money." (Micah 3:5, 11.) "But the laborer in Zion shall labor for Zion; for if they labor for money they shall perish." (2 Ne. 26:31.) Need we say more on this point?

11. *False prophets do not raise the warning voice and cry repentance.*

True prophets preach repentance; they invite men to forsake their sins and be baptized; their voice is a warning voice, one that sets forth the sorrow and desolation reserved for the rebellious. But how can the ministers of Christendom speak thus boldly against sin and evil and iniquity when their livelihood is in the hands of the sinners in their congregation?

Speaking of prophets who have forsaken the Lord to serve another master, Isaiah leaves us this graphic imagery: "His watchmen are blind: they are all ignorant, they are all dumb dogs, they cannot bark; sleeping, lying down, loving to slumber. Yea, they are greedy dogs which can never have enough, and they are shepherds that cannot understand: they all look to their own way, every one for his gain, from his quarter." (Isa. 56:10-11.)

12. *False prophets prophesy falsely.*

The primary sin of false prophets is false teaching—teaching that does not lead men to God and salvation. But when they do attempt to prophesy, in the sense of foretelling the future, their words fail and their prophecies do not come to pass. "A wonderful and horrible thing is committed in the land; The prophets prophesy falsely, and the priests bear rule by their means; and my people love to have it so." (Jer. 5:30-31.)

Professors of religion in our day undertake so-called radio ministries or conduct great televised revivals, all with a view to solving the problems of men and of nations. They speak great swelling words to explain the visions of Daniel and of the Apocalypse. They apply selected scriptures to national and international events and postulate this or that calendar schedule, including oftentimes even the very time of the Second Coming. The great pyramid in Egypt is often woven into their preaching as though it were a book of scripture in stone. By the time one prophecy fails, another takes its place in the minds of their devotees, so that the cycle of mysticism and fablizing goes on in almost one eternal round. It is marvelous what darkened minds will accept in the name of religion!

13. *False prophets perform false ordinances that have no efficacy, virtue, or force in and after the resurrection.*

Think of the rituals and imagery that have supplanted the simple sacrament of the Lord's supper as found among the primitive saints.

Think of the prayers offered to St. Genevieve, St. Barbara, St. Joan, and an endless retinue of canonized persons, all with the thought that they will intercede with the Lord for and on behalf of the petitioners.

Think of baptism by pouring and sprinkling rather than by immersion in similitude of the death, burial, and resurrection of Him whom the ordinance is designed to typify.

Think of infant baptism and be reminded of the Holy Word which says: "It is solemn mockery before God, that ye should baptize little children. . . . He that supposeth that little children need baptism is in the gall of bitterness and in the bonds of iniquity, for he hath neither faith, hope, nor charity; wherefore, should he be cut off while in the thought, he must go down to hell. . . . Wo be unto them that shall pervert the ways of the Lord after this manner, for they shall perish except they repent. . . . And he that saith that little children need baptism denieth the mercies of Christ, and setteth at naught the atonement of him and the power of his redemption. Wo unto such, for they are in danger of death, hell, and an endless torment." (Moro. 8:9-21.)

Think also of Nadab and Abihu, who offered "strange fire"— ordinances of their own devising—upon the altar of the Lord, and wonder if the fire from heaven that devoured them was not a type and a shadow of the spiritual destruction awaiting all who pervert the right ways of the Lord with ordinances of their own. (Lev. 10:1-2.)

14. *False prophets do not receive revelation, see visions, entertain angels, and see the face of God.*

"These are wells without water, clouds that are carried with a tempest; to whom the mist of darkness is reserved for ever." (2

Pet. 2:17.) Wells without water! Prophets who do not prophesy, seers who do not see the future, ministers who receive no revelation, teachers who are lost in a mist of darkness!

They are they of whom the Lord says: "Night shall be unto you, that ye shall not have a vision; and it shall be dark unto you, that ye shall not divine; and the sun shall go down over the prophets, and the day shall be dark over them. Then shall the seers be ashamed, and the diviners confounded: yea, they shall all cover their lips; for there is no answer of God." (Micah 3:6-7.)

This is the day of wonder and amazement. Men rely upon themselves and imagine in their own minds what is to be; they seek not the Lord, to learn from him the providences he hath ordained. "Stay yourselves, and wonder; cry ye out, and cry: they are drunken, but not with wine; they stagger, but not with strong drink. For the Lord hath poured out upon you the spirit of deep sleep, and hath closed your eyes: the prophets and your rulers, the seers hath he covered." (Isa. 29:9-10.)

Oh, if men would but turn unto Him who is the same yesterday, today, and forever, who is no respecter of persons, and who treats all men alike, he would speak unto them as he spoke unto their fathers! Once again his prophets and saints would see his face and converse with their fellowservants beyond the veil.

15. *False prophets deny the gifts of the Spirit and latter-day miracles.*

They "deny the revelations of God, and say that they are done away, that there are no revelations, nor prophecies, nor gifts, nor healing, nor speaking with tongues, and the interpretation of tongues." And among them none of these are found, for they have dwindled in unbelief, and departed from the right way, "and know not the God in whom they should trust." (Morm. 9:7, 20.)

16. *False prophets do not have the testimony of Jesus, which is the spirit of prophecy.*

Joseph Smith said: "According to John, the testimony of Jesus is the spirit of prophecy; therefore, if I profess to be a witness or teacher, and have not the spirit of prophecy, which is the testimony of Jesus, I must be a false witness; but if I be a true teacher and witness, I must possess the spirit of prophecy, and that constitutes a prophet; and any man who says he is a teacher or a preacher of righteousness, and denies the spirit of prophecy, is a liar, and the truth is not in him; and by this key false teachers and impostors may be detected." (*Teachings*, p. 269.)

17. *False prophets promote carnal and evil causes that are not of God.*

"The land is full of adulterers, . . . For both prophet and priest are profane." (Jer. 23:10-11.) And thus it ever is. Adultery and a profane priesthood go hand and hand. Harlots are the desires of the great and abominable church. Every form of sin and evil abounds when spiritual leaders go astray. Lucifer's ministers teach worldly concepts and encourage carnal practices. They ordain homosexuals and women to a priesthood they pretend to hold. They profess to forgive sins for money. They stamp out heresies, as they assume, by an inquisition. Their faith is propagated by the sword. Religious wars sweep through nations and kingdoms. They persecute those who do not believe as they do. The whole history of Christendom from the day the apostles fell asleep to the present hour has been one unending course of war and blood and carnage and plague and immorality and evil, in all of which the spiritual rulers of the people have guided men in their carnal course.

18. *False prophets do not hold priesthood.*

They are not legal administrators with power and authority to bind on earth and seal in heaven. The ordinances they perform have whatever validity man can give them for this life, but they have no efficacy, virtue, or force in the life to come. They have "a form of godliness, but they deny the power thereof." (JS-H 1:19.) Most of them have scarcely heard that there is a Melchizedek Priesthood, or have assumed that Christ alone held such a delegation of divine power. Where are their apostles, high priests, patriarchs, and seventies? As to the Aaronic Priesthood, that, they suppose, ceased when the law of Moses was fulfilled. And as to the keys of the kingdom, well, they are just something to argue and wonder about.

19. *False prophets engage in priestcrafts.*

We look back upon the priest-ridden societies of the past and wonder how whole nations and kingdoms had their wealth and means and power put at the disposal of their religious rulers. And yet, how many there are even in our day who are subject to the same dominion. How great is the number of ministers who engage—openly, blatantly, even proudly—in priestcrafts, for, by definition, "Priestcrafts are that men preach and set themselves up for a light unto the world, that they may get gain and praise of the world; but they seek not the welfare of Zion." (2 Ne. 26:29.)

20. *False prophets work false miracles and engage in sorceries, witchcrafts, and magic.*

We have seen the priests of Pharaoh perform false miracles by the power of the devil. Among the Nephites in their darkest hour "there were sorceries, and witchcrafts, and magics; and the power of the evil one was wrought upon all the face of the land." (Morm. 1:19.) Witchcraft and sorcery and false miracles are not things of the past. Today also there are mediums and wizards who chirp and mutter as they arrange for their devotees to hear from the dead. Today also there are those who pretend to engage in great healing ministries. And what we now see is only the beginning. As the hour of the Second Coming draws nearer, and Satan gains greater power over more of his followers, we shall see even greater outpourings of evil power. Indeed, the day is not far distant when the evil one will make "fire come down from heaven on earth in the sight of men" (Rev. 13:13), and "the spirits of devils, working miracles," will "go forth unto the kings of the earth and of the whole world, to gather them to the battle of that great day of God Almighty" (Rev. 16:14).

21. *False prophets are leaders of apostate groups that have broken away from the true Church.*

Peter climaxes his denunciation of false prophets by speaking of traitors to the truth, deluded persons who are more to be despised and pitied than any of the false prophets of the world. He speaks of apostates who leave the true church to follow their own wayward and ill-conceived courses. "If after they have escaped the pollutions of the world through the knowledge of the Lord and Saviour Jesus Christ," he says, "they are again entangled therein, and overcome, the latter end is worse with them than the beginning. For it had been better for them not to have known the way of righteousness, than, after they have known it, to turn from the holy commandment delivered unto them. But it is happened unto them according to the true proverb, The dog is turned to his own vomit again; and the sow that was washed to her wallowing in the mire." (2 Pet. 2:20-22.)

Would it be amiss for us to conclude this portion of our analysis by applying to the Latter-day Saints the words of the Beloved John, who wrote relative to the former-day saints. "We are of God," he said. "He that knoweth God heareth us; he that is not of God heareth not us. Hereby know we the spirit of truth, and the spirit of error." (1 Jn. 4:6.)

Chapter 8

THE TIMES OF RESTITUTION

The Promised Age of Restoration

Shortly after the ascension of the Lord Jesus into heaven, where he now sits on the right hand of God the Father Almighty, Peter took it upon himself to do what he had seen his Master do. Peter healed a man without reference to the faith of the decrepit person. Jesus had opened the eyes of one who was born blind in order to gain a congregation and to set the stage for a glorious proclamation of his own divine Sonship. All this is set forth in the sermon about the Good Shepherd. (John 9-10.) Peter healed "a certain man lame from his mother's womb" for a similar reason.

The man, begging at the gate of the temple, asked for alms from Peter and John. Peter said, "Look on us," which the man did. Then from the lips of the Chief Apostle came these divine words: "Silver and gold have I none; but such as I have give I thee: In the name of Jesus Christ of Nazareth rise up and walk." The man arose, walked, leaped, praised God, and showed himself to all the people in the temple. The people, knowing the man was born lame, "were filled with wonder and amazement," and all ran together in Solomon's porch.

Peter had his congregation. As when Jesus opened the blind eyes, the people could not do other than listen to the one who had wrought so great a miracle in their presence. "Ye men of Israel, why marvel ye at this?" Peter asked. "Or why look ye so earnestly on us, as though by our own power or holiness we had made this man to walk?"

Then came the kind of a sermon that no false prophet would ever preach. Peter's words were not designed to tickle their ears, or to please their vanity, or to encourage them to pay him for preaching. "The God of our fathers, hath glorified his Son Jesus," Peter said, "whom ye delivered up, and denied him in the presence of Pilate, when he was determined to let him go. But ye denied the Holy One and the Just, and desired a murderer to be granted unto you; and killed the Prince of life, whom God hath raised from the dead; whereof we are witnesses."

That is: 'You caused his arrest; you delivered him to Pilate; you denied him. You chose Barabbas, the murderer, to be released; you are guilty of the death of one who was holy and just and innocent. His blood is upon your hands. You are murderers.' These things must be made clear if we are to understand what follows. Peter is speaking to murderers. "I wot [know] that through ignorance ye did it, as did also your rulers," he then added. They did not know that Jesus was their Lord—on that point they were ignorant; but he was a man who had done nothing worthy of death, and they caused his death. Pilate, on their behalf, issued a legal decree that resulted in a judicial murder.

And because "no murderer hath eternal life abiding in him" (1 Jn. 3:15), Peter is not going to ask them to repent and be baptized. Instead he says: "*Repent ye therefore, and be converted*"— 'Repent and believe; convert your flinty hearts of stone into hearts of flesh; change from your awful state of disbelief and rebellion to one of glorious faith'—"*that your sins may be blotted out*"—'that you may, in the providences of Him who is merciful to those who repent, gain a forgiveness of your sin of shedding innocent blood'—"*when the times of refreshing shall come from the presence of the Lord*"—'when the earth shall be renewed and receive its paradisiacal glory; when all things shall be made new; when there shall be a new heaven and a new earth; when the millennial era shall commence'—"*And he shall send Jesus Christ, which before was preached unto you*"—'when the Lord shall send his Son again; when Jesus shall return to live and reign with men; when the glorious day of the Second Coming of the Son of Man arrives; when Jesus comes again, even the same Jesus whose gospel we now preach'—"*Whom the heaven must receive until the times of restitution of all things, which God hath spoken by the mouth of all his holy prophets since the world began*"—'Which Jesus must remain in heaven until the age of restoration; until the period of time begins in which the Lord shall restore all things; until God commences the restoration of all things known to and predicted by all the holy prophets from the beginning.' (Acts 3:1-21. Italics added.)

That is to say: Christ came once. He was crucified, died, and rose again. He ascended into heaven where he now is. And he shall come again to usher in the Millennium, to refresh the earth, to make of it a new earth, to restore its paradisiacal glory. But he cannot come, and the promised day will not arrive, until a period of time commences which is named the Age of Restoration.

Peter does not say that all things will be restored before the Lord comes. What he does say is: Christ cannot come until the Age of Restoration has its beginning. That age commenced in the spring of 1820 and is now shedding its light and truth abroad, and it will continue to do so until well into the millennial era. That age will include the events incident to the Second Coming and will continue after that glorious and dread day. Indeed, the great reservoir of revealed truth will not be made available until after the Lord comes and destroys the unbelieving and rebellious. "When the Lord shall come, he shall reveal all things," our scripture recites, "things which have passed, and hidden things which no man knew, things of the earth, by which it was made, and the purpose and the end thereof—things most precious, things that are above, and things that are beneath, things that are in the earth, and upon the earth, and in heaven." (D&C 101:32-34.)

What is it that shall be restored in the times of restitution of all things? What is it that God hath spoken by the mouth of all his holy prophets since the world began?

It is everything pertaining to the salvation and exaltation of his children. God's eternal purposes are to bring to pass the immortality and eternal life of man. He has no others. His plan of salvation is the gospel of God. By obedience to its laws and conditions, men have power to advance and progress and become like him. By such obedience, they have power to gain eternal life, which is the kind of life he lives.

It is everything pertaining to the divine Sonship of the Lord Jesus Christ—how he was chosen and foreordained in the councils of eternity to be the Savior of the world and the Redeemer of men; how he was born as the Son of God, inheriting from his Father the power of immortality; how he took upon himself the sins of all men, beginning in Gethsemane as he sweat great drops of blood from every pore, and continuing on the cross when the sufferings of Gethsemane were renewed; how he abolished death and brought life and immortality to light through the gospel; how he burst the bands of death and brought to pass the resurrection for all men; and how he will come in glorious immortality to live and reign on earth for a thousand years.

It is all of the gifts of the Spirit—the miracles, signs, and wonders of the past. It is revelation and visions and a knowledge of the wonders of eternity. It is the way and the means and the power whereby the Holy Spirit of God can make of man a new creature— can burn dross and evil out of him as though by fire; can bring him forth in a newness of life, free from carnality and sin; and can sanctify his soul and make him a fit companion for Gods and angels.

It is the fulness of the everlasting gospel. It is priesthoods, and keys, and powers, and authorities. It is the truths of salvation as they were taught in wondrous glory in the City of Holiness where Enoch dwelt. It is the covenant God made with Abraham that in him and in his seed all generations should be blessed.

It is the keys of creation as used by Jehovah and Michael in the creation of the earth. It is the keys of presidency over all men as used by Adam and Noah, the fathers of all men from their days onward. It is the keys to gather Israel and lead them from the darkness of their present Egyptian bondage into the light of their promised land. It is the sealing power possessed by a lowly Tishbite who became a mighty prophet. It is the apostolic commission vested in Peter, James, and John, and their fellows. It is every key, power, and authority ever possessed by any prophet and seer in any location and in any age. All are to come again in the dispensation of the fulness of times.

But it is more. It is also governments and kingdoms. It is lands and properties and peoples. The church and kingdom of God on earth is to be set up again. Israel is to be gathered into the church. In due course the political kingdom is to be restored to Israel. The Book of Mormon shall come forth, including the sealed portion. The lost portions of the Bible shall again be read from the housetops. The gospel is to go to the Lamanites, and they shall become again a pure and a delightsome people. Jerusalem of old shall be rebuilt in its old place, and a New Jerusalem shall arise in America. The knowledge of God shall cover the earth as the waters cover the sea, and once again men shall speak a pure language. Men shall be resurrected, and all of the eternal purposes of the Lord shall come to pass.

Was this earth once a garden fair, without thorns, thistles, briers, and noxious weeds? It shall be renewed and receive again its paradisiacal glory. The burning desert shall blossom as the rose and become once again like the garden of the Lord. Was it once blessed with rolling hills, pleasant valleys, and rivers of splendor? In the promised day every mountain shall be made low, every valley shall be exalted, and the rough places shall be made smooth.

Was there a day when the continents were one land and the islands were not separated from them? Such shall come again. The great deep shall be driven back into the north and the land surfaces of the earth shall be one again as they were in the days before they were divided.

Did Enoch's Zion, filled with righteous souls, once grace the earth? So shall it yet be. He and all his city shall return to dwell in peace on earth with those who once again can abide the laws which caused the ancient ones to be translated. Was the earth once new, glorious, and paradisiacal in nature? So shall it be again. The earth shall be renewed. There will be a new heaven and a new earth whereon dwelleth righteousness.

All things pertaining to the creation and peopling and destiny of the earth—these are the things that God hath spoken by the mouth of all his holy prophets. This revealed knowledge shall be restored, and the events of which they spoke shall come to pass, all during that age of the earth known as the times of restitution. Of all these things we shall speak more particularly hereafter in their proper settings.

The Age of Renaissance and Preparation

The times of restitution—the age of restoration—was not born without a long period of gestation. This glorious and wondrous age, in which floods of celestial light were destined to shine again in the hearts of men, did not spring into being full grown. The Age of Restoration did not burst forth unannounced in the midst of the dark ages; there was no sudden flash or blaze of heavenly light in the midnight sky. Its dawning came gradually as rays of light and truth and understanding pierced the eastern sky. The stranglehold of the great and abominable church on the minds and souls of men was not broken with one burst of Sampsonian strength. And even now, in modern times, the iron grasp of evil keeps the masses of men from seeing through the mists of darkness that yet cover the earth.

The times of restitution in which the Lord shall "do his work, his strange work; and bring to pass his act, his strange act" (Isa. 28:21), had its forerunners. As Elias went before Messias, so the Renaissance and then the Reformation prepared the way for the Restoration. Beginning in the 14th century (the 1300s) there was a new birth of learning. An inquiring spirit spread forth among men. Universities sprang up. There were splendid achievements in art and architecture, and scientific discoveries began to shake the creeds of darkness. By about 1450 printing presses were spreading the ideas of the new intellectuals. The Gutenberg Bible came forth in 1456.

"The urge to inquire, to debate, and seek new explanations spread from the field of classical learning into that of religious studies," the astute Winston Churchill tells us. "Greek and even Hebrew texts, as well as Latin, were scrutinised afresh. Inevitably this led to the questioning of accepted religious beliefs. The Renaissance bred the Reformation. In 1517, at the age of thirty-four, Martin Luther, a German priest, denounced the sale of Indulgences, nailed his theses on this and other matters on the door of Wittenberg Castle church, and embarked on his venturesome intellectual foray with the Pope. What began as a protest against Church practices soon became a challenge to Church doctrine. In this struggle Luther displayed qualities of determination and conviction at the peril of the stake which won him his name and fame. He started or gave an impulse to a movement which within a decade swamped the Continent, and proudly bears the general title of the Reformation. It took different forms in different countries, particularly in Switzerland under Zwingli and Calvin. The latter's influence spread from Geneva across France to the Netherlands and Britain, where it was most strongly felt in Scotland. . . .

"Heresies there had always been, and over the centuries feeling against the Church had often run strong in almost every country of Europe. But the schism that had begun with Luther was novel and formidable. All the actors in it, the enemies and the defenders of Rome alike, were still deeply influenced by medieval views. They thought of themselves as restorers of the purer ways of ancient times and of the early Church. But the Reformation added to the confusion and uncertainty of an age in which men and states were tugging unwillingly and unwittingly at the anchors that had so long held Europe. After a period of ecclesiastical strife between the Papacy and the Reformation, Protestantism was established over a great part of the Continent under a variety of sects and schools, of which Lutheranism covered the larger area. The Church in Rome, strengthened by the heart-searching Catholic revival known as the Counter-Reformation and in the more worldly sphere by the activities of the Inquisition, proved able to maintain itself through a long series of religious wars."

Then Churchill, quoting Charles Beard, poses some blunt questions: " 'Was, then, the Reformation, from the intellectual point of view, a failure? Did it break one yoke only to impose another? We are obliged to confess that, especially in Germany, it soon parted company with free learning; that it turned its back upon culture, that it lost itself in a maze of arid theological controversy, that it held out no hand of welcome to awakening

91

science. . . . Even at a later time it has been the divines who have most loudly declared their allegiance to the theology of the Reformation who have also looked most askance at science, and claimed for their statements an entire independence of modern knowledge. I do not know how, on any ordinary theory of the Reformation, it is possible to answer the accusations implied in these facts. The most learned, the profoundest, the most tolerant of modern theologians, would be the most reluctant to accept in their fullness the systems of Melancthon and of Calvin. . . . The fact is, that while the services which the Reformers rendered to truth and liberty by their revolt against the unbroken supremacy of medieval Christianity cannot be over-estimated, it was impossible for them to settle the questions which they raised. Not merely did the necessary knowledge fail them, but they did not even see the scope of the controversies in which they were engaged. It was their part to open the flood-gates; and the stream, in spite of their well-meant efforts to check and confine it, has since rushed impetuously on, now destroying old landmarks, now fertilising new fields, but always bringing with it life and refreshment. To look at the Reformation by itself, to judge it only by its theological and ecclesiastical development, is to pronounce it a failure; to consider it as part of a general movement of European thought, to show its essential connection with ripening scholarship and advancing science, to prove its necessary alliance with liberty, to illustrate its slow growth into toleration, is at once to vindicate its past and to promise it the future.' " (Winston S. Churchill, *A History of the English-Speaking People* [New York: Dodd, Mead & Co., 1956], vol. 2, pp. 4-8.)

As they view things, the scholars of the world know that the Reformers and the Reformation did not solve the problems of an ancient religion or of an awakening science. From our vantage point, we gain a clearer perspective. We know that Christ in his day brought the bright light of the glorious gospel; that thereafter there was darkness; pure truths were twisted into evil heresies; godly conduct degenerated into carnal lewdness. Then came the Renaissance, as the light of Christ refreshed the consciences of men; as art and architecture and learning were born anew; as science and a search for truth outside the creeds found place in the hearts of men. Then came the Reformation; the Catholic yoke was broken; Protestantism arose and commanded the allegiance of peoples and nations. And thus for half a millennium the Lord channeled the thinking of men and prepared them spiritually for the day of revelation and restoration, the day when the bright light would shine again.

America: The Land of Liberty

America was discovered, colonized, and made into a great nation so that the Lord would have a proper place both to restore the gospel and from which to send it forth to all other nations. As a prelude to his coming, and so the promised work of restoration would roll forward, the foundations of the American nation were laid in the days of the Renaissance and the Reformation. "The Spirit of God," meaning the light of Christ, rested upon "a man among the Gentiles," meaning Columbus. He discovered America in 1492. Then other Gentiles, guided from on high in like manner, "went forth out of captivity" to colonize the New World. Then came the Revolutionary War in which "the Gentiles that had gone out of captivity were delivered by the power of God out of the hands of all other nations." (1 Ne. 13:12-19.) Nephi saw all this in vision, and through it the foundations were laid for the establishment of the United States of America.

Be it noted that those who colonized America "went forth out of captivity." That is, they left the Catholic and Protestant nations of Europe in search of religious freedom; they, as pilgrims and separatists, sought a place where they could worship God according to the dictates of their conscience rather than as decreed by the reigning monarchs of the moment.

The Protestant churches of Europe freed themselves from the yoke of Rome, only to create their own state churches, which in turn compelled all nationals to worship as decreed by the particular brand of Protestantism that prevailed in their nation. There was no religious freedom as such, nor could there be as long as the civil law dictated forms and systems of worship.

But in America it was different. No one colony had power to

force all others to worship its way. Out of political necessity the Thirteen Colonies, when they united to form a new nation, were forced to approve religious freedom and to let each church in each colony go its own way. Thus, in the providences of the Lord, freedom of worship was guaranteed in the new nation. And thus, speaking of this and other freedoms, Jesus, after his resurrection, said to the Nephites: "It is wisdom in the Father" that the Gentiles "should be established in this land, and be set up as a free people by the power of the Father," that the Book of Mormon and the gospel might be taken to the Lamanites, "that the covenant of the Father may be fulfilled which he hath covenanted with his people." (3 Ne. 21:4.)

The Constitution of the United States is the political document that guarantees to men their freedom; it is the supreme law of the land; it is the standard by which all laws are measured. "I established the Constitution of this land," the Lord says, "by the hands of wise men whom I raised up unto this very purpose." The Constitution and the laws enacted in harmony therewith "should be maintained for the rights and protection of all flesh, according to just and holy principles." (D&C 101:76-80.) "And that law of the land which is constitutional, supporting that principle of freedom in maintaining rights and privileges," the Lord also says, "belongs to all mankind, and is justifiable before me." (D&C 98:4-10.)

There is, thus, one great nation on earth that exalts and protects freedom and liberty and the right to worship as one chooses. "This land," the land of America, "shall be a land of liberty," saith the Lord, "and there shall be no kings upon the land. . . . For I, the Lord, the king of heaven, will be their king, and I will be a light unto them forever, that hear my words." (2 Ne. 10:10-14.) And further, in Moroni's language: "This is a choice land, and whatsoever nation shall possess it shall be free from bondage, and from captivity, and from all other nations under heaven, if they will but serve the God of the land, who is Jesus Christ." (Ether 2:12.)

This is the land of prophecy and of destiny. Here the gospel was restored; here men are free to worship; here they have the talents and the means to carry the word to other nations. This is the Lord's base of operations in the last days. From here the word of

94

truth shall go forth to prepare a people for the Second Coming of the Son of Man. This land, Isaiah says, "sendeth ambassadors"—the elders of Israel—to all the "inhabitants of the world, and dwellers on the earth." They shall say: "See ye, when he lifteth up an ensign on the mountains; and when he bloweth a trumpet, hear ye." (Isa. 18:1-3.) That call is now going forth.

Chapter 9

THE RESTORATION OF THE GLORIOUS GOSPEL

Restoration and the Eternal Plan

In the eternal providences of Him whose work and glory it is to save his children, an immutable decree went forth in the beginning. The Eternal One swore, with his own voice and in his own name—with a certainty that is as firm as the pillars of heaven—that in the last days he would restore the fulness of his everlasting gospel.

This restoration of the glorious gospel of God would prepare a people for the Second Coming of the Son of Man. This restoration of the plan of salvation would make eternal life available to more of his children—more? ten thousand times ten thousand more—than all the preaching and all the labors of all the prophets of all the ages. This restoration of all the truths, and all the powers, and all the graces ever enjoyed and possessed by any people would be the most glorious and wondrous event ever to occur on planet earth, save only the atoning sacrifice of the Son of God. And it was destined to take place in "the times of restitution" and to be part of the promised "restitution of all things, which God hath spoken by the mouth of all his holy prophets since the world began." (Acts 3:21.)

In the beginning when men were few and times were simple, the Lord revealed the fulness of his everlasting gospel. To Adam

96

and his children the command came: "Believe on his Only Begotten Son, even him who he declared should come in the meridian of time, who was prepared from before the foundation of the world." Men thus came to know that salvation is in Christ and that to gain such a great reward they must believe and obey his law. "And thus the Gospel began to be preached, from the beginning, being declared by holy angels sent forth from the presence of God, and by his own voice, and by the gift of the Holy Ghost. And thus all things were confirmed unto Adam, by an holy ordinance, and the Gospel preached, and a decree sent forth, that it should be in the world [in a series of dispensations], until the end thereof." (Moses 5:57-59.)

And thus also was the pattern set for the giving of the gospel to men in whatever age and under whatever circumstances it was destined to come. Three means of divine direction were and are required:

1. Men must hear the voice of God. Those holy beings whom it is life eternal to know must reveal themselves from heaven. God stands revealed or he remains forever unknown. The heavens must rend; revelations must rain forth; and the things of God must be manifest in plainness and purity to those who dwell on earth.

2. Holy angels must minister to mortals. They must confer priesthoods and keys; they must reveal truths and doctrines; they must identify themselves as the fellow servants of the preachers of righteousness who dwell on earth.

3. Men must receive the gift of the Holy Ghost. Thereby revelation comes, for the Holy Ghost is a revelator; he knows all things and gives them freely to all who attune themselves to his eternal broadcasts. Thereby dross and evil is burned out of human souls as though by fire, for the Holy Ghost brings the baptism of fire. Thereby men are born again and their souls sanctified, for the Holy Ghost is a sanctifier. Thereby all of the gifts and signs and miracles are found among the faithful, for the Holy Ghost, who is no respecter of persons, gives to all in accordance with their faith. And by the power of the Spirit—the Holy Spirit of Promise—men are sealed up unto eternal life.

What, then, is the gospel that is dispensed from heaven to

men? It is the great and eternal plan of salvation. It is the way and the means provided by the Father whereby his spirit children—Christ included—can advance and progress and become like him. It is the trials and training of preexistence, the problems and probation of this mortality, and the glory and honor of a future day. It is the atonement of Christ, the ransom from the fall, the plan of redemption. It is "the gospel of God," as Paul said, "Concerning his Son Jesus Christ our Lord, which was made of the seed of David according to the flesh; And declared to be the Son of God with power, according to the spirit of holiness, by the resurrection from the dead. . . . It is the power of God unto salvation." (Rom. 1:1-4, 16.)

And because it is the power of God that saves men, it includes both what the Lord does for us and what we must do for ourselves to be saved. On his part it is the atonement; on our part it is obedience to all that is given us of God. Thus the gospel includes every truth, every principle, every law—all that men must believe and know. Thus it includes every ordinance, every rite, every performance—all that men must do to please their Maker. Thus it includes every priesthood, every key, every power—all that men must receive to have their acts bound on earth and sealed eternally in the heavens.

The fulness of the everlasting gospel, meaning all that is needed to enable men to gain a fulness of everlasting salvation, has been given of God in successive dispensations. The Adamic age set the pattern, and there has been a partial or total restoration in each succeeding dispensation. Jesus thus restored the gospel of the kingdom in his day. He brought back again much of what the ancient prophets and saints had enjoyed in their days. The total apostasy following his day calls for a total restoration in the last days.

This promised, destined, and decreed latter-day restoration is so replete with glory and wonder; it is so infinite and eternal in scope and importance; it is destined to affect so many of the spirit hosts of heaven, all children of the Eternal Father; it does and will mean so much to so many—that all of the holy prophets knew it would come to pass, and almost all who wrote prophetically have had more or less to say about it. "Surely the Lord God will do nothing, but he revealeth his secret unto his servants the prophets." (Amos 3:7.)

Whenever prophets so live as to receive a knowledge of things past, present, and future, such is showered upon them. All that they have said about the gathering of Israel, the return of the Ten Tribes, the coming forth of the Book of Mormon, the establishment of Zion, the building of a New Jerusalem and the restoration of the Old Jerusalem, of the Second Coming of the Lord, and of the millennial era—all these things and more—are part of what is involved in the restoration of the gospel in the last days. We shall consider them all, each in its place and position in the eternal scheme of things. First, however, we shall note a few of the promises, given in general terms, relative to the restoration of the gospel as such.

Moroni and the Other Angelic Ministrants

John, the Beloved Revelator, banished on Patmos for the love of God and the testimony of Jesus, saw in vision the restoration of the glorious gospel in the last days. "And I saw another angel fly in the midst of heaven," he said, "having the everlasting gospel to preach unto them that dwell on the earth, and to every nation, and kindred, and tongue, and people."

How the sects of Christendom must shake in their hollow shells! God Almighty, by the mouth of his prophet, says there is to be revelation in the last days, in a day subsequent to New Testament times, in a day following the great apostasy. An angelic ministrant descends from the courts of glory. What message does he bring? Behold, it is the everlasting gospel, the eternal plan of salvation, the same saving truths had in all dispensations. It is given again to men. The age of restoration sheds forth its brilliant light.

And to whom shall this same gospel, this gospel had of old, this gospel which is everlasting, to whom shall it be preached when the angel comes? To all who dwell upon the earth, to the inhabiters of every nation, to all the kindreds of men, to those who speak every tongue, and to every people on the face of the globe—all are to hear the message. And if it is to be offered to all, do any of them already have it? Truly, John is seeing the heavens rend, revelation is commencing anew, the angels of God are coming again as they did of old; but John is doing more—he is testifying of the absolute, total spiritual darkness that covers the earth. The new gospel, which is the old gospel, which is the everlasting gospel, is being restored for the blessing of all men. None have it; it is coming again for the benefit and blessing of all.

With a loud voice—there is no fear, nothing is hidden, nothing is done in secret—with the trump of God, the angel says: "Fear God, and give glory to him; for the hour of his judgment is come: and worship him that made heaven, and earth, and the sea, and the fountains of waters." Immediately thereafter another angel announces the fall of Babylon, which is the destruction of the great and abominable church. (Rev. 14:6-8.)

Once again men are invited—nay, commanded—to worship the true and living God who is the Creator of all things. The Second Coming is soon to be, and evil Babylon is about to be burned with unquenchable fire. Worship God! "Worship the Father in spirit and in truth; for the Father seeketh such to worship him. For unto such hath God promised his Spirit. And they who worship him, must worship in spirit and in truth." (JST, John 4:25-26.)

No longer does it suffice to rely on the creeds that make of God a spirit essence filling immensity, which has neither body, parts, or passions. To every man who has thus made "gods unto himself, and they are no gods," to all who have thus "inherited lies, vanity, and things wherein there is no profit," to all who will hear his voice, he now acclaims: "Behold, I will this once cause them to know, I will cause them to know mine hand and my might; and they shall know that my name is The Lord." (Jer. 16:19-21.) That this new knowledge of the ancient God was first manifest in the spring of 1820, with the appearance of the Father and the Son to the first prophet of this dispensation, is, of course, known to all the saints.

Truly, as the scripture saith, murder and tyranny and oppression, during the long days of spiritual darkness, have been "supported and urged on and upheld by the influence of that spirit which hath so strongly riveted the creeds of the fathers, who have inherited lies, upon the hearts of the children, and filled the world with confusion, and has been growing stronger and stronger, and is now the very mainspring of all corruption, and the whole earth groans under the weight of its iniquity. It is an iron yoke, it is a strong band; they are the very handcuffs, and chains, and shackles, and fetters of hell." (D&C 123:7-8.)

But thanks be to God, in this age of restoration, the voice of God is heard again. He speaks. His angel descends and the mighty restoration is underway. Moroni, the first great angel of the restoration, came many times. His first appearance was during the night of September 21-22, 1823. He revealed the hiding place of the Nephite scriptures, instructed Joseph Smith relative to their translation, and gave him the care and custody of the gold plates for an appointed season. The Book of Mormon was published to the world in 1830. This volume of holy scripture contains the fulness of the everlasting gospel, meaning that it is a record of God's dealings with a people who had the fulness of the gospel, and in it is an inspired account of what men must do to gain eternal life in our Father's kingdom. It contains the "word" of the gospel.

In November 1831, addressing himself to the "inhabitants of the earth," the Lord said: "I have sent forth mine angel flying through the midst of heaven, having the everlasting gospel, who hath appeared unto some and hath committed it unto man, who shall appear unto many that dwell on the earth." (D&C 133:36.) Up to this point in time, Moroni had come with the Book of Mormon, John the Baptist had restored the Aaronic Priesthood and its keys, and Peter, James, and John had conferred upon mortal men the Melchizedek Priesthood and the keys of the kingdom, and the Church had been organized. Other angels would thereafter bring their keys. The Lord's angels were bringing to pass the promised restoration, a restoration of the "word" of the gospel and a restoration of the "power" of the gospel. (1 Thes. 1:5.) Of the preaching of this gospel in all the world before the Second Coming we shall speak more particularly hereafter.

Elias of the Restoration

In one or many ancient scriptures, none of which have been preserved for us, the word of the Lord, spoken with prophetic fervor, acclaimed that Elias would come and restore all things before the Second Coming of the Lord. Would God that we now had this ancient prophetic word as someday we shall. Whether it is revealed anew to us before or after the Second Coming may well depend upon our spiritual preparation to receive it. But thanks be to Him from whom revelations come, we do have enough scriptural references to it so that we can envision with some clarity the doctrine relative to Elias of the Restoration.

It is perfectly clear that the Jews in the day of Jesus knew that Elias was to come and restore all things. "When the Jews sent priests and Levites from Jerusalem" to Bethabara to inquire of John the Baptist what right he had to baptize, the inquisitors asked: "Who art thou?" They also raised the issue as to whether he was Elias. "And he confessed, and denied not that he was Elias; but confessed, saying; I am not the Christ." Then came the query: "How then art thou Elias?" His answer: "I am not that Elias who was to restore all things." Next came his great pronouncement that he was sent to prepare the way before the Lord as foretold by Isaiah. But his interrogators still persisted. "Why baptizest thou then," they asked, "if thou be not the Christ, nor Elias who was to restore all things?" In answer, John testified that Christ himself was the Elias who was to restore saving truths for their day. "I baptize with water," he said, "but there standeth one among you, whom ye know not; He it is of whom I bear record. He is that prophet, even Elias, who, coming after me, is preferred before me, whose shoe's latchet I am not worthy to unloose, or whose place I am not able to fill; for he shall baptize, not only with water, but with fire, and with the Holy Ghost." (JST, John 1:20-28.)

Peter, James, and John, the chosen three, smitten with wondering awe, saw Moses and Elijah (Elias) minister to their Lord and Friend on the Mount of Transfiguration. Coming down from the heights of Hermon, they pondered how it was that the prophetic word said Elias would come *before* the Messiah to prepare the way, and yet here on the Holy Mount he had come *after*. They asked: "Why then say the scribes that Elias must first come?" Jesus confirmed the verity of the ancient word. He said: "Elias truly shall first come, and restore all things, as the prophets have written." There would be a day of restoration in the last days. Then the ancient word about Elias would be fulfilled.

As pertaining to their day, Jesus then said: "And again I say unto you that Elias has come already, concerning whom it is written, Behold, I will send my messenger, and he shall prepare the way before me; and they knew him not, and have done unto him whatsoever they listed. Likewise shall also the Son of man suffer of them. But I say unto you, Who is Elias? Behold, this is Elias, whom I send to prepare the way before me." Two Eliases are involved, one who went before and another who came after. "Then the disciples understood that he spake unto them of John the Baptist, and also of another who should come and restore all things, as it is written by the prophets." (JST, Matt. 17:9-14.)

There is no valid reason for confusion as to the identity and mission of Elias. There was a man named Elias who came to Joseph Smith and Oliver Cowdery on April 3, 1836, in the Kirtland Temple to restore "the gospel of Abraham." (D&C 110:12.) Whether he was Abraham himself or someone else from his dispensation, we do not know. Elias is one of the names of Gabriel who is Noah, and it was in this capacity that Gabriel visited Zacharias the father of John the Baptist. (D&C 27:6-7.) Elias is the Greek form of the Hebrew Elijah, and in this sense has reference to the prophet from Tishbe. Elias is also the title or name of a forerunner who goes before to prepare the way for someone who is greater; this is the doctrine of Elias, and in this sense John the Baptist was both Elias and an Elias. John came in the way that Gabriel (who is Elias) promised, that is, "in the spirit and power of Elias, . . . to make ready a people prepared for the Lord." (Luke 1:17.) In this sense also, the Aaronic Priesthood is the Priesthood of Elias because it prepares men for the greater priesthood. We shall hereafter speak of Joseph Smith as the Elias who came to prepare the way for the Second Coming.

But, as we have seen, there is also an Elias of the Restoration, meaning that there is also a doctrine of Elias that pertains not to preparation alone, but to restoration. Christ was Elias in his day because he restored the gospel for those then living. In our revelations the Lord says that Gabriel (Noah) is the "Elias, to whom I have committed the keys of bringing to pass the restoration of all things spoken by the mouth of all the holy prophets since the world began, concerning the last days." (D&C 27:6.) The one who holds the keys is the one who directs the work; keys are the right of presidency. Thus Gabriel, who stands next to Michael (Adam) in the heavenly hierarchy, has a great directing and supervising work in connection with the restoration of all things.

John the Revelator not only saw an "angel fly in the midst of heaven, having the everlasting gospel to preach unto them that dwell on the earth" (Rev. 14:6) in the last days, but he also "saw four angels standing on the four corners of the earth, holding the four winds of the earth, that the wind should not blow on the earth, nor on the sea, nor on any tree." (Rev. 7:1.) The mission of these four angels is not as apparent as is the mission of the angelic ministrant who is named as bringing the gospel to all men. That our understanding of the restoration of the gospel might be perfected, however, the Prophet Joseph Smith, writing by the spirit of revelation, said of them: "We are to understand that they are four angels sent forth from God, to whom is given power over the four parts of the earth, to save life and to destroy; these are they who have the everlasting gospel to commit to every nation, kindred, tongue, and people; having power to shut up the heavens, to seal up unto life, or to cast down to the regions of darkness." (D&C 77:8.) Thus there is more than one angel involved in the restoration of the gospel in the last days.

Then John saw yet another heavenly ministrant come forth to play his part in the strange act of the Lord of heaven. "And I saw another angel ascending from the east," he said, "having the seal of the living God: and he cried with a loud voice to the four angels, to whom it was given to hurt the earth and the sea, Saying, Hurt not the earth, neither the sea, nor the trees, till we have sealed the ser-

104

vants of our God in their foreheads." (Rev. 7:2-3.) This refers to sealing the servants of God up unto eternal life so "they shall pass by the angels, and the gods, . . . to their exaltation and glory in all things, as hath been sealed upon their heads, which glory shall be a fulness and a continuation of the seeds forever and ever. Then shall they be gods." (D&C 132:19-20.) And, be it noted, it was Elijah the prophet who restored the sealing power in this dispensation.

Again, so that the divine commission involved might be understood by those who are spiritually literate, the Prophet, as guided by the Spirit, gave this explanation: "We are to understand that the angel ascending from the east is he to whom is given the seal of the living God over the twelve tribes of Israel; wherefore, he crieth unto the four angels having the everlasting gospel, saying: Hurt not the earth, neither the sea, nor the trees, till we have sealed the servants of our God in their foreheads. And, if you will receive it, this is Elias which was to come to gather together the tribes of Israel and restore all things." (D&C 77:9.) Some of this sealing has already occurred—a few of Ephraim and a sprinkling of Manasseh have been sealed up unto eternal life; but the great day of fulfillment, where all Israel is concerned, lies ahead. And again, be it noted, there is more to the labors of Elias of the Restoration than the works of one angel only.

Continuing his inspired exegesis of the hidden truths in the Apocalypse, the Prophet asked: "What are we to understand by the little book which was eaten by John, as mentioned in the 10th chapter of Revelation?" His answer: "We are to understand that it was a mission, and an ordinance, for him to gather the tribes of Israel; behold, this is Elias, who, as it is written, must come and restore all things." (D&C 77:14.) Thus John himself is another of these enigmatic Eliases, all of whose ministries combine to fulfill the ancient word that Elias shall come and restore all things in the times of restitution, which "times" began in the spring of 1820 and shall continue until after the Lord Jesus reigns again among men. We shall have more to say about Elias of the Restoration in chapters 10 and 11.

The Ancient Prophets and the Restored Gospel

We are inclined to believe that all of the ancient prophets knew about the restoration of the gospel in the last days. We know they all had the plan of salvation; they all knew that salvation is in Christ; they all knew he would come to atone for the sins of the world; and they all knew about the Second Coming. Those who were prophets in Israel knew about the latter-day gathering of that chosen people, and some of them knew about the Nephite nation and the coming forth of the Book of Mormon. Implicit in all this is the fact that they must have known about the restoration of that gospel which would gather Israel and prepare a people for the Second Coming of Him in whose name they worshipped the Father.

Our purpose here is simply to sample a few slivers of the prophetic word so as to have the concept before us that the restoration of the gospel in the last days was one of the great wonders toward which the ancients looked with anxious expectation. The Lord's purposes were not hidden from them any more than they are from us. They knew as we know that the day of final triumph and glory for the Lord's people was reserved for the last days.

Joel, for instance, had many things to say about the gathering of Israel, about the wars and desolations of the last days, and about the Second Coming. By his mouth the Lord said: "I will pour out my spirit upon all flesh; and your sons and your daughters shall prophesy, your old men shall dream dreams, your young men shall see visions: And also upon the servants and upon the handmaids in those days will I pour out my spirit." Then, he continues, shall come to pass the wonders in the heavens and on earth, the blood and fire and vapors of smoke, and the sun turning to darkness that shall attend "the great and the terrible day of the Lord." (Joel 2:28-31.) Can there be any doubt that these dreams and visions preceding the Lord's return will come to those who believe and obey the same gospel laws that qualified their forebears to receive like heavenly manifestations? Indeed, when Moroni first came to the Prophet, he quoted these very words from Joel and said they would soon be fulfilled. (JS-H 1:41.)

When Isaiah promised that the Lord would "set up an ensign

106

for the nations" and gather the dispersed of Israel, the ensign, the standard, the divine flag around which all men should rally was to be the holy gospel. (Isa. 5:26; 11:12.) When the Lord said, as Isaiah records, "Forasmuch as this people draw near me with their mouth, and with their lips do honour me, but have removed their heart far from me, and their fear toward me is taught by the precept of men: Therefore, behold, I will proceed to do a marvellous work among this people, even a marvellous work and a wonder: for the wisdom of their wise men shall perish, and the understanding of their prudent men shall be hid" (Isa. 29:13-14)— when these divine words were uttered, they had reference to the restoration of the gospel in our day. And some of these very words were quoted by the Son of God in the First Vision. (JS-H 1:19.) Many latter-day revelations identify the marvelous work here named as the restored gospel.

When the Lord said, "A law shall proceed from me, and I will make my judgment to rest for a light of the people" (Isa. 51:4); when the call shall go forth, "Arise, shine; for thy light is come, and the glory of the Lord is risen upon thee" (Isa. 60:1); when the pronouncement was made, "The Lord God will cause righteousness and praise to spring forth before all the nations" (Isa. 61:11); when the divine word shall say, "Lift up a standard for the people," and the call shall go forth "unto the end of the world, . . . Behold, thy salvation cometh" (Isa. 62:10-11)—when all these and many like pronouncements were and shall be made, be it known that they all refer to the Lord's great latter-day work of restoration. His purposes were known to his ancient friends.

When the Lord promised to reveal unto scattered Israel "the abundance of peace and truth" (Jer. 33:6), and when he said, "I will give them one heart, and I will put a new spirit within you . . . That they may walk in my statutes, and keep mine ordinances, and do them" (Ezek. 11:17-20)—when all this comes to pass, it will be in and through and because of the restored gospel. His statutes, his laws, and his ordinances make up the gospel. Through them men are born again and receive a new spirit.

Among the Book of Mormon prophets, the word relative to the restoration of the gospel came with that clarity and perfectness for which the Nephite record is renowned. To illustrate: "I will be merciful unto the Gentiles," the Lord told Nephi, for, in the last days, "I will bring forth unto them, in mine own power, much of my gospel, which shall be plain and precious." (1 Ne. 13:34.) Much of the gospel as here used means the fulness of the gospel as we use the term. We have the fulness of the gospel, meaning we have all of the powers and sufficient of the doctrines to enable us to gain a fulness of salvation. We do not have all of the truths and doctrines possessed by the Nephites in their golden era.

One added illustration will suffice. An angel, speaking in the name of the Lord, as prophets on both sides of the veil are wont to do, said to Nephi: "For the time cometh, saith the Lamb of God, that I will work a great and marvelous work among the children of men; a work which shall be everlasting, either on the one hand or on the other—either to the convincing of them unto peace and life eternal, or unto the deliverance of them to the hardness of their hearts and the blindness of their minds unto their being brought down into captivity, and also into destruction, both temporally and spiritually, according to the captivity of the devil." (1 Ne. 14:7.) The gospel saves and the gospel damns. It saves those who believe and obey; it damns those who reject it and continue to walk in carnal ways. It is the standard by which all men, both the great and the small, shall be judged. And thus it is.

Chapter 10

THE DISPENSATION OF THE FULNESS OF TIMES

Elias Restores the Truths and Doctrines

Let us reason by way of analogy. Let us personify two of the greatest events of history. Let us thereby show the relationship that exists between the "times of restitution" and "the dispensation of the fulness of times."

The "times of restitution" has, as it were, a close friend, a relative, someone begotten by the same father, carried in the same womb, and born in the same family. His name is "the dispensation of the fulness of times." These two are not identical twins, but they are brothers in a closely knit family. The times of restitution was born first; he came to prepare the way for his younger brother, the dispensation of the fulness of times. With this second son came the greater power and glory. In his hands we find the fulness of the everlasting gospel, which itself is the power of God unto salvation.

These twain were born in the household of faith, and their names were selected by revelation. The times of restitution is so named because he is the age of restoration, the age in which God has promised to restore all things, all truths, all powers, all that he hath spoken by the mouth of all his holy prophets since the world began, all this and more. It is the age in which the Lord designs to restore the earth itself to its primeval and paradisiacal state. The dispensation of the fulness of times gains his divine name because he is the dispensation of the fulness of dispensations, or the time of the fulness of times, or the gospel age in which every truth and every power possessed in any dispensation of the past shall be restored.

The times of restitution is a special friend of Peter. Indeed, we heard the Chief Apostle say that the Lord Jesus, who has all power, must remain in heaven and cannot return in glory to reign mightily among his saints, until after this age of restoration commences. The dispensation of the fulness of times developed an especial fondness for Paul, and the Apostle to the Gentiles prophesied about him. Among other things, he said that "the God and Father of our Lord Jesus Christ" has "made known unto us the mystery of his will, according to his good pleasure which he hath purposed in himself." The "mystery of his will," his strange act, the glorious events reserved by him to take place in the last days are these: "That in the dispensation of the fulness of times he might gather together in one all things in Christ, both which are in heaven, and which are on earth; even in him." (Eph. 1:3, 9-10.)

All things! O how glorious is the promise! Already the heavens have been rent and the saving truths of the gospel are with men. However dark it may be among the cults of men and in the halls where false doctrines are taught, the light of heaven shines in the hearts of the saints. And the promised outpouring of divine truth has scarcely begun. To his saints who have made everlasting covenant with him, to the faithful who have received the gift of the Holy Ghost, to all those who love and serve him "in righteousness and in truth," the promises are infinite and eternal. "To them will I reveal all mysteries, yea, all the hidden mysteries of my kingdom from days of old," the Lord says, "and for ages to come, will I make known unto them the good pleasure of my will concerning all things pertaining to my kingdom." How glorious is this word!

Of them the heavenly Voice acclaims: "Yea, even the wonders of eternity shall they know, and things to come will I show them, even the things of many generations. And their wisdom shall be great, and their understanding reach to heaven; and before them the wisdom of the wise shall perish, and the understanding of the prudent shall come to naught."

How can all this be? The Lord continues: "For by my Spirit will I enlighten them, and by my power will I make known unto them the secrets of my will—yea, even those things which eye has not seen, nor ear heard, nor yet entered into the heart of man." (D&C 76:5-10.) Truly, the things of God are known only by the power of his Spirit!

When shall all this be? To his saints the divine word is: "God shall give unto you knowledge by his Holy Spirit, yea, by the unspeakable gift of the Holy Ghost"—note it well, knowledge "that has not been revealed since the world was until now." It shall be knowledge "which our forefathers have awaited with anxious expectation to be revealed in the last times." It shall be knowledge "which their minds were pointed to by the angels, as held in reserve for the fulness of their glory." It is destined to be revealed in "a time to come in the which nothing shall be withheld, whether there be one God or many gods, they shall be manifest. All thrones and dominions, principalities and powers, shall be revealed and set forth upon all who have endured valiantly for the gospel of Jesus Christ."

Nor is even this all. The divine word continues: "And also, if there be bounds set to the heavens or to the seas, or to the dry land, or to the sun, moon, or stars—All the times of their revolutions, all the appointed days, months, and years, and all their glories, laws, and set times, shall be revealed in the days of the dispensation of the fulness of times—According to that which was ordained in the midst of the Council of the Eternal God of all other gods before this world was, that should be reserved unto the finishing and the end thereof, when every man shall enter into his eternal presence and into his immortal rest." (D&C 121:26-32.)

"And not only this, but those things which never have been revealed from the foundation of the world, but have been kept hid from the wise and prudent, shall be revealed unto babes and sucklings in this, the dispensation of the fulness of times." (D&C 128:18.) "For I deign to reveal unto my church," the Lord says, "things which have been kept hid from before the foundation of the world, things that pertain to the dispensation of the fulness of times." (D&C 124:41.)

The door to the dispensation of the fulness of times was opened in the spring of 1820 when the Father and the Son appeared to Joseph Smith, and it will not be closed until "the Lord shall come" and "reveal all things." (D&C 101:32.) On that glorious spring morning, traditionally believed to be the sixth of April, the Gods of heaven revealed themselves again. "I saw a pillar of light exactly over my head, above the brightness of the sun, which descended gradually until it fell upon me," the Lord's great latter-day prophet tells us. "When the light rested upon me I saw two Personages, whose brightness and glory defy all description, standing above me in the air. One of them spake unto me, calling me by name and said, pointing to the other—*This is My Beloved Son. Hear Him!*"

From them, by the mouth of the Son, the word came that all the churches were wrong; "that all their creeds were an abomination in his sight"; that the ministers of religion "were all corrupt"; and that the worship of the day had "a form of godliness," but not "the power" to save a human soul. (JS-H 1:16-19.)

Thus, as the door of the dispensation opened, revelation commenced anew; the musty creeds of a creaking Christendom were swept aside; the Father and the Son were seen as personal beings in whose image man is made; the fact of universal apostasy was confirmed; and a promise was given that the fulness of the everlasting gospel would soon be restored through Joseph Smith. From that dawning day, the light of truth has grown brighter and brighter, and before the dispensation ends it will be as when the sun shines in its strength.

In due course the Book of Mormon came forth and the unsealed portion was translated and published to bring salvation to all those who will believe it and the testimony it bears of Him by whom salvation comes. Many revelations came through the prophet and seer of our day, of whom the Lord said: "Thou shalt give heed unto all his words and commandments which he shall give unto you as he receiveth them, walking in all holiness before me; for his word ye shall receive, as if from mine own mouth, in all patience and faith." (D&C 21:4-5.)

A portion of the Lord's word that came through Joseph Smith and that has been partially ignored by many Latter-day Saints is found in the revisions he made by the spirit of revelation in the Bible itself. He prepared his New Translation for publication in his day, but the power of evil was so great, and the persecutions and drivings of the saints were so extensive and severe, that the work as then prepared did not come forth in that day. We have since published in the Pearl of Great Price the portions known as the Book of Moses and as the 24th chapter of Matthew. In 1979 the Church also published in the footnotes and appendix of their official Bible many of the major changes. There will, of course, be a future day when added revisions, made with prophetic power, will become part of the Stick of Judah.

In this connection, be it also remembered that the brass plates that Nephi took from Jerusalem contain more of the word of the Lord for the comparable period than does our present Old Testament. They, of course, will also come forth in due time as part of the restoration of all things. Indeed, Lehi prophesied "that these plates of brass should go forth unto all nations, kindreds, tongues, and people who were of his seed. Wherefore, he said that these plates of brass should never perish; neither should they be dimmed any more by time." (1 Ne. 5:18-19.)

Without any question, however, the scripture that is yet to come forth, which will reveal more of the mind and will and purposes of the Lord than any other, is the sealed portion of the Book of Mormon. Moroni says that "there never were greater things made manifest than those which were made manifest unto the brother of Jared." All of these things are recorded in the sealed portion of the book. Of them, the Lord said to Moroni: "They shall not go forth unto the Gentiles until the day that they shall repent of their iniquity, and become clean before the Lord. And in that day that they shall exercise faith in me, saith the Lord, even as the brother of Jared did, that they may become sanctified in me, then will I manifest unto them the things which the brother of Jared saw, even to the unfolding unto them all my revelations, saith Jesus Christ, the Son of God, the Father of the heavens and of the earth, and all things that in them are." (Ether 4:4-7.)

Nephi spoke similarly. He said: "The book shall be sealed; and in the book shall be a revelation from God, from the beginning of the world to the ending thereof. Wherefore, because of the things which are sealed up, the things which are sealed shall not be delivered in the day of the wickedness and abominations of the people. Wherefore the book shall be kept from them."

And further: "The book shall be sealed by the power of God, and the revelation which was sealed shall be kept in the book until the own due time of the Lord, that they may come forth; for behold, they reveal all things from the foundation of the world unto the end thereof." This causes us to ask: How would the worldly-wise react if they learned from the book the falsity of their evolutionary theories and how damning their views are about the creation of the world? How would they react if they found detailed prophecies about Joseph Smith and the dispensation in which we live? What if men found in them the mysteries of the kingdom that are revealed in the temples? Would the Lord thus be casting pearls before swine? Our present revelations do, of course, have many allusions to things that are most assuredly set forth extensively and with clarity in the sealed scriptures.

It seems apparent, under all the circumstances, that the sealed portion of the Book of Mormon will not come forth until after the Lord Jesus comes. Nephi's prophetic word is: "And the day cometh that the words of the book which were sealed shall be read upon the house tops; and they shall be read by the power of Christ; and all things shall be revealed unto the children of men which ever have been among the children of men, and which ever will be even unto the end of the earth." (2 Ne. 27:7-11.)

To those who suppose they believe the Bible but who do not now believe and accept all that the Lord has given to the world, we simply quote what he has to say on the subject: "Wherefore murmur ye, because that ye shall receive more of my word?" (2 Ne. 29:8.) Can men know too much of the mind and will and purposes of their God?

And to those who do not seek for added light and knowledge from on high, our sorrowful word is: From you shall be taken away even that which ye have received.

Elias Restores the Powers and Priesthoods

When the prophetic word calls for the restoration of the fulness of the everlasting gospel in the last days, such includes the restoration of the power and keys and priesthoods that were part and portion of that eternal plan of salvation. The gospel fulness cannot be restored if a vital part is left out.

When the promise is made that Elias must return before the Second Coming and restore all things, that restoration of necessity includes the conferral again upon mortal men of every priesthood held anciently; of every divine and eternal commission ever given to the prophets of old; of the keys of the kingdom, the holy apostleship, and the power to bind on earth and have it sealed everlastingly in the heavens.

If ours is the dispensation in which God has promised to "gather together in one all things in Christ," if this includes "all things . . . which are in heaven, and which are on earth" (Eph. 1:10), and if the priesthood is in heaven and men are on earth, then these two must come together again. Angelic ministrants must bring back the ancient powers.

If "the Holy Priesthood . . . continueth in the church of God in all generations, and is without beginning of days or end of years," and if "this greater priesthood administereth the gospel and holdeth the key of the mysteries of the kingdom" (D&C 84:6, 17-19), then that priesthood must accompany the restoration of the eternal truths comprising the gospel. Otherwise, who would administer the Lord's work on earth, and how would his earthly kingdom be governed? The Lord's house is a house of order and not a house of confusion. Unless there are legal administrators to identify and proclaim his gospel and to govern and control all of his affairs, there would be anarchy.

If, as Paul reasoned, the law of Moses was administered by the lesser priesthood; if the divine word called for Christ and others, coming after Moses and the law, to minister in the greater priesthood; and if, "the priesthood being changed, there is made of necessity a change also of the law" (Heb. 7:12), it follows that the Lord's affairs on earth, in all generations, must be administered by those holding power and authority.

The Aaronic Priesthood administers the law of Moses; the Melchizedek Priesthood, always and everlastingly, administers the gospel. It cannot be otherwise. Thus, if the gospel comes again, the priesthood must come also; otherwise, the revealed system would not be the true gospel, and even if it were, there would be none to administer its affairs on earth.

Thus, none can escape this conclusion: When God Almighty restores the fulness of his everlasting gospel, he restores also the fulness of his everlasting priesthood.

Priesthood is the power and authority of God delegated to man on earth to act in all things for the salvation of men. The keys of the priesthood and of the kingdom are the right of presidency; they are the right to direct the manner in which others use their priesthood; they are the right to preside over and govern all the affairs of the Church, which is the kingdom; they are the right, power, and responsibility to use the priesthood to do all things necessary to save and exalt fallen man, and to carry out all of the purposes of the Lord on earth.

All this being true, we should expect the ancient prophets, as they prophesied of the restoration of the gospel, also to speak of the legal administrators who are destined to administer the Lord's affairs in the last days. And such is the case.

In the last days, when "Zion shall be redeemed with judgment, and her converts with righteousness," the Lord promised Israel: "I will restore thy judges as at the first, and thy counsellers as at the beginning." (Isa. 1:26-27.) Those who serve as bishops are common judges in Israel, and they labor "among the inhabitants of Zion." (D&C 107:74.) "Counsellers" are other priesthood leaders who guide the destinies of the Lord's people.

In the age of restoration the cry shall go forth: "Awake, awake; put on thy strength, O Zion; put on thy beautiful garments, O Jerusalem, the holy city." (Isa. 52:1.) And in answer to the question "What people had Isaiah reference to" in this passage, the Prophet said: "He had reference to those whom God should call in the last days, who should hold the power of priesthood to bring again Zion, and the redemption of Israel; and to put on her strength is to put on the authority of the priesthood, which she, Zion, has a right to by lineage; also to return to that power which she had lost." (D&C 113:7-8.)

These priesthood brethren "shall build the old wastes, they shall raise up the former desolations, and they shall repair the waste cities, the desolations of many generations." Of them the prophetic word acclaims: "Ye shall be named the Priests of the Lord: men shall call you the Ministers of our God." (Isa. 61:4-6.) "They shall declare my glory among the Gentiles," the Lord says. They shall gather Israel, "And I will also take of them for priests and for Levites, saith the Lord." (Isa. 66:19-21.) Through Jeremiah the Lord said of gathered Israel: "And I will set up shepherds over them which shall feed them." (Jer. 23:4.) And the promise is that when the Lord comes, "he shall purify the sons of Levi, and purge them as gold and silver, that they may offer unto the Lord an offering in righteousness." (Mal. 3:3.)

The dispensation of the fulness of times is the greatest of all the dispensations. In it the gospel shall be preached to more people than in all previous dispensations combined. In it the saving ordinances will be performed for the endless hosts of men who lived without a true knowledge of Christ and his saving truths. In it Israel shall be gathered and a people prepared for our Lord's return.

This dispensation of restoration and glory now has all of the power and authority ever possessed by any people in any age. It shall receive in due course all of the light and truth ever revealed. It may be pictured as a great ocean into which all the dispensation-rivers of the past flow. Representatives have come from each of the great biblical dispensations to restore the keys and powers they possessed. It is of them that we shall now speak. Each of them played his part in the restoration of all things, and each, in this sense, came as the Elias of the Restoration.

John the Baptist, our Lord's Elias, came first. On May 15, 1829, he descended from the courts of glory, laid his hands upon

Joseph Smith and Olivery. Cowdery, and said: "Upon you my fellow servants, in the name of Messiah I confer the Priesthood of Aaron, which holds the keys of the ministering of angels, and of the gospel of repentance, and of baptism by immersion for the remission of sins; and this shall never be taken again from the earth, until the sons of Levi do offer again an offering unto the Lord in righteousness." (D&C 13.)

Thus mortal men received both the lesser priesthood and the keys that go with it. They received an endowment of heavenly power, together with the right to use it for the benefit and blessing of their fellowmen. They could now begin to preach the gospel; they could baptize for the remission of sins; but they could not confer the gift of the Holy Ghost. In due course, by the authority they then received, the sons of Levi will offer again their sacrificial performances before the Lord, as Malachi promised.

Shortly thereafter the First Presidency of the Church as it existed in the meridian of time also visited Joseph and Oliver and conferred priesthood and keys upon them. In specifying the mission they performed, the Lord says: "Peter, and James, and John, whom I have sent unto you, by whom I have ordained you and confirmed you to be apostles, and especial witnesses of my name, and bear the keys of your ministry and of the same things which I revealed unto them; Unto whom I have committed the keys of my kingdom, and a dispensation of the gospel for the last times; and for the fulness of times, in the which I will gather together in one all things, both which are in heaven, and which are on earth." (D&C 27:12-13.)

Referring to this glorious visitation, Joseph Smith testifies: "Peter, James, and John [came] in the wilderness between Harmony, Susquehanna county, and Colesville, Broome county, on the Susquehanna river, declaring themselves as possessing the keys of the kingdom, and of the dispensation of the fulness of times." (D&C 128:20.)

What did these ancient apostles restore? They brought back the Melchizedek Priesthood, which administers the gospel and governs the Church and includes the holy apostleship. They conferred the keys of the kingdom and the keys of the dispensation of the fulness of times. As a result, the Church was organized again among men on April 6, 1830. They restored the apostolic commission to go into all the world and preach the gospel with signs following those who believe.

Three ancient prophets came on April 3, 1836, to Joseph Smith and Oliver Cowdery in the Kirtland Temple. Moses committed unto them "the keys of the gathering of Israel from the four parts of the earth, and the leading of the ten tribes from the land of the north." Thus the priesthood was to be used for those purposes.

Elias "committed the dispensation of the gospel of Abraham, saying that in us and our seed all generations after us should be blessed." That is, he brought back the authorization to use the priesthood to perfect eternal family units, even as this commission and covenant was had by Abraham and those who followed after him.

Then Elijah came and restored the sealing power, the power that binds on earth and seals in heaven, the power by which all ordinances have efficacy beyond the grave, the power that turns the hearts of children to their fathers and fathers to their children. It is a power that operates for the living and the dead. (D&C 110:11-16.)

Gabriel who is Noah also came. He "committed the keys of bringing to pass the restoration of all things." (D&C 27:6.) We assume that the continents were divided, beginning in his day, and that he also brought back the power by which the great deep will be commanded to return to its own place in the north so that the islands will become one land again. (D&C 133:23.)

Raphael, whom we assume to have been Enoch or someone from his dispensation, came and committed such keys as appertained to that day. No doubt these included the power to use the priesthood to translate men, as will be the state of all those who abide the day of the Second Coming.

Michael who is Adam came. The keys he brought are not named. But we know he was the presiding high priest over all the earth and that he held the keys of creation and participated in the creation of this earth. We suppose these are the rights and powers he restored. The holy priesthood will be used in eternity as well as

119

in time. It is not only the power and authority to save men here and now; it is also the power by which the worlds were made and by which all things are. It also could well be that Adam, who brought mortality and death into the world, was also permitted to restore the power that brings immortality and life to his descendants. Christ, of course, in the ultimate sense holds the keys of the resurrection and of raising souls in immortality, but, as we also know, it is his practice to operate through his servants, and righteous persons will, in due course, participate in calling their loved ones forth in the resurrection.

These holy angels whom we have named, all taken together, are the Elias of the Restoration. It took all of them to bring to pass the restoration of all the keys and powers and authorities needed to save and exalt man. "For it is necessary in the ushering in of the dispensation of the fulness of times, which dispensation is now beginning to usher in," the Prophet Joseph Smith says, "that a whole and complete and perfect union, and welding together of dispensations, and keys, and powers, and glories should take place, and be revealed from the days of Adam even to the present time." (D&C 128:18.)

All of the keys, powers, and authorities conferred by holy angels upon Joseph Smith and others have been given to each person called to the holy apostleship and set apart to serve in the Council of the Twelve of The Church of Jesus Christ of Latter-day Saints. "For unto you, the Twelve, and those, the First Presidency, who are appointed with you to be your counselors and your leaders, is the power of this priesthood given," the Lord says, "for the last days and for the last time, in the which is the dispensation of the fulness of times. Which power you hold, in connection with all those who have received a dispensation at any time from the beginning of the creation; for verily I say unto you, the keys of the dispensation, which ye have received, have come down from the fathers, and last of all, being sent down from heaven unto you." (D&C 112:30-32.)

And thus it is that there are many now on earth—including all who have received the fulness of the priesthood and who are magnifying their callings therein—to whom this word comes from the

120

Lord: "Ye are lawful heirs, according to the flesh, and have been hid from the world with Christ in God—Therefore your life and the priesthood have remained, and must needs remain through you and your lineage until the restoration of all things spoken by the mouths of all the holy prophets since the world began. Therefore, blessed are ye if ye continue in my goodness, a light unto the Gentiles, and through this priesthood, a savior unto my people Israel. The Lord hath said it." (D&C 86:9-11.)

Chapter 11

THE CHURCH IN THE LAST DAYS

The Eternal Church

How little the world knows about the Church, the eternal Church, the Church of the living God! How microscopic is the knowledge of most men as to the Church which administers the gospel, the Church by which salvation comes, the Church through which the Lord Omnipotent regulates all his affairs in all worlds and throughout all eternity!

Even the saints ofttimes see only small struggling congregations—a few faithful souls here and a few there, encompassed by the evils of the world—and they wonder how the Church will survive and what destiny it has. What are even a few million humble followers of the Lamb as compared to billions of unbelievers? How can these few withstand the combined powers and pressures of communism and Islam, of Buddhism and Confucianism, and of all the sects of a worldly Christendom? How can they preserve their integrity and ways of worship in the face of atheism and infidelity and organized crime, and when subject to governmental controls of education and of employment and of families? How will they escape the pestilence and plagues and wars that a wicked world brings upon itself?

If we are to envision what is involved in the Second Coming of the Son of Man, we must know the place and mission of the Church in the eternal scheme of things. We must know why and by what power it has been restored. We must know that there is no single organization that will have as much influence for good upon men and nations in our day as will that church which the Lord has set up anew to be a light to the world and "a standard for the nations." (D&C 115:5.)

The Church on earth is patterned after the Church in heaven, where God himself is its President, Lawgiver, and King. The Church there is the administrative agency through which the Almighty governs the universe. Members of the earthly Church "who overcome by faith" shall be members of "the church of the Firstborn" in the highest heaven of the celestial world. (D&C 76:53-54.) Such persons, however, need not await that celestial day to gain a perfect knowledge of God and his heavenly kingdom. Through "the power and authority of the higher, or Melchizedek Priesthood," they "have the privilege of receiving the mysteries of the kingdom of heaven, to have the heavens opened unto them, to commune with the general assembly and church of the Firstborn, and to enjoy the communion and presence of God the Father, and Jesus the mediator of the new covenant." (D&C 107:18-19.)

Our gracious God gave his church to Adam, the first man of all men. It was an earthly church patterned after its parent in heaven. It was an earthly kingdom designed to prepare men to return to their heavenly home. The Church as we have it is the kingdom of God on earth; those who make themselves worthy of all its blessings here and now will be inheritors of all its blessings in the kingdom of God hereafter.

The Melchizedek Priesthood "continueth in the church of God in all generations" (D&C 84:17), which is to say that whenever and wherever men have the Melchizedek Priesthood, there is the Church and kingdom of God on earth. Conversely, when and where there is no Melchizedek Priesthood, there is no true Church and no earthly kingdom which is the Lord's, and consequently, no way to prepare men to go to the eternal church in heaven. The purpose of the Church on earth is to prepare men for membership in the eternal Church in heaven.

The priesthood is God's power, and it administers the gospel; the gospel is the plan of salvation; the Church is an organized body of believers who have the gospel. The purpose of the Church is to make salvation available to men through the gospel and by the power of the priesthood.

Adam, Seth, Enos, Cainan, Mahalaleel, Jared, Enoch, Methuselah, Lamech, and Noah all held presiding positions in the Church in their days. They were all righteous high priests. So also was it with Shem and Melchizedek—for whom "the church, in ancient days" (D&C 107:4) named the priesthood—and with Abraham, Isaac, and Jacob. The congregations of Israel were the congregations of the Church in their day. Isaiah, Jeremiah, Ezekiel, Daniel, and all the holy prophets prized their membership in the Lord's earthly kingdom and have gone on to receive their inheritances in his heavenly kingdom. Nephi speaks of "the brethren of the church" (1 Ne. 4:26) near the year 600 B.C., and the Church as such was established among the Nephites whenever they were faithful enough to receive it.

Our conclusion: The Church is eternal. Priesthood is eternal. Keys are eternal. Apostolic power is eternal. And all of these have been, are now, and always will be found together whenever the true Church is on earth. With this understanding, we are ready to view the setting up anew of the Church on earth as a prelude to the Second Coming of Him whose witnesses we are.

Elias Restores the Church and Kingdom

When the ancient revelations foretell the restoration of the gospel in that day of darkness preceding the return of the Eternal Light, they are speaking also of the setting up anew among men of the true Church and kingdom of God on earth. The gospel and the priesthood and the Church go together. They are one in spirit and purpose. All that we have said about the restoration of the gospel in the last days and about the giving again of power and keys to mortals applies also to the organizing again of the Church on earth. To all this let us now append a few prophetic words that speak of the restoration of the Church and kingdom as such.

In one of the most abused and misinterpreted passages in the whole Bible, Jesus promised to give Peter certain keys and powers, which would enable the ancient apostle to build up the Church and kingdom in the meridian of time. The apostolic party

124

was near Caesarea Philippi, up north of the Sea of Galilee and near Mount Hermon, at the time. Jesus asked: "Whom do men say that I the Son of man am?" He was told of the various views of Herod Antipas and the priests and the people. "But whom say ye that I am?" he queried. Peter, being moved upon by the Holy Ghost, and receiving utterance by the power of the Spirit, testified: "Thou art the Christ, the Son of the living God."

Jesus commended and blessed Peter for his witness. "Flesh and blood hath not revealed it unto thee, but my Father which is in heaven," he said, "and upon this rock"—the rock of revelation— "I will build my church; and the gates of hell shall not prevail against it." Then came what to the world is an enigmatic promise: "And I will give unto thee the keys of the kingdom of heaven: and whatsoever thou shalt bind on earth shall be bound in heaven: and whatsoever thou shalt loose on earth shall be loosed in heaven." (Matt. 16:13-19.)

These keys, as we are aware, are the right and power to preside over the kingdom which is the Church. They enable the legal administrators who hold them to perform the ordinances of salvation so they will be binding on earth and sealed in heaven. Unless, for instance, a baptism performed on earth has efficacy and force in heaven, it will not admit the penitent person into the eternal heaven, which his soul desires. These sealing keys were, in fact, given to Peter, James, and John about a week later, when they climbed nearby Mount Hermon to meet with Moses and Elijah and to participate in the glory of the Transfiguration. Later they were given to all of the Twelve, so that all had the power to bind and loose both on earth and in heaven. (Matt. 18:18.)

And as we have heretofore recited, Peter, James, and John restored their keys and powers and their apostolic commission to Joseph Smith and Oliver Cowdery, thereby enabling them to organize the same church and kingdom that Peter and the apostles presided over in their day. The initial organization took place on April 6, 1830, with the perfecting of the kingdom coming as added keys were received from heavenly ministrants and as the growth of the work warranted.

There are many false churches, but there can be only one true

Church. There are many false gospels, false prophets, and false Christs, but there can be only one true system of religion, only one gospel that has power to save and exalt fallen man. Christ is not divided; truth is not at variance with itself; conflicting doctrines and ordinances cannot all be right. The Divine Voice in the spring of 1820 said of all the sects of men: 'They are all wrong.' (JS-H 1:19.) After he had restored his own church, "The Church of Jesus Christ of Latter-day Saints" (D&C 115:4), he called it "the only true and living church upon the face of the whole earth." (D&C 1:30.)

His great latter-day proclamation was: "If this generation harden not their hearts, I will establish my church among them." And establish it he did! And how comforting are his words: "Whosoever belongeth to my church need not fear, for such shall inherit the kingdom of heaven," if, of course, they keep the commandments. "But it is they who do not fear me, neither keep my commandments but build up churches unto themselves to get gain, yea, and all those that do wickedly and build up the kingdom of the devil—yea, verily, verily, I say unto you, that it is they that I will disturb, and cause to tremble and shake to the center."

His church will have his gospel. "Behold, this is my doctrine —whosoever repenteth and cometh unto me, the same is my church. Whosoever declareth more or less than this, the same is not of me, but is against me; therefore he is not of my church." Men either come to the true Church and sustain it and all its views and teachings or they are not of God. Only those who are of God and of his church shall be saved.

"And now, behold, whosoever is of my church," saith the Lord, "and endureth of my church to the end, him will I establish upon my rock, and the gates of hell shall not prevail against them." (D&C 10:53-56, 67-69.)

The Lord's rock is his gospel. He commands all those who are established thereon to proclaim his message, saying: "Repent, repent, and prepare ye the way of the Lord, and make his paths straight; for the kingdom of heaven is at hand; yea, repent and be baptized, every one of you, for a remission of your sins; yea, be baptized even by water, and then cometh the baptism of fire and of the Holy Ghost."

Such is his message of salvation to all men. Of it he says, "Behold, verily, verily, I say unto you, this is my gospel; and remember that they shall have faith in me or they can in nowise be saved; and upon this rock I will build my church; yea, upon this rock ye are built, and if ye continue, the gates of hell shall not prevail against you." (D&C 33:10-13.) The true Church is built upon the rock of his gospel, upon the rock of faith in the Lord Jesus Christ, upon the rock of personal revelation, which, coming by the power of the Holy Ghost, reveals that he is the Son of the living God, who was crucified for the sins of the world.

The Latter-day Kingdom of the God of Heaven

There is scarcely a more dramatic account in ancient writ than the interpretation by Daniel the prophet of the dream of Nebuchadnezzar the king. Daniel and the children of Judah were in captivity in Babylon, in bondage to Gentile overlords who were evil and wicked and merciless. So vile and carnal were the Babylonians, so corrupt and evil was their nation, so filled with the power of Satan were their priests and religionists, that from then until now, the very name Babylon has caused the prophetic mind to wince with horror. Indeed, it has become the prophetic symbol for all that is evil and antichrist in the world, and for all that comes from Satan. Babylon is the world; Babylon is the church of the devil; Babylon is all that is evil and degenerate and vile on this benighted globe. And Babylon in that day ruled the world.

And so, it was into this dark hell of hatred, into this place of persecution for the Lord's people, into this realm where naught but evil reigned and where Satan was worshipped, that the Lord Jehovah chose to send a few rays of heavenly light that would ease the burdens of his people. To Nebuchadnezzar there came a dream—call it the dream of dreams, if you will, for it forecast God's dealings with nations and kingdoms for the next two and a half millenniums. Out of it came some surcease from toil and trouble for the Jewish exiles in Babylon, because the king made

Daniel "ruler over the whole province of Babylon, and chief of the governors over all the wise men of Babylon." (Dan. 2:48.)

Nebuchadnezzar first dreamed his dream of awful import—shall we not say it was a vision?—and then the remembrance of the thing was taken from him. Troubled in spirit, he called upon the magicians, astrologers, sorcerers, and Chaldeans to reveal and then interpret his dream. If they could tell him the dream, he would then believe their interpretation. Their failure was predestined, and the king in anger commanded that they and all the wise men of Babylon be cut in pieces and their houses made into a dunghill. When the soldiers came to slay Daniel and his fellows, the prophet persuaded the captain of the king's guard to give him time and he would make the interpretation. The secret was then revealed to Daniel in a night vision.

Taken before the king, Daniel said: "The secret which the king hath demanded cannot the wise men, the astrologers, the magicians, the soothsayers, shew unto the king." Their power was from beneath; they were servants of Satan; their religion was not founded on the rock of revelation; visions and the things of the Spirit were far from them. "But there is a God in heaven that revealeth secrets," Daniel said, "and [he] maketh known to the king Nebuchadnezzar what shall be in the latter days."

The dream and its meaning pertain to our day, "the latter days," the days just preceding the Second Coming of Him who gave the dream. "Thy dream, and the visions of thy head upon thy bed, are these; As for thee, O king," Daniel said, "thy thoughts came into thy mind upon thy bed, what should come to pass hereafter: and he that revealeth secrets maketh known to thee what shall come to pass."

Standing in the most awesome mortal presence then on earth, speaking boldly before all of the imperial court, relying upon prophetic insight and seeric assurance, Daniel then gave forth the divine word: "Thou, O king, sawest, and behold a great image." Doubt is absent; Daniel knows. "This great image, whose brightness was excellent, stood before thee; and the form thereof was terrible." No artist has yet gained the inspiration to paint the terrible form nor the awesome visage of this great image, nor do we suppose that mortal skill could record on canvas what the Lord placed first in the mind of the wicked king and then in the heart of the righteous prophet. Providentially we have a few descriptive words from that prophet, the prophet in whose presence even the roaring lions closed their mouths.

"This image's head was of fine gold," Daniel continued, "his breast and his arms of silver, his belly and his thighs of brass, his legs of iron, his feet part of iron and part of clay." Such was the wondrous image chosen by divine wisdom to represent the successive and great kingdoms of men. Looking back we can identify with ease the respective earthly powers whose periods of supremacy were molded and sculptured into the terrible image.

"Thou, O king, art a king of kings: for the God of heaven hath given thee a kingdom, power, and strength, and glory," Daniel said to Nebuchadnezzar. "And wheresoever the children of men dwell, the beasts of the field and the fowls of the heaven hath he given into thine hand, and hath made thee ruler over them all. Thou art this head of gold." Babylonia was indeed the first world-kingdom. She held sway from about 605 to 538 B.C., with Nebuchadnezzar's prosperous reign lasting from about 606 to 562 B.C. His voice was as the voice of God to the millions who trembled at his word. His armies traversed the earth, conquered kingdoms, and transported whole nations from one land to another by the sharpness of their swords and the piercing power of their spears. On the roof of his vast palace in Babylon were the famous hanging gardens, ranked as one of the Seven Wonders of the World.

"And after thee shall arise another kingdom inferior to thee," Daniel told Nebuchadnezzar, "and another third kingdom of brass, which shall bear rule over all the earth." These kingdoms are the Medo-Persian or second world-kingdoms, whose dominion prevailed from about 538 to 333 B.C. and the Grecian powers that prevailed beginning with the conquest of the Persian Empire by Alexander the Great in 332 B.C.

"And the fourth kingdom shall be strong as iron: forasmuch as iron breaketh in pieces and subdueth all things: and as iron that breaketh all these, shall it break in pieces and bruise." Here we see the powers of Rome, beginning with the Caesars, particularly

Augustus, who ruled when the Lord Jesus was born, and continuing until the first barbarian king ruled in Italy in A.D. 476. The two legs of iron symbolize perfectly the division into an eastern and a western Roman Empire, with Constantine the Great (in whose day the Nicene Creed was written) establishing a new capital at Byzantium and giving it the new name of Constantinople (now Istanbul).

"And whereas thou sawest the feet and toes, part of potters' clay, and part of iron, the kingdom shall be divided; but there shall be in it of the strength of the iron, forasmuch as thou sawest the iron mixed with miry clay. And as the toes of the feet were part of iron, and part of clay, so the kingdom shall be partly strong, and partly broken. And whereas thou sawest iron mixed with miry clay, they shall mingle themselves with the seed of men: but they shall not cleave one to another, even as iron is not mixed with clay." Clearly these are the numerous, divided, warring kingdoms—some strong, others weak—that grew out of the mighty Roman Empire. That they did not "cleave one to another" has resulted in the death and misery of many people during the long ages from the fall of Rome to the day of restoration with which the dream is now prepared to concern itself.

Having thus described the terrible image, Daniel tells the king: "Thou sawest till that a stone was cut out without hands, which smote the image upon his feet that were of iron and clay, and brake them to pieces. Then was the iron, the clay, the brass, the silver, and the gold, broken to pieces together, and became like the chaff of the summer threshingfloor; and the wind carried them away, that no place was found for them: and the stone that smote the image became a great mountain, and filled the whole earth."

By way of interpretation, Daniel's divine word is: "And in the days of these kings"—those of divers sorts, powers, and strengths, which grew out of the Roman Empire—"shall the God of heaven set up a kingdom, which shall never be destroyed: and the kingdom shall not be left to other people, but it shall break in pieces and consume all these kingdoms, and it shall stand for ever. Forasmuch as thou sawest that the stone was cut out of the mountain without hands, and that it brake in pieces the iron, the brass, the clay, the silver, and the gold; the great God hath made known to the king what shall come to pass hereafter: and the dream is certain, and the interpretation thereof sure." (Dan. 2:27-45.)

How wondrous are the ways of the Lord! How glorious are the mysteries of this kingdom! And how sweet is the word he sends by dreams and visions and seeric interpretations! Here we have seen the kingdoms of this world, kingdoms drenched in blood and held together by the arm of flesh, one following another until the set time for the great latter-day restoration of all things. Then a stone is cut out of the mountain without hands and a kingdom is set up by the God of heaven. It is a new kind of kingdom. The arm of flesh plays no part in its creation. It is created without man's hand. It comes from God. It is established by revelation. It is the Church and kingdom of God on earth.

And it grows until it fills the whole earth, until the knowledge of God covers the earth as the waters cover the sea, until every living soul on earth is converted. And what of the other kingdoms? This eternal kingdom, this kingdom which shall never be destroyed, this kingdom which is the new and everlasting kingdom, shall break in pieces and consume all kingdoms. It shall make a full end of all nations; they shall vanish as the chaff before the summer breeze and shall not be found on earth. And the new kingdom shall not be left to any other people; never again will there be a general apostasy; the Church of the God of heaven will be set up on earth to stand forever. Thus saith Daniel. Thus saith the Lord. "And the dream is certain, and the interpretation thereof sure." (Dan. 2:45.)

This kingdom was set up on April 6, 1830, by revelation and commandment from on high. It is "called by a new name, which the mouth of the Lord" has named. (Isa. 62:2.) For, as the prophets foretold, "the Lord God shall . . . call his servants by another name" (Isa. 65:15) in that day when Israel is restored and her people are prepared for his coming. It is The Church of Jesus Christ of Latter-day Saints, and its eternal destiny is assured. For thus saith the Lord: "The keys of the kingdom of God are committed unto man on the earth, and from thence shall the gospel roll forth unto the ends of the earth, as the stone which is cut out of the mountain without hands shall roll forth, until it has filled the whole earth."

And further, by way of invitation, the revealed word says: "Call upon the Lord, that his kingdom may go forth upon the earth, that the inhabitants thereof may receive it, and be prepared for the days to come, in the which the Son of Man shall come down in heaven, clothed in the brightness of his glory, to meet the kingdom of God which is set up on the earth. Wherefore, may the kingdom of God go forth, that the kingdom of heaven may come, that thou, O God, mayest be glorified in heaven so on earth, that thine enemies may be subdued; for thine is the honor, power and glory, forever and ever." (D&C 65:2, 5-6.)

The Mission of the Church and Kingdom

When we say, as say we must with all the power and persuasion at our command, that the Almighty promised to set up his Church and kingdom again on earth before his millennial return; when we speak of the restoration of the everlasting gospel in the last days; and when we testify that the ancient keys and powers must once again be vested in mortal men—such pronouncements mean that everything that appertains to, is connected with, or is part of the gospel shall be restored and shall be administered by the Church. God's Church and kingdom can accomplish its destined mission only if it is restored in all its glory, beauty, and perfection. That mission divides into three parts:

1. *Preaching the gospel to the world.*

The Church must—for that Lord whose church it is has so commanded—the Church must proclaim the fulness of the everlasting gospel in all the world and to every creature, for it is an imperative duty God has laid upon us. All men are children of the Father. They are entitled to hear the warning voice. Israel must be gathered out of Babylon into the earthly kingdom so that all who will may believe and obey and be saved.

2. *Perfecting the saints.*

No unclean thing can enter into the Eternal Presence and final eternal rest. Repentant souls must retain a remission of their sins. They must go from grace to grace until they perfect their souls. It is our privilege to obtain and perfect the attributes of godliness so they may be restored to us again in the resurrection. We are to build up a Zion composed of the pure in heart. We are to prepare a people for the coming of the Sinless One with whom the saints, being themselves free from sin, can then associate.

3. *Saving the dead.*

Thanks be to God for his mercy and grace! How pleasing it is to know that the Merciful One, who desires to see all his children saved, has made provision for the preaching of the gospel in the world of spirits, for the performance for them of vicarious ordinances in holy temples, and for the planting in the hearts of the children the promises made to the fathers.

We shall speak more particularly of all these things, each in its proper place, as we open to view the designs and purposes of the Lord as pertaining to the last days. We mention them here to make it clear to all that the restoration of the gospel and the Church embraces, includes, and was intended to include all that the Church now has or shall hereafter receive. The Church is God's earthly kingdom, and he will continue to do with it whatsoever is pleasing unto himself. And blessed be his holy name for all that he has given and does give and shall give unto his saints.

Chapter 12

PREACHING THE EVERLASTING WORD

Preaching in All Nations

Let it be written with a pen of steel on plates of gold. Let the sound go forth with the trump of God so as to shake the earth and cause every ear to tingle. It is the eternal decree of the Great Jehovah. The fulness of the everlasting gospel, as restored by the Prophet Joseph Smith, shall be preached to every nation, and kindred, and tongue, and people. Then, and only then, shall the Lord Jesus Christ descend in the clouds of glory with ten thousand of his saints. But first the everlasting word must and shall go forth. Such is the will of heaven.

Jesus said: "This Gospel of the Kingdom shall be preached in all the world, for a witness unto all nations, and then shall the end come, or the destruction of the wicked." (JS-M 1:31.) What is the gospel of which our Lord speaks?

It is the gospel that he taught, the gospel of Peter, James, and John, the gospel of Paul and the primitive saints—not the gospel of an apostate Christendom.

It is the gospel that God is our Father and we are his children; that we dwelt in his presence in preexistence; that he is a Holy Man, having a body of flesh and bones; that he is a personage of tabernacle in whose image man is made—not the gospel that God is a spirit that fills immensity and is everywhere and nowhere in particular present.

It is the gospel that Christ, as the Lamb slain from the founda-

134

tion of the world, atoned for the sins of all men on condition of repentance; that he brought life and immortality to light through his gospel; that immortality is a free gift for all men, but that eternal life comes only to those who believe and obey—not the gospel that men are saved by grace alone, without works, simply by confessing the Lord Jesus with their lips.

It is the gospel that men will be punished for their own sins and not for Adam's transgression—not the gospel that infants must be baptized to free them from Adam's sin; not the gospel that chosen souls are predestined to gain salvation through the grace and goodness of God, for reasons known to him alone, without reference to the deeds done in the flesh.

It is the gospel that men must be born again; that the Holy Ghost is a revelator and a sanctifier; that the gifts of the Spirit and miracles of every sort are always poured out upon the faithful— not the gospel that the Lord has done his work and that gifts and miracles ceased with the ancient apostles.

It is the gospel that the heavens are open; that God speaks today; that angels minister as of old; and that holy men can see the face of their Maker in the same way as did their forebears—not the gospel that the heavens are as brass, that revelation is not needed in this scientific age, and that the Bible contains all that is needed for the salvation of man.

It is the everlasting gospel, the gospel of God, the gospel that saved Adam and the ancients, the gospel that can make of man a god and of this earth a heaven—not the gospel of mystery, and of vagaries, and of the philosophies of men.

It is the restored gospel. It is the gospel brought back by angelic ministration, as we have already seen. And now it shall go forth and be offered to all men. Of this gospel, restored by Moroni and other angelic ministrants, the holy word says: "And this gospel shall be preached unto every nation, and kindred, and tongue, and people." This is a prophetic utterance that is not yet fulfilled, but will be in due course. For "the servants of God shall go forth, saying with a loud voice: Fear God and give glory to him, for the hour of his judgment is come; And worship him that made heaven, and earth, and the sea, and the fountains of waters—Calling upon the name of the Lord day and night, saying: O that thou wouldst rend the heavens, that thou wouldst come down, that the mountains might flow down at thy presence." (D&C 133:37-40.)

This restored gospel will reveal the true God and make his laws known. It shall go to all men before the hour of his judgment arrives. It will prepare a people for that dreadful day. And with reference to it, we say, as did Paul of old: "Though we, or an angel from heaven, preach any other gospel unto you than that which we have preached unto you, let him be accursed." (Gal. 1:8.)

When the prophetic word says the gospel shall be preached in every nation, it means every nation. It includes Russia and China and India. When it speaks of every kindred and people, it embraces the people of Islam and the believers in Buddha. When it mentions every tongue, it includes all the confusing dialects of all the sects and parties of men. The gospel is to go to them all. And the Lord will not come until it does.

Manifestly there is an assigned order in which the various nations and peoples shall hear the word. There is a divine timetable known to God and made manifest to his servants, little by little, as their strength and means increase, thus enabling them to go to new and added places. Nations rise and nations fall, kindreds and peoples come and go, the earth is inhabited here and there at one time or another, all according to the divine will.

Paul acclaimed that God "hath made of one blood all nations of men"—all men are brothers, all are the children of Adam—"for to dwell on all the face of the earth"; also, that the Lord "hath determined the times before appointed, and the bounds of their inhabitation." And all of this he hath done, "That they should seek the Lord," and that "haply they might feel after him, and find him." (Acts 17:26-27.) Indeed, the very purpose of life itself is for men to come unto God and to worship him in spirit and in truth. This can be done only when they learn his laws and believe his gospel.

We have commenced the preaching processes in most of the free world; the voice of warning is beginning to go forth; and a few of Ephraim and a sprinkling of Manasseh have begun to gather into the true fold. But the great day of missionary work lies ahead. We must go to all nations and do far more in those nations where the work has begun. In due course the Lord will break down the barriers among men. The iron curtain will rise; the prohibitions against preaching in the Islamic world will fade away; the Jews will be free to believe or not as they choose—and the everlasting word will go forth as He has decreed.

Preaching amid War and Desolation

The preaching of the everlasting word is for the purpose of saving souls. The servants of the Lord, the elders of his kingdom, the missionaries who carry the message are called to labor in his fields. They go forth to reap; they are to gather the wheat into barns and bind up the tares for the day of burning. And as it has always been, the harvest is great and the laborers are few, and we must plead with the Lord of the harvest to send us more witnesses of his holy name. "Behold, the field is white already to harvest," he says, "therefore, whoso desireth to reap, let him thrust in his sickle with his might, and reap while the day lasts, that he may treasure up for his soul everlasting salvation in the kingdom of God. Yea, whosoever will thrust in his sickle and reap, the same is called of God." (D&C 6:3-4.)

Those who labor with their might "shall be laden with many sheaves." (D&C 75:5.) These sheaves are then carried to the threshing floor where the chaff is blown away and the wheat made ready for the granary. These threshing processes are now going on for the last time on earth. The Lord of the harvest has sent laborers into his fields to gather in the wheat before he burns the tares with unquenchable fire. The day is rapidly approaching when every corruptible thing will be consumed and there will be a new heaven and a new earth whereon dwelleth righteousness.

But what is not as well understood among us as it should be is that the harvest is to go forward under increasingly difficult circumstances. It could not be otherwise in a world that is ripening in iniquity. War and pestilence and desolation shall cover the earth before the Lord comes, and the preaching of his holy word must and shall go forward in the midst of these. "I call upon the weak things of the world," the Lord says, "those who are unlearned and despised, to thrash the nations by the power of my Spirit." To thrash is to thresh; they are one and the same.

How and under what circumstances shall this preaching go forward? "Their arm shall be my arm," the Lord says of his servants, "and I will be their shield and their buckler; and I will gird up their loins, and they shall fight manfully for me; and their enemies shall be under their feet; and I will let fall the sword in their behalf, and by the fire of mine indignation will I preserve them." This promise to let the sword fall in behalf of his servants must of necessity mean that the Lord will use the wars that are fomented and fought by the wicked to open nations and kingdoms to the preaching of the gospel. Thus, by the weak and the simple, laboring in the midst of tribulation, "the poor and the meek shall have the gospel preached unto them, and they shall be looking forth for the time of my coming," saith the Lord, "for it is nigh at hand." (D&C 35:13-15.)

Let us, then, look at the prophetic word which associates the preaching of the gospel in the last days with a time of war and desolation. Micah, after saying "the house of the Lord shall be established in the top of the mountains," with Israel gathering thereto, says that "many nations" shall then gather against the Lord's people. "But they know not the thoughts of the Lord," he says, "neither understand they his counsel: for he shall gather them as the sheaves into the floor." That is to say: When nations and peoples gather to oppose us, we must preach the saving truths to them as Ammon and his brethren did to the Lamanites. There is nothing but the gospel that will soften the hearts of men and cause them to turn away from war, and from evil, and from opposition to God.

It is in this setting, then, that the Lord commands: "Arise and thresh, O daughter of Zion"—stand forth, proclaim my word, thrust in your sickles, carry many sheaves to the threshing floor—"for I will make thine horn iron, and I will make thy hoofs brass: and thou shalt beat in pieces many people: and I will consecrate their gain unto the Lord, and their substance unto the Lord of the whole earth." (Micah 4:1, 11-13.) The laborers in the Lord's fields will come off triumphant; they will make many converts whose substance will be used to further the work.

Joseph Smith poured forth these eloquent words relative to the preaching of the gospel in our day: "The servants of God will not have gone over the nations of the Gentiles, with a warning voice, until the destroying angel will commence to waste the inhabitants of the earth, and as the prophet hath said, 'It shall be a vexation to hear the report.' I speak thus because I feel for my fellow men; I do it in the name of the Lord, being moved upon by the Holy Spirit. Oh, that I could snatch them from the vortex of misery, into which I behold them plunging themselves, by their sins; that I might be enabled by the warning voice, to be an instrument of bringing them to unfeigned repentance, that they might have faith to stand in the evil day!" (*Teachings*, p. 87.)

The prophet who spoke of the vexation here mentioned was Isaiah. To vex is to trouble grievously; it is to harass; it is to afflict as with a disease. Vexation is a state of trouble; it is a cause of trouble and of affliction. Speaking of the Lord's latter-day people and of the desolations promised in their day, Isaiah said: "The overflowing scourge shall pass through, then ye shall be trodden down by it. From the time that it goeth forth it shall take you: for morning by morning shall it pass over, by day and by night: and it shall be a vexation only to understand the report." Or, as it is otherwise translated, "It shall be nought but terror to understand the message." Then, Isaiah continues, "the Lord shall rise up . . . that he may do his work, his strange work; and bring to pass his act, his strange act. Now therefore be ye not mockers, lest your bands be made strong: for I have heard from the Lord God of hosts a consumption, even determined upon the whole earth." (Isa. 28:18-22.)

In latter-day revelation, speaking of the day when the times of the Gentiles shall be fulfilled, the Lord says: "There shall be men standing in that generation, that shall not pass until they shall see an overflowing scourge; for a desolating sickness shall cover the land. But my disciples shall stand in holy places, and shall not be moved; but among the wicked, men shall lift up their voices and curse God and die." (D&C 45:31-32.) And through it all, we must and shall continue to preach, morning after morning, day after day, and night after night.

The Lord's Controversy with the Nations

The ancient prophets speak of the Lord Jehovah engaging in a controversy with his people and with all the nations of the earth in the last days. He will discuss with them a controverted matter; he will dispute and debate a controversial issue; and the views of the contending parties will be proclaimed in a setting of strife. The issue at stake will be whether men believe his gospel, repent of their sins, keep his commandments, and gain salvation; or whether they rebel against him, reject the light of truth, walk in darkness, do wickedly, and are damned. It will be the greatest controversy of the ages.

Hosea, speaking of "the Lord and his goodness in the latter days," proclaims: "Hear the word of the Lord, ye children of Israel: for the Lord hath a controversy with the inhabitants of the land, because there is no truth, nor mercy, nor knowledge of God in the land." How aptly he describes the day of apostasy, the day when darkness covers the earth and gross darkness the minds of the people! "By swearing, and lying, and killing, and stealing, and committing adultery, they break out, and blood toucheth blood. Therefore shall the land mourn, and every one that dwelleth therein shall languish." (Hosea 3:5; 4:1-3.) Such is the setting in which the great controversy shall wage.

Micah prophesies of "the remnant of Jacob" that "shall be among the Gentiles" in the last days. (Micah 5:8-15.) His words, in their entirety and with some additions, are quoted by the Risen Lord to the Nephites. (3 Ne. 21:12-19.) Then Jesus says: "For it shall come to pass, saith the Father, that at that day"—the day of restoration and of gathering, the day in which we live—"whosoever will not repent and come unto my Beloved Son, them will I cut off from among my people, O house of Israel; And I will execute vengeance and fury upon them, even as upon the heathen, such as they have not heard. But if they will repent and hearken unto my words, and harden not their hearts, I will establish my church among them, and they shall come in unto the covenant and be numbered among this the remnant of Jacob, unto whom I have given this land for their inheritance." (3 Ne. 21:20-22.) Such shall be the result of the great controversy—men shall save or damn themselves depending upon the part they play in the warfare between truth and error.

And so it is that we hear Micah proclaim: "Hear ye now what the Lord saith; Arise, contend thou before the mountains, and let the hills hear thy voice. Hear ye, O mountains, the Lord's controversy, and ye strong foundations of the earth:for the Lord hath a controversy with his people, and he will plead with Israel." (Micah 6:1-2.)

The Lord's controversy! The Lord pleading with men— pleading by the mouths of his servants—to repent and be saved, and men rejecting the message! And so we turn to the words of Jeremiah to learn what will happen to the nations of men who reject the truth in the last days. In words descriptive of Armageddon-like scenes, Jeremiah says: "I will call for a sword upon all the inhabitants of the earth, saith the Lord of hosts. Therefore prophesy thou against them all these words, and say unto them, The Lord shall roar from on high, and utter his voice from his holy habitation; he shall mightily roar upon his habitation; he shall give a shout, as they that tread the grapes, against all the inhabitants of the earth."

The scene thus depicted is one descriptive of the Second Coming. Having so asserted, the prophetic word continues: "A noise shall come even to the ends of the earth; for the Lord hath a controversy with the nations, he will plead with all flesh; he will give them that are wicked to the sword, saith the Lord. Thus saith the Lord of hosts, Behold, evil shall go forth from nation to nation, and a great whirlwind shall be raised up from the coasts of the earth. And the slain of the Lord shall be at that day from one end of the earth even unto the other end of the earth: they shall not be lamented, neither gathered, nor buried; they shall be dung upon the ground." (Jer. 25:29-33.)

In the midst of his great prophecy about the worldwide war during which the Lord Jesus will return, the prophet Joel inserts

141

these words about offering, even then, the saving word to wicked men. Thus saith the Lord: "Put ye in the sickle, for the harvest is ripe: come, get you down; for the press is full, the fats overflow; for their wickedness is great. Multitudes, multitudes in the valley of decision: for the day of the Lord is near in the valley of decision." (Joel 3:13-14.)

Of the wars and destructions, and of Armageddon itself, we shall speak more particularly hereafter. The issue with which we now wrestle is the one of preaching the everlasting word in the midst of war and desolation and pestilence and evil of every sort. And in the light of all that the prophets have said, some conclusions seem inescapable. The gospel shall be preached. It shall go to every nation, and it shall go in the day of vengeance and of evil. It may be that millions of preachers will be needed to raise the warning voice in every ear. Certainly billions of worldly men will oppose the message. Indeed, all the forces of evil men, all the subtleties of Satan, and all the horrors of hell shall rise to fight the truth. The controversy shall cover the whole earth, and the servants of the Lord will plead with men everywhere to repent and believe the gospel. Knowing these things, we cannot permit opposition, however powerful and severe, to deter us from complying with the divine commission to proclaim the gospel to every creature.

Making Converts in All Nations

What will be the result of the great controversy—the Lord's controversy, the controversy between truth and error, the warfare between the saints and the world—that shall be waged in all nations and among all people before the Second Coming? What choice will men make in the valley of decision? Will they choose to believe in the Only Begotten or go their own way to sorrow and destruction and death? And if but few believe; if all the voices of earth and hell cry out for the destruction of the Lord's people— what then? Will the saints be preserved, and if so, how?

Let there be no mistake on these matters. The gospel shall be preached everywhere; success will attend the labors of those who

142

proclaim the truth; converts by the thousands and the millions will be made in all nations. There is no question about this; none can stay the hand of the Lord or of his servants; the message shall go forth. Comparatively speaking, however, a few only in all nations will believe the restored truth; the masses of men in all nations will mock and scorn the true ministers and their message; the battle lines of the controversy will be tightly drawn.

Then, when the saints have done all that in their power lies, both to preach the everlasting word and to build up the eternal kingdom; when they of themselves can no longer go forward with the decreed success attending their labors; when the wars and desolations and carnality of men are about to overwhelm them—then the Lord will take over. By his own power he will destroy the wicked, complete his strange act, and pour out the consumption decreed.

These things are set forth by Nephi in this manner. He is speaking of the last days. An angel has just shown him "that great and abominable church, which is the mother of abominations, whose foundation is the devil." He has learned that "she is the whore of all the earth," and that in the last days "she sat upon many waters; and she had dominion over all the earth, among all nations, kindreds, tongues, and people." These are the very nations, kindreds, tongues, and peoples to whom the gospel must go; these are the nations where the Lord's controversy shall be waged; these are the peoples who stand in the valley of decision.

In this setting Nephi says: "I beheld the church of the Lamb of God"—The Church of Jesus Christ of Latter-day Saints!—"and its numbers were few, because of the wickedness and abominations of the whore who sat upon many waters." This is the day when "there are save two churches only; the one is the church of the Lamb of God, and the other is the church of the devil." This is the day when "whoso belongeth not to the church of the Lamb of God belongeth to that great church, which is the mother of abominations." The evil forces on earth, which control nations and kingdoms, false religions of all sorts and kinds, the communistic powers, and every worldly organization which opposes the cause of truth and righteousness—all these are gathered under one banner, the banner of Lucifer. All these are united in an evil cause, the cause that opposes the saints of the Lamb.

"Nevertheless," Nephi continues, meaning in spite of all this opposition, "I beheld that the church of the Lamb, who were the saints of God, were also upon all the face of the earth." The Church of Jesus Christ of Latter-day Saints will be established in all nations and among every people before the Lord comes. There will be a few saints everywhere. Success in this sense shall attend the labors of those who go forth to preach the gospel.

However, Nephi continues, "their dominions upon the face of the earth were small, because of the wickedness of the great whore whom I saw." These dominions, comparatively speaking, are small now; they will be small in days to come; great and glorious as the Church shall become before the appointed dreadful day, its rulership and influence in the world will be immeasurably less than that of the combined evil forces of earth and hell that taken together are the church of the devil.

How, then, will the Lord's controversy fare? Nephi says: "I beheld that the great mother of abominations did gather together multitudes upon the face of all the earth, among all the nations of the Gentiles, to fight against the Lamb of God." Those who oppose the Lord's Church oppose him. To reject the apostles and prophets who are sent to preach the gospel is to reject him who sent them. To be in opposition to The Church of Jesus Christ of Latter-day Saints on moral issues is to link arms with Satan and to fight against God. On this point we must speak plainly and bluntly—there is no middle ground; men are either for him or against him, and those who are not for him are against him.

And the Lord will not let his people fail. "I, Nephi, beheld the power of the Lamb of God," the scriptural account continues, "that it descended upon the saints of the church of the Lamb, and upon the covenant people of the Lord, who were scattered upon all the face of the earth; and they were armed with righteousness and with the power of God in great glory. And it came to pass that I beheld that the wrath of God was poured out upon the great and abominable church, insomuch that there were wars and rumors of wars among all the nations and kindreds of the earth."

This is the day in which we live. These wars and rumors of wars have been, now are, and yet will be. The worldwide wars of the recent past, and the never-ending rumors and reports of the present now, in all of which the communications media so delight, are but a type and a shadow of the wars and rumors of wars that soon shall be poured out without measure.

Nephi saw our day. He described it as a day in which "there began to be wars and rumors of wars among all the nations which belonged to the mother of abominations." As he viewed the awful scene, the angelic ministrant who presided over the visions then being given to a mortal man said these solemn words: "Behold, the wrath of God is upon the mother of harlots; and behold, thou seest all these things—And when the day cometh that the wrath of God is poured out upon the mother of harlots, which is the great and abominable church of all the earth, whose foundation is the devil, then, at that day, the work of the Father shall commence, in preparing the way for the fulfilling of his covenants, which he hath made to his people who are of the house of Israel." (1 Ne. 14:9-17.)

This word speaks of us. We are of Israel, and the covenants made with our fathers are now being fulfilled. We are called to preach the everlasting word in all the world that our scattered brethren of the house of Jacob may all hear the message, be gathered into the fold of their Ancient Shepherd, and there find refreshment with all his sheep. And it matters not that the warning voice must go forth in the midst of war and desolation. That it would be thus was foreseen and foreknown from the beginning. So be it.

Chapter 13

THE BOOK OF MORMON
AND THE
SECOND COMING

What Think Ye of the Book of Mormon?

We have some truths to tell and some testimony to bear about a volume of latter-day scripture—the Book of Mormon—which does now and yet shall shake the very foundations of Christendom. We intend to state, with a plainness that defies misunderstanding, how this holy book prepares the way for the Second Coming of the Son of Man; how it makes ready a people for that dread and glorious day; how all men on earth will be saved or damned because they believe or disbelieve its words; and how the ancient prophets foretold that the Lord Jesus would not come in the clouds of glory until this book of books, this American Bible, this voice from the dust, came forth and was offered to all men in all nations.

The coming forth of the Book of Mormon and its publication to the world is one of the signs of the times. It is one of the great events destined to occur before the Second Coming. Prophets and preachers of righteousness spent four thousand years recording the truths it contains. Civilizations rose and fell as they accepted or rejected the teachings on its pages. And the world today will rise or fall, nations will survive or perish, men will gain celestial glory or suffer with the damned in hell, all depending upon their reaction to this volume of holy writ.

This holy book, this Nephite record, this voice of God speaking, as it were, with seven thunders, came forth to bear testimony of the divine Sonship of Christ and to teach the doctrines of salvation to every nation, and kindred, and tongue, and people. It is the very volume of holy scripture that has been prepared by the Lord to take his message of salvation to a wicked world in the last days. Its message is for the Lamanites, and for the whole house of Israel, and for the Gentiles, and for every living soul upon the face of the whole earth.

And no man—great or small, wise or ignorant, theologian or atheist—no man who lives on the earth in the last days can be saved in the kingdom of heaven unless and until he comes to know, by the power of the Holy Ghost, that this holy book is the mind and will and voice of God to the world. And all who reject its message will be damned. This is as plain and blunt a declaration as the one made by the Lord Jesus with reference to the heaven-sent baptism that he commanded his apostles to preach to the world. It is one of the great foundation stones of revealed religion in modern times. Men will stand or fall—eternally—because of what they think of the Book of Mormon.

Before we can identify the time and the season of our Lord's triumphant return, we must learn what part the Book of Mormon has played and yet will play relative to that coming day. The book itself is an inspired history of God's dealings with the ancient inhabitants of the Americas. It was written by prophets and seers upon plates of gold and other metals in their own tongues and languages. The many prophetic records that came into being were condensed, abridged, and quoted by the prophet-historian Mormon as he wrote the book that now bears his name.

The accounts deal primarily with the prophet Lehi and his descendants who lived and labored in the Western Hemisphere for about a thousand years—from shortly after 600 B.C. to almost A.D. 421. There is also a brief abridgment of the history of the Jaredite people who left the Old World at the time of the confusion of tongues at the tower of Babel (about 2247 B.C.), were led to the Americas by the hand of the Lord, and lived as a great people and a mighty nation until their destruction in Nephite times.

But the Book of Mormon is more, far more, than an inspired history. It is a volume of holy scripture comparable in scope, in doctrine, and in literary excellence to that greatest of all books, the holy Bible. Indeed, it is an American Bible, which was written "by the spirit of prophecy and of revelation." (Title page.) It expounds the doctrines of salvation in plainness and perfection. It contains the fulness of the everlasting gospel, meaning that it is a record of God's dealings with a people who had the fulness of the gospel, and meaning also that in it is a divine delineation of the laws and truths and powers by which salvation may be gained. It sets forth the covenants God has made with his people. It was translated by the gift and power of God by the great seer of latter days. And it is now published to the world "to the convincing of the Jew and Gentile that Jesus is the Christ, the Eternal God, manifesting himself unto all nations." (Title page.)

As we inquire into the second coming of that eternal God of whom the Book of Mormon testifies, we must ask and answer such questions as these: What is the relationship between the Book of Mormon and the Second Coming? How is this book involved in the restoration of all things? In what way does it help to prepare a people for millennial peace and righteousness? What effect does it have on the gathering of Israel? Does it, in fact, prove the reality of the restoration and the presence of the glorious gospel among men? What is its relationship to the Bible and the other scriptures that have lighted and will light the way to eternal life? And what does the prophetic word have to say about its coming forth and the part it will play in the eternal scheme of things?

Let every man who loves truth and cherishes goodness ponder in his heart the great query: *What think ye of the Book of Mormon?* And further: *Whence came it? Is it of God or of man? And if it be of God, what is my responsibility with reference to it?*

"Truth Shall Spring Out of the Earth"

No man can speak too highly of the Holy Bible, that volume of divine writ which came down from heaven to light the path back to those celestial realms. The Bible contains the mind and will and voice of God to all men everywhere; it is a record of his dealings with some of his children during the four thousand years from the first Adam, by whom the fall came, to the Second Adam, by whom the ransom was paid.

In its original and perfect form the Bible was a transcript of those celestial records which the Lord designed, in his infinite wisdom, to reveal to his earthly children. It bears witness of Christ and teaches the doctrines of salvation. It charts the course leading to eternal life. It tells men how and in what way they can attain peace in this life and eternal glory in the realms ahead.

The King James Version of the Bible is by all odds the best and plainest rendition of the original records that the translators of the world have produced. It is the Bible version prepared by the Lord for use by his modern prophet, Joseph Smith, when he translated the Book of Mormon, brought forth the revelations in the Doctrine and Covenants, and laid the foundations of the great work of restoration in the latter days. The Joseph Smith Translation, commonly called the Inspired Version, has added to and perfected much of the King James Version, and someday—we suppose it will be a millennial day—the work of perfecting the Bible will be completed, and men will then have again the scriptural knowledge possessed by their forebears.

All that is said of the Bible applies with equal force to the Book of Mormon. It too is a volume of holy writ; it too is an inspired history of God's dealings with ancient civilizations; it too contains the fulness of the everlasting gospel. The peoples with whom it deals dwelt for some twenty-six hundred years in the Americas, where they developed civilizations and a religious zeal comparable to any of the races and nations of the Old World.

In the Book of Mormon is found a new witness for Christ; in it the doctrines of salvation are set forth with a clarity and plainness that surpass the Bible; and in it is found the proof that God has spoken again in these last days. No man can speak too highly of the Book of Mormon or testify with excessive power of its truth and divinity. It too is a transcript from the eternal records of heaven, and in its original form it contained much more than a wise Father has permitted to be translated and published among us. And in a yet future day—and again we suppose it will be millennial— the fulness of the Book of Mormon accounts will be preached from the housetops.

In the eternal providences of the Lord, known and revealed from the beginning, the Book of Mormon was destined to make its appearance in the last days as part of the glorious restoration of all things. This fact he revealed to many of his ancient prophets— Enoch, Joseph who was sold into Egypt, Isaiah, Ezekiel, Zenos, and no doubt many others whose prophecies are on the brass plates or in other books yet to come forth.

As part of those eternal providences of which we speak, the Lord designed from the beginning to bring the Book of Mormon forth from the ground as a voice from the dust, as truth springing out of the earth. The symbolism and imagery in this are beautiful. As revelation pours down from above to water the earth, so the gospel plant grows out of the earth to bear witness that the heavenly rains contain the life-giving power. Heaven and earth join hands in testifying of the truths of salvation. Their combined voices are the voice of restoration, the voice of glory and honor and eternal life, the voice from heaven, and the voice out of the earth. Such is part of the Lord's act, his strange act, the act in which all who are willing to forsake the world and come unto him with full purpose of heart may play a part. "And out of small things proceedeth that which is great." (D&C 64:33.)

Enoch, whose mortal ministry preceded by five thousand years the coming forth of the Book of Mormon, saw in vision both the Second Coming and the coming forth of the volume of holy scripture that would prepare the way for that glorious day. To him the Lord said: "And righteousness will I send down out of heaven"—that is, revelation shall commence anew and the gospel shall be restored—"and truth will I send forth out of the earth, to bear testimony of mine Only Begotten; his resurrection from the dead; yea, and also the resurrection of all men." (Moses 7:62.) The Book of Mormon shall come forth from American soil, from plates buried in Cumorah, from the soil that supported the people of whom it speaks. The Book of Mormon shall come forth containing the *word* of the gospel which will unite with the *power* of the gospel that comes down from heaven. The Book of Mormon shall come forth to testify of Christ and his resurrection and the resurrection of all men. It was to be the Lord's way of bringing to light anew his saving truths.

David, whose doings preceded by almost three thousand years the coming forth of the Book of Mormon, was led by the Spirit to say: "I will hear what God the Lord will speak"—oh, that all men would open their hearts to hear and believe and obey—"for he will speak peace unto his people, and to his saints." His gospel is a message of peace, peace in this life, and peace everlasting in the kingdom of peace. "Surely his salvation is nigh them that fear him." Salvation is always nigh when the Lord speaks; his voice, coming by revelation or recorded in the scriptures, is the voice of salvation. "Mercy and truth are met together; righteousness and peace have kissed each other. Truth shall spring out of the earth; and righteousness shall look down from heaven. Yea, the Lord shall give that which is good." (Ps. 85:8-12.) Such is the manner in which the restoration shall be brought to pass. Heaven shall reveal her wonders, and earth shall bear an echoing testimony. God shall speak to his prophets, and the Book of Mormon shall proclaim the same words. The same words that flow down from above shall spring forth in the record of a civilization long dead.

Isaiah, whose voice was heard some twenty-six hundred years before the voice spoke from the dust, received these words from the Lord: "Drop down, ye heavens, from above, and let the skies pour down righteousness: let the earth open, and let them bring forth salvation, and let righteousness spring up together; I the Lord have created it." It is the age-old message of heaven and earth uniting to testify of the truth. Having given these words of truth to his great prophet, the Lord then, as a warning to the disbelievers of the last days, acclaims: "Woe unto him that striveth with his Maker!" (Isa. 45:8-9.) Our Maker's words as they come down from heaven and as they spring forth out of the earth must not be treated lightly.

A Voice Speaks from the Dust

Behold what wonders God hath wrought! Truth springs out of the earth; the gold plates are translated by the gift and power of

God; and the voice we hear is one that whispers from the dust. It is the voice of all the Nephis, of Alma and Amulek and Abinadi, of Ether and Mormon and Moroni—of all the Nephite and Jaredite prophets. It is the voice of the Lord Jesus Christ, who ministered among the Nephites, inviting them to feel the prints of the nails in his hands and in his feet and to thrust their hands into his riven *split* side. It is the voice of doctrine and testimony and miracles. It is the voice of God speaking to men through the Book of Mormon.

Knowing beforehand what should come to pass in the last days, the Lord Jehovah spoke by the mouth of Isaiah relative to the Nephite peoples who should "be visited of the Lord of hosts with thunder, and with earthquake, and great noise, with storm and tempest, and the flame of devouring fire." Because they forsook the Lord and fought against Zion, it should be with them "as when an hungry man dreameth, and, behold, he eateth; but he awaketh, and his soul is empty: or as when a thirsty man dreameth, and, behold, he drinketh; but he awaketh, and, behold, he is faint, and his soul hath appetite." Because they rejected the gospel and fought against the truth, they should be destroyed.

But a record would be preserved, and through it the great things revealed to their prophets would be known again. "And thou shalt be brought down," the prophetic word intones, "and shalt speak out of the ground, and thy speech shall be low out of the dust, and thy voice shall be, as of one that hath a familiar spirit, out of the ground, and thy speech shall whisper out of the dust." The spirit and tone and tenor of the message shall be familiar. A like account, one dealing with the same truths, the same laws, and the same ordinances, is found in the Bible.

In this setting Isaiah speaks of the universal apostasy; of the words of a sealed book being delivered to one who is learned, but who confesses that he cannot read a sealed book; of the Lord piercing the spiritual darkness and doing a marvelous work and a wonder among men, which work is the restoration of the gospel; and of the influence the book—the Book of Mormon—will then have in all the world. We shall note some of this shortly. (Isa. 29:1-24.)

Isaiah's words were engraved on the brass plates. Nephi pondered their meaning and learned by revelation that they applied to the descendants of Lehi in their American promised land and also to the Gentiles in the last days. In expounding them, Nephi taught that the seed of Lehi would dwindle in unbelief after the destruction of the Nephites, "after the Lord God shall have camped against them round about, and shall have laid siege against them with a mount, and raised forts against them." Herein is the destruction of the Nephite peoples foretold. "And after they shall have been brought down low in the dust, even that they are not, yet the words of the righteous shall be written, and the prayers of the faithful shall be heard, and all those who have dwindled in unbelief shall not be forgotten." How the faithful had pled with the Lord that the gospel would come again in the last days and go to their seed and to all men!

"For those who shall be destroyed," who are the Nephites, "shall speak unto them out of the ground, and their speech shall be low out of the dust, and their voice shall be as one that hath a familiar spirit; for the Lord God will give unto him power, that he may whisper concerning them, even as it were out of the ground; and their speech shall whisper out of the dust."

The Nephite voice shall never cease. It shall be trumpeted in every ear until the end of time. The whisper from the dust shall build up to a mighty crescendo which shall reverberate from one end of heaven to the other. What began as a whisper will soon sound like roll upon roll of thunder. "For thus saith the Lord God: They shall write the things which shall be done among them, and they shall be written and sealed up in a book, and those who have dwindled in unbelief [the Lamanites in the day of their degeneracy] shall not have them, for they seek to destroy the things of God.

"Wherefore, as those who have been destroyed [the Nephites] have been destroyed speedily; and the multitude of their terrible ones shall be as chaff that passeth away—yea, thus saith the Lord God: It shall be at an instant, suddenly—And it shall come to pass, that those who have dwindled in unbelief shall be smitten by the hand of the Gentiles." That is, the American Indians shall be smitten and driven by the American people. At this point Nephi speaks of the dire apostasy of the last days, of the many false churches and secret combinations, and of the priestcrafts that lead men astray. (2 Ne. 26:1-33.)

"In the last days," Nephi continues, when those in "all the nations" and "upon all the lands of the earth" are "drunken with iniquity and all manner of abominations," then once again shall the wrath of God rest upon them as it did upon the Nephites at the time of their destruction. "And when that day shall come they shall be visited of the Lord of Hosts, with thunder and with earthquake, and with the flame of devouring fire. And all the nations that fight against Zion, and that distress her, shall be as a dream of a night vision."

Nephi continues by quoting the words of Isaiah about the hungry and thirsty who dream their needs are satisfied and who awake to find their bellies gnawing with hunger and their thirst unquenched. He notes Isaiah's words about those—about all men—who are drunken, but not with wine, and who stagger, but not with strong drink, and then he comes to the book, the Book of Mormon.

"And it shall come to pass that the Lord God shall bring forth unto you the words of a book, and they shall be the words of them which have slumbered. And behold the book shall be sealed; and in the book shall be a revelation from God, from the beginning of the world to the ending thereof." Such were the gold plates delivered by Moroni, not to the world, but to a prophet called of God to translate and proclaim a portion of the divine word engraved by the ancients upon the sacred plates. In part the plates were sealed. "Wherefore, because of the things which are sealed up, the things which are sealed shall not be delivered in the day of the wickedness and abominations of the people. Wherefore the book shall be kept from them."

When wickedness ends, when abominations are no more, when the Lord comes and the wicked are destroyed—which is the end of the world—then shall the book itself come forth for the edification of all. "For the book shall be sealed by the power of God, and the revelation which was sealed shall be kept in the book until the own due time of the Lord, that they may come forth; for behold, they reveal all things from the foundation of the world unto the end thereof."

The restoration of all things cannot be completed until all things are restored. As we have seen, the Lord Jesus cannot come until the era of restoration commences, but the full restoration will not occur until after he comes. "And the day cometh that the words of the book which were sealed shall be read upon the house tops; and they shall be read by the power of Christ; and all things shall be revealed unto the children of men which ever have been among the children of men, and which ever will be even unto the end of the earth."

Nephi's account then speaks of the translation of the portion of the book that men in our day are able to receive; of the witnesses who "shall testify to the truth of the book and the things therein"; and of the learned one (Professor Charles Anthon) to whom some of the words were delivered, and who said, "I cannot read a sealed book." (JS-H 1:63-65.)

Next the inspired writing records the commandment given to Joseph Smith: "Touch not the things which are sealed." And also, "When thou hast read the words which I have commanded thee, and obtained the witnesses which I have promised unto thee, then shalt thou seal up the book again, and hide it up unto me, that I may preserve the words which thou hast not read, until I shall see fit in mine own wisdom to reveal all things unto the children of men. For behold, I am God; and I am a God of miracles; and I will show unto the world that I am the same yesterday, today, and forever; and I work not among the children of men save it be according to their faith."

Then there follows the prophecy about a marvelous work and a wonder—the restored gospel—which is to come forth after the Book of Mormon as we have it is translated, followed by the prophetic words relative to the effect our present Book of Mormon shall have upon men when we proclaim its message to the world. (2 Ne. 27:1-35.) We shall speak of this in chapter 14.

Ephraim Holds the Stick of Joseph

Ezekiel, who was carried captive into Babylon and who lived in the days of Lehi, received the divine word that there would be two great books of scripture in the last days—the Bible and the

Book of Mormon. The one should come from the kingdom of Judah and the other should have its source in the kingdom of Ephraim, the two nations that comprised divided Israel anciently.

To this great prophet of Judah, the Lord said: "Take thee one stick, and write upon it, For Judah, and for the children of Israel his companions." The designation and title thus recorded on the stick symbolized the word of the Lord that came to the prophets of Judah, some of whose words are preserved for us in the Bible. The people of Judah, among whom Ezekiel then ministered, knew of such prophetic writings and such seeric sayings as had thus far been received. Their contents were taught in every household.

"Then take another stick, and write upon it, For Joseph, the stick of Ephraim, and for all the house of Israel his companions." The message so inscribed symbolized the divine word that would come through the house of Joseph, that Joseph who was sold into Egypt and whose sons, Ephraim and Manasseh, each held tribal status in Israel. Of these words the people of Judah had no knowledge in that day, for the divine sayings were yet to find utterance through prophetic lips. Ezekiel's hearers could not have done other than wonder what great sayings were yet to come through another people, a people to whom but little of the word of the Lord had thus far been revealed.

Then came the divine injunction: "And join them one to another into one stick; and they shall become one in thine hand." The two sacred books, the two volumes of holy scripture, the word of the Lord as it came to Judah and his fellows on the one hand, and the same word as it came to Joseph and his fellows on the other— these accounts were to become one in Ezekiel's hand.

Each would bear witness of Christ. Each would teach sound doctrine. Each would chart the course to eternal life in the Everlasting Presence. Each would be the mind and will and voice of God to the world. One would be a witness from the Old World, the other from the New World. And they would be one, for there is one God and one Shepherd over all the earth, and he speaks the same words to all who will attune their souls so as to hear his eternal message.

"And when the children of thy people shall speak unto thee,

saying, Wilt thou not shew us what thou meanest by these? Say unto them, Thus saith the Lord God; Behold, I will take the stick of Joseph, which is in the hand of Ephraim, and the tribes of Israel his fellows, and will put them with him, even with the stick of Judah, and make them one stick, and they shall be one in mine hand. And the sticks whereon thou writest shall be in thine hand before their eyes."

Thus the Lord foretold his purposes relative to the written records which would testify of him and of his goodness unto men. Ezekiel was then to use the two sticks that became one as a means of teaching the gathering of Israel, the restoration of the gospel, the building of temples in the last days, and the millennial reign of the Eternal David, concerning all of which we shall have more to say hereafter. (Ezek. 37:15-28.)

The stick of Joseph—the prophetic word that has come through his seed—is now in the hands of Ephraim. Joseph Smith was of Ephraim; we are of Ephraim; and Moroni has given to us "the keys of the record of the stick of Ephraim." (D&C 27:5.) Ephraim receives the blessings of the firstborn, and as such he is gathering first in the last days. The Book of Mormon, which gathers Israel, is in our hands and is one with the Bible in presenting the truths of salvation to the world.

All of these things were known to Lehi; in addition, he knew they would be fulfilled through his seed. "I am a descendant of Joseph who was carried captive into Egypt," Lehi said. "And great were the covenants of the Lord which he made unto Joseph." These covenants are written on the brass plates, from which source Lehi learned them, and they will in due course come forth in their fulness and perfection for all men to read.

"Joseph truly saw our day," the day of the Nephites, Lehi continues. "And he obtained a promise of the Lord, that out of the fruits of his loins the Lord God would raise up a righteous branch unto the house of Israel; not the Messiah"—one of whose titles is the Branch, signifying he would be born as a branch of that olive tree which is Israel—"but a branch which was to be broken off, nevertheless, to be remembered in the covenants of the Lord that the Messiah should be made manifest unto them in the latter days, in the spirit of power, unto the bringing of them out of darkness unto light—yea, out of hidden darkness and out of captivity unto freedom."

To Joseph the Lord said: "The fruit of thy loins shall write; and the fruit of the loins of Judah shall write; and that which shall be written by the fruit of thy loins, and also that which shall be written by the fruit of the loins of Judah, shall grow together, unto the confounding of false doctrines and laying down of contentions, and establishing peace among the fruit of thy loins, and bringing them to the knowledge of their fathers in the latter days, and also to the knowledge of my covenants, saith the Lord."

Also to Joseph of old, but speaking of Joseph Smith, the seer of the latter days, the Lord said: "I will give unto him that he shall write the writing of the fruit of thy loins, unto the fruit of thy loins." That is, Joseph Smith will translate the Book of Mormon and send it forth to the Lamanites, who are the seed of Joseph. "And the words which he shall write shall be the words which are expedient in my wisdom should go forth unto the fruit of thy loins. And it shall be as if the fruit of thy loins had cried unto them from the dust; for I know their faith.

"And they shall cry from the dust; yea, even repentance unto their brethren, even after many generations have gone by them. And it shall come to pass that their cry shall go, even according to the simpleness of their words. Because of their faith their words shall proceed forth out of my mouth unto their brethren who are the fruit of thy loins; and the weakness of their words will I make strong in their faith, unto the remembering of my covenant which I made unto thy fathers." (2 Ne. 3:1-21.)

We are witnesses that all of these things have or shall come to pass, and we testify that the Book of Mormon, both as now constituted and as it shall hereafter be, shall change the whole history of the world.

Chapter 14

THE BOOK
THAT WELCOMES
THE SECOND COMING

The Divine Mission of the Divine Book

Few men on earth, either in or out of the Church, have caught the vision of what the Book of Mormon is all about. Few are they among men who know the part it has played and will yet play in preparing the way for the coming of Him of whom it is a new witness. Few are they who believe its truths and abide by its precepts to such a degree that they would qualify to read the sealed portion of the plates and learn the full account of what the Lord has in store for the people of the world.

Guarding carefully against the use of unwarranted superlatives, let us summarize the divine mission of the Book of Mormon under these headings:

1. *The Book of Mormon bears witness of Christ.*

This holy book, this sacred record, this divine transcript copied from celestial pages which are filed in the libraries above, this book bears solemn witness of Him by whom salvation comes. Above all else it acclaims the divine sonship of the Son of God; it speaks of the Holy Messiah who came to save his people; it tells of his birth, ministry, crucifixion, and resurrection. Having the prints of the nails in his hands and in his feet, and carrying the gashing wound made by a Roman spear in his side, he himself ministered, in love and compassion, to his other sheep in their

American promised land. Christ the Lord stands at the heart and core and center of the book. And the witness it bears of him shall go forth to every nation, and kindred, and tongue, and people, before he comes to rule and reign on earth for a thousand years.

The Bible itself, which recounts much of his life and many of his doings, does not bear a sweeter or purer testimony of his infinite goodness and grace than does this companion volume of holy writ. Why should any who profess to love the Lord and to seek his face have aught but praise for a work that acclaims so perfectly the majesty and glory of the one who is Lord of all?

2. *The Book of Mormon reveals and proclaims the everlasting gospel to the world.*

Salvation is in Christ and in his holy gospel. Moroni, in glorious immortality, flew through the midst of heaven to bring again the everlasting word; Joseph Smith translated the ancient record; and it is now going forth in many languages to all who will receive it. The Book of Mormon contains the fulness of the everlasting gospel. When the revealed word says the gospel restored through Joseph Smith shall be preached in every nation and to every people before the Lord comes, it includes the directive that the Book of Mormon shall go forth to all people and then shall the end come. This book is the way and the means, prepared by the Lord, to preach his gospel in all the world for a witness unto all people.

3. *The Book of Mormon teaches the true doctrines and proclaims the saving truths.*

Truth, diamond truth, pure truth, the truth of heaven, leads men to salvation. True doctrines save; false doctrines damn. In the midst of darkness and apostasy the Book of Mormon came forth to proclaim the doctrines of salvation in plainness and purity, so that all men may know what they must believe to be saved in God's kingdom.

4. *The Book of Mormon sustains and clarifies the Bible.*

The Bible bears true witness of God and his gospel as far as it is translated correctly. Many plain and precious things have been deleted, however; and the Book of Mormon is the means, provided by divine wisdom, to pour forth the gospel word as it was given in

160

perfection to the ancients. It has come to preserve and sustain the Bible, not to destroy or dilute its message.

5. *The Book of Mormon gathers scattered Israel into the true fold and to the appointed places.*

Is the Book of Mormon accomplishing its divine purpose? How else can we account for the fact that those who believe its words forsake all that they have and join with the saints to build up the kingdom? Hundreds of thousands have forsaken lands, homes, families, and the nations of their ancestors to start anew, in poverty and in weakness, with the Lord's people in a desert wasteland. Hundreds of thousands now assemble in stakes of Zion in nation upon nation because they know by the power of the Holy Ghost that the Book of Mormon is true. And endless hosts shall yet place the beauty of its message ahead of the wealth and prestige of the world.

6. *The Book of Mormon proves the truth and divinity of the Lord's great latter-day work.*

If the Book of Mormon is true, then Jesus Christ is the Son of the living God, because that book bears repeated witness of this eternal verity. If the Book of Mormon is true, then Joseph Smith was called of God to usher in the dispensation of the fulness of times and to set up again on earth the Church and kingdom of God. The book proves he was a prophet. If he received the plates from an angel; if he translated them by the gift and power of God; if he received revelations from the Almighty—all of which is a reality if the Book of Mormon is true—who can say he was not a prophet? If the Book of Mormon is true and Joseph Smith is a prophet, who can deny that The Church of Jesus Christ of Latter-day Saints, which he set up by divine direction, is in fact the kingdom of God on earth?

7. *The Book of Mormon came to prepare a people for the second coming of the Son of Man.*

This is implicit in all we have said. It is the restored gospel and the gathering of Israel that prepare men to meet their Lord. It is repentance and right living and keeping the commandments that qualify them to abide the day of his coming. And it is the Book of

Mormon that preaches the gospel and invites men to believe and repent.

8. *The Book of Mormon came to save (or damn) the souls of men.*

Such is the grand conclusion. Men will gain celestial rest or welter with the damned in hell depending on how they view the Nephite record. He that believeth shall be saved! Believeth what? Men must believe the everlasting gospel; they must accept the prophets and legal administrators sent in their day; they must cleave unto the word of truth given of God in the day of their probation. All of this requires that they believe the Lord's word as found in the Book of Mormon—in the Book of Salvation, if you will.

Much of the summary of the power and purpose, the mission and influence, of the Book of Mormon has already been discussed in one connection or another. We shall now expand our bare-bones outline on the remaining points.

The Book of Mormon Perfects the Biblical Message

The Holy Bible has done more to preserve the culture and civilization of Christendom than any other single thing. The invention of printing and the publishing of the Bible did more to lift the shroud of darkness that covered the earth than anything else ever did. The King James Version of the Bible has preserved the English tongue and kept the English-speaking peoples anchored to those standards of decency and morality without which men become animals and nations crumble and decay. And yet neither this Bible nor any Bible has been preserved in sufficient purity to enable men to find the course leading to eternal life and then to walk therein. To gain this end—so devoutly to be desired—the world had to await the coming forth of the Book of Mormon.

Nephi saw in vision both the Bible and the Book of Mormon. As to the Bible he was told by an angel: "When it proceeded forth from the mouth of a Jew it contained the plainness of the gospel of the Lord, of whom the twelve apostles bear record; and . . . these things go forth from the Jews in purity unto the Gentiles." Then came the day of darkness, of apostasy, and of evil.

162

Then, after the gospel truths went forth "by the hand of the twelve apostles of the Lamb, from the Jews unto the Gentiles," the angel said, "thou seest the foundation of a great and abominable church, which is most abominable above all other churches." This evil church, this church of the devil, this outgrowth of primitive Christianity, was the most wicked and satanic church then on earth. It pretended to make salvation available while following Lucifer rather than the Lord. Of those in this dire church the angel continued: "They have taken away from the gospel of the Lamb many parts which are plain and most precious; and also many covenants of the Lord have they taken away."

Why did they do this evil thing? The angelic answer was: "And all this have they done that they might pervert the right ways of the Lord, that they might blind the eyes and harden the hearts of the children of men." When the scriptures are perverted, it becomes easy to find ways to walk after the manner of the world and revel in ungodliness. The philosophies of men, mingled with scripture, soon replace the pure word as it was once written in the holy record. "Wherefore, thou seest that after the book hath gone forth through the hands of the great and abominable church," the angelic word continues, "that there are many plain and precious things taken away from the book, which is the book of the Lamb of God."

Thus in the earliest days of the apostasy, the church that once was the Lord's forsook him and worshipped and served what its fancy chose. Then Nephi saw the perverted Bible go forth among all the nations of the Gentiles, including the people in America. In this setting the angel said: "Because of the many plain and precious things which have been taken out of the book, which were plain unto the understanding of the children of men, according to the plainness which is in the Lamb of God—because of these things which are taken away out of the gospel of the Lamb, an exceeding great many do stumble, yea, insomuch that Satan hath great power over them."

But through it all a brighter day lay ahead. The Lord God promised that he would not "suffer that the Gentiles shall forever remain in that awful state of blindness, which thou beholdest they are in, because of the plain and most precious parts of the gospel of

163

the Lamb which have been kept back by that abominable church, whose formation thou hast seen."

There was to be a day of restoration; the light of heaven was to pierce the darkness covering the earth; new scripture was to lift the gross darkness enshrouding the hearts of men. For thus saith the Lord: "After the Gentiles do stumble exceedingly, because of the most plain and precious parts of the gospel of the Lamb which have been kept back by that abominable church, which is the mother of harlots, saith the Lamb—I will be merciful unto the Gentiles in that day, insomuch that I will bring forth unto them, in mine own power, much of my gospel, which shall be plain and precious, saith the Lamb."

The promise is then made of the coming forth of the Book of Mormon. Lehi's seed shall keep the record; they shall be destroyed and dwindle in unbelief; and their records shall be hidden in the earth. In due course these records shall "come forth unto the Gentiles, by the gift and power of the Lamb. And in them shall be written my gospel, saith the Lamb, and my rock and my salvation." (1 Ne. 13:20-36.)

And thus, the Lord be praised, we have his eternal promise that the Bible will be added to, clarified, perfected, as it were, by the Nephite scripture—that glorious volume, the Book of Mormon—before the second coming of the Son of Man!

Lucifer Wages War Against the Book of Mormon

Satan guided his servants in taking many plain and precious things, and many of the covenants of the Lord, from the Bible, so that men would stumble and fall and lose their souls. When these truths and doctrines and covenants are restored through the Book of Mormon, what may we expect from Satan and from his servants? Their natural reaction—their craft is in danger!—will be to poison the minds of men against the Nephite scripture, so they will continue to stumble as they rely on the Bible alone.

One obvious approach is for them to write in their creeds, to preach from their pulpits, and to use all their powers of learning and sophistry to proclaim such doctrines as these: revelation has ceased; the gifts of the Spirit are no longer needed; the Bible suffices; it contains all that is needed for salvation; what was good enough for Paul and Peter is good enough for us. To all such who should arise in the last days, and their numbers are many, this word came from the Lord to Nephi: "Wo be unto him that hearkeneth unto the precepts of men, and denieth the power of God, and the gift of the Holy Ghost!" What blessing is there in a religion where the power of God is not manifest and where the gifts of the Spirit are not found? Can a religion without power to heal the sick and raise the dead have power to exalt a mortal soul in celestial glory?

"Yea, wo be unto him that saith: We have received, and we need no more!" How unthinkable it is that man can close the mouth of God! If the Great God is the same yesterday, today, and forever; if he is no respecter of persons and he spoke in times past; if a soul is just as precious in his sight today as it ever was, how dare anyone presume to close the heavens and say, "Our God is dead; his voice is stilled; revelation was for the ancients, not for us"? Are all the problems of the earth solved? Is there no need for divine guidance to direct the affairs of men today?

"Wo unto all those who tremble, and are angry because of the truth of God! For behold, he that is built upon the rock receiveth it with gladness; and he that is built upon a sandy foundation trembleth lest he shall fall." Why should men be angry because God spoke to Joseph Smith? If they do not believe he did so, then why rise up in wrath? If they are right, and there is no revelation, they have nothing to fear. But the devil knows who the Lord's prophets are and where the work of the Almighty is found. And all who are built on false and sandy foundations rise up in fear. Only those who belong to false churches fear and deride the prophets; only those without the light and guidance of heaven rise up to fight the Lord's work.

"Wo be unto him that shall say: We have received the word of God, and we need no more of the word of God, for we have enough!" How devilish and evil it is to say: "We want no new truths; we choose to remain in darkness; we prefer ignorance as a way of life. The light of this candle suffices; let no man discover electricity. We have enough."

The Lord's own condemnation of all such small, bigoted, and prejudiced souls is set forth in these words: "Thus saith the Lord God: I will give unto the children of men line upon line, precept upon precept, here a little and there a little; and blessed are those who hearken unto my precepts, and lend an ear unto my counsel, for they shall learn wisdom; for unto him that receiveth will I give more; and from them that shall say, We have enough, from them shall be taken away even that which they have." How plain and pure is this word! How it accords with all that God has said in all ages! Surely the day shall come when all those who find fault with the revelations given to Joseph Smith and who deny the divine status of the Book of Mormon shall have cause to fear and tremble. Surely their souls shall be in turmoil and their minds filled with anxieties as they stand before the judgment bar.

"Cursed is he that putteth his trust in man," the divine word continues, "or maketh flesh his arm, or shall hearken unto the precepts of men, save their precepts shall be given by the power of the Holy Ghost." Unless the power of God attends the teaching of doctrine, unless the Holy Spirit bears witness of the truths expressed, unless the words spoken have divine approval, they have no saving power. And where there is no salvation, there must of necessity be damnation.

"Wo be unto the Gentiles, saith the Lord God of Hosts! For notwithstanding I shall lengthen out mine arm unto them from day to day, they will deny me." How many things there are on every hand that invite and entice men to believe the word found in modern scripture. One scientific discovery after another bears witness of what God by his prophets has proclaimed to the world. Every jot and tittle of reason and logic and sense combine to show the excellence of the Lord's way as recorded in holy writ. And yet men deny and disbelieve.

"Nevertheless, I will be merciful unto them, saith the Lord God, if they will repent and come unto me; for mine arm is lengthened out all the day long, saith the Lord God of Hosts." (2 Ne. 28:26-32.) Thanks be to God there is hope—even for those who thus far have fought the truth—if they will repent of their false doctrines and false teachings; if they will forsake the master who heretofore has guided their thinking and desires; and if they will worship the Lord and fellowship his saints.

Having laid this foundation, the Lord goes on to a glorious climax. In doing so, he both reasons with men and announces his own views. And who can deny his word or refute the divine logic it sets forth? "My words shall hiss forth unto the ends of the earth," saith the Lord God, "for a standard unto my people, which are of the house of Israel; And because my words shall hiss forth"—note it well, it is one of the signs of the times; one of the things that must and shall occur before the Second Coming; one of the things that lets us know the day is near—"many of the Gentiles shall say: A Bible! A Bible! We have got a Bible, and there cannot be any more Bible." How vain, how foolish, how arrogant for man to tell God what he can and cannot do. Are there no new truths to be revealed? Were the Jews the only people to whom God ever spoke? Who but Satan would teach such a doctrine?

"But thus saith the Lord God: O fools, they shall have a Bible"—strong language this!—"and it shall proceed forth from the Jews, mine ancient covenant people." The Bible is the book of the Jews; salvation is of the Jews; they are the source of Gentile knowledge about God and his laws. "And what thank they the Jews for the Bible which they receive from them? Yea, what do the Gentiles mean? Do they remember the travails, and the labors, and the pains of the Jews, and their diligence unto me, in bringing forth salvation unto the Gentiles?"

Jesus, who was crucified, and Peter, who died in like manner, were Jews. Isaiah, who was sawn asunder, and Jeremiah, who languished in a foul dungeon, were Jews. Daniel, who was cast into a den of lions, and Ezekiel, who was carried captive into Babylon, were Jews. "O ye Gentiles, have ye remembered the Jews, mine ancient covenant people? Nay; but ye have cursed them, and have hated them, and have not sought to recover them. But behold, I will return all these things upon your own heads; for I the Lord have not forgotten my people."

How severe is the condemnation of those who suppose they believe part of the Lord's word, but who openly reject the re-mainder. "Thou fool, that shall say: A Bible, we have got a Bible, and we need no more Bible. Have ye obtained a Bible save it were by the Jews?" And if the world received its Bible from the Jews, wherein does this differ from receiving the Book of Mormon from the Nephites?

"Know ye not that there are more nations than one? Know ye not that I, the Lord your God, have created all men, and that I remember those who are upon the isles of the sea; and that I rule in the heavens above and in the earth beneath; and I bring forth my word unto the children of men, yea, even upon all the nations of the earth? Wherefore murmur ye, because that ye shall receive more of my word?" (2 Ne. 29:2-8.) And thus it is. Let those who reject the Book of Mormon know that, like their counterparts in Jerusalem who rejected the Lord Jesus when he ministered among them, they are fulfilling the prophetic word and are bringing to pass one of the signs of the times.

Chapter 15

THE BOOK THAT PREPARES THE WAY

The Divine Power of the Divine Book

The written word—how great it is! The divine word—how it has shaped the destiny of men and governed the course of nations! The holy scriptures—how they have brought to pass the purposes of the Lord, among both believers and unbelievers!

Nephi, at the peril of his own life, slew Laban and gained the brass plates for himself and his people. Because of them, the Nephites knew and lived the law of Moses; because of them, they preserved their language, their culture, their civilization, and even their religion. The Mulekites, on the other hand, being without the written word, dwindled in unbelief, lost their language and culture and religion, and degenerated to a low and uncivilized state. So also was it with the Lamanites after they destroyed the Nephite nation. They were degenerate, slothful, and without God in the world; they enjoyed none of the gifts of the Spirit and had no hope of eternal life.

Such decency and civilization as prevailed during the dark ages came because a few biblical truths were taught and a handful of people had access to the written word itself. The revival of learning and the breaking of the shackles of ignorance came to pass because the Bible was published to the people. Protestant churches exist because members of the Catholic Church began to read the Bible and compare what they learned with the practices of their church. There were wars and battles and crusades; there were compacts and alliances and treaties; there were nations and kingdoms and peoples—all of which played their part in history because men felt this or that way about the written word. The whole history of the the English-speaking peoples in particular has been one of religious wars and religious conflicts.

Nor has it been nor shall it be any different where the Book of Mormon is concerned. Like the Bible, it is a volume of holy writ that speaks forth the mind and will of the Almighty. Like the Bible, it invites men to forsake the world and live as becometh saints. Like the Bible, it has such an impact upon the hearts of men that they are prepared to die in defense of their beliefs. Already the ten thousands of Ephraim and the thousands of Manasseh have left Babylon and come to Zion with songs of everlasting joy because of it. And before the end of the world, which is the premillennial destruction of the wicked, and before the end of the earth, which shall not occur until after the Millennium, the Book of Mormon shall so affect men that the whole earth and all its peoples will have been influenced and governed by it.

What says the prophetic word with reference to the divine power that shall attend this divine book?

After the Lord told Enoch that in the last days righteousness would come down out of heaven (meaning the gospel would be restored), and that truth would come out of the earth to bear testimony of Christ and his gospel (meaning the Book of Mormon would come forth), then the divine word acclaimed: "And righteousness and truth will I cause to sweep the earth as with a flood." That is to say: The restored gospel and the Book of Mormon will surge forth in a tide that cannot be stayed. As flooding rains and surging rivers sweep bridges and obstacles before them; as houses and lands and even mountains flow down by the power of a flood; as water cleanses and washes away the filth of the world—so shall the divine word go forth. There is no power like the power of a flood; nothing can stay its swirling, surging, sweeping waves. So shall it be with the spread of truth in the last days.

And why shall the flood of truth—the gospel and the Book of Mormon—go forth? "To gather out mine elect from the four quarters of the earth," the Lord says, "unto a place which I shall prepare, an Holy City, that my people may gird up their loins, and be looking forth for the time of my coming; for there shall be my tabernacle, and it shall be called Zion, a New Jerusalem." (Moses 7:62.)

What then is the power of the Book of Mormon? It will proclaim the everlasting gospel; it will gather Israel; it will build the New Jerusalem; it will prepare a people for the Second Coming; it will usher in the Millennium—at least it will play such an important part in all of these that its value and power can scarcely be overstated.

Ezekiel bears a like witness. It is part of his prophecy about the Stick of Judah and the Stick of Joseph. When he was asked, "Wilt thou not shew us what thou meanest by these?" the Lord directed him to answer that even as the Bible and the Book of Mormon became one in his hand, so should the divided kingdoms of Judah and Ephraim become one kingdom in the last days. "Say unto them," he was told, "Thus saith the Lord God; Behold, I will take the children of Israel from among the heathen, whither they be gone, and will gather them on every side, and bring them into their own land: And I will make them one nation in the land upon the mountains of Israel." One nation, one people, one gospel, one set of standard works, one doctrine (that in the Bible and the Book of Mormon)—such shall be their heritage in that day.

"And one king shall be king to them all," and he shall be the Lord Jesus Christ, the Son of David, the King of Israel. "And they shall be no more two nations, neither shall they be divided into two kingdoms any more at all," for those who come unto Christ "are no more strangers and foreigners, but fellowcitizens with the saints, and of the household of God." (Eph. 2:19.) They are members of one kingdom, the kingdom of their King.

"Neither shall they defile themselves any more with their idols, nor with their detestable things, nor with any of their transgressions: but I will save them out of all their dwellingplaces, wherein they have sinned, and will cleanse them: so shall they be my people, and I will be their God." They will believe in Christ, repent of their sins, be cleansed in the waters of baptism, and become the Lord's people.

"And David my servant"—the Eternal David, the Son of David, the one of whom David of old was a type and a shadow— "shall be king over them; and they all shall have one shepherd." This is the day of which the angel said to Nephi: "These last records, which thou hast seen among the Gentiles [the Book of Mormon and other latter-day scripture], shall establish the truth of the first, which are of the twelve apostles of the Lamb [the Bible], and shall make known the plain and precious things which have been taken away from them; and shall make known to all kindreds, tongues, and people, that the Lamb of God is the Son of the Eternal Father, and the Savior of the world; and that all men must come unto him, or they cannot be saved. And they must come according to the words which shall be established by the mouth of the Lamb; and the words of the Lamb shall be made known in the records of thy seed [the Book of Mormon], as well as in the records of the twelve apostles of the Lamb [the Bible]; wherefore they both shall be established in one; for there is one God and one Shepherd over all the earth." (1 Ne. 13:40-41.)

"They shall also walk in my judgments, and observe my statutes, and do them." They shall keep the commandments; they shall live the gospel; they shall walk in the light. They shall dwell in the appointed place, "and my servant David"—the Eternal David—"shall be their prince for ever." Christ will reign among them, and he will be their everlasting King.

"Moreover I will make a covenant of peace with them; it shall be an everlasting covenant with them." They shall have the gospel; it is the covenant of peace; it is the new and everlasting covenant, the covenant of salvation.

"And I will place them, and multiply them, and will set my sanctuary [my temple] in the midst of them for evermore. My tabernacle also shall be with them: yea, I will be their God, and they shall be my people. And the heathen shall know that I the Lord do sanctify Israel, when my sanctuary [temple] shall be in the midst of them for evermore." (Ezek. 37:15-28.)

What is it that shall happen when the Bible and the Book of Mormon become one in the Lord's hand? Israel shall gather both spiritually and temporally. They shall become one people, and division and disunity among them shall cease. "Ephraim shall not envy Judah, and Judah shall not vex Ephraim." (Isa. 11:13.) The Lord himself, the Eternal David, shall be their King and their Shepherd. They will repent and be baptized and keep the commandments. The everlasting gospel shall be their most prized possession, and the Lord's houses of worship and his holy temple will be in their midst.

And how will all this be brought to pass? Not by a dead and dying Christendom; not by a people without power and authority; not by those who do not even know what the Lord's sanctuary is; not by the Bible, from which many plain and precious things and many covenants of the Lord have been lost. These things will come to pass in the day of restoration, when righteousness comes down from heaven and truth springs out of the earth. They will be brought to pass by the power of God, by his holy gospel, by the Book of Mormon, wherein the gospel is recorded, and which is sent forth to testify of Christ, to teach doctrine, and to prove the truth and divinity of the Lord's great latter-day work.

Isaiah's great prophecy about the Book of Mormon and the restoration of the gospel speaks of the destruction of the Nephite nation; of their voice speaking from the dust with a familiar spirit; of the day of apostasy when men are drunken but not with wine, and when they stagger but not with strong drink; of the vision of all being as the words of a book that is sealed; of the Lord restoring the gospel; of their land becoming a fruitful field; and, then, of the Book of Mormon going forth to play its part in the great work of the latter days. "And in that day"—when all these things come to pass—"shall the deaf hear the words of the book, and the eyes of the blind shall see out of obscurity and out of darkness." (2 Ne. 27:29.)

"Bring forth the blind people that have eyes, and the deaf that have ears." (Isa. 43:8.) Bring forth those who are blind to the light of the gospel, who cannot see that which is shown before them in the Bible; bring forth those who are deaf to the voice of the Spirit, who do not hear the voice of the Lord as it speaks from the ancient scriptures. Let them see and hear the words of the Book of Mormon where the precious truths are set forth with such plainness that none need err. Then will their eyes be opened and their ears un-stopped, and the deaf shall hear and the blind see.

"And the meek also shall increase, and their joy shall be in the Lord, and the poor among men shall rejoice in the Holy One of Israel." (2 Ne. 27:30.) The meek are the God-fearing and the righteous; they come unto the Lord because of the Book of Mormon; they rejoice in his glorious goodness and shout praises to the Holy One of Israel.

Then the holy word speaks of what shall be at the Second Coming. "For assuredly as the Lord liveth they"—his saints, the meek among men, those who have believed the words of the book— "shall see that the terrible one is brought to naught, and the scorner is consumed, and all that watch for iniquity are cut off," as also will be the case with those "that make a man an offender for a word, and lay a snare for him that reproveth in the gate, and turn aside the just for a thing of naught." (2 Ne. 27:31-32.) This is the day when every corruptible thing shall be consumed. Those who believe the Book of Mormon and turn unto the Lord shall be saved in the day of burning, for the book came to prepare a people to meet their God.

"Therefore thus saith the Lord, who redeemed Abraham, concerning the house of Jacob, Jacob shall not now be ashamed, neither shall his face now wax pale." Those who accept the gospel and live the law no longer fear the day when the wicked shall be consumed. "But when he seeth his children, the work of mine hands, in the midst of him, they shall sanctify my name, and sanctify the Holy One of Jacob, and shall fear the God of Israel." Israel and her children and her children's children shall worship and serve the true and living God.

"They also that erred in spirit shall come to understanding, and they that murmured shall learn doctrine." (Isa. 29:1-24.) Such is the purpose of the Book of Mormon. Members of false churches who err in spirit, who think they have the truth, are brought by the Book of Mormon to the fulness of the gospel. Those who have based their beliefs on isolated verses and obscure passages, and who have wondered and murmured at seeming biblical conflicts, come to learn sound doctrine. No longer do they worry about the atonement, salvation by grace alone, infant baptism, the priest-hood, the gifts of the Spirit, the passages about an apostasy, a gospel restoration, and the gathering of Israel. All things fall into place because of this new witness for Christ and his gospel, this witness which bears the name of the prophet Mormon.

Proving the Second Coming

We are mindful of Peter's prophecy that in the last days scoff-ers shall rise up, "walking after their own lusts, And saying, Where is the promise of his coming?" (2 Pet. 3:3-4.) We are aware that few only among us mortals, including even those who call themselves Christians, believe that he will come, clothed with im-mortal glory, having a body of flesh and bones, to live and walk and be among men again. This brings us face to face with such questions as these: How do you prove there will be a second com-ing? How can anyone know he will come again? Are the views of various religionists on this matter simply legend, folklore, and myth?

A special standard of judgment is needed to prove anything in the spiritual realm. No scientific research, no intellectual inquiry, no investigative processes known to mortal man can prove that God is a personal being, that all men will be raised in immortality, and that repentant souls are born of the Spirit. There is no way to perform an experiment in a laboratory that will duplicate the appearance of the Father and the Son in the spring of 1820, or the coming of Moroni or Moses or Elijah to the Prophet Joseph Smith, or the vision of the degrees of glory opened to the view of Joseph Smith and Sidney Rigdon. Spiritual verities can be proven only by spiritual means. The visions of eternity can be duplicated only by those who abide the laws that enable them to attune their souls to the infinite. This is as yet beyond the spiritual capacity of most weak and faltering mortals.

The Lord has given to us all, however, a standard of judgment that is both unique and perfect. By using it we may gain a perfect knowledge as to the Second Coming or any other gospel verity. In the ultimate and final sense of the word, this standard of judgment is to receive the Holy Spirit, whose mission is to reveal and bear witness of the truth. In practice it is something else; it is the Book of Mormon. This book is the volume of divine truth that the Lord has given to the world to prove all else that he has ever said.

How and in what way does the Book of Mormon prove there will be a second coming of Christ? Or, for that matter, how does it give absolute certainty where any great spiritual verity is concerned? In principle, when we are able to determine one spiritual verity with absolute certainty, that determination carries with it an irrefutable witness of many other truths. For instance, if we know there is a Son of God, we of necessity also know there is a God; otherwise he could not have had a Son. If we know that the Holy Messiah redeemed men from the fall of Adam, we also know that there was an Adam and that he brought temporal and spiritual death into the world. If we know that God is the same yesterday, today, and forever, and that he sent angels to minister to men anciently, we also know that under the same circumstances and in like situations he will send angels to minister to men today.

Thus, if we know by revelation from the Holy Ghost that the Book of Mormon is a volume of holy scripture that came forth by the gift and power of God; if we know that it was translated by a man who communed with angels and saw visions; if we know that it is the voice of God to a degenerate world—we thereby know that Joseph Smith was a prophet and that the doctrines taught by the Nephite prophets are true.

These realizations bring us to a consideration of certain revealed concepts that show the position of the Book of Mormon in the eternal scheme of things. After saying that the Book of Mormon persuades men to do good, to believe in Jesus, and to endure to the end, and after saying it speaks harshly against sin, Nephi acclaimed: "No man will be angry at the words which I have written save he shall be of the spirit of the devil." And further: "Believe in Christ. . . . And if ye shall believe in Christ ye will believe in these words, for they are the words of Christ, and he hath given them unto me; and they teach all men that they should do good." (2 Ne. 33:4-5, 10.)

The Lord Jesus spoke these words to Moroni: "He that will

176

contend against the word of the Lord, let him be accursed; and he that shall deny these things"—the things then spoken, the things written in the Book of Mormon—"let him be accursed; for unto them will I show no greater things. . . . And he that believeth not my words believeth not my disciples. . . . But he that believeth these things which I have spoken"—and which are recorded in the Book of Mormon—"him will I visit with the manifestations of my Spirit, and he shall know and bear record. For because of my Spirit he shall know that these things are true; for it persuadeth men to do good. And whatsoever thing persuadeth men to do good is of me; for good cometh of none save it be of me. I am the same that leadeth men to all good; he that will not believe my words will not believe me—that I am; and he that will not believe me will not believe the Father who sent me." (Ether 4:8-12.)

Mormon addressed these words to the Lamanites living in the last days: "Repent, and be baptized in the name of Jesus, and lay hold upon the gospel of Christ, which shall be set before you, not only in this record [the Book of Mormon] but also in the record which shall come unto the Gentiles from the Jews [the Bible], which record shall come from the Gentiles unto you. For behold, this is written for the intent that ye may believe that; and if ye believe that ye will believe this also; and if ye believe this ye will know concerning your fathers, and also the marvelous works which were wrought by the power of God among them." (Morm. 7:8-9.)

From these passages we reach certain clear conclusions relative to believing in Christ and in his holy word. Among them are these: A belief in Christ and a belief in the Book of Mormon go together; they are locked in each other's arms; they cannot be separated. Like Ezekiel's two sticks, they are one in the hands of the Father. Those who believe in Christ also believe the Book of Mormon because it contains the words of Christ. Those who believe the words of Christ, as given by his disciples and as recorded in the Book of Mormon, believe in Christ. And those who do not believe these words do not believe in him. The Book of Mormon bears witness of Christ and of the Bible; it is written to persuade men to believe in their Lord and in his ancient word. Those who believe the Book of Mormon believe the Bible, and those who believe the Bible believe the Book of Mormon.

Having set forth these concepts from the Book of Mormon itself, we are now prepared to put the capstone on the whole matter by catching the vision of these words of latter-day revelation. They are in the revelation commanding Joseph Smith and his associates to organize again on earth that eternal church which is the kingdom of God on earth. The revealed word says: "God ministered unto him [Joseph Smith] by an holy angel [Moroni], whose countenance was as lightning, and whose garments were pure and white above all other whiteness." God, who is the Lord Jesus Christ, by the hand of Moroni, during the whole night of September 21-22, 1823, revealed to his chosen prophet the hiding place of the ancient record and a knowledge of much that was destined to be in the last days before his glorious return.

And God "gave unto him commandments which inspired him." The word poured forth by the mouth of the angel, by the power of the Spirit, by the opening of the heavens, by the audible voice of God himself—all speaking peace, all giving direction, all laying the foundation for the work that now has commenced.

And God "gave him power from on high, by the means which were before prepared [the Urim and Thummim], to translate the Book of Mormon." Truth must spring out of the earth; a voice must whisper from the dust; the testimony of a people long dead must be heard. Joseph Smith must translate the Book of Mormon, "which contains a record of a fallen people"—it is an inspired history—"and the fulness of the gospel of Jesus Christ to the Gentiles and to the Jews also." Here then is the promised record prepared from ages past, prepared by the unwearying diligence of a whole congregation of prophets, prepared by God himself that his gospel, the plan of salvation, might be known again among men.

The newly called prophet must translate the Book of Mormon, "which was given by inspiration"—to Nephi, Alma, Mormon, and the ancient prophets—"and is confirmed to others by the ministering of angels"—angelic ministrants bore record to their fellow servants on earth that the ancient word was true—"and is declared unto the world by them." Joseph Smith, the Three Witnesses, all who gained the knowledge from heaven-sent messengers then presented the message to the world and testified to all men that it was true.

The Book of Mormon came forth "proving to the world that the holy scriptures [those in the holy Bible] are true, and that God does inspire men and call them to his holy work in this age and genera- tion, as well as in generations of old; thereby showing that he is the same God yesterday, today, and forever." (D&C 20:6-12.) Thus the Nephite record came forth to prove that the Bible is true; it came forth to prove that Joseph Smith, its translator, was and is a prophet; it came forth to prove that God calls men again in this day "to his holy work," which holy work, being the Lord's, is itself eternally and everlastingly true.

In the absolute and eternal sense, the greatest and most impor- tant issue in the field of revealed religion in all ages is this: Is there a God in heaven who ordained and established a plan of salvation to enable his children to advance and progress and become like him?

Also in the absolute and eternal sense, because that eternal plan of salvation is based upon and made operative by the atoning sacrifice of God's Son, we can properly say that the heart and cen- ter of revealed religion in all ages is: Was Jesus Christ the Son of the living God who was crucified for the sins of the world, did he bring life and immortality to light through the gospel, and is his the only name given under heaven whereby man may come unto God and find that eternal life so devoutly desired by the righteous?

In a nearer and more pointed sense, we can with propriety, in this day and dispensation, say that the great and eternal issue to be resolved is: Was Joseph Smith called of God? For if he was, then the witness he has borne of the Lord Jesus is true, and the church he organized administers the eternal plan of salvation of the Father.

And even more pointedly, let us say that there is no greater issue ever to confront mankind in modern times than this: Is the Book of Mormon the mind and will and voice of God to all men? For if it is, then Joseph Smith was a prophet, the testimony of Jesus he gave is true, and the plan of salvation of the Great God is in full operation.

It is no wonder, then, that we find the Prophet himself saying: "I told the brethren [the modern Twelve Apostles of the Lamb] that the Book of Mormon was the most correct of any book on earth, and the keystone of our religion, and a man would get nearer to God by abiding by its precepts, than by any other book." (*Teachings*, p. 194.)

The keystone is the central stone at the top of an arch which binds the whole structure together. When it is firmly in place, the arch stands; when it is removed, the structure falls. Thus "our religion," the whole system of revealed truth that has come to us by the opening of the heavens, stands or falls depending upon the truth or falsity of the Book of Mormon. This holy volume proves the divinity of the work as a whole and of every part and portion individually.

And so the prophetic word, having set forth the general concept that the Book of Mormon came forth to prove the divinity of the work itself, begins to particularize. "By these things"—the coming forth of a record written anciently by the spirit of prophecy; its translation by the gift and power of God; the confirmation of its truth by angelic ministration—"By these things we know" the verity of all that has been revealed to us. Among the items then and there listed are these: "That there is a God in heaven"; that he created all things; that he revealed his holy truths to man; that Adam fell and men became carnal, sensual, and devilish; that the Only Begotten atoned for the sins of the world; and that those who believe and obey shall be saved. (D&C 20:17-31.) These truths are but illustrations; the application of the principle knows no bounds.

Every accountable person on earth—there is no exception; this principle has universal application; no living soul is exempt—every such person who will read the Book of Mormon, ponder its truths in his heart, and ask God the Eternal Father in the name of Christ, in sincerity and with real intent, "having faith in Christ," shall come to know, "by the power of the Holy Ghost," that the book is true. (Moro. 10:3-5.) All such persons can then, by the same power, testify to the truth of all things pertaining to the glorious restoration now in process. They can say:

We know that the Father and the Son appeared to Joseph Smith because the Book of Mormon is true.

We know that the angelic ministrants conferred priesthoods and keys upon mortals in this day because the Book of Mormon is true.

We know that Joseph Smith is a prophet of God because the Book of Mormon is true.

We know that The Church of Jesus Christ of Latter-day Saints is the kingdom of God on earth, the one place where salvation may be found, because the Book of Mormon is true.

We know that the Lord Jesus Christ will come in the clouds of glory in due course because the Book of Mormon is true.

The truth and divinity of the Book of Mormon is an absolute and unshakable witness that there will be a second coming of Christ!

Chapter 16

ISRAEL:
THE CHOSEN PEOPLE

The Israel of God

Blessed Israel, the people favored by the Father—who are they and what part do they play in the eternal scheme of things?

For the last four thousand years the whole history of the world—the rise and fall of nations; the discovery of islands and continents; the peopling of all lands and the fates which have befallen all people—for four millenniums the whole earth has been governed and controlled for the benefit of the children of Israel. And now the day of their glory and triumph is at the door.

The concept of a chosen and favored people, a concept scarcely known in the world and but little understood even by the saints of God, is one of the most marvelous systems ever devised for administering salvation to all men in all nations in all ages. Israel, the Lord's chosen people, were a congregation set apart in preexistence. In large measure, the spirit children of the Father who acquired a talent for spirituality, who chose to heed the divine word then given, and who sought, above their fellows, to do good and work righteousness—all these were foreordained to be born in the house of Israel. They were chosen before they were born. This is the doctrine of election. They were true and faithful in the premortal life, and they earned the right to be born as the Lord's people and to have the privilege, on a preferential basis, of believing and obeying the word of truth. Believing blood, the blood of Abraham, flows in their veins. They are the ones of whom Jesus said:

"My sheep hear my voice, and I know them, and they follow me: And I give unto them eternal life; and they shall never perish, neither shall any man pluck them out of my hand." (John 10:27-28.)

Because their numbers were known and the days of their mortal probation were selected in advance, Moses was able to say: "When the most High divided to the nations their inheritance, when he separated the sons of Adam, he set the bounds of the people according to the number of the children of Israel. For the Lord's portion is his people; Jacob is the lot of his inheritance." (Deut. 32:8-9.) And thus Jehovah said to Israel anciently: "If ye will obey my voice indeed, and keep my covenant, then ye shall be a peculiar treasure unto me above all people: for all the earth is mine: And ye shall be unto me a kingdom of priests, and an holy nation." (Ex. 19:5-6.) "For thou art an holy people unto the Lord thy God: the Lord thy God hath chosen thee to be a special people unto himself, above all people that are upon the face of the earth." (Deut. 7:6; 14:2.) And thus Peter said to Israel in his day: "Ye are a chosen generation, a royal priesthood, an holy nation, a peculiar people; that ye should shew forth the praises of him who hath called you out of darkness into his marvellous light." (1 Pet. 2:9.) And as it was in those days, so it is today. Gathered Israel is now and everlastingly shall be a holy nation, a peculiar people, and a kingdom of priests who minister salvation to the peoples of the world.

Israel are the seed of Abraham; they are the children of the prophets; and they associate with the Lord's seers. Israel are the friends of apostles and revelators; they are the children of God by faith; they are the sons and daughters of the Lord Jesus Christ in whose name they worship the Father. Paul acclaims that they are the ones "to whom pertaineth the adoption, and the glory, and the covenants, and the giving of the law, and the service of God, and the promises." They are the nation "of whom as concerning the flesh Christ came."

But "they are not all Israel, which are of Israel: Neither, because they are the seed of Abraham, are they all children: but, In Isaac shall thy seed be called. That is, They which are the children

183

of the flesh, these are not the children of God." And all this, Paul says, was determined of God beforehand, "that the purpose of God according to election might stand, not of works, but of him that calleth." (Rom. 9:4-11.)

Adam came to be the father of all living; Noah succeeded to this high status and became the father of all living from his day onward; and Abraham came to be the father of the faithful, the father of all who believe and obey the gospel from his day onward as long as the earth shall stand. Of this we shall speak more particularly when we set forth the promises made to the fathers, which must be planted in the hearts of the children before the Lord comes. For our present purposes it will suffice to know that the seed of Abraham, and then the seed of Isaac, and then the seed of Jacob (who is Israel) comprise the chosen people, a people who first save themselves and who then offer salvation to all men. Salvation is of Israel; or, as Jesus said of the portion of Israel yet unscattered in his day, "Salvation is of the Jews." (John 4:22.)

Israel, anciently, went down into Egypt to find corn lest they die of hunger; they came out of Egyptian bondage to worship God without the interference of the world, and they then became a mighty people in their promised land. Thereafter, for rebellion, they were scattered in all the nations of the earth. The scriptures abound with prophetic statements relative to them, to their scattering in ancient days and their gathering again in latter days, to their restoration as a people and a kingdom; and to their ultimate glory, honor, and renown among the nations of men. It is of these things that we shall now speak.

Scattering the Chosen Ones

The gathering of Israel, now commenced and now in progress, is one of the signs of the times. It is one of the marvels of the ages, one of the worldwide and earth-shaking occurrences destined to come before and to continue after the Second Coming. It is written that "all Israel shall be saved"—all who return and are faithful—all shall be saved by the Deliverer who shall come out of Zion, for he "shall turn away ungodliness from Jacob," and in the appointed day, he "shall take away their sins." (Rom. 11:26-27.)

No man, in these last days, can be saved unless he gathers with Israel and casts his lot with the chosen people. No man can gather with the elect unless and until he knows who they are and where they reside. Nor can any person identify Israel and fully envision what is involved in the doctrine of the gathering unless he knows how, and why, and in what manner, and where Israel was scattered. The gathering grows out of the scattering, and the reasons for the scattering will reveal how the gathering will be brought to pass.

During the almost two thousand years from the birth of Jacob in 1837 B.C. to the destruction of Jerusalem and the scattering of the Jews in A.D. 71, Israel swung back and forth like a pendulum, manifesting exceedingly great righteousness on the one hand and the most abominable wickedness and perversion on the other. When she was righteous, the Lord Jehovah poured out his gifts and powers upon her and she triumphed over all her enemies. In the days of her rebellion, she was overrun by alien nations; her fair sons and daughters fell by the sword; pestilence and disease swept through her cities; and captive remnants were carried into other nations to serve the gods of men and of devils.

Israel was governed by the law of Moses, which was the preparatory gospel, and at times portions of her people had the fulness of the gospel. The Nephites had both the gospel and the law of Moses as did those, from time to time, who followed the counsels of Elijah and Isaiah and various of the prophets. Thus the people —not always but during periods of especial righteousness—enjoyed the gifts of the Spirit and walked in a pleasing way before their God. And that God, the God of Israel, was the Lord Jehovah who is the Lord Jesus Christ. This we must know if we are to understand the scattering and the gathering.

It was faith in Christ of which Paul spoke when he recited the glories and grandeurs of Israelitish history. It was faith in Christ that parted the Red Sea, broke down the walls of Jericho, put to flight the armies of aliens, raised the dead, and rent the heavens. (Heb. 11:23-40.) Indeed, "all the holy prophets . . . believed in Christ and worshiped the Father in his name." (Jacob 4:4-5.)

Having these things in mind, we are prepared to ask why Israel was scattered and where and in what places the elect and chosen ones found new places of abode. On these points the prophets speak *in extenso*; many passages deal with these issues; there is no dearth of revealed knowledge as to the *why* and the *where* of the scattering. And we must not be deceived on the points at issue.

1. *Why was Israel scattered?*

Israel was scattered from time to time during some fifteen hundred years of her history. Why? It is a sad and sorry tale. But the record is clear; the divine word is specific; the passages giving the reasons are numerous. Israel was rejected, cursed, smitten, and scattered for her sins and because she rebelled against the God of Israel.

Israel, from time to time and on many occasions, sank back into the bondage of Egypt, into the bondage of Babylon, into the bondage of the world, because she forsook the Lord Jehovah and worshipped and lived after the manner of the world. As a people she reveled in all of the abominations of the carnal nations that preceded her in Canaan. She trusted in the arm of flesh as did the Canaanites and Hittites. She found pleasure in the astrology and necromancy of the Amorites and the Perizzites. She looked with favor on the practices of the Hivites and the Jebusites.

Israel was cursed because she partook of all the evils of the world in which she dwelt. Her young men visited the temple prostitutes of Ashtoreth, and her young women defiled themselves as harlots with the heathen. Her priests sacrificed on the altars of Baal, and Solomon himself built an altar to Molech whereon Ahaz and others sacrificed children. Portions and groups of Israel in Palestine sank to the same depths of depravity and evil that prevailed among the Lamanites in that day when murder and adultery and human sacrifices became their way of life.

Israel was scattered because she apostatized; because she broke the Ten Commandments; because she rejected the prophets and seers and turned to wizards that peep and mutter; because she forsook the covenant; because she gave heed to false ministers and joined false churches; because she ceased to be a peculiar people and a kingdom of priests. When she became as the world, the Lord left her to suffer and live and be as the world then was.

"Hath a nation changed their gods?" Jehovah asked his people. Have they accepted gods "which are yet no gods"? he asked. "My people have changed their glory for that which doth not profit," he said. "Be astonished, O ye heavens, at this, and be horribly afraid, be ye very desolate, saith the Lord. For my people have committed two evils; they have forsaken me the fountain of living waters, and hewed them out cisterns, broken cisterns, and that can hold no water." (Jer. 2:11-13.) Israel forsook Jehovah, from whom living waters flow, and worshipped other gods. Israel no longer drank the living water, which, if men drink, they shall never thirst more. Rather she made her own churches, her own cisterns—"broken cisterns," false churches—which can hold none of the waters of life.

Lehi and his family left Jerusalem for their American promised land in 600 B.C. In about 588 B.C. Nebuchadnezzar overran Jerusalem and took the people captive into Babylon. At this time Mulek led another colony to the Americas, where in due course they founded the great city of Zarahemla. Seventy years after the fall of Jerusalem, Cyrus the Persian, having first conquered Babylon, permitted a remnant of the Jews to return to Jerusalem and build again their city and temple. These were the forebears of the Jews of Jesus' day, which Jews were finally scattered to the four winds after the destruction of Jerusalem by Titus in A.D. 70.

All of these historical events, and others of which we have little or no knowledge, came to pass in complete conformity with the prophetic word.

Jacob himself, the father of all Israel, prophesied of one of his sons: "Joseph is a fruitful bough, even a fruitful bough by a well; whose branches run over the wall" (Gen. 49:22), thus foreshadowing the establishment of the Lehite civilization in the Americas. Lehi was of the tribe of Manasseh.

This same Joseph is the one who said: "The Lord hath visited me, and I have obtained a promise of the Lord, that out of the fruit of my loins, the Lord God will raise up a righteous branch out of my loins." He then spoke of the deliverance of Israel from Egyptian bondage. "And it shall come to pass that they shall be scattered again," he said, "and a branch shall be broken off, and shall be carried into a far country; nevertheless they shall be remembered in the covenants of the Lord, when the Messiah cometh." (JST, Gen. 50:24-25.) All of this speaks of Lehi and his seed, a mighty people in the Americas, and of the visit of the Lord Jesus to them after his mortal ministry in Jerusalem.

Moses, speaking to all of the twelve tribes, said: "If thou wilt not hearken unto the voice of the Lord thy God, to observe to do all his commandments and his statutes, . . . [then] shalt [thou] be removed into all the kingdoms of the earth. . . . And ye shall be plucked from off the land whither thou goest to possess it. And the Lord shall scatter thee among all people, from the one end of the earth even unto the other; and there thou shalt serve other gods, which neither thou nor thy fathers have known." (Deut. 28:15, 25, 63-64.)

To Amos the Lord said: "I will sift the house of Israel among all nations, like as corn is sifted in a sieve, yet shall not the least grain fall upon the earth." (Amos 9:9.) Micah recorded the promise that "the remnant of Jacob shall be among the Gentiles in the midst of many people." (Micah 5:8.) And the Lord's word preserved by Zechariah is: "I scattered them with a whirlwind among all the nations whom they knew not." (Zech. 7:14.)

Nephi bears a concurring testimony. "The house of Israel, sooner or later," he says, "will be scattered upon all the face of the earth, and also among all nations." Then speaking of the Ten Tribes he acclaims: "And behold, there are many who are already lost from the knowledge of those who are at Jerusalem. Yea, the more part of all the tribes, have been led away; and they are scattered to and fro upon the isles of the sea; and whither they are none of us knoweth, save that we know that they have been led away."

Then he speaks of the Jews who shall crucify Christ. Because they harden their hearts against the Holy One of Israel, he says, "they shall be scattered among all nations and shall be hated of all men." And then he turns to the scattering of Lehi's seed: "After all the house of Israel have been scattered and confounded, . . . the Lord God will raise up a mighty nation among the Gentiles, yea, even upon the face of this land; and by them shall our seed be scattered." (1 Ne. 22:3-7.)

So speak the scriptures, and what we have written is but a small part of what the prophets have said. And from it all we conclude: Israel—all Israel, every tribe, including the Ten Tribes, who for the moment are lost because we cannot identify them—all Israel is now scattered in all nations and among all peoples. Unless we know this, we cannot catch the vision of the gathering that is to be.

Ephraim—The Wanderer in Israel

Ephraim is the presiding tribe in Israel. He plays the chief role in both the scattering and the gathering of the chosen seed. It is his privilege to lay the foundation for the Second Coming, and the part he is to play has already commenced.

All of the tribes have played and shall play their part in the Lord's strange act. Each has provided and shall provide prophets and seers, and the members of each stand equally before the Lord in seeking and obtaining eternal life. Christ came of Judah as did most of the prophets and apostles of old. Moses and Aaron were of Levi, Paul of Benjamin, and the Nephite prophets of Manasseh. Joseph Smith and the latter-day apostles and prophets are of Ephraim. The Book of Mormon is the Stick of Joseph in the hands of Ephraim. And it is Ephraim who is to guide the destiny of the kingdom in the last days and to bring the blessings of the gospel to the other tribes in the family of Jacob.

Manasseh and Ephraim, born in that order to Joseph, were adopted by their grandfather, Jacob. "And now, of thy two sons, Ephraim and Manasseh," Jacob said to Joseph, "behold, they are mine, and the God of my fathers shall bless them; even as Reuben and Simeon they shall be blessed, for they are mine; wherefore they shall be called after my name. (Therefore they were called Israel.) And thy issue which thou begettest after them, shall be thine, and shall be called after the name of their brethren in their inheritance, in the tribes; therefore they were called the tribes of Manasseh and of Ephraim." Even Joseph's other children were to become the seed of these first two sons.

Then Israel's great patriarch gave Joseph this promise: "The God of thy fathers shall bless thee, and the fruit of thy loins, that

189

they shall be blessed above thy brethren, and above thy father's house"—Manasseh and Ephraim were to take precedence over the other tribes of Israel—"For thou hast prevailed, and thy father's house hath bowed down unto thee, even as it was shown unto thee, before thou wast sold into Egypt by the hands of thy brethren; wherefore thy brethren shall bow down unto thee, from generation to generation, unto the fruit of thy loins forever; For thou shalt be a light unto my people, to deliver them in the days of their captivity, from bondage; and to bring salvation unto them, when they are altogether bowed down under sin." (JST, Gen. 48:5-11.) It is Ephraim and Manasseh who shall administer salvation unto the whole house of Israel in the last days.

Joseph then took Manasseh and Ephraim to Jacob, whose eyes were dim with age, to receive a patriarchal blessing. The young lads were so placed that Jacob's right hand would be placed on Manasseh's head and his left on Ephraim's. But Jacob, "guiding his hands wittingly," reversed the order of precedence. With his right hand on Ephraim and his left on Manasseh, he said: "The Angel which redeemed me from all evil"—meaning the Lord Jehovah, who is the Lord Jesus—"bless the lads; and let my name be named on them, and the name of my fathers Abraham and Isaac; and let them grow into a multitude in the midst of the earth."

Joseph was displeased with the placement of his father's hands. "Not so, my father," he said, "for this is the firstborn; put thy right hand upon his head." Jacob refused. "I know it, my son, I know it," he replied; "he also shall become a people, and he also shall be great: but truly his younger brother shall be greater than he, and his seed shall become a multitude of nations."

Continuing as guided by the Spirit, Jacob "blessed them that day, saying, In thee"—or, better, by thee—"shall Israel bless, saying, God make thee as Ephraim and as Manasseh: and he set Ephraim before Manasseh." (Gen. 48:14-20.)

Reuben, the firstborn, through sin forfeited his right to rule in Israel, and the birthright, by divine direction, passed to Ephraim, an adopted son. Thus, as the Lord promised to gather Israel, he said: "I am a father to Israel, and Ephraim is my firstborn." (Jer.

31:9.) Ephraim shall stand supreme and shall be a guide and a light to his fellows.

In keeping with this concept is the latter-day promise that when the Ten Tribes return, "they shall bring forth their rich treasures unto the children of Ephraim" who are the Lord's "servants." And these other tribes shall "fall down" before Ephraim "and be crowned with glory, even in Zion, by the hands of the servants of the Lord, even the children of Ephraim. . . . Behold, this is the blessing of the everlasting God upon the tribes of Israel, and the richer blessing upon the head of Ephraim and his fellows." (D&C 133:30-34.)

Speaking of the day of gathering and of the people who should bring it to pass, Moses said: "Joseph . . . shall push the people together to the ends of the earth." The tribe of Joseph shall do it! And who is Joseph? Moses continues: "And they are the ten thousands of Ephraim, and they are the thousands of Manasseh." (Deut. 33:16-17.)

Thus, if Israel is to be scattered in all nations upon all the face of the earth; if she is to be gathered by the tribe of Joseph; if Ephraim has the birthright and is the presiding tribe; if the other tribes are to receive their blessings from Ephraim—then Ephraim must also be in all nations upon all the face of the earth, and Ephraim must be the first tribe to gather in the last days. And so it is.

Of the scattering of Ephraim—not alone the Kingdom of Ephraim, but more particularly the tribe itself—the prophetic word says many things, of which these are but a sample: "Ephraim, he hath mixed himself among the people. . . . Strangers have devoured his strength." (Hosea 7:8-9.) "Ephraim hath hired lovers. . . . Because Ephraim hath made many altars to sin, altars shall be unto him to sin." (Hosea 8:9-11.) He has worshipped and served other gods. "Ephraim shall return to Egypt"; he shall leave the true God and return to the worship of the world. "As for Ephraim, their glory shall fly away like a bird. . . . Ephraim is smitten, their root is dried up, they shall bear no fruit. . . . My God will cast them away, because they did not hearken unto him: and they shall be wanderers among the nations." (Hosea 9:3, 11, 16-17.) And there is more, much, much more in similar vein.

Such was the day of scattering. But ours is the day of gathering, a gathering that must commence and has commenced with Ephraim. This is the day when "the rebellious are not of the blood of Ephraim." (D&C 64:36.) This is the day when the cry is going forth:

Come home, ye wanderers; turn to the Lord, ye prodigals; leave the husks and the swine and feast upon the fatted calf! Come home, O Ephraim, and fill thy appointed place in pushing together thy fellows from the ends of the earth!

Chapter 17

ISRAEL: GATHERING HIS CHOSEN ONES

God Guarantees the Gathering

Has the Lord Omnipotent, who has all might, all power, and all dominion, spoken with absolute finality with reference to the destiny of his people? Most assuredly he has. Is the decree of the Almighty relative to Israel immutable? Verily it is so. It is his eternal word; it shall come to pass as surely as he lives; it is the decree of his own mouth. Though heaven and earth pass away, not one jot or tittle of his holy word shall fail. Israel shall be gathered; the kingdom shall be restored to the chosen people; Zion shall rise again, for the mouth of the Lord hath spoken it.

It shall be a literal gathering. The seed of Abraham, those in whose veins flows the blood of Jacob, those who are the children of the prophets after the manner of the flesh, shall find their place in the family of their fathers. Though they are separated from their parents by a thousand generations, yet shall they claim their inheritance among the elect. Israel shall be gathered and become one family. In all eternity there is nothing more sure than this. It carries the seal and the guarantee of the Lord God himself.

"For there shall be a day," saith the Lord—and that day is today; it is now; its dawning sun has already risen—"that the watchmen upon the mount Ephraim shall cry, Arise ye, and let us go up to Zion unto the Lord our God." Hear it again, O ye scattered ones, and let it be written in every heart. Ephraim shall bring salvation to you in the last days. Ephraim shall hear the word from the Lord and proclaim it to you. In his hands shall be the Stick of Joseph, which is the Stick of Ephraim, which is the Book of Mormon, which contains the fulness of the everlasting gospel, which is the standard around which all men must either rally or be damned. The call shall come unto you from the mountains of Ephraim. Be wise and give heed.

"For thus saith the Lord; Sing with gladness for Jacob, and shout among the chief of the nations: publish ye, praise ye, and say, O Lord, save thy people, the remnant of Israel." Salvation now goes forth to the scattered remnants in all the nations of their habitation. Publish the word; praise the Lord. Cry Salvation, and Glory, and Honor. The promised day of restoration is here.

"Behold, I will bring them from the north country," saith the Lord—meaning from all the country north of Palestine, north of their original promised land, north of where they were when for their sins they were scattered—"and gather them from the coasts of the earth." Yea, and they shall come not only from the north country, but from all the coasts and regions of the earth, from all the lands where the whirlwind of scattering has carried them. "And with them [are] the blind and the lame, the woman with child and her that travaileth with child together; a great company shall return thither."

So sure is the sound of the trumpet—God does not deal in uncertainties—that even the lame and the blind shall walk with stumbling steps in the caravan of the gathered; even women with children and those travailing in birth shall suffer whatever need be rather than be left behind. Numerous babies were, in fact, born the very night the driven saints, leaving their homes in Nauvoo, crossed the frozen Mississippi River to seek a refuge known only to that God who led their fathers through the Red Sea in ancient days.

"They shall come with weeping, and with supplications, will I lead them." How sweet and tender is the relationship between the Lord and his people. How often the strong weep as they testify of his goodness to them. How he pleads with them to press forward and endure to the end. "I will cause them to walk by the rivers of waters in a straight way, wherein they shall not stumble: for I am a

194

father to Israel, and Ephraim is my firstborn." Let the saints come to Zion, whence streams of living water flow, yea, rivers of water give that refreshment of which, if men drink, they shall never thirst more. The way is straight and the course is narrow, but the Lord shall be a father to all who heed the call of Ephraim and walk therein.

"Hear the word of the Lord, O ye nations, and declare it in the isles afar off, and say, He that scattered Israel will gather him, and keep him, as a shepherd doth his flock. For the Lord hath redeemed Jacob, and ransomed him from the hand of him that was stronger than he. Therefore they shall come and sing in the height of Zion, and shall flow together to the goodness of the Lord." Let all the ends of the earth know that this is the mind and will and purpose of the Almighty; it is his decree, and none can stay his hand.

"Thus saith the Lord, which giveth the sun for a light by day, and the ordinances of the moon and of the stars for a light by night, which divideth the sea when the waves thereof roar; The Lord of hosts is his name: If those ordinances depart from before me, saith the Lord, then the seed of Israel also shall cease from being a nation before me for ever. Thus saith the Lord; If heaven above can be measured, and the foundations of the earth searched out beneath, I will also cast off all the seed of Israel for all that they have done, saith the Lord." (Jer. 31:6-12, 35-37.)

And thus it is. With this principle Isaiah and all the prophets accord, and none can stay the hand that brings it to pass. As there is night and day, as there is heaven and earth, as there is life and death, just so surely will God gather Israel in the last days. Yea, he that scattereth Israel is now gathering her.

Israel Gathers to Jehovah

Jehovah is the God of Israel who led his people out of Egypt and to whom they then gathered in the land of Palestine. Thereafter they were scattered when they forsook him and his laws and worshipped and served false gods. The gathering of Israel—guaranteed as we have seen by Jehovah himself—consists primarily, chiefly, and above all else in the acceptance of and the return to the Lord Jehovah and his laws.

The Lord Jehovah and the Lord Jesus Christ are one and the same person. That person is the Son of God; he is the Savior of men and the Redeemer of the world; he is the Holy One of Israel, the Holy Messiah by whom redemption comes. True religion consists in worshipping the Father, in the name of the Son, by the power of the Holy Ghost. Such was the case with Israel of old in the days of their enlightenment. It was a departure from this course that caused the scattering, and it will be a return to this perfect worship that will bring to pass the gathering.

We have heretofore quoted the word of Jehovah, as given to Jeremiah, that Israel was scattered because they forsook him and worshipped false gods, and that they would continue so to worship in their scattered state in all nations. Then, in this setting, and speaking of the wonders that will attend his great latter-day work—wonders so great that even the parting of the Red Sea will seem insignificant in comparison—in this setting the Lord speaks of the gathering of his people and how and in what way it will be brought to pass.

"Behold, the days come, saith the Lord, that it shall no more be said, The Lord liveth, that brought up the children of Israel out of the land of Egypt; But, The Lord liveth, that brought up the children of Israel from the land of the north, and from all the lands whither he had driven them: and I will bring them again into their land that I gave unto their fathers." This is the promise. Such of the gathering of Israel as has come to pass so far is but the gleam of a star that soon will be hidden by the splendor of the sun in full blaze; truly, the magnitude and grandeur and glory of the gathering is yet to be.

"Behold, I will send for many fishers, saith the Lord, and they shall fish them"—a few here and a few there, in this stream and that, with a large catch occasionally filling the gospel net when it is cast into some favored lake—"and after will I send for many hunters, and they shall hunt them from every mountain, and from every hill, and out of the holes of the rocks." This is the great missionary work of the kingdom. The elders of Ephraim go forth to find the elect of God, hidden as they are from the knowledge of men.

These lost sheep of the fold of Israel shall be found among the Gentiles. Seeing all this in vision, Jeremiah exclaimed: "O Lord, my strength, and my fortress, and my refuge in the day of affliction"—thus using the words and expressing the feelings that would be in the hearts of those who gather—"the Gentiles shall come unto thee from the ends of the earth." That is, those who are not Jews in the sense of being the nationals of the Kingdom of Judah shall be gathered again unto their God.

When they are gathered, they will say: "Surely our fathers have inherited lies, vanity, and things wherein there is no profit. Shall a man make gods unto himself, and they are no gods?" Let that which men worship be made with the axe and saw, with the hammer and chisel, with the furnace and mold; or let it be made in the minds of men and be written in the creeds of apostasy—no matter: men cannot create God. Whatever comes from their hands or springs from their minds is nothing more than a poor, shriveling shadow of the Eternal Reality. God is the Almighty, not an idol made by the hands of man, not a spirit essence dreamed up by fertile brains and described in decadent creeds. God is not what the Christians describe in their creeds; he is not what the Buddhists worship in their temples, nor is he what the heathen bow before in their groves.

God is the Lord Jehovah, and there is none else to whom men must come for salvation.

"Therefore," thus saith Jehovah, "behold, I will this once cause them to know"—'I will identify myself again to men for the last time'—"I will cause them to know mine hand and my might." Once again men will be able to worship Him who made heaven and earth and the sea and the fountains of waters, as he shall be identified by the angelic ministrant who restores the everlasting gospel; once again the true knowledge of God shall be proclaimed in the ears of all living; once again men shall know that God stands revealed or he remains forever unknown.

"And they shall know that my name is The Lord." (Jer. 16:14-21.) 'They shall know that I am Jehovah; that I am the Eternal One; that I am the God of Israel; that I am the God of Abraham, Isaac, and Jacob; that I am the Lord Jesus Christ, the Son of God, the

Redeemer and Savior. And knowing me, they shall of necessity know my word, which is my law, which is my gospel.'

Is it any wonder, then, that the Personage who addressed young Joseph on that spring morning in 1820 commanded him to join none of the sects of the day? Or that the divine lips "said that all their creeds were an abomination in his sight"? (JS-H 1:19.)

Lies, vanity, and things wherein there is no profit! What does it profit a man to worship a cow or a crocodile? The creeds of men and of devils! Can a spirit essence or the laws of nature bring to pass the immortality and eternal life of man? Let uninspired men define God as an incorporeal, uncreated nothingness; let them say he is everywhere and nowhere in particular present; let them prattle about a being who is without body, parts, and passions—so be it: the holy word says these concepts are lies.

Jehovah is the Son; he has a body of flesh and bones as tangible as his Father's. This once, for the final time, to usher in the dispensation of the fulness of times and to prepare gathering Israel for the Second Coming of their ancient God, he has manifest himself and his laws to men on earth. Jehovah be praised!

Israel Gathers to the Gospel

The gathering of Israel—both that which comes *before* and that which comes *after* the Second Coming of the Son of Man—consists of two things. It consists, first, of receiving the restored gospel and of joining The Church of Jesus Christ of Latter-day Saints. Next it consists of assembling to whatever places are appointed for the worship of the Lord and the receipt of the fulness of his blessings.

Thus, the gathering is both spiritual and temporal. The spiritual gathering makes us members of the Church and kingdom of God on earth; it gives us a new birth, a new heart, a new allegiance. Through it we become fellow-citizens with the saints; we forsake the world; we come into the marvelous light of Christ. The temporal gathering consists of assembling physically to an appointed place where we can be strengthened in our determination to serve God and keep his commandments, and where we can receive the ordinances of salvation in their eternal fulness. There was not and could not be a gathering until the gospel was restored; and there is not and cannot be a gathering to specific locations without continuing revelation to name the places and appoint the times of assembly.

The promises to scattered Israel are glorious indeed. "I will gather them out of all countries, whither I have driven them," saith the Lord. "And they shall be my people, and I will be their God"—Jehovah is speaking—"and I will give them one heart, and one way, that they may fear me for ever, for the good of them, and of their children after them: And I will make an everlasting covenant with them." (Jer. 32:37-40.) The gospel is the everlasting covenant, the covenant of salvation that the Lord makes with all who come unto him.

Gathered Israel shall no longer walk in darkness and rebellion as did their fathers. "I will give them one heart," saith the Lord, "and I will put a new spirit within you; and I will take the stony heart out of their flesh, and will give them an heart of flesh." Why? "That they may walk in my statutes, and keep mine ordinances, and do them: and they shall be my people, and I will be their God." (Ezek. 11:19-20.)

And after they keep his commandments, they shall see his face as did the prophets of old. "There"—in your places of gathering—"will I plead with you face to face," he promises. "And I will cause you to pass under the rod, and I will bring you into the bond of the covenant." (Ezek. 20:35-37.) Is not this the promise he has given us? "Every soul who forsaketh his sins and cometh unto me, and calleth on my name, and obeyeth my voice, and keepeth my commandments, shall see my face and know that I am." (D&C 93:1.)

Old Testament prophecies about the gathering use language that means Israel shall gather to their ancient inheritances in Palestine. This, of course, will come to pass, and it is also descriptive of the phase of the gathering that enabled the ancients to envision clearly the literal nature of what was to be. The Book of Mormon prophets speak similarly, although their emphasis is on the Americas—the land of Joseph—as the gathering place for Ephraim and Manasseh. In addition, the Book of Mormon, with repeated emphasis, speaks not of a gathering to one place only, but of a gathering to appointed lands, meaning to all of the appointed places.

"The Lord God will proceed to make bare his arm in the eyes of all the nations, in bringing about his covenants and his gospel unto those who are of the house of Israel," Nephi says. "Wherefore, he will bring them again out of captivity, and they shall be gathered together to the lands of their inheritance; and they shall be brought out of obscurity and out of darkness; and they shall know that the Lord is their Savior and their Redeemer, the Mighty One of Israel." (1 Ne. 22:11-12.)

It is not the *place* of gathering that will save the scattered remnants, but the *message* of salvation that comes to them in their Redeemer's name. When he issues the call—"Assemble yourselves and come; draw near together, ye that are escaped of the nations"—what is important is that men turn to him in whatever nation and place they find themselves. "Look unto me, and be ye saved, all the ends of the earth," he says, "for I am God, and there is none else." Salvation is not in a *place* but in a *person*. It is in Christ; he alone ransoms men from death and redeems them from the grave; he alone grants them eternal life in his Father's kingdom; no man cometh unto the Father but by him. "Unto me every knee shall bow, [and] every tongue shall swear," saith Jehovah who is Christ. (Isa. 45:20-23.)

The Lord "has covenanted with all the house of Israel," Jacob says, in what amounts to a perfect summary of the whole matter, "that they shall be restored to the true church and fold of God; when they shall be gathered home to the lands of their inheritance, and shall be established in all their lands of promise." (2 Ne. 9:1-2.) We shall consider this matter more fully when we set forth that the gathering of Israel consists in coming to Zion or to any of her stakes no matter where they are located. It suffices for the present to know, with certainty and clarity, that the true gathering is to the true gospel that is proclaimed by the true Christ.

"Ye Are My Witnesses"

Who and how and by what means will Israel be gathered in the last days? Who among men can so much as identify a single lost sheep from the fold of the chosen ones? What man is there who would dare say to another: Come, assemble here; leave houses and wives and lands and properties, and come; cast your lot here in this desert wasteland with a handful of pilgrims?

How can anyone learn who Jehovah is? Or which among the religions of the world has the true gospel? And even if he could, where would he get the power to work the miracles and wonders that shall surpass the parting of the Red Sea?

Israel is to be gathered by the power of God, by the authority of the priesthood, by the preaching of the gospel, by the servants of the Lord going forth two by two into all the nations of the earth. The Lord's sheep hear his voice, and they follow him, and another they will not follow. Israel is gathered by the missionaries of the kingdom.

It is not a matter of armies assembling and marching under great banners to an ancient homeland. It is not a matter of earthly kings moving masses of men as Nebuchadnezzar did when Judah went into captivity. It will not be done by kings and parliaments and rulers. The gathering of Israel results from the Holy Spirit of God working in the hearts of contrite souls. "Ye shall be gathered one by one, O ye children of Israel," Isaiah acclaimed. (Isa. 27:12.) Converts come one at a time; people are baptized as individuals; every person must make his own decision.

"Turn, O backsliding children, saith the Lord; for I am married unto you: and I will take you one of a city, and two of a family, and I will bring you to Zion: And I will give you pastors according to mine heart, which shall feed you with knowledge and understanding." Such is the Lord's way for gathering his people. So shall Judah and Israel—the Jews and the Ten Tribes—"come together out of the land of the north." (Jer. 3:14-18.)

Six souls were gathered into the sheepfold of Israel by Jehovah himself on the 6th day of April in 1830. By heaven-sent revelation and divine commandment they set up the new kingdom whose destiny it is to fill the whole earth. These few followers of the true Shepherd were appointed pastors to find others of the lost sheep and to lead them into the fold—one by one, one of a city and two of a family.

These new pastors, the first legal administrators on earth since the meridian of time, became the first elders in the new kingdom. To them and to others who soon joined with them, the Lord gave this commission: "Ye are called to bring to pass the gathering of mine elect; for mine elect hear my voice and harden not their hearts." (D&C 29:7.) He commanded them: "Gather mine elect from the four quarters of the earth, even as many as will believe in me, and hearken unto my voice." (D&C 33:6.) Their instructions were: "Push the people together from the ends of the earth." (D&C 58:45.)

Truly, as the Lord had said of old, "I will save the house of Joseph, . . . And they of Ephraim shall be like a mighty man, and their heart shall rejoice." This is that Ephraim of whom he said: "I will sow them among the people: and they shall remember me in far countries; and they shall live with their children, and turn again," and concerning whom his promise is: "I will hiss for them, and gather them; for I have redeemed them: and they shall increase as they have increased." (Zech. 10:6-9.)

Thus, the ten thousands of Ephraim, and thereafter the thousands of Manasseh, began to return to their ancient God and to live as had their faithful fathers. By the 3rd of April in 1836 many thousands had come out of the Egypt of the world into a promised land of gospel peace. And then the heavens were rent, the Great God sent Moses back to confer keys and powers upon mortals, and the way was prepared for the full gathering that would make the first flight out of Egypt seem as nothing. The millions of our fathers who escaped the bondage of Pharaoh would be but the seed from which a bounteous harvest of billions would be reaped when the final harvest was ripe.

Moses came. He conferred upon Joseph Smith and Oliver Cowdery "the keys of the gathering of Israel from the four parts of the earth, and the leading of the ten tribes from the land of the north." (D&C 110:11.) Keys are the right of presidency; they are divine authorization to use the priesthood for a specified purpose; they empower those who hold them to use the power of God to do the work of Him whose power it is.

How was Israel gathered the first time? In what way came they out of Egypt, free from bondage, carrying the riches of the land with them? Truly it was by the power of God. With a mighty hand and a stretched-out arm and with fury poured out, Jehovah led his ancient people. And he did it by the hand of Moses, his servant, who held the keys of the gathering, the keys and power to use the priesthood to part the Red Sea and do all else that must needs be.

When "the Lord shall set his hand again the second time to recover the remnant of his people" (Isa. 11:11) from all the countries whither he hath driven them, how shall the work be done? It shall be again as it was before. His prophets, holding again the keys and powers possessed by Moses, shall lead Israel out of the bondage of a modern Egypt. Again Jehovah will move among the people with a mighty hand and a stretched-out arm and with fury poured out.

Thus Israel returns at the direction of the president of The Church of Jesus Christ of Latter-day Saints. Thus when the Ten Tribes come forth from the lands of the north to receive their blessings in the temples of God, they will come at the command of the presiding officer in the true Church. When they fall down before Ephraim, as their fathers did before Joseph of old, and when they are blessed by the children of Ephraim, it will be because the one who holds the keys of the kingdom of God on earth turns the key in their behalf. He alone is empowered to use all of the keys in their eternal fulness. There is never but one on earth at a time who can preside over and direct all of the affairs of the Lord among mortals, and this includes the gathering of all Israel as well as all else involved in the heaven-directed work.

Let no one suppose that the Ten Tribes, having been gathered by the elders of Israel so as to return in a body; let no one suppose that because they bring their scriptures with them; let no one suppose that because prophets mingle among them—let no one suppose that any of this shall happen independent of the senior apostle of God on earth who holds the keys of gathering and who is authorized to use them as the Spirit directs. There is one God and one Shepherd over all the earth, and there is one prophet and one presiding officer of the earthly kingdom, and he has rule over all of the Lord's affairs in all the earth.

This brings us to a consideration of how the lost sheep shall come to know that Jehovah is their God; how he will this once cause them to know that his name is The Lord; how they will be led to forsake the lies, vanities, and unprofitable things of their fathers—how they will be led to come unto Christ and believe his gospel in the last days.

The answer is: They will be guided by testimony. Their souls will vibrate—even as one tuning fork does with another that is similarly calibrated—when they hear the witness borne relative to the restoration of eternal truth in the last days. They will respond with glad acclaim to the written testimony in the Book of Mormon and will cry out in joyous tones: "The Stick of Joseph in the hands of Ephraim is the mind and will and voice of the Lord to us and to all Israel and to all men. Come, let us go up to the mountain of the Lord where his house is found and there receive our eternal blessings."

Let us now hear how Isaiah gives the word of the Lord on this matter. "I am the Lord thy God, the Holy One of Israel, thy Saviour," the ancient word acclaims. And it is the Lord Jehovah who is speaking. "I will bring thy seed from the east, and gather thee from the west; I will say to the north, Give up; and to the south, Keep not back: bring my sons from far, and my daughters from the ends of the earth; Even every one that is called by my name." It is the Lord Jesus who is speaking. He is calling his sons and his daughters from the ends of the earth; he is speaking to those who have received his gospel and who have exercised the power thus given them to become the sons of God by faith; he is naming those who have been spiritually born of him. He is speaking to those who have been adopted into his family and have taken upon them his name, which is the name of Christ. He is saying what he said through Hosea: "The number of the children of Israel shall be as the sand of the sea, which cannot be measured nor numbered; and it shall come to pass, that in the place where it was said unto them, Ye are not my people, there it shall be said unto them, Ye are the sons of the living God. Then shall the children of Judah and the children of Israel be gathered together, and appoint themselves

204

one head, and they shall come up out of the land." (Hosea 1:10-11.)

To his sons and daughters thus gathered into his fold in all nations, the Lord acclaims: "Ye are my witnesses, saith the Lord, and my servant whom I have chosen: that ye may know and believe me, and understand that I am he." It is the Lord's servants who proclaim his divinity to the world; they are the ones who testify that salvation is in Christ; it is their witness that brings in converts and is binding on earth and in heaven. "I, even I, am the Lord; and beside me there is no saviour. I have declared, and have saved, and I have shewed, when there was no strange god among you: therefore ye are my witnesses, saith the Lord, that I am God." (Isa. 43:3-12.) He alone is the Saviour; he alone is that Jehovah who this once will cause men to know his name and his might. And the word so affirming shall go forth to all men in the last days by the mouths of his servants the prophets.

Truly, as all the scriptures attest: Faith cometh by hearing the word of God taught by a legal administrator who teaches and testifies by the power of the Holy Ghost. And thus it is that the word is going and shall go forth whereby Israel shall know their God and come again to his eternal truths.

Chapter 18

THE LAMANITES
AND THE SECOND
COMING

The Lehites: A Case Study

We know enough about the Lehite peoples, during the twenty-five hundred years of their existence as an identifiable branch of the house of Israel, to enable us to use them as an ideal case study of the scattering and gathering of Israel. Their days of faith and devotion, their nights of sorrow and darkness, their travels and trials—all these are set forth in the Book of Mormon with sufficient detail to enable us to learn how the Lord Jehovah treats his people when they are righteous and when they are wicked. Knowing what he did with reference to Lehi and his seed and those who joined with them, we can envision how and in what manner he is dealing with all the branches of the olive tree that is Israel.

Lehi was a Jew of Jerusalem, a loyal subject of Zedekiah king of Judah, a member of the house of Joseph and of the tribe of Manasseh. He and his family, along with Ishmael the Jew and his family, and Zoram the Jew, neither of whose tribal affiliations are named but who also may have been of Manasseh, left Jerusalem in about 600 B.C. After some ten years of travel and preparation, climaxed by a long and tempestuous ocean voyage, they landed somewhere on the west coast of South America. They were thus scattered from their original homeland but gathered to their new promised land, the land promised to Joseph and his seed forever.

Mulek, the son of Zedekiah, together with his friends and followers, who also were Jews and who well may have had among

206

them representatives from many tribes, particularly the tribe of Judah, made a similar journey to the Western Hemisphere. In due course they joined with the Nephites and were adopted into and swallowed up by that branch of the Lehite civilization. They also were thus scattered from Jerusalem but gathered to the land of Joseph.

Lehi's seed divided into two nations—the Nephites, who maintained their membership in the true Church and who worshipped the true God, and the Lamanites, who forsook the faith, rejected the gospel, and turned to the worship of false gods. These latter were cursed by the Lord for their rebellion, and he placed a mark upon them—a dark skin—lest the Nephites should intermarry with them and sink into their loathsome and degraded state.

For a thousand years these Lehite peoples alternately flourished and prospered on the one hand, or dwindled in darkness and struggled without civilization and decency on the other. In the main the Nephites were righteous and the Lamanites were wicked, though on occasions this was reversed. Ordinarily when Nephites apostatized and joined the Lamanites, they became Lamanites, but there was one glorious period when the Lamanites were converted, when they joined with and became Nephites, and when they received back skins that were white.

During the Golden Era, after the ministry of the Risen Lord among them, there were no dissenters, neither Lamanites "nor any manner of -ites; but they were in one, the children of Christ, and heirs to the kingdom of God." (4 Ne. 1:17.) When apostasy began again among them, however, the old tribal claims were revived, and the warfare and ways of old prevailed once more.

The Nephites as a people were destroyed by the Lamanites by about A.D. 400. Thereafter the Lamanites—the American Indians—apparently joined by a few wanderers from Asia or elsewhere, broke up into warring factions, continued to degenerate, and became what Columbus and subsequent European Gentiles found in the Americas. These American Indians are descendants primarily of Laman and Lemuel, though they also include some of the seed of Nephi and Ishmael and Zoram and others of the ancient worthies. They are Lamanites because of lineage, and they are Lamanites because of apostasy and disbelief and wayward living.

Providentially the Book of Mormon preserves for us the prophecies and promises made to and about Lehi and his seed and those who were adopted, as it were, into his family. By the simple expedient of studying the Lamanite scattering and gathering, we shall learn the concepts that will enable us to understand, in principle, what is happening to every branch of that nation which sprang from righteous Jacob.

The Lamanite Scattering

The Lamanites were cursed, scattered, and scourged; they became an evil, loathsome, and degenerate people; their skins turned black and their hearts became as flint—all because they forsook the Lord and chose to walk after the manner of the world. They left the Church; they apostatized; they rejected the gospel; they made gods unto themselves which were no gods. They treated the truths of salvation the same way their kindred in Jerusalem were doing in the day the vengeance of Babylon fell upon them.

Nephi was told by his angelic associate that the Lamanites would "dwindle in unbelief." Then he saw in vision that "after they had dwindled in unbelief they became a dark, and loathsome, and a filthy people, full of idleness and all manner of abominations." (1 Ne. 12:22-23.) And the angel said that "the wrath of God" rested upon them. (1 Ne. 13:11.)

Why did such an evil fate befall children born in the house of Israel, children whose inheritance was with the chosen people, children whose right it was to obtain all the blessings of Abraham, Isaac, and Jacob? Nephi gives answer in this way. He says the Lord "caused the cursing to come upon them, yea, even a sore cursing, because of their iniquity. For behold, they had hardened their hearts against him, that they had become like unto a flint; wherefore, as they were white, and exceeding fair and delightsome, that they might not be enticing unto my people the Lord God did cause a skin of blackness to come upon them."

Righteousness brings blessings, and wickedness spawns cursings. "And thus saith the Lord God: I will cause that they shall be loathsome unto thy people, save they shall repent of their iniquities. And cursed shall be the seed of him that mixeth with their seed; for they shall be cursed even with the same cursing." To this Nephi adds, "And the Lord spake it, and it was done." And also: "Because of their cursing which was upon them they did become an idle people, full of mischief and subtlety, and did seek in the wilderness for beasts of prey." (2 Ne. 5:21-24.)

Mormon picks up the same theme, using even stronger language. He speaks of the Lamanite destiny as the final great conflict between them and the Nephites draws near. "For this people shall be scattered," he prophesies, "and shall become a dark, a filthy, and a loathsome people, beyond the description of that which ever hath been amongst us, yea, even that which hath been among the Lamanites, and this because of their unbelief and idolatry. For behold, the Spirit of the Lord hath already ceased to strive with their fathers; and they are without Christ and God in the world; and they are driven about as chaff before the wind. They were once a delightsome people, and they had Christ for their shepherd; yea, they were led even by God the Father. But now, behold, they are led about by Satan, even as chaff is driven before the wind, or as a vessel is tossed about upon the waves, without sail or anchor, or without anything wherewith to steer her; and even as she is, so are they."

Nor is this all. These Lamanites, even in the days of the colonizing and settling of the Americas by the Gentiles, shall continue to be driven and slaughtered. In the United States, in Mexico, in Peru, in Uruguay, and in every place from one end of the Americas to the other, the sword of vengeance has spilled the blood of Father Lehi's children. "And behold, the Lord hath reserved their blessings, which they might have received in the land, for the Gentiles who shall possess the land," Mormon continues. "But behold, it shall come to pass that they shall be driven and scattered by the Gentiles; and after they have been driven and scattered by the Gentiles, behold, then will the Lord remember the covenant which he made unto Abraham and unto all the house of Israel." (Morm. 5:15-20.)

Such is the scattering of the Lamanites. The key words and phrases of holy writ are: unbelief, filthy, idleness, abominations, iniquities, mischief, subtlety, idolatry, without Christ and God in the world, led about by Satan, and the consequent cursings and wrath. And from our case study we are expected to learn that these same things led to the scattering of all branches of the chosen people.

The Lamanite Gathering

Our case study now turns to the day of Lamanite gathering. The long night of apostate darkness that left the remnants of Lehi's seed in their low and fallen and loathsome state is drawing to an end. Already the rays of gospel light are rising in the eastern sky and the day of gathering is dawning. Lamanites in the United States and Canada, in Mexico and Central America, and in the various nations of South America, together with the Lamanites in the islands of the South Pacific, whom we call Polynesians—all these are coming back, one by one as the divine decree requires. And when the day has fully dawned, as soon it must, they will be a glorious people indeed.

Indeed, that day—the day of the Lamanite—shall dawn before the Second Coming. Its arrival will be one of the signs of the times, and all those who can read the promised signs will thereby know that the coming of their Lord is nigh at hand. Pending that day, the Lord's command to his people is: "Be not deceived, but continue in steadfastness, looking forth for the heavens to be shaken, and the earth to tremble and to reel to and fro as a drunken man, and for the valleys to be exalted, and for the mountains to be made low, and for the rough places to become smooth—and all this when the angel shall sound his trumpet."

Having so announced, the Lord then relates all this to the gathering of Israel, including the Lamanite gathering. "But before the great day of the Lord shall come," he says, "Jacob shall flourish in the wilderness, and the Lamanites shall blossom as the rose. Zion shall flourish upon the hills and rejoice upon the mountains, and shall be assembled together unto the place which I have appointed." (D&C 49:23-25.) The physical gathering here alluded to is the assembling of the Latter-day Saints in the tops of the mountains in western America. It is there that Zion shall flourish upon the hills and rejoice upon the mountains. The wilderness referred to is the then-uninhabited areas that were colonized by Brigham Young less than a score of years later. And as to the day when the Lamanites shall blossom as the rose, it has scarcely commenced. They are not yet, except in a beginning degree, the pure and delightsome people of whom the scriptures speak. It is to these promises relative to their gathering that we shall now give attention.

Both the Lamanites and the Nephites were of the tribe of Manasseh, whose father, Joseph, was sold by his brethren into Egyptian slavery. This Joseph, one of the greatest of the ancient seers, saw in vision his Lehite descendants and their civilization in the Western Hemisphere. He saw them as "a branch . . . broken off" from the olive tree of Israel, a branch separated from their kinsmen in the Old World; and he saw that they would "be remembered in the covenants of the Lord." He saw them gathered back to the ancient standards when "the Messiah should be made manifest unto them in the latter days, in the spirit of power, unto the bringing of them out of darkness unto light—yea, out of hidden darkness and out of captivity unto freedom." This restoration, Joseph of old testified, would be brought to pass through a seer—Joseph the seer of latter days—whom the Lord would raise up to commence the restoration of all things and to bring the remnants of Israel "to the knowledge of the covenants" that the Lord made with their fathers. (2 Ne. 3:5-7.)

Lehi and Nephi both had similar spiritual insights relative to that portion of Joseph's seed which inhabited the Americas. "The house of Israel was compared unto an olive-tree, by the Spirit of the Lord which was in our fathers," Nephi said. Then he asked: "Are we not broken off from the house of Israel, and are we not a branch of the house of Israel?" Then, "concerning the grafting in of the natural branches" to the parent tree, Nephi prophesied: It shall be "in the latter days, when our seed shall have dwindled in unbelief." It shall be "many generations after the Messiah shall be manifested in body unto the children of men." When it comes to pass, "then shall the fulness of the gospel of the Messiah come unto the Gentiles, and from the Gentiles unto the remnant of our seed." Thus shall the gospel bring to pass the gathering of Israel.

"And at that day shall the remnant of our seed know that they are of the house of Israel," Nephi continues to prophesy, "and that they are the covenant people of the Lord; and then shall they know and come to the knowledge of their forefathers, and also to the knowledge of the gospel of their Redeemer, which was ministered unto their fathers by him; wherefore, they shall come to the knowledge of their Redeemer and the very points of his doctrine, that they may know how to come unto him and be saved." Such is the prophetic word. How plainly the Book of Mormon prophets speak. Can anyone mistake the true intent and meaning and reality of the Lamanite gathering?

"And then at that day," Nephi continues, "will they not rejoice and give praise unto their everlasting God, their rock and their salvation? Yea, at that day, will they not receive the strength and nourishment from the true vine? Yea, will they not come unto the true fold of God?" In answer the son of Lehi acclaims: "Behold, I say unto you, Yea; they shall be remembered again among the house of Israel; they shall be grafted in, being a natural branch of the olive-tree, into the true olive-tree." (1 Ne. 15:12-16.)

How is the gospel to go to the Lamanites and to all Israel in the latter days? It shall be through Joseph Smith and the Book of Mormon. The angelic word on this point to Nephi was couched in these words: "These last records [the Book of Mormon and the revelations given in the latter days], which thou hast seen among the Gentiles, shall establish the truth of the first [the Bible], which are of the twelve apostles of the Lamb, and shall make known the plain and precious things which have been taken away from them; and shall make known to all kindreds, tongues, and people, that the Lamb of God is the Son of the Eternal Father, and the Savior of the world; and that all men must come unto him, or they cannot be saved." (1 Ne. 13:40.)

Thereafter Nephi prophesies: "For after the book of which I have spoken [the Book of Mormon] shall come forth, and be written unto the Gentiles, and sealed up again unto the Lord [all of which has now transpired], there shall be many which shall believe the words which are written; and they shall carry them forth unto the remnant of our seed." The Book of Mormon is going forth, not only to the seed of Lehi, but to the whole world, as rapidly as our strength and means enable us to place it in the hands of receptive persons.

"And then shall the remnant of our seed know concerning us, how that we came out from Jerusalem, and that they are descendants of the Jews. And the gospel of Jesus Christ shall be declared among them; wherefore, they shall be restored unto the knowledge of their fathers, and also to the knowledge of Jesus Christ, which was had among their fathers. And then shall they rejoice; for they shall know that it is a blessing unto them from the hand of God; and many generations shall not pass away among them, save they shall be a pure and delightsome people." (2 Ne. 30:3-6.) These words are now in process of fulfillment. The scales of darkness have fallen from a few eyes and shall fall from many; and, ere long, the pure and delightsome status shall be attained by this remnant of the covenant people.

Thus we learn that the Lamanites shall come out of apostate darkness into the light of the gospel; they shall escape from the captivity of sin and gain the freedom of the gospel; they shall be grafted in to the natural olive tree again—because they worship the Father in the name of the Son by the power of the Spirit.

Thus we learn that they shall blossom as the rose and become a pure and a delightsome people, because they return unto the Lord their God; because they accept Christ as their Savior; because they glory once again in their Redeemer—the Redeemer of Israel— who has bought them with his blood and whose atoning sacrifice brings immortality to all men and the hope of eternal life to those who believe and obey.

Thus we learn that they shall come into the fold of the Good Shepherd—the Shepherd of Israel—when they believe the Book of Mormon, when they come to a knowledge of the covenants made with their fathers, when they reject the false doctrine of Laman and turn to the true doctrine of Nephi.

The Lamanites—A Pattern for All Israel

Our knowledge of the Lamanite gathering lets us know how and in what manner all Israel will return again to Him who has

chosen them as his own. Through it we learn how all the tribes—
Ephraim and Manasseh wherever they are; the Jews who are scattered and mocked in all nations; the Ten Tribes who are lost and
hidden among all the nations of the Gentiles—thus we learn how
and in what manner they too shall be gathered. It is with Ephraim
as it is with Manasseh; it is with Joseph as it is with Judah; and it
shall be with Reuben and Simeon as with all the other tribes. All
are alike unto God. All shall gather on the same terms and conditions.

It is, of course, the most natural thing in the world for the Book
of Mormon prophets to take the words spoken by Isaiah and the
other prophets—words spoken relative to the whole house of
Israel—and show how they are fulfilled in their own seed whom
we and they know as the Lamanites. Where better should their interests have been centered than in their own family members?
Should we not do the very same thing and make a specific application of the prophetic word to our own children who also are of
Israel, though, in fact, they are only a small part of the whole
nation?

But the Nephite prophets knew and repeatedly testified that
what they said about the Lamanite gathering applied also to the
gathering of all Israel. "After our seed is scattered," Nephi said,
"the Lord God will proceed to do a marvelous work among the
Gentiles, which shall be of great worth unto our seed"—the marvelous work is the restoration of the gospel to the Gentiles, to a
people who were not nationals of the kingdom of Judah—
"wherefore, it is likened unto their being nourished by the Gentiles
and being carried in their arms and upon their shoulders." (1 Ne.
22:8.) The allusion here is to Isaiah's great prophecy—made to all
the house of Israel, and which Nephi had previously quoted—that
when the Lord raised his standard and restored his gospel to the
Gentiles, their kings would be nursing fathers and their queens
nursing mothers in bringing the Israelites back to the lands of their
inheritance. (1 Ne. 21:22-23.) In applying these words, Nephi's
first emphasis is on the Lamanite gathering. It takes precedence,
even as our own families are more important to us than are others.
Then, as he continues to speak of the gathering in the day of resto-

ration, he broadens the view to include all Israel. "And it shall also be of worth unto the Gentiles; and not only unto the Gentiles but unto all the house of Israel, unto the making known of the covenants of the Father of heaven unto Abraham, saying: In thy seed shall all the kindreds of the earth be blessed." All the house of Israel means all the house of Israel. The words mean what they say and include the Ten Tribes.

Because the house of Israel is scattered in all nations, the gathering must take place on all the surface of the earth. Hence the prophetic word acclaims: "And I would, my brethren, that ye should know that all the kindreds of the earth cannot be blessed unless he shall make bare his arm in the eyes of the nations. Wherefore, the Lord God will proceed to make bare his arm in the eyes of all the nations, in bringing about his covenants and his gospel unto those who are of the house of Israel." The gospel shall go to all Israel in all nations in all the earth. "Wherefore, he will bring them again out of captivity, and they shall be gathered together to the lands of their inheritance"—which lands (a plural word) we shall define and identify more particularly hereafter—"and they shall be brought out of obscurity and out of darkness; and they shall know that the Lord is their Savior and their Redeemer, the Mighty One of Israel." (1 Ne. 22:9-12.)

One other of the many like passages will suffice for our purposes. Our friend Mormon, as he nears the end of his divinely appointed work, that of preserving the everlasting word as it was had among the Nephites, says: "I write unto you, Gentiles, and also unto you, house of Israel, when the work shall commence, that ye shall be about to prepare to return to the land of your inheritance." Then, as though this salutation was not sufficient, and lest any should be confused as to the people to whom the Book of Mormon shall go, Mormon wrote: "Yea, behold, I write unto all the ends of the earth; yea, unto you, [the] twelve tribes of Israel." _The Book of Mormon is written to the twelve tribes of Israel_. And this includes the lost Ten Tribes. For that matter, the New Testament itself is addressed "to the twelve tribes which are scattered abroad." (James 1:1.)

"And these things doth the Spirit manifest unto me; therefore I

215

write unto you all"—all the house of Israel. Why? "That ye may believe the gospel of Jesus Christ, which ye shall have among you; and also that the Jews, the covenant people of the Lord, shall have other witness besides him whom they saw and heard, that Jesus, whom they slew, was the very Christ and the very God. And I would that I could persuade all ye ends of the earth to repent and prepare to stand before the judgment-seat of Christ." (Morm. 3:17-22.) That is to say, all Israel, the Lamanites and the Ten Tribes included, shall be gathered if and when they believe the Book of Mormon. The Ten Tribes shall return after they accept the Book of Mormon; then they shall come to Ephraim to receive their blessings, the blessings of the house of the Lord, the blessings that make them heirs of the covenant God made with their father Abraham.

But, says one, *are they not in a body somewhere in the land of the north?* Answer: They are not; they are scattered in all nations. The north countries of their habitation are all the countries north of their Palestinian home, north of Assyria from whence they escaped, north of the prophets who attempted to describe their habitat. And for that matter, they shall also come from the south and the east and the west and the ends of the earth. Such is the prophetic word.

But, says another, *did not Jesus visit them after he ministered among the Nephites?* Answer: Of course he did, in one or many places as suited his purposes. He assembled them together then in exactly the same way he gathered the Nephites in the land Bountiful so that they too could hear his voice and feel the prints of the nails in his hands and in his feet. Of this there can be no question. And we suppose that he also called twelve apostles and established his kingdom among them even as he did in Jerusalem and in the Americas. Why should he deal any differently with one branch of Israel than with another?

Query: *What happened to the Ten Tribes after the visit of the Savior to them near the end of the thirty-fourth year following his birth?* Answer: The same thing that happened to the Nephites. There was righteousness for a season, and then there was apostasy and wickedness. Be it remembered that darkness was destined to cover the earth—all of it—before the day of the restoration, and that the restored gospel was to go to every nation and kindred and tongue and people upon the face of the whole earth, including the Ten Tribes of Israel.

But, says yet another, *what about their scriptures—will they not bring them when they return?* Answer: Yes, they will bring the Book of Mormon and the Bible, both of which were written to them and must be received by them before they gather. And further, as we devoutly hope, they will also have other records that will give an account of the ministry of the resurrected Lord among them—records that will come forth in a marvelous manner, at the direction of the president of The Church of Jesus Christ of Latter-day Saints, who is a revelator and a translator and who holds the keys of the kingdom of God on earth as pertaining to all men, the Ten Tribes included.

And, finally, says yet another, *will they not come with their prophets and seers?* Answer: There is no other way they or any people can be gathered. Of course they will be led by their prophets, prophets who are subject to and receive instructions from, and prophets who report their labors to the one man on earth who holds and exercises all of the keys of the kingdom in their fulness. Did not Paul say that "the spirits of the prophets are subject to the prophets," and that "God is not the author of confusion"? (1 Cor. 14:32-33.) The Lord's house is a house of order; it has only one head at one time; Christ is not divided. In this day when the head of the Church can communicate with all men on earth, there is no longer any need for one kingdom in Jerusalem and another in Bountiful and others in whatever place or places the Ten Tribes were when Jesus visited them. This is the promised day when there shall be one God, one Shepherd, one prophet, one gospel, one church, and one kingdom for all the earth. This is the day when one man shall direct all of the Lord's work in all the earth; the day when he shall bring all Israel into one fold; the day when one man will give an account of his stewardship over all the earth at Adam-ondi-Ahman just before the great day of the Lord arrives.

Come, Ye Lamanites

Mormon himself issues the great call to the Lamanites of the latter days. It is a call to gather into the sheepfold of their ancient fathers and to receive again the protecting care of the Shepherd of Israel. It is a call to come out of the deserts of sin and find rest in a pleasant land that flows with milk and honey. It is a call to receive again the gifts and blessings of those upon whom the face of the Lord once shone. It is a divine proclamation that sets the pattern for the call that must go forth to all the scattered remnants of the Lord's covenant people. What he says unto one applies to all: all shall return and gain divine approval on the same basis.

Come, ye Lamanites; come, ye Jews; come, ye lost tribes of Israel—come. Come and drink of the waters of life; come feast on the manna from heaven; come bask in the light of the Lord. Return, O backsliding Israel; return unto Him whom your fathers served; return unto the Lord your God. His arm is not shortened that he cannot save; his voice is heard again; the word of salvation, now in the hands of Ephraim and Manasseh, is for all the seed of Jacob.

"Know ye that ye are of the house of Israel." The blood of Abraham, Isaac, and Jacob flows in your veins. Ye are their seed after the manner of the flesh. "Know ye that ye must come unto repentance, or ye cannot be saved." Ye cannot be saved in your sins. Repent, repent; why will ye perish? Ye cannot live after the manner of worldly men and find favor with God.

"Know ye that ye must come to the knowledge of your fathers, and repent of all your sins and iniquities, and believe in Jesus Christ, that he is the Son of God, and that he was slain by the Jews, and by the power of the Father he hath risen again, whereby he hath gained the victory over the grave; and also in him is the sting of death swallowed up." Salvation is in Christ. Beside him there is no Savior. It is now as it was in the days of your fathers. "And he"—Christ the Lord—"bringeth to pass the resurrection of the dead, whereby man must be raised to stand before his judgment-seat. And he hath brought to pass the redemption of the world, whereby he that is found guiltless before him at the judgment day hath it given unto him to dwell in the presence of God in his kingdom, to sing ceaseless praises with the choirs above, unto the Father, and unto the Son, and unto the Holy Ghost, which are one God, in a state of happiness which hath no end."

Jehovah who is Christ scattered his people because they rejected him and his law. Christ who is Jehovah shall gather his people when they return unto him and believe again his holy gospel. "Therefore," ye Lamanites, ye Jews, ye twelve tribes of Israel, "repent, and be baptized in the name of Jesus, and lay hold upon the gospel of Christ, which shall be set before you, not only in this record [the Book of Mormon] but also in the record which shall come unto the Gentiles from the Jews [the Bible], which record shall come from the Gentiles unto you."

Thus we say: Come, all ye house of Israel, all ye scattered sheep, all ye lost and fallen ones; come, ye of every tribe and family; believe the testimony of Joseph Smith and those upon whom his prophetic mantle has fallen. Come out of the world, out of the bondage of Egypt, and join The Church of Jesus Christ of Latter-day Saints, for this church administers the gospel, and the gospel is the plan of salvation. Come to the Lord's house and receive your blessings and inherit thereby the same blessings given to Abraham, Isaac, and Jacob and promised to all of their righteous children. All ye who "are a remnant of the seed of Jacob," know that "ye are numbered among the people of the first covenant; and if it so be that ye believe in Christ, and are baptized, first with water, then with fire and the Holy Ghost, following the example of our Savior, according to that which he hath commanded us, it shall be well with you in the day of judgment. Amen." (Morm. 7:1-10.)

Chapter 19

THE JEWS
AND THE SECOND
COMING

Who Are the Jews?

When he made flesh his tabernacle, our blessed Lord—Mary's Son, one Jesus by name—came to the Jews of his day. They were his own people when he dwelt among the sons of men. He himself was a Jew. And when he comes again—as the Son of God, as the Incarnate Jehovah—it will be to his own, to the Jews; and he himself will be a Jew, a Jew of the Jews, the Chief Jew of the chosen race.

It was Jewish blood that was shed for the sins of the world. It was Jewish blood that oozed in great gouts from every pore as he suffered beyond compare in Gethsemane. It was Jewish blood that clotted around the nails in his hands, dripped from the wounds in his feet, and gushed from his riven side. It was a Jew who died on a cross that all men might be freed from the agonies of the flesh and the terrors of death. And it will be a Jew—the Rejected Jew, the Chief Jew, the King of the Jews, risen in glorious immortality—who shall come again, in all the glory of his Father's kingdom, as the remnant of that once great nation cries out: 'Blessed be he who cometh in the name of the Lord. Hosanna in the highest. All glory to his everlasting name.'

The second coming of the Son of Man will be a day of Jewish glory and triumph. As they were singled out to see his face and hear his voice when he came to atone for the sins of the world, so—after long centuries of being cursed and scourged and slain—

they will be chosen again to see the wounds in his flesh, to accept the salvation of the cross, and to find at long last their Promised Messiah. They will yet play the role assigned them for that glorious day when he comes to complete the salvation of man and to crown his work before delivering the kingdom spotless to his Father. And even as we study the Jewish religion and the Jewish way of life in order to understand what Jesus did and said in the Palestine of the past, so we must know the part the Jews are to play in his glorious return, if we ourselves are to abide the day and find ourselves numbered with those of the chosen race.

Who, then, are the Jews, and what part shall they yet play in the gathering of Israel and the return of their King? There is a maze of fuzzy thinking and shoddy scholarship, both in the world and in the Church, that seeks to identify the Jews, both ancient and modern, and to expound upon what they have believed and do believe. It is not strange that the divines of the day—not knowing that the kingdom is to be restored to Israel at that glorious day; not having the Book of Mormon and latter-day revelation to guide them—it is not strange that they come up with false and twisted views about the mission and destiny of the Jews. It is a little sad that church members sometimes partake of these false views and of this secular spirit so as to misread the signs of the times.

The term *Jew* is a contraction of the name *Judah*, but the Jews are not the members of the tribe of Judah as such. After the reign of Solomon, the Lord's people divided into the *kingdom of Israel* and the *kingdom of Judah*. Nearly ten tribes served Jeroboam in Israel and two and a half tribes served Rehoboam in Judah. The Levites were scattered among all the tribes. Judah, Simeon, and part of Benjamin comprised the kingdom of Judah. In actual fact, and considering blood lineage only, both kingdoms had in them people from all of the tribes. Lehi, who lived in Judah and was a Jew, was of the tribe of Manasseh. The Jews were nationals of the kingdom of Judah without reference to tribal ancestry. Thus the descendants of Lehi, both the Nephites and the Lamanites, were Jews because they came out from Jerusalem and from the kingdom of Judah. (2 Ne. 33:8.)

The Jews today are also those whose origins stem back to the kingdom of their fathers. Clearly the dominant tribe—dominant, however, only in the sense of political power and rulership—was Judah. As to the bloodlines, who knows whether there are more of Judah or of Simeon or of Benjamin or of some other tribe among the Jews as we know them? Paul, a Jew, was of the tribe of Benjamin. The name *Judea*, now used as a noun, is actually an adjective meaning *Jewish* and is the Greek and Roman designation for the land of Judah.

Since the Ten Tribes were taken into Assyria and lost from the knowledge of their fellows more than a century before the Jews went into Babylonian captivity, the prophets began to speak of Jews and Gentiles and to consider as a Gentile everyone who was not a Jew. This classifies Ephraim and the rest of scattered Israel as Gentiles. Everyone, in this sense, who is not a Jew is a Gentile, a concept that will enable us, in due course, to set forth what is meant by the fulness of the Gentiles.

As to their ancient beliefs, the Jews had either the fulness of the gospel or the preparatory gospel as their religious zeal and devotion of the moment warranted. They were always subject to the law of Moses, but whenever, as among the Nephites, their prophets held the Melchizedek Priesthood, they also had the fulness of the gospel. Both under the gospel and under the law—this latter, at least, in their more righteous days—they had a hope in Christ and understood that salvation would come through his atoning sacrifice. And as our studies will now show, the Jews were scattered when they forsook their Messiah, and they will be gathered when they return to him.

The Jewish Scattering

The Jews, the Lord's ancient covenant people! Would God that today they might be as were their righteous forebears, when David drove the Jebusites from Jerusalem, when Solomon reigned in splendor with great wisdom and compassion, when Isaiah extended the life of Hezekiah! Oh, that once again a Daniel might close the mouths of the lions that roar against them, and a Zerubbabel might arise to build again an holy sanctuary in their own Jerusalem! Oh, that a Peter, James, and John might once more be found among them who could stand on a modern Mount of Transfiguration, converse with Moses and Elias, and hear the voice of God as the divine Shekinah spreads its luminous brilliance over the heights of Hermon!

For three thousand years the history of the Jews—and God's dealings with them—has been the history of mankind. Never in all history has any people been treated, even in small measure, as have these ancient covenant ones. For half the time mortal man has dwelt on earth; for one hundred and fifty generations of fathers and sons; from the day the first David ascended the throne of Israel until the Second David shall come to reign on earth for a thousand years—during all this length of days, the history of the earth has revolved and will revolve around the seed of Abraham to whom the promises were made. In the days of their faith they have climbed one Sinai after another and seen Jehovah face to face. In the days of their rebellion they have suffered the eternal burnings of one Gehenna after another and been subject to that evil spirit who dwells in Sheol. Those who saw the face of their Maker dwelt in the Holy City and have gone on to dwell in the Eternal Presence. Those who loved darkness rather than light, because their deeds were evil, spent their days outside the city walls in the Valley of Hinnom, and they now dwell among the servants of the one whom they listed to obey.

Moses the man of God placed before all Israel heavenly blessings and hellish cursings, the blessings being conditioned upon faith and obedience and righteousness, the curses, upon rebellion and disobedience and wickedness. In the days of their cursings the seed of Jacob were promised desolation and disease and bondage. Wars and plagues and famines would be their common lot. Tender and delicate women would eat their own children in the siege against Jerusalem, and then, finally, speaking particularly of Jewish-Israel, the divine word affirmed: "Ye shall be plucked from off the land whither thou goest to possess it. And the Lord shall scatter thee among all people, from the one end of the earth even unto the other; and there thou shalt serve other gods, which neither thou nor thy fathers have known." How far the ancient people have departed from the pure worship of the Father, in the name of the Son, by the power of the Holy Ghost, which existed among their fathers!

"And among these nations shalt thou find no ease, neither shall the sole of thy foot have rest: but the Lord shall give thee there a trembling heart, and failing of eyes, and sorrow of mind: And thy life shall hang in doubt before thee; and thou shalt fear day and night, and shalt have none assurance of thy life." As the full significance of these words sinks into our souls, our minds turn to Russia and Germany and all the nations that have slain the Jews because they were Jews, by the thousands, and the tens of thousands, and the hundreds of thousands, and by the millions. Truly of these Jews the prophetic word acclaims: "In the morning thou shalt say, Would God it were even! and at even thou shalt say, Would God it were morning! for the fear of thine heart wherewith thou shalt fear, and for the sight of thine eyes which thou shalt see." (Deut. 28:15-68.)

Knowing all these things, and having in mind particularly the siege when human flesh will be all that is left to satisfy the pangs of hunger, we are not surprised to hear Jesus say, on the Mount of Olives, speaking of the then imminent destruction of Jerusalem by Titus in A.D. 70, "Then, in those days, shall be great tribulation on the Jews, and upon the inhabitants of Jerusalem, such as was not before sent upon Israel, of God, since the beginning of their kingdom until this time; no, nor ever shall be sent again upon Israel." And then, as though the famine and blood and death of the Roman siege were not enough, the Voice on Olivet adds: "All things which have befallen them are only the beginning of the sorrows which shall come upon them." (JS-M 1:18-19.)

Why were the Jews scattered and scourged and slain? From the beginning of their kingdom—from the day Rehoboam taxed the people into bondage to the day of Pilate, when they were still rendering unto Caesar the things that are Caesar's—they were scattered because they forsook the Lord Jehovah and his laws. And from the day Pilate said "Take ye him, and crucify him," they were scattered because they crucified their King.

Let this fact be engraved in the eternal records with a pen of steel: the Jews were cursed, and smitten, and cursed anew, because they rejected the gospel, cast out their Messiah, and cruci-fied their King. Let the spiritually illiterate suppose what they may, it was the Jewish denial and rejection of the Holy One of Is-rael, whom their fathers worshipped in the beauty of holiness, that has made them a hiss and a byword in all nations and that has taken millions of their fair sons and daughters to untimely graves.

What saith the holy word? "They shall be scourged by all peo-ple, because they crucify the God of Israel, and turn their hearts aside, rejecting signs and wonders, and the power and glory of the God of Israel. And because they turn their hearts aside, . . . and have despised the Holy One of Israel, they shall wander in the flesh, and perish, and become a hiss and a by-word and be hated among all nations." (1 Ne. 19:13-14; 2 Ne. 6:9-11.) Such is the prophetic word of Nephi. His brother Jacob speaks in like lan-guage. "There is none other nation on earth that would crucify their God," he says. "But because of priestcrafts and iniquities, they at Jerusalem will stiffen their necks against him, that he be crucified. Wherefore, because of their iniquities, destructions, famines, pestilences, and bloodshed shall come upon them; and they who shall not be destroyed shall be scattered among all na-tions." (2 Ne. 10:3-6; 25:12-15.)

The Jewish Gathering

Why and how and in what manner shall the Jews be gathered again in the last days? It shall be with them as it is with the Laman-ites, who unbeknown to the world are, in fact, Jews, and as it is with Ephraim and all the house of Israel. The Jews shall be gathered one of a city and two of a family, a favored person here and an elect soul there. They shall come back because they believe the Book of Mormon and when they accept the gospel. They shall return, a few to Palestine, most of them to the folds of their An-cient Shepherd as these are found in all the nations of the earth. They shall come again to the Holy One of Israel, wait no longer for a Messiah who is to come, but accept Christ as their Savior and plead with the Father in the name of the Son for the cleansing pow-er of his blood. They shall return when they join the true Church, The Church of Jesus Christ of Latter-day Saints.

Truly, as Isaiah promised, the cry shall go forth—nay, is even now going forth: "Awake, awake, stand up, O Jerusalem, which hast drunk at the hand of the Lord the cup of his fury; thou hast drunken the dregs of the cup of trembling [staggering], and wrung them out." Thy sons have suffered "desolation, and destruction, and the famine, and the sword. . . . Therefore hear now this, thou afflicted, and drunken, but not with wine: Thus saith thy Lord the Lord, and thy God that pleadeth the cause of his people, Behold, I have taken out of thine hand the cup of trembling [staggering], even the dregs of the cup of my fury; thou shalt no more drink it again." (Isa. 51:17-22.)

Isaiah's poetic imagery is added upon and given anew in plain words by the Book of Mormon prophets. Moroni, who wrote the title page of this volume of holy scripture, said that it was sent forth "to the convincing of the Jew and Gentile that JESUS is the CHRIST, the ETERNAL GOD, manifesting himself unto all nations." His father Mormon said, "These things," meaning the Book of Mormon, "are written unto the remnant of the house of Jacob. . . . And behold, they shall go unto the unbelieving of the Jews; and for this intent shall they go—that they may be persuaded that Jesus is the Christ, the Son of the living God; that the Father may bring about, through his most Beloved, his great and eternal purpose, in restoring the Jews." (Morm. 5:12-14.) The Book of Mormon gathers Israel, including the Jews, who are part of Israel. It "contains the truth and the word of God." It came forth by way of "the Gentile," that "it may go to the Jew, of whom the Lamanites are a remnant, that they may believe the gospel, and look not for a Messiah to come who has already come." (D&C 19:26-27.) Such is the word of the Lord given in this day.

Jacob recounts that after the Jews crucify Christ, "they shall be scattered, and smitten, and hated; nevertheless, the Lord will be merciful unto them, that when they shall come to the knowledge of their Redeemer, they shall be gathered together again to the lands of their inheritance. . . . The Messiah will set himself again the second time to recover them; wherefore, he will manifest himself unto them in power and great glory, unto the destruction of their enemies, when that day cometh when they shall believe in him. . . . For the Mighty God shall deliver his covenant people." (2 Ne. 6:9-17.)

Nephi prophesies of the coming of the Only Begotten of the Father in the flesh; of his rejection by the Jews "because of their iniquities, and the hardness of their hearts, and the stiffness of their necks"; of his crucifixion, resurrection, and the salvation he thus brings; of his resurrected appearances; of the subsequent destruction of Jerusalem; and of the scattering of the Jews "among all nations." Then come these prophetic words: "And after they have been scattered, and the Lord God hath scourged them by other nations for the space of many generations, yea, even down from generation to generation until they shall be persuaded to believe in Christ, the Son of God, and the atonement, which is infinite for all mankind—and when that day shall come that they shall believe in Christ, and worship the Father in his name, with pure hearts and clean hands, and look not forward any more for another Messiah, then, at that time, the day will come that it must needs be expedient that they should believe these things."

How awful has that scourging been! Like the Chief Jew whose flesh was torn by the beads of lead and the sharp bones in the Roman flagellum, as he was scourged for sins that were not his, so a whole nation has cringed beneath the lacerating whip, for their own sins and those of their fathers. And as it has been for generations, so shall it be until they repent and come unto Him whom their fathers slew and hanged on a tree, which faith and repentance shall come to pass when, and only when, they believe the Book of Mormon and turn to Joseph Smith, through whom the gospel has been restored in and for our day.

"And the Lord will set his hand again the second time to restore his people from their lost and fallen state." Once he led them out of Egyptian bondage into a promised land, with a mighty hand and with power poured out; and he will yet again lead them out of the Egypt of the world into the only true and living Church upon the face of the whole earth. "Wherefore, he will proceed to do a marvelous work and a wonder among the children of men. Wherefore, he shall bring forth his words unto them, which words shall judge them at the last day, for they shall be given them for the purpose of convincing them of the true Messiah, who was rejected by them; and unto the convincing of them that they need not look forward any more for a Messiah to come, for there should not any come, save it should be a false Messiah which should deceive the people; for there is save one Messiah spoken of by the prophets, and that Messiah is he who should be rejected of the Jews." (2 Ne. 25:12-18.) When that day comes, they shall, as Jacob said, "be restored to the true church and fold of God." (2 Ne. 9:2.)

The Day of Jewish Conversion

When will Jewish Israel be gathered again into the true Church and fold of their ancient Messiah? When will they accept the Lord Jesus Christ as the Savior of the world and worship the Father in his holy name? When will they believe the Book of Mormon, be cleansed from their sins in the waters of Judah, and come and receive their blessings under the hands of Ephraim, the firstborn? Will these things come to pass before or after their ancient and once rejected King returns in power and great glory to reign gloriously among his saints?

Nephi prophesies that the gospel of Jesus Christ shall be taken to the remnant of Lehi's seed in the last days; that they shall believe and obey and gain anew the knowledge and blessings enjoyed by their fathers; and that "their scales of darkness shall begin to fall from their eyes; and many generations shall not pass away among them, save they shall be a pure and delightsome people." In this setting of Lehite conversion, and of the newness of life that shall be theirs after the Book of Mormon comes forth, our ancient friend prophesies also of the Jews. "And it shall come to pass that the Jews which are scattered also shall begin to believe in Christ; and they shall begin to gather in upon the face of the land; and as many as shall believe in Christ shall also become a delightsome people." Then the prophetic word continues—and the chronological order of events is of great import—then Nephi talks at length about millennial conditions and the triumph and glory of the Lord's people in that blessed day. (2 Ne. 30:3-18.)

That is to say, the Jews "shall begin to believe in Christ" before he comes the second time. Some of them will accept the gospel and forsake the traditions of their fathers; a few will find in Jesus the fulfillment of their ancient Messianic hopes; but their nation as a whole, their people as the distinct body that they now are in all nations, the Jews as a unit shall not, at that time, accept the word of truth. But a beginning will be made; a foundation will be laid; and then Christ will come and usher in the millennial year of his redeemed.

As all the world knows, many Jews are now gathering to Palestine, where they have their own nation and way of worship, all without reference to a belief in Christ or an acceptance of the laws and ordinances of his everlasting gospel. Is this the latter-day gathering of the Jews of which the scriptures speak? No! It is not; let there be no misunderstanding in any discerning mind on this point. This gathering of the Jews to their homeland, and their organization into a nation and a kingdom, is not the gathering promised by the prophets. It does not fulfill the ancient promises. Those who have thus assembled have not gathered into the true Church and fold of their ancient Messiah. They have not received again the saving truths of that very gospel which blessed Moses their lawgiver, and Elijah their prophet, and Peter, James, and John, whom their fathers rejected.

This gathering of the unconverted to Palestine—shall we not call it a political gathering based on such understanding of the ancient word as those without the guidance of the Holy Spirit can attain, or shall we not call it a preliminary gathering brought to pass in the wisdom of him who once was their God?—this gathering, of those whose eyes are yet dimmed by scales of darkness and who have not yet become the delightsome people it is their destiny to be, is nonetheless part of the divine plan. It is Elias going before Messias; it is a preparatory work; it is the setting of the stage for the grand drama soon to be played on Olivet. A remnant of the once-chosen people must be at the proper place, at the appointed time, to fulfill that which aforetime has been promised relative to the return of the Crucified One to the people who once chanted, in a delirious chorus, as Pilate sought to free him at the fourth Passover, "Crucify him, crucify him."

Seated on the Mount of Olives, surrounded by the Twelve, in

the Olivet Discourse Jesus said of his glorious return: "And the remnant"—those Jews who have come out of the nations of the earth to live again in the land of Judah—"shall be gathered unto this place." This place is Palestine; it is Jerusalem; it is the Mount of Olives on the east of the holy city. "And then they shall look for me, and, behold, I will come; and they shall see me in the clouds of heaven, clothed with power and great glory; with all the holy angels." (D&C 45:43-44.) This coming—and there will be many appearances which taken together comprise the second coming of the Son of Man—this coming will be in the midst of war; it will be preceded by the destruction of the wicked; it will be to those Jews "that remain" after the day of burning, as Zechariah so aptly identifies them.

Foretelling and describing that day and that appearance, Jehovah said of olden time: "And I will pour upon the house of David, and upon the inhabitants of Jerusalem"—meaning upon those that remain after the wars, after the burning of the vineyard, after the destruction of the wicked—"the spirit of grace and of supplications: and they shall look upon me whom they have pierced, and they shall mourn for him, as one mourneth for his only son, and shall be in bitterness for him, as one that is in bitterness for his firstborn."

There follows a pronouncement relative to the inconsolable grief of those whose eyes are now open and who now know their fathers have walked in darkness, choosing to lose their souls rather than accept their Savior. Then comes this gladsome word: "In that day there shall be a fountain opened to the house of David and to the inhabitants of Jerusalem for sin and for uncleanness." They shall be baptized and receive the Holy Ghost! Sin and dross and evil will be burned out of them as though by fire. False worship shall cease. It is the millennial day. Their King is among them, and they know it. "And one shall say unto him, What are these wounds in thine hands? Then he shall answer, Those with which I was wounded in the house of my friends." (Zech. 12:10-14; 13:1, 6.)

The holy word that has come to us speaks of that day in these words: "And then shall the Jews look upon me and say: What are these wounds in thine hands and in thy feet? Then shall they know that I am the Lord; for I will say unto them: These wounds are the wounds with which I was wounded in the house of my friends. I am he who was lifted up. I am Jesus that was crucified. I am the Son of God." (D&C 45:51-52.)

And thus cometh the day of the conversion of the Jews. It is a, millennial day, a day after the destruction of the wicked, a day when those who remain shall seek the Lord and find his gospel. And, for that matter, so shall it be with reference to the gathering and triumph of all Israel. What we do now in preparation for the Second Coming is but a prelude. The great day of gathering and glory lies ahead. It will be in that age when men beat their swords into plowshares and their spears into pruning hooks, and there is peace in all the earth.

Chapter 20

THE GENTILES
AND THE SECOND
COMING

Who Are the Gentiles?

We have spoken and shall yet speak in glowing terms of Israel and her destiny as we rejoice in the goodness of God to his chosen people. But what of the aliens, what of those in whose veins none of the blood of father Jacob flows, what of the Gentiles? Shall they not play some part in the Lord's strange act, that act which is now being performed on the stage of the world? Have they no part to play in preparing a people for the second coming of the Son of Man?

Would it be amiss to take a Pauline approach to the Israel-Gentile relationship and ask: What? "Is he the God of the Jews only? is he not also of the Gentiles? Yes, of the Gentiles also." (Rom. 3:29.) And does not the Father of us all love all his children? Has he no work for his less-favored seed in that day when the whole earth and the people in every nation must hear the announcement of the return of the God of Israel, who is also the God of the whole earth? Is salvation reserved for the Jews only, or for Israel only? Did no one but Abraham have seed deserving of reward? God forbid. Such cannot be. Salvation is for all men, and there is work enough in the vineyards of the Lord for ministers chosen from every nation. None have more talents than they can use, and none have so few that they cannot perform some service for their King. As it was when Jesus first came, so it is today: the harvest truly is plenteous, but the laborers are few.

232

Truly, God "hath made of one blood all nations of men for to dwell on all the face of the earth" (Acts 17:26), and hath determined, in his own infinite wisdom, how and when they can best serve him and what they should do to further his interests. In it the Gentiles shall play their part, as we are about to see. But first, who are the Gentiles of whom we shall speak? Where are they found, and what relationship do they have both to Jewish Israel and to all Israel?

We have heretofore identified the Jews as both the nationals of the kingdom of Judah and as their lineal descendants, all this without reference to tribal affiliation. And we have said, within this usage of terms, that all other people are Gentiles, including the lost and scattered remnants of the kingdom of Israel in whose veins the precious blood of him whose name was Israel does in fact flow. Thus Joseph Smith, of the tribe of Ephraim, the chief and foremost tribe of Israel itself, was the Gentile by whose hand the Book of Mormon came forth, and the members of The Church of Jesus Christ of Latter-day Saints, who have the gospel and who are of Israel by blood descent, are the Gentiles who carry salvation to the Lamanites and to the Jews. The Lamanites, having come out from Jerusalem, are in fact Jews, although they are not the Jews of whom we speak when we divide mankind into the two camps of Jews and Gentiles.

There were, of course, Gentiles before there were Jews and before there was a kingdom of Judah. They were simply the aliens, the people of other nations, the citizens of other kingdoms, the worshippers of other gods than the Lord. In that day they were outside the pale of saving grace because they had neither the gospel in its fulness nor the law of Moses. It was proper then, and it is proper now, to refer to the Gentiles as those unbelievers who do not serve the Lord Jehovah (the God of Israel), and to refer to Israel as the believers who accept him as their God and who strive to do his will.

Israel in her scattered state is made up of those who are the literal seed of Jacob, even though they are now serving other gods than the Lord, and the Gentiles are those who have not descended from this ancient patriarchal house. Manifestly Israel and the alien nations have intermarried and many of earth's inhabitants are of mixed blood. With these concepts before us we are prepared to set forth the word of scripture relative to the Gentiles and their great latter-day work.

The Gospel Goes to the Gentiles

To envision why and under what circumstances the gospel was and is destined to go to the Gentiles, in preference to the Jews, we must take a brief overview of the dealings of God with mortals through the ages. We must open to view the hoary facts of antiquity and pierce the prophetic curtain that veils the future. We must come to know that the Father of us all, in his infinite goodness and grace, desires to save all his children; that he offers his saving truths to men under those circumstances in which the greatest possible number will believe and obey; and that he blesses those who seek his face and curses those who choose to walk in worldly ways.

Accordingly, a gracious God first gave his gospel to Adam and commanded him to teach his children—all his children from generation to generation—that salvation is in Christ and comes because of his atoning sacrifice. This our first mortal father did. And soon the pattern for all ages was set. The Abels among men sought the Lord, and the Cains served Satan. Men built cities of holiness wherein Enoch and his converts became pure in heart, and cities of sin in which the wicked and ungodly gratified the lusts of the flesh. There were righteous nations where the saints strengthened each other in the holy faith, and wicked nations in which none of the truths of heaven were found. Truly, the law of agency was and is in active operation in all ages and among all people.

Men are born into mortality with the talents and abilities acquired by obedience to law in their first estate. Above all talents—greater than any other capacities, chief among all endowments—stands the talent for spirituality. Those so endowed find it easy to believe the truth in this life. In large measure they are sent to earth in the households of faith where the gospel is known and taught and where they will have a better chance to gain salvation. In large measure, since the day of Abraham, they have been

234

born in Israel where the Lord's will is known. Even now the scattered and lost sheep of that favored house find it easier to accept the gospel than is the case with the residue of men. True it is that "all mankind"—Jew and Gentile alike—"may be saved, by obedience to the laws and ordinances of the Gospel." (A of F 3.) But the word of truth is sent to some before it goes to others because they earned the right to such preferential treatment in preexistence.

Thus some nations had the gospel before the flood and others did not. In that day "the seed of Cain," for instance, "were black, and had not place" among the people of God. (Moses 7:22.) Converts, however, were sought and made from among the balance of Adam's posterity. Similarly, after the flood, in the days of Abraham, the seed of Ham were "cursed . . . as pertaining to the Priesthood," and thus could not receive the fulness of the ordinances of the house of the Lord. (Abr. 1:26.) But when Abraham and his family left Ur to dwell in Canaan, he says they took with them "the souls that we had won in Haran." (Abr. 2:15.) Then, as now, the servants of the Lord were seeking to save their fellowmen.

From the day Israel was led out of Egypt and established as a nation until the ministry of their Messiah among them, the blessings of salvation were reserved almost exclusively for them. During that entire time the aliens had no claim upon Jehovah and his goodness. He was the God of Israel alone in the true sense of the word. But even then such Gentiles as took the yoke of the law upon them became Israelites by adoption and were blessed equally with the natural seed of Abraham. "The stranger that dwelleth with you shall be unto you as one born among you," the Lord commanded, "and thou shalt love him as thyself." (Lev. 19:34.)

Jesus made himself subject to this same law during his mortal ministry. With minor exceptions he confined his ministerial labors to "the lost sheep of the house of Israel." During a brief stay near Gentile Tyre and Sidon, he withheld his healing goodness from "a woman of Canaan" until she importuned with exceedingly great faith. "It is not meet to take the children's bread, and to cast it to dogs," he said. (Matt. 15:21-28.) During a short visit to the half-Jew, half-Gentile area of Decapolis, he proclaimed the gospel to all who there abode. But the great burden of his labors were with the Jews only. And when he sent the Twelve forth, they were similarly restricted. "Go not into the way of the Gentiles," he said, "But go rather to the lost sheep of the house of Israel." (Matt. 10:5-6.)

But all of this was simply to give the Jews the first opportunity to receive the gospel. Thereafter the divine word was to go to the Gentiles, as the prophetic word so eloquently attests. "I am sought of them that asked not for me," saith the God of Israel; "I am found of them that sought me not: I said, Behold me, behold me, unto a nation that was not called by my name." (Isa. 65:1.) "I will gather all nations and tongues; and they shall come, and see my glory." My ministers "shall declare my glory among the Gentiles. . . . And I will also take of them"—the Gentiles!—"for priests and for Levites, saith the Lord." (Isa. 66:18-21.) "For from the rising of the sun even unto the going down of the same my name shall be great among the Gentiles; . . . my name shall be great among the heathen, saith the Lord of hosts." (Mal. 1:11.)

It was to the Jews that the Messiah came, but he also came to save all men, both Jew and Gentile alike. The Messianic word affirms: "He shall bring forth judgment to the Gentiles," and shall be "a light of the Gentiles." (Isa. 42:1, 6.) Matthew interprets Isaiah's words to mean: "And in his name shall the Gentiles trust." (Matt. 12:21.) And saintly Simeon, in the temple, holding the Christ Child in his arms, was guided by the Spirit to testify that the newly born Messiah had come as "a light to lighten the Gentiles," as well as to be the glory of Israel. (Luke 2:32.)

The ancient word from Israel's God was: "Look unto me, and be ye saved, all the ends of the earth: for I am God, and there is none else." He is the one unto whom "every knee shall bow" and "every tongue shall swear." (Isa. 45:22-23.) And that all men might come unto him and be saved, he, after his resurrection, commanded his ancient apostles, "Go ye into all the world, and preach the gospel to every creature." (Mark 16:15.) At long last the promises to the Gentiles were to be fulfilled. His word, his gospel, his salvation was, eventually, for all men of every race, culture, and creed.

This new course of inviting all men to come and eat at the table of the Lord ushered in a new era of hope and salvation for all the seed of Adam. It was indeed a vision so broad and a concept so glorious that even the ancient Twelve were slow to understand its full import. They were Jews trained in Jewish theology and had seen their Master limit his work to their own kindred. The token of the covenant that set them apart from all nations had been cut into the very flesh of their bodies. They had yet to learn that circumcision, which they had supposed was an eternal and everlasting rite, had been done away in Christ, and that the sun of Jewish separateness was setting.

Hence, God gave Peter the vision of the unclean creatures and commanded: "What God hath cleansed, that call not thou common." Peter was then sent to Cornelius, where that Lord who is no respecter of persons, in the presence of his chief apostle, gave the Holy Ghost to Gentiles even before baptism, to the great astonishment of those "of the circumcision." (Acts 10:1-48.) From that day, the gospel went to both the Jews and the Gentiles, with a lessening emphasis on the Jews and an increasing call to the erstwhile aliens. After Paul and Barnabas had been rejected by the Jews, they said: "It was necessary that the word of God should first have been spoken to you: but seeing ye put it from you, and judge yourselves unworthy of everlasting life, lo, we turn to the Gentiles. For so hath the Lord commanded us, saying, I have set thee"— meaning the God of Israel—"to be a light of the Gentiles, that thou shouldest be for salvation unto the ends of the earth." (Acts 13:46-47.) After the destruction of Jerusalem and the scattering of her people, the *times of the Jews* drew to an end; thereafter the gospel went mainly to the Gentiles.

The Gospel Restored to the Gentiles

There were, in effect, three peoples, three different religious worlds, in the day of Jesus. These were:

1. The Jews, who had the Aaronic Priesthood, the law of Moses, the words of the prophets, and the hope of a messianic deliverer. It was among them that the Lord Jesus ministered as a mortal.

2. The other branches of the house of Israel, meaning (a) the Nephites, who had the Melchizedek Priesthood, the law of Moses, and the fulness of the gospel, and (b) the lost tribes of Israel, whom the Lord centuries before had led away into the lands northward, and who were not then known to have either the priesthood or the divine law. It was among these—the Nephites and the Ten Tribes—that Jesus ministered as a resurrected personage.

3. The Gentiles, meaning all other races of men, who dwelt wherever the nations of men were found. All these were without priesthood and authority and had none of the saving truths. Among them the Lord Jesus did not minister either as a mortal or an immortal, and to them the gospel was destined to go by the power of the Holy Ghost.

Jesus first took the gospel to the Jews, and it was by them rejected. Few indeed were the true believers among them. Then he took the very same truths and the very same powers to the rest of the house of Israel, whom we believe to have been faithful for many years thereafter. We know the Nephites hewed to the line of righteousness for two hundred years as did no other people of whom we know save only those in Enoch's Zion. Then the word of truth went to the Gentiles who were "converted through" the preaching of the Jews. These Gentiles did not "at any time" hear the Lord's voice, and he was not manifest unto them "save it were by the Holy Ghost." (3 Ne. 15:22-23.)

It is to those who are not Jews that the Lord promised to give his gospel first in the last days. "In the latter days, when our seed" —now known as Lamanites—"shall have dwindled in unbelief, yea, for the space of many years," Nephi said, "and many generations after the Messiah shall be manifested in body unto the children of men, then"—and this is to be in the glorious age of restoration in which we now live—"then shall the fulness of the gospel of the Messiah come unto the Gentiles, and from the Gentiles unto the remnant of our seed." This gospel shall come to them "by way of the Gentiles." Why? "That the Lord may show his power unto the Gentiles," Nephi continues, "for the very cause that he shall be rejected of the Jews, or of the house of Israel." (1 Ne. 15:13-17.)

We are those Gentiles of whom Nephi speaks. We have re-

238

ceived in this age of restoration the fulness of the everlasting gospel. It is now beginning to go from us to the Lamanites and to the Jews. But the great day of the Lamanites and the great day of the Jews both lie ahead. In the full and true sense of the word, the day of their worldwide glory, the day of the triumph and glory of both the Lamanites and the Jews, in all nations—that day will be millennial.

Jesus spoke many things to the Nephites, for their benefit and for ours, about these things. His words let us know what is to happen relative to the house of Israel both before and after he comes in glory to usher in the great Millennium. Speaking of the Jews, whom he identified as "my people at Jerusalem, they who have seen me and been with me in my ministry"—and they were to be scourged and scattered in all nations—of them Jesus said: "Through the fulness of the Gentiles, the remnant of their seed, . . . may be brought to a knowledge of me, their Redeemer." These dissident and rebellious souls whose fathers had cried: "His blood be on us, and"—God help us!—"on our children" (Matt. 27:25); these Jews who have not yet accepted the Lord Jesus as the Son of God and as their Promised Messiah, these descendants of those with whom God made covenant in olden times —they "shall be scattered forth upon the face of the earth because of their unbelief," Jesus says.

But when they accept Him whom their fathers rejected; when they believe in the one whom they slew and hanged on a tree; when they turn to the very Messiah who was born of Mary in Bethlehem of Judea and accept him as their King—then shall they be heirs of salvation along with faithful Abraham their father. "Then will I gather them in from the four quarters of the earth," Jesus promises, "and then will I fulfill the covenant which the Father hath made unto all the people of the house of Israel." The great day of glory for any people comes after they believe, after they are converted, after they obey the law upon which the receipt of the promised blessings is predicated. As with all Israel, so with the Jews; they shall be blessed after they believe and obey.

"And blessed are the Gentiles," Jesus testifies, "because of their belief in me, in and of the Holy Ghost, which witnesses unto them of me and of the Father." The holy gospel comes to us not because Jesus ministered among us in the days of his flesh, as he did to the Jews; not because he appeared and taught us as a resurrected personage, as he did to the Nephites and the Ten Tribes; rather, the gospel comes to us "in and of the Holy Ghost." We are in a like category with those in Jesus' day of whom he said: "The Gentiles should not at any time hear my voice," and "I should not manifest myself unto them save it were by the Holy Ghost." (3 Ne. 15:23.)

Of the Gentiles in the last days, our Lord continues: "Behold, because of their belief in me, saith the Father, and because of the unbelief of you, O house of Israel, in the latter day shall the truth come unto the Gentiles, that the fulness of these things shall be made known unto them." We shall receive again the gospel; we shall know what the ancients knew; we shall have the words Jesus spoke to the Nephites.

That the Gentiles of our day do not believe in the one and only Savior of mankind is one of the most self-evident truths of history. A few Jews believed when he came to them, but most of them rejected him and his salvation. So it is today. A few Gentiles believe, but the masses of men continue on in their carnal courses as worldly men have in all ages. Hence: "Wo, saith the Father, unto the unbelieving of the Gentiles—for notwithstanding they have come forth upon the face of this land [America], and have scattered my people [the Lamanites] who are of the house of Israel; and my people who are of the house of Israel have been cast out from among them, and have been trodden under feet by them; And because of the mercies of the Father unto the Gentiles, and also the judgments of the Father upon my people who are of the house of Israel, verily, verily, I say unto you, that after all this, and I have caused my people who are of the house of Israel to be smitten, and to be afflicted, and to be slain, and to be cast out from among them, and to become hated by them, and to become a hiss and a byword among them— . . . And then will I remember my covenant which I have made unto my people, O house of Israel, and I will bring my gospel unto them." In the last days the gospel goes first to the Gentiles and then to the Jews and Lamanites.

Why will the Lord take the gospel from the unbelieving Gentiles? Jesus answers: "At that day when the Gentiles shall sin against my gospel"—he is speaking here more particularly of the United States of America, of the nation that has scattered the Lamanites, of the nation that esteems itself greater than any other nation—"and shall be lifted up in the pride of their hearts above all nations, and above all the people of the whole earth, and shall be filled with all manner of lyings, and of deceits, and of mischiefs, and all manner of hypocrisy, and murders, and priestcrafts, and whoredoms, and of secret abominations; and if they shall do all those things, and shall reject the fulness of my gospel, behold, saith the Father, I will bring the fulness of my gospel from among them."

When will the Lord take the gospel from the unbelieving Gentiles? It will be when the fulness of the Gentiles is come in, when he remembers the covenant made with his own people, when the hour for millennial glory has arrived. "And then . . . I will show unto thee, O house of Israel, that the Gentiles shall not have power over you; but I will remember my covenant unto you, O house of Israel, and ye shall come unto the knowledge of the fulness of my gospel. But if the Gentiles will repent and return unto me, saith the Father, behold they shall be numbered among my people, O house of Israel."

The Gentiles as a whole and as a people will not repent and be numbered with the house of Israel. They are ripening in iniquity and the end is near, for the destruction of the wicked, which is the end of the world, shall soon come. But any portion of the Gentiles who do repent will be blessed and will not be destroyed in the coming day. Such shall inherit the blessings next spoken of by Jesus: "And I will not suffer my people, who are of the house of Israel, to go through among them, and tread them down, saith the Father."

Next Jesus speaks of the day when the wicked shall be cut off from among the people, when they will be burned as stubble, when every corruptible thing will be consumed. In doing so he uses some graphic imagery. "But if they will not turn unto me, and hearken unto my voice, I will suffer them, yea, I will suffer my people, O house of Israel, that they shall go through among them, and shall tread them down, and they shall be as salt that hath lost its savor, which is thenceforth good for nothing but to be cast out, and to be trodden under foot of my people, O house of Israel." In the full and true sense, Israel shall triumph over her foes only when the Millennium is ushered in, only when her Messiah comes to deliver them from the aliens, only when the wicked are destroyed and the Lord reigns gloriously among his saints.

It is in this setting—a millennial setting; a day of millennial glory; the day when peace prevails because the wicked have been destroyed—it is in this setting that Jesus says: "Then"—in the day of which we speak—"the words of the prophet Isaiah shall be fulfilled." These are the words: "Thy watchmen shall lift up the voice; with the voice together shall they sing, for they shall see eye to eye when the Lord shall bring again Zion." We are establishing Zion now, but our Zion is only the foundation for that which is to be. We are laying a foundation; the promises relative to the glorious Zion of God which shall yet stand upon the earth shall be fulfilled after the Lord comes. "Break forth into joy, sing together, ye waste places of Jerusalem," Isaiah continues, "for the Lord hath comforted his people, he hath redeemed Jerusalem." The true and full redemption of Jerusalem must await the day of the Lord's return. "The Lord hath made bare his holy arm in the eye of all the nations; and all the ends of the earth shall see the salvation of God." (3 Ne. 16:4-20.) Again, we have made a beginning, but the glorious fulfillment lies ahead.

We shall pick up and amplify these thoughts in the next chapter as we consider the Gentile fulness. At this point, as we speak of the gospel going to the Gentiles before the Second Coming, it but remains for us to bear one added solemn witness.

I was present, together with my Brethren of the Twelve and the counselors in the First Presidency, when the voice of God, speaking from the midst of eternity by the power of the Spirit, revealed a glorious truth to his servant the prophet. The message then confirmed in the heart and soul of President Spencer W. Kimball was that the time, long desired and devoutly sought for, had now come to offer to all men of every race and color, solely on the basis of personal worthiness, the fulness of the blessings of the Holy

242

Priesthood, including celestial marriage and all of the blessings of the house of the Lord.

All of us then present in the holy temple on that blessed occasion became living witnesses of the reality of the revealed word that then came to the one appointed to receive revelation for the Church and for the world. Each of us received a confirming witness in our souls—the Holy Spirit of God speaking to the spirits within us—so that we can and do testify to the world that the revelation came and that it is the mind and will and voice of the Lord.

The receipt of this revelation is one of the signs of the times. It lets us know that the coming of the Lord Jesus Christ to usher in the great Millennium is not far distant. It opens the door so that we can truly preach the gospel to every nation and kindred and tongue and people. Now there are no restrictions as to where Zion can be established or to the people who can become heirs of full salvation.

Having borne this witness and laid this foundation, we are now ready to build upon the foundations here laid and turn our attention to that rather enigmatic expression "the fulness of the Gentiles," which we shall do in chapter 21.

THE TIMES
OF THE GENTILES

The Gentiles and the Abrahamic Covenant

As we rejoice in the goodness of a gracious God to the Gentiles; as we marvel to see him give the blessings of the chosen people to the aliens; as we realize that the gospel blessings are for all men, Jew and Gentile alike—we must yet keep in proper perspective the favored status of blessed Israel. It was to Abraham that the promises came; it was Isaac who inherited all things from Abraham; and it was Jacob upon whom the fulness fell in his day. It is the God of Israel who, having first blessed the chosen seed, became the God of the whole earth and offered his gospel unto all who would believe and obey.

How glorious is the word that the Lord Jehovah chose Abraham, his friend, above all the inhabitants of the earth, to be the father of the faithful for all generations—not the father of the faithful in the house of Israel only, but the father of the faithful in all nations. "In thy seed shall all the nations of the earth be blessed" was the divine decree. (Gen. 22:18.)

How glorious is the word, given to Abraham, "In Isaac shall thy seed be called." (Gen. 21:12.) 'In this Sarah's son shall the promises be fulfilled. He shall inherit the blessings given to thee, Abraham, his father. Through him shall come the chosen and favored seed who shall believe the gospel and worship the true God and be saved in his kingdom.'

How glorious is the word that the God of Israel chose Jacob,

244

who is Israel, to inherit the blessings of his fathers—the blessings of life and salvation through the atonement of the Son of God.

And how glorious is the word that the Gentiles may be adopted into the family of Abraham and receive, inherit, and possess equally with the literal seed. "As many as receive this Gospel shall be called after thy name," the Lord Jehovah promised Abraham, "and shall be accounted thy seed, and shall rise up and bless thee, as their father." And further: "In thy seed after thee (that is to say, the literal seed, or the seed of the body) shall all the families of the earth be blessed, even with the blessings of the Gospel, which are the blessings of salvation, even of life eternal." (Abr. 2:10-11.)

Thus, salvation comes because of the covenant God made with Abraham. It was Jesus himself who said, "Salvation is of the Jews." (John 4:22.) It must go from Israel to others. If the Gentiles are to gain such a blessed boon, they must become Israelites; they must be adopted into the fold of Abraham; they must rise up and bless him as their father. It was to the natural seed of Jacob that Isaiah said these words of the Lord, and they are equally true with reference to the adopted seed: "Hearken to me, ye that follow after righteousness, ye that seek the Lord: look unto the rock whence ye are hewn, and to the hole of the pit whence ye are digged. Look unto Abraham your father, and unto Sarah that bare you: for I called him alone, and blessed him, and increased him." (Isa. 51:1-2.) Abraham alone is the father of us all, speaking after the manner of the flesh, and all who receive the blessings of the gospel are either natural or adopted sons in his everlasting family.

Thus, also, Nephi says: "As many of the Gentiles as will repent are the covenant people of the Lord; and as many of the Jews as will not repent shall be cast off; for the Lord covenanteth with none save it be with them that repent and believe in his Son, who is the Holy One of Israel." (2 Ne. 30:2.) The covenant here involved is the Abrahamic covenant. It is, Nephi says, the "covenant the Lord made to our father Abraham, saying: In thy seed shall all the kindreds of the earth be blessed." And it shall "be fulfilled in the latter days." (1 Ne. 15:18.)

And thus Jesus, ministering among the Nephite portion of Israel, tells them of their favored status. "Ye are the children of the prophets; and ye are of the house of Israel," he says. They were the natural seed of the ancient patriarch, and so he says: "Ye are of the covenant which the Father made with your fathers, saying unto Abraham: And in thy seed shall all the kindreds of the earth be blessed." Because of this favored status, because they were heirs of promise, because they were the literal seed and the blood of Israel flowed in their veins, they had preference over the aliens. Thus Jesus said to them: "The Father having raised me up unto you first, and sent me to bless you in turning away every one of you from his iniquities; and this because ye are the children of the covenant—And after that ye were blessed then fulfilleth the Father the covenant which he made with Abraham, saying: In thy seed shall all the kindreds of the earth be blessed—unto the pouring out of the Holy Ghost through me upon the Gentiles, which blessing upon the Gentiles shall make them mighty above all, unto the scattering of my people, O house of Israel." (3 Ne. 20:25-27.)

It is Israel first and the Gentiles second. It is the chosen seed ahead of the alien nations. The natural sons are already in the family when the adopted sons take upon themselves the name of him whom they choose as their father. But all men, in or out of the house of Israel, are freed from their iniquities in the same way. If they "walk in the light," as God "is in the light," if they have "fellowship one with another," as becometh true saints, then "the blood of Jesus Christ his Son cleanseth [them] from all sin." (1 Jn. 1:7.) There is no other way. All are alike unto God.

Israel's Millennial Gathering and Glory

Knowing that Israel and the aliens shall join in one fold and have one Shepherd, we are prepared to pick up again, as he himself did, the threads of Jesus' preaching to the Nephites about the chosen seed and those who join with them. In 3 Nephi 16, Jesus spoke of the gospel coming to the Gentiles in the latter days; of the gathering of Israel from the four quarters of the earth; of the Gentiles, drenched in wickedness and abominations, sinning against the gospel; and then of the gospel going to others of the house of Israel. He spoke of the triumph of Israel as the Millennium was ushered in, and said that in that millennial day the words in Isaiah

52:8-10 would be fulfilled. All this we considered in chapter 20.

Now, after an interval of teaching on other matters, the Risen Lord returns to his prior theme—the part Israel and the Gentiles are to play in his strange act in the dispensation of the fulness of times. "Ye remember that I spake unto you, and said that when the words of Isaiah should be fulfilled—behold they are written, ye have them before you, therefore search them—And verily, verily, I say unto you, that when they shall be fulfilled then is the fulfilling of the covenant which the Father hath made unto his people, O house of Israel."

With this introduction we are back to the general subject of the latter-day gathering of Israel and to the specific passage in Isaiah that is to find fulfillment in the Millennium. This is Isaiah 52:8-10, which Jesus will soon quote again. But first, in this setting among the Nephites, our Lord says: "And then"—that is, in the millennial day—"shall the remnants, which shall be scattered abroad upon the face of the earth, be gathered in from the east and from the west, and from the south and from the north; and they shall be brought to the knowledge of the Lord their God, who hath redeemed them."

Israel shall be gathered in part before the Millennium, and that gathering is now going forward apace, with particular reference to Ephraim, the firstborn, and Manasseh, his twin. But Israel shall be gathered in full after the Millennium commences, and that gathering will include the Jews and, as we are about to see, the Ten Tribes. What Jesus now says is not all intended to be chronological. He will make interpretive comments as he goes forward, but there is ample explanation to enable us to conclude with some certainty much of what is to precede and what is to follow his millennial return.

"And I say unto you, that if the Gentiles do not repent after the blessing which they shall receive, after they have scattered my people"—our Lord announces by way of introduction to what is to follow. He is saying that if the Gentiles—the non-Jews—to whom the gospel has been restored in the last days do not accept that gospel, then, after they have scattered the Lamanites, as they have now done, certain things will happen. These are:

"Then"—in the day of our Lord's return—"Then shall ye, who are a remnant of the house of Jacob, go forth among them; and ye shall be in the midst of them who shall be many; and ye shall be among them as a lion among the beasts of the forest, and as a young lion among the flocks of sheep, who, if he goeth through both treadeth down and teareth in pieces, and none can deliver. Thy hand shall be lifted up upon thine adversaries, and all thine enemies shall be cut off."

These words of our Lord to the Nephites are quoted from Micah 5:8-9 and have reference to the desolations and ultimate burning that shall destroy the wicked at the Second Coming. Except for a few who are the humble followers of Christ, the Gentiles will not repent. They will revel in their abominations and sin against the restored gospel, and they will be burned by the brightness of our Lord's coming while the righteous—here called the remnant of Jacob—shall abide the day. And then, in the prophetic imagery, it will be as though the remnant of Israel overthrew their enemies as a young lion among the flocks of sheep.

It is in this setting, a setting that has ushered in the Millennium, that the promise is made: "And I will gather my people together as a man gathereth his sheaves into the floor." This is the great gathering destined to occur after our Lord's return. By way of further explanation of the triumphant events involved, Jesus now says: "For I will make my people with whom the Father hath covenanted, yea, I will make thy horn iron, and I will make thy hoofs brass. And thou shalt beat in pieces many people; and I will consecrate their gain unto the Lord, and their substance unto the Lord of the whole earth. And behold, I am he who doeth it." Again the prophetic imagery comes from the Old Testament. It is taken from Micah 4:13.

"And it shall come to pass, saith the Father, that the sword of my justice shall hang over them at that day; and except they repent it shall fall upon them, saith the Father, yea, even upon all the nations of the Gentiles." Again Jesus is speaking of the complete separation of the righteous and the wicked that will take place when he comes. "And it shall come to pass," in that millennial day, "that I will establish my people, O house of Israel." The Millennium is Israel's day.

"And behold, this people"—the Nephites, the Lamanites, the descendants of Lehi—"will I establish in this land [America], unto the fulfilling of the covenant which I made with your father Jacob; and it shall be a New Jerusalem. And the powers of heaven shall be in the midst of this people; yea, even I will be in the midst of you." Christ will reign personally upon the earth in that millennial day when the remnant of Lehi becomes a mighty people in America and when the New Jerusalem is the capital of the kingdom of God on earth.

A little later Jesus speaks of the Gentiles and the Jews and places the Jewish gathering after his Second Coming. Of the Gentiles he says: "When they shall have received the fulness of my gospel, then if they shall harden their hearts against me I will return their iniquities upon their own heads, saith the Father." They will suffer for their own sins; the Lord's blood will not cleanse them because they do not repent. And we repeat, most of the Gentiles will reject the truth and be bundled with the tares to be burned at that great day.

Of the Jews he says: "And I will remember the covenant which I have made with my people; and I have covenanted with them that I would gather them together in mine own due time, that I would give unto them again the land of their fathers for their inheritance, which is the land of Jerusalem, which is the promised land unto them forever, saith the Father." The Jews shall dwell again in Jerusalem of old, and in all Judea, and in all Palestine. "And it shall come to pass that the time cometh, when the fulness of my gospel shall be preached unto them; And they shall believe in me, that I am Jesus Christ, the Son of God, and shall pray unto the Father in my name."

At this point he returns again to Isaiah 52:8-10—which we have heretofore quoted and which we have seen is a passage reserved for millennial fulfillment—quoting it this time as the word of the Father, for "the Father and I are one," he says. "And then"—the time, be it remembered, is millennial—"shall be brought to pass that which is written," Jesus says, quoting three passages, all from this same 52nd chapter of Isaiah, and all relative to the gathering, rejoicing, and triumph of his people. These are Isaiah 52:1-3, 6; Isaiah 52:7; and Isaiah 52:11-15, which the astute student will desire to read and ponder in the setting here given. "Verily, verily, I say unto you, all these things"—those things Jesus has just said and those he has quoted from Isaiah— "shall surely come, even as the Father hath commanded me," Jesus says. "Then shall this covenant which the Father hath covenanted with his people be fulfilled; and then shall Jerusalem be inhabited again with my people, and it shall be the land of their inheritance." (3 Ne. 20:10-46.)

Jesus then gives a sign whereby all men "may know the time" when all these things he has told them about Israel and the Gentiles "shall be about to take place." The sign is the establishment of a free people in the United States of America; it is the restoration of the gospel in the last days; it is the carrying of the gospel to the Lamanites; it is the martyrdom of the Prophet Joseph Smith and his eternal triumph in the kingdom above. After this sign has been given, "it shall come to pass that whosoever will not believe in my words, who am Jesus Christ," he says, "which the Father shall cause him [the latter-day seer] to bring forth unto the Gentiles, and shall give unto him power that he shall bring them forth unto the Gentiles, (it shall be done even as Moses said) they shall be cut off from among the people who are of the covenant."

Then Jesus quotes again Micah's words about the remnant of Jacob being among the Gentiles as a young lion among the flocks of sheep, equating such with the wicked being cut off from among the people as Moses said. But this time he continues the Old Testament quotation to include Micah 5:10-15, which deals with the social and religious changes that will occur at the Second Coming. To the imagery and doctrine of Micah he adds: "It shall come to pass, saith the Father, that at that day"—the day of our Lord's return—"whosoever will not repent and come unto my Beloved Son, them will I cut off from among my people, O house of Israel; And I will execute vengeance and fury upon them, even as upon the heathen, such as they have not heard." This is the great day of burning when the wicked shall be as stubble.

Jesus' next statements seem to be commentary and explanation relative to events that will happen both before and after his coming. It is not always possible for us in our present state of spiritual enlightenment to put every event into an exact category or time frame. We are left to ponder and wonder about many things, perhaps to keep us alert and attentive to the commandments should the Lord come in our day. And some of the prophetic utterances apply to both pre- and post-millennial events; some have an initial and partial fulfillment in our day and shall have a second and grander completion in the days ahead.

And so we now hear Jesus say of the Gentiles: "If they will repent and hearken unto my words, and harden not their hearts, I will establish my church among them, and they shall come in unto the covenant and be numbered among this the remnant of Jacob." There follows an announcement of the building of a New Jerusalem in America and the gathering of the elect into its sacred walls. "And then shall the power of heaven come down among them; and I also will be in the midst." This, of course, is millennial. (3 Ne. 21:1-25.)

Jesus now speaks of the work among all the dispersed of Israel, with particular reference to the Ten Tribes. We are left to wonder whether he means they shall return before or after his own coming in the clouds of glory. The inference is that they will return during the Millennium, which is also the apparent meaning of the recitations in D&C 133:22-35, which we shall hereafter consider. In any event we know that the great day of gathering and glory for Israel and for the believing Gentiles lies ahead. It is reserved for the millennial day when the Lord Jesus dwells and reigns among his covenant people.

The Fulness of the Gentiles

Oh, that the Jews, the Lord's ancient covenant people, had received their Messiah when he came unto his own!

Oh, that they had believed his words and obeyed his law when he taught in their streets and preached in their synagogues!

Oh, that they had believed and obeyed in the day appointed for their salvation, in the day which was the times of the Jews!

Glory and honor and blessing, peace and joy and salvation—for them and for their children—was offered to them, offered without money and without price. They were invited to feast on the good word of God and to drink of the waters of life. But they would not.

They rejected the gospel, gave no heed to the Divine Voice, and crucified their King—all because their deeds were evil. And so God sent upon them sore destructions. Their house—both the temple and the city—was left unto them desolate; they were scourged and slaughtered and slain; they were condemned and cursed and crucified. And a remnant, a few captives of a once great nation, was scattered upon all the face of the earth and among every people.

"These be the days of vengeance," Jesus said. "There shall be great distress in the land, and wrath upon this people. And they shall fall by the edge of the sword, and shall be led away captive into all nations." Well might we ask: How long, how long, O Lord, shall the curse rest upon these Jews? When will they return to the ancient standard and be counted again among the sheep of their once-rejected Shepherd? Jesus answers: "Jerusalem shall be trodden down of the Gentiles, until the times of the Gentiles be fulfilled." (Luke 21:22-24.)

With the destruction of Jerusalem in A.D. 70; with the tearing apart of the temple, stone by stone, as the Romans made its gold and riches their own; with the scattering of the Jews in all nations—the times of the Jews ended. Their day to receive the glad tidings of salvation on a preferential basis was past. At that hour the times of the Gentiles dawned upon the earth. And from that hour the apostles and prophets began to turn to the aliens to find those who would believe in the God of the whole earth, who is Jesus Christ.

For almost two thousand years; for almost two millenniums; for as long a time as from Abraham, who fathered Israel, to Jesus, who came to save the seed of that ancient patriarch—Jerusalem has been and is "trodden down of the Gentiles." In 1917 Field Marshal Edmund Allenby of Great Britain captured the city almost without opposition, and a measure of political freedom thus came to the site where once Melchizedek was king and which David took from the Jebusites. Since then the once holy city, and its environs, and all of Palestine, have been available for the temporal return of the Jews. An initial and preparatory political gathering is now underway. But the city is still a Gentile stronghold, and it is still trodden down by forces alien to those true believers who one day will build anew its walls and erect therein again a holy temple to Jehovah. That many who now gather there are of the loins of Israel is of little moment, "For they are not all Israel, which are of Israel: Neither, because they are the seed of Abraham, are they all children," as Paul said. (Rom. 9:6-7.) And also: "Blindness in part is happened to Israel, until the fulness of the Gentiles be come in." (Rom. 11:25.) The true Israelites and the true Jews believe in the true Messiah and worship his Father in spirit and in truth. And so it is that the times of the Gentiles is not yet fulfilled, and so it is that the city where our Lord was crucified shall be trodden down by Gentile unbelievers until that day of fulfillment dawns upon the earth.

Jesus, on the Mount of Olives, alone with the Twelve, as we suppose, as they gazed upon the glittering brilliance of Herod's Temple in the distance, said: "And now ye behold this temple which is in Jerusalem, which ye call the house of God, and your enemies say that this house shall never fall. But, verily I say unto you, that desolation shall come upon this generation as a thief in the night, and this people shall be destroyed and scattered among all nations. And this temple which ye now see shall be thrown down that there shall not be left one stone upon another." This is the destruction and scattering of the Jews in A.D. 70, which ended the times of the Jews and commenced the times of the Gentiles.

"And it shall come to pass, that this generation of Jews"—those then living who had rejected their Messiah and were ripened in iniquity and ready for destruction—"shall not pass away until every desolation which I have told you concerning them shall come to pass." Their fate was to suffer an overflowing scourge and

253

to feel the intolerable weight of the abomination of desolation, all of which was a type of the scourges and desolations that shall yet precede the Second Coming.

What is the relationship of these events, all now part of the hoary records of antiquity, to the yet future Second Coming? Jesus continues to speak: "Ye say that ye know that the end of the world cometh; ye say also that ye know that the heavens and the earth shall pass away; And in this ye say truly, for so it is; but these things which I have told you shall not pass away until all shall be fulfilled. And this I have told you concerning Jerusalem; and when that day shall come, shall a remnant be scattered among all nations; But they shall be gathered again; but they shall remain until the times of the Gentiles be fulfilled." The true gathering of the Jews to their homeland shall not occur until the day—yet future— when the times of the Gentiles is fulfilled.

"And in that day"—the day when the times of the Gentiles is about to be fulfilled—"shall be heard of wars and rumors of wars, and the whole earth shall be in commotion, and men's hearts shall fail them, and they shall say Christ delayeth his coming until the end of the earth. And the love of men shall wax cold, and iniquity shall abound. And when the times of the Gentiles is come in"— when it begins anew, as it were, for this is the second time the true gospel shall go to the Gentiles (the first was in Paul's day, and the second is in our day, a day in which the same gospel preached by Paul has been restored), and thus—"when the times of the Gentiles is come in, a light shall break forth among them that sit in darkness, and it shall be the fulness of my gospel; But they"—the Gentiles—"receive it not; for they perceive not the light, and they turn their hearts from me because of the precepts of men. And in that generation shall the times of the Gentiles be fulfilled." (D&C 45:18-30.)

When Moroni appeared to Joseph Smith in 1823, he "stated that the fulness of the Gentiles was soon to come in." (JS-H 1:41.) Those who love the Lord and believe his gospel await that day with anxious expectation and ponder the words of the Lord Jesus, also spoken on Olivet: "In the generation in which the times of the Gentiles shall be fulfilled," he said, "there shall be signs in the sun, and

254

in the moon, and in the stars; and upon the earth distress of nations with perplexity, like the sea and the waves roaring. The earth also shall be troubled, and the waters of the great deep; Men's hearts failing them for fear, and for looking after those things which are coming on the earth. For the powers of heaven shall be shaken. And when these things begin to come to pass, then look up and lift up your heads, for the day of your redemption draweth nigh. And then shall they see the Son of man coming in a cloud, with power and great glory." (JST, Luke 21:25-28.)

The Call to the Gentiles

We have now set forth, in weakness and with fumbling phrases, and yet with such clarity and plainness as our weakness permits, the glorious doctrine that the Gentiles also are heirs of the covenant God made with Abraham. Shall we not add to our words a call, coupled with a warning, to the Gentiles everywhere?

We testify that God has in these times, the times of the Gentiles, restored the fulness of his everlasting gospel to prepare a people for the second coming of the Son of Man. The Book of Mormon has now "come unto the Gentiles" as a sign "that the covenant which the Father hath made with the children of Israel . . . is already beginning to be fulfilled."

Therefore, by way of testimony and exhortation, we say to the Gentiles: "Ye may know that the words of the Lord, which have been spoken by the holy prophets, shall all be fulfilled; and ye need not say that the Lord delays his coming unto the children of Israel." Behold, he will come as he hath said, and none can say him nay.

"And ye need not imagine in your hearts that the words which have been spoken are vain, for behold, the Lord will remember his covenant which he hath made unto his people of the house of Israel." And he will also remember all who join with Israel to further his work in this final dispensation. They shall be blessed with the faithful and made heirs of all the promises.

"And when ye shall see these sayings"—the Book of Mormon —"coming forth among you, then ye need not any longer spurn at the doings of the Lord, for the sword of his justice is in his right hand." Truly, the Book of Mormon has come forth in such plainness and perfection that all men are expected to believe its pure truths and to give heed to the wondrous witness it bears. "And behold, at that day"—when the true doctrines of Christ are set forth before men in such a glorious way in the Book of Mormon—"if ye shall spurn at his doings he will cause that it [the sword of his justice] shall soon overtake you."

And so, by way of warning, we say to the Gentiles: "Wo unto him that spurneth at the doings of the Lord; yea, wo unto him that shall deny the Christ and his works!

"Yea, wo unto him that shall deny the revelations of the Lord, and that shall say the Lord no longer worketh by revelation, or by prophecy, or by gifts, or by tongues, or by healings, or by the power of the Holy Ghost!" And oh, how many of the great churches in Christendom, to say nothing of the religious groups who do not even profess to believe in Christ, fall under this condemnation!

"Yea, and wo unto him that shall say at that day"—when, we repeat, all things are so wondrously and clearly set forth, so much so that no person who has arrived at the years of accountability is justified in misunderstanding the terms and conditions of the great plan of redemption that is in Christ—"wo unto him that shall say at that day, to get gain, that there can be no miracle wrought by Jesus Christ; for he that doeth this shall become like unto the son of perdition, for whom there was no mercy, according to the word of Christ!" Those who deny the great miracles of the opening of the heavens, of the appearance of the Great God, of the coming forth of the Book of Mormon, of the ministering of angels to men, of the pouring out of the Holy Ghost upon the faithful, and of an endless retinue of accompanying blessings—those who deny these miracles do so at their peril.

"Yea, and ye need not any longer hiss, nor spurn, nor make game of the Jews"—and oh, how common this has been and is among the self-appointed pious ones of a decadent Christendom!—"nor any of the remnant of the house of Israel; for behold, the Lord remembereth his covenant unto them, and he will do unto them according to that which he hath sworn. Therefore ye need not suppose that ye can turn the right hand of the Lord unto the left, that he may not execute judgment unto the fulfilling of the covenant which he hath made unto the house of Israel." (3 Ne. 29:1-9.)

By way of commandment we say to the Gentiles: "Hearken, O ye Gentiles, and hear the words of Jesus Christ, the Son of the living God, which he hath commanded me [Mormon] that I should speak concerning you, for, behold he commandeth me that I should write, saying:

"Turn, all ye Gentiles, from your wicked ways; and repent of your evil doings, of your lyings and deceivings, and of your whoredoms, and of your secret abominations, and your idolatries, and of your murders, and your priestcrafts, and your envyings, and your strifes, and from all your wickedness and abominations, and come unto me, and be baptized in my name, that ye may receive a remission of your sins, and be filled with the Holy Ghost, that ye may be numbered with my people who are of the house of Israel." (3 Ne. 30:1-2.)

And, finally, by way of invitation and exhortation to the Gentiles and to the house of Israel, we say: "Come unto Christ, and lay hold upon every good gift, and touch not the evil gift, nor the unclean thing.

"And awake, and arise from the dust, O Jerusalem; yea, and put on thy beautiful garments, O daughter of Zion; and strengthen thy stakes and enlarge thy borders forever, that thou mayest no more be confounded, that the covenants of the Eternal Father which he hath made unto thee, O house of Israel, may be fulfilled.

"Yea, come unto Christ, and be perfected in him, and deny yourselves of all ungodliness; and if ye shall deny yourselves of all ungodliness and love God with all your might, mind and strength, then is his grace sufficient for you, that by his grace ye may be perfect in Christ; and if by the grace of God ye are perfect in Christ, ye can in nowise deny the power of God.

"And again, if ye by the grace of God are perfect in Christ, and deny not his power, then are ye sanctified in Christ by the grace of God, through the shedding of the blood of Christ, which is in the covenant of the Father unto the remission of your sins, that ye become holy, without spot." (Moro. 10:30-33.)

Chapter 22

THE PROMISES MADE TO THE FATHERS

The General Promises

Certain promises made by the prophets of the past must come to pass before the return of earth's Chief Prophet. As the children of these ancient prophets, we may well ask: What are the promises made of old to our fathers, and what is their relationship to the Second Coming? Indeed, who are the prophetic fathers, and what was said by them that does or should affect us their children? And what obligations rest upon us with respect to these ancient promises?

Thoughtful analysis and careful study of the prophetic word enable us to put these promises into two categories: general promises relative to the chosen seed as a people, and specific promises centered in those families who, when taken together, form the chosen race. The general promises involve nations and kingdoms and lands and peoples. They include within their bounds the dealings of the Lord with Israel and the Gentiles and the peopling of the lands of the earth. The specific promises bring the blessings of the gospel, and the glories possessed by them of the past, into the souls and lives of the families of the present.

First, then, let us make a brief overview of the general promises of the Lord to the chosen people and to all men. And then we shall see that these general promises were given so that certain specific blessings might come to those who pledged their allegiance to the great worldwide movements that a divine providence is now causing to occur among all the races of men.

On Mount Olivet, eastward from Jerusalem, in the intimate circle of those whom he had chosen to stand as apostolic witnesses of his holy name, the Lord Jesus said: "As ye have asked of me concerning the signs of my coming, in the day when I shall come in my glory in the clouds of heaven, to fulfil the promises that I have made unto your fathers, For as ye have looked upon the long absence of your spirits from your bodies to be a bondage, I will show unto you how the day of redemption shall come, and also the restoration of the scattered Israel." (D&C 45:16-17.) Then followed the great Olivet Discourse on the destructions destined for their day, on the signs of the times of our day, and on his glorious return in the latter days.

But what are "the promises that I"—he, be it remembered, is Jehovah, the God of their fathers—"have made unto your fathers"? Clearly they are the promises relative to his second coming and the worldwide events that shall attend that dreadful day. He names two of them, the day of redemption and the gathering of scattered Israel. Having this perspective, we immediately know what the general promises are; and of them, in this work, we have spoken or yet will speak in detail. To have the Lord's eternal perspective ever before us we shall, at this point, simply allude to some of them.

The promises made to the fathers include the glorious reality that the Messiah of Israel will come again, as the great Deliverer, to save his people from the bondage of Babylon. They include the immutable decree that he will take vengeance on the wicked and slay the ungodly with the breath of his lips, and that his redeemed, whose year it shall be, will find millennial rest for a thousand years and then eternal peace forever. They include the sure word— God's eternal promise—that there will be a day of refreshing, a day of a new heaven and a new earth, a day when the wolf and the lamb will feed together and the lion shall eat straw like the bullock.

The promises made to the fathers include utterances without end of a day of restoration in which all things fore-announced by all the holy prophets of all the ages shall come to pass. There is the promise of dire and evil apostasy between the two comings of the Lord of glory. There are all the promises about false prophets, false churches, false worship, and false gods—all to spread their evil venom in the last days. There are the promises that iniquity shall abound and abominations cover the earth. Men everywhere are to be drunken with blood; war and carnage are to cover the earth; and evil men, led by evil leaders, shall do evil deeds.

The promises made to the fathers are that the Book of Mormon shall come forth; that Israel shall gather to the ancient standard and believe in their ancient God; that in a yet future day the political kingdom shall be restored to Israel, and they shall rule the whole earth; that Zion shall arise and shine; and that the Gentiles shall come to her light. There are the promises that in the days of certain kings the God of heaven shall set up his own eternal kingdom, which will grow and increase until it breaks in pieces all other kingdoms and fills the whole earth. There are the promises about salvation for the dead, that the prisoners shall go free, and that those who did not have the opportunity to receive the gospel in this life shall have that glorious privilege in the spirit world. There is the promise of a New Jerusalem to be built upon the American continent, to be a companion and a sister city to the Old Jerusalem which shall rise again in glory on the ancient site. There are the promises that the earth itself will receive again its paradisiacal glory and become as it was in the days before the fall.

The promises indeed are many. We mention but a few that the concept may be before us. And as pertaining to these promises, those named and unnamed—God himself by his own mouth and in his own name has sworn that they shall surely come to pass. And all these promises—there are no exceptions—have been given with one object and intent in view. That purpose is to enable the Abrahamic promises to live in the lives of those who are the seed of the father of the faithful. It is through the Abrahamic covenant that salvation is made available to Jew and Gentile alike.

The Abrahamic Promises

Christians, Jews, and Moslems—three races and cultures, almost as diverse and varied as the races of men can be—all claim

Abraham as their father, all look upon him as the ancient patriarchal giant among men, all give a certain lip service to the common concept that God made some sort of a covenant with him that somehow blesses his seed after him.

The Jews claim him as their ancestor and suppose that the law of Moses and the word of the prophets have come to them because of their heirship in Abraham's family. But Jesus excoriated them with these cutting words: "If ye were Abraham's children, ye would do the works of Abraham." (John 8:39.) Whatever their natural bloodline was, they had been cut off from the family and house of their ancient progenitor because their lives no longer conformed to the Abrahamic standard.

Christians, whether of Jewish or Gentile blood, suppose they are heirs of Abraham's blessings because Paul said of the ancient saints who believed the true gospel: "Ye are all one in Christ Jesus. And if ye be Christ's, then are ye Abraham's seed, and heirs according to the promise." (Gal. 3:28-29.) They suppose that Israel is now some kind of a spiritual kingdom composed of all the warring and bickering sects of a divided Christendom, to whom by the grace of God, with little or no reference to the works of righteousness, the blessings of salvation shall come. But as with the Jews, so with the Christians: "If ye were Abraham's children, ye would do the works of Abraham." (John 8:39.)

Our brethren of Islam are even farther removed from any vestige of reality. They suppose that the promises came down, not through Isaac as the scriptures say, but through Ishmael, and that he, the son of the bondwoman, was the one Abraham came near to sacrificing on Moriah. And as to their doctrinal beliefs, they are even farther removed from fact and truth than are their views of history. Indeed, they scarcely have any theology that resembles or is patterned after the teachings of the true prophets. One of the chief purposes of their Koran—perhaps, in the eternal perspective, the chief purpose—is to deny affirmatively the divine Sonship of him through whom salvation comes. Their general concept is: 'Allah had no need for a son to redeem men; he has but to speak and it is done.' And so again we are faced with the same test of true Abrahamic descent that applies to apostate Jewry and to that

Christendom which has lost the fulness of the everlasting word. Those who do the works of Abraham, those who believe what he believed and worship as he worshipped, those who have the fulness of the everlasting gospel, those who "are of faith, the same are the children of Abraham." (Gal. 3:7.) None others qualify.

What, then, are the promises made to Abraham for himself and for his seed? And are there now any among men who can qualify as his true seed in the full sense? Brief fragments of truth, a sliver here and a twig there, have come down to us in the records of the past. The accounts in Genesis let us know that the Lord said to Abraham: "I will make of thee a great nation, and I will bless thee, and make thy name great; and thou shalt be a blessing: And I will bless them that bless thee, and curse him that curseth thee: and in thee shall all families of the earth be blessed." (Gen. 12:2-3.) Here indeed is a promise for Abraham and for all the families of the earth whether they sprang from the loins of the great patriarch or not.

Later the Lord said to his friend Abraham: "I will make thy seed as the dust of the earth: so that if a man can number the dust of the earth, then shall thy seed also be numbered." (Gen. 13:16.) And again: "Look now toward heaven, and tell the stars, if thou be able to number them: and he said unto him, So shall thy seed be." (Gen. 15:5.) And yet again: "Thou shalt be a father of many nations." (Gen. 17:4.) And finally: "By myself have I sworn, saith the Lord, . . . That in blessing I will bless thee, and in multiplying I will multiply thy seed as the stars of the heaven, and as the sand which is upon the sea shore; and thy seed shall possess the gate of his enemies; And in thy seed shall all the nations of the earth be blessed." (Gen. 22:16-18.)

All of these are biblical promises. Their full meaning, as there found, is hidden from the spiritually illiterate and can, in fact, be known only by revelation. As we are about to see, they pertain to the continuation of the family unit in the highest heaven of the celestial world. But first, be it noted, the same promises were renewed to Isaac and to Jacob in their days. To Isaac the Lord said: "I will make thy seed to multiply as the stars of heaven, and will give unto thy seed all these countries; and in thy seed shall all the nations of the earth be blessed." (Gen. 26:4.) And to Jacob the promise came in these words: "And thy seed shall be as the dust of the earth, and thou shalt spread abroad to the west, and to the east, and to the north, and to the south: and in thee and in thy seed shall all the families of the earth be blessed." (Gen. 28:14.)

In the providences of the Lord, there has come to us in the Book of Abraham a broader and more carefully delineated account of the Abrahamic covenant, which includes these words: "And I will make of thee a great nation, and I will bless thee above measure, and make thy name great among all nations, and thou shalt be a blessing unto thy seed after thee, that in their hands they shall bear this ministry and Priesthood unto all nations." It is the seed of Abraham who themselves hold the same priesthood held by their noble forebear who will take salvation to all the nations of the earth.

"And I will bless them through thy name; for as many as receive this Gospel shall be called after thy name, and shall be accounted thy seed, and shall rise up and bless thee, as their father." This promise we have considered in connection with the part the Gentiles are playing and shall play incident to the Second Coming. Now the great covenant reaches its climax in these very express words: "And I will bless them that bless thee, and curse them that curse thee; and in thee (that is, in thy Priesthood) and in thy seed (that is, thy Priesthood), for I give unto thee a promise that this right shall continue in thee, and in thy seed after thee (that is to say, the literal seed, or the seed of the body) shall all the families of the earth be blessed, even with the blessings of the Gospel, which are the blessings of salvation, even of life eternal." (Abr. 2:9-11.)

All the families of the earth, Jew and Gentile alike—whether composed of blood descendants or adopted sons—shall receive the blessings of the gospel only when it is taken to them by Abraham's seed. His seed are the ministers of Christ; they hold the holy priesthood; they have received the divine commission to preach the gospel in all the world and to every creature. And what are the blessings they offer mankind? They are salvation and eternal life.

And what is salvation? Joseph Smith's definition is: "Salvation consists in the glory, authority, majesty, power and dominion which Jehovah possesses and in nothing else; and no being can possess it but himself or one like him." (*Lectures on Faith*, lecture 7, para. 9.) And what is eternal life? It is the name of the kind of life God lives. It consists of two things: life in the family unit, and the receipt of the fulness of the Father, meaning the fulness of the power, glory, and dominion of God himself.

What, then, is the promise made to Abraham and to his seed, meaning to that portion of his seed who, rising up and blessing him as their father, in fact do Abraham's works and qualify for the rewards he received? The blessings of Abraham and his seed are the blessings of celestial marriage, which order of matrimony is the gate to exaltation in the mansions on high.

What a wondrous thing it is to behold mortal men—Abraham, Isaac, and Jacob, our patriarchal fathers—receiving the divine word that in them and in their seed all generations shall be blessed, and that their posterity, through the continuation of the eternal family unit, shall be as the dust of the earth in number, as the sands upon the seashore in multitude, as the stars in the sidereal heavens in endless continuance! As we ponder such a glorious thought, may we ask: Is it conceivable that such a mighty seer as Joseph Smith might also have received this promise? As we shall see shortly, he did; it was the same promise given to Abraham, Isaac, and Jacob. Would we dare go further and ask if the president of The Church of Jesus Christ of Latter-day Saints might also be in this category? He is, as are his counselors. And what of the Twelve? They too have been so blessed, as have all the First Quorum of the Seventy. And as the crowning cause for wonderment, that God who is no respecter of persons has given a like promise to every elder in the kingdom who has gone to the holy temple and entered into the blessed order of matrimony there performed. Every person married in the temple for time and for all eternity has sealed upon him, conditioned upon his faithfulness, all of the blessings of the ancient patriarchs, including the crowning promise and assurance of eternal increase, which means, literally, a posterity as numerous as the dust particles of the earth.

That none of these things would or could be known except by revelation scarcely needs to be stated. And the crowning revelation in our day on the promises made to the fathers is couched in these words: "Abraham received all things, whatsoever he received, by revelation and commandment, by my word, saith the Lord, and hath entered into his exaltation and sitteth upon his throne. Abraham received promises concerning his seed, and of the fruit of his loins—from those whose loins ye are, namely, my servant Joseph—which were to continue so long as they were in the world; and as touching Abraham and his seed, out of the world they should continue; both in the world and out of the world should they continue as innumerable as the stars; or, if ye were to count the sand upon the seashore ye could not number them. This promise is yours also, because ye are of Abraham, and the promise was made unto Abraham; and by this law is the continuation of the works of my Father, wherein he glorifieth himself. Go ye, therefore, and do the works of Abraham; enter ye into my law and ye shall be saved." (D&C 132:29-32.)

And thus it is that the restoration of celestial marriage, the Lord's holy and perfect order of matrimony, has come into the world as one of the required events that must occur before the second coming of the Son of Man.

Elias and Elijah Prepare the Way

No tradition was more firmly planted in the hearts of Jewish Israel in Jesus' day than the firm belief that Elijah the prophet would come again to prepare the way before the expected Messiah. Both John and Jesus were assumed by some to be this ancient prophet come again. To this day devout Jews set a vacant chair at their table for Elijah when they celebrate the feast of the Passover. In part, at least, this universal belief grew out of Jehovah's promise given by the mouth of Malachi: "Behold, I will send you Elijah the prophet before the coming of the great and dreadful day of the Lord: And he shall turn the heart of the fathers to the children, and the heart of the children to their fathers, lest I come and smite the earth with a curse." (Mal. 4:5-6.)

Moroni, ministering to Joseph Smith during the whole of the night of September 21-22, 1823, rendered a plainer translation of these words: "Behold, I will reveal unto you the Priesthood, by the hand of Elijah the prophet, before the coming of the great and dreadful day of the Lord. And he shall plant in the hearts of the children the promises made to the fathers, and the hearts of the children shall turn to their fathers. If it were not so, the whole earth would be utterly wasted at his coming." (D&C 2:1-3.)

Both of these translations are correct; both convey the mind and will of the Lord; and both teach sound and true doctrine. Taken together, they give us an expanded and comprehensive view of the mission of Elijah that we would not gain from either of them alone. As a matter of fact, both the Book of Mormon (3 Ne. 25:5-6) and the Doctrine and Covenants (D&C 128:17-18), in scripture given after Moroni's visit, use the less perfect though true translation.

By combining the concepts found in both versions of these prophetic words we learn:

1. Elijah the Tishbite, a strange and unusual prophet, who ministered in Israel more than nine hundred years before the coming of the Lord Jesus Christ in the flesh; Elijah, who called down fire from heaven in the confrontation with the priests of Baal and on other occasions; Elijah, who sealed the heavens that there was no rain in all the land for three and a half years; Elijah, who raised from death the son of the widow of Zarephath; Elijah, at whose word her barrel of meal did not waste nor her cruse of oil fail until the Lord sent again rain on the earth; Elijah, who smote the river Jordan with his mantle to divide the waters and enable him and Elisha to pass over on dry ground; Elijah, who was translated and taken up into heaven in a chariot of fire without tasting death; Elijah, than whom, save Moses only, there was scarcely a greater prophet in all Israel; Elijah, who came again in a body of flesh and bones on the Mount of Transfiguration to join with translated Moses and the mortal Jesus in conferring upon Peter, James, and John the keys of the kingdom; Elijah, than whom few have been greater in all the long history of this earth—Elijah shall come again before the great and dreadful day of the Lord, before the earth burns as an oven, and before all the proud and they who do wickedly shall be as stubble. Elijah shall come again before the second coming of the Son of Man.

2. Elijah will reveal unto men the priesthood. He will bring again the sealing power. He will authorize mortals to use the priesthood to bind on earth and seal everlastingly in the heavens. He will give the same keys to Joseph Smith and Oliver Cowdery that he gave to Peter, James, and John on the holy mount.

3. Elijah shall plant in the hearts of the children the promises made to the fathers. As Joseph Smith expressed it, "He shall reveal the covenants of the fathers in relation to the children, and the covenants of the children in relation to the fathers." (*Teachings*, p. 321.) Who are the fathers? They are Abraham, Isaac, and Jacob, to whom the promises were made. What are the promises? They are the promises of a continuation of the family unit in eternity; of posterity in numbers as the dust of the earth and the stars in the firmament; of eternal increase; and of the consequent glory, and honor, and exaltation, and eternal life inherent in such a way of eternal existence.

4. Elijah shall turn the hearts of the fathers to the children, and the hearts of the children to their fathers. His coming shall unite families, unite them in this life and unite them in eternity. Because he comes, all of the ordinances of salvation and exaltation shall be binding on earth and in heaven, both for the living and for the dead. Because he comes, we can be sealed together as husband and wife in the holy temple so that our marriage union shall endure both in time and throughout all eternity. Because he comes, the living children will seek after their dead fathers, identifying them through genealogical research, so that the sealing ordinances may be performed for them vicariously in the holy temples.

5. Elijah's coming will keep the earth from being smitten with a curse and from being utterly wasted at our Lord's return. "The hearts of the children of men will have to be turned to the fathers, and the fathers to the children, living or dead," the Prophet said, "to prepare them for the coming of the Son of Man. If Elijah did not come, the whole earth would be smitten." (*Teachings*, p. 160.) Because of his coming, men will be saved and exalted. If the sealing power—the power that binds on earth and seals in heaven—was not given to men, there would be no harvest of saved souls when the Lord reaps in his fields. Thus, the vineyard would be

cursed; it would be wasted; it would have failed to serve the useful purpose for which it was created.

But praise God, Elijah has come, as has Elias. On the 3rd day of April in 1836, in the Kirtland Temple, both of these ancient worthies appeared to Joseph Smith and Oliver Cowdery. As the holy account attests: "Elias appeared, and committed the dispensation of the gospel of Abraham"—that is to say, he gave them the great commission given of God to Abraham, which pertained to the family unit and its eternal continuance in the realms ahead— "saying that in us and our seed all generations after us should be blessed." Who Elias was when he dwelt in mortality, we do not know. He may have been Abraham himself. But no matter; what is important is that he brought back the eternal covenant, with all its promises, that Jehovah had given to Abraham, Isaac, and Jacob.

"After this vision had closed," the sacred writing continues, "another great and glorious vision burst upon us; for Elijah the prophet, who was taken to heaven without tasting death"—but who attained his resurrected glory when Jesus rose from the grave—"stood before us, and said: Behold, the time has fully come, which was spoken of by the mouth of Malachi—testifying that he [Elijah] should be sent, before the great and dreadful day of the Lord come—To turn the hearts of the fathers to the children, and the children to the fathers, lest the whole earth be smitten with a curse—Therefore, the keys of this dispensation are committed into your hands; and by this ye may know that the great and dreadful day of the Lord is near, even at the doors." (D&C 110:12-16.)

Elias, who lived, as we suppose, some four thousand years ago, and Elijah, who underwent his mortal probation some three thousand years ago, these two, mighty prophets of old, have come again to play their part in preparing a people for the second coming of him whom they and we accept as our Savior. Line upon line the promised miracles that prepare the way of the Lord in the last days are truly coming to pass.

Salvation for the Dead and the Second Coming

Much might be said about the doctrine of salvation and exaltation for our dead ancestors. It is well known among us that all who do not have the privilege to believe and obey the holy gospel in this life shall have that blessed privilege in the world of spirits as they await the day of the resurrection. All who would have accepted the holy word with all their hearts had they been permitted to hear it in this life, all such shall receive this opportunity in the spirit world; we shall perform the saving ordinances for them vicariously; and together, if we are all true and faithful, we shall attain an inheritance in the Eternal Presence. How glorious is the concept here involved. A gracious God will save all who believe and obey whether they heard the gospel in this life or in the spirit world.

Our present concern, however, is to make it clear—crystal clear so that none can doubt—that the principles of salvation for the dead had to be revealed before the Second Coming as part of the preparation for that great day. We have spoken of the coming of Elijah and know that he came to prepare men to do this very work. Of this infinitely great and glorious work the Prophet said: "The greatest responsibility in this world that God has laid upon us is to seek after our dead." (*Teachings*, p. 356.) It is a work that exceeds in magnitude even the preaching of the gospel in all nations, for it will go forward and be one of the dominant undertakings of the Millennium itself.

We do not know all things pertaining to the purposes and plans of the Lord in the salvation of his children. But this we do know: His system for offering salvation to the dead as well as for the living must go forward to prepare the way for his return.

"And saviours shall come up on mount Zion," Obadiah prophesied, "and the kingdom shall be the Lord's." (Obad. 1:21.) That is to say, 'Saviors shall come up upon Mount Zion to prepare the way for the Lord.' The Lord's counsel on this matter is given by the Prophet Joseph Smith in these words: "The keys are to be delivered, the spirit of Elijah is to come, the Gospel to be established, the Saints of God gathered, Zion built up, and the Saints to come up as saviors on Mount Zion.

"But how are they to become saviors on Mount Zion? By building their temples, erecting their baptismal fonts, and going forth and receiving all the ordinances, baptisms, confirmations, washings, anointings, ordinations and sealing powers upon their heads, in behalf of all their progenitors who are dead, and redeem them that they may come forth in the first resurrection and be exalted to thrones of glory with them; and herein is the chain that binds the hearts of the fathers to the children, and the children to the fathers, which fulfills the mission of Elijah. . . .

"The Saints have not too much time to save and redeem their dead, and gather together their living relatives, that they may be saved also, before the earth will be smitten, and the consumption decreed falls upon the world.

"I would advise all the Saints to go with their might and gather together all their living relatives to this place, that they may be sealed and saved, that they may be prepared against the day that the destroying angel goes forth; and if the whole Church should go to with all their might to save their dead, seal their posterity, and gather their living friends, and spend none of their time in behalf of the world, they would hardly get through before night would come, when no man can work." (*Teachings*, pp. 330-31.)

The promises made to the fathers! How wondrous and great they are! Promises to gather Israel, to restore the gospel, to build up Zion anew! Promises to plant in our hearts the desires to gain the blessings of Abraham himself! And promises that we can turn the key in behalf of our dead ancestors so that we with them may be inheritors of the fulness of our Father's kingdom!

Chapter 23

TEMPLES AND THE SECOND COMING

Temples: Their Nature and Use

Holy temples of our God—what are they? What purposes do they serve? Who knows how and in what manner to build them? Who knows the use to which they should be put?

Holy temples of our God—sacred sanctuaries set apart from the world, unique and unusual buildings into which only a favored few may enter—what part shall they play in the second coming of him whose houses they are?

With reference to the not-far-distant day when the Son of Righteousness shall rend the veil and come down to dwell with men again on earth, the ancient word attests: "The Lord, whom ye seek, shall suddenly come to his temple." (Mal. 3:1.) Like witness is borne in the modern word: "I am Jesus Christ, the Son of God," he says, "wherefore, gird up your loins and I will suddenly come to my temple." (D&C 36:8.)

Now, if the Lord is soon to come with unexpected suddenness to his temple, where is that sacred sanctuary? If it is yet to be built, who is to do it, and where is the construction site? How and in what manner shall the work go forward, and what will the glorious edifice look like when it is finished? And how, except by revelation, can any people choose the site, prepare the house, and have it in readiness when the time comes for the Heavenly Visitant to rend the veil and come to that holy of holies which he will accept as his own?

271

These are vital questions, and if we can find a people who know the answers, we will have identified the true saints on earth. How can any stewards be the Lord's true servants unless they labor in his vineyards, dwell in his house, and are keeping all things in readiness for their Lord's return? True it is that if a people know and practice the true law of temple construction and use, they are the Lord's people, and they have the power of God unto salvation which Paul called the gospel. And true it is also that if a church is without a knowledge of these mysterious matters, it is not composed of the Lord's people, and in it there is no power to save souls.

There is, of course, a sense in which the world itself is the temple to which the Lord will come, although in its low and fallen state it is far from the type of sanctuary fit for a heavenly King. We have, in fact, a rather enigmatic scripture, the full depth and meaning of which we cannot plumb, in which we are commanded: "Prepare for the revelation which is to come, when the veil of the covering of my temple, in my tabernacle, which hideth the earth, shall be taken off, and all flesh shall see me together." (D&C 101:23.) But as will be increasingly clear from the analysis now to be set forth, the Lord will come to his temples in the sense of specific buildings erected and dedicated to his holy name.

A temple is a house of the Lord, literally and in the full sense of the word. He owns it. It is sacred and clean and pure—a fit abode for the Holy One. Where else would he come except to the purest and most sacred places on earth? When he has no houses on earth, he comes to his servants on mountaintops, in groves of trees, or in desert places. But when there is a holy house fit for his presence, such is the place where his servants see his face—all of which is a type of what shall be when he comes to rule and reign on earth. He will appear in many places, chief among which will be the holy houses built and dedicated to him.

Thus, as Haggai records of the latter-day temple to which the True Owner will come: "Thus saith the Lord of hosts; Yet once, it is a little while, and I will shake the heavens, and the earth, and the sea, and the dry land; And I will shake all nations, and the desire of all nations shall come: and I will fill this house with glory, saith the

Lord of hosts. . . . The glory of this latter house shall be greater than of the former, saith the Lord of hosts: and in this place will I give peace, saith the Lord of hosts." (Hag. 2:6-9.) And thus Isaiah, writing of the day when the Lord will come with fire, tells Israel, "He shall appear to your joy," and there shall be "a voice from the temple"—his voice—"a voice of the Lord that rendereth recompence to his enemies." (Isa. 66:5-6.)

A temple is also a sanctuary to which those who are striving with all their hearts to become like the Holy One may come to enter into sacred covenants with him. It is the place where baptisms for the dead are performed; where the faithful are endowed with power from on high; where the sealing power restored by Elijah unites worthy couples in the bonds of eternal matrimony; where the fulness of the priesthood is received; and where those who are true and faithful in all things receive the assurance of eternal life in the Eternal Presence. A temple is a place where the saints make the same covenants made by Abraham and receive for themselves the promises made to the fathers.

Thus, the Lord, as Ezekiel records, said to scattered Israel: "I will take you from among the heathen, and gather you out of all countries, and will bring you into your own land. Then will I sprinkle clean water upon you"—in my holy temples—"and ye shall be clean: from all your filthiness, and from all your idols, will I cleanse you. A new heart also will I give you, and a new spirit will I put within you: and I will take away the stony heart out of your flesh, and I will give you an heart of flesh. And I will put my spirit within you, and cause you to walk in my statutes, and ye shall keep my judgments, and do them." (Ezek. 36:24-27.) Truly, temples prepare a people to meet their God.

The Mountains of the Lord's Houses

Lift up thine eyes, O Israel, lift up thine eyes "unto the hills," whence cometh thy help. (Ps. 121:1.) Gaze not in the valleys below; look not toward the low and the mean; view not what is carnal and evil. Look now to the mountains of Israel; fix thy gaze upon the mount of the Lord; view now those heaven-kissed heights, whence cometh thy help. Lift up thine eyes unto the mountains of the Lord.

The mountains of the Lord! The mountains of the Great Jehovah! The holy places where the soles of his feet have trod! How grand they are! And they are the towering peaks and the cloud-topped summits where the temples of the Lord—all of them—shall be built in the last days.

In all the days of his goodness, mountain heights have been the places chosen by the Lord to commune with his people. The experiences of Enoch, and of Moriancumer, and of Moses show how the Lord deigned to deal with his servants when they lifted themselves temporally and spiritually toward heaven's heights.

"Turn ye, and get ye upon the mount Simeon," was the divine command to Enoch. "And it came to pass that I turned and went up on the mount," he said, "and as I stood upon the mount, I beheld the heavens open, and I was clothed upon with glory; And I saw the Lord; and he stood before my face, and he talked with me, even as a man talketh one with another, face to face." (Moses 7:2-4.)

Jared's brother, Moriancumer, scarcely a whit behind Enoch in faith and righteousness, took sixteen small stones "upon the top of the mount," there to plead with the Lord to touch the stones that they might give light in the Jaredite barges. There followed the grandest and most comprehensive revelation of the Lord Jesus Christ that had ever been given to any man up to that time. The mighty Jaredite prophet then saw the spirit body of Him who would one day take upon himself flesh and blood, that he might redeem his people, and he was shown things that are to this day hidden from us for want of the spiritual capacity to understand them. (Ether 3:1-28.)

Moses, in like manner, "was caught up into an exceedingly high mountain, And he saw God face to face, and he talked with him, and the glory of God was upon Moses," and he saw the wonders of eternity and received the account of the creation and redemption of our planet and of worlds without number. (Moses 1–3.)

And also, in like manner, Nephi received glorious visions on the mountain heights; Peter, James, and John, with their Lord on the Mount of Transfiguration, saw in vision the millennial earth and received from heavenly visitants keys and powers; and Elijah, on Horeb, the mount of God, received some of his great spiritual experiences. On one occasion anciently, "the glory of the Lord abode upon mount Sinai, . . . And the sight of the glory of the Lord was like devouring fire on the top of the mount in the eyes of the children of Israel." (Ex. 24:16-17.)

Is it any wonder, then, that in prophetic imagery the term "mountains of the Lord" has become a symbol to identify the places where spiritual blessings are received? The restored gospel is "a banner upon the high mountain" (Isa. 13:2); when we preach the gospel, we "publish it upon the mountains" (D&C 19:29); and the Lord's promise to Zion is that she "shall flourish upon the hills and rejoice upon the mountains" (D&C 49:25). The highest accolade of praise bestowed upon a preacher of righteousness is the sweet expression: "How beautiful upon the mountains are the feet of him that bringeth good tidings, that publisheth peace; that bringeth good tidings of good, that publisheth salvation; that saith unto Zion, Thy God reigneth!" (Isa. 52:7.)

Singling out the righteous from among men, the Psalmic word asks: "Who shall ascend into the hill of the Lord?" Is not the hill of the Lord the place where salvation is found? "Or who shall stand in his holy place?" (Ps. 24:3.) Is not his holy place his temple on earth and his eternal kingdom hereafter? Indeed, those who gain exaltation in the highest heaven hereafter are said to "come unto Mount Zion." (D&C 76:66.) Truly, the mountains of the Lord are the places of greatest spiritual refreshment in this life and the places of the fulness of spiritual enjoyment in the life to come.

All of this is but prelude to saying that all of the holy temples of our God in the latter days shall be built in the mountains of the Lord, for his mountains—whether the land itself is a hill, a valley, or a plain—are the places where he comes, personally and by the power of his Spirit, to commune with his people. If he has no house on earth, he comes to a mountaintop or other places of his own choosing, but when his people have built him a place "where to lay his head" (Matt. 8:20), as it were, then he comes to that holy house.

Isaiah names the building of latter-day temples as a sign both of the gathering of Israel and of the second coming of Christ. Israel, as we are aware, is to gather to places where there are temples so her municipals may gain the blessings made available in these holy houses, and these blessings prepare their recipients to meet the Lord, who will suddenly come to his temple.

Isaiah introduces his pronouncement relative to temples by saying: "The word that Isaiah, the son of Amoz, saw concerning Judah and Jerusalem." That is, the subject under consideration is the kingdom of Judah and her capital city, Jerusalem. "And it"—what he is about to say concerning Judah and Jerusalem— "shall come to pass in the last days, when the mountain of the Lord's house shall be established in the top of the mountains, and shall be exalted above the hills, and all nations shall flow unto it." The building of a temple in both the mountain of the Lord and the tops of the mountains, unto which the elect of the Lord shall come out of all nations, is the promised sign. This is first and foremost the temple, capped with six spires and crowned with an angelic ministrant sounding the trump of God, that now stands in Salt Lake City in the tops of the mountains of America. All of the temples now built or that may be built in the high mountains of America also do or will fulfill this prophetic word.

"And many people," Isaiah continues, "shall go and say, Come ye, and let us go up to the mountain of the Lord, to the house of the God of Jacob; and he will teach us of his ways, and we will walk in his paths; for out of Zion shall go forth the law, and the word of the Lord from Jerusalem." Then the ancient seer proceeds to speak of the Second Coming and its effect upon Judah and Jerusalem. (2 Ne. 12:1-22; Isa. 2:1-22.) His words about the gathering have received a partial fulfillment in the gathering of Israel from many nations to the American Zion in the tops of the mountains, but their complete realization is for another day and another location, as we shall soon see. And the statement about the law going forth from Zion and the word of the Lord from Jerusalem will come to pass during the Millennium, as we shall also see in due course. At this point our concern is to know with surety that latter-day temples must arise in the mountains of the Lord before the

Second Coming; that none can build such holy houses unless divinely commissioned to do so; and that when they are built—in proof, as it were, of their divine status—all nations will flow unto them.

We shall now turn our attention to the temples yet to be built in Old Jerusalem and in the New Jerusalem, both of which also are to be built in the mountains of the Lord.

Temples in the New and Old Jerusalems

We expect to see the day when temples will dot the earth, each one a house of the Lord; each one built in the mountains of the Lord; each one a sacred sanctuary to which Israel and the Gentiles shall gather to receive the blessings of Abraham, Isaac, and Jacob. Perhaps they will number in the hundreds, or even in the thousands, before the Lord returns. During the Millennium their presence will be everywhere, for the billions of church members will all be entitled to the fulness of the ordinances and blessings of the Lord's holy houses. But there are two great temples in particular, two glorious houses of the Great Jehovah, that must be built by his people before he comes—one in Jerusalem of old, the other in the New Jerusalem.

Old Jerusalem, the ancient holy city, has been and will again be a temple city. On three occasions of which we know, the Lord's own earthly house, as a priceless gem in a heaven-set crown, has graced the ground that is now claimed by the Jews and trodden down of the Gentiles. Solomon built a majestic mansion for the Lord in the day of Israel's glory. Zerubbabel built it anew when the remnant returned from bondage in Babylon. And Herod—a wretched, evil man whose every act bore Satan's stamp—built it for the final time in the day our Lord made flesh his tabernacle. This is the temple—one of the architectural wonders of the world, whose marble blocks were covered with gold, and whose influence upon the people cannot be measured—this is the temple that was torn apart, stone by stone, by Titus and his minions.

Thus Herod's temple became a refuse heap, and with its destruction ancient Judaism died also. Sacrifices ceased; the Jews, as a nation, gave up the ghost; the law of Moses, the man of God, became a curse; and the Jews were driven into every nation, there to struggle and suffer until the voice of their Messiah shall call them home to build anew his holy house in the city of his choice. For "it shall come to pass," according to the holy word, that the Lord shall return them to their ancient soil. "Ye shall be gathered one by one, O ye children of Israel," saith the divine word. Ye shall be gathered when "the great trumpet shall be blown, . . . and shall worship the Lord in the holy mount at Jerusalem." (Isa. 27:12-13.)

As to Herod's Temple, the disciples presented this petition: "Master, show us concerning the buildings of the temple." From Jesus came this answer: "Behold ye these stones of the temple, and all this great work, and buildings of the temple? Verily I say unto you, they shall be thrown down and left unto the Jews desolate. . . . See ye not all these things, and do ye not understand them? Verily I say unto you, There shall not be left here upon this temple, one stone upon another, that shall not be thrown down." (JST, Mark 13:1-5.)

So it was promised, and so it came to pass. And thus ended temple work in Jerusalem, in the old temple with its Mosaic ordinances, in the temple whose work, like the law of Moses of which it was a symbol, was fulfilled. And thus was it to be in Jerusalem until the promised day when a new temple should arise—perhaps on the very site of the old one—in which the gospel ordinances of the new kingdom shall be performed.

This new temple shall be the one of which Ezekiel spoke. "I will make a covenant of peace" with Jewish Israel when they return to the ancient fold, saith the Lord. "It shall be an everlasting covenant with them"—even the fulness of the everlasting gospel, which is the new and the everlasting covenant—"and I will place them, and multiply them, and will set my sanctuary [my temple] in the midst of them for evermore. My tabernacle also shall be with them: yea, I will be their God, and they shall be my people. And the heathen shall know that I the Lord do sanctify Israel, when my sanctuary shall be in the midst of them for evermore." (Ezek. 37:26-28.)

This is the day of which Zechariah spoke: "Thus saith the

Lord; I am returned to Jerusalem with mercies: my house shall be built in it, saith the Lord of hosts. . . . My cities through prosperity shall yet be spread abroad; and the Lord shall yet comfort Zion, and shall yet choose Jerusalem." (Zech. 1:16-17.) And then shall the Millennium be ushered in, for, saith the Lord, "I will bring forth my servant the BRANCH. . . . I will remove the iniquity of that land in one day," the day of burning when every corruptible thing shall be consumed. "In that day, saith the Lord of hosts, shall ye call every man his neighbour under the vine and under the fig tree." (Zech. 3:8-10.)

Who shall build this temple? The Lord himself shall do it by the hands of his servants the prophets. "Behold the man whose name is The BRANCH; . . . he shall build the temple of the Lord"—and, be it remembered, the Branch is one of the Messianic designations by which the Promised Messiah is known—"Even he shall build the temple of the Lord; and he shall bear the glory, and shall sit and rule upon his throne." And whence shall the workmen come to build the sanctuary? "They that are far off shall come and build in the temple of the Lord." (Zech. 6:12-15.)

Who are those "that are far off" who shall come to Jerusalem to build the house of the Lord? Surely they are the Jews who have been scattered afar. By what power and under whose authorization shall the work be done? There is only one place under the whole heavens where the keys of temple building are found. There is only one people who know how to build temples and what to do in them when they are completed. That people is the Latter-day Saints. The temple in Jerusalem will not be built by Jews who have assembled there for political purposes as at present. It will not be built by a people who know nothing whatever about the sealing ordinances and their application to the living and the dead. It will not be built by those who know nothing about Christ and his laws and the mysteries reserved for the saints. But it will be built by Jews who have come unto Christ, who once again are in the true fold of their ancient Shepherd, and who have learned anew about temples because they know that Elijah did come, not to sit in a vacant chair at some Jewish feast of the Passover, but to the Kirtland Temple on April 3, 1836, to Joseph Smith and Oliver

Cowdery. The temple in Jerusalem will be built by The Church of Jesus Christ of Latter-day Saints. "They that are far off," they that come from an American Zion, they who have a temple in Salt Lake City will come to Jerusalem to build there another holy house in the Jerusalem portion of "the mountains of the Lord's house." (D&C 133:13.)

Then "many people and strong nations shall come to seek the Lord of hosts in Jerusalem, and to pray before the Lord." (Zech. 8:22.) "And it shall be in that day, that living waters shall go out from Jerusalem; . . . And the Lord shall be king over all the earth: in that day shall there be one Lord, and his name one." (Zech. 14:8-9.) These are the waters of which the scripture saith: "They shall be healed." (Ezek. 47:9.)

All of this brings us to that inspired statement of the Prophet Joseph Smith relative to the temple in Jerusalem and the Second Coming: "Judah must return," he said, "Jerusalem must be rebuilt, and the temple, and water come out from under the temple, and the waters of the Dead Sea be healed. It will take some time to rebuild the walls of the city and the temple, etc.; and all this must be done before the Son of Man will make His appearance." (*Teachings*, p. 286.)

From the temple in Old Jerusalem we now turn to a consideration of the temple in the New Jerusalem. Neither of the Jerusalems—neither the Old Jerusalem, which shall be built up again, nor the New Jerusalem yet to rise on the American continent—can be a holy city, a city of Zion, until a house of the Lord graces that Mount Zion upon which each is located. The Lord will not reign in or send forth his law from a city in which he has no house of his own. And so, in July 1831 the Prophet Joseph Smith, then in Jackson County, Missouri, importuned the Lord in these words: "When will the wilderness blossom as the rose? When will Zion be built up in her glory, and where will thy Temple stand, unto which all nations shall come in the last days?" (Introductory heading, D&C 57.) In answer the Lord said: "This is the land of promise, and the place for the city of Zion. . . . Behold, the place which is now called Independence is the center place; and a spot for the temple is lying westward, upon a lot which is not far from the court-house." (D&C 57:1-3.)

It is of this city, a city that shall be built before the Second Coming, that the Lord said to Enoch: "I shall prepare, an Holy City, that my people may gird up their loins, and be looking forth for the time of my coming; for there shall be my tabernacle, and it shall be called Zion, a New Jerusalem." (Moses 7:62.) It is in this city, the New Jerusalem in Jackson County, that the house of the Lord unto which all nations shall come in the last days shall be built, "which temple," the Lord said in September 1832, "shall be reared in this generation. For verily this generation shall not all pass away until an house shall be built unto the Lord, and a cloud shall rest upon it, which cloud shall be even the glory of the Lord, which shall fill the house." (D&C 84:1-5.)

Because the saints were "hindered by the hands of their enemies, and by oppression," the Lord withdrew the time limitation (D&C 124:49-54), and the command now in force is: "Zion shall be redeemed in mine own due time." (D&C 136:18.) When that is to be remains to be seen, but that it will surely come to pass, as part of the preparation of the Lord's people for his glorious return, is as certain as that the sun shines or that the Great God is Lord of all. When the appointed time comes, the Lord will reveal it to his servants who preside over his kingdom from Salt Lake City, and then the great work will go forward. They will direct the work; they hold the keys of temple building; the temple will be built by gathered Israel and particularly by Ephraim, for it is unto Ephraim that the other tribes shall come to receive their temple blessings in due course. Some Lamanites may assist and some Gentiles may bring their wealth to adorn the buildings, but the keys are with Ephraim, and it is Ephraim that is now stepping forth and that yet shall step forth to bless the rest of the house of Israel.

Chapter 24

THE HOLY ZION
OF GOD

What Is Zion?

Zion, Zion, blessed Zion—Zion concerning whom all of the prophets from the beginning have spoken—what shall we now say of thee? O thou choice and favored one, what part art thou destined to play in the second coming of thy King, the King of Zion?

Shall we not say that thou hast been chosen above all others to prepare a people for earth's true King? Shall we not say that only a pure people will be fit companions for the Holy One who has said he will yet reign in Zion? Shall we not say that the Lord will not come until Zion is built up by his people; that when he comes he will also bring Zion with him; and that then Zion in its fulness shall flourish and prosper beyond any comprehension we now have? And shall we not say that those who gain celestial rest itself shall do so because they come unto Mount Zion, the Heavenly Jerusalem, and to the general assembly and Church of the Firstborn?

What then is Zion, and how is she to be esteemed? Our first contact with the Zion of God comes in the day of Enoch. That seer of seers, whose faith was so great that at his word the earth trembled, mountains fled, and rivers turned out of their courses, converted great hosts to the gospel. These saints of the Most High kept the commandments and attained such unity and perfection that "the Lord came and dwelt with his people, and they dwelt in righteousness." It was then as it shall be when he comes again. In Enoch's day, "The fear of the Lord was upon all nations, so great was the glory of the Lord, which was upon his people." So shall it be with the enemies of God when the great Millennium is ushered in: the fear of the Lord shall be upon all those who fight against his saints. Nor is this all. As to the ancient Zion, the account says: "And the Lord blessed the land, and they were blessed upon the mountains, and upon the high places, and did flourish." And again so shall it be in the latter end of the earth. Again the Lord will bless the land; indeed, so great shall be the blessing that the whole earth shall become as it was in the day of the Garden of Eden.

It is in this setting that the holy word records: "And the Lord called his people ZION, because they were of one heart and one mind, and dwelt in righteousness; and there was no poor among them." And it is from these words that we gain our basic concept of Zion. Zion is those who have overcome the world and who are fit companions for him who said: "Be holy, for I am holy" (Lev. 11:45), and "Ye shall be holy: for I the Lord your God am holy" (Lev. 19:2).

"And Enoch continued his preaching in righteousness unto the people of God. And it came to pass in his days, that he built a city that was called the City of Holiness, even ZION." And so we learn that Zion became also a place. The place where the people named Zion dwelt became the place named Zion. The city bore the title of the people, and of course it was a City of Holiness, for all of its inhabitants were holy. And because they were holy, the Lord preserved them from their enemies, even as he shall do in the latter days. This marvelous manifestation of preserving care caused Enoch to say to the Lord: "Surely Zion shall dwell in safety forever." To this the Lord replied: "Zion have I blessed, but the residue of the people have I cursed," even as it shall also be when Zion comes in the last days. And that his servant might know the state of Zion, "the Lord showed unto Enoch all the inhabitants of the earth; and he beheld, and lo, Zion, in process of time, was taken up into heaven. And the Lord said unto Enoch: Behold mine abode forever." (Moses 7:13-21.)

Later in the scriptural account this general summary is made relative to the saints of ancient days: "And all the days of Zion, in the days of Enoch, were three hundred and sixty-five years."

When the Millennium comes, Zion will continue for a thousand years. "And Enoch and all his people walked with God, and he dwelt in the midst of Zion; and it came to pass that Zion was not, for God received it up into his own bosom; and from thence went forth the saying, ZION IS FLED." (Moses 7:68-69.) Such is the divine word relative to the Zion of old, the original Zion, the first Zion, the Zion of Enoch, the Zion taken by God into his own bosom. Why was she taken? Because all her municipals were fit to dwell with the Lord; because all of them were too pure, too holy to remain longer in this carnal and wicked world. And it shall yet be, when the Lord brings again Zion in her fulness and glory, that all his people will walk with him, and he shall dwell on earth with them for a thousand years. And then it shall be said: The Lord hath brought again Zion, his own city, the City of Holiness, the City of our God.

Zion Through the Ages

After those in the City of Holiness were translated and taken up into heaven without tasting death, so that Zion as a people and a congregation had fled from the battle-scarred surface of the earth, the Lord sought others among men who would serve him. From the days of Enoch to the flood, new converts and true believers, except those needed to carry out the Lord's purposes among mortals, were translated, "and the Holy Ghost fell on many, and they were caught up by the powers of heaven into Zion." (Moses 7:27.) "And men having this faith"—the faith of Enoch and his people— "coming up unto this order of God"—the holy order of priesthood which we call the Melchizedek Priesthood—"were translated and taken up into heaven." (JST, Gen. 14:32.)

After the flood, righteous men, knowing what had been before their day, continued to seek a place in Zion. Of those who lived in the days of Melchizedek it is written: "And now, Melchizedek was a priest of this order; therefore he obtained peace in Salem, and was called the Prince of peace. And his people wrought righteousness, and obtained heaven, and sought for the city of Enoch which God had before taken, separating it from the earth, having reserved it unto the latter days, or the end of the world; And hath said, and sworn with an oath, that the heavens and the earth should come together; and the sons of God should be tried so as by fire." (JST, Gen. 14:33-35.)

But thereafter except in a few isolated instances—those of Moses, Elijah, Alma the son of Alma, John the Beloved, and the Three Nephites are the only ones of which we know—except in these cases, each involving a special purpose, the Lord ceased translating faithful people. Rather, they were permitted to die and go into the spirit world, there to perform the ever-increasing work needed in that sphere. We are led to believe that Abraham, Isaac, and Jacob, and some of the faithful of old continued to seek an inheritance in the City of Enoch. Paul says they "looked for a city which hath foundations, whose builder and maker is God," and that they "confessed . . . they were strangers and pilgrims on the earth. For they . . . declare plainly that they seek a country." (Heb. 11:10, 13-14.)

There has been no perfect Zion on earth since the flood. There have been many righteous congregations of saints upon whom the Lord has poured out rich blessings, but none of these has attained the degree of perfection that would enable the Lord to dwell among the people. These numerous congregations, however, have contained the choicest and most favored of earth's inhabitants. Such congregations have included and do include the faithful among the Jaredites; those who served the Lord in ancient Israel; the believing Lehite congregations; the so-called primitive saints who believed the words of Peter and Paul; certainly some groups of believers among the Ten Tribes, to whom Jesus went after his resurrection; and, of course, the various congregations of Latter-day Saints in our day. All these have sought the Lord, have struggled to perfect their lives, and—knowing they were strangers and pilgrims in a strange land, far from their heavenly home— have looked forward, with an eye of faith, to an inheritance in that city whose builder and maker is God.

Certain of the capital cities and chief places of worship of the saints in various ages have been used to crystallize in the minds of the people the concept that there is a Zion where the pure in heart shall dwell. Foremost among all of these was Jerusalem of old. It was Zion in its day. From it the word of the Lord went forth, and to it every male in Israel was commanded to come three times each year to appear before the Lord and there to worship him in spirit and in truth. Salt Lake City in our day, with its conferences and administrative offices, serves a similar purpose. It is a modern Zion. But none of these compare with the New Jerusalem yet to be built in Missouri, or to the coming millennial Zion with all its grandeur and splendor.

Our Present Zion

Our present Zion is the one whose mission it is to prepare a people for the return of the Lord. We are appointed, in due course, to build the New Jerusalem and to erect therein the holy temple to which he shall come. We are now in process of building up the stakes of Zion and of striving to perfect our lives so we will be able to build Zion itself in the appointed day.

And as we seek to build up Zion we are brought back to the Lord's definition of Zion. Our revelation says: "This is Zion—THE PURE IN HEART." (D&C 97:21.) Again the message comes through loud and clear. Zion is people. Zion is those whose sins are washed away in the waters of baptism. Zion is those out of whose souls dross and evil have been burned as though by fire. Zion is those who have received the baptism of fire so as to stand pure and clean before the Lord. Zion is those who keep the commandments of God.

Zion is the pure in heart. "And blessed are all the pure in heart, for they shall see God." (3 Ne. 12:8.) That is to say: If and when the latter-day Zion becomes like the original Zion, then the Lord will come and dwell with his people as he did in the ancient Zion. That we have not yet attained this high state of righteousness is clear, for few among the saints see the face of the Lord while they are in mortality, to say nothing of the Lord coming and dwelling with the whole body of his people as he did anciently.

Thus, Zion is built up by righteousness and destroyed by wickedness, for Zion is composed of righteous people, and if they cease to keep the commandments, they are no longer Zion. It was of the labors of rebellious Israel in times past that the Lord said: "They build up Zion with blood, and Jerusalem with iniquity. The heads thereof judge for reward, and the priests thereof teach for hire, and the prophets thereof divine for money: yet will they lean upon the Lord, and say, Is not the Lord among us? none evil can come upon us. Therefore shall Zion for your sake be plowed as a field, and Jerusalem shall become heaps, and the mountain of the house as the high places of the forest." (Micah 3:10-12.) And it is of the building of Zion in the last days that the Lord says: "And Zion cannot be built up unless it is by the principles of the law of the celestial kingdom; otherwise I cannot receive her unto myself." (D&C 105:5.)

On August 2, 1833, the Lord gave his saints—his small band of struggling, striving saints—such a promise, relative to the establishment of Zion, as none but he could fulfill. If Zion is true and faithful in all things, he said, "she shall prosper, and spread herself and become very glorious, very great, and very terrible. And the nations of the earth shall honor her, and shall say: Surely Zion is the city of our God, and surely Zion cannot fall, neither be moved out of her place, for God is there, and the hand of the Lord is there; And he hath sworn by the power of his might to be her salvation and her high tower." That is, if Zion in the last days becomes like Zion was in the early days, the same preserving care from on high will rest upon her, the Lord will dwell in her midst, and the wicked of the world will have no power over her.

But Zion did not become again as she once was, for reasons we shall note, and the Lord's promise has been reserved for millennial fulfillment. Indeed, when it was given, the Lord accompanied it with a solemn warning. "Let Zion rejoice," he said, "while all the wicked shall mourn. For behold, and lo, vengeance cometh speedily upon the ungodly as the whirlwind; and who shall escape it? The Lord's scourge shall pass over by night and by day, and the report thereof shall vex all people; yea, it shall not be stayed until the Lord come; For the indignation of the Lord is kindled against their abominations and all their wicked works." Vengeance has rested, is resting, and will rest upon all the nations of the earth. Their inhabitants have been, are now, and yet will be scourged and cursed and driven and slain because of their abominations. Such will not cease until the wicked are destroyed when the Lord comes.

And now, to Zion the Lord gives this warning: "Nevertheless, Zion shall escape if she observe to do all things whatsoever I have commanded her. But if she observe not to do whatsoever I have commanded her, I will visit her according to all her works, with sore affliction, with pestilence, with plague, with sword, with vengeance, with devouring fire." (D&C 97:18-26.) Zion in that day did not keep the commandments and gain the promised blessings, nor have we, their successors in interest, risen to the standard set by them of old. The saints sought to build up Zion in Missouri and failed. Some of the promised scourging fell upon them, and more of it will yet fall upon us if we do not keep the commandments more fully than in the past.

On December 16, 1833, the Lord revealed why our early brethren failed. "At this time the Saints who had gathered in Missouri were suffering great persecution. Mobs had driven them from their homes in Jackson County, and some of the Saints had tried to establish themselves in Van Buren County, but persecution followed them. The main body of the Church was at that time in Clay County, Missouri. Threats of death against individuals of the Church were many. The people had lost household furniture, clothing, livestock and other personal property, and many of their crops had been destroyed." (D&C 101; introductory heading.)

Why, oh why, did the Lord permit these persecutions and drivings? His answer, which contained also an assurance of salvation for those so chastened, came in these words: "I, the Lord, have suffered the affliction to come upon them, wherewith they have been afflicted, in consequence of their transgressions; . . . Behold, I say unto you, there were jarrings, and contentions, and envyings, and strifes, and lustful and covetous desires among them; therefore by these things they polluted their inheritances." (D&C 101:1-9.)

Zion shall be redeemed and built up at the appointed time—a time yet future—and she "shall not be moved out of her place." (D&C 101:17.) The saints are to "wait for a little season"—as the

Lord measures time—"for the redemption of Zion. . . . First let my army become very great," the Lord says, "and let it be sanctified before me. . . . And let those commandments which I have given concerning Zion and her law be executed and fulfilled, after her redemption." (D&C 105:9, 31, 34.) As men measure time, the period of waiting is "many years." (D&C 58:44.) Meanwhile we are appointed to strengthen the stakes and sanctify our souls—all in preparation for the great day ahead.

"And blessed are they who shall seek to bring forth my Zion at that day"—the day in which we live and the day that is yet to be—"for they shall have the gift and the power of the Holy Ghost; and if they endure unto the end they shall be lifted up at the last day, and shall be saved in the everlasting kingdom of the Lamb; and whoso shall publish peace, yea, tidings of great joy, how beautiful upon the mountains shall they be." (1 Ne. 13:37.)

Israel Gathers to Zion

"There shall be a day"—and thanks be to God, that day is now—"that the watchmen upon the mount Ephraim shall cry, Arise, ye, and let us go up to Zion unto the Lord our God." We who are of Ephraim, who have received the fulness of the everlasting gospel by the opening of the heavens, we send forth the cry. We stand on the mount Ephraim and blow the trump of God; our voices mingle with the angels beyond the veil, as we say to all Israel: "Come home; come to Zion; be one with us; wash away your sins in the waters of baptism; be clean; turn to the Lord and serve him as in days of old. Know ye that Zion is the pure in heart." And we know that success will attend our labors and that the scattered ones "shall come and sing in the height of Zion, and shall flow together to the goodness of the Lord." (Jer. 31:6, 12.) As the Lord lives, scattered Israel is coming and shall come to Zion.

Our divine commission to bring Israel to Zion is recorded in our revelations. But it can also be read in the inspired decisions of the living oracles who send forth the elders of Israel, duly and properly instructed, to tell the people in all nations where and under what circumstances they shall gather in their day and situation. One of the greatest of the written calls came in a revelation to the Prophet Joseph Smith on November 3, 1831, a mere nineteen months after the Church and kingdom of God had been set up again on earth in this final gospel dispensation. It is to this wondrous document of superlative worth, and one filled with dynamic expression, that we shall first give our attention. Then we shall note some other revealed statements and weave them all into the inspired procedures ordained by those who hold the keys of gathering and who are thereby empowered to specify the place and direct the manner in which each soul in scattered Israel shall gather.

Speaking to his newly established church, to the little flock gathered into his latter-day sheepfold, to those who already believed his word and sought to learn and do his will, the Lord said: "Prepare ye, prepare ye, O my people; sanctify yourselves; gather ye together, O ye people of my church, upon the land of Zion, all you that have not been commanded to tarry." The Lord always gathers his people. In this wicked world they must come together to strengthen each other in the holy faith. They must assemble in congregations to teach one another the doctrines of the kingdom. They must use their united strength to bear the burdens of each other, to mourn with those who mourn, and to comfort those who stand in need of comfort. They must come where the temples of God stand so as to be endowed with power from on high. Where but among themselves can they worship the Lord in spirit and in truth? Where else can they work out their salvation with fear and trembling before the Lord? Truly, if the Lord's people do not gather, they cannot and will not be saved. Alone in the world, each unprotected sheep would soon be destroyed by the wolves of wickedness.

Hence the Lord says to his saints: "Go ye out from Babylon. Be ye clean that bear the vessels of the Lord." Forsake the world; cleave unto the kingdom; no longer live as other men live. You are a people set apart. "Call your solemn assemblies, and speak often one to another." Teach, train, counsel, instruct, exhort, and testify; join one with another in sacred meetings. "And let every man call upon the name of the Lord." All are alike unto God. All are to believe; all are to pray; all are to preach. Every man is to stand as a minister of Christ. "Yea, verily I say unto you again, the time has come when the voice of the Lord is unto you: Go ye out of Babylon; gather ye out from among the nations, from the four winds, from one end of heaven to the other." Israel was scattered to the four winds; and as was the scattering, so shall the gathering be; the believing remnant must separate themselves from the world in every nation.

"Send forth the elders of my church unto the nations which are afar off; unto the islands of the sea; send forth unto foreign lands; call upon all nations, first upon the Gentiles, and then upon the Jews." This we are now doing to a modest extent; this we shall continue to do to a greater extent until the Lord comes; and even then the voice of the Lord, by the mouths of his servants, shall continue to cry out until every living soul on earth is converted and gathered into the true fold.

"And behold, and lo, this shall be their cry"—in this present world—"and the voice of the Lord unto all people: Go ye forth unto the land of Zion, that the borders of my people may be enlarged, and that her stakes may be strengthened, and that Zion may go forth unto the regions round about." In November 1831, and for many years thereafter, the gathering of Israel was to the United States of America, where Zion and her stakes needed strengthening. The Church was young; its numbers were few; the armies of the Lord yet needed to become very great, very strong, and very powerful. To come off victorious over Babylon, all of the strength of the whole kingdom needed to be centered in one place, centered in the mountain where the Lord's house would be exalted above the hills.

The gathering of Israel to the Zion of God is to prepare them for the Second Coming. And so the divine word continues: "Yea, let the cry go forth among all people: Awake and arise and go forth to meet the Bridegroom; behold and lo, the Bridegroom cometh; go ye out to meet him." Men go forth to meet the Bridegroom when they join the Church and fill their lamps with that Holy Spirit which the world cannot receive, but which is the priceless possession of every true believer. "Prepare yourselves for the great day of the Lord. Watch, therefore, for ye know neither the day nor the hour."

Where, then, shall Israel assemble to prepare for that great day? "Let them, therefore, who are among the Gentiles flee unto Zion." This they began to do as soon as the warning voice was raised in their hearing. "And let them who be of Judah flee unto Jerusalem, unto the mountains of the Lord's house." This is yet future; Judah has yet to begin to believe in such numbers that they can assemble in the land of their fathers to build the destined temple there. This will be one of the final events before the coming again of their Messiah.

But the call now is to all men, Jew and Gentile alike: "Go ye out from among the nations, even from Babylon, from the midst of wickedness, which is spiritual Babylon." There is a great key hidden in these words. The gathering is both temporal and spiritual. Israel gathers spiritually by joining the Church; she gathers temporally by assembling where church congregations are found. The great issue is one of leaving Babylon, leaving the world, leaving wickedness; it is one of becoming pure in heart so as to be part of Zion.

Such a glorious and worldwide movement as the gathering of Israel to Zion must not occur in a haphazard way; it must not be left to chance; the Lord's work always goes forward in an organized and systematized way. And so the Lord cautions—cautions? nay, commands—his saints: "Let not your flight be in haste, but let all things be prepared before you; and he that goeth, let him not look back lest sudden destruction shall come upon him." Is it not written elsewhere, "No man, having put his hand to the plough, and looking back, is fit for the kingdom of God"? (Luke 9:62.)

"Hearken and hear, O ye inhabitants of the earth. Listen, ye elders of my church together, and hear the voice of the Lord; for he calleth upon all men, and he commandeth all men everywhere to repent." (D&C 133:4-16.) This, then, is the message of gathering: Come unto Christ; repent and be baptized; receive the gift of the Holy Ghost and become pure, as pure and untainted from the sins of the world as is a newly born babe. Then assemble with the saints that the sanctifying processes may work in your life and you become a fit subject to stand before the King of Zion when he comes to reign in his glory.

Where Is Zion?

Building on the foundations heretofore laid, we are now ready to inquire: Where shall the temporal gathering of Israel be? Where shall scattered Israel assemble in the last days? Are all converts to the kingdom destined to come to western America? Where is Zion? To all of these, and to all like questions, there are answers from the Lord that no man need misunderstand.

Be it remembered that Zion is people; Zion is the pure in heart; Zion is the saints of the living God. And be it also remembered that the people called Zion build the places called Zion. Thus wherever the saints build an old or a new Jerusalem, wherever they establish cities of holiness, wherever they create stakes of Zion, there is Zion; and where these things are not, Zion is not.

It is clear that the gathered remnants of Judah shall build a holy city, the Jerusalem of old. Here then is Zion—Zion as a capital city—to which, as the prophets foretold, Israel shall return. Will they all live in Jerusalem itself? Obviously not; they did not do so anciently, and they will not do so in the last days. Zion will reach out and embrace the whole land of Palestine.

It is also clear that the gathered remnants of Joseph will build a holy city, a New Jerusalem in Jackson County, Missouri. Here also is Zion—Zion as a capital city—to which, again as the holy word records, Israel shall gather. Once again we ask: Will they all dwell in this Zion itself? Again the answer is clear. This will be a city whence the law goes forth. Gathered Israel shall dwell in various places; one place alone would never be able to contain them all.

These capital cities will be glorious indeed. Of them the psalmic and prophetic word acclaims: "Great is the Lord, and greatly to be praised in the city of our God, in the mountain of his holiness. Beautiful for situation, the joy of the whole earth, is mount Zion, . . . the city of the great King. God is known in her palaces." (Ps. 48:1-3.) And also: "The Lord loveth the gates of

Zion more than all the dwellings of Jacob. Glorious things are spoken of thee, O city of God. . . . And of Zion it shall be said, This and that man was born in her: and the highest himself shall establish her." (Ps. 87:2-5.) But with it all, they are but types and shadows of a much greater Zion that shall have like glory and whose inhabitants shall reap equal praise.

As we are aware, the building of the New Jerusalem lies in the future, at a time yet to be designated by revelation. There is no present call for the saints to purchase land or to live in Jackson County or in any place connected therewith. The revealed word relative to the gathering to Independence and its environs will come through the prophet of God on earth. When it does come—with the consequent return of the saints to that Zion which shall not be moved out of its place—that call will not be for the saints in general to assemble there. The return to Jackson County will be by delegates, as it were. Those whose services are needed there will assemble as appointed. The rest of Israel will remain in their appointed places. The Lord's house is a house of order, and faithful saints do as they are told and go at the bidding of their prophet, for his voice is the voice of the Lord. And as with the New Jerusalem, so with the Jerusalem of old. Those assigned will build up the city. It certainly will not be the abiding place of all converted Jews.

Zion will be built up in many places. Jesus said that "the covenant which the Father hath made with the children of Israel" was one involving "their restoration to the lands of their inheritance" (3 Ne. 29:1)—not one land but many. Speaking of "all the house of Israel," Nephi prophesied, "they shall be gathered together to the lands of their inheritance" (1 Ne. 22:9-12)—not one land but many. Both the house of Israel and the Jews, Jacob promised, "shall be gathered home to the lands of their inheritance, and shall be established in all their lands of promise" (2 Ne. 9:1-2; 10:7)—not in one location, or in several, but in many. In the day of gathering the Lehite remnants of Joseph are to receive the land of America as their inheritance. (3 Ne. 20:13-14.)

The law of gathering as given to us has varied to meet the needs of an ever-growing Church that one day will have dominion over all the earth. In 1830 the saints were commanded to assemble in "one place." (D&C 29:8.) How could it have been otherwise? They were told to "assemble together at the Ohio" (D&C 37:3) and to go forth to Zion in "the western countries" (D&C 45:64). In 1833 they were told to gather in the Zion of Missouri, "Until the day cometh when there is found no more room for them; and then I have other places which I will appoint unto them," saith the Lord, "and they shall be called stakes, for the curtains or the strength of Zion." They were to worship the Lord "in holy places." (D&C 101:21-22.) In the revealed prayer dedicating the Kirtland Temple (1836), the Prophet importuned for the righteous, "that they may come forth to Zion, or to her stakes, the places of thine appointment, with songs of everlasting joy." (D&C 109:39.) In 1838 the Lord spoke of "the gathering together upon the land of Zion, and upon her stakes." (D&C 115:6.) In 1844 the prophetic word acclaimed: "The whole of America is Zion itself from north to south, and is described by the Prophets, who declare that it is the Zion where the mountain of the Lord should be, and that it should be in the center of the land." (*Teachings*, p. 362.)

We now have stakes of Zion in many nations, in Europe and Asia and South America and upon the islands of the sea. Before the Lord comes, there will be stakes in all lands and among all peoples. Any portion of the surface of the earth that is organized into a stake of Zion—a City of Holiness, as it were—becomes a part of Zion. A stake of Zion is a part of Zion—it is just that simple. And every stake becomes the place of gathering for the saints who live in the area involved.

We now have temples at the ends of the earth. Many more will be built before the dread day when the Lord comes to his temple. In these houses of the Lord every priesthood, key, power, endowment, and gospel blessing is available. There is nothing the saints of God can receive in the Salt Lake Temple that is not also available in the Sao Paulo Temple.

How well Isaiah spoke when he said: "He shall cause them that come of Jacob to take root: Israel shall blossom and bud, and fill the face of the world with fruit." (Isa. 27:6.)

Where then is Zion? It is wherever there are congregations of the pure in heart. And where is Israel to gather? Into the stakes of

Zion, there to perfect themselves as they wait patiently for the Lord. How glorious is the word that the God of Israel is the God of the whole earth, and that he who hath chosen Jacob hath also chosen all those who will repent and come unto him and live his laws.

Chapter 25

THE TWO JERUSALEMS AND THE SECOND COMING

Jerusalem Falls from Grace

Zion and Jerusalem, as cities, are or should be one and the same. The original Zion was the City of Holiness wherein the pure in heart dwelt. All her inhabitants were of one heart and one mind, and they lived together in love and in righteousness. Anciently Jerusalem was appointed by the Lord to be the *City of Peace*. The name itself apparently derives from the Hebrew *shalom (shalem)* meaning peace. Melchizedek was king of Salem, and like Enoch, whose converts worshipped the Lord in the *City of Holiness*, so the converts of Melchizedek worshipped in the *City of Peace* where Melchizedek reigned as the Prince of peace. (JST, Gen. 14:33.)

But whereas Zion was taken up into heaven, Jerusalem, following a long and tempestuous history in which she both ascended to the heights and sank to the depths, was thrust down to hell, as it were, there to await a future day of restoration and glory. Commonly called the *Holy City*, because the House of the Lord was there and the Son of God ministered in her streets and synagogues, she is now known to the saints as "the great city, which spiritually is called Sodom and Egypt, where also our Lord was crucified." (Rev. 11:8.) She is the one concerning whom the divine decree went forth. Thus saith the Lord, "I will remove Judah also out of my sight, as I have removed Israel, and will cast off this city Jerusalem which I have chosen, and the house of which I said, My name shall be there." (2 Kgs. 23:27.) And as it was promised, so it

297

came to pass. Titus destroyed the city, tore down the temple stone by stone, slew more than a million Jews with the sword, and made slaves of the rest.

Why, why, oh why, did the Holy City become a vile and pestilent hole? Why did the Great Jehovah permit his holy house to be desecrated by the Gentiles and made by them into a dung hill? Why were the chosen people scourged and slain and scattered and made a hiss and a byword in all nations? The answer is clear and certain. It was because they crucified their King. It was because they rejected the God of their fathers. It was because they did not believe the gospel of salvation when it was taught to them by legal administrators sent of God. Truly the Lord said by the mouth of his ancient prophet: "They build up Zion with blood, and Jerusalem with iniquity. The heads thereof judge for reward, and the priests thereof teach for hire, and the prophets thereof divine for money: yet will they lean upon the Lord, and say, Is not the Lord among us? none evil can come upon us. Therefore shall Zion for your sake be plowed as a field, and Jerusalem shall become heaps, and the mountain of the house [the mountain of the temple] as the high places of the forest." (Micah 3:10-12.) And as it was promised, so it came to pass, both in the day of Nebuchadnezzar and again in the meridian of time.

Jerusalem Shall Rise Again

Though there may be many Jerusalems—each a Zion in its own right, because its inhabitants dwell in righteousness—yet there are two in particular that concern us because of the part they are destined to play in the Second Coming of the one who shall yet reign in the Jerusalem of His choice. These two are the Jerusalem now standing in Palestine and the New Jerusalem yet to be built in Jackson County, Missouri. Both will house a holy temple, and each will serve as a world capital during the Millennium. Biblical prophecies relative to the Second Coming make frequent reference to Zion and Jerusalem as two cities, not one. As a prelude to specifying how both Jerusalems, the Old and the New, fit into our Lord's return, we should ponder and interpret at least a few of the relevant passages from the Old Testament.

298

Isaiah—the great prophet of the restoration, the one who seems to have known as much about our day as we ourselves know—Isaiah cried out: "Oh that thou wouldest rend the heavens, that thou wouldest come down, that the mountains might flow down at thy presence." Then he speaks other words about that glorious day which will usher in the era of righteousness to follow. In them he inserts one of the reasons why the Lord cannot yet come. "Thy holy cities are a wilderness," he says, "Zion is a wilderness, Jerusalem a desolation. Our holy and our beautiful house [the temple], where our fathers praised thee, is burned up with fire: and all our pleasant things are laid waste." (Isa. 64:1-12.) That is, two holy cities must be prepared to receive the Lord when he comes. As long as Zion is a wilderness, where a city is yet to be built, and as long as Jerusalem, having been destroyed, is yet a desolation, the Lord will not rend the heavens and cause the mountains to flow down at his glorious advent.

Both Isaiah and Micah prophesied of the building of temples in the last days, of the gathering of Israel to those holy houses, and of the gospel teaching they would there receive. "For out of Zion shall go forth the law," they both said, "and the word of the Lord from Jerusalem"—thus naming the two great world capitals and indicating the authoritative decrees to go forth from each. Isaiah put his words in a millennial context by saying that "he [Christ] shall [then] judge among the nations, and shall rebuke many people: and they shall beat their swords into plowshares, and their spears into pruninghooks: nation shall not lift up sword against nation, neither shall they learn war any more." Micah says all this and more. He speaks in addition of the millennial gathering of Israel and says, "The Lord shall reign over them in mount Zion from henceforth, even for ever." (Isa. 2:1-5; Micah 4:1-7.)

Joel, whose words were quoted by Moroni to Joseph Smith, told of the "wonders in the heavens and in the earth," and of the "blood, and fire, and pillars of smoke" that would precede the Second Coming. "The sun shall be turned into darkness, and the moon into blood, before the great and the terrible day of the Lord come," he said. When these things fall upon the earth, there will be no security and no salvation except for those who believe and obey the everlasting gospel. "And it shall come to pass, that whosoever shall call on the name of the Lord shall be delivered: for in mount Zion and in Jerusalem shall be deliverance, as the Lord hath said, and in the remnant whom the Lord shall call." (Joel 2:30-32.) Two great cities of deliverance, Zion and Jerusalem; two great world capitals, Jerusalem of the Jews and the New Jerusalem of all Israel! In that day, "The sun and the moon shall be darkened, and the stars shall withdraw their shining. The Lord also shall roar out of Zion, and utter his voice from Jerusalem; and the heavens and the earth shall shake: but the Lord will be the hope of his people, and the strength of the children of Israel." In that day, "Judah shall dwell for ever, and Jerusalem from generation to generation," and it shall be said, "The Lord dwelleth in Zion." (Joel 3:15-16, 20-21.)

Truly, truly shall it be. Jerusalem shall rise again. As she fell from grace because she forsook the living God, so shall she rise again when she once more worships her Eternal King in the beauty of holiness. As she fell because of iniquity, so shall she be restored through righteousness. When the Jews receive the fulness of the everlasting gospel as it has been restored through the Prophet Joseph Smith, they will return to Jerusalem as the Lord's true legal administrators to build up Jerusalem as a Zion and to place again on the ancient site the temple of the new kingdom. And then when the Lord comes, the ancient city will shine forth with a glory and a splendor never before known among mortals.

How gloriously speaks the prophetic word of that day! "Thus saith the Lord; I am returned unto Zion, and will dwell in the midst of Jerusalem" for a thousand years, "and Jerusalem shall be called a city of truth; and the mountain of the Lord of hosts the holy mountain." It shall be the mountain where the temple stands.

And what of the inhabitants of the Holy City? "Thus saith the Lord of hosts; There shall yet old men and old women dwell in the streets of Jerusalem, and every man with his staff in his hand for very age." It is the day when men shall live to the age of a tree and then be changed from mortality to immortality in the twinkling of an eye. "And the streets of the city shall be full of boys and girls playing in the streets thereof." It is the day when the children of the prophets shall grow up without sin unto salvation.

It is also the day of the final great and glorious gathering of Israel. "Thus saith the Lord of hosts; Behold, I will save my people from the east country, and from the west country; And I will bring them, and they shall dwell in the midst of Jerusalem: and they shall be my people, and I will be their God, in truth and in righteousness." And it shall not be with the gathered ones as it was with those who were scattered. "But now I will not be unto the residue of this people as in the former days, saith the Lord of hosts. For the seed shall be prosperous; the vine shall give her fruit, and the ground shall give her increase, and the heavens shall give their dew; and I will cause the remnant of this people to possess all these things." It is the day of the new heaven and of the new earth, when the desert blossoms as the rose and all the earth becomes as the garden of the Lord.

And what manner of conduct shall prevail among men? "These are the things that ye shall do," the holy word affirms: "Speak ye every man the truth to his neighbour; execute the judgment of truth and peace in your gates: And let none of you imagine evil in your hearts against his neighbour; and love no false oath: for all these are things that I hate, saith the Lord." And in that day "many people and strong nations shall come to seek the Lord of hosts in Jerusalem, and to pray before the Lord. Thus saith the Lord of hosts; In those days it shall come to pass, that ten men shall take hold out of all languages of the nations, even shall take hold of the skirt of him that is a Jew, saying, We will go with you: for we have heard that God is with you." (Zech. 8:1-23.)

The New Jerusalem

"We believe . . . that Zion (the New Jerusalem) will be built upon the American continent." So specified the seer of latter days in our tenth Article of Faith. Zion, the New Jerusalem, on American soil! And we hasten to add, so also shall there be Zions in all lands and New Jerusalems in the mountains of the Lord in all the earth. But the American Zion shall be the capital city, the source whence the law shall go forth to govern all the earth. It shall be the city of the Great King. His throne shall be there, and from there he shall reign gloriously over all the earth. And so, let us now drink deeply from some of those passages in holy writ which tell of our American Zion. As we do so we must rightly divide the word of God, as Paul might have cautioned, lest we become confused as to what shall happen before and what after the Second Coming.

To Enoch the Lord swore with an oath in his own name, because, as Paul would say, he could swear by no greater, that he would come a second time "in the last days, in the days of wickedness and vengeance. . . . And the day shall come that the earth shall rest," he said, speaking of the Millennium, "but before that day the heavens shall be darkened, and a veil of darkness shall cover the earth." This is the evil and universal apostasy that has prevailed for nearly two thousand years and that even now covers the earth except where the faithful among the saints are concerned. "And the heavens shall shake, and also the earth," the Lord continues, "and great tribulations shall be among the children of men, but my people will I preserve." Then he speaks of the glorious restoration, of the coming forth of the Book of Mormon, and of righteousness and truth sweeping the earth as with a flood. To what purpose? "To gather out mine elect from the four quarters of the earth, unto a place which I shall prepare, an Holy City, that my people may gird up their loins, and be looking forth for the time of my coming." The Holy City of which he speaks shall be built before the Second Coming. Of this city the Lord says: "There shall be my tabernacle"—the place where my saints shall worship —"and it shall be called Zion, a New Jerusalem."

The saints of the living God, the true believers who worship the God of Enoch, the righteous souls who receive revelation and know how and where and in what manner to build the Holy City—they shall build the New Jerusalem before the Lord comes. "Then"—that is, after the city is built—"Then shalt thou [Enoch] and all thy city meet them there, and we will receive them into our bosom, and they shall see us; and we will fall upon their necks, and they shall fall upon our necks, and we will kiss each other." It is the Lord who is speaking. He continues: "And there"—in the New

Jerusalem—"shall be mine abode, and it shall be Zion, which shall come forth out of all the creations which I have made; and for the space of a thousand years the earth shall rest." (Moses 7:60-64.)

Our Lord, risen in glorious immortality, taught his Nephite saints about the latter-day gathering of all Israel. "I will gather my people together as a man gathereth his sheaves into the floor," he said. "And behold, this people"—the Lehite civilization who were of the house of Joseph—"will I establish in this land [America], unto the fulfilling of the covenant which I made with your father Jacob; and it"—apparently the whole land—"shall be a New Jerusalem. And the powers of heaven shall be in the midst of this people; yea, even I will be in the midst of you." (3 Ne. 20:18, 22.) Clearly Jesus is speaking of the New Jerusalem during its millennial existence, for it is then that he shall dwell on earth among the righteous.

A short while later in the same discourse, still speaking of the latter days, Jesus said the rebellious would be cut off from the house of Israel, but that among the righteous he would establish his church. "And they shall come in unto the covenant and be numbered among this the remnant of Jacob, unto whom I have given this land for their inheritance." It is these righteous people, these believing ones who have made covenant with the Lord, who shall build the New Jerusalem. "And they shall assist my people, the remnant of Jacob, and also as many of the house of Israel as shall come, that they may build a city, which shall be called the New Jerusalem." The gathered elect of Israel shall build the city under the direction of the President of The Church of Jesus Christ of Latter-day Saints. "And then shall they assist my people that they may be gathered in, who are scattered upon all the face of the land, in unto the New Jerusalem." Note it, there is to be a great and glorious day of gathering after the New Jerusalem is built. And after this gathering "shall the power of heaven come down among them; and I also will be in the midst," meaning that the Lord will reign personally upon the earth during the Millennium. (3 Ne. 21:20-25.)

This New Jerusalem is to be built in Jackson County, Missouri, and its glory and power shall be known in all the earth. "And it shall be called the New Jerusalem, a land of peace, a city of refuge, a place of safety for the saints of the Most High God; And the glory of the Lord shall be there, and the terror of the Lord also shall be there, insomuch that the wicked will not come unto it, and it shall be called Zion. And it shall come to pass among the wicked, that every man that will not take his sword against his neighbor must needs flee unto Zion for safety. And there shall be gathered unto it out of every nation under heaven; and it shall be the only people that shall not be at war one with another. And it shall be said among the wicked: Let us not go up to battle against Zion, for the inhabitants of Zion are terrible; wherefore we cannot stand. And it shall come to pass that the righteous shall be gathered out from among all nations, and shall come to Zion, singing with songs of everlasting joy." (D&C 45:66-71.) All this lies in the future. The city has yet to be built, and it will not be built and cannot be built except by a people who are living a celestial law. And after it is built, the fear and dread of the Lord will rest upon the wicked as they see how and in what manner the Lord preserves its righteous inhabitants.

As we might surmise, the sealed portion of the Book of Mormon contains a full and complete account of all things pertaining to the New Jerusalem and the second coming of Christ. From the writings of Ether, preserved in full on those plates, Moroni digested for us a few salient facts that enable us to glimpse what is to be. He tells us the American continent "was the place of the New Jerusalem, which should come down out of heaven, and [the place of] the holy sanctuary [temple] of the Lord." This New Jerusalem is the City of Enoch, which shall return after the Lord comes again. "Behold, Ether saw the days of Christ [the days of his glorious Second Coming], and he spake concerning a New Jerusalem upon this land." This New Jerusalem seems to be the one built by the saints in the latter days to which the New Jerusalem from heaven shall come.

"And he," meaning Ether, Moroni continues, "spake also concerning the house of Israel, and the Jerusalem from whence Lehi should come—after it should be destroyed it should be built up

304

again, a holy city unto the Lord; wherefore, it could not be a new Jerusalem for it had been in a time of old; but it should be built up again, and become a holy city of the Lord; and it should be built unto the house of Israel." Moroni, summarizing Ether, says that "a New Jerusalem should be built upon this land"—the land of America, built up in the same way Old Jerusalem shall be rebuilt, that is, by mortal hands—built up "unto the remnant of the seed of Joseph, for which things," he says, "there has been a type."

The type is then given in these words: "For as Joseph brought his father down into the land of Egypt, even so he died there; wherefore, the Lord brought a remnant of the seed of Joseph out of the land of Jerusalem, that he might be merciful unto the seed of Joseph that they should perish not, even as he was merciful unto the father of Joseph that he should perish not. Wherefore, the remnant of the house of Joseph shall be built upon this land; and it shall be a land of their inheritance; and they shall build up a holy city unto the Lord, like unto the Jerusalem of old; and they shall no more be confounded, until the end come when the earth shall pass away." We who are of Ephraim (and of Manasseh) into whose hands the Church and kingdom has now been given shall build the city in due course, and we and our children after us shall never be confounded or lose the faith; for our dispensation, the promise is that the gospel shall remain with us to prepare a people for the second coming of Him whose servants we are.

And when our Lord returns, Moroni continues, "there shall be a new heaven and a new earth; and they shall be like unto the old save the old have passed away, and all things have become new." These words are descriptive of the millennial earth, the paradisiacal earth, the transfigured earth that shall be again as it was in the days of the Garden of Eden.

"And then"—after there is a new heaven and a new earth— "cometh the New Jerusalem"—in all its millennial glory, joined as it will be with Enoch's city—"and blessed are they who dwell therein, for it is they whose garments are white through the blood of the Lamb; and they are they who are numbered among the remnant of the seed of Joseph, who are of the house of Israel. And then also cometh the Jerusalem of old; and the inhabitants thereof, blessed are they, for they have been washed in the blood of the Lamb; and they are they who were scattered and gathered in from the four quarters of the earth, and from the north countries, and are partakers of the fulfilling of the covenant which God made with their father, Abraham." (Ether 13:3-11.) This glorious destiny for Old Jerusalem is clearly millennial. There will be a beginning before the Lord comes, but the great day shall be when he is here to send forth his word from his ancient holy city.

The millennial setting of the New Jerusalem is nowhere seen better than in the biblical words of the Beloved Disciple. He records: "And I saw a new heaven and a new earth"—he is seeing the millennial earth—"for the first heaven and the first earth were passed away; and there was no more sea." The continents and islands have become one land and are no more divided by the oceans of the earth. "And I John saw the holy city, new Jerusalem [the City of Enoch], coming down from God out of heaven, prepared as a bride adorned for her husband." Christ is the husband, and the robes with which his beloved ones are adorned are the robes of righteousness. "And I heard a great voice out of heaven saying, Behold, the tabernacle of God is with men, and he will dwell with them, and they shall be his people, and God himself shall be with them, and be their God." Christ, who is the Lord God, shall reign on earth. "And God shall wipe away all tears from their eyes; and there shall be no more death, neither sorrow, nor crying, neither shall there be any more pain: for the former things are passed away." (Rev. 21:1-4.) All these things, as we shall see in a later context, are descriptive of life during the Millennium.

This indeed shall be the glorious day when "the graves of the saints shall be opened; and they shall come forth and stand on the right hand of the Lamb, when he shall stand upon Mount Zion, and upon the holy city, the New Jerusalem; and they shall sing the song of the Lamb, day and night forever and ever." (D&C 133:56.) Among other things they shall sing:

The Lord hath brought again Zion;
The Lord hath redeemed his people, Israel,
According to the election of grace,
Which was brought to pass by the faith

306

And covenant of their fathers.
The Lord hath redeemed his people;
And Satan is bound and time is no longer.
The Lord hath gathered all things in one.
The Lord hath brought down Zion from above.
The Lord hath brought up Zion from beneath.
The earth hath travailed and brought forth her strength;
And truth is established in her bowels;
And the heavens have smiled upon her;
And she is clothed with the glory of her God;
For he stands in the midst of his people.
Glory, and honor, and power, and might,
Be ascribed to our God; for he is full of mercy,
Justice, grace and truth, and peace,
Forever and ever, Amen.

—D&C 84:99-102

The Celestial Jerusalem

When this earth becomes a celestial sphere; when it becomes the eternal heaven for exalted beings; when the Father and the Son abide, as occasion requires, on its resurrected surface—then again shall the holy city come down from God in heaven to be with men on earth. Or, rather, of that day of celestial rest, shall we not say that the whole earth shall be a heavenly Jerusalem?

It is Paul who tells us that the saved saints shall "come unto mount Zion, and unto the city of the living God, the heavenly Jerusalem, and to an innumerable company of angels, . . . and to God the Judge of all." (Heb. 12:22-23.) And our revelations speak of exalted beings as "they who are come unto Mount Zion, and unto the city of the living God, the heavenly place, the holiest of all." (D&C 76:66.) But it is John to whom we turn to read the grand imagery, also literal, that describes that celestial Jerusalem.

John saw "the holy Jerusalem, descending out of heaven from God, having the glory of God." He saw the celestial light that blazed forth in her streets, showing that God himself was there. He saw the great wall with twelve gates, guarded by twelve angels, with the names of the twelve tribes of Israel inscribed thereon, showing that saved Israel and all who are adopted into Abraham's family shall dwell therein. He saw the twelve foundations on which were the names of the twelve apostles of the Lamb, showing that all who dwell in the sacred city have believed the witness and obeyed the counsel of those who testified of Christ. He saw the great size of the city, the enormous length and breadth and height, signifying that it encompassed the whole planet. He saw the jewels and precious stones and gates of pearl and streets of gold, letting him know that those who dwell therein inherit all things and nothing is withheld.

"I saw no temple therein," he said, "for the Lord God Almighty and the Lamb are the temple of it. And the city had no need of the sun, neither of the moon, to shine in it: for the glory of God did lighten it, and the Lamb is the light thereof." This is the day when the earth, as a sea of glass, exists in its sanctified, immortal, and eternal state. "And the nations of them which are saved shall walk in the light of it," John says, "and the kings of the earth do bring their glory and honour into it." Only exalted beings shall reign within its walls. "And the gates of it shall not be shut at all by day: for there shall be no night there. And they shall bring the glory and honour of the nations into it. And there shall in no wise enter into it any thing that defileth, neither whatsoever worketh abomination, or maketh a lie: but they which are written in the Lamb's book of life." (Rev. 21:10-27.)

Truly Zion is the *City of Holiness* and Jerusalem is the *City of Peace*, and in them none but the righteous shall dwell.

Chapter 26

RESTORING
THE KINGDOM
TO ISRAEL

Israel: Her Kingdom and Power

Jesus ministered among men, taught them the gospel, and appointed pastors to feed his flock, but he did not restore the kingdom to Israel. Our Lord worked out the infinite and eternal atonement in Gethsemane and on Calvary; he rose in glorious immortality from the Arimathean's tomb; and he commanded the Twelve to go into all the world, preach the gospel to every creature, baptize believers, and give them the gift of the Holy Ghost—but he did not restore the kingdom to Israel.

The restoration of the kingdom to Israel—that was the thing uppermost in the minds of Jewish Israel in our Lord's day. They had even tried to take him by force, coronate him with an earthly crown, and put a sword wielded by the arm of flesh into his hands. They sought freedom from Roman bondage with a fanatical passion. Their blood drenched the great altar in Jehovah's house and flowed in rivulets in the streets of the Holy City as a witness that freedom from Gentile rule was worth more to them than life itself.

And so even the Twelve—after spending three years with Jesus in his mortal ministry; after associating with him for forty days as a resurrected being; and after being taught all that it was expedient for them to know to perform the labor that then was theirs—even the apostles sought yet to learn of the fulfillment of the prophetic word concerning Israel the chosen. "When they therefore were come together," at the time appointed for the ascension of Jesus into heaven, to sit down on the right hand of the Majesty on high, "they asked of him, saying, Lord, wilt thou at this time restore again the kingdom to Israel?"

They had received the keys of the kingdom of heaven; they presided over the Church and kingdom of God on earth; they held the holy apostleship, than which there is no higher power and authority on earth. They knew that theirs was an earthwide commission to carry the hope of salvation to all men. But what of the volumes spoken by the prophets of old about the glory and triumph of Israel? When would the scattered remnants of Jacob return? When would Jerusalem become a holy city whence the word of the Lord would go to all people? When would the Gentiles—Rome included!—bow beneath Israel's rod? And when would Israel govern all the earth?

To all this there was an answer, but it was not theirs to learn. Their ears were not to hear the glad tidings that have now been heralded in ours. To them Jesus said: "It is not for you to know the times or the seasons, which the Father hath put in his own power." That knowledge was reserved for another people in a future day. "But ye shall receive power," Jesus told them, "after that the Holy Ghost is come upon you: and ye shall be witnesses unto me both in Jerusalem, and in all Judea, and in Samaria, and unto the uttermost part of the earth." The kingdom was not to be restored to Israel in their day. Let them preach the gospel and save souls before the dire day of darkness that soon would cover the earth. The promised day of restoration, the day of Israel's triumph and glory, the day of millennial glory—all this lay ahead. It was scheduled for the last days. "And when he had spoken these things, while they beheld, he was taken up; and a cloud received him out of their sight." (Acts 1:6-9.) Thus Jesus' last words to his mortal ministers reaffirmed their great commission for the meridian of time, and they refrained from revealing the set time for favoring Israel and putting the ancient kingdom once again in her hands.

In her righteous days Israel prevailed over all opposing powers. Her armies put the aliens to flight; Jehovah fought her battles;

and David reigned on a stable throne. King David, then a man after the Lord's own heart, "executed judgment and justice unto all his people" (2 Sam. 8:15), and they prospered temporally and spiritually. Prophets dwelt among them, the heavens were open to the faithful, and the gifts of the Spirit blessed whole congregations. But in the days when they forsook the Lord and walked after the manner of the world, they were scourged and cursed and scattered. Through it all, however, the prophetic word held forth the hope of a gathering and a day of glory and triumph beyond anything ever known by them. Once again, according to the promises, Israel, as a theocracy, would receive laws from on high and administer them for the blessing of mankind. Once again there would be officers and judges and peace and prosperity.

This kingdom of which the apostles and prophets have spoken has not yet been restored to Israel but soon will be. The age of restoration has commenced, and the ecclesiastical kingdom—which is the Church—has been set up again. For the present there is a separation of church and state; the Church administers salvation and gives laws to its people on moral and spiritual issues, and the state administers civic matters and enacts such laws as are needed to govern in the affairs of men. But when the Lord comes and takes over the governments of the earth, he will place all things, both ecclesiastical and civic, in the hands of his own true kingdom. Then, as it is written, "the saints of the most High shall take the kingdom, and possess the kingdom for ever, even for ever and ever. . . . And the kingdom and dominion, and the greatness of the kingdom under the whole heaven, shall be given to the people of the saints of the most High, whose kingdom is an everlasting kingdom, and all dominions shall serve and obey him [the Lord]." (Dan. 7:18, 27.) Such is the kingdom that shall be restored to Israel in due course.

Gathering the Remainder of the Elect

Much of the prophetic word relative to the gathering of Israel in the last days has a dual fulfillment. It is descriptive of the gathering now in process, which is premillennial, but it has a far greater and more expanded application to the gathering after the ushering in of the Millennium when the earth shall be cleansed by fire. This final gathering will occur after the wicked masses of carnal men have been burned as stubble and after the barriers now separating the nations of the earth have been broken down.

The premillennial gathering is going forward and shall continue to go forward in the midst of war and desolation and persecution. All of the forces of evil do and shall oppose it, for it is of God and they are of the devil. But the gathering destined to come after the Second Coming shall be by power—divine power—and shall take place after Satan is bound and after the wicked have been destroyed. In that day hell will no longer be able to fight against God, and Zion will triumph and flourish to the full.

Few have written as clearly and plainly about these matters as did Nephi. He prophesied that "the Lord God will proceed to make bare his arm in the eyes of all the nations, in bringing about his covenants and his gospel unto those who are of the house of Israel." Israel "shall be gathered," he said, when they come to know "that the Lord is their Savior and their Redeemer, the Mighty One of Israel." That evil powers shall oppose this gathering and fight against Zion is so axiomatic it scarcely needs stating. Evil men always oppose righteous causes. The church of the devil always does the bidding of its master. But over this church, in due course, righteousness shall prevail. "And the blood of that great and abominable church," Nephi says, "which is the whore of all the earth, shall turn upon their own heads; for they shall war among themselves"—as they are even now doing—"and the sword of their own hands shall fall upon their own heads, and they shall be drunken with their own blood." Can anyone with spiritual insight look upon the nations of the earth today, in this day when we are struggling with all our might to gather Israel into the stakes of Zion, and not see a beginning fulfillment of Nephi's words?

"And every nation which shall war against thee, O house of Israel," the inspired word continues, "shall be turned one against another, and they shall fall into the pit which they digged to ensnare the people of the Lord." This is not yet, but soon shall be. "And all that fight against Zion shall be destroyed"—such is their eventual destiny—"and that great whore, who hath perverted the right ways of the Lord, yea, that great and abominable church, shall tumble to the dust and great shall be the fall of it."

When shall this come to pass? "For behold, saith the prophet, the time cometh speedily that Satan shall have no more power over the hearts of the children of men; for the day soon cometh that all the proud and they who do wickedly shall be as stubble; and the day cometh that they must be burned." That day is the great and dreadful day of the Lord. "For the time soon cometh that the fulness of the wrath of God shall be poured out upon all the children of men; for he will not suffer that the wicked shall destroy the righteous."

Of course, Satan will slay some of the righteous that their blood—with the blood of all the martyrs of all the ages—may cry from the ground as a witness against those who fight against God. Yet, as a people the true saints shall prevail. The Lord "will preserve the righteous by his power, even if it so be that the fulness of his wrath must come, and the righteous be preserved, even unto the destruction of their enemies by fire." This refers to the day of burning that shall attend the Second Coming. "Wherefore, the righteous need not fear; for thus saith the prophet, they shall be saved, even if it so be as by fire."

Nephi continues to use language descriptive of the Second Coming; promises that "the time surely must come that all they who fight against Zion shall be cut off"; says that "the righteous need not fear"; and speaks of the destruction of the kingdom of the devil. Then he says: "And the time cometh speedily that the righteous must be led up as calves of the stall, and the Holy One of Israel must reign in dominion, and might, and power, and great glory." Such shall be in the Millennium. In this setting our prophetic friend says: "And he gathereth his children from the four quarters of the earth; and he numbereth his sheep, and they know him; and there shall be one fold and one shepherd; and he shall feed his sheep, and in him they shall find pasture." Do we not see in this a millennial gathering of the elect from the four quarters of the earth?

"And because of the righteousness of his people"—his people are gathered Israel—"Satan has no power; wherefore, he cannot be loosed for the space of many years; for he hath no power over the hearts of the people, for they dwell in righteousness, and the Holy One of Israel reigneth." (1 Ne. 22:11-26.)

Those of Israel who live on earth and are worthy, and who are not gathered before the Lord comes, shall be gathered thereafter. "And they shall see the Son of Man coming in the clouds of heaven, with power and great glory," Jesus said, "and he shall send his angels before him with the great sound of a trumpet, and they shall gather together the remainder of his elect from the four winds, from one end of heaven to the other." (JS-M 1:36-37.) How shall this work be performed, and who shall do the actual gathering in of the lost sheep? As we are aware, the scriptural promise announced that an angel would fly through the midst of heaven having the everlasting gospel to preach unto all men. And as we have seen, this restoration was brought to pass by many angels, as each restored knowledge and keys and priesthood, and then mortal men proclaimed the angelic message to their fellowmen. So shall it be, as we suppose, in this final gathering of the elect by the angels. The message itself shall come from on high, and the Lord, as his custom is, will work through his servants on earth. They will do the work as they are now doing it. The elders of Israel will gather Israel after the Lord comes, on the same basis as at present.

Truly, saith the Psalmist, "Our God shall come, and shall not keep silence: a fire shall devour before him, and it shall be very tempestuous round about him. He shall call to the heavens from above, and to the earth, that he may judge his people." And what shall his call be? He shall say: "Gather my saints together unto me; those that have made a covenant with me by sacrifice." So shall it be in the day of judgment. "And the heavens shall declare his righteousness: for God is judge himself." (Ps. 50:3-6.)

Gathered Israel Governs the Earth

It will serve our purposes well to analyze selected prophetic utterances about the gathering of Israel. We shall choose a few

314

whose chief fulfillment is millennial, and we shall seek to learn from them the governing status of the chosen people in that blessed day. We have already seen that Jesus put chapter 52 of Isaiah in a millennial context. In it is found the cry: "Awake, awake; put on thy strength, O Zion; put on thy beautiful garments, O Jerusalem, the holy city: for henceforth there shall no more come into thee the uncircumcised and the unclean." In the day of which we speak there will be none who are unclean in the telestial sense of the word, for the wicked will be destroyed by the brightness of His coming. And there will be none who are uncircumcised, as it were, for all who seek the blessings of the Holy City will be in harmony with the plans and purposes of Him whose city it is.

"Break forth into joy, sing together, ye waste places of Jerusalem: for the Lord hath comforted his people, he hath redeemed Jerusalem." (Isa. 52:1, 9.) It is the millennial Old Jerusalem, rebuilt in the cause of righteousness, of which the prophet here speaks. It is the same consoling word that the Lord gave by the mouth of Isaiah in these words: "Comfort ye, comfort ye my people, saith your God. Speak ye comfortably to Jerusalem, and cry unto her, that her warfare is accomplished, that her iniquity is pardoned: for she hath received of the Lord's hand double for all her sins." (Isa. 40:1-2.)

It is Isaiah, speaking of the Second Coming, who says: "And the light of Israel shall be for a fire, and his Holy One for a flame: and it shall burn and devour his thorns and his briers in one day." So it is said of the day of burning when the vineyard is cleansed. "And [the fire] shall consume the glory of his forest, and of his fruitful field, both soul and body," the account continues. "And the rest of the trees of his forest shall be few, that a child may write them." The wickedness of men is so widespread, and their evils are so great, that few—comparatively—shall abide the day. "And it shall come to pass in that day"—the day of burning, the day when every corruptible thing is consumed, the day when few men are left—"that the remnant of Israel, and such as are escaped of the house of Jacob, shall no more again stay upon him that smote them; but shall stay upon the Lord, the Holy One of Israel, in truth.

The remnant shall return, even the remnant of Jacob, unto the mighty God." (Isa. 10:17-21.) They shall be gathered after the coming of the Lord.

We also learn from Isaiah that in the millennial day, when "the whole earth is at rest, and is quiet," then Israel shall "break forth into singing." Why? Because "the Lord will have mercy on Jacob, and will yet choose Israel, and set them in their own land: and the strangers shall be joined with them, and they shall cleave to the house of Jacob." Such spiritual blessings as come to the Gentiles shall be theirs because they cleave unto Israel. "And the people"—the Gentiles—"shall take them, and bring them to their place: and the house of Israel shall possess them"—the Gentiles— "in the land of the Lord for servants and handmaids: and they shall take them captives, whose captives they were; and they shall rule over their oppressors." (Isa. 14:1-7.) Israel shall rule; the Gentiles shall serve; the kingdom is the Lord's. His people are the governing ones—such is the meaning of Isaiah's imagery.

When Israel receives her latter-day glory; when she gains again the kingdom that once was hers; when she attains her ultimate supremacy over all the earth—it will be in response to the divine call: "Arise, shine; for thy light is come, and the glory of the Lord is risen upon thee." Christ has come, and his glory is with Israel. And then shall the ancient promise be fulfilled: "The Gentiles shall come to thy light, and kings to the brightness of thy rising." The Gentiles shall bring their wealth and their power. As the sons of Jacob return to the ancient fold, they shall be helped on their way by the great and the good and the mighty of the earth. "And the sons of strangers shall build up thy walls, and their kings shall minister unto thee," saith the holy word. "For the nation and kingdom that will not serve thee shall perish; yea, those nations shall be utterly wasted. . . . The sons also of them that afflicted thee shall come bending unto thee; and all they that despise thee shall bow themselves down at the soles of thy feet; and they shall call thee, The city of the Lord, The Zion of the Holy One of Israel." (Isa. 60:1-22.) What better words could Isaiah have chosen to bear record of the preeminence and power and rulership of Israel in the day of the Lord Jesus Christ?

316

And yet he has more to say. "They shall build the old wastes, they shall raise up the former desolations, and they shall repair the waste cities, the desolations of many generations," he says. "And the strangers shall stand and feed your flocks, and the sons of the alien shall be your plowmen and your vinedressers. But ye shall be named the Priests of the Lord: men shall call you the Ministers of our God: ye shall eat the riches of the Gentiles, and in their glory shall ye boast yourselves." (Isa. 61:4-6.)

"For, behold, the Lord will come with fire, and with his chariots like a whirlwind, to render his anger with fury, and his rebuke with flames of fire." It is the great and dreadful day of the Lord. "For by fire and by his sword will the Lord plead with all flesh: and the slain of the Lord shall be many." And then what? What comes after his dreadful coming? Why, "I will gather all nations and tongues," he says, "and they shall come, and see my glory." (Isa. 66:15-18.)

Micah prophesies of the Second Coming and describes the millennial era of peace that will then commence. In it, he says, "they shall sit every man under his vine and under his fig tree; and none shall make them afraid: for the mouth of the Lord hath spoken it. For all people will walk every one in the name of his god, and we will walk in the name of the Lord our God for ever and ever." There will be freedom of worship in that day; until all men receive the everlasting gospel, they will continue to worship as they choose. Unbelievers will still need to come to a knowledge of the truth and to gather into the stakes of Zion with the Lord's people. "In that day"—the millennial day—"saith the Lord, will I assemble her that halteth, and I will gather her that is driven out, and her that I have afflicted; And I will make her that halted a remnant, and her that was cast far off a strong nation: and the Lord shall reign over them in mount Zion from henceforth, even for ever." (Micah 4:3-7.)

We need not pursue this course of inquiry further. Isaiah said many other things about it; Jeremiah and Ezekiel and Joel and others of the prophets added their concurring witnesses. We are all under obligation to search the scriptures, to ponder what is found in them, and to gain a correct understanding of all their various parts. It suffices for our present purposes to know that the premillennial gathering of Israel, in which the true believers come to Zion, "one of a city, and two of a family" (Jer. 3:14), shall one day reach such proportions that men will say: "Who hath heard such a thing? who hath seen such things? Shall the earth be made to bring forth in one day? or shall a nation be born at once? for as soon as Zion travailed, she brought forth her children" (Isa. 66:8).

We have before us, then, the doctrine and the witness that the great day of Israel's gathering and glory lies ahead; that the prophetic word can never find complete fulfillment in this wicked world; and that in the better day which lies ahead, all things shall come to pass as the prophets have foretold. In this setting we are now ready to turn our attention to the return of the Ten Tribes and the reign of the Second David.

Chapter 27

THE RESTORATION
OF THE
TEN TRIBES

Why They Shall Come from the North Countries

"We believe in the literal gathering of Israel and in the restoration of the Ten Tribes." (A of F 10.) This inspired language leaves the clear impression that the gathering of Israel is one thing and the restoration of the Ten Tribes is another. Why this distinction? Are not the Ten Tribes a part of Israel? And if Israel is to be gathered, surely in the very nature of things this would include the gathering of the major portion of that ancient and favored people.

An immortal Moses, appearing in resurrected glory on the 3rd day of April, 1836, in the Kirtland Temple, committed unto his mortal fellowservants, Joseph Smith and Oliver Cowdery, "the keys of the gathering of Israel from the four parts of the earth, and the leading of the ten tribes from the land of the north." (D&C 110:11.) Again there is a distinction between Israel as a whole and the Ten Tribes who are the dominant portion of Jacob's seed. All scripture comes by the power of the Holy Ghost and is verily true. When special and unusual language is used, there is a reason. Holy writ is not idle chatter; it is the mind and will of the Lord; it says what he wants said. And so it now behooves us to learn why it is one thing to gather Israel from the four parts of the earth and yet another to lead the Ten Tribes from the land of the north.

We have already seen that all Israel, including specifically and pointedly the Ten Tribes, is scattered in all the nations of the earth, upon all the islands of the sea, and among every people who dwell

319

on this planet. It is absolutely basic and fundamental to know this. We cannot understand the gathering of Israel, we cannot envision what is meant by the restoration of the Ten Tribes, and we cannot properly relate these two things to the Second Coming of our Lord unless we know where Israel and the Ten Tribes now are.

We are also aware that the Ten Tribes were first taken as a body into Assyria; that they went out from Assyria, northward, in a body, under prophetic guidance; and that they were then splintered and driven and scattered into all places and among all peoples. These Ten Tribes, no matter where they are located, are in nations and places known in the days of Isaiah and Jeremiah and the ancient prophets as the north countries. Hence, their return to Palestine at least will be from the land of the north.

The tribe of Ephraim is one of the Ten Tribes; and her people became wanderers in the nations, where they now reside and where they are now being found and gathered, one of a city and two of a family, into the stakes of Zion in those nations. This gathering of Israel is not to an American Zion; it is not to Palestine and the ancient holy land; it is not to any central place or location. Rather, it is to the holy places of safety that are now being set up in all nations as rapidly as our strength and means permit. As we have seen, this gathering of Ephraim falls in the category of the gathering of Israel and not of the leading of the Ten Tribes from the land of the north. This gathering of Ephraim is into the stakes of Zion in all the nations of the earth. There are, of course, isolated and unusual instances of people from the other lost tribes gathering with Ephraim, but these are few and far between. The gathering of these other tribes is not yet, but by and by.

What, then, is meant by the leading of the Ten Tribes from the land of the north? Our answer is: Just what the words say. We are gathering Israel now in all nations and counseling them to stay where they are, there to enlarge the borders of Zion, there to build up stakes of Zion in their own lands and among their own people. But with the Ten Tribes, in part at least, it will be another thing. They are destined to return (at least in large and representative numbers) to the same soil where the feet of their forebears walked during the days of their mortal pilgrimage. They are to return to

Palestine. At least a constituent assembly will congregate there in the very land given of God to Abraham their father. Others will, of course, be in America and in all lands, but the formal return, the return from the north countries, will be to the land of their ancient inheritance.

Why They Shall Return to Palestine

Abraham went into the land of Canaan, where the Lord said unto him: "Unto thy seed will I give this land." (Gen. 12:7.) "For all the land which thou seest, to thee will I give it, and to thy seed for ever. . . . Arise, walk through the land in the length of it and in the breadth of it; for I will give it unto thee." (Gen. 13:15-17.) "Unto thy seed have I given this land, from the river of Egypt unto the great river, the river Euphrates." (Gen. 15:18.) "And I will give unto thee, and to thy seed after thee, the land wherein thou art a stranger, all the land of Canaan, for an everlasting possession; and I will be their God." (Gen. 17:8.) All these promises, made to Abraham, were renewed to Isaac, unto whom the Lord said: "Sojourn in this land, and I will be with thee, and will bless thee; for unto thee, and unto thy seed, I will give all these countries." (Gen. 26:3.) Then to Jacob came the same promise: "The land whereon thou liest, to thee will I give it, and to thy seed." (Gen. 28:13.) "And the land which I gave Abraham and Isaac, to thee I will give it, and to thy seed after thee will I give the land." (Gen. 35:12.) And also: "Behold, I will make thee fruitful, and multiply thee, and I will make of thee a multitude of people; and will give this land to thy seed after thee for an everlasting possession." (Gen. 48:4.)

Paul, pleading before Agrippa, hearkened back to these ancient promises—that Israel, in time and in eternity, as mortal men and as immortal beings, should inherit everlastingly the land of Abraham—and said: "Now I stand and am judged for the hope of the promise made of God unto our fathers: Unto which promise our twelve tribes, instantly serving God day and night, hope to come. For which hope's sake, king Agrippa, I am accused of the Jews." And what was that hope, the hope of the twelve tribes of Israel? It was that even in eternity, as resurrected beings, they

321

should have this blessed soil where once their fathers dwelt. Hence, Paul asked: "Why should it be thought a thing incredible with you, that God should raise the dead?" (Acts 26:6-8.)

It is clear; it is plain; it is certain: God gave ancient Canaan to Abraham, Isaac, and Jacob, and the twelve tribes of Israel, of whom the Ten Tribes are the dominant part. It is their land, in time and in eternity. It is their land now whenever they are worthy to tread its blessed surface. And it shall be theirs again in that everlasting eternity that lies ahead. "It is decreed that the poor and the meek of the earth shall inherit it," in that celestial day when it shall be crowned with the presence of God, even the Father. (D&C 88:17-19.) Where else, then, would we expect to see the Ten Tribes return? Where else would we expect them to assemble to worship the God of their fathers and to be inheritors of the promises made to the ancient ones whose seed they are?

Thus it is that we see why the revelations speak of the gathering of Israel from the four parts of the earth into the Church and kingdom of God on earth, and also of the leading of the Ten Tribes from the land of the north back again to their promised Canaan. The gathering of Israel is one thing, the return of the Ten Tribes to a specified place is another; and Moses gave to men in our day the keys and power to perform both labors. This means that Israel is gathered at the direction and pursuant to the power and authority vested in the legal administrators who preside over The Church of Jesus Christ of Latter-day Saints. And it also means that the Ten Tribes—scattered, lost, unknown, and now in all the nations of the earth—these Ten Tribes, with their prophets, with their scriptures, in faith and desiring righteousness, shall return to blessed Canaan at the direction of these same legal administrators. The President of the Church is the only person on earth at any given time who does or can exercise these or any other priesthood keys in their eternal fulness. He will direct the return of the Ten Tribes. It will not come to pass in any other way.

Before we can envision what is involved in the final gathering of Israel and the return of her King to reign over the house of Jacob and over all men, we must learn (1) where the Ten Tribes now are, and why they are scattered in all nations; (2) the place to which they shall return, and the moving power that will sweep them into old Canaan again; (3) where the keys are vested that will direct such a worldwide movement, and how they came to be held by the President of the Church; and (4) when these lost tribes are appointed to journey back to the land of their fathers, meaning whether it is before or after the coming of Him in whose name they shall then worship the Father. We have set forth the answers to the first three of these matters and shall now turn our attention to the time of the return of the lost tribes of Israel.

The Ten Tribes—Their Millennial Return

We do not say that occasional blood descendants of Reuben or Naphtali or others of the other tribal heads shall not return to their Palestinian Zion, or assemble in an American Zion, or find their way into the stakes of Zion in all nations, all before the Second Coming of Christ. Some shall no doubt return to Canaan as true believers and members of the true Church, with the intent and purpose of fulfilling the scriptures and building up the ancient cities of Israel. This may well happen in some small measure, and to it there can be no objection. Great movements have small beginnings, and floods that sweep forth from bursting dams are first forecast when small rivulets trickle from the pent-up reservoirs. But we do say that the great day of the return of the Ten Tribes, the day when the assembling hosts shall fulfill the prophetic promises, shall come after our Lord's return. In this connection let us turn to the word of scripture.

We have had much to say relative to the teachings of the Risen Lord to the Nephites about the last days. In Third Nephi, chapter 20, he speaks of the millennial gathering of Israel. Then in chapter 21, he tells of the establishment of the United States of America; of the coming forth of the Nephite word in the Book of Mormon; of the restoration of his everlasting gospel; of the triumph of Israel over their Gentile foes when the Millennium is ushered in; and of the end of evil and wickedness in that glorious day of peace and righteousness. Then he speaks of the New Jerusalem in America; of the gathering of people to it before he comes; and of his coming to dwell in the midst of his people. "And then"—after the gathering of Israel to the New Jersualem—"shall the power of heaven come down among them." This refers to the Second Coming. "And I also will be in the midst." He shall reign personally upon the earth. "And then"—after his return and during the Millennium—"shall the work of the Father commence at that day, even when this gospel shall be preached among the remnant of this people." There is to be a millennial gathering of the Lehite people. "Verily I say unto you, at that day"—note it well, the day involved is millennial—"shall the work of the Father commence among all the dispersed of my people, yea, even the tribes which have been lost, which the Father hath led away out of Jerusalem." The Ten Tribes are to return after the Second Coming. Their establishment in their land of promise shall not come to pass until there is a new heaven and a new earth wherein dwelleth righteousness. They were led away in à day of war and wickedness; they shall return in a day of peace and righteousness.

"Yea," and it is in that day that "the work shall commence among all the dispersed of my people, with the Father, to prepare the way whereby they may come unto me, that they may call on the Father in my name." Our present endeavors offer the gospel to all those whom the hunters and fishers can find in the forests and streams of the world. In the coming day the word will go to "all the dispersed," and none shall escape hearing its word of peace and salvation.

"Yea, and then shall the work commence, with the Father, among all nations, in preparing the way whereby his people may be gathered home to the land of their inheritance." This is a specific gathering back to Palestine. "And they shall go out from all nations"—note that his people, including as he said the tribes which have been lost, who are the Ten Tribes, who have been scattered in all nations, shall go out therefrom—"and they shall not go out in haste, nor go by flight, for I will go before them, saith the Father, and I will be their rearward." (3 Ne. 21:1-29.)

Isaiah's Prophecy of Their Millennial Return

We shall now turn to two parallel passages, D&C 133:25-35 and Isaiah 35:1-10, and weave them together into one consecutive account. They both speak of the same events, and each one supplements and enlarges upon the concepts revealed in the other. Their united voice teaches and testifies of what is to be in the coming day when the Ten Tribes of Israel are led back to their ancient homeland.

"And the Lord, even the Savior, shall stand in the midst of his people, and shall reign over all flesh." So proclaims our modern revelation. The setting of what is to follow is thus millennial. Christ is among his people and is King over all the earth. It is the day of the new heaven and the new earth. Thus, of it, Isaiah says: "The wilderness and the solitary place shall be glad for them"— that is, for those who then dwell on earth and who shall possess it from generation to generation—"and the desert shall rejoice, and blossom as the rose. It shall blossom abundantly, and rejoice even with joy and singing: the glory of Lebanon shall be given unto it, the excellency of Carmel and Sharon, they shall see the glory of the Lord, and the excellency of our God." The whole earth shall be as the Garden of Eden, for the earth has been renewed and received its paradisiacal glory. And those who dwell on earth shall see the glory of God, for he shall dwell among them.

In that day, "They who are in the north countries shall come in remembrance before the Lord." The lost tribes of Israel, the Ten Tribes whose members are scattered among the northern nations, shall be remembered. The set time to favor them will have dawned. The work of the Father will then commence among them; converts will be made; they will believe the everlasting gospel taken to them by the elders of Ephraim; and they will be baptized and receive the gift of the Holy Ghost. They will become again the Lord's people. "And their prophets shall hear his voice, and shall no longer stay themselves."

Their prophets! Who are they? Are they to be holy men called from some unknown place and people? Are they prophets unbeknown to the presiding officers of "the only true and living church upon the face of the whole earth"? (D&C 1:30.) Perish the thought! The President of the Church, who holds the keys to lead the Ten Tribes from the nations of the north wherein they now reside, holds also the keys of salvation for all men. There are not two true churches on earth, only one; there are not two gospels or two plans of salvation, only one; there are not two competing organizations, both having divine approval, only one. "Is Christ divided?" (1 Cor. 1:13.) God forbid. Their prophets are members of The Church of Jesus Christ of Latter-day Saints. They are stake presidents and bishops and quorum presidents who are appointed to guide and direct the destinies of their stakes and wards and quorums.

The true Church is or should be made up of prophets without number. "Would God that all the Lord's people were prophets, and that the Lord would put his spirit upon them!" Moses exclaimed to ancient Israel. (Num. 11:29.) "Ye may all prophesy one by one, that all may learn, and all may be comforted," Paul said. Every man should be a prophet for his family and for those over whom he is called to preside in the Church and kingdom of God on earth. But there is to be no diversity of views, no differences of opinion, among the prophets. A prophet is a prophet only because he receives revelation from the Holy Ghost and is in tune with the Spirit of God. Anarchy is foreign to a heaven-sent organization. The Lord's house is a house of order and not a house of confusion. And so "the spirits of the prophets are subject to the prophets." (1 Cor. 14:29-32.)

There is only one presiding prophet on earth at any one time, and he is the President of the Church. All other prophets are subject to him and his direction. There is not now on earth and there shall not be—as long as the earth shall stand or there is one man on the face thereof—a prophet who is not subject to and whose acts are not governed by the presiding prophet. Who, then, shall the prophets be among the Ten Tribes? They shall be the worthy and faithful members of the great latter-day kingdom who serve as all faithful elders now serve. Thus saith the Lord: "It shall not be given to any one to go forth to preach my gospel, or to build up my church, except he be ordained by some one who has authority, and it is known to the church that he has authority and has been regularly ordained by the heads of the church." (D&C 42:11.)

"And they [their prophets] shall smite the rocks, and the ice shall flow down at their presence." Presumably, when our sphere becomes a new earth; when every valley is exalted and every mountain is made low; when the islands become one land, and the great deep is driven back into the north countries—when all these and other changes occur, then there will also be changes in the climate, and the ice masses of the polar areas will no longer be as they now are.

"And an highway shall be cast up in the midst of the great deep." The revelation to Joseph Smith says no more on this point than these words convey. Isaiah gives a somewhat more expansive view in these words: "And an highway shall be there, and a way, and it shall be called The way of holiness; the unclean shall not pass over it; but it shall be for those [who are worthy, and]: the wayfaring men, though fools, shall not err therein. No lion shall be there, nor any ravenous beast shall go up thereon, it shall not be found there; but the redeemed shall walk there." It appears that a way will be provided to assemble the outcasts of Israel again in their promised land. The safe and secure physical arrangements, whatever they may be, will, in fact, be but symbolical of the way of holiness whereon only the righteous can find footing. The way of holiness cannot be other than the strait and narrow path. The wayward tribes, having forsaken the ancient holy way, having been scattered for their wickedness, shall now be gathered because they forsake the world and seek again that whereon the footprints of their fathers are found.

Our revelation says: "Their enemies shall become a prey unto them." Isaiah gives meaning to this assurance by saying: "Strengthen ye the weak hands, and confirm the feeble knees." The people themselves will need the assurance that God is with them and that they will be preserved. "Say to them that are of a fearful heart," the ancient prophet continues, "Be strong, fear not: behold, your God will come with vengeance, even God with a recompence; he will come and save you." Once forsaken, left alone, now they shall be enfolded in the arms of his love. And oh, what blessings await them! "Then the eyes of the blind shall be opened, and the ears of the deaf shall be unstopped. Then shall the lame man leap as an hart, and the tongue of the dumb sing." The miracles of the mortal ministry of the Holy One will be but a type and a shadow of those that shall attend the immortal ministry of the same Holy One.

Isaiah then says: "In the wilderness shall waters break out, and streams in the desert. And the parched ground shall become a pool, and the thirsty land springs of water: in the habitation of dragons, where each lay, shall be grass with reeds and rushes." We do not doubt that this is temporal, for the deserts of this old earth, in its fallen and barren state, shall become the gardens and flowering fields of the new earth in the millennial day. But it is also spiritual, for the latter-day revelation says: "And in the barren deserts there shall come forth pools of living water; and the parched ground shall no longer be a thirsty land." In that day all Israel shall drink from streams of living water, streams that flow direct from the great Fountain Head, streams filled with the words of eternal life of which men may drink and never thirst more.

The climax of Isaiah's prophetic utterances relative to the millennial return of the many tribes of Israel is: "And the ransomed of the Lord shall return, and come to Zion with songs and everlasting joy upon their heads: they shall obtain joy and gladness, and sorrow and sighing shall flee away." The latter-day word tells us: "They shall bring forth their rich treasures unto the children of Ephraim, my servants. And the boundaries of the everlasting hills shall tremble at their presence. And there shall they fall down and be crowned with glory, even in Zion, by the hands of the servants of the Lord, even the children of Ephraim." Thus they will assemble, not alone in their ancient lands—as a representative constituency, at least, must assemble—but in the latter-day Zion where the headquarters of Ephraim is found. And once again we learn that this glorious return is not of a people receiving independent revelation, not of a people with independent prophets, not of a people who are independent of the constituted authorities of the great latter-day kingdom that has already been set up on earth. Ephraim will be their head. They will come to Ephraim, at the direction of Ephraim, and they will receive the blessings of the house of the Lord that are now administered by those of us who are of Ephraim. Indeed, they will come because they believe what is written in the Stick of Ephraim, which is the Book of Mormon.

"And they shall be filled with songs of everlasting joy. Behold, this is the blessing of the everlasting God upon the tribes of Israel, and the richer blessing upon the head of Ephraim and his fellows. And they also of the tribe of Judah, after their pain shall be sanctified in holiness before the Lord, to dwell in his presence day and night, forever and ever." (D&C 133:25-35; Isa. 35:1-10.) Thus the ancient kingdom of Ephraim with its Ten Tribes and the kingdom of Judah with the smaller portion of Israel shall once again become "one nation in the land upon the mountains of Israel; . . . and they shall be no more two nations, neither shall they be divided into two kingdoms any more at all: . . . so shall they be my people, and I will be their God." (Ezek. 37:22-23.)

Chapter 28

JOSEPH SMITH AND THE SECOND COMING

Joseph Smith: The Seer of Latter Days

Think now of the concepts set forth so far in our study of the Second Coming of the Desire of All Nations. Think of that wondrous age of restoration in which the Great God has sent down righteousness from heaven and caused truth to spring out of the earth. Remember that once again God's eternal plan of salvation—it is the fulness of the everlasting gospel—is resident with mortal men. Name over in your mind the holy angels who have come from the courts of glory to give power and authority, priesthood and keys, knowledge and intelligence, to fallen man. Look around you and see the hosts of gathered Israel who have come out of Babylon into the latter-day kingdom of Him whom their fathers served.

Rejoice with the saints in the gifts and signs and miracles that are everywhere to be seen in the households of faith. Savor once again that sweet spirit which overshadowed you when you knelt at a holy altar in a sacred sanctuary built in the mountains of Israel. Weep again as you recall the blood of modern martyrs mingled with that of their ancient fellows to cry against the wicked and ungodly.

And as you ponder these verities and recall these scenes, as your feelings are mellowed and awed by the immensity and glory of it all, ask yourself: Who among men has brought all this to pass? To whom was the gospel restored, and to whom were the keys and powers committed? Where is the one for whom the heavens were rent, and who drank in the revealed word as the scorched earth absorbs the gentle rain? Can all these things take place without a living prophet?

Those with spiritual insight know the answer, an answer that comes to them by revelation from the Holy Spirit of God. The man involved is Joseph Smith. He is the mighty restorer, the head of the dispensation of the fulness of times, the seer of latter days. Truly, as it is written: "Joseph Smith, the Prophet and Seer of the Lord, has done more, save Jesus only, for the salvation of men in this world, than any other man that ever lived in it." (D&C 135:3.)

How and in what way did this modern Moses, this latter-day Abraham, this seer among seers, accomplish such a great work for so many of the sons of men? The mighty mission, given of God to our chief modern prophet, falls into two categories:

1. Joseph Smith was the revealer of the knowledge of Christ and of salvation to men on earth, the revealer who brought the ancient truths back again after a long night of spiritual darkness. Unless and until men know and believe the true religion, they cannot be saved. Truth is the rock foundation upon which all progress and ultimate salvation rest.

2. Joseph Smith was a legal administrator who received power and authority from heavenly visitants, by virtue of which he was authorized to preach the gospel and administer all of its ordinances so they would be binding on earth and sealed everlastingly in the heavens. Like Peter, he held the keys of the kingdom of heaven so that whatsoever he bound on earth would be bound in heaven, and whatsoever he loosed on earth would be loosed in heaven.

Viewed from the eternal perspective, Joseph Smith ranks among the dozen or score of the greatest and mightiest souls so far sent to earth. Christ is first, Adam second, and, in the priestly hierarchy, Noah is third. "Adam is the father of the human family, and presides over the spirits of all men," and Noah "stands next in authority to Adam in the Priesthood." (*Teachings*, p. 157.) We have no way of ranking Enoch and Moses and Abraham and the other dispensation heads; we can only say they all were among the noble and great in the councils of eternity, and that the Lord sent the greatest spirits he had to head his gospel dispensations. All of the other apostles and prophets in any dispensation are but echoes and shadows of the one who ushers in the Lord's work for that day and age. It is no wonder, then, that the saints of latter days have received this command from the Lord with reference to Joseph Smith: "Thou shalt give heed unto all his words and commandments which he shall give unto you as he receiveth them, walking in all holiness before me; For his word ye shall receive, as if from mine own mouth, in all patience and faith." (D&C 21:4-5.)

Every prophecy about any of the great and glorious events destined to take place in the dispensation of the fulness of times is in its nature a prophecy about Joseph Smith. If the gospel is to be restored, there must be a living prophet to receive the old yet new message. If Elijah is to come before the great and dreadful day of the Lord, there must be an appointed person to receive his message. If Israel is to be gathered, according to the ancient word, someone must be empowered to identify the chosen people, to name the places of gathering, and to specify when and under what circumstances the children of the prophets shall assemble.

One of the most expressive and pointed prophetic utterances relative to the one chosen to head the dispensation of the fulness of times comes to us from Joseph who was sold into Egypt. "A seer shall the Lord my God raise up, who shall be a choice seer unto the fruit of my loins," he testified. To Joseph of old, the Lord said: "A choice seer will I raise up out of the fruit of thy loins; and he shall be esteemed highly among the fruit of thy loins. And unto him will I give commandment that he shall do a work for the fruit of thy loins, his brethren, which shall be of great worth unto them, even to the bringing of them to the knowledge of the covenants which I have made with thy fathers." In expounding upon this promise, the son of Jacob said: "His name shall be called after me; and it shall be after the name of his father. And he shall be like unto me; for the thing, which the Lord shall bring forth by his hand, by the power of the Lord shall bring my people unto salvation." (2 Ne. 3:6-15.) Joseph Smith was foreordained in the councils of eternity to come to earth in the last days, to set up again on earth the true Church and the Lord's kingdom, and to prepare a people for the second coming of the Lord.

Joseph Smith: The Revelator Who Brings Salvation

Salvation is in Christ. There is no other by whom it comes. He is the Redeemer of men and the Savior of the world. He alone worked out the infinite and eternal atonement whereby all men are raised in immortality while those who believe and obey are raised also unto eternal life. "Salvation was, and is, and is to come, in and through the atoning blood of Christ, the Lord Omnipotent." None other has ever lived on earth, none other now lives among us, and none other will ever breathe the breath of life who can compare with him. None other, among all the billions of our Father's children, will ever deserve such eternal praise as all the hosts of heaven heap upon him. Yea, "There shall be no other name given nor any other way nor means whereby salvation can come unto the children of men, only in and through the name of Christ, the Lord Omnipotent." (Mosiah 3:17-18.)

But Christ and his laws can be known only by revelation. His gospel must come from heaven or remain forever unknown. And his word must go forth by the mouths of his servants the prophets, or the message will never be heard. Christ calls prophets. They represent him. Their voice is his voice; their words are his words; and they say what he would say if he were personally present. "I am the vine, ye are the branches," he says to his legal representatives on earth. "He that abideth in me, and I in him, the same bringeth forth much fruit: for without me ye can do nothing." (John 15:5.)

And thus, for this dispensation of grace, we come to Joseph Smith. He was called of God to reveal anew the doctrines of salvation. He was called of God to stand as the Lord's legal administrator, dispensing salvation to all men—repeat: *all men*—in the last days. Christ is the True Vine; Joseph Smith is the chief branch for our day. Moroni told him that his "name should be had for good and evil among all nations, kindreds, and tongues, or that it should be both good and evil spoken of among all people." (JS-H 1:33.)

333

And as the Prophet, years later, suffered in the jail at Liberty, Missouri, for the testimony of Jesus and the love of the Lord that was his, the voice of the Lord comforted him with these words: "The ends of the earth shall inquire after thy name, and fools shall have thee in derision, and hell shall rage against thee; While the pure in heart, and the wise, and the noble, and the virtuous, shall seek counsel, and authority, and blessings constantly from under thy hand." (D&C 122:1-2.)

And thus, all men—every living soul who has lived or shall live on earth between the spring of 1820 and that glorious future day when the Son of God shall return to reign personally on earth—all men in the latter days must turn to Joseph Smith to gain salvation. Why? The answer is clear and plain; let it be spoken with seven thunders. He alone can bring them the gospel; he alone can perform for them the ordinances of salvation and exaltation; he stands, as have all the prophets of all the ages in their times and seasons, in the place and stead of the Heavenly One in administering salvation to men on earth.

The Father is the author and originator of the gospel. It is his plan of salvation; he ordained and established its terms and conditions so that his spirit children, Christ included, might advance and progress and become like him. The Son is the Savior and Redeemer who, through his great atoning sacrifice, put all of the provisions of his Father's plan into full operation. It is the atonement of Christ that gives efficacy, virtue, and force to all things in the gospel. They are operative because the Holy Messiah took upon himself the sins of all men on condition of repentance and because he laid down his life to ransom men from eternal death. And it is the Lord's prophets who take the word of salvation to their fellowmen. It was to Joseph Smith that the Lord said: "This generation shall have my word through you." (D&C 5:10.) There is none other who will bring it. Joseph Smith is the man. It is the word of the Lord, but it comes by the mouth of his latter-day prophet.

Every person who is called of God to preach the gospel and build up his kingdom in the latter days is but an echo of Joseph Smith. The latter-day Twelve "are called to go unto all the world" and "to preach my gospel unto every creature," the Lord says.

(D&C 18:28.) What gospel? The everlasting gospel, the same gospel preached by Paul and Peter, the gospel that has been revealed anew to Joseph Smith. And by what power do they preach? By the power of the Holy Ghost and the Holy Priesthood, both of which powers have come to them from the head of our dispensation. Can they bind on earth and seal in heaven as did the ancient apostles? They can! Whence came their power to do so? From Joseph Smith, who received the keys of the kingdom from angelic ministrants. And what of all the elders of Israel and all the ministers of the kingdom? They all preach the same gospel and administer the same ordinances, and are endowed with the same power. To all his servants the Lord says: "You shall"—it is mandatory—"declare the things which have been revealed to my servant, Joseph Smith, Jun." (D&C 31:4.)

We do not pretend to have authority and gospel knowledge because we read in holy writ that those anciently were so endowed. Ours is a modern commission; ours is a present-day power; the message we declare has been revealed anew to us. That it conforms to the ancient word is apparent, for it is the same gospel given again. To all of us the Lord says: "Teach the principles of my gospel, which are in the Bible and the Book of Mormon, in the which is the fulness of the gospel." (D&C 42:12.) We are to "remember the new covenant, even the Book of Mormon." The divine decree to us is: "Remain steadfast in your minds in solemnity and the spirit of prayer, in bearing testimony to all the world of those things which are communicated unto you." (D&C 84:57, 61.) We are to go forth, to proclaim the gospel, and to prune the vineyard; we are not to tarry, but to labor with our might. The Lord tells us to lift up our voices as with the sound of a trump, "proclaiming the truth according to the revelations and commandments" he has given us. (D&C 75:2-4.)

Our message is a living, vibrant, modern message. We speak of the appearance of the Father and the Son to Joseph Smith in our day. We tell of Moroni and the Book of Mormon. We testify that holy angels came from the courts of glory and gave priesthoods and keys to mortals. We bear witness of the truth and divinity of the revelations given to Joseph Smith and his successors. We de-

335

clare the things that have come to us. Of course, we believe what the ancients believed; of course, we enjoy the same gifts of the Spirit that enriched their lives; of course, we have the same hope of eternal life that filled their souls. Their doctrine is our doctrine. The Bible as well as the Book of Mormon is true: both are the mind and will and voice of the Lord; both are accounts of a people who had the fulness of the gospel. But our commission, our authority, our message for mankind has come to us by the opening of the heavens. And Joseph Smith is the mighty prophet through whom it came.

Joseph Smith: The Messenger Before His Face

Our Blessed Lord did not come unannounced when he made flesh his tabernacle and dwelt as a man among men. Neither will he conceal the day of preparation for his resplendent second coming. He will announce his imminent return. Those with ears to hear will know he is soon to come, clothed in glorious immortality, to rule and reign among the sons of men. John the Baptist, of blessed memory, was his forerunner in the meridian of time. Joseph Smith, the prophet and seer of latter days, whose innocent blood was mingled with that of the Blessed Baptist, is his forerunner in the fulness of times.

There are two great prophecies about the messengers who shall prepare the way before the face of the Lord. One is by Isaiah, the other comes from Malachi. Each of them refers both to the meridian and to the millennial advents, but more especially to the latter. By the mouth of Malachi the Lord said: "Behold, I will send my messenger, and he shall prepare the way before me: and the Lord, whom ye seek, shall suddenly come to his temple, even the messenger of the covenant, whom ye delight in: behold, he shall come, saith the Lord of hosts." (Mal. 3:1.) What follows speaks solely and exclusively of the Second Coming and the day of judgment and burning that will accompany it.

Through Isaiah the Lord speaks of comfort to Jerusalem that shall be fulfilled after the Second Coming. In that setting (as the full and amplified account is quoted in Luke) Isaiah's prophetic words say: "The voice of one crying in the wilderness, Prepare ye the way of the Lord, and make his paths straight. For behold, and lo, he shall come, as it is written in the book of the prophets, to take away the sins of the world, and to bring salvation unto the heathen nations, to gather together those who are lost, who are of the sheepfold of Israel; Yea, even the dispersed and afflicted; and also to prepare the way, and make possible the preaching of the gospel unto the Gentiles; And to be a light unto all who sit in darkness, unto the uttermost parts of the earth; to bring to pass the resurrection from the dead, and to ascend up on high, to dwell on the right hand of the Father, Until the fullness of time, and the law and the testimony shall be sealed, and the keys of the kingdom shall be delivered up again unto the Father; To administer justice unto all; to come down in judgment upon all, and to convince all the ungodly of their ungodly deeds, which they have committed; and all this in the day that he shall come; For it is a day of power; yea, every valley shall be filled, and every mountain and hill shall be brought low; the crooked shall be made straight, and the rough ways made smooth; And all flesh shall see the salvation of God." (JST, Luke 3:4-11.) The next words in the Isaiah account add: "And the glory of the Lord shall be revealed, and all flesh shall see it together: for the mouth of the Lord hath spoken it." (Isa. 40:1-5.)

These two prophetic pronouncements are applied to John the Baptist by the New Testament writers, and truly he came to prepare the way for our Lord's mortal ministry. But each of the inspired accounts has an infinitely greater and grander fulfillment in the last days. John came to prepare the way for the atoning ministry, the ministry of reconciliation, as Paul calls it, the ministry that brought life and immortality to light through the gospel. Joseph Smith came to prepare the way for the triumphal coming, the coming in power and glory with all the hosts of heaven, the coming when the vineyard will be burned and the wicked destroyed, the coming when righteousness and peace shall be established among those who abide the day.

How do messengers prepare the way before the Lord? First, they identify Him whose forerunners they are; they testify of his divine Sonship; they introduce him to the world—all with a view to persuading men to come unto him and be saved. Second, and equally important, they prepare a people to receive him. They qualify a people to abide the day of his coming, to see his face when he arrives, to enjoy his presence, and to dwell with him and enjoy the gifts and graces that are his.

And how is a people prepared to meet their God? What must they do to stand in his presence and hear the blessed word: "Well done, thou good and faithful servant; enter into the joy of thy Lord"? To be so blessed, they must receive the message of the messenger. They must believe in that Lord who sent him. They must accept the gospel and live its laws. They must forsake the world, repent of all their sins, be baptized, and receive the gift of the Holy Ghost. They must become pure in heart, for all the pure in heart shall see God. They must (in our day) join The Church of Jesus Christ of Latter-day Saints and become the saints of the Most High.

There are none in our day to whom the Lord has given the power of language to set forth the goodness and grace of Christ, or the beauty and holiness of his everlasting gospel, or the mighty strength and spiritual stature of the latter-day prophet sent to prepare the way before the Lord. Perhaps these things can be known in full only by the power of the Spirit.

But this we know: The Lord sends men to match the message, and Joseph Smith, as a revealer of Christ and a restorer of eternal truth, has been the instrument in the hands of the Lord of preparing the way before him. Thus, from that Lord who shall soon come, we hear this word: "I have sent mine everlasting covenant into the world, to be a light to the world, and to be a standard for my people, and for the Gentiles to seek to it, and to be a messenger before my face to prepare the way before me." (D&C 45:9.)

The everlasting covenant is the latter-day messenger before the Lord. It is the ancient standard raised anew. It is an ensign upon Mount Zion around which the honest in heart from all nations may rally. The everlasting gospel itself is the messenger. And whereas the gospel came through Joseph Smith, he becomes and is the messenger. He it is who raised the Lord's standard; he it is who raised the ensign to the nations; he it is who waved the banner of truth and righteousness in the sight of all men—all as promised in the ancient word.

What says the ancient word on these points? It says that the Great Jehovah will make an everlasting covenant with his people when he comes to reign gloriously among them. "I will make a new covenant with the house of Israel, and with the house of Judah," saith the Lord. It shall be made with both kingdoms, with all Israel, with the Jews and the Ten Tribes. And "this shall be the covenant that I will make," saith the Lord, "I will put my law in their inward parts, and write it in their hearts; and will be their God, and they shall be my people." (Jer. 31:31-33.) "Behold, I will gather them out of all countries, whither I have driven them in mine anger, and in my fury, and in great wrath; and I will bring them again unto this place, and I will cause them to dwell safely: And they shall be my people, and I will be their God: And I will give them one heart, and one way, that they may fear me for ever, for the good of them, and of their children after them: And I will make an everlasting covenant with them." (Jer. 32:37-40.) "I will bring you into the bond of the covenant." (Ezek. 20:37.) The new covenant, the everlasting covenant, the new and everlasting covenant is the fulness of the everlasting gospel. It is to this that the Lord's people will come in the last days.

"My people are gone into captivity, because they have no knowledge," saith the Lord. Yet they shall return. For "he will lift up an ensign to the nations from far, and will hiss unto them from the end of the earth: and, behold, they shall come with speed swiftly." (Isa. 5:13, 26-30.) Israel shall gather again to the gospel covenant. "And in that day there shall be a root of Jesse, which shall stand for an ensign of the people; to it shall the Gentiles seek: and his rest shall be glorious [or, better, glory shall be his resting place]." (Isa. 11:10.) "What is the root of Jesse spoken of in the 10th verse of the 11th chapter? Behold, thus saith the Lord, it is a descendant of Jesse, as well as of Joseph, unto whom rightly belongs the priesthood, and the keys of the kingdom, for an ensign, and for the gathering of my people in the last days."

Are we amiss in saying that the prophet here mentioned is Joseph Smith, to whom the priesthood came, who received the keys of the kingdom, and who raised the ensign for the gathering of the Lord's people in our dispensation? And is he not also the "servant in the hands of Christ, who is partly a descendant of Jesse as well as of Ephraim, or of the house of Joseph, on whom there is laid much power"? (D&C 113:4-6.) Those whose ears are attuned to the whisperings of the Infinite will know the meaning of these things.

Truly, "the Lord shall set his hand again the second time"—he set it the first time when he led Israel out of Egypt, and also when he brought back a few scattered ones from Babylon—"to recover the remnant of his people," who are in all the nations of the earth and upon "the islands of the sea. And he shall set up an ensign for the nations, and shall assemble the outcasts of Israel, and gather together the dispersed of Judah from the four corners of the earth." (Isa. 11:11-12.) Israel (the Ten Tribes) and Judah (the kingdom of Judah, whose descendants are known as Jews) are now in all the earth, but shall soon return to the lands of their inheritance, as we have already set forth.

How glorious it is to know that there shall be a literal gathering of Israel—all Israel—as the Lord has appointed! Can we not feel the exulting joy and sense of triumph in Isaiah's repeated words about that gathering? Is it not satisfying to know that it is going forward and shall continue to go forward by virtue of the keys given by Moses to Joseph Smith? "All ye inhabitants of the world, and dwellers on the earth, see ye, when he lifteth up an ensign on the mountains; and when he bloweth a trumpet, hear ye." (Isa. 18:3.) That ensign now floats in the cooling breezes of a modern Zion, and that trumpet is now sounding forth the gladsome tidings of glory and salvation to all men.

"Thus saith the Lord God, Behold, I will lift up mine hand to the Gentiles, and set up my standard to the people." (Isa. 49:22.) "I will make an everlasting covenant with them." (Isa. 61:8.) And those of us with whom this covenant has been made have this word from the Lord: "Lift up a standard for the people. Behold, the Lord hath proclaimed unto the end of the world, Say ye to the daughter of Zion, Behold, thy salvation cometh; behold, his reward is with him, and his work before him." Christ the Lord cometh. "And they shall call them, The holy people, The redeemed of the Lord: and thou shalt be called, Sought out, A city not forsaken." (Isa. 62:10-12.) "For thus shall my church be called in the last days, even The Church of Jesus Christ of Latter-day Saints. Verily I say unto you all: Arise and shine forth, that thy light may be a standard for the nations; And that the gathering together upon the land of Zion, and upon her stakes, may be for a defense, and for a refuge from the storm, and from wrath when it shall be poured out without mixture upon the whole earth." (D&C 115:4-6.)

Thank God for the gospel. Thank the Lord for Joseph Smith and the great restoration of eternal truth in our day. Jehovah be praised that his messenger has delivered his message.

Chapter 29

THE PARABLES OF THE SECOND COMING

The Three Great Parables of His Coming

Our Blessed Lord, who spake as none other ever has spoken or shall speak, included in his parables numerous allusions to and pronouncements about his Second Coming. Our present purpose is to extract from these gems of literary excellence the teachings they set forth relative to that great and coming day. The parables involved teach many lessons. Our arrangement of the subject matter is simply to help us put in a proper perspective all things concerning the coming of Him whose parables they are. First, then, we shall consider what are probably the three greatest parables pertaining to the Second Coming.

1. *The Parable of the Wheat and the Tares*

The Lord Jesus, and his holy apostles, and the legal administrators whom they call—all these sow good seeds in all the world. The good seeds are the children of the kingdom, the true saints, those who are faithful and true. They are the wheat. This sowing took place first in the meridian of time and then again "in the last days, even now," when "the Lord is beginning to bring forth the word" anew. (D&C 86:4.)

Lucifer and his ministers oversow the field. Their seeds are the children of the wicked one, the children of disobedience, those who live after the manner of the world. They

342

are the tares. And the tares seek to smother the wheat, lest any should ripen and be harvested and find place in the barns of the householder, for the enemy seeks to destroy the souls of men.

He whose vineyard it is decrees that the tares shall not be rooted up lest the wheat also be destroyed. They are to grow together until the day of harvest. Then the reapers shall gather the wheat unto salvation, the tares shall be bound in bundles, and the field shall be burned. (Matt. 13:24-43; D&C 86:1-11.) And even now, for the day of His coming is at hand, "the angels are waiting the great command to reap down the earth, [and] to gather the tares that they may be burned." (D&C 38:12.)

2. *The Parable of the Ten Virgins.*

In the last days, before the Son of Man comes, his church is likened unto ten virgins, all of whom have accepted the gospel invitation to attend the marriage feast of the Lamb. But the bridegroom delays his coming; the hour for the marriage is uncertain; it is late and darkness covers the earth. Surely he will not come at such an unseemly hour.

Five of the virgins are wise and have taken the Holy Spirit for their guide; their lamps are lighted and they await the coming of Him whose feast it is. But five are foolish; they do not put first in their lives the things of their Lord; other interests consume their attention. Their lamps are without oil, for they have not made the Holy Ghost their constant companion.

At midnight the cry goes forth: "Behold, the bridegroom cometh; go ye out to meet him." While the foolish virgins seek to make themselves worthy—for salvation is a personal matter, and no man can claim the good works of another—the wise virgins enter into eternal reward and the door is shut. And so the Lord counsels his people: "Watch therefore, for ye know neither the day nor the hour wherein the Son of man cometh." (Matt. 25:1-13.)

"At that day, when I shall come in my glory," the Lord

343

says, "shall the parable be fulfilled which I spake concerning the ten virgins. For they that are wise and have received the truth, and have taken the Holy Spirit for their guide, and have not been deceived—verily I say unto you, they shall not be hewn down and cast into the fire, but shall abide the day." (D&C 45:56-57.) "And until that hour there will be foolish virgins among the wise; and at that hour cometh an entire separation of the righteous and the wicked." (D&C 63:54.) Therefore, "let the cry go forth among all people: Awake and arise and go forth to meet the Bridegroom; behold and lo, the Bridegroom cometh; go ye out to meet him. Prepare yourselves for the great day of the Lord. Watch, therefore, for ye know neither the day nor the hour." (D&C 133:10-11.)

3. *The Parable of the Fig Tree.*

When men see the tender leaves of the fig tree begin to shoot forth, they know that summer is near. In like manner, when the elect see the signs of the times, they know that the Lord's coming "is near, even at the doors." (Matt. 24:32-33.) We live in the day when the signs are coming to pass. This is the day when "the poor and the meek shall have the gospel preached unto them, and they shall be looking forth for the time of my coming," the Lord says, "for it is nigh at hand—And they shall learn the parable of the fig-tree, for even now already summer is nigh." (D&C 35:15-16.) "And it shall come to pass that he that feareth me shall be looking forth for the great day of the Lord to come, even for the signs of the coming of the Son of Man." (D&C 45:39.)

The Parables of Judgment and Vengeance

The Second Coming is a day of judgment, a day of vengeance, a day of burning. "I will come near to you to judgment," is the Messianic promise. (Mal. 3:5.) In that day the wicked shall be destroyed; the righteous shall find eternal peace; and the Great Judge of all the earth shall measure to every man as his works merit. And so we find

Jesus speaking parables that will cause men to ponder these truths, parables that will encourage them to do good and work righteousness so they will be numbered with the true saints in that dread day.

1. *The Parable of the Gospel Net.*

The Church and kingdom of God on earth, which both preaches and administers the holy gospel, is like a great draw net or seine that sweeps through large areas of the sea. Fish of every kind are caught. The good are gathered into vessels and the bad are cast away. And thus it shall be when the Lord Jesus returns in glory to judge and rule. The wicked—though caught in the gospel net, though in the Church, though gathered with the Israel of God—shall be severed from among the just and shall be cast "into the furnace of fire." (Matt. 13:47-53.) Church membership alone is no guarantee of salvation. Only the God-fearing and the righteous shall sit down in the kingdom of God with Abraham, Isaac, and Jacob, and all the holy prophets.

2. *The Parable of the Wicked Husbandmen.*

The Divine Householder plants his earthly vineyard and lets it out to husbandmen. In due season he sends his servants to receive the fruits. They are rejected, beaten, stoned, and slain. Last of all he sends his Son, whom the wicked husbandmen slay—all of which brings forth the promise that the wicked husbandmen will be destroyed and the vineyard let out to other husbandmen who will bring forth fruits in due season. At this point Jesus said: "Did ye never read in the scriptures, The stone which the builders rejected, the same is become the head of the corner: this is the Lord's doing, and it is marvellous in our eyes? . . . And whosoever shall fall on this stone shall be broken: but on whomsoever it shall fall, it will grind him to powder." (Matt. 21:33-46.)

To his disciples, by way of interpretation, Jesus said: "I am the stone, and those wicked ones reject me, and shall be broken. And the kingdom of God shall be taken from them, and shall be given to a nation bringing forth the fruits thereof; (meaning the Gentiles.) Wherefore, on whomsoever this stone shall fall, it shall grind him to powder. And when the Lord therefore of the vineyard cometh, he will destroy those miserable, wicked men, and will let again his vineyard unto other husbandmen, even in the last days, who shall render him the fruits in their seasons. And then understood they the parable which he spake unto them, that the Gentiles should be destroyed also, when the Lord should descend out of heaven to reign in his vineyard, which is the earth and the inhabitants thereof." (JST, Matt. 21:51-56.)

3. *The Parable of the Great Supper.*

According to Jewish tradition, the resurrection of the just, and the subsequent setting up of the kingdom of God, was to be ushered in by a great festival in which all of the chosen people would participate. Hence their saying: "Blessed is he that shall eat bread in the kingdom of God." As a response to this very statement, Jesus tells of a certain man who gives a great supper. The guests who are bidden excuse themselves for frivolous and foolish reasons. Thereupon the master of the house, being angry, turns away from the covenant people, to whom he first offered the good things of his gospel table. Now he invites the Gentiles, in their spiritually halt and lame and blind status, as well as the pagans and foreigners who live at a great distance—he invites all these to come and eat at his table. (Luke 14:12-24.)

And thus it is reaffirmed that the blessings of the gospel profit only those who feast upon the eternal word, and that the alien and the foreigner who feast on the good work of God shall be blessed when the Supper of the Great God is prepared to usher in his millennial reign. It is of that feast of good things that the elders of Israel are now inviting all men to partake.

4. *The Parable of the Marriage of the King's Son.*

A certain king (who is God) prepares a marriage for his son (who is Christ), Jesus says, thus confirming the Jewish

346

tradition that the Messianic kingdom will be ushered in by a great feast in which God and his people will be united, symbolically, in marriage. The wedding is ready, but the invited guests do not come. They make light of the invitation and even slay the servants who bring them the word. Hence, other people (the Gentiles) are invited and the feast goes forward. But when one comes without a wedding garment (the robes of righteousness), the king says: "Bind him hand and foot, and take him away, and cast him into outer darkness; there shall be weeping and gnashing of teeth." (Matt. 22:1-14.)

And so it is, as the millennial day approaches, that the servants of the Lord go forth, inviting all men, Jew and Gentile alike, to come to "the supper of the Lamb," to "make ready for the Bridegroom," to come to "a feast of fat things," and "of wine on the lees well refined," to come to "a supper of the house of the Lord, well prepared, unto which all nations shall be invited." (D&C 58:6-11; 65:3.) And it shall yet come to pass that those who accept the invitation and come to the feast, but who do not wear the approved wedding garments and are not clothed in the robes of righteousness, shall be cast into outer darkness. In that day only the pure and the clean shall feast at the eternal table.

5. *The Parable of the Unjust Judge.*

A certain widow whose cause is just importunes for redress before an unjust judge. He cares nothing for right and justice but grants her petition lest she weary him with her continuing pleas. Thus Jesus teaches that "men ought always to pray, and not to faint. . . . And shall not God avenge his own elect, which cry day and night unto him, though he bear long with them? I tell you that he will come, and when he does come, he will avenge his saints speedily." (Luke 18:1-8; JST, Luke 18:8.)

However the saints are treated in this life, whatever burdens are strapped to their aching backs, whatever wrongs are inflicted upon them by evil men—all will be made right in the coming day of judgment. Let them importune for redress of grievances, here and now. If their pleas go unheeded by unjust men, yet the Great Judge shall render a right decision in his own due time.

It was this very parable that that Judge used to teach his Latter-day Saints to importune at the feet of judges, governors, and presidents for the righting of many wrongs. If these pleas went unheeded—and they did—he promised to "arise and come forth out of his hiding place, and in his fury vex the nation"—which he did, in part at least, in the Civil War—"And in his hot displeasure, and in his fierce anger, in his time, [he] will cut off those wicked, unfaithful, and unjust stewards, and appoint them their portion among hypocrites, and unbelievers; Even in outer darkness, where there is weeping, and wailing, and gnashing of teeth." (D&C 101:81-92.) What an awful burden rests upon governmental officers to enact, administer, and interpret laws—all in harmony with the mind and will of the Eternal Judge.

The Parables of Ministerial Service

If those who bear rule in earthly governments shall give account of their man-delegated stewardships before the Eternal Bar, how much more so shall it be with those stewards who bear rule in the earthly kingdom of him who is Eternal. Shall they not give an account before the Eternal One relative to their heaven-delegated stewardships? Three of the parables bear a solemn witness in this respect.

1. *The Parable of the Laborers in the Vineyard.*

Laborers are called to serve in the vineyards of the Lord—some as the sun rises, others as late as the eleventh hour, when there remains but little daylight. Their promised pay is a penny for the day, and yet each is paid the same. Those who bear the heat and burden of the day receive no more than the new converts who come into the kingdom during their latter years. (Matt. 20:1-16.)

There is no mercenary calculation of payment scales in

the celestial realms. The venerable apostle and the lowly elder each receives all that the Father hath if he magnifies his calling in the Holy Order. The seed of Cain, from whom the blessings of the priesthood and the fulness of the ordinances of the house of the Lord have been withheld for nearly six thousand years, shall now, in the eleventh hour, be paid their penny and enter into the fulness of reward hereafter. In the providences of the Lord, none of his ministers shall receive less than is promised, and none need feel that others of seemingly lesser service have been overpaid. There is no jealousy among those who abide the day of his coming and who sit down with him in his kingdom. "And he makes them equal in power, and in might, and in dominion." (D&C 76:95.)

2. *The Parable of the Pounds.*

A certain nobleman (Christ) goes into a far country (his heavenly home) to receive for himself a kingdom (all power in heaven and on earth) and then to return (the second coming of the Son of Man). He leaves his servants (the apostles and others) to care for his affairs. To each of his ministers he gives a pound to use in his work. His citizens (the wicked and rebellious in general) hate him and send a message after him, saying, "We will not have this man to reign over us."

He returns; he calls his servants; he asks for an accounting. Those in whose hands his affairs were left make their reports. One has multiplied his pound into ten, another into five, and they are commended and given rule over ten and five cities respectively. Another returns only the pound he received. He made no profit; he saved no souls during his ministry. "I feared thee," he said, "because thou art an austere man: thou takest up that thou layedst not down, and reapest that thou didst not sow."

The nobleman sits in judgment upon his slothful servant, classifies him with the wicked, takes from him the original pound, and gives it to the one with ten pounds. The Lord's ministers are all endowed with the same blessings;

all have the gift of the Holy Ghost; all hold the Holy Melchizedek Priesthood; all are promised an inheritance of eternal life; all are to search the same scriptures and learn the same doctrines of salvation; all must live the same laws to be saved; all are commanded to bring souls to Christ. Those who do nothing damn themselves and lose their own salvation.

And what of those who sent a message deriding the claims of the Nobleman? "Those mine enemies, which would not that I should reign over them," he now decrees—it is the Second Coming, when the wicked shall be destroyed—"bring [them] hither, and slay them before me." (Luke 19:11-28.)

3. *The Parable of the Talents.*

Again, as the parabolic account recites, the Lord Jesus is going to travel to his heavenly home; this time the ministers who are left to govern his affairs are endowed with various talents, every man according to his several abilities, and after a long time the Lord is to return and have a reckoning with his servants. No two men are of like talent and ability; none are equal; all have a variety of capacities and aptitudes. And each is appointed to use all his powers in the service of the Master. Each is called to serve him with all his heart, might, mind, and strength. Nothing less will do. The gifts came from God, and they are to be used in his service.

When the Lord returns—it is his Second Coming— each servant who had many talents and who doubled them receives the blessed benediction: "Well done, thou good and faithful servant: thou hast been faithful over a few things, I will make thee ruler over many things: enter thou into the joy of thy lord." But the servant with little ability, who feared the Lord and hid his talent, is adjudged as wicked and slothful. His talent is taken from him and given to one with ten talents, and the Lord decrees: "Cast ye the unprofitable servant into outer darkness: there shall be weeping and gnashing of teeth." (Matt. 25:14-30.) Those who do not use their talents to save souls are damned.

The Parables of Hope

The Second Coming shall be a day of peace and joy and reward for the righteous. They look forward in hope to the day of their Lord's return. No greater joy can come to them than to see his face, dwell in his presence, and be as he is.

1. *The Eagles of Israel Assemble.*

Unto what shall the Lord liken the gathering of Israel in the last days? What figure shall he use to remind all men how and why and under what circumstances the lost and scattered ones will come to their appointed places?

He is seated with the Twelve on Olivet, unfolding before them the mysteries of the kingdom, the hidden things pertaining to his second coming and the triumph of his chosen Israel. "And now I show unto you a parable," he says. "Behold, wheresoever the carcass is, there will the eagles be gathered together; so likewise shall mine elect be gathered from the four quarters of the earth." (JS-M 1:27.)

The soaring, free eagles, the mightiest of the birds of the air, whose choice of domain knows no bounds, these free-spirited ones choose to come to the carcass. Such is our Lord's illustration, chosen with divine insight. It compares in graphic imagery with his sweet words about the lilies of the valley that neither toil nor spin, and yet are more grandly arrayed than even Solomon in all his glory, thus showing the living care of a gracious God over all created things. It is like his saying that the foxes have holes and the birds of the air have nests, but the Son of Man hath not where to lay his head, thus testifying that he had forsaken all worldly things that he might be about his Father's business. It is akin to his likening the full and white heads of barley, crying out for the reaper, to the souls of men, souls also ready to be harvested.

How often the Twelve, and all whose lives have been

blessed with the joys of a pastoral people, had seen the eagles assemble from all directions and descend from their aerial heights to satisfy their pangs of hunger by ripping the flesh from a sheep or a goat that was slain. In our American deserts we see the great vultures of the air seeking food for themselves and their young from the carcasses of animals that have died. In their hunger they fly in great soaring circles around dying and decrepit earthbound forms of life, awaiting the moment when the morsels of flesh shall be theirs.

And so we see the eagles of Israel scattered by the four winds from one end of heaven to the other. We see them flying in the skies of all nations in search of spiritual food, waiting for a day when life-assuring morsels will come into view. They are free, independent thinkers, anxious to escape the darkness of the night and to soar into the dawn of a new day. The creeds of men do not feed their souls. They are not at rest in the lands of their scattering. They yearn for that which their fathers enjoyed in the days of their ancient glory.

Then the food that will feed their souls is made available. The gospel is restored; the Book of Mormon comes forth; the gifts and graces enjoyed by the ancients are again found on earth. It is time for Israel to come home. The eagles are invited to feast upon the good word of God. They seek the food that satisfies the soul. They descend from their lofty heights of worldliness and feast upon those things of which men may eat and never hunger more. The gospel gathers Israel, and where it is, there the eagles of Israel shall be found.

2. *The Parable of Our Lord's Dwelling with His People.*

With reference to the various kingdoms of his creating, to the planets and worlds that roll in their orbits, inhabited as they are with the children of the Father, the Lord in our day has given us this parable:

"Behold, I will liken these kingdoms unto a man having

a field, and he sent forth his servants into the field to dig in the field." Thus they went forth to labor in all the kingdoms he had created, some on this earth, others on another. But none of his servants were to be forgotten, none were to be left alone without his guidance and direction. "And he said unto the first: Go ye and labor in the field, and in the first hour I will come unto you, and ye shall behold the joy of my countenance. And he said unto the second: Go ye also into the field, and in the second hour I will visit you with the joy of my countenance. And also unto the third, saying: I will visit you; And unto the fourth, and so on unto the twelfth." There is order and system in all the Lord's doings. He visits in one part of his fields today and in another part tomorrow. All shall see his countenance in due course.

"And the lord of the field went unto the first in the first hour, and tarried with him all that hour, and he was made glad with the light of the countenance of his lord. And then he withdrew from the first that he might visit the second also, and the third, and the fourth, and so on unto the twelfth." Such is the course he is now pursuing with our millennial visitation almost at hand.

"And thus they all received the light of the countenance of their lord, every man in his hour, and in his time, and in his season—Beginning at the first, and so on unto the last, and from the last unto the first, and from the first unto the last; Every man in his own order, until his hour was finished, even according as his lord had commanded him, that his lord might be glorified in him, and he in his lord, that they all might be glorified." Those who dwell with their lord in the day he visits in their field shall be glorified. They are the meek who shall inherit the earth; they are the God-fearing and the righteous. And they in turn glorify their Lord, for they bring forth much fruit unto him.

"Therefore, unto this parable I will liken all these kingdoms," he says, "and the inhabitants thereof—every kingdom in its hour, and in its time, and in its season, even according to the decree which God hath made."

What, then, is the application of the parable? "I leave these sayings with you to ponder in your hearts," he says, "with this commandment which I give unto you, that ye shall call upon me while I am near." (D&C 88:51-62.) Truly, the time draws near and the day will soon arrive when he will visit us in our field, and if we are to find joy in his presence and glory in the light of his countenance, we must make ourselves worthy.

Chapter 30

THE SIMILITUDES OF THE SECOND COMING

The Earth and Its Five Transformations

From the day of its temporal creation to the day when it becomes a celestial sphere, planet earth has passed or will pass through five transformations. Each of these is or will be of such a magnitude as to change the whole course of the lives of all or of major portions of the inhabitants of the earth. As the future home of mortal man, this earth was created first spiritually and then temporally. In the pristine day, before the fall, before death entered the scheme of things, the earth was in a paradisiacal or Edenic state. It was then a glorious garden and a fit abode for Adam and Eve, whose bodies of flesh and bones had been made from the dust of the earth, even as ours have been.

In order for our first parents—the first man and the first woman—to have children, however, a change had to be made in their bodies. It was decreed that they fall from their then deathless state to a state of mortality; death itself must enter the world. Procreation must needs commence among all created things, and procreation, in the sense of mortal offspring who are born and die, requires mortal bodies. The life of the body is in the blood, and blood must begin to flow in the veins of man and beast.

Being thus reminded of the nature of this earth when it was first brought into temporal existence, and being thus

355

reminded of the immortal existence that then prevailed among all the creations of our gracious God, we are in a position to list the five transformations that have since befallen the earth. We are ready to be made aware of the effect each one has had or will have upon man and all forms of life.

1. This earth was created in a terrestrial state, an Edenic state, a paradisiacal state. It was pronounced very good by its Creator. All of the land masses were in one place and the waters in another. There was no death or sorrow or disease. Then came the fall of Adam, which brought temporal and spiritual death into the world. And the effects of the fall passed upon the earth and all forms of life on its surface. It became a telestial or fallen orb as at present, a world in which death and disease, sorrow and suffering, and all of the ills of the flesh are everywhere to be found. Adam and Eve, earth's sole human inhabitants, became mortal so they could begin the process of providing bodies for the spirit children of the Eternal Father.

2. In the days of Noah came the flood, a universal flood, a flood that immersed the earth and destroyed men and beasts. We suppose that at this time the continents and islands were divided, with the division becoming complete in the days of Peleg.

3. At the time of the crucifixion there was a great earthquake. In the Americas this was of such immeasurable proportions that the whole surface of the continents was changed. Mountain ranges arose, valleys disappeared, cities sank into the sea, and almost a whole civilization was destroyed.

4. When the Millennium is ushered in, there will be a new heaven and a new earth. It will be renewed and will receive again its paradisiacal glory. The islands and continents will come together again, and there will be one land mass, as it was in the days before it was divided. It will become again a terrestrial sphere. As it was baptized in water in the days of Noah, so it shall be baptized by fire in

the day of the Lord Jesus Christ. The entire vineyard will be burned and the wicked will be as stubble.

5. Finally, when all things relative to the salvation of men are completed, it will become a celestial sphere, to be inhabited by saved beings to all eternity.

We are approaching the day of burning when the promised new heaven and new earth will be created. And as we shall now see, the transformation in the days of Noah, and all that attended it, is a similitude and type of that which is to be in the day of burning that is soon to be.

Noah and the Second Coming

"The Son of Man shall come," Jesus said. "But of that day, and hour, no one knoweth; no, not the angels of God in heaven, but my Father only." Then he gave one of the great signs whereby the general time of his return might be known. "But as it was in the days of Noah, so it shall be also at the coming of the Son of Man," he continued, "For it shall be with them, as it was in the days which were before the flood; for until the day that Noah entered into the ark they were eating and drinking, marrying and giving in marriage; and knew not until the flood came, and took them all away; so shall also the coming of the Son of Man be." (JS-M 1:37-43.)

This similitude lets us know that the normal activities of life will continue unabated until the day of cleansing comes, and also that these ordinary activities will be as evil and wicked as they were in that day when men were drowned by the flood lest their evil deeds further offend their Maker.

Wickedness and evil commenced in the days of Adam; it spread and increased until, by the time of the flood, it covered the earth and contaminated every living soul save Noah and his family. When Adam preached the gospel to his seed, Satan came among them and taught false doctrines, "and they loved Satan more than God. And men began from that time forth to be carnal, sensual, and devilish." (Moses 5:13.) As it was then, so it is today. Satan

357

rages in the hearts of men, and wickedness and carnality are almost the norm of life.

As the number of men increased, their evil deeds grew in magnitude. In the days of Seth, "the children of men were numerous upon all the face of the land. And in those days Satan had great dominion among men, and raged in their hearts; and from thenceforth came wars and bloodshed; and a man's hand was against his own brother, in administering death, because of secret works, seeking for power." (Moses 6:15.) And so it is today. The power of Satan is everywhere. "Signs and lying wonders" are poured forth on every hand. (2 Thes. 2:9-12.) Men give heed "to seducing spirits, and doctrines of devils." They speak "lies in hypocrisy; having their conscience seared with a hot iron." (1 Tim. 4:1-2.) War and bloodshed are now a way of life. We expect them; they are the norm.

In the day of these evils, Enoch was sent forth to cry repentance, even as the Lord's servants go forth today. "I am angry with this people," the Lord said, "and my fierce anger is kindled against them; for their hearts have waxed hard, and their ears are dull of hearing, and their eyes cannot see afar off." How like this is the generality of mankind today. "And for these many generations, ever since the day that I created them, have they gone astray, and have denied me, and have sought their own counsels in the dark; and in their own abominations have they devised murder, and have not kept the commandments, which I gave unto their father, Adam." And as Enoch cried repentance and said, "Choose ye this day, to serve the Lord God who made you" (Moses 6:27-33), so we go forth crying, "Repent ye, for the great day of the Lord is come" (D&C 43:22).

And so wickedness spread and iniquity prevailed until the Lord said to Enoch, "They are without affection, and they hate their own blood." And also: "There has not been so great wickedness as among thy brethren," no, not in all the worlds of the Lord's creating. Therefore, saith the Lord, "will I send in the floods upon them, for my fierce anger is kindled against them. . . . Satan shall be their father, and misery shall be their doom; and the whole heavens shall weep over them."

As Enoch felt the weight and the terror of all this evil, he pled for the seed of Noah. "I ask thee, O Lord, in the name of thine Only Begotten, even Jesus Christ," he prayed, "that thou wilt have mercy upon Noah and his seed, that the earth might never more be covered by the floods." Then the Lord covenanted with Enoch that he would stay the floods, and that a remnant of Noah's seed "should always be found among all nations, while the earth should stand."

With continuing pleas, Enoch asked: "When shall the earth rest? . . . Wilt thou not come again [a second time] upon the earth?" The divine reply: "As I live, even so will I come in the last days, in the days of wickedness and vengeance, to fulfill the oath which I have made unto you concerning the children of Noah; And the day shall come that the earth shall rest." (Moses 7:33-61.)

From Adam to Noah, like rolling crashes of thunder, each louder than the one before, evil and carnality and wickedness increased until "every man was lifted up in the imagination of the thoughts of his heart, being only evil continually." In that day, "The earth was corrupt before God, and it was filled with violence. And God looked upon the earth, and, behold, it was corrupt, for all flesh had corrupted its way upon the earth. And God said unto Noah: The end of all flesh is come before me, for the earth is filled with violence, and behold I will destroy all flesh from off the earth." (Moses 8:22-30.)

In like manner, from the days of martyrdom and death when Rome slew the saints and sent the faithful followers of the lowly Nazarene into the gladiatorial arenas, from then until now, and from now until Armageddon, the roaring thunders of evil and the piercing lightnings of iniquity have been and are and will increase. In consequence, at the appointed time the Lord will burn the wicked with unquenchable fire. It will be a day of burning and desolation and death. As the earth was cleansed once by water, so it shall be cleansed a second time by fire.

What was it in Noah's day that caused such an outpouring of evil to cover the earth? Note it and note it well: it was their marriage discipline, their disregard of proper family relations, their gluttony and their drunkenness—all of which led to wars and carnality and corruption. When Noah cried repentance to the people, they said: "Behold, we are the sons of God"—they claimed for themselves the blessings of true religion, though they lived after the manner of the world—"have we not taken unto ourselves the daughters of men?" Men were marrying out of the Church because they preferred a lewd and lascivious way of life rather than the one decreed in proper matrimony. "And are we not eating and drinking, and marrying and giving in marriage?" Theirs was a life of gluttony and drunkenness. "And our wives bear unto us children, and the same are mighty men, which are like unto men of old, men of great renown." (Moses 8:21.)

Is it any different today? Never in the entire history of the world has there ever been such an assault on the family unit as there is now. In some nations women work and the state rears their children. Under the cloak of supposed equal rights, college dormitories and athletic shower rooms are opened to male and female students alike. Women are handed rifles and taught the ways of war, and they are employed alongside men in drudgery and labor that destroys feminine sensitivities. Male homosexuals marry each other. Millions of couples live together in sin. Death-dealing abortions have legal approval. Courses given in public schools encourage and approve immoral practices. Prostitution is legal in some jurisdictions. All this and all else prevailing in our social structure make us wonder how much worse things must become before the burning fires of destruction shall cover the earth.

Truly, "by the word of God," the earth in Noah's day was "overflowed with water," and its inhabitants "perished." And so, "the heavens and the earth, which are now, by the same word are kept in store, reserved unto fire against the day of judgment and perdition of ungodly men." (2 Pet. 3:5-7.) So says the holy word, and so shall it be.

Shadows, Similitudes, and Types of His Coming

Israel's prophets used the current events with which the people were familiar to teach great truths relative to the Second Coming. Their wars and calamities were pointed to as types and shadows of what would be in that great day. The brutality and bloodshed and carnage that wrought havoc in Israel became a similitude of the greater warfare and destructions destined to overrun the earth in the last days. To the extent that we have prophetic insight as to what will transpire when our Lord returns, we can do the same thing with reference to the wars and plagues of our day. Such similitudes as the following are worthy of note:

1. *The Destruction of Sodom and Gomorrah.*

It was Jesus himself, after using the similitude about Noah and the Second Coming, who said: "Likewise also as it was in the days of Lot; they did eat, they drank, they bought, they sold, they planted, they builded; But the same day that Lot went out of Sodom it rained fire and brimstone from heaven, and destroyed them all. Even thus shall it be in the day when the Son of man is revealed. . . . Remember Lot's wife." (Luke 17:28-32.)

In Sodom and Gomorrah there was such lewdness and immorality and perversion and wickedness and evil as is seldom found on earth. All the people were as those who lived in the days of Noah, and all deserved the same fate. When Lot and his loved ones left Sodom, all who remained were carnal, sensual, and devilish; all were ripened in iniquity; all were ready for the burning. Among them there was not the slightest intimation of the destructions that lay ahead. As they continued the normal activities of life reveling in their evil ways, of a sudden, coming as it were from the midst of eternity, fire and brimstone destroyed them and their cities. As for Lot's wife, she looked back; that is, she turned again to the things of the world, and she too was destroyed with the wicked. So also shall it be at the end of the world.

Even now the generality of men love Satan more than God; even now sodomic practices—immorality, homosexuality, and all manner of perversions—are found among great segments of our society; even now the righteous are leaving the world and finding place in the stakes of Zion. And as the residue of men go forward in their normal activities, reveling in their wickedness as did they of old, the day of burning, coming, as it were, from the midst of eternity, shall come upon them. And should any of the saints look back as did Lot's wife, they will be burned with the wicked.

2. *Assyria, the Enemy of Israel.*

What better similitude could Isaiah choose, to show the destructions incident to the last days, than to point to the warlike ways of the neighboring kingdom of Assyria? Assyria was the great world power that invaded the land of Israel and carried the Ten Tribes into captivity and bondage. The slaughter and sorrow, the death and destruction, and the evil religious influences of the Assyrian invasion can scarcely be overstated. When a whole nation is transported to another area of the earth, it is, for them, a day of gloominess and dark despair. When the invasion is, in fact, a holy war against Jehovah and his people; when it is directed by an Assyrian king who acts as regent on earth for the national god Ashur; when the false religion of the pagans overthrows the true kingdom of Jehovah—when these things happen, surely the Lord must come out of his hiding place and fight the battles of his people. And such is the message Isaiah delivers.

Though earth and hell combine to fight against the true believers who have the true gospel; though there is apostasy and darkness and the saints are carried away to a spiritual Assyria; though the cause of Satan triumphs for a season—surely the Lord will come again in the last days to save his people and destroy their enemies. Such is the similitude with which we are dealing.

"And what will ye do in the day of visitation, and in the desolation which shall come from far?" Isaiah asks. "To whom will ye flee for help? and where will ye leave your glory?" In answer the Lord promises to punish Assyria, even as he will punish the wicked enemies of his people in the last days. As the Assyrians conquer nations and kingdoms, with power and might, so that none stand against them, even so shall the Lord send destruction and burning at his coming. "Therefore shall the Lord, the Lord of hosts . . . kindle a burning like the burning of a fire. And the light of Israel shall be for a fire, and his Holy One for a flame: and it shall burn and devour his thorns and his briers in one day." The vineyard shall be burned at his coming, and the latter-day "Assyrian," the one who opposes his people in that great day, shall be burned as are thorns and briers. "And the rest of the trees of his forest shall be few, that a child may write them." (Isa. 10:3-19.) Comparatively few will remain on earth to enjoy the millennial bliss.

3. *Moab: A Type of All Nations.*

When the Lord comes, he will make a full end of all nations; none shall abide the day; all shall be destroyed. There will be no law but his law when he comes. Isaiah's prophecy about the destruction of Moab in the last days taught this to ancient Israel.

In the midst of a prophetic account as to what would happen to Moab, Isaiah uttered these Messianic words: "And in mercy shall the throne be established: and he shall sit upon it in truth in the tabernacle of David, judging, and seeking judgment, and hasting righteousness.'' (Isa. 16:5.) Later, in the midst of a glorious Messianic sermon about the resurrection and the Second Coming, Isaiah said: "And it shall be said in that day, Lo, this is our God; we have waited for him, and he will save us: this is the Lord; we have waited for him, we will be glad and rejoice in his salvation.'' Christ shall save his people when he comes again. At this point the scripture says: "For in this mountain shall the hand of the Lord rest, and Moab shall be trodden down under him, even as straw is trodden down for the dunghill.'' (Isa. 25:9-10.) And as with Moab, so with all nations in the great and coming day.

4. *Egypt: First Smitten, Then Healed.*

In the last days all nations shall be smitten and destroyed and the wicked among them shall be burned. But what of those who remain? They shall turn unto the Lord and be saved with his people Israel. Isaiah made Egypt the illustration of this concept.

After setting forth the woes that would come upon Egypt, Isaiah then promised: "They shall cry unto the Lord because of the oppressors, and he shall send them a saviour, and a great one, and he shall deliver them.'' Is there deliverance for any people except in and through the Savior of mankind? Are any ever freed from oppression in the full sense until they cleave unto the Lord of hosts? Next Isaiah says: "And the Lord shall be known to Egypt, and the Egyptians shall know the Lord in that day.'' Such has never yet been the case in Egypt, but it shall soon be. They, along with all nations, shall be opened to the preaching of the gospel, and a foothold will be gained. Then cometh the end, and then shall those who remain rally to the standard set up before them. "And the Lord shall smite Egypt: he shall smite and heal it: and they shall return even to the Lord, and he shall be intreated of them, and shall heal them.'' Egypt shall have the blessings of the gospel.

And as with Egypt, so with all nations. A residue shall turn unto the Lord and be blessed of him. Then shall be

fulfilled that which is written: "Blessed be Egypt my
people," saith the Lord, "and Assyria the work of my
hands, and Israel mine inheritance." (Isa. 19:20-25.)

5. *Modern Similitudes of His Coming.*

Those who know what lies ahead, and who have
prophetic insight as to the future, find it easy to devise
similitudes that are as plain and graphic as those used by
Isaiah or any of the prophets. They can compare the desolations poured out upon Jerusalem in A.D. 70 with those
that will fall upon all men in the last days. They can compare the destructions of the Jaredite and Nephite peoples
with the destructions that shall befall the wicked in all
nations at that great and dreadful day. They can look to the
bloodshed and horrors of two world wars and see in them a
type and a shadow of what shall be as the Armageddon of
the future rears its ugly head of horror before us. They can
speak of atomic holocausts and of hydrogen bombs that
will desolate whole nations and peoples. All these things
are but types of what is yet to be.

Out of this horrible picture there is only one ray of
hope. Those who believe and obey, whether in life or in
death, shall have eternal life. The God-fearing and the
righteous who remain, together with those who rise from
their graves to meet our Lord at his coming, shall have joy
everlasting with him in his kingdom. However awesome is
the future, the promised reward is worth the price, and the
promised glory will swallow up all sorrows. It is the Lord's
work, and he will bring it off triumphant.

Chapter 31

THE WORLD OF WICKEDNESS IN THE LAST DAYS

Satan Reigns on Earth

These are the days of evil and abominations destined to precede the coming of the Holy One. We have no words at our command, nor do we have the ability to coin phrases descriptive of the wickedness of the modern world, nor would we use such words or coin such phrases if it lay in our power to do so. We do not desire to dwell on devilish and degenerate conduct. Of these our days, Jesus said simply: "And in that day shall be heard of wars and rumors of wars, and the whole earth shall be in commotion, and men's hearts shall fail them, and they shall say that Christ delayeth his coming until the end of the earth. And the love of men shall wax cold, and iniquity shall abound." (D&C 45:26-27.)

Of our present world, a world of carnality and corruption, the holy word attests: "Enoch saw the day of the coming of the Son of Man, in the last days, to dwell on the earth in righteousness for the space of a thousand years; But before that day he saw great tribulations among the wicked; and he also saw the sea, that it was troubled, and men's hearts failing them, looking forth with fear for the judgments of the Almighty God, which should come upon the wicked." (Moses 7:65-66.)

And Nephi bore this testimony: "Behold, in the last

days, . . . all the nations of the Gentiles and also the Jews, both those who shall come upon this land and those who shall be upon other lands, yea, even upon all the lands of the earth, behold, they will be drunken with iniquity and all manner of abominations—And when that day shall come they shall be visited of the Lord of Hosts, with thunder and with earthquake, and with a great noise, and with storm, and with tempest, and with the flame of devouring fire." (2 Ne. 27:1-2.)

Who can deny that these things are now upon us? We shall speak hereafter of the natural disasters and the eventual fire that shall cleanse the earth. But we must first set forth why there is so much evil in all the world. It is one of the signs of the times. It comes because of lust and carnality in the hearts of men. It comes because men love Satan more than God and choose to worship at his altars. We have seen that this was the case before the flood when the earth was cleansed by water, and now we see it in our day when the earth will soon be cleansed by fire.

In the early days of our dispensation, when the Lord was laying the foundations of his great latter-day work, he said: "The day speedily cometh; the hour is not yet, but is nigh at hand, when peace shall be taken from the earth"— that time has now come, and peace has been taken from the earth—"and the devil shall have power over his own dominion." That day also is now with us, and Lucifer reigns in the hearts of his own. "And also the Lord shall have power over his saints"—and thanks be to God, this too is a present reality—"and shall reign in their midst, and shall come down in judgment upon Idumea, or the world." (D&C 1:35-36.) And the day is soon to be when he shall come down in judgment and be in our midst.

How then does Satan reign over men? Where is his kingdom, and what is his dominion? We have already spoken of the apostasy, of the false worship, false prophets, and false churches of the last days. These are his kingdom. There his dominion is found. He is the author of apostasy, the lord of false worship, and the prophet of false churches. He is the founder of secret combinations and the spreader of lies. And so we have this inspired account of the coming forth of the Lord's work in the last days: "It shall come in a day when the blood of saints shall cry unto the Lord, because of secret combinations and the works of darkness." We have seen some of this; Joseph and Hyrum fell in Carthage jail, and thousands of the saints met untimely deaths because of the drivings and persecutions in Missouri and the bitter cold of their snow-impeded journeys to the valleys of the mountains. Their blood cries unto the Lord for vengeance against those who denied them further mortal experience.

"Yea, it shall come in a day when the power of God shall be denied, and churches become defiled and be lifted up in the pride of their hearts; yea, even in a day when leaders of churches and teachers shall rise in the pride of their hearts, even to the envying of them who belong to their churches." These churches are part of that great church which is not the Lord's church, which is abominable and evil and which shall be burned with the tares when the Lord of the vineyard comes.

"Yea, it shall come in a day when there shall be heard of fires, and tempests, and vapors of smoke in foreign lands; And there shall also be heard of wars, rumors of wars, and earthquakes in divers places." These are part of the signs of the times, as we shall hereafter note. Our chief present concern, however, is in these graphic words: "Yea, it shall come in a day when there shall be great pollutions upon the face of the earth; there shall be murders, and robbing, and lying, and deceivings, and whoredoms, and all manner of abominations; when there shall be many who will say, Do this, or do that, and it mattereth not, for the Lord will uphold such at the last day." The account then speaks of the wickedness of the churches that have "transfigured the holy word of God" to the point that their adherents feel comfortable in living godless lives because they suppose, falsely, that they will be saved.

If churches sell indulgences remitting the penalties for sins that will be committed in the future, what incentive is there to live righteously? If they say, "Come unto me, and for your money you shall be forgiven of your sins," why worry about doing good or working righteousness? (Morm. 8:27-33.) If salvation is for sale for a few pence, why should even those who profess to be religious concern themselves with the struggles and labors that will enable them to gain faith like the ancients? If churches can save souls by grace alone, without works, what is to deter men from living after the manner of the world while they suppose their eternal inheritance shall be with God and Christ and holy beings?

If even the professors of religion can live in sin and be saved, what of those who openly rebel against God and his laws? How may we expect to see them live? And if, as the evolutionists suppose, life is all chance and happenstance, without the guidance of a Divine Providence, what is there to worry about? Life will cease with death anyway. And so with the atheists. If there is no God and no eternal judgment, is not a life of greed and sin and lust and murder as acceptable as one of religious privation?

Truly, these last days are days of wickedness and abomination, and they have become such through and because of apostasy from the truth. They have become such because the allegiance of men is pledged to Lucifer. Men choose to believe false doctrines—whether these doctrines bear the name of science or religion—and as a consequence, their way of life is evil. This is how and why they worship as Satan dictates. This is what is meant by loving Satan more than God.

What better illustrations are there than these as to why men must believe the truth in order to live godly lives? False beliefs invite wicked deeds. True beliefs lead to a life of righteousness. "The Messiah will set himself again the second time to recover" his people, Jacob said. And "when that day cometh when they shall believe in him"— believe with all the fervor and devotion manifest in ancient days—then "he will manifest himself unto them in power and great glory, unto the destruction of their enemies." This has reference to his second coming. "And none will he destroy that believe in him." They shall abide the day and not be burned with the wicked. "And they that believe not in him shall be destroyed, both by fire, and by tempest, and by earthquakes, and by bloodsheds, and by pestilence, and by famine." (2 Ne. 6:14-15.) These are the judgments of a just God that shall fall upon the world in the last days.

Wars and Rumors of Wars in the Last Days

What is the crowning evil on earth, the one that spreads the greatest suffering, the one that spawns all other evils? Surely it is war. Murder is the most wicked of all sins, and war is mass murder. Millions among men have suffered untimely deaths in the wars of the past; and before the coming desolations are ended, the number will be in the billions. The souls of most of those slain by the sword have gone where Lucifer laughs at their misery and rejoices in their remorse of conscience.

Next to murder in the category of personal sins comes immorality—adultery, homosexuality, fornication, and unchastity in all its forms. After these abominations, in no known order, come all the ills and evils of our day. And all of these grow out of and are multiplied by war. Surely war is the greatest evil that has or can spread its soul-destroying power over all the earth.

Wars have been waged from the beginning. Nations and kingdoms and civilizations have been destroyed. Bloodshed and carnage have made men insensitive to every instinct of decency and refinement. For instance, the Nephites, in the day of their greatest degeneracy, took the daughters of the Lamanites as prisoners, robbed them of their "chastity and virtue," and, then, in Mormon's language, "they did murder them in a most cruel manner, torturing their bodies even unto death; and after they have done this, they devour their flesh like unto wild beasts, because of the hardness of their hearts; and they do it for a token of bravery." (Moro. 9:9-10.)

How do the wars of the past compare with those destined to be fought in the last days? They were but preparation and prologue for the present and the future. The great and dreadful wars have been reserved for the last days, the days after the invention of the machine, the days when the number of wicked persons would swell into the billions. This is the day when a new order of war would be instituted, and that new order began with the Civil War in America. It was then that modern armaments had their birth. Already they have grown into a hideous monster, and the end is nowhere to be seen.

Thus it is that the prophetic word speaks of wars and rumors of wars as being among the signs of the times. Jesus set the stage for our consideration of these matters when, discoursing on Olivet, he said of the gathered ones of Israel in the last days: "And they shall hear of wars, and rumors of wars. Behold I speak for mine elect's sake"—he is speaking of those in our day who will be able to distinguish what the scriptures say about the ancient wars from what they say relative to those of the present; they are the ones who shall catch the vision of a new order of blood and carnage reserved for the last days—"for nation shall rise against nation, and kingdom against kingdom; there shall be famines, and pestilences, and earthquakes, in divers places." (JS-M 1:28-29.) And also: "And there shall be earthquakes also in divers places, and many desolations; yet men will harden their hearts against me, and they will take up the sword, one against another, and they will kill one another." (D&C 45:33.) He is here giving the wars of the last days a place of preeminence and standing among all the wars of the ages.

"I, the Lord, am angry with the wicked," he said to

Joseph Smith. "I am holding my Spirit from the inhabitants of the earth. I have sworn in my wrath, and decreed wars upon the face of the earth, and the wicked shall slay the wicked, and fear shall come upon every man; And the saints also shall hardly escape; nevertheless, I, the Lord, am with them, and will come down in heaven from the presence of my Father and consume the wicked with unquenchable fire. And behold, this is not yet, but by and by." (D&C 63:32-35.) The decreed wars have commenced; they are in progress; but the day of burning is by and by, in the day when he comes again.

These latter-day wars had their beginning in 1861. "I prophesy, in the name of the Lord God, that the commencement of the difficulties which will cause much bloodshed previous to the coming of the Son of Man will be in South Carolina. . . . This a voice declared to me, while I was praying earnestly on the subject, December 25th, 1832." (D&C 130:12-13.) Such is the inspired pronouncement of the seer of our day. Indeed, it was on that very Christmas day in 1832 when he received the revelation and prophecy on war. This revelation specifies: "Verily, thus saith the Lord concerning the wars that will shortly come to pass, beginning at the rebellion of South Carolina, which will eventually terminate in the death and misery of many souls; And the time will come that war will be poured out upon all nations, beginning at this place."

The end of these wars is not yet, far from it. After repeating that "war shall be poured out upon all nations," the revealed word attests: "With the sword and by bloodshed the inhabitants of the earth shall mourn; and with famine, and plague, and earthquake, and the thunder of heaven, and the fierce and vivid lightning also, shall the inhabitants of the earth be made to feel the wrath, and indignation, and chastening hand of an Almighty God, until the consumption decreed hath made a full end of all nations." (D&C 87:1-6.) These wars and plagues and desolations shall continue—and increase—until the kingdoms of this world are destroyed and He reigns whose right it is.

This is quite a different preparatory period than some, even among the elect, have supposed would exist prior to the Second Coming. This coming will not be ushered in by righteousness, but by wickedness. It will not come when the saints have converted the world and prepared men to meet their God. It will not come because the generality of mankind is ready to receive the Second David. Indeed, the great battle of Armageddon itself will be in progress when the Lord comes. And thus we read in the prophetic word: "Proclaim ye this among the Gentiles; Prepare war, wake up the mighty men, let all the men of war draw near; let them come up: Beat your plowshares into swords, and your pruninghooks into spears: let the weak say, I am strong." This is said of the last days; it is the opposite of what shall be in the millennial day when men shall beat their swords into plowshares and their spears into pruning hooks and shall not learn war anymore at all. But for the premillennial period the call is: "Assemble yourselves, and come, all ye heathen, and gather yourselves together round about: thither cause thy mighty ones to come down, O Lord. Let the heathen be wakened, and come up to the valley of Jehoshaphat: for there will I sit to judge all the heathen round about." (Joel 3:9-12.) It is Christ the Lord who thus speaks. He will come in the day of war and desolation; then he will judge all men and divide the sheep from the goats.

Isaiah's great prophecy relative to the fire and desolation that will attend the Second Coming is preserved for us in these words: "For, behold, the Lord will come with fire, and with his chariots like a whirlwind, to render his anger with fury, and his rebuke with flames of fire. For by fire and by his sword will the Lord plead with all flesh: and the slain of the Lord shall be many. . . . And they [those who are left] shall go forth, and look upon the carcases of the men that have transgressed against me," saith the

Lord, "for their worm shall not die, neither shall their fire be quenched; and they shall be an abhorring unto all flesh." (Isa. 66:15-16, 24.)

Truly, in the last days men "shall be drunken with their own blood, as with sweet wine." (Isa. 49:26.) All these things have begun; they are now underway, and they shall increase in intensity and in horror until that dreadful day when the God of battles himself shall descend from heaven with a shout and with the trump of the archangel.

The Earth Itself Cries Repentance

This earth was created for us, to be our abiding place during a mortal probation. It was made in such a way as to best serve our needs. The Lord had power to arrange the earth, the elements, and all created things in the way that would best serve man, his crowning creation. Why did he make provision for natural disasters, acts of God, as they are called in legal parlance? What purpose is served by earthquakes, floods, volcanic eruptions, storms, tempests, heat waves that burn the crops of men, and cold waves that freeze the fruits of the earth? These have all been woven into the continuing existence of our earth, an earth designed to serve us. Why?

It seems clear that we are here in mortality to gain experiences that could not be gained in any other way. We need to combat and overcome the forces of nature. We must face up to the sorrows and vicissitudes of mortality if we are to appreciate the eternal joys of immortality. And in addition, the disasters of earth—controlled as they are in the infinite wisdom of that Lord who knoweth all things— are used by him to temper and train us. He uses natural disasters to bring to us the conscious realization that we are dependent upon a Supreme Being for all things. He uses them as a means of judgment to punish us for evil deeds done in the flesh. He uses them to humble us so that perchance we will repent and live as he would have us live.

"Except the Lord doth chasten his people with many afflictions, yea, except he doth visit them with death and with terror, and with famine and with all manner of pestilence, they will not remember him." (Hel. 12:3.) And all of this has particular application in this day of wickedness when the world is being prepared to receive its rightful King.

There is an account, in the visions and revelations of Enoch, in which our very planet is personified and delivers a message. This method of divine teaching lets us know that the earth itself is used to get men to do what they must do to gain salvation. "Enoch looked upon the earth; and he heard a voice from the bowels thereof, saying: Wo, wo is me, the mother of men; I am pained, I am weary, because of the wickedness of my children. When shall I rest, and be cleansed from the filthiness which is gone forth out of me? When will my Creator sanctify me, that I may rest, and righteousness for a season abide upon my face?" This is a sweet and poignant expression that alludes to the great millennial day when the earth will rest because wickedness ceases among men who were made from the dust of the earth. "And when Enoch heard the earth mourn, he wept, and cried unto the Lord, saying: O Lord, wilt thou not have compassion upon the earth?" (Moses 7:48-49.)

In some of our latter-day scriptures the Lord uses a like teaching technique. "Hearken ye, for, behold, the great day of the Lord is nigh at hand," he says to his servants. Then he commands them: "Lift up your voices and spare not. Call upon the nations to repent, both old and young, both bond and free, saying: Prepare yourselves for the great day of the Lord; For if I, who am a man, do lift up my voice and call upon you to repent, and ye hate me, what will ye say when the day cometh when the thunders shall utter their voices from the ends of the earth, speaking to the ears of all that live, saying—Repent, and prepare for the great day of the Lord? Yea, and again, when the lightnings shall streak forth from the east unto the west, and shall utter forth their voices unto all that live, and make the ears of all tingle that hear, saying these words—Repent ye, for the great day of the Lord is come?" The very elements of the earth echo, as it were, the message of the servants of the Lord.

"And again, the Lord shall utter his voice out of heaven, saying: Hearken, O ye nations of the earth, and hear the words of that God who made you. O, ye nations of the earth, how often would I have gathered you together as a hen gathereth her chickens under her wings, but ye would not!" How beautiful this imagery is. In the literal sense the words will be spoken by the servants of the Lord; in the eternal sense they will be his words, for when his servants speak by the power of his Spirit, their words are his words.

Our Lord's graphic expression continues: "How oft have I called upon you by the mouth of my servants, and by the ministering of angels, and by mine own voice, and by the voice of thunderings, and by the voice of lightnings, and by the voice of tempests, and by the voice of earthquakes, and great hailstorms, and by the voice of famines and pestilences of every kind, and by the great sound of a trump, and by the voice of judgment, and by the voice of mercy all the day long, and by the voice of glory and honor and the riches of eternal life, and would have saved you with an everlasting salvation, but ye would not!" (D&C 43:17-25.)

Can there be any question that the Lord has woven the disasters of nature into his program for a purpose? Can we doubt that he uses them for our benefit and blessing? In the midst of a great revelation concerning his coming, he says to us, the elders of his kingdom: "And after your testimony cometh wrath and indignation upon the people." We shall preach the gospel to the world, and if they do not believe and obey, they will be cursed. "For after your testimony cometh the testimony of earthquakes, that shall cause groanings in the midst of her, and men shall fall upon the ground and shall not be able to stand." There are greater earthquakes ahead than there have ever been in the past. "And also cometh the testimony of the voice of thunderings, and the voice of lightnings, and the voice of tempests, and the voice of the waves of the sea heaving themselves beyond their bounds. And all things shall be in commotion; and surely, men's hearts shall fail them; for fear shall come upon all people."

After the disasters and terrors of the last days, "Angels shall fly through the midst of heaven, crying with a loud voice, sounding the trump of God, saying: Prepare ye, prepare ye, O inhabitants of the earth; for the judgment of our God is come. Behold, and lo, the Bridegroom cometh; go ye out to meet him." (D&C 88:88-92.)

Chapter 32

PLAGUES AND PESTILENCE IN THE LAST DAYS

Plagues and Pestilence Prepare the Way of the Lord

Before this earth becomes a fit habitat for the Holy One, it must be cleansed and purified. The wicked must be destroyed; peace must replace war; and the evil imaginations in the hearts of men must give way to desires for righteousness. How shall this be brought to pass? There are two ways: (1) By plagues and pestilence and wars and desolation. The wicked shall slay the wicked, as did the Nephites and the Lamanites in the day of the extinction of the Nephites as a nation. Plagues will sweep the earth, as the Black Death ravaged Asia and Europe in the fourteenth century. The carcasses of the dead will be stacked in uncounted numbers to rot and decay and fill the earth with stench. (2) Then, at his coming, the vineyard will be burned. The residue of the wicked will be consumed. No corruptible thing will remain. And this earth will then become a fit abode for the Prince of Peace.

Thus Jesus on Olivet said: "There shall be famines, and pestilences, and earthquakes, in divers places." (JS-M 1:29.) And the Lord, in March of 1829, said to Joseph Smith: "A desolating scourge shall go forth among the inhabitants of the earth, and shall continue to be poured out from time to time, if they repent not''—and they will not repent, as we know from other revelations—''until the earth is empty, and the inhabitants thereof are consumed away and utterly destroyed by the brightness of my coming. Behold, I tell you these things, even as I also told the people of the destruction of Jerusalem; and my word shall be verified at this time as it hath hitherto been verified.'' (D&C 5:19-20.) Then in September 1832 this word came from the Lord: ''I, the Almighty, have laid my hands upon the nations, to scourge them for their wickedness. And plagues shall go forth, and they shall not be taken from the earth until I have completed my work, which shall be cut short in righteousness—Until all shall know me, who remain.'' (D&C 84:96-98.)

Thus, all men have a choice. They can repent, or they can suffer. They can believe and obey, or they can reject the truth and live in disobedience. They can prepare themselves to abide the day and to stand when he appeareth, or they can bow in submission to the plagues and pestilences that lie ahead; and, should they escape these, they can then be numbered with the great host who will be burned at his coming.

John Reveals the Signs of the Times

Many prophets speak of the plagues and woes to be poured out without measure upon men in the last days. None do so, however, with such vivid imagery and in such graphic language as did the Beloved John. His divine commission was to see in vision ''all things . . . concerning the end of the world'' and to write them for the blessing and enlightenment of men. (1 Ne. 14:18-27.)

John's visions are not chronological—deliberately so—and we cannot, with our present knowledge, place on a chronological chart each thing of which he speaks. Some of the woes proclaimed are of such a nature as to have a continuing or a repeated fulfillment. We shall, therefore, consider them in the order in which they are recorded in the book of Revelation, interspersing as we go along such commentary and explanation as seems needed. Many of the specific things to which John alludes are considered in extenso in other contexts in this book.

John saw a book, sealed on the back with seven seals, which "contains the revealed will, mysteries, and the works of God; the hidden things of his economy concerning this earth during the seven thousand years of its continuance, or its temporal existence." Each seal contains the things of a thousand-year period beginning at the time of Adam's fall and continuing until the end of the Millennium. (D&C 77:6-7.)

The Lamb of God opened each seal to show forth the great things of each succeeding thousand years, things that would begin or occur during that period. When he opened the sixth seal—and we are now living near the end of the sixth period of a thousand years—"lo, there was a great earthquake; and the sun became black as sackcloth of hair, and the moon became as blood; And the stars of heaven fell unto the earth, even as a fig tree casteth her untimely figs, when she is shaken of a mighty wind." (Rev. 6:12-13.) There may be more than one occasion when the light of the sun and the moon shall be withheld from men, and when it will seem as though the very stars in the firmament are being hurled from their places. What is here recited could mean that the light of the sun is blotted out by smoke and weather conditions, which would also make the moon appear "as blood." This falling of the stars "unto the earth" could be meteoric showers, as distinguished from the stars, on another occasion, appearing to fall because the earth itself reels to and fro. Perhaps the passage has reference to both types of falling stars. The latter-day revelation that seems to parallel John's words has come to us in this language: "Not many days hence and the earth shall tremble and reel to and fro as a drunken man; and the sun shall hide his face, and shall refuse to give light; and the moon shall be bathed in blood; and the stars shall become exceedingly angry, and shall cast themselves down as a fig that falleth from off a fig-tree." (D&C 88:87.)

Next, in language that may refer to what shall be during the seventh seal, John says: "And the heaven departed as a scroll when it is rolled together; and every mountain and island were moved out of their places." Surely this has reference to the continents becoming one land again. "And the kings of the earth, and the great men, and the rich men, and the chief captains, and the mighty men, and every bondman, and every free man, hid themselves in the dens and in the rocks of the mountains; And said to the mountains and rocks, Fall on us, and hide us from the face of him that sitteth on the throne, and from the wrath of the Lamb: For the great day of his wrath is come; and who shall be able to stand?" (Rev. 6:14-17.) These events must surely be destined to occur during the wars and terrors of the last days and before the day of burning when the wicked are consumed. As to their chronology, they are listed in latter-day revelation as coming after the half hour of silence in heaven (D&C 88:95), which silence is designated in Revelation 8:1 as occurring after the seventh period of one thousand years has commenced.

Plagues Poured Out in the Seventh Seal

We are now living in the Saturday night of time; the millennial morning will soon dawn. This is the end of the sixth seal, and the seventh seal will soon be opened. Our modern revelation tells us plainly that Christ will come sometime after the opening of seventh seal; it will be during the seventh thousand years and after the events listed in the eighth chapter of John's writings. The plagues and woes there recited shall all take place during the seventh seal, and they are "the preparing of the way before the time of his coming." (D&C 77:12.) Will he come ten or fifty or a

381

hundred years after the opening of the seventh seal? Or will his various appearances be interspersed with the signs of the times that are reserved for that future day? Answers to these and like questions have been withheld from us and will be known only as the various events transpire.

And when the Lamb "had opened the seventh seal, there was silence in heaven about the space of half an hour." If the time here mentioned is "the Lord's time" in which one day is a thousand years, the half hour would be some twenty-one of our years. (Abr. 3:4; 2 Pet. 3:8.) Could this be interpreted to mean that such a period will elapse after the commencement of the seventh thousand-year period and before the outpouring of the woes about to be named?

"And I saw the seven angels which stood before God; and to them were given seven trumpets," John continues. "And there were voices, and thunderings, and lightnings, and an earthquake." Would that we knew, as John apparently did, what the voices said. "And [then] the seven angels which had the seven trumpets prepared themselves to sound." And thus the scene is set for the recitation of the plagues and woes and sorrows that are to sweep the earth after the opening of the seventh seal.

1. *The First Angel: Hail and Fire Descend.*

"The first angel sounded, and there followed hail and fire mingled with blood, and they were cast upon the earth: and the third part of trees was burnt up, and all green grass was burnt up." Is this the "overflowing rain, and great hailstones, fire, and brimstone," of which Ezekiel spoke? (Ezek. 38:22.) Could all this be brought to pass through atomic warfare, or will it come by natural disasters, as when God rained fire and brimstone upon Sodom and Gomorrah? Speculatively, most of the plagues and destructions here announced could be brought to pass by men themselves as they use the weapons and armaments they have created.

2. *The Second Angel: The Sea Is Smitten.*

"And the second angel sounded, and as it were a great mountain burning with fire was cast into the sea: and the third part of the sea became blood; And the third part of the creatures which were in the sea, and had life, died; and the third part of the ships were destroyed." We have no way of conceiving what kind of a natural calamity would destroy a third part of the sea life and of all ships. Will it be a volcanic eruption of such magnitude as to involve whole continents? Or will it be a rain of atomic bombs sent forth by warring nations?

3. *The Third Angel: Earth's Waters Are Polluted.*

"And the third angel sounded, and there fell a great star from heaven, burning as it were a lamp, and it fell upon the third part of the rivers, and upon the fountains of waters; And the name of the star is called Wormwood: and the third part of the waters became wormwood; and many men died of the waters, because they were made bitter." Could this result from atomic fallout or pollutions from the factories of the world? Or will it be brought to pass by some law of nature beyond our control?

4. *The Fourth Angel: The Light-Bearing Luminaries Are Smitten.*

"And the fourth angel sounded, and the third part of the sun was smitten, and the third part of the moon, and the third part of the stars; so as the third part of them was darkened, and the day shone not for a third part of it, and night likewise." Perhaps a merciful God withholds from us the ways and the means whereby the very luminaries of heaven will cease to serve their ordained purposes for a third part of the time.

"And I beheld, and heard an angel flying through the midst of heaven," John here interjects, "saying with a loud voice, Woe, woe, woe, to the inhabiters of the earth by reason of the other voices of the trumpet of the three angels, which are yet to sound!" (Rev. 8:1-13.) Four angels have trumpeted their woes upon a wicked world, and it is scarcely a beginning of what is to be.

5. *The Fifth Angel: Modern Warfare Curses the World.*

The whole of the ninth chapter of Revelation is a recitation of the woes pronounced by the fifth angel. "They are to be accomplished after the opening of the seventh seal, before the coming of Christ." (D&C 77:13.) They are, thus, perils and destructions that lie ahead, although in small measure some like woes have already befallen large portions of mankind.

"And the fifth angel sounded, and I saw a star fall from heaven unto the earth: and to him was given the key of the bottomless pit [or, better, the pit of the abyss]." Lucifer, who was cast out of heaven, now has his new abode, an endless hell where he holds the keys of power and dominion over his fellow demons and over all mortals who bow before him as their master.

"And he opened the bottomless pit; and there arose a smoke out of the pit, as the smoke of a great furnace; and the sun and the air were darkened by reason of the smoke of the pit." Lucifer opens the doors of hell, and every vile influence ascends from its evil depths as does smoke from a great furnace. So dark is the smoke and so widespread is the evil that the sun and the air are darkened.

"And there came out of the smoke locusts upon the earth: and unto them was given power, as the scorpions of the earth have power." Men as locusts—evil, wicked, guided by Satan and filled with the spirit of the times— begin their warfare.

"And it was commanded them that they should not hurt the grass of the earth, neither any green thing, neither any tree; but only those men which have not the seal of God in their foreheads. And to them it was given that they should not kill them, but that they should be tormented five months: and their torment was as the torment of a scorpion, when he striketh a man. And in those days shall men seek death, and shall not find it; and shall desire to die, and death shall flee from them.'' We can only speculate as to how this will be fulfilled. The warriors of the world apparently attack men without destroying the fruits of the ground. Only those in Zion who are sealed up unto eternal life have power to withstand the onslaught. Could it be that John is seeing the effects of poisonous gas, or bacteriological warfare, or atomic fallout, which disable but do not kill?

"And the shapes of the locusts were like unto horses prepared unto battle; and on their heads were as it were crowns like gold, and their faces were as the faces of men. And they had hair as the hair of women, and their teeth were as the teeth of lions. And they had breastplates, as it were breastplates of iron; and the sound of their wings was as the sound of chariots of many horses running to battle. And they had tails like unto scorpions, and there were stings in their tails: and their power was to hurt men five months.'' John is seeing warfare and armaments so foreign to his experience that he has no language to describe to the people of his day the horror and destructive power of it all. We suppose the Lord is showing him machine guns and cannons, tanks and airplanes, flame throwers and airborne missiles, to say nothing of other weapons of which we ourselves have as yet no knowledge.

"And they had a king over them, which is the angel of the bottomless pit, whose name in the Hebrew tongue is Abaddon, but in the Greek tongue hath his name Apollyon. One woe is past; and, behold, there come two woes more hereafter.'' Satan is king. He rules in the hearts of men. He commands the armies of mortal men who wage these wicked wars among themselves.

6. *The Sixth Angel: Armageddon Spreadeth Destruction.*

"And the sixth angel sounded, and I heard a voice from the four horns of the golden altar which is before God, Saying to the sixth angel which had the trumpet, Loose the four angels which are bound in the great river Euphrates [or, rather, as the Inspired Version has it, in the bottomless pit]. And the four angels were loosed, which were prepared for an hour, and a day, and a month, and a year, for to slay the third part of men.'' Four angels of the devil, demons from the depths of hell, are given free reign to lead the armies of men in destroying a third of the population of the earth. If, as is not improbable, the earth by then has, say, twelve or fifteen billion inhabitants, then the magnitude of the slaughter in this Armageddon of the future will be such as to destroy more people than now live on earth.

''And the number of the army of the horsemen were two hundred thousand thousand: and I heard the number of them.'' No such armed forces—two hundred million strong—have ever yet drawn the sword of battle at any one time on earth, nor could that number of armed combatants ever have been assembled until these last days in which we now live.

''And thus I saw the horses in the vision, and them that sat on them, having breastplates of fire, and of jacinth, and brimstone: and the heads of the horses were as the heads of lions; and out of their mouths issued fire and smoke and brimstone. By these three was the third part of men killed, by the fire, and by the smoke, and by the brimstone, which issued out of their mouths. For their power is in their mouth, and in their tails: for their tails were like unto serpents, and had heads, and with them they do hurt.'' In this divine summary is seen again, as we suppose, an account of guns and armored tanks, of flame throwers and airplanes, and of airborne missiles and the smoke of atomic bombs.

''And the rest of the men which were not killed by these plagues yet repented not of the works of their hands, that they should not worship devils, and idols of gold, and silver, and brass, and stone, and of wood: which neither can see, nor hear, nor walk: Neither repented they of their murders, nor of their sorceries, nor of their fornication, nor of their thefts.'' (Rev. 9:1-21.) Neither the Nephites nor the Jaredites repented when rivers of blood flowed on their battlefields and millions of their number were slain by the sword. Neither shall these carnal and evil inhabiters of a weary and wicked world repent when the abomination that maketh desolate is poured out upon them.

The war they shall wage is a religious war. It will be against the Lord's covenant people, as we shall hereafter see. It will be waged by men who "worship devils"; they will be in conflict with others whose God is Jehovah. And the blood and carnage and death will not bring the carnal and wicked warriors to repentance. Repentance is a gift of God; it follows faith; and the tares among men, who are being prepared for the burning, are without God in the world and have no faith.

7. *The Seventh Angel: Christ Comes and Destroys the Wicked.*

Before the sounding of the trump of the seventh angel, John was permitted to see the part he was destined to play in the latter-day restoration of all things (Rev. 10:1-11), and to learn of the two prophets to be slain in Jerusalem just before the battle of Armageddon, of which battle the sixth angel spoke. After recounting the ministry of these two prophets, of whom we shall speak more particularly hereafter, the account says: "The second woe is past; and, behold, the third woe cometh quickly." (Rev. 11:14.)

With reference to these three woes, the present author has written: "After showing John the woes that would befall mankind before the Second Coming (Rev. 6:9-17; 7; 8:1-13), the Lord by an angelic ministrant promised three more woes, which were to attend and usher in the reign of the Great King (Rev. 8:13). The first of these was the unbelievably destructive series of wars leading up to the final great holocaust. (Rev. 9:1-12.) The second was the final great war itself in which one-third of the hosts of men should be slain. (Rev. 9:12-21; 10; 11:1-14.) And now the third woe is to be the destruction of the remainder of the wicked when the vineyard is burned by divine power and the earth changes from its telestial to its terrestrial state. In destructive power and effect this woe is to surpass all others many times over." (*Commentary* 3:511.)

It is in this setting, then, that we read: "And the seventh angel sounded; and there were great voices in heaven, saying, The kingdoms of this world are become the kingdoms of our Lord, and of his Christ; and he shall reign for ever and ever." Christ the Lord reigneth. After the plagues and pestilences, after the destruction of the wicked, after the burning of the vineyard—then cometh the great day. Earth's rightful King reigneth.

"And the four and twenty elders, which sat before God on their seats, fell upon their faces, and worshipped God, Saying, We give thee thanks, O Lord God Almighty, which art, and wast, and art to come; because thou hast taken to thee thy great power, and hast reigned." What a glorious day it is for the saints when their King reigneth. All evil shall then cease, and naught but righteousness and peace shall prevail on all the earth.

"And the nations were angry, and thy wrath is come, and the time of the dead, that they should be judged, and that thou shouldest give reward unto thy servants the prophets, and to the saints, and them that fear thy name, small and great; and shouldest destroy them which destroy the earth. And the temple of God was opened in heaven, and there was seen in his temple the ark of his testament: and there were lightnings, and voices, and thunderings, and an earthquake, and great hail." (Rev. 11:15-19.) When the Lord comes, he will destroy those who destroyed the earth. He is angry with the wicked, and in his wrath he will cleanse his vineyard by fire, and in his mercy he will reward his prophets and his saints. The wicked who remain after the first woe and the second woe shall be destroyed in the third.

Chapter 33

THE SEVEN
LAST PLAGUES

The Two Prophets: Martyred in Jerusalem

Our setting for the slaughter of the two prophets in Jerusalem and for the seven last plagues is not only in the seventh seal, but also just before and during the time when the seventh angel is announcing the plague of burning and destruction that will usher in the Second Coming. "In the days of the voice of the seventh angel, when he shall begin to sound," John tells us, "the mystery of God should be finished, as he hath declared to his servants the prophets." (Rev. 10:7.) That is, the great winding-up scene will come to pass during the time the plagues and events pronounced by this angel are occurring. These events are heralded by the ministry and death of the two witnesses in Jerusalem; then the seventh angel will sound his trump to proclaim the outpouring of the seven last plagues, the battle of Armageddon, the fall of Babylon, and the burning of the vineyard with fire.

John is given a reed and told to measure the temple in Jerusalem, but not the court of the Gentiles, which is part of the holy site, "for it is given unto the Gentiles: and the holy city shall they tread under foot forty and two months." That is to say, there will be a day of universal apostasy. It will commence when the apostles and prophets cease to minister among men and will continue until the opening of the heavens again in the spring of 1820. A part of this apostasy calls for Jerusalem to be trodden down of the Gentiles. The detailed application of the period of forty-two months has not as yet been revealed.

In this setting, however, the word that comes from the Lord is: "I will give power unto my two witnesses, and they shall prophesy a thousand two hundred and three score days, clothed in sackcloth." Who are these witnesses, and when will they prophesy? "They are two prophets that are to be raised up to the Jewish nation in the last days, at the time of the restoration, and to prophesy to the Jews after they are gathered and have built the city of Jerusalem in the land of their fathers." (D&C 77:15.) Their ministry will take place after the latter-day temple has been built in Old Jerusalem, after some of the Jews who dwell there have been converted, and just before Armageddon and the return of the Lord Jesus. How long will they minister in Jerusalem and in the Holy Land? For three and a half years, the precise time spent by the Lord in his ministry to the ancient Jews. The Jews, as an assembled people, will hear again the testimony of legal administrators bearing record that salvation is in Christ and in his gospel. Who will these witnesses be? We do not know, except that they will be followers of Joseph Smith; they will hold the holy Melchizedek Priesthood; they will be members of The Church of Jesus Christ of Latter-day Saints. It is reasonable to suppose, knowing how the Lord has always dealt with his people in all ages, that they will be two members of the Council of the Twelve or of the First Presidency of the Church.

How will their witness be received by the people? This we do know. It will be with these two witnesses as it was with their Lord some two millenniums before. The righteous will believe their words, and the wicked will thirst for their blood. "And if any man will hurt them, fire proceedeth out of their mouth, and devoureth their enemies: and if any man will hurt them, he must in this manner be killed. These have power to shut heaven, that it rain not in the days of their prophecy: and have power over waters to turn them to blood, and to smite the earth with all plagues, as often as they will." It will be with them as it was with Elijah, who both called down fire from heaven to consume his enemies and sealed the heavens that there was neither dew nor rain for three and a half years. And it will be with them as it was with Moses, who turned the rivers and waters of Egypt into blood and who smote the Egyptians with many plagues.

"And when they shall have finished their testimony, the beast that ascendeth out of the bottomless pit shall make war against them, and shall overcome them, and kill them." Satan shall slay them by the hands of his ministers, even as he slew their Lord by the hands of the Jews and the Romans who hearkened to his will.

"And their dead bodies shall lie in the street of the great city, which spiritually is called Sodom and Egypt, where also our Lord was crucified. And they of the people and kindreds and tongues and nations shall see their dead bodies three days and an half, and shall not suffer their dead bodies to be put in graves." There will not be so much as a Pilate to authorize a Joseph of Arimathea to take their bodies and place them in a borrowed grave.

"And they that dwell upon the earth shall rejoice over them, and make merry, and shall send gifts one to another; because these two prophets tormented them that dwelt on the earth." The rejoicing of the wicked at the death of the righteous constitutes a witness, written in blood, that the rebels of the world have ripened in iniquity and are fit and ready for the burning.

"And after three days and an half the Spirit of life from God entered into them, and they stood upon their feet; and great fear fell upon them which saw them. And they heard a great voice from heaven saying unto them, Come up hither. And they ascended up to heaven in a cloud; and their enemies beheld them." As with their Lord, whose witnesses they were, the two prophets arise from the dead on the third day and ascend into heaven.

"And the same hour was there a great earthquake, and the tenth part of the city fell, and in the earthquake were slain of men seven thousand: and the remnant were affrighted, and gave glory to the God of heaven." Jerusalem is shaken by a mighty earthquake even as it was at the crucifixion of Christ. This time many of the wicked are slain, while the saints—those Jews who have accepted Christ and his gospel, those who have participated in building the temple, those who have received the ordinances of the house of the Lord and are waiting for his return—they shall give glory to the God of heaven.

"The second woe is past; and, behold, the third woe cometh quickly." (Rev. 11:1-14.) The third woe, the burning of the vineyard, shall soon commence.

Plagues Manifest the Wrath of God

"And I saw another sign in heaven, great and marvelous," our apostolic friend and colleague tells us, "seven angels having the seven last plagues; for in them is filled up the wrath of God." (Rev. 15:1.) These are seven other angels whose plagues shall be poured out in the day of the seventh angel of whom we have been speaking. Their plagues shall fulfill all that has been written and promised that should fall upon the wicked before the war of Armageddon and the day of burning.

At this late date in the history of the world, the warning voice has been raised in every nation and to every people; the gospel has been preached in every tongue and among every kindred. All have been invited—nay, commanded—to come unto Christ, to repent, to believe and obey his gospel, to join with the saints, and to become inheritors of eternal life. The masses of men have rejected the gospel message, have persecuted the saints and slain the prophets, and have continued to walk in worldly paths. They are now ripened in iniquity. The servants of the Lord who have gone forth proclaiming the glad tidings of salvation for the last time have now exercised the power given them "to seal both on earth and in heaven, the unbelieving and rebellious; Yea, verily, to seal them up unto the day when the wrath of God shall be poured out upon the wicked without measure—Unto the day when the Lord shall come to recompense unto every man according to his work, and measure to every man according to the measure which he has measured to his fellow man." (D&C 1:8-10.)

"I looked, and, behold, the temple of the tabernacle of the testimony in heaven was opened," John continues, "And the seven angels came out of the temple, having the seven plagues, clothed in pure and white linen, and having their breasts girded with golden girdles." The ceremonies of the earthly temple with which John was familiar are being reenacted in heaven to teach with great power and eternal impact the marvelous truths involved. "And one of the four beasts gave unto the seven angels seven golden vials full of the wrath of God, who liveth for ever and ever." The vials are bowls or small vessels to hold liquids. "And the temple was filled with smoke from the glory of God, and from his power; and no man was able to enter into the temple, till the seven plagues of the seven angels were fulfilled." (Rev. 15:5-8.)

And so it is that the day has arrived and the hour is at hand. Let the plagues come in their fulness. All the plagues of the past are but a prelude. Now, with the burning just ahead, the wrath of God will be manifest in the greatest plagues of the ages.

What Are the Seven Last Plagues?

"And I heard a great voice out of the temple saying to the seven angels, Go your ways, and pour out the vials of the wrath of God upon the earth." These, then, are the seven last plagues, the plagues that pour out the fulness of the wrath of God upon the wicked, the plagues that usher in the second coming of the Son of Man:

1. *A Noisome and Grievous Sore.*

"And the first went, and poured out his vial upon the earth; and there fell a noisome and grievous sore upon the men which had the mark of the beast, and upon them which worshipped his image." Could this be the same plague of which Zechariah speaks when he says that men's "flesh shall consume away while they stand upon their feet, and their eyes shall consume away in their holes, and their tongue shall consume away in their mouth"? (Zech. 14:12.) Does it have reference to these words of latter-day revelation: "And their flesh shall fall from off their bones, and their eyes from their sockets"? (D&C 29:19.) Is this a plague that will result from atomic fallout? Or from some worldwide pollution of the air we breathe, the food we eat, and the water we drink? It is to come upon those who worship at the altars of evil, leaving the inference that those only will escape who have faith in the Lord and who exercise the power of the priesthood to rebuke the evils that otherwise would afflict them.

2. *The Seas Become Blood and Their Life Dies.*

"And the second angel poured out his vial upon the sea; and it became as the blood of a dead man: and every living soul died in the sea." This will be a plague of unbelievable breadth and depth. When all the oceans of the world are so polluted that all life in them dies, how can anyone measure the effect this will have on mankind?

3. *All Water Turns to Blood and Is Diseased.*

"And the third angel poured out his vial upon the rivers and fountains of waters; and they became blood." The plague that contaminated the great waters of the saline seas is now extended to include the rivers and streams and springs from which thirst is quenched and crops are watered. What an awful thing it is to be cursed by the Almighty!

Perhaps the horror of all this caused John to marvel that the Great Judge of all the earth would deal thus with men.

And yet wherein does it differ in principle from the destruction of man by the flood of Noah or the burning of the world at the Second Coming? In any event, John records: "And I heard the angel of the waters say, Thou art righteous, O Lord, which art, and wast, and shalt be, because thou hast judged thus." The wicked are receiving that which they merit and deserve. "For they have shed the blood of saints and prophets"—two of whom are the martyrs to be slain in Jerusalem—"and thou hast given them blood to drink; for they are worthy. And I heard another out of the altar say, Even so, Lord God Almighty, true and righteous are thy judgments."

4. *The Sun Scorches Men and the Earth.*

"And the fourth angel poured out his vial upon the sun; and power was given unto him to scorch men with fire. And men were scorched with great heat, and blasphemed the name of God, which hath power over these plagues: and they repented not to give him glory." This appears to be a plague of nature, one that the Lord will impose upon the world. Occasional brief heat waves destroy the crops of an area of the earth. What will it be like when the whole earth is afflicted with heat at the same time? Suppose temperatures rose to a hundred and ten, or a hundred and twenty, or a hundred and thirty degrees Fahrenheit—what effect would this have on all forms of life?

5. *Darkness, Pain, and Sores in the Kingdoms of the World.*

"And the fifth angel poured out his vial upon the seat of the beast; and his kingdom was full of darkness; and they gnawed their tongues for pain, and blasphemed the God of heaven because of their pains and their sores, and repented not of their deeds." We have spoken of darkness covering the earth and gross darkness the minds of the people. We see, even now, the grossly wicked ways of men because they believe a lie. We shudder at the abominations on every hand because men love darkness rather than light. We ask:

Can things get worse than they are before a just God will destroy men as he did in the days of Noah? We answer: They can, and they will.

In the day when the fifth angel pours out his vial upon the earth, darkness will increase. The great and abominable church, who is the whore of all the earth, will be full of darkness. Its doctrines will partake more and more of the evils of the world. There will be less and less light and truth, and more and more darkness and error. Hence, sin and evil will increase. And this process will go on until Babylon falls, and when she falls she will have attained a state and a degree of wickedness beyond anything in her long and evil history. The saints can expect to see more cultism, more false doctrines in the world, a greater emphasis in educational fields upon false scientific theories, more evil practices among the ungodly, more abominations among sex-obsessed men, and more of all that is evil everywhere—and then cometh the end of the world. What a horrible plague is the plague of darkness!

6. *False Miracles as the World Prepares for Armageddon.*

"And the sixth angel poured out his vial upon the great river Euphrates; and the water thereof was dried up, that the way of the kings of the east might be prepared. And I saw three unclean spirits like frogs come out of the mouth of the dragon, and out of the mouth of the beast, and out of the mouth of the false prophet. For they are the spirits of devils, working miracles, which go forth unto the kings of the earth and of the whole world, to gather them to the battle of that great day of God Almighty." Devils—of whom the frogs are a type and a shadow—shall work miracles. The world will be so degenerate that men will choose to follow magicians and politicians who deceive and defraud rather than turn to prophets who have power to move mountains and save souls.

And what greater miracle can these evil spirits perform, working as they always have through receptive mortals, than to indoctrinate men in all nations with that hate and lust for power which will cause them to assemble (in an age of atomic warfare!) with a view to the utter destruction of civilization? Then, as that great day of God Almighty arrives, and as the war of wars is being waged, Christ will come. "Behold, I come as a thief. Blessed is he that watcheth, and keepeth his garments, lest he walk naked, and they see his shame." He will come to save his saints, those who have kept their garments, and to destroy the wicked, those whose hearts are only evil continually.

"And he gathered them together into a place called in the Hebrew tongue Armageddon." The center of the battle will be on the mount and in the valley of Megiddo and on the plains of Esdraelon, though, since all nations are involved, it cannot be other than a worldwide conflict.

7. *War, Upheavals of Nature, and the Fall of Babylon.*

"And the seventh angel poured out his vial into the air; and there came a great voice out of the temple of heaven, from the throne, saying, It is done. And there were voices, and thunders, and lightnings; and there was a great earthquake, such as was not since men were upon the earth, so mighty an earthquake, and so great." This is the time when earth's land masses shall unite; when islands and continents shall become one land; when every valley shall be exalted and every mountain shall be made low; when the rugged terrain of today shall level out into a millennial garden; when the great deep shall be driven back into its own place in the north. It is no wonder that the earthquake shall exceed all others in the entire history of the world.

"And the great city was divided into three parts, and the cities of the nations fell: and great Babylon came in remembrance before God, to give unto her the cup of the wine of the fierceness of his wrath. And every island fled away, and the mountains were not found." The cities of the world shall be destroyed. Babylon shall fall, of which we shall speak more particularly hereafter. The wicked shall taste the fulness of the wrath of God.

"And there fell upon men a great hail out of heaven, every stone about the weight of a talent: and men blasphemed God because of the plague of the hail; for the plague thereof was exceeding great." (Rev. 16:1-21.) We shall speak of this hail when we consider Ezekiel's prophecies about the battle of Armageddon. But we should here observe that Armageddon is a holy war. In it men will blaspheme God. They will be in rebellion against Jehovah. The armies that face each other will have opposing philosophies of life. It will be religious instincts that cause them to assemble to the battle. And the plagues poured out upon them will not cause them to repent.

Such—sadly—is the destiny that lies ahead.

And such—providentially—is not right at hand. It is some years away. It shall come to pass by and by.

Chapter 34

THE SIGNS
OF THE TIMES

What Are the Signs of the Times?

In the days of his flesh, our blessed Lord preached the gospel, spake as never man spake, and wrought an endless array of miracles. Blind eyes saw, lame men leaped, and deaf ears heard. Lepers became clean, and dead corpses rose from their biers. He walked on a tempestuous sea, silenced a raging storm, and fed thousands with a little fish savory and a few small loaves of barley bread.

Yet those who hated him demanded "that he would shew them a sign from heaven." They wanted to see something that fitted their ideas of what the Promised Messiah would do. Let him rain fire and brimstone on Rome or dry up the Jordan with a wave of the hand. Let him leap from the pinnacle of the temple and be caught by a legion of angels before he crushed his feet on the rocks below. Let him do some spectacular thing that would identify him to their Gentile overlords and send waves of terror through the ranks of the wicked.

In answer Jesus said: "When it is evening, ye say, It will be fair weather: for the sky is red. And in the morning, It will be foul weather to day: for the sky is red and lowring. O ye hypocrites, ye can discern the face of the sky; but can ye not discern the signs of the times?" (Matt. 16:1-3.) The true signs of his divinity were before them. Let them pay attention to the doctrine he preached. Let them ask the lame and the blind and the deaf, who now leaped and saw and heard, let them learn from those whom he had healed whether he was the Son of God or not. Let them view the true signs of the times, not seek for something they had imagined in their evil hearts should be the case. The true signs were before them, and they could be read as easily as the signs foretelling the day's weather.

And so it is today. The Lord has poured and is pouring out the signs of the times on every hand. He is showing forth the very things, promised of old, that are to herald the coming of the Son of Man. And the issue before all men is whether they are able to read the signs of the times or whether they will ignore the divine warnings and continue on their godless course to an assured destruction. The true saints have this promise: "Unto you it shall be given to know the signs of the times, and the signs of the coming of the Son of Man." (D&C 68:11.) What, then, are these signs? Let us consider them under the following headings:

1. *The Preparatory Signs.*

When the apostles fell asleep, save only John who was translated, the gospel sun soon set upon a wicked world. Almost immediately a dark night of apostate darkness covered the earth. Early in the coming dawn, before the gospel sun rose again, certain preparatory work was under way to herald that glorious day. The Lord began to pour out his Spirit—the Light of Christ—upon men everywhere. As guided thereby, an age of renaissance and reformation began. The dark gloom of the long night began to give way before a destined dawn. Printing was discovered, the Bible was published, and learning increased. Columbus discovered America; its colonization followed; and an inspired constitution was adopted for the United States. The King James Version of the Holy Bible was translated to bring the ancient word to the people among whom the gospel would soon be restored. All these things, and many more that were companion to them, constitute the preparatory, initial signs that set the stage for the other and greater signs that were and are to be. These preparatory signs were but prelude to the promised day when young men would see visions and old men would dream dreams and the Lord would pour out his Spirit upon all flesh.

2. *The Signs That Prepare a People for Their Lord.*

This is the group of signs, above all others, that men must see and understand if they are to know the generation of their Lord's return. These signs include the opening of the heavens so that revelation pours forth anew as it did in ancient days; the coming forth of the Book of Mormon, that ancient record which testifies of Christ and his gospel; and the restoration, for the last time, of the fulness of the everlasting gospel, with all its graces, powers, and glories.

These signs include the setting up again on earth of the only true and living Church, the establishment of the Zion of God once more among men, and the preaching of the restored gospel in all the world as a witness unto all nations. They include the restoration of keys and powers and priesthoods, the coming of angelic ministrants from former days to confer upon mortals their rights and prerogatives, and the restitution of all things spoken by the mouths of all the holy prophets since the world began. They include the coming of John the Baptist, and Peter, James, and John; of Moses and Elijah and Elias; of Raphael and Gabriel and Michael; and of divers angels—all bringing back again their ancient powers and glories.

These signs include the sending of a messenger before the face of the Lord to prepare his way; the great and wondrous ministry of Joseph Smith, the prophet and seer of the Lord, who has done more save Jesus only for the salvation of men in this world than any other man who ever lived in it; and the total and complete establishment again on earth of all that appertains to the dispensation of the fulness of times. These, and all that grows out of them, constitute the great and glorious signs of the times. And they have already been shown forth that believing souls might be prepared by righteousness to abide the day of the Lord's coming.

3. *The Signs Involving the Chosen Ones of Israel.*

Surely these are signs that even the wicked and ungodly can discern in the face of the sky, as it were. Many scattered ones in all nations shall forsake families and friends and moneys and lands and gather to the houses of the Lord in the tops of the mountains of Israel. Others shall come together and live as people set apart; they shall make the stakes of Zion in all nations their refuge. The Jews shall go to Jerusalem preparatory to accepting Him whom their fathers crucified. The Ten Tribes—long lost from the knowledge of men—shall take up an abode in their ancient Palestine; the times of the Gentiles shall be fulfilled; and the Lamanites shall blossom as the rose. And accompanying it all, persecution shall be the heritage of the faithful. All who forsake the world and begin to live as becometh true saints shall feel the scourge of Satan, whether they are the seed of Abraham or the children of the aliens. Surely when people assemble in great numbers, when new nations are born in a day, and when whole congregations change their way of life, surely these are signs that can be read by all.

4. *The Temple-centered Signs.*

What ought the world to think when temples begin to dot the earth? When men begin to talk again of salvation for the dead as did Peter? When they begin anew to baptize for the dead as did Paul? Is not the coming of Elijah one of the signs of the times? And does not the fact that genealogical research, for all practical purposes, was born on the 3rd day of April in 1836 prove that he came? Every temple built in the last days, every new wave of genealogical interest and research, every baptism performed for the dead, every vicarious ordinance performed in a house of the Lord—all these are signs of the times, witnesses that the Lord's coming is near, even at the door.

5. *The Signs Involving Present World Conditions.*

How and in what way do worldliness and apostasy and

false worship become signs of the times? The answer is self-evident. The world itself is the social circumstances created by the acts of worldly people; it is the society in which carnal and sensual and devilish people dwell, and the end of the world is the destruction of the wicked. As the end draws near, wickedness and worldliness will increase until all the proud and they who do wickedly shall be ready for the burning.

Thus the signs of the times include the prevailing apostate darkness in the sects of Christendom and in the religious world in general. False churches, false prophets, false worship—breeding as they do a way of life that runs counter to the divine will—all these are signs of the times. As men's consciences are seared with the hot iron of sin, the Spirit of the Lord ceases to strive with them, sorrow and fear increase in their hearts, and they are prone, increasingly, to do that which is evil—all of which things are signs of the times. Robbery, plunder, murder, and violent crimes of all sorts; many of the strikes and labor disputes in the industrial world; much of the litigation that clogs the courts of the nations; drug abuse and indecent and immoral conduct; the spreading plague of evil abortions; the abominations of incest and homosexuality—all these things are signs of the times. Satan is not dead, and his influence is increasing and shall increase in the world until the end comes.

6. *The Signs of Wars and Plagues and Disasters.*

These are the signs toward which men generally look as they try to discern the face of the latter-day skies, and yet these are the lesser signs, those of relatively little moment when compared to the great signs involving the restoration of the saving truths. Nonetheless they are part of the signs of the times, and they are now being shown forth in power and with sorrowful results.

They include wars and rumors of wars. Probably there has been no single moment since South Carolina rebelled in 1861 when there has been peace on earth. We do not anticipate even a scant duration of time in the future when all armed conflict and all bloodshed will cease, until the Great Millennium arrives. Until then there will be wars and desolation and death; until then disease and plagues and pestilence will sweep the earth from time to time; until then there will be famines and hunger and men dying for want of bread. In these last days all things shall be in commotion. The waves of the seas will spread death; the volcanoes in many lands will belch forth their fire and brimstone; and earthquakes will increase in number and intensity. Woes shall rest upon men as the Lord by the voice of the forces of nature calls upon them to repent and be as he would have them be.

7. *The Signs That Lie in the Future.*

In the very nature of things, the signs of the times will not cease until the Lord comes. Those that involve chaos and commotion and distress of nations will continue in the future with even greater destructive force. Men's hearts will fail them for fear in greater degree hereafter than heretofore. Wars will get worse. Moments of armistice and peace will be less stable. Viewed in the perspective of years, all worldly things will degenerate. There will be an increasing polarization of views. There will be more apostasy from the Church, more summer saints and sunshine patriots who will be won over to the cause of the adversary. Those who support the kingdom because of the loaves and the fishes will find other bread to eat. While the faithful saints get better and better, and cleave more firmly to the heaven-sent standards, the world will get worse and worse and will cleave to the policies and views of Lucifer.

Among the specific signs that lie ahead are the building of the New Jerusalem and the rebuilding of the Jerusalem of old. The great conference at Adam-ondi-Ahman must yet be held. The two prophets must minister and be martyred in Jerusalem. The gloom and despair and death of Armageddon must yet cover the earth; Babylon must fall; the vineyard must be burned; and then the earth shall rest and the Lord Jesus shall rule and reign for the space of a thousand years. But before that great day there shall be signs and wonders of a marvelous and miraculous kind shown forth in heaven and on earth. These we shall consider in the next chapter.

Our souls cry out: "God hasten the day of the coming of thy Son," and yet we know that such cannot be. The day is fixed and the hour is set. The signs have been, are now, and will hereafter be shown forth. Our obligation is to discern the signs of the times lest we, with the world, be taken unawares.

Chapter 35

THE PROMISED
SIGNS AND WONDERS

Signs and Wonders in Heaven and on Earth

We come now to those great signs of mystery and wonder, the signs that cause even the faithful to marvel and to wonder how and under what circumstances they will come to pass. They are to be shown forth in heaven above and on the earth beneath. They involve forces and powers beyond the control of man, except possibly in a few instances, and they all are in the future. None of them have yet transpired, nor will they for some years. There are, as we shall see, a number of specific things that must precede the manifestation of these signs to men. These signs and wonders of which we speak are indeed the crowning and culminating signs of the times, and their occurrence will be almost or actually concurrent with the great and dreadful day of the Lord.

Various passages of scripture tie these signs together and speak of them in such a way that it seems the course of wisdom for us to follow substantially the same course. The signs of which we speak are:

1. *Manifestations of blood, and fire, and vapors of smoke.*

2. *The sun shall be darkened and the moon turn into blood.*

3. *The stars shall hurl themselves from heaven.*

4. *The rainbow shall cease to appear in the mists and rains of heaven.*

5. *The sign of the Son of Man shall make its appearance.*

6. *A mighty earthquake, beyond anything of the past, shall shake the very foundations of the earth.*

As we consider these coming signs, our concern will be twofold: to identify what is involved so there will be no doubt as to the occurrences themselves, and to place each ' sign in its relationship to other known events so we can pinpoint, insofar as the revealed word allows, the actual time when it shall come to pass.

These various signs are alluded to, defined, and set forth in many passages of scripture. Each passage gives only a partial view of what is involved, and each adds a perspective not found in any of the others. All of them taken together let us know, insofar as can be, what the realities are. There remains, of course, much that we do not yet know about these signs. It is, however, a moral certainty—perhaps it is even a prophetic certainty—that more will be revealed about them before the time when they are manifest. Certainly, for instance, the two prophets who shall minister in Jerusalem for three and a half years, preaching and prophesying, shall make inspired utterances about that which is to come after their day and before the coming of their Lord. But let us now look to that prophetic word available to us and learn what we can of the mysterious signs and wonders that are yet to be shown forth by divine power in heaven and on earth.

Jesus said, as Luke records it: "And there shall be signs in the sun, and in the moon, and in the stars." The luminaries of the skies, in some marvelous way, shall bear a witness of the Lord's return. "And upon the earth" there shall be "distress of nations, with perplexity." The nations and kingdoms of the world, with all their leadership and power, shall not know where to turn or what to do. Their leaders will be perplexed. Shall they align themselves with these nations or with those? What alliances will best serve their own national interests? Rumors of war are everywhere. What is to be done to find peace and security? Or to add glory and renown to their nation? No human power can give the answers.

And amid it all, natural disasters shall be everywhere, "the sea and the waves roaring"—there shall be no safety upon the waters in the last days—"men's hearts failing them for fear, and for looking after those things which are coming on the earth: for the powers of heaven shall be shaken." Ought not men's hearts to fail them for fear when they see the volcanic eruptions, the earthquakes, the famine, the pestilence, the plagues, and the disease? It is as though the very human race is about to be destroyed. Is this to be the end of the earth and of all life upon its face? "And then shall they see the Son of man coming in a cloud with power and great glory." And among all the inhabitants of the earth, only the Latter-day Saints will have any peace of mind. Jesus' next words are addressed to them: "And when these things begin to come to pass"—and we are seeing some of them now, though the great day of fulfillment lies ahead—"then look up, and lift up your heads; for your redemption draweth nigh." (Luke 21:25-28.)

In revealing to us some of the things he said to the apostles on Olivet, the Lord said: "And it shall come to pass that he that feareth me"—meaning the faithful saints—"shall be looking forth for the great day of the Lord to come, even for the signs of the coming of the Son of Man." With all our hearts we seek to know and understand these signs. "And they shall see signs and wonders, for they shall be shown forth in the heavens above, and in the earth beneath." Some of these signs we have seen; most of them lie in futurity. "And they shall behold blood, and fire, and vapors of smoke." The blood and fire and vapors of smoke could all be man-made. Atomic bombs— dealing death, shedding blood, spreading fire, and rising in great clouds of smoke—could bring this to pass. In full measure it must refer to the fire and brimstone to be rained upon men at Armageddon, but it may be that even this will be the result of man's doings. "And before the day of the Lord shall come, the sun shall be darkened, and the moon be turned into blood, and the stars fall from heaven. . . . And then they shall look for me, and, behold, I will come." (D&C 45:39-44.)

These words are more specific than those in Luke. One, at least, of the "signs in the sun" is that it shall be darkened. It is not hard to envision how this shall come to pass. Samuel the Lamanite gave the Nephites a sign—separated as they were by an ocean from the actual events—whereby they would know of the death of Christ. "In that day that he shall suffer death," was the prophetic word; "the sun shall be darkened and refuse to give his light unto you; and also the moon and the stars; and there shall be no light upon the face of this land, even from the time that he shall suffer death, for the space of three days, to the time that he shall rise again from the dead." (Hel. 14:20.)

The fulfillment of Samuel's prophetic word is recorded in these words of scripture: "There was thick darkness upon all the face of the land, insomuch that the inhabitants thereof who had not fallen could feel the vapor of darkness; And there could be no light, because of the darkness, neither candles, neither torches; neither could there be fire kindled with their fine and exceedingly dry wood, so that there could not be any light at all; And there was not any light seen, neither fire, nor glimmer, neither the sun, nor the moon, nor the stars, for so great were the mists of darkness which were upon the face of the land. And it came to pass that it did last for the space of three days that there was no light seen." (3 Ne. 8:19-23.) This darkness came upon the Americas along with the great destructions that caused the whole continents to become deformed and changed. It is reasonable to suppose that some equivalent thing will cause darkness to cover the earth in the last days.

One, at least, of the signs "in the moon" is that the

moon shall be turned into blood. It is not difficult to envision a scene, amid the fires and burnings that shall ravage the earth, in which the moon, viewed through the smoke and polluted atmospheric conditions, would appear as red as blood. Little previews of this, when conditions are just right, are occasionally seen on earth even now. As to the stars falling from heaven, we shall have more to say shortly.

To what we have already seen about the signs shown forth by the sun, moon, and stars, let us add this verse from an early revelation: "Behold, I say unto you," saith the Lord, "that before this great day"—'my second coming'—"shall come the sun shall be darkened, and the moon shall be turned into blood, and the stars shall fall from heaven, and there shall be greater signs in heaven above and in the earth beneath." (D&C 29:14.) This divine word seems to say that yet unnamed signs—to be shown forth in heaven above and on the earth beneath—shall exceed in magnitude and glory even those of which we have been speaking. What these are remains to be seen.

Both Isaiah and Joel speak of these signs to be shown forth in the sun, moon, and stars, and seem to place the promised events in the midst of war and desolation. Isaiah says: "Behold, the day of the Lord cometh, cruel both with wrath and fierce anger, to lay the land desolate: and he shall destroy the sinners thereof out of it." Truly, it is the great and dreadful day of the Lord, the day of vengeance that was in his heart, the day when the wicked shall be burned. "For the stars of heaven and the constellations thereof shall not give their light: the sun shall be darkened in his going forth, and the moon shall not cause her light to shine." The new emphasis here, for our purposes, is on the moon and the stellar constellations being darkened as well as the sun. Obviously, if the sun is darkened, such will be the case also with the moon, for this lesser light is but a reflection of the greater; and if great darkening mists blot out the nearby brilliance of the sun, they will surely do the same for the twinkling glimmerings of the distant stars. "And I will punish the world for their evil, and the wicked for their iniquity," the holy word continues, thus keeping the heavenly signs in their setting, "and I will cause the arrogancy of the proud to cease, and will lay low the haughtiness of the terrible." (Isa. 13:9-11.)

Joel adds a new dimension by giving the word in this way: "And I will shew wonders in the heavens and in the earth, blood, and fire, and pillars of smoke." All this we have heretofore considered. "The sun shall be turned into darkness, and the moon into blood." This, too, we have duly noted. But then Joel says, with reference to the whole matter, that it shall come to pass "before the great and terrible day of the Lord come." (Joel 2:30-31.) Then, almost immediately, he launches into a prophecy about Armageddon and its dire destructions. This lets us know that although, as Isaiah seems to say, the desolations are in progress when the signs are given, yet the fulness of the day of wrath, meaning the final day of burning and destruction, shall not come until after the signs are shown forth. This accords with and amplifies what we have quoted from latter-day revelation.

Now let us come to the matter of the stars falling or being hurled from heaven. Our latter-day revelation speaks of the coming of the Lord and says that "so great shall be the glory of his presence that the sun shall hide his face in shame, and the moon shall withhold its light, and the stars shall be hurled from their places." (D&C 133:49.) From this account we conclude that the stars shall fall from heaven at the time of his arrival rather than before. In another passage, heretofore quoted in another connection, the Lord says: "Not many days hence and the earth shall tremble and reel to and fro as a drunken man; and the sun shall hide his face, and shall refuse to give light; and the moon shall be bathed in blood; and the stars shall become exceedingly angry, and shall cast themselves down as a fig falleth from off a fig-tree." (D&C 88:87.) Other passages also speak of the earth trembling and reeling to and fro and specify that it shall be when the Lord sets his foot again upon the Mount of Olives. (D&C 45:48.) Employing the strong language and graphic imagery that he alone can use with such power, Isaiah says: "The earth is utterly broken down, the earth is clean dissolved, the earth is moved exceedingly." He is talking of the new heaven and the new earth that shall come into being when the elements melt with fervent heat. "The earth shall reel to and fro like a drunkard, and shall be removed like a cottage; and the transgression thereof shall be heavy upon it." This, we repeat, is in the day of burning. "And it shall come to pass in that day, that the Lord shall punish the host of the high ones that are on high, and the kings of the earth upon the earth." (Isa. 24:19-21.)

Knowing that the earth is to reel to and fro, knowing that the mighty deep shall return to its place in the north, knowing that the continents and islands shall join again, what about the stars and their fall from heaven? Our answer is that it will seem to men on earth as though the stars—those great suns in the sidereal heavens around which other planets revolve—are falling because the earth reels. The great fixed stars will continue in their assigned orbits and spheres. The sun also will continue to give light, but it will appear to men to be darkened; and the moon will remain as she has been since the creation, but it will seem to mortal eyes as though she is bathed in blood.

Many scriptures speak of earthquakes as one of the signs of the times. We have noted this, somewhat repetitiously, as it has been associated with other matters. The clear inference is that for some reason as yet unknown to man, earthquakes have been and are destined to increase both in number and intensity in the last days. Certainly they shall increase in terror and destructive power simply because there are more people and more man-made structures on earth than at any previous time. And clearly the crowning earthquake—the earthquake of earthquakes—is

412

the one that shall occur as the earth reels to and fro and the stars seem to fall from their places in the sidereal heavens.

As we consider the reeling of the earth to and fro and the total realignment of its land masses incident to the Second Coming, and as we consider the burning of the vineyard by fire to destroy the wicked, as they were once destroyed by water in the days of Noah, we are faced with a somewhat difficult problem relative to the rainbow. We say difficult because not all things relative to it have been revealed, and we have only a few slivers of divine truth upon which to build our house of understanding. In the eternal sense nothing is difficult once the whole matter has been revealed to minds prepared and qualified to receive and understand. Let us lay a foundation for the place the rainbow is destined to play in the Second Coming by recounting the circumstances under which it apparently came into being.

Seed time and harvest, in the sense of one season following another, exist because the axis of the earth is tilted twenty-three and a half degrees from the upright. This is the reason we have summer and winter, spring and fall. The first reference in the scriptures to seasons as we know them is in connection with the flood of Noah. There is a presumption that prior to the flood there were no seasons because the axis of the earth was upright, and a similar presumption that when the Millennium comes and the earth returns to its original paradisiacal state, once again the seasons as we know them will cease and that seed time and harvest will go on concurrently at all times. The whole earth at all times will be a garden as it was in the days of Eden.

Whatever the case may be with reference to these things, something apparently happened with reference to the rainbow in Noah's day, and something is certainly going to happen with reference to it in connection with the Lord's return. We are left to speculate relative to some of these matters, which is not all bad as long as any expressed views are clearly identified for what they are. In fact, in our present state of spiritual enlightenment the Lord deliberately leaves us to ponder and wonder about many things connected with his coming; in this way our hearts are centered upon him so that we will qualify in due course to receive absolute and clear revelation on many things.

After the flood Noah offered sacrifices, worshipped the Lord, and said in his heart: "I will call on the name of the Lord, that he will not again curse the ground any more for man's sake, for the imagination of man's heart is evil from his youth; and that he will not again smite any more everything living, as he hath done, while the earth remaineth." Man had been destroyed once, meaning every living soul save the eight who were on the ark. Such a slaughter staggers the imagination. Conceive of cities and nations buried under mountains of water and of millions of dead bodies tossed about by the watery waves. What was more natural than for Noah to plead with his God that such should never come to pass again?

With these thoughts, Noah coupled the sincere and devout prayer "that seed-time and harvest, and cold and heat, and summer and winter, and day and night, may not cease with man." Question: Why this prayer? Answer: If man was to survive in a world provided with days and nights and cold and heat, he must also have summer and winter and their consequent seed time and harvest. The seasons, as then given, must continue so that man might provide for himself food, clothing, and shelter.

In reply God told Noah and his sons: "I will establish my covenant with you, which I made unto your father Enoch, concerning your seed after you." This covenant, as we have seen, was that a remnant of the seed of Noah, after the flood, should inhabit the earth forever. At this point in the account the Lord promises that the various forms of life in the ark shall survive and multiply. And also: "Neither shall all flesh be cut off any more by the waters of a flood; neither shall there any more be a flood to destroy the earth.'' Thus the Lord granted Noah's petition in part only. He received no promise that man—wicked men—should not thereafter be destroyed, only that there would be no future destruction of all life by a flood.

Truly there was to be another day of death and destruction. But it would be a day of burning, a day when every corruptible thing should be consumed, a day when every living soul, save the few who were righteous, should be destroyed. ''And I will establish my covenant with you,'' the Lord promised, ''which I made unto Enoch, concerning the remnants of your posterity.'' Not all of Noah's seed would be burned. The God-fearing and the righteous would abide the day. A remnant—eight souls, as it were—would enter into the ark of the kingdom, shut the doors against the rain of wickedness in the world, and save themselves from the untoward generation of men among whom they had dwelt.

''And God made a covenant with Noah, and said, This shall be the token of the covenant I make between me and you, and for every living creature with you, for perpetual generations; I will set my bow in the cloud; and it shall be for a token of a covenant between me and the earth.'' The inference is that the rainbow is being shown forth for the first time and that for some reason unknown to us it had not been manifest before. However this may be, again for reasons unknown to us, the rainbow will soon cease to show its glimmering rays of color in the mists and clouds of the air.

''And it shall come to pass, when I bring a cloud over the earth''—the Lord is continuing to speak to Noah—''that the bow shall be seen in the cloud; and I will remember my covenant, which I have made between me and you, for every living creature of all flesh.'' This is the testimony the rainbow bears as pertaining to the flood of Noah, a flood that is past.

But that same rainbow also bears a witness about something that lies in the future. ''And the bow shall be in the cloud," the divine word continues, "and I will look upon it, that I may remember the everlasting covenant, which I made unto thy father Enoch; that, when men should keep all my commandments, Zion should again come on the earth, the city of Enoch which I have caught up unto myself." The rainbow bears record that God will send again the Zion of Enoch, that the ancient holy city, the ancient City of Holiness, will descend out of heaven and be with men again on earth.

"And this is mine everlasting covenant, that when thy posterity shall embrace the truth"—when remnants of Noah's seed accept the gospel in the last days—"and look upward, then shall Zion look downward, and all the heavens shall shake with gladness, and the earth shall tremble with joy; And the general assembly of the church of the firstborn shall come down out of heaven, and possess the earth, and shall have place until the end come. And this is mine everlasting covenant, which I made with thy father Enoch." All this is part of the Second Coming. We shall build a New Jerusalem in Jackson County, Missouri, and Enoch's city shall descend and join with it.

Having stated these glorious truths, the Lord's very next words are: "And the bow shall be in the cloud, and I will establish my covenant unto thee, which I have made between me and thee, for every living creature of all flesh that shall be upon the earth. And God said unto Noah, This is the token of the covenant which I have established between me and thee; for all flesh that shall be upon the earth." (JST, Gen. 9:6-25.)

It is clear from the foregoing that there is some relationship between the destruction of the world by water in Noah's day, the destruction by fire in the day of the Lord Jesus Christ, and the placing of the rainbow in the heavens as a token of a covenant that involved both the flood and the Second Coming. Joseph Smith, with characteristic spiritual insight, ties the whole matter together by statements made on two different occasions. "The Lord deals with this people as a tender parent with a child," the Prophet said, "communicating light and intelligence and the knowledge of his ways as they can bear it. The inhabitants of the earth are asleep; they know not the day of their visitation. The Lord hath set the bow in the cloud for a sign that while it shall be seen, seed time and harvest, summer and winter shall not fail; but when it shall disappear, woe to that generation, for behold the end cometh quickly." (*Teachings*, p. 305.)

"I have asked of the Lord concerning His coming," the Prophet also said, "and while asking the Lord, He gave a sign and said, 'In the days of Noah I set a bow in the heavens as a sign and token that in any year that the bow should be seen the Lord would not come; but there should be seed time and harvest during that year: but whenever you see the bow withdrawn, it shall be a token that there shall be famine, pestilence, and great distress among the nations, and that the coming of the Messiah is not far distant.' But I will take the responsibility upon myself to prophesy in the name of the Lord, that Christ will not come this year, . . . for we have seen the bow." (*Teachings*, pp. 340-41.)

When shall all these things come to pass? When will the sun and the moon and the stars play their portentous part in the coming of Christ? When will the glimmering beauty of the bow in heaven cease to portray its span of colors to men? When will the sign of the coming of the Son of Man be given? We have already shown that the seven last plagues shall be poured out after the opening of the seventh seal, and thus in the beginning of the seventh thousand years. It is then that Armageddon shall be fought; it is then that Jerusalem shall again reap the fate that once was hers; it is then that the abomination that maketh desolate shall utterly destroy the wicked within her walls. All this, of course, will come after Judah returns, after the Jerusalem temple is built, after the Jews have begun to believe in their true Messiah.

Thus, Jesus on Olivet spoke of the gospel of the kingdom being preached in all the world in the last days and of a second "abomination of desolation" being "fulfilled." Then, using language that establishes a definite time frame and that sets forth an order of chronology, he said: "And immediately after the tribulation of those days"—the plagues and wars and abominable desolation that shall destroy again the city of Jerusalem in the final great war—"the sun shall be darkened, and the moon shall not give her light, and the stars shall fall from heaven, and the powers of heaven shall be shaken." He is speaking thus of the final great signs, the wonders and marvels that are yet to be, the final signs that shall be shown forth in heaven and on earth.

And then comes this word: "And, as I said before, after the tribulation of those days, and the powers of heaven shall be shaken"—with some deliberation and by emphasis born of repetition he is identifying the time frame—"then shall appear the sign of the Son of Man in heaven, and then shall all the tribes of the earth mourn; and they shall see the Son of Man coming in the clouds of heaven, with power and great glory." (JS-M 1:31-36.)

The sign of the coming of the Son of Man—what is it? We do not know. Our revelation says simply: "And immediately there shall appear a great sign in heaven, and all people shall see it together." (D&C 88:93.) In 1843 someone by the name of Redding claimed to have seen this promised sign. In response to this claim, the Prophet Joseph Smith said: "I shall use my right"—his right as a prophet to know and identify the signs of the times—"and declare that, notwithstanding Mr. Redding may have seen a wonderful appearance in the clouds one morning about sunrise (which is nothing very uncommon in the winter season) he has not seen the sign of the Son of Man, as foretold by Jesus; neither has any man, nor will any man, until after the sun shall have been darkened and the moon bathed in blood; for the Lord hath not shown me any such sign." (*Teachings*, p. 280.) Then the Prophet quoted the famous statement from Amos, "Surely the Lord God will do nothing, but he revealeth his secret unto his servants the prophets" (Amos 3:7), indicating that when the sign is given, the Lord's servants the prophets, including all the faithful saints, will know it for what it is, and thus be made aware that the long-expected day has arrived.

On another occasion the Prophet, after reciting that before our Lord returns, Jerusalem and her temple must be built and the waters of the Dead Sea healed, continued by saying: "There will be wars and rumors of wars, signs in the heavens above and on the earth beneath, the sun turned into darkness and the moon to blood, earthquakes in divers places, the seas heaving beyond their bounds; then"— meaning after all these things—"then will appear one grand sign of the Son of Man in heaven. But what will the world do? They will say it is a planet, a comet, etc. But the Son of Man will come as the sign of the coming of the Son of Man, which will be as the light of the morning cometh out of the east." (*Teachings*, pp. 286-87.)

All people shall see it together! It shall spread over all the earth as the morning light! "For as the light of the morning cometh out of the east, and shineth even unto the west, and covereth the whole earth, so shall also the coming of the Son of Man be." (JS-M 1:26.) Surely this is that of which Isaiah said: "And the glory of the Lord shall be revealed, and all flesh shall see it together: for the mouth of the Lord hath spoken it." (Isa. 40:5.) Surely this is that of which our revelation speaks: "Prepare for the revelation which is to come, when the veil of the covering of my temple, in my tabernacle, which hideth the earth, shall be taken off, and all flesh shall see me together." (D&C 101:23.) Surely this is that day of which Zechariah prophesied: "The Lord my God shall come, and all the saints with thee. And it shall come to pass in that day, that the light shall not be clear, nor dark: But it shall be one day which shall be known to the Lord, not day, nor night: but it shall come to pass, that at evening time it shall be light. . . .

And the Lord shall be king over all the earth." (Zech. 14:5-9.)

And thus all the promised signs shall come to pass and the Great God, who is Lord of all, shall come and reign on earth; and for the space of a thousand years the earth shall rest.

Chapter 36

BABYLON: A SIMILITUDE OF THE CHRISTIAN ERA

Babylon of Babylonia

It is our hope now to show how and in what way the fall of Babylon is related to the second coming of Him whose return will burn all those in Babylon. In order to do so, we must have some background information about Babylon herself and the part she played in the history of Israel anciently. Only in this way can we envision fully why she was chosen as a type and a figure for the downfall of evil organizations and the overthrow of worldliness in the last days.

We are so far removed in point of time from ancient Babylon that any impact she has on us and our lives seems to be no greater than that of a dim shadow cast by a passing cloud. We know so little about her evil power and man-made glory that we no longer fear and tremble at the mere mention of her name as did our forebears in ancient Israel. We have ceased to recoil in revulsion at her evil practices, and seldom equate them anymore with the sodomic vices of Gomorrah. We have lost sight of the great underlying reasons why the ancient prophets made Babylon and her fall a similitude for apostate religions, for evil governments, and for the world in general, all of which are destined to fall as Babylon fell.

It was in the days of Isaiah and Jeremiah that the prophetic word began to deal at great length with Babylon of Babylonia and her impact upon the ancient saints in Israel. As Jerusalem was the holy city where Jehovah's word was law, so Babylon was the evil metropolis from which the will of Satan went forth. As Palestine was the holy land where remnants of Israel still dwelt and where prophets still parted the heavenly veil, so Babylonia was a worldly kingdom where the priests of sin sought direction from that master whose servants they were. As Jerusalem was the sacred site of the house of the Lord in which the Jews worshipped their God in the name of Jehovah, so in Babylon there were more than fifty temples in which false gods received the meaningless incantations and worship of apostate peoples. Jerusalem was the capital city of the Lord's earthly kingdom; Babylon held a like status in the earthly kingdom of Lucifer.

Located astride the Euphrates, some fifty miles south of modern Baghdad in Iraq, Babylon was the most splendid city of antiquity. In size and magnitude it was overwhelming. Within its walls, on two hundred square miles of land, in closely spaced buildings, dwelt hosts of the Gentile hordes. During the reign of Nebuchadnezzar, who overran Judah and destroyed Jerusalem, it became the largest and most elaborate city in the ancient world. Also within its walls were the famous hanging gardens, rated by the Greeks as among the seven wonders of the world. Its engineers and artisans both bridged over and tunneled under the great Euphrates, and the city had extensive parks, magnificent buildings, navigable canals, and splendid streets. Chariots could be driven on its dual walls, and its municipals found it easy to believe that the works of their hands had been made by Omnipotence itself.

In the course of a long and stormy history, many other nations and kingdoms were subject to and bowed before Babylon. After Lehi left Jerusalem in 600 B.C., Nebuchadnezzar in successive invasions, in 597, 586, and 581 B.C., overran the kingdom of Judah, destroyed Jerusalem, and took the Jews captive and transported them to Babylon, there to live in bondage. How filled with tears and sorrow are these sad words of the ancient covenant people, serving as slaves to Gentile overlords in Babylon, the center of worldliness: "By the rivers of Babylon, there we sat down, yea, we wept, when we remembered Zion. We hanged our harps upon the willows in the midst thereof. For there they that carried us away captive required of us a song; and they that wasted us required of us mirth, saying, Sing us one of the songs of Zion. How shall we sing the Lord's song in a strange land?" (Ps. 137:1-4.)

Then, in the providences of the Lord, Cyrus the Persian in 539 B.C. conquered Babylon and freed the captive Jews that they might go back to Jerusalem and build anew, as they then did under Zerubbabel, the holy sanctuary of the Great Jehovah. Their temple vessels, taken into Babylon along with their blinded king Zedekiah, were returned. And the Jews began a new life in their homeland, albeit in large part an apostate way of life, which prepared them for what they were when the Lord Jesus came among them.

But with Cyrus the Persian began the decline and fall of Babylon. Never again did it regain the glory and splendor of the days of Nebuchadnezzar, all of which is reminiscent of the statement made by Daniel to that great king, while interpreting for him his dream of the great image: "Thou, O king, art a king of kings: for the God of heaven hath given thee a kingdom, power, and strength, and glory. And wheresoever the children of men dwell, the beasts of the field and the fowls of the heaven hath he given into thine hand, and hath made thee ruler over them all. Thou art this head of gold. And after thee shall arise another kingdom inferior to thee." (Dan. 2:37-39.)

Babylon was also destroyed by Xerxes in 478 B.C. and again after Alexander the Great overran the Persian empire in 330 B.C. A rival city was soon built on the Tigris, and Babylon never recovered. Today the greatest world city of antiquity is a mound of desert earth that will not rise again. Babylon the great has fallen forever.

Ancient Babylon Prefigures Modern Babylon

In prophetic imagery, Babylon is the world with all its carnality and wickedness. Babylon is the degenerate social order created by lustful men who love darkness rather than light because their deeds are evil. Babylon is the almighty governmental power that takes the saints of God into captivity; it is the false churches that build false temples and worship false gods; it is every false philosophy (as, for instance, organic evolution) that leads men away from God and salvation. Babylon is false and degenerate religion in all its forms and branches. Babylon is the communistic system that seeks to destroy the freedom of people in all nations and kingdoms; it is the Mafia and crime syndicates that murder and rob and steal; it is the secret combinations that seek for power and unrighteous dominion over the souls of men. Babylon is the promoter of pornography; it is organized crime and prostitution; it is every evil and wicked and ungodly thing in our whole social structure.

Conditions in the world today are as they were in ancient Babylon. What, then, is more natural than for the prophets, aware of the sins and evils and final destruction of Babylon, to use her as a symbol of that which now is and which shall soon be. The things that happened with reference to the ancient Jews in Babylon of Babylonia were in similitude of what was destined to be with reference to the Lord's people and the spiritual Babylon of the world after the coming of Christ. Let us consider the similitudes involved under four headings.

1. *As the Jews were carried as captives into Babylon, so the Church and kingdom set up by the Lord Jesus has been overcome by the world.*

If the Jews had lived in all respects as becometh saints, walking uprightly before the Lord and keeping his commandments, he would have preserved them in their own land with their own king. Israel was scattered and the Jews went into captivity because of disobedience. Such was the punishment decreed for their rebellion. The Lord pours plagues upon the wicked in consequence of their sins, and so the outpourings of pestilence and sorrow fulfill his purposes.

The Babylonian captivity of the Jews was thus in harmony with the mind and will of the Lord. And so with reference to it, the Lord said to Jeremiah: "I have made the earth, the man and the beast that are upon the ground, by my great power and by my outstretched arm, and have given it unto whom it seemed meet unto me. And now have I given all these lands into the hand of Nebuchadnezzar the king of Babylon, my servant; and the beasts of the field have I given him also to serve him. And all nations shall serve him. . . . And it shall come to pass, that the nation and kingdom which will not serve the same Nebuchadnezzar the king of Babylon, and that will not put their neck under the yoke of the king of Babylon, that nation will I punish, saith the Lord, with the sword, and with the famine, and with the pestilence, until I have consumed them by his hand." (Jer. 27:5-8.)

In like manner the saints in the early days of the Christian era soon forsook the faith. Tares were sown in the gospel fields. And "the apostate, the whore, even Babylon, that maketh all nations to drink of her cup, in whose hearts the enemy, even Satan, sitteth to reign"—even he took over the kingdom. (D&C 86:3.) The apostasy was complete and universal. All nations and kingdoms served the king of Babylon. But in the eternal providences of Him who gives nations and kingdoms to whomsoever he chooses, the ascendancy of Babylon will not last forever. The Jews were in Babylon for seventy years, and Babylon has now ruled the world for nearly two thousand years since the early apostles fell asleep, but her kingdom will soon fall. Thus saith the Lord: "They have strayed from mine ordinances, and have broken mine everlasting covenant; They seek not the Lord to establish his righteousness, but every man walketh in his own way, and after the image of his own God, whose image is in the likeness of the world, and whose substance is that of an idol, which waxeth old and shall perish in Babylon, even Babylon the great, which shall fall." (D&C 1:15-16.)

2. *As false prophets arose in Israel to cry peace and safety and to announce, falsely, that the Jews would soon be free from Babylonian bondage, so false ministers in an apostate Christendom profess to make salvation available to men on terms and conditions of their own.*

False prophets always arise to oppose the truth. There must needs be an opposition in all things. Whenever the Lord sends his true ministers, Satan sends his priests. It appears that almost a whole congregation of false prophets stepped forth to deceive the people relative to the Babylonian captivity. The situation became so serious that the Lord gave this commandment: "Hearken not ye to your prophets, nor to your diviners, nor to your dreamers, nor to your enchanters, nor to your sorcerers, which speak unto you, saying, Ye shall not serve the king of Babylon: For they prophesy a lie unto you, . . . For I have not sent them, saith the Lord, yet they prophesy a lie in my name; . . . that ye might perish, ye, and the prophets that prophesy unto you." (Jer. 27:9-10, 15.)

One of these false prophets was Hananiah, who had a great confrontation with Jeremiah "in the house of the Lord, in the presence of the priests and of all the people." Using the Lord's name, Hananiah prophesied that the yoke of the king of Babylon had been broken and that the vessels of the Lord's house would be returned to Jerusalem within two years. To dramatize his sayings, Hananiah broke a yoke of wood. The word of the Lord that then came through Jeremiah acclaimed that the king of Babylon would "put a yoke of iron upon the neck of all these nations,"

426

which could not be broken. As to the false prophet, Jeremiah said: "Hear now, Hananiah; The Lord hath not sent thee; but thou makest this people to trust in a lie. Therefore thus saith the Lord; Behold, I will cast thee from off the face of the earth: this year thou shalt die, because thou hast taught rebellion against the Lord. So Hananiah the prophet died the same year in the seventh month." (Jer. 28:1, 14-17.)

Wherein does this differ from what goes on today in the religious world? False ministers, in their houses of worship, before their fellows, and in the presence of the people, profess to tell what the Lord has said about salvation, when he has said no such thing. They speak, as it were, in his name—on the authority of the Holy Book, as they express it—telling men who live in Babylon to do this or that and be saved. Their doctrines are false; they teach people to trust in a lie. God has not sent them; they are blind guides who lead blind followers into pits of despair.

3. *As the Jews came out of Babylon, freed from captivity, so the call goes forth today to flee from Babylon and the chains of worldliness and to come into that liberty wherewith Christ hath made men free.*

Scriptures that commanded the ancient Jews to arise, leave Babylon, and go back to their homeland, and those scriptures that command modern Israel to leave the world and come to a latter-day Zion, are almost identical in thought content. Ancient Babylon was the world, with all its evil and wickedness, from which the Jews of old must flee to be saved; Jerusalem was their Zion where the faithful must assemble to worship the Lord. And the world, all of it, with its Babylonish carnality, is the spiritual Babylon from which all who love the Lord must flee; they too must come to Zion, a latter-day Zion, there to worship the Lord their God and become heirs of salvation.

The Lord's call to his ancient covenant people to leave Babylon and return to Jerusalem contained such commands and exhortations as these: "Flee and escape out of

427

the land of Babylon, . . . declare in Zion the vengeance of the Lord our God." (Jer. 50:28.) "Flee out of the midst of Babylon, and deliver every man his soul: be not cut off in her iniquity; for this is the time of the Lord's vengeance. . . . Come, and let us declare in Zion the work of the Lord our God. . . . My people, go ye out of the midst of her, and deliver ye every man his soul from the fierce anger of the Lord. . . . Remember the Lord afar off, and let Jerusalem come into your mind." (Jer. 51:6, 10, 45, 50.)

Could we not, with propriety, use these very words in calling upon men to come into the kingdom today? Indeed, some of the words used with reference to the ancient gathering again in Jerusalem seem to have been chosen so as to have a dual application. For instance: "In those days, and in that time, saith the Lord"—and the time and the day, with equal propriety, can be the return from Babylon and the coming out of the world and into the latter-day kingdom—"the children of Israel shall come, they and the children of Judah together, going and weeping: they shall go, and seek the Lord their God. They shall ask the way to Zion with their faces thitherward, saying, Come, and let us join ourselves to the Lord in a perpetual covenant that shall not be forgotten." (Jer. 50:4-5.)

As it was anciently, so it is today. The ancient call is going forth in a modern setting. Those who flee from the Chaldeans, as did their fathers, shall be saved in Zion, as were their fathers. Those who loiter by the way and who remain in whole or in part in Babylon shall be destroyed in the coming day of burning. "Go ye forth of Babylon," Isaiah says to us in the last days, "flee ye from the Chaldeans, with a voice of singing declare ye, tell this, utter it even to the end of the earth; say ye, The Lord hath redeemed his servant Jacob." (Isa. 48:20.) The great day of gathering is at hand.

How joyous is the day! What glories and wonders attend its arrival! It is the dawning of that day of which Isaiah acclaimed: "Break forth into joy, sing together, ye waste places of Jerusalem: for the Lord hath comforted his people, he hath redeemed Jerusalem." This is not yet, but is soon to be. "The Lord hath made bare his holy arm in the eyes of all the nations; and all the ends of the earth shall see the salvation of our God." This also is soon to be. "Depart ye, depart ye, go ye out from thence, touch no unclean thing; go ye out of the midst of her; be ye clean, that bear the vessels of the Lord." (Isa. 52:9-11.)

With these words of poetic majesty calling to us over a span of two and a half millenniums, we hear also the like strains of melody made in our day. To us, the Lord our God—"who shall come down upon the world with a curse to judgment; yea, upon all the nations that forget God, and upon all the ungodly" among his people—the Lord says that "he shall make bare his holy arm in the eyes of all the nations, and all the ends of the earth shall see the salvation of their God." He is confirming the word given anciently through Isaiah. "Wherefore, prepare ye, prepare ye, O my people," the divine voice continues. "Sanctify yourselves; gather ye together, O ye people of my church. . . . Go ye out from Babylon. Be ye clean that bear the vessels of the Lord. . . . Yea, verily I say unto you again, the time has come when the voice of the Lord is unto you: Go ye out of Babylon; gather ye out from among the nations, from the four winds, from one end of heaven to the other. . . . Go ye out from among the nations, even from Babylon, from the midst of wickedness, which is spiritual Babylon." (D&C 133:2-5, 7, 14.)

4. *As Babylon was destroyed with violence, never to rise again, so shall it soon be with spiritual Babylon; she too shall be swept from the earth, and hell will be filled with her municipals.*

Here is a truism that all men should hear: Babylon fell, and her gods with her; and Babylon shall fall, and her gods with her. False gods create an evil society. The world is the world, and Babylon is Babylon, because they worship false gods. When men worship the true God according to gospel standards, their social conditions rival those in Enoch's city; when men worship false gods, they fall into the ways of the world, and their social conditions become as those in Babylon. When we view the fall of Babylon anciently, what we see is the destruction of her idols and ways of worship; and when we shall come to the fall of Babylon in the last days, it will be—oh, blessed day—the destruction of false worship. The Athanasian creed will return to the realms of darkness where it was spawned. The doctrine of salvation by grace alone without works shall be anathema. The great and abominable church shall tumble to the dust. False worship shall cease.

It comes as no surprise, then, to find the accounts of the destruction of ancient Babylon interspersed with expressions about the fate of her false gods. "Declare ye among the nations, and publish, and set up a standard," the Lord said to Jeremiah; "publish, and conceal not: say, Babylon is taken, Bel is confounded, Merodach is broken in pieces; her idols are confounded, her images are broken in pieces." Merodach (Marduk) was king of the gods of Babylon. Bel was one of the principal deities. According to apocryphal sources, it was the image of Bel-Marduk that Daniel and his companions were asked to worship.

Babylon's sins befell her because she was "proud against the Lord, against the Holy One of Israel." Hers was a "land of graven images," and the people were "mad upon their idols." (Jer. 50:2, 29, 38.) Babylonians were wicked because their gods had no power to lift them to righteousness. "Every man is brutish by his knowledge; every founder is confounded by the graven image: for his molten image is falsehood, and there is no breath in them. They are vanity, the work of errors: in the time of their visitation they shall perish." And so the Lord says: "I will punish Bel in Babylon, . . . and the nations shall not flow together any more unto him: yea, the wall of Babylon shall fall. . . . Therefore, behold, the days come, that I will do judgment upon the graven images of Babylon: and her whole land shall be confounded, and all her slain shall fall in the midst of her." (Jer. 51:17-18, 44, 47.) Truly, false worship is the root of all evil.

When John the Revelator wrote the account of his vision of the future fall of Babylon, we suppose he had before him chapters 50 and 51 of Jeremiah, chapter 13 of Isaiah, and other scriptures that tell of the fall of old Babylon. At least John picked up the language and emphasis of the old scriptures and gave them new meanings and impact in the new scripture that flowed from his pen. All of this ancient word is deserving of an in-depth study. For our purposes, however, that we may have a feel at least of what is involved, we select out the following expressions.

Babylon is to be overthrown by "an assembly of great nations from the north country," and she shall become "a wilderness, a dry land, and a desert." And, "Because of the wrath of the Lord it shall not be inhabited, but it shall be wholly desolate: every one that goeth by Babylon shall be astonished, and hiss at all her plagues." Of her it shall be said: "How is the hammer of the whole earth cut asunder and broken! how is Babylon become a desolation among the nations!" What is her destiny? "The wild beasts [wolves, or howling creatures] of the desert with the wild beasts of the islands shall dwell there, and the owls [ostriches] shall dwell therein: and it shall be no more inhabited for ever; neither shall it be dwelt in from generation to generation. As God overthrew Sodom and Gomorrah and the neighbour cities thereof, saith the Lord; so shall no man abide there, neither shall any son of man dwell therein. . . . At the noise of the taking of Babylon the earth is moved, and the cry is heard among the nations." (Jer. 50:9, 12-13, 23, 39-40, 46.)

"Babylon hath been a golden cup in the Lord's hand, that made all the earth drunken: the nations have drunken of her wine; therefore the nations are mad. Babylon is suddenly fallen and destroyed: howl for her. . . . O thou that dwellest upon many waters, abundant in treasures,

thine end is come, and the measure of thy covetousness. . . . And Babylon shall become heaps, a dwelling-
place for dragons [jackals], an astonishment, and an hiss-
ing, without an inhabitant. . . . Thus shall Babylon sink,
and shall not rise." (Jer. 51:7-8, 13, 37, 64.)

We know of no prophet whose ability to create similitudes and use them to teach great and eternal truths
equals that of Isaiah. When he speaks of the fall of Babylon
and of the second coming of Him who overthrew Babylon
once and will do so again, there is no way of knowing
where one account ends and the other begins. Indeed, in
his presentation the fall of Babylon becomes the destruction of the wicked in the last days, and "the day of the
Lord" that overthrew the wicked anciently is the same day
that shall crush them into nothingness in the days that lie
ahead. The fall of Babylon anciently, with all its blood and
horror, becomes and is the similitude whereby those with
spiritual insight come to know what will be involved in the
future fall of the kingdom of the same name.

There is, Isaiah says, "a tumultuous noise of the kingdoms of nations gathered together: the Lord of hosts mus-
tereth the host of the battle. They come from a far country,
from the end of heaven, even the Lord, and the weapons of
his indignation, to destroy the whole land." When and in
what age shall this occur? The application is to both falls of
both Babylons. Having so stated, Isaiah next says: "Howl
ye; for the day of the Lord is at hand; it shall come as a
destruction from the Almighty. Therefore shall all hands be
faint, and every man's heart shall melt: And they shall be
afraid: pangs and sorrows shall take hold of them; they
shall be in pain as a woman that travaileth: they shall be
amazed one at another; their faces shall be as flames." As
far as we are concerned, he is speaking of the Second
Coming, but the facts and the imagery had their beginning
in the ancient destructions.

Then Isaiah speaks of the Lord's wrath, the destruction
of the wicked, and the sun being darkened, which we have

quoted in other connections, all of which refer to the Second Coming. This is followed by descriptive language that occurred anciently and will be repeated in due course. Then comes the famous passage about the fate of Babylon: "And Babylon, the glory of kingdoms, the beauty of the Chaldees' excellency," the seeric word proclaims, "shall be as when God overthrew Sodom and Gomorrah. It shall never be inhabited, neither shall it be dwelt in from generation to generation: neither shall the Arabian pitch tent there; neither shall the shepherds make their fold there. But wild beasts of the desert shall lie there; and their houses shall be full of doleful creatures; and owls [ostriches] shall dwell there, and satyrs [he-goats] shall dance there. And the wild beasts of the islands shall cry in their desolate houses, and dragons [jackals] in their pleasant palaces: and her time is near to come, and her days shall not be prolonged." (Isa. 13:4-8, 19-22.)

Then come these words, which have a dual meaning: "How hath the oppressor ceased! the golden city ceased! The Lord hath broken the staff of the wicked, and the sceptre of the rulers. He who smote the people in wrath with a continual stroke, he that ruled the nations in anger, is persecuted, and none hindereth. The whole earth is at rest, and is quiet: they break forth into singing." (Isa. 14:4-7.) The whole earth is at rest! It is the Millennium. Truly, "Babylon is fallen, is fallen; and all the graven images of her gods he hath broken unto the ground." (Isa. 21:9.) The Lord is King, and he alone is worshipped.

Chapter 37

THE FALL
OF BABYLON

The Time of the Fall of Babylon

When, oh, when will Babylon fall? When will wickedness cease and the earth rest? Must the saints forever face and fight the abominations in this present fallen and carnal world? Every faithful soul cries out: "Thy kingdom come. Thy will be done in earth, as it is in heaven." (Matt. 6:10.) And come it must, and come it will; and it shall be ushered in by the fall of Babylon. There is no concord between Christ and Belial; and when the Lord comes to reign, the world and its wickedness must be cast into the lake of fire.

Our insight into the fall and utter destruction of this great whore of all the earth, who sitteth upon many waters and exerciseth dominion over the kings of the earth, our insight into her death and the burning of her disease-ridden body, comes from the pen of John. And nowhere else in all his writings—not in his Gospel, not in his epistles, not elsewhere in the Apocalypse—nowhere does he delve so deeply and write so plainly and with such incisive particularity as he does in recording the fall and destruction of Babylon. Oh, how he and all the saints have longed for the day when this earth, free from Babylon and her abominations, shall be a fit abode for the King of Peace and Righteousness!

In setting forth what shall soon transpire with reference to false churches, false governments, and false ways of worship, all being part and portion of Babylon, we shall simply follow the recitations of the Beloved John, interspersing them with such explanations as are needed to put them in their relationship to the whole of that strange act which the Lord is performing on the stage of the world. Our first reference follows the announcement of the restoration of the everlasting gospel by an angelic ministrant. This angel—who we have seen was, in fact, many angels, all of whom combined to bring again the doctrines, powers, and keys that taken together comprise the fulness of the everlasting gospel—this angel, who has already come, shall be followed by two more. The next one to come shall issue the great proclamation: "Babylon is fallen, is fallen, that great city, because she made all nations drink of the wine of the wrath of her fornication." Fornication, adultery, and whoredoms, these are the terms the prophets use to describe the false worship, the devil's way of worship, the worship that is not of God. They are the most grievous of all sins save murder only, and they are used to denote the most degenerate of all states that can befall man save only his death and destruction, and that state is to worship false gods and thereby to be cut off from any hope of salvation. Thus Babylon is fallen because she imposed false religion, false worship, and thereby a degenerate way of life upon men in all nations.

False worship brings damnation. And so we hear the next angel say, of those in Babylon: "If any man worship the beast and his image, and receive his mark in his forehead, or in his hand"—whoso readeth let him understand—"The same shall drink of the wine of the wrath of God, which is poured out without mixture into the cup of his indignation; and he shall be tormented with fire and brimstone in the presence of the holy angels, and in the presence of the Lamb: And the smoke of their torment ascendeth up for ever and ever: and they have no rest day nor night, who worship the beast and his image, and whosoever receiveth the mark of his name." (Rev. 14:8-11.)

Babylon shall fall after the gospel has been restored, and those in Babylon shall suffer the fires of eternal torment, the burning anguish of cloudy and seared consciences, in that hell which is prepared for the wicked. Why? Their fate befalls them because they worshipped—not the Father, in the name of the Son, by the power of the Spirit—but the beast and his image. They sacrificed at evil altars. Theirs was a worldly way of life. They did not overcome the world, and put off the natural man, and become saints through the atonement of Christ the Lord. They dwelt in Babylon in the day of her fall, in the day when the sword of vengeance fell upon her.

When will Babylon fall? We have already set forth that which is known about the seven last plagues and shown that they will take place in the beginning of the seventh thousand years. One of these, the sixth, involved "the spirits of devils, working miracles"; it resulted in the gathering together of all nations to "the battle of that great day of God Almighty" at Armageddon. Then, still in the day of the seventh seal, the seventh angel poured out his vial, and there followed the greatest earthquake of the ages, the one in which "every island fled away, and the mountains were not found." It is in this setting that John records: "And the great city was divided into three parts [he is speaking of Jerusalem], and the cities of the nations fell [this is all the great cities in all nations]: and great Babylon came in remembrance before God, to give unto her the cup of the wine of the fierceness of his wrath." Then John speaks of the "great hail out of heaven" that shall destroy those in the battle of Armageddon. (Rev. 16:14-21.)

That is to say, Babylon shall fall during the battle of Armageddon. She shall fall in the very hour when the Lord returns. She shall fall when the vineyard is burned and every corruptible thing is consumed. Until then, Satan shall have power over his own dominion and abominations shall abound. But thanks be to God, when the hour of his judgment is come, the wicked shall be destroyed, millennial rest will commence, and he shall reign gloriously among his saints for the space of a thousand years.

Babylon: The Church of the Devil

Babylon the great has been arraigned before the bar of the Great Jehovah; many witnesses have borne record of her sins; and the blood of the martyred saints has cried out against her. She has been weighed in the balance and found wanting, and the Great God has issued his eternal decree. The penalty is death. Babylon shall be burned with fire. The execution date is set and shall not be delayed.

Our friend John, by divine appointment, is about to see her fall and describe the cleansing fires that shall consume the corruptions within her walls. But first he must see her in all her wickedness and degeneracy. After an angelic ministrant sets forth her sins and shows him the iniquities in which she is ensnared, his voice will join the great chorus that cries, Amen, to the judgment rendered by the Just Judge against all that is evil and carnal and devilish in the world.

"One of the seven angels which had the seven vials," out of which were poured the seven last plagues, said to John: "Come hither; I will shew unto thee the judgment of the great whore that sitteth upon many waters: With whom the kings of the earth have committed fornication, and the inhabitants of the earth have made drunk with the wine of her fornication." What sins must men commit to be found deserving of death? The sins of Babylon—what are they? Why is she to be burned with fire? The angelic reply cries out: Because of her fornication; that is, because of false worship, false religion, and a false plan of salvation, because she guides men to worship false gods. And if the Judge of all the earth, whose judgments are just, decrees the death penalty, who shall question the wisdom of the verdict, or say him nay on the day of the execution?

"So he carried me away in the spirit into the wilderness," John says, "and I saw a woman sit upon a scarlet coloured beast, full of names of blasphemy, having seven heads and ten horns." This woman is the great and abominable church. "The seven heads are seven mountains"—the seven hills of Rome—"on which the woman sitteth." John is seeing that which Nephi saw.

"And the woman was arrayed in purple and scarlet colour, and decked with gold and precious stones and pearls, having a golden cup in her hand full of abominations and filthiness of her fornication." When Nephi saw in vision these same things, an angel—perhaps the same one who appeared to John—said to the American seer: "Look, and behold that great and abominable church, which is the mother of abominations, whose founder is the devil." (1 Ne. 14:9.) "And it came to pass that I beheld this great and abominable church," Nephi said, "and I saw the devil that he was the founder of it. And I also saw gold, and silver, and silks, and scarlets, and fine-twined linen, and all manner of precious clothing; and I saw many harlots. And the angel spake unto me, saying: Behold the gold, and the silver, and the silks, and the scarlets, and the fine-twined linen, and the precious clothing, and the harlots, are the desires of this great and abominable church." (1 Ne. 13:6-8.)

"And upon her forehead," John continues, "was a name written, MYSTERY, BABYLON THE GREAT, THE MOTHER OF HARLOTS AND ABOMINATIONS OF THE EARTH." What a name this is for a church—no, not a church, but rather a particular church—the church of the devil. Names among the Hebrews bore witness of the chief characteristics of those upon whose heads they were placed. This church—glorifying the mysterious and unknown; aping the conduct of those in the great city of Nebuchadnezzar; herself a harlot and also the mother of other apostate churches—this church was the mother of the abominations of the earth. Her theology and her practices fostered sin and encouraged men to walk in a Babylonish path without fear of divine retribution. "Come unto me," she proclaimed, "and for your money you shall be forgiven of your sins." (Morm. 8:32.) Wars were fought at her command and converts were made, not by the sweet voice of persuasion, not by inspired preaching, but by the edge of the sword and the point of the spear. Inquisitions took the lives of her heretics, and religion became an arm of the state so that sovereign lords could enforce religious rites and force men to believe approved doctrines.

"And I saw the woman"—the great and abominable church, the church of the devil—"drunken with the blood of the saints, and with the blood of the martyrs of Jesus: and when I saw her, I wondered with great admiration." Nephi's views were similar. "I saw among the nations of the Gentiles," the American prophet said, "the formation of a great church. And the angel said unto me: Behold the formation of a church which is most abominable above all other churches, which slayeth the saints of God, yea, and tortureth them and bindeth them down, and yoketh them with a yoke of iron, and bringeth them down into captivity. . . . And also for the praise of the world do they destroy the saints of God, and bring them down into captivity." (1 Ne. 13:4-5, 9.)

John's account makes it clear that both church and state are involved in the abominations that shall bring to pass the fall of Babylon. As the angel has already intoned, "the kings of the earth have committed fornication," with "the great whore that sitteth upon many waters." Now in the hidden and half-understood imagery in which the whole concept is couched, the angel speaks of ten kings, symbolical, as we suppose, of all the kings of the earth. "These have one mind, and shall give their power and strength unto the beast. These shall make war with the Lamb, and the Lamb shall overcome them: for he is Lord of lords, and King of kings: and they that are with him are called, and

439

chosen, and faithful. And he saith unto me, The waters which thou sawest, where the whore sitteth, are peoples, and multitudes, and nations, and tongues." In the ultimate sense it is the church and not the state that has responsibility for the abominations of the last days, for the moral standards come from religion. The state is an arm, a tool, a part of Babylon; the state operates on the basis of the low and evil standards of the church.

The nations and parts of Babylon shall war among themselves. These nations "shall hate the whore, and shall make her desolate and naked, and shall eat her flesh, and burn her with fire." So spake the angel to John. "For God hath put in their hearts to fulfill his will, and to agree, and give their kingdom unto the beast, until the words of God shall be fulfilled. And the woman which thou sawest is that great city"—Rome, the capital city of the Babylonish church—"which reigneth over the kings of the earth." (Rev. 17:1-18.)

Our understanding of what John saw and taught is confirmed and clarified by the parallel accounts of the same things written by Nephi. Speaking of this same latter-day period, when the day for the burning of the tares is near, an angel said to Nephi: "Behold there are save two churches only; the one is the church of the Lamb of God, and the other is the church of the devil." At this late date, after the restoration of the gospel, after the setting up again on earth of the church and kingdom of God, after abominations had reigned for centuries—after all this, men are divided into two camps. There is polarization; the righteous are on one hand and the wicked on the other. "Wherefore, whoso belongeth not to the church of the Lamb of God belongeth to that great church, which is the mother of abominations; and she is the whore of all the earth."

Having heard this angelic pronouncement, Nephi then said: "And it came to pass that I looked and beheld the whore of all the earth"—the time frame is now the latter days—"and she sat upon many waters; and she had dominion over all the earth, among all nations, kindreds, tongues, and people.'' Babylon is everywhere; the evil power controls the world. Worldliness is supreme; carnality reigns in the hearts of people in all nations. It cannot be otherwise, for no standard of righteousness is raised by those who have long since lost the pure and perfect gospel of the lowly Nazarene. In this period there are but few members of ''the church of the Lamb of God.''

But the downfall of the great and abominable church is at hand. The fall of Babylon is about to come to pass. And thus Nephi sets forth in plain words what John has preserved for us in imagery and figures. ''And it came to pass that I beheld that the wrath of God was poured out upon the great and abominable church,'' Nephi says, ''insomuch that there were wars and rumors of wars among all the nations and kindreds of the earth.'' Surely this is our day, and surely the intensity and horror of what is to be shall increase as the days go by. ''And as there began to be wars and rumors of wars among all the nations which belonged to the mother of abominations, the angel spake unto me, saying: Behold, the wrath of God is upon the mother of harlots; and behold, thou seest all these things—And when the day cometh that the wrath of God is poured out upon the mother of harlots, which is the great and abominable church of all the earth, whose founder is the devil, then, at that day, the work of the Father shall commence, in preparing the way for the fulfilling of his covenants, which he hath made to his people who are of the house of Israel.'' (1 Ne. 14:10-17.)

This is the day in which the Lord ''will preserve the righteous by his power, even if it so be that the fulness of his wrath must come, and the righteous be preserved, even unto the destruction of their enemies by fire. Wherefore, the righteous need not fear; for thus saith the prophet, they shall be saved, even if it so be as by fire.'' (1 Ne. 22:17.) This is the day in which Babylon shall fall, to which fall we shall now turn our attention.

"Babylon Is Fallen, Is Fallen"

Babylon was conceived by Satan, gestated in hell, born in sin, and lives in lust and lewdness. She has grown into a horrible two-headed monster. Hers is an ecclesiastical kingdom, and hers is a political kingdom. We shall now view, through the eyes of John, the fall of the ecclesiastical kingdom; and when we recount what the revelations say about the battle of Armageddon, we shall tell of the fall of the political kingdom. The church of the devil is both an ecclesiastical and a political kingdom; it reigns in the hearts of men by imposing false doctrines upon them, and it uses the power of the state to enforce its hellish decrees. John's account of the fall of Babylon speaks of both kingdoms, but dramatizes the greatness of the fall and the severity of the judgments by speaking particularly of the fall of the ecclesiastical kingdom.

John's account primarily speaks of the same thing Nephi told about in these words: "Behold, that great and abominable church, the whore of all the earth, must tumble to the earth, and great must be the fall thereof. For the kingdom of the devil must shake, and they which belong to it must needs be stirred up unto repentance, or the devil will grasp them with his everlasting chains, and they be stirred up to anger, and perish." (2 Ne. 28:18-19.)

What is it, then, that the ancient apostle has to say about the fall of the great and abominable church? "I saw another angel come down from heaven, having great power," he says, "and the earth was lightened with his glory." The devil's kingdom on earth, which is his church, is "full of darkness." (Rev. 16:10.) How fitting that the angel who comes to announce its fall is of such standing and stature and glory that the whole earth is lightened by his very presence. When Babylon falls, darkness flees and light shines forth.

"And he cried mightily with a strong voice, saying, Babylon the great is fallen, is fallen, and is become the habitation of devils, and the hold of every foul spirit, and a

cage of every unclean and hateful bird." What is this declaration but an application of Isaiah's prophecy about ancient
Babylon. Wild beasts and doleful creatures, satyrs and
dragons, were to take over forever what was once the
mightiest and grandest city ever built. So shall it be, the
angel said, with spiritual Babylon in the last days.

"For all nations have drunk of the wine of the wrath of
her fornication, and the kings of the earth have committed
fornication with her, and the merchants of the earth are
waxed rich through the abundance of her delicacies." The
Babylonish church falls; the church that caused kings and
nations to worship false gods—which false worship is
spiritual fornication!—lo, she falls. As our latter-day revelation has it: "That great church, the mother of abominations, that made all nations drink of the wine of the wrath
of her fornication, that persecuteth the saints of God, that
shed their blood—she who sitteth upon many waters, and
upon the islands of the sea—behold, she is the tares of the
earth; she is bound in bundles; her bands are made strong,
no man can loose them; therefore, she is ready to be
burned." (D&C 88:94.)

At this point John "heard another voice from heaven,
saying, Come out of her, my people, that ye be not partakers of her sins, and that ye receive not of her plagues.
For her sins have reached unto heaven, and God hath
remembered her iniquities." As it was in the days of Cyrus,
so shall it be in the day of Christ. The cry shall go forth:
'Go ye out from Babylon; flee ye from the Chaldeans;
forsake the world; turn your face to Zion; come, worship
the Lord in his holy mount. Believe the gospel and partake
not of the promised plagues.'

And as to Babylon: "Reward her even as she rewarded
you, and double unto her double according to her works: in
the cup which she hath filled fill to her double. How much
she hath glorified herself, and lived deliciously, so much
torment and sorrow give her: for she saith in her heart, I sit
a queen, and am no widow, and shall see no sorrow." How

marvelous to the carnal mind is the religion of the world! Those who worship at its shrines and who mouth its doctrines thereby drink an opiate that dulls the conscience. They are free to live in lust, free to savor deliciously the fleeting fancies of the flesh, and yet to have a hope of salvation as they suppose.

"Therefore shall her plagues come in one day, death, and mourning, and famine; and she shall be utterly burned with fire: for strong is the Lord God who judgeth her." Plagues first, the burning second—and those who escape the disease and pestilence shall be consumed in the fires. For "all the proud and they that do wickedly shall be as stubble; and I will burn them up, for I am the Lord of Hosts; and I will not spare any that remain in Babylon." (D&C 64:24.)

In this setting we hear a great dirge; mournful sounds fill the air; the kings and merchants and great ones of the earth lament and weep over the fall of all those things in which they trusted. "And the kings of the earth, who have committed fornication and lived deliciously with her, shall bewail her, and lament for her, when they shall see the smoke of her burning, Standing afar off for the fear of her torment, saying, Alas, alas, that great city Babylon, that mighty city! for in one hour is thy judgment come." When the religions of men and of devils fail; when the churches of men and of devils are shown forth for what they are; when the ways of men and of devils come to naught—then, oh then, what howling and lamentation shall arise from ten thousand times ten thousand throats!

"And the merchants of the earth shall weep and mourn over her; for no man buyeth their merchandise any more: The merchandise of gold, and silver, and precious stones, and of pearls, and fine linen, and purple, and silk, and scarlet, and all thyine wood, and all manner vessels of ivory, and all manner vessels of most precious wood, and of brass, and iron, and marble, And cinnamon, and odours, and ointments, and frankincense, and wine, and oil, and fine flour, and wheat, and beasts, and sheep, and horses, and chariots, and slaves, and souls of men.'' The riches of this world—how little value they shall have in eternity. The precious baubles of gold and the granaries filled with corn—of what worth shall they be in that great day? And that great and abominable church, which thrives on merchandising and which sells the souls of men for any price the market will bear—of what profit will it all be to her in the day of burning?

''And the fruits that thy soul lusted after are departed from thee, and all things which were dainty and goodly are departed from thee, and thou shalt find them no more at all. The merchants of these things, which were made rich by her, shall stand afar off for the fear of her torment, weeping and wailing, And saying, Alas, alas, that great city, that was clothed in fine linen, and purple, and scarlet, and decked with gold, and precious stones, and pearls! For in one hour so great riches is come to nought.'' The city is Babylon; she is the similitude. The city is Rome; but she too is only a type and a figure. The city is all the cities of the world—San Francisco, Chicago, and New York City; London, Paris, and Berlin; Moscow, Tokyo, and Sao Paulo—all of which are subject to the rule and dominion of evil and carnality.

''And every shipmaster, and all the company in ships, and sailors, and as many as trade by sea, stood afar off, And cried when they saw the smoke of her burning, saying, What city is like unto this great city! And they cast dust on their heads, and cried, weeping and wailing, saying, Alas, alas, that great city, wherein were made rich all that had ships in the sea by reason of her costliness! for in one hour is she made desolate.'' How the commerce of the world will be affected when the hearts of men are no longer centered on the delicacies and merchandise that are carried in ships.

''Rejoice over her, thou heaven, and ye holy apostles and prophets; for God hath avenged you on her.'' God hath done it; it is the day of his vengeance. No longer need the righteous wear out their lives in the war with worldliness; it is the day of righteousness and peace in which all evil has fled. It is the millennial day.

"And a mighty angel took up a stone like a great millstone, and cast it into the sea, saying, Thus with violence shall that great city Babylon be thrown down, and shall be found no more at all." As Isaiah said: "It shall never be inhabited, neither shall it be dwelt in from generation to generation." (Isa. 13:20.) "And the voice of harpers, and musicians, and of pipers, and trumpeters, shall be heard no more at all in thee; and no craftsman, of whatsoever craft he be, shall be found any more in thee; and the sound of a millstone shall be heard no more at all in thee; And the light of a candle shall shine no more at all in thee; and the voice of the bridegroom and of the bride shall be heard no more at all in thee: for thy merchants were the great men of the earth; for by thy sorceries were all nations deceived." Thy sorceries, thy magic incantations, thy masses and rites and mysterious recitations—thy substitutes for that pure religion, with its simplicity of worship, that was found among the primitive saints—all these have deceived all nations.

"And in her was found the blood of prophets, and of saints, and of all that were slain upon the earth." (Rev. 18:1-24.) Murder, martyrdom, and war, these three, the death-dealing tools of the evil one—all such that have occurred in all the earth are laid at the door of the mother of abominations whose end is soon to be.

"And after these things I heard a great voice of much people in heaven, saying, Alleluia; Salvation, and glory, and honour, and power, unto the Lord our God: For true and righteous are his judgments: for he hath judged the great whore, which did corrupt the earth with her fornication, and hath avenged the blood of his servants at her hand. And again they said, Alleluia. And her smoke rose up for ever and ever." (Rev. 19:1-3.)

446

And thus it shall be with Babylon, Babylon the great who is fallen, is fallen. And when she falls, God grant that we may join in the heavenly chorus of Alleluia, the chorus of praise and adoration to the Lord our God, who hath wrought her destruction.

Chapter 38

ARMAGEDDON: FORETOLD BY THE PROPHETS

Armageddon: A Day of Blood and Horror and Death

Surely the Lord God who revealeth his secrets unto his servants·the prophets, and who maketh known unto them all things which it is expedient for them to know, according to the heed and diligence they give unto him, surely he will tell them of that great Armageddon that lies ahead. Surely, if the God of Battles is destined to return, destroy the wicked, and bring peace on earth, all at the very moment when the greatest war of the ages is in progress, surely he will tell his prophets about that coming war. If he has been at pains to speak of wars and rumors of wars in the last days, surely he will not overlook revealing all we are able to bear about the final great war that will usher in the Millennium. If prophetic voices—rising early, crying out during the heat of the day, and refusing to be silenced when the night comes—if these voices have told us about lesser wars and smaller plagues, surely they will cry out, in advance, about the plague of plagues and the war of wars.

Be it remembered that both Nephi and John saw in vision the evil and dire apostasy and the formation of the great and abominable church in post-apostolic days. Be it

448

remembered that to each of them was shown how this wretched harlot and mother of abominations, this wicked whore of all the earth who was like unto Babylon of old, gained power over the kings of the earth and those who dwelt in all nations. Recall also that they both beheld the restoration of the gospel in the last days, the gathering again of the Lord's ancient covenant people, and the frightful plagues and final war that would usher in the Second Coming. Be it remembered also that the Lord God hath shown all these things unto "others who have been," and that "they have written them; and they are sealed up to come forth in their purity, according to the truth which is in the Lamb, in the own due time of the Lord, unto the house of Israel." (1 Ne. 14:26.)

We have already quoted at some length from Nephi and John and some others on these matters. Let us now, however, pick up a few additional slivers of revealed truth from various of the prophets. Let us drink as deeply as our spiritual thirst permits from the fountains of inspiration and wisdom. When the seventh seal is opened, all these things relative to Armageddon and the great winding-up scene will come to pass in their eternal fulness. Can any of us know too much or envision too fully what lies ahead? Perhaps if our cup of knowledge is full and our obedience runneth over, we shall escape some of the plagues and sorrows that shall fall upon the wicked when the cup of their iniquity is full.

As we search the scriptures for prophetic statements about Armageddon, we must have the promised coming events in their true perspective. Armageddon is the final great battle in a war that covers the earth and involves all nations. We suppose it will be the first and only time, until the armies of Gog and Magog clash for a second time after the Millennium, when no nation in any land will be neutral. This coming conflict will be universal, and out of it will come the final day of destruction and burning. It will exceed in horror, intensity, and scope all prior wars. It is only in the last days that there are enough people on earth to field armies of the required size, and only now do we have the weapons to slay millions at a single blast. What, then, say the prophets about Armageddon?

Approaching this matter, as he so often did in his Messianic utterances, David said: "The Lord trieth the righteous. . . . Upon the wicked he shall rain snares, fire and brimstone, and an horrible tempest." (Ps. 11:5-6.) "He shall judge among the heathen, he shall fill the places with the dead bodies." (Ps. 110:6.) "All nations compassed me about: but in the name of the Lord will I destroy them." (Ps. 118:10.) Fire and brimstone are to be rained upon all nations; all of their ungodly inhabitants shall be destroyed in the name of the Lord; dead bodies will be everywhere; it is a day of judgment.

"Thy men shall fall by the sword, and thy mighty in the war," Isaiah says of a latter-day Zion in which there are some wicked and wanton people. "And her gates shall lament and mourn." (Isa. 3:25-26.) "And I will punish the world for their evil, and the wicked for their iniquity; and I will cause the arrogancy of the proud to cease, and will lay low the haughtiness of the terrible. . . . Every one that is found shall be thrust through; and every one that is joined unto them shall fall by the sword. Their children also shall be dashed to pieces before their eyes; their houses shall be spoiled, and their wives ravished." (Isa. 13:11, 15-16.) These expressions are part of a recitation of what is to be at the Second Coming.

"Come near, ye nations, to hear; and hearken, ye people: let the earth hear, and all that is therein; the world, and all things that come forth of it." Let all men know of the coming wars and desolations; let them know that Armageddon is at the door; let them know that the sword of the Lord's justice hangs heavily over all men. Let not these things be hidden from them. They are entitled to be warned, and God, by the mouth of Isaiah, raises the warning voice.

"For the indignation of the Lord is upon all nations, and his fury upon all their armies: he hath utterly destroyed them, he hath delivered them to the slaughter. Their slain also shall be cast out, and their stink shall come up out of their carcases, and the mountains shall be melted with their blood." How horrible is the day. The destruction of the Jaredites and of the Nephites is as nothing in comparison. The dropping of atomic bombs on Hiroshima and Nagasaki, and the Lord only knows where else, is only the beginning of sorrows, as it were. This coming war shall involve all nations, and the dead shall not be numbered.

When shall all this be? When shall all nations come to the slaughter, when shall the carcasses of their great ones raise such a stench as has never before choked the nostrils of men? It shall be when "all the host of heaven shall be dissolved"—when the elements shall melt with fervent heat—"and the heavens shall be rolled together as a scroll"—one of the great events incident to the Second Coming—"and all their host shall fall down, as the leaf falleth off from the vine, and as a falling fig from the fig tree." The prophetic word is sure; the eventuality is certain; the war is decreed, and the war shall come.

"For my sword shall be bathed in heaven: behold, it shall come down upon Idumea, and upon the people of my curse, to judgment." Of these same things our latter-day revelation says: "Wherefore the voice of the Lord is unto the ends of the earth, that all that will may hear: Prepare ye, prepare ye for that which is to come, for the Lord is nigh; And the anger of the Lord is kindled, and his sword is bathed in heaven, and it shall fall upon the inhabitants of the earth. . . . And also the Lord shall . . . come down in judgment upon Idumea, or the world." (D&C 1:11-13, 36.) And it is just such newly revealed pronouncements as this—picking up and interpreting the very words and phrases of the ancient word as they do—that, among other things, enable us to know with unshakable certainty the true meaning of much that the ancient prophets said.

But back to Isaiah and the great and last war of which he is speaking. "The sword of the Lord is filled with blood, . . . for the Lord hath a sacrifice in Bozrah, and a great slaughter in the land of Idumea. . . . For it is the day of the Lord's vengeance, and the year of recompences for the controversy of Zion. And the streams thereof shall be turned into pitch, and the dust thereof into brimstone, and the land thereof shall become burning pitch. It shall not be quenched night nor day." (Isa. 34:1-10.) After this, Isaiah speaks of the coming of the Lord, of the desert blossoming as the rose, and of the ransomed of the Lord returning to Zion with songs of everlasting joy.

From yet another passage, in which Isaiah is speaking of the Second Coming and the Millennium, we select these words relative to the final great war: "For by fire and by his sword will the Lord plead with all flesh: and the slain of the Lord shall be many. . . . I will gather all nations and tongues. . . . And they shall go forth, and look upon the carcases of the men that have transgressed against me: for their worm shall not die, neither shall their fire be quenched; and they shall be an abhorring unto all flesh." (Isa. 66:16, 18, 24.) Not only shall the dead bodies of the slain pollute the earth, but their spirits shall also be cast into hell, there to suffer the torments of the damned.

By the mouth of Jeremiah, the Lord sent a message to "all the kingdoms of the world, which are upon the face of the earth." The ancient prophet was to "take the wine cup" of the Lord's "fury" and "cause all the nations . . . to drink it." He was to say to them: "Thus saith the Lord of hosts, the God of Israel; Drink ye, and be drunken, and spue, and fall, and rise no more, because of the sword which I will send among you."

It is to the nations of the earth that are and shall be in our day that these dire words are addressed. They shall all fall by the sword, and none shall remain, or rise again, or be a nation or a kingdom thereafter. "For I will call for a sword upon all the inhabitants of the earth, saith the Lord of hosts." Lo, at long last, all men in all nations in all the world are to feel the wrath of the Lord.

"Therefore prophesy thou against them all these words, and say unto them, The Lord shall roar from on high, and utter his voice from his holy habitation; he shall mightily roar upon his habitation; he shall give a shout, as they that tread the grapes, against all the inhabitants of the earth. A noise shall come even to the ends of the earth; for the Lord hath a controversy with the nations, he will plead with all flesh; he will give them that are wicked to the sword, saith the Lord." Almost all men upon all the face of the earth will be wicked; a few only will stand in holy places and find a covert to shield them from the terrible storm. As to the others, the wicked shall slay the wicked until there are few men left. It shall be an awful day.

"Thus saith the Lord of hosts, Behold, evil shall go forth from nation to nation, and a great whirlwind shall be raised up from the coasts of the earth. And the slain of the Lord shall be at that day from one end of the earth even unto the other end of the earth: they shall not be lamented, neither gathered, nor buried; they shall be dung upon the ground." (Jer. 25:14-33.) How many will be slain, and who shall count the number of dead bodies? When we come to the revealed description of the battle itself, we shall see that the slain will be a third of the inhabitants of the earth itself, however many billions of people that may turn out to be.

Armageddon: A Day for Repentance and Hope

So far we have spoken more particularly of the blood and horror and death that shall cover the earth as part of the final great conflict that ushers in the Millennium. Words fail us and prophetic pens shake with palsy as those who see the future seek to record the bestiality and wickedness, the plagues and the sorrows of that coming day. And yet, amid it all, there are a few rays of hope for some of the saints in whose day the great desolations shall come. And there is ultimate triumph and glory and honor—either in life or in death—for all the faithful. For, be it remembered, it is on the mount and in the valley of Meggido, and on the plains of Esdraelon, and on the Mount of Olives—at which places the great battle of Armageddon shall center—that the Millennium will be born.

Let us, then, turn to the prophetic words of Joel, who includes in his inspired writings an added dimension, a dimension of hope and salvation for a favored few, where the final war is concerned. He speaks of the dread and death that shall attend it. But he also issues a call of repentance to Israel, coupled with a promise that some few, through righteousness, may escape the horrors of that dread day. And he restates what all the prophets affirm, that in the millennial day Israel and all the faithful shall finally triumph over all their enemies and ever thereafter live in joy and peace before the Lord.

Joel speaks first of the plagues that have destroyed the fruits of the earth, and then of the armies—"strong, and without number, whose teeth are the teeth of a lion"—that have come against Israel. The land is wasted and their social order is in complete disarray. But the chosen people have a responsibility; the defenders of Jerusalem must do all they can to save themselves; the cause of freedom must still have its champions. And so the prophetic call goes forth: "Gird yourselves, and lament, ye priests: howl, ye ministers of the altar: come, lie all night in sackcloth, ye ministers of my God." There is work to be done; repentance is needed; perhaps the Lord will still hear our cry. If the God of Battles is to come down and fight for Israel as he did in the days of their fathers, he must be importuned. The people must unite in mighty faith. It was by faith that the mouths of lions were closed anciently, and so shall it be again when the teeth of lions afflict the Lord's people.

"Sanctify ye a fast, call a solemn assembly, gather the

elders and all the inhabitants of the land into the house of the Lord your God, and cry unto the Lord, Alas for the day! for the day of the Lord is at hand, and as a destruction from the Almighty shàll it come." Surely if there is any hope for any people in that day, it will be in the Lord of Hosts. Who can stay the rain of atomic bombs? How can any be healed from the atomic fallout, except by the power of faith? How can the crops of the earth grow and the beasts of the field survive in the days of the plagues, except by the power of faith?

"How do the beasts groan! the herds of cattle are perplexed, because they have no pasture; yea, the flocks of sheep are made desolate. O Lord, to thee will I cry: for the fire hath devoured the pastures of the wilderness, and the flame hath burned all the trees of the field. The beasts of the field cry also unto thee: for the rivers of waters are dried up, and the fire hath devoured the pastures of the wilderness." (Joel 1:1-20.) Faith and faith alone will prevail in that dread day. For all others there will be naught but sorrow and suffering and death.

As to Armageddon itself, Joel waxes eloquent. He sees in vision our modern warfare and describes it in terms of the weaponry and combatants of his day. "Blow ye the trumpet in Zion, and sound an alarm in my holy mountains," saith the Lord. "Let all the inhabitants of the land tremble: for the day of the Lord cometh, for it is nigh at hand." The Great Jehovah shall return; all men must be warned; the war-of-his-return is at hand; let the trumpet sound the alarm.

Unless men are warned they shall perish, for it is "a day of darkness and of gloominess, a day of clouds and of thick darkness, as the morning spread upon the mountains." Never has there been a day like unto this day. Even in the days of Noah there was not so great wickedness as in this gloomy and mournful hour. Men are prepared for the slaughter, and the armies are assembling. "There hath not been ever the like, neither shall be any more after it, even to the years of many generations." Not until the war of Gog and Magog after the Millennium, plus a little season, will there be another conflict like unto it.

"A fire devoureth before them; and behind them a flame burneth." Are these the flame-throwers, the incendiary bombs, and other means yet to be devised by men that shall be used to burn and destroy? "The land is as the garden of Eden before them, and behind them a desolate wilderness; yea, and nothing shall escape them." It is as when Rome planted Carthage with salt. It is as when the Medes and the Persians put a torch to Babylon. It is as when an atomic bomb fell upon Hiroshima.

How can Joel, who has seen nothing but swords and spears and shields, describe the warriors and their weapons? "The appearance of them is as the appearance of horses; and as horsemen so shall they run." Are these the tanks and trucks and mechanized vehicles used by a modern army? "Like the noise of chariots on the tops of mountains shall they leap, like the noise of a flame of fire that devoureth the stubble, as a strong people set in battle array." Is he seeing airplanes and helicopters and intercontinental ballistic missiles? Or does the vision show weapons and armaments yet to be invented?

"Before their face the people shall be much pained: all faces shall gather blackness." How fearful modern weaponry has become. How horrendous is the slaughter, which no soldier in the ranks can avoid. "They shall run like mighty men; they shall climb the wall like men of war; and they shall march every one on his ways, and they shall not break their ranks: Neither shall one thrust another; they shall walk every one in his path: and when they fall upon the sword, they shall not be wounded. They shall run to and fro in the city; they shall run upon the wall, they shall climb up upon the houses; they shall enter in at the windows like a thief." How disciplined and invincible are the warriors. How safely they stand behind their armor. How rapid is their movement from one scene of conflict to another. Their spies are everywhere. To Joel it is beyond anything he has imagined or supposed in his wildest dreams.

Their thunderous power cannot be resisted. "The earth shall quake before them; the heavens shall tremble: the sun and the moon shall be dark, and the stars shall withdraw their shining." It is the great and dreadful day; it is the day of the Second Coming; and the Lord himself shall descend from heaven with a shout and with the voice of the archangel.

"And the Lord shall utter his voice before his army: for his camp is very great: for he is strong that executeth his word: for the day of the Lord is great and very terrible; and who can abide it?" One host opposes the other. One host is for God and his cause; the other fights against him. Both hosts are comprised of wicked and worldly men, but one is defending freedom, and the other would destroy liberty and enslave men. One defends free institutions, freedom in government, freedom to worship the god of one's choice according to one's own conscience, and the other, Lucifer-like, seeks to overthrow liberty and freedom in all its forms. And the Lord himself is interceding to bring to pass his own purposes.

But if the Lord is to fight the battles of his people, ought they not turn to him and plead for his help? "Therefore also now, saith the Lord, turn ye even to me with all your heart, and with fasting, and with weeping, and with mourning." Armageddon is in progress; the dreadful day has arrived; but still the Lord's arm is not shortened that he will not save the penitent. There is still hope for those who believe and repent and obey. Therefore, let the cry go forth: "Rend your heart, and not your garments, and turn unto the Lord your God: for he is gracious and merciful, slow to anger, and of great kindness, and repenteth him of the evil." With this call comes the quiet assurance couched by Joel in question form: "Who knoweth if he will return and repent, and leave a blessing behind him?" Truly he will do so for those who seek him with all their hearts; truly his saints will be blessed, whether in life or in death, no matter how dire and gloomy the day.

Members of the Church will have a special need to seek the Lord in those days. "Blow the trumpet in Zion," the divine word commands, yea, "sanctify a fast, call a solemn assembly; Gather the people, sanctify the congregation, assemble the elders, gather the children, and those that suck the breasts: let the bridegroom go forth of his chamber, and the bride out of her closet. Let the priests, the ministers of the Lord, weep between the porch and the altar, and let them say, Spare thy people, O Lord, and give not thine heritage to reproach, that the heathen should rule over them: wherefore should they say among the people, Where is their God?" Let the members of The Church of Jesus Christ of Latter-day Saints keep the commandments, stand fast in the day of doom, and prepare for the day of their redemption.

When the Lord has tested their faith to the full, he will give his answer. Then his help will come. For his saints there shall be a great reward. It is millennial peace. Because they sought the Lord with all their hearts in an evil and gloomy day, they in turn shall abide the day of his coming. "Then will the Lord be jealous for his land, and pity his people. Yea, the Lord will answer and say unto his people, Behold, I will send you corn, and wine, and oil, and ye shall be satisfied therewith: and I will no more make you a reproach among the heathen."

In that day those who fight on the Lord's side shall come off victorious. "I will remove far off from you the northern army," saith the Lord, "and will drive him into a land barren and desolate, with his face toward the east sea, and his hinder part toward the utmost [western] sea, and his stink shall come up, and his ill savour shall come up, because he hath done great things." All of these things shall not happen in an hour or a day or, we suppose, a few years. The final war will be long and perilous, with many battles and much bloodshed and continuing horrors. But in the end the proper cause will triumph.

Then will the Lord's word as given through Joel come to pass: "Fear not, O land; be glad and rejoice: for the Lord will do great things. Be not afraid, ye beasts of the field: for the pastures of the wilderness do spring, for the tree beareth her fruit, the fig tree and the vine do yield their strength. Be glad then, ye children of Zion, and rejoice in the Lord your God. . . . And the floors shall be full of wheat, and the fats shall overflow with wine and oil. . . . And ye shall eat in plenty, and be satisfied, and praise the name of the Lord your God, that hath dealt wondrously with you: and my people shall never be ashamed." All this shall come to pass in the millennial day.

"And ye shall know that I am in the midst of Israel, and that I am the Lord your God, and none else: and my people shall never be ashamed." In that day the Lord shall dwell personally upon the earth. "And it shall come to pass, that whosoever shall call on the name of the Lord shall be delivered: for in mount Zion and in Jerusalem shall be deliverance, as the Lord hath said, and in the remnant whom the Lord shall call." (Joel 2:1-32.) O glorious, wondrous day! O blessed millennial day!

By way of summary and recapitulation Joel, speaking in the first person for the Lord, says: "For, behold, in those days, and in that time, when I shall bring again the captivity of Judah and Jerusalem"—when Judah returns to Palestine, and when old Jerusalem is rebuilt by the true saints, and when her promised temple sits again on the ancient sacred site—then "I will also gather all nations, and will bring them down into the valley of Jehoshaphat, and will plead with them there for my people and for my heritage Israel, whom they have scattered among the nations, and parted my land." This is the promised day of Armageddon when all nations are involved in the final war. Jehoshaphat, meaning Jehovah judges, is a valley near Jerusalem.

Then, in that day, the cry shall go forth: "Proclaim ye

this among the Gentiles; Prepare war, wake up the mighty men, let all the men of war draw near; let them come up: Beat your plowshares into swords, and your pruninghooks into spears: let the weak say, I am strong. Assemble yourselves, and come, all ye heathen, and gather yourselves together round about: thither cause thy mighty ones to come down, O Lord." The might of the world and the mighty among men shall be assembled. The day of the war of wars has arrived.

It shall be a day of judgment. "Let the heathen be wakened, and come up to the valley of Jehoshaphat: for there will I sit to judge all the heathen round about." In that day there will be a complete separation between the righteous and the wicked. In that day the great Judge shall issue his decrees. The wicked shall be destroyed and faithful Israel shall be saved.

It shall also be a day of missionary work. Men shall not be judged and found wanting until they have had opportunity to hear the gospel and forsake the world. The voice of warning shall be raised by the elders of Israel. They shall preach the everlasting gospel with a loud voice and with the sound of a trump. The names of Jesus Christ and Joseph Smith shall be trumpeted in every ear. "Put ye in the sickle, for the harvest is ripe: come, get you down; for the press is full, the fats overflow; for their wickedness is great. Multitudes, multitudes in the valley of decision: for the day of the Lord is near in the valley of decision." All men, from one end of the earth to the other, must then decide whether they are for God or against him, whether they will obey his gospel law or continue to live after the manner of the world, whether they will come unto Christ or continue to serve Satan.

Then "the sun and the moon shall be darkened, and the stars shall withdraw their shining." Then "the Lord also shall roar out of Zion, and utter his voice from Jerusalem; and the heavens and the earth shall shake: but the Lord will be the hope of his people, and the strength of the children of Israel.'' Then shall the great Millennium pour forth its blessings upon all who remain. ''So shall ye know that I am the Lord your God dwelling in Zion, my holy mountain,'' saith the Lord. ''Then shall Jerusalem be holy, and there shall no strangers pass through her any more.'' Only the pure and the clean and the worthy shall walk through her streets in that day.

''And it shall come to pass in that day, that the mountains shall drop down new wine, and the hills shall flow with milk, and all the rivers of Judah shall flow with waters, and a fountain shall come forth of the house of the Lord, and shall water the valley of Shittim.'' It is the day appointed for the redemption of Zion and for the glory of the chosen people. ''Egypt shall be a desolation,'' however, ''and Edom shall be a desolate wilderness, for the violence against the children of Judah, because they have shed innocent blood in their land.'' Those in Egypt and in Edom who remain, and those in every nation who have not received the gospel and bowed the knee to Him whose gospel it is, shall not as yet receive the fulness of the promised blessings.

''But Judah shall dwell for ever, and Jerusalem from generation to generation. For I will cleanse their blood that I have not cleansed: for the Lord dwelleth in Zion.'' (Joel 3:1-21.) The great day of redemption and of salvation for the Jews is reserved for the Second Coming. Then, when the Lord dwells among his people—among those who remain—they shall be cleansed by baptism and saved by righteousness.

Chapter 39

JERUSALEM
AND ARMAGEDDON

Armageddon: Jerusalem Besieged

Jerusalem is the Holy City, the city of David, the city of the Great King. It is the city where Melchizedek, the king of Salem and the prince of peace, reigned in righteousness and with his people served the Lord in spirit and in truth. Jerusalem, captured by David from the Jebusites, became the capital city in Israel and later the capital of the kingdom of Judah.

In her environs the Son of God was born; in her streets the Holy Messiah ministered; and in her temple the witness was borne of his divine Sonship. Outside her walls, in a garden called Gethsemane, suffering in agony beyond compare, he took upon himself the sins of all men on conditions of repentance. Outside her walls at a place called Golgotha, he was nailed to a cross and crucified for the sins of the world. Outside her walls in a quiet garden, he burst the bands of death, arose from the Arimathean's tomb, and brought life and immortality to light.

Jerusalem, in the days of her sorrow, was sacked by Nebuchadnezzar, conquered by Rome, put to the torch by Titus. And now for nearly two millenniums she has been trodden down of the Gentiles, and the end of her sorrow is not yet. In the days ahead some of the faithful will gather again within her walls and shall build the promised temple, a temple whose functions and uses will be patterned after the house of the Lord in Salt Lake City. Thereafter two prophets—valiant, mighty witnesses of the Lord Jesus Christ—will teach and testify and prophesy in her streets for three and a half years, at which time they will be slain, resurrected, and caught up to heaven. In the midst of the great war of Armageddon then in progress, Jerusalem will fall, the Lord will come, and the remnant of Judah that remains will accept the Nazarene as their King.

Jerusalem has ascended to the heights and descended to the depths. The Lord Omnipotent, who was and is from everlasting to everlasting, made the dust of her streets holy because the soles of his feet found footing there. The blood of prophets cries from that same dust for vengeance against godless wretches to whom innocent blood was of no more worth than sour wine. Jerusalem has been and yet again will be destroyed for her iniquities. When Nebuchadnezzar pillaged and burned and slew and carried the Jews into Babylon, it was because they had rejected Jeremiah and Lehi and the prophets. It was because they walked in an evil course. When Titus tore her asunder, slew most of her citizens, and made slaves of the rest, it was a just retribution because she had crucified her King. And when she falls again, amid the horror and brimstone and blood and fire of Armageddon, it will be because she has again slain the prophets and chosen to worship Baal and Bel and Merodach and all the idols of the heathen rather than the Lord Jehovah.

Wars come because of sin. They are born of lust and evil. The great tribulations sent upon the Jews in the days of Titus exceeded anything ever sent of God upon them from the beginning of their kingdom until that time. The tribulations parallel the sins. The Just One was slain, and the unjust murderers paid the penalty. So shall it be at Armageddon. The whole world will be wallowing in wickedness, but Jerusalem will be, as it were, the capital of all the wretched evils of the world. Once again the cup of her iniquity will be full, and she shall fall as she fell before. Then, having been cleansed by blood, she shall rise to become the millennial capital from which the word of the Lord shall go forth to all the earth.

Jehoshaphat, meaning Jehovah judges, is the valley between Jerusalem and the Mount of Olives. It is in this valley that the returning Lord will sit to judge the heathen nations. The Mount of Olives (also, Olivet) is a mountain of modest size on the east of the Holy City. It is there that the Lord will set his foot when this same Jesus who ascended from Olivet returns again.

The valley of Megiddo (once Megiddon), meaning place of troops, is part of the plain of Esdraelon (or plain of Jezreel), which is some twenty miles long and fourteen miles wide. It was on the plain of Esdraelon that Elijah had his confrontation with the priests of Baal. The valley of Megiddo has been a famous battleground through the centuries. It is in Samaria, a few miles south of Nazareth of Galilee. Armageddon is the hill of the valley of Megiddo west of Jordan on the plain of Jezreel. And Armageddon is the place where the final war will be fought, meaning, as we suppose, that it will be the focal point of a worldwide conflict, and also that as a place of ancient warfare, it will be a symbol of the conflict that will be raging in many nations and on many battlefronts.

Having these things in mind, let us turn to the prophetic word relative to Jerusalem and the final great battle during which our Lord will return. "Behold, I will make Jerusalem a cup of trembling unto all the people round about," saith the Lord, "when they shall be in the siege both against Judah and against Jerusalem." Armageddon is in process; all nations are at war; some are attacking Jerusalem and others are defending the once holy city. She is the political prize. Three world religions claim her—Christianity, Islam, and Judaism. Emotion and fanaticism run high; it is a holy war as such have been called through the ages. Men are fighting for their religion. They are in siege against the city of Jerusalem and the land of Judah.

"And in that day will I make Jerusalem a burdensome stone for all people: all that burden themselves with it shall be cut in pieces, though all the people of the earth be gathered together against it." What though all the nations of the earth come up to battle against Jerusalem, yet, in due course, and after the fall of the city and the destruction of the wicked, all shall fail and fall and their venture shall come to naught. "In that day, saith the Lord, I will smite every horse with astonishment, and his rider with madness: and I will open mine eyes upon the house of Judah, and will smite every horse of the people with blindness." (Zech. 12:2-4.) The warring hosts shall be smitten with madness, and a blind rage will overrule all reason. Men will say, "Let us eat and drink; for tomorrow we shall die," and the answering word will be: "Surely this iniquity shall not be purged from you till ye die, saith the Lord God of hosts." (Isa. 22:13-14.)

How will the battle go, and who will come off victorious? What chance for life will any have, considering the destructive power of the weapons then in the hands of the madmen who command the armies? In answer we are told: "And it shall come to pass, that in all the land, saith the Lord, two parts therein shall be cut off and die; but the third shall be left therein." This is Israel of whom he speaks. These are the armies who are defending Jerusalem and whose cause, in the eternal sense, is just. Two-thirds of them shall die.

"And I will bring the third part through the fire, and will refine them as silver is refined, and will try them as gold is tried: they shall call on my name, and I will hear them: I will say, It is my people: and they shall say, The Lord is my God." (Zech. 13:8-9.) We repeat: It is a religious war. The forces of antichrist are seeking to destroy freedom and liberty and right; they seek to deny men the right to worship the Lord; they are the enemies of God. The one-third who remain in the land of Israel are the Lord's people. They believe in Christ and accept Joseph Smith as his prophet and revealer for the last days.

But what of the wicked among the defenders of Jerusalem? They shall be destroyed. "Behold, the day of the Lord cometh, and thy spoil shall be divided in the midst of thee," saith the Lord. "For I will gather all nations against Jerusalem to battle"—remember, this is Armageddon, and all the nations of the earth are at war—"and the city shall be taken, and the houses rifled, and the women ravished; and half of the city shall go forth into captivity, and the residue of the people shall not be cut off from the city." So shall it be with Jerusalem when she falls again.

But what of the fate of those who fought against her? In spite of her fall, Jerusalem shall be victorious. Though she is taken and pillaged and her women ravished, yet in the end she shall be victorious. As to her enemies the account says: "And this shall be the plague wherewith the Lord will smite all the people that have fought against Jerusalem; Their flesh shall consume away while they stand upon their feet, and their eyes shall consume away in their holes, and their tongue shall consume away in their mouth." Already man has created weapons that will have this very effect upon those upon whom the death-dealing powers are sent forth. And lest any assume that the ancient word shall not be fulfilled in the full and literal sense, the Lord in our day acclaims: "I the Lord God will send forth flies upon the face of the earth, which shall take hold of the inhabitants thereof, and shall eat their flesh, and shall cause maggots to come in upon them; And their tongues shall be stayed that they shall not utter against me; and their flesh shall fall from off their bones, and their eyes from their sockets; And it shall come to pass that the beasts of the forest and the fowls of the air shall devour them up." (D&C 29:18-20.)

These things boggle the mind and dull our sensitivities.

We can scarcely conceive the full horror of what is involved, and what we do envision shall be only the beginning of sorrows, as it were. "And it shall come to pass in that day, that a great tumult from the Lord shall be among them; and they shall lay hold every one on the hand of his neighbour, and his hand shall rise up against the hand of his neighbour." It is as though the whole world shall become one great arena of anarchy, with every man wielding his own sword and seeking to betray and slay his brother. "And Judah also shall fight at Jerusalem"—Jerusalem shall be defended manfully—"and the wealth of all the heathen round about shall be gathered together, gold, and silver, and apparel, in great abundance. And so shall be the plague of the horse, of the mule, of the camel, and of the ass, and of all the beasts that shall be in these tents, as this plague." (Zech. 14:1-2, 12-15.) Man and beast alike shall suffer and die, and the whole earth shall be one great Gehenna, where the worms and rats and creeping things feast on the carcasses of the slain.

The Jewish Conversion and Cleansing

Out of Armageddon will come great blessings, in the eternal sense, to those Jews and others who abide the day. "In that day"—when all nations are gathered together against Jerusalem and she has become a cup of trembling unto all the people—"shall the Lord defend the inhabitants of Jerusalem; and he that is feeble among them at that day shall be as David; and the house of David shall be as God, as the angel of the Lord before them." This is the day when two shall put their tens of thousands to flight, when divine intervention will scatter the hosts of the wicked, when in weakness and by faith the Lord's people will wax valiant and put to flight the armies of the aliens.

"And it shall come to pass in that day, that I will seek to destroy all the nations that come against Jerusalem," saith the Lord. (Zech. 12:8-9.) "Then shall the Lord go forth, and fight against those nations, as when he fought in the day of battle.'' The battles will be fought by the warriors of earth, but the Lord's hand will be in it. It shall be with the defenders of Jerusalem as it was with Gideon and his three hundred soldiers when they put the Midianites to flight. It shall be as when Samson burst the cords with which he was bound, found a new jawbone of an ass, and with it slew a thousand Philistines. It shall be as when Israel prevailed over the armies of Amalek as long as Aaron and Hur held up the hands of Moses. The Lord will fight for Israel as he fought times without number for them during the long years of their sorrow and travail.

And then he shall come in person. The Great God shall appear. ''And his feet shall stand in that day upon the mount of Olives, which is before Jerusalem on the east, and the mount of Olives shall cleave in the midst thereof toward the east and toward the west, and there shall be a very great valley; and half of the mountain shall remove toward the north, and half of it toward the south.'' This shall be part of the upheavals which cause every valley to be exalted and every mountain to be made low. This shall be the immeasurably great earthquake foreseen by John and spoken of by the prophets.

Then, with reference to the people, the account continues: ''And ye shall flee to the valley of the mountains; . . . yea, ye shall flee, like as ye fled from before the earthquake in the days of Uzziah king of Judah: and the Lord my God shall come, and all the saints with thee.'' (Zech. 14:3-5.)

And further, with reference to the people—meaning those who remain, for by this time the wicked will have been destroyed by the plagues and the war and the burning—with reference to the people the Lord says: ''And I will pour upon the house of David, and upon the inhabitants of Jerusalem, the spirit of grace and of supplications.'' Lo, at long last the Jews shall turn to their Messiah and believe in him who was born of Mary in Bethlehem of Judea. They will supplicate the Lord their God, in the name of Christ who is the Deliverer, even as their forebears did, and the Lord will hear their cry. They will pray to the Father in the name of the Son, having faith in Christ, to gain the witness, borne of the Spirit, that the Book of Mormon is the mind and will and voice of the Lord to a fallen world. They will come to know by the revelations of the Holy Spirit of God that the Book of Mormon is a Jewish book that deals with Jews who went out from Jerusalem in the days of Zedekiah king of Judah.

"And they shall look upon me whom they have pierced." (Zech. 12:10.) The pierced one appears; the Prophet of Nazareth of Galilee stands before them; the Carpenter's Son whom they rejected comes in immortal glory. Now they know whether any good thing can come out of Nazareth and whether a true prophet shall arise from Galilee. The riven side of the Son of Man retains the wound whence came blood and water as his dead body hung on the cross of Calvary. "And one shall say unto him, What are these wounds in thine hands? Then he shall answer, Those with which I was wounded in the house of my friends." (Zech. 13:6.)

Oh, what sorrow, what mourning, what wailing shall rise in that day from the lips of all men in all nations, from all who have not made Christ—the true Christ—their King. How the Jews will mourn because they crucified their King. What sorrow will be in the hearts of the Mohammedans because they acclaimed him as one of the prophets and denied his divine Sonship. What tears will water the faces of all those whose fathers bequeathed false forms of worship to them. And how the Christians will wail—wail until it will seem their very souls shall dissolve into nothingness—for they, favored above all the kindreds of the earth, had the Holy Scriptures and could read the words of the ancient prophets and the holy apostles, and yet they did not believe the true gospel of the lowly one by whom salvation came. As Jesus said on Olivet, "Then shall all the tribes of the earth mourn; and they shall see the Son of Man coming in the clouds of heaven, with power and great glory." (JS-M 1:36.)

Zechariah, himself a Jew and writing to the Jews, and speaking of his own nation, said: "They shall mourn for him, as one mourneth for his only son, and shall be in bitterness for him, as one that is in bitterness for his firstborn." How apt is this language. The only Son of God, the Firstborn of the Father, is the one who was slain. If men mourn over the loss of an only son, who is their heir and firstborn, how much more ought they to mourn for the firstborn and heir of the Father, his Only Son, who, having come to bring salvation, was rejected and crucified by his friends.

"In that day shall there be a great mourning in Jerusalem, as the mourning of Hadadrimmon in the valley of Megiddon. And the land shall mourn, every family apart; the family of the house of David apart, and their wives apart; the family of the house of Nathan apart, and their wives apart; The family of the house of Levi apart, and their wives apart; the family of Shimei apart, and their wives apart; All the families that remain, every family apart, and their wives apart." (Zech. 12:10-14.) Then shall be fulfilled that which is written: "Behold, he cometh with clouds; and every eye shall see him, and they also which pierced him: and all kindreds of the earth shall wail because of him." (Rev. 1:7.)

We have received by revelation an amplified account of what the Lord Jesus said in the great Olivet discourse. Of his return to the Jews, which we are here considering, this holy word says: "Then shall the arm of the Lord fall upon the nations. And then shall the Lord set his foot upon this mount [the Mount of Olives], and it shall cleave in twain, and the earth shall tremble, and reel to and fro, and the heavens also shall shake. And the Lord shall utter his voice, and all the ends of the earth shall hear it; and the nations of the earth shall mourn, and they that have laughed shall see their folly. And calamity shall cover the mocker, and the scorner shall be consumed; and they that have watched for iniquity shall be hewn down and cast into the fire. And then shall the Jews look upon me and say: What are these wounds in thine hands and in thy feet? Then shall they know that I am the Lord; for I will say unto them: These wounds are the wounds with which I was wounded in the house of my friends. I am he who was lifted up. I am Jesus that was crucified. I am the Son of God. And then shall they weep because of their iniquities; then shall they lament because they persecuted their king." (D&C 45:47-53.)

"In that day there shall be a fountain opened to the house of David and to the inhabitants of Jerusalem for sin and for uncleanness." (Zech. 13:1.) A fountain, the cleansing fountain, the fountain of the Lord! What is it? It is a baptismal font. The house of David, the inhabitants of Jerusalem, the upright and noble in all nations, good men at the ends of the earth and among every kindred—all shall be baptized for the remission of sins. All shall receive the gift of the Holy Ghost, that baptism of fire which burns dross and evil out of a human soul as though by fire. In that day all men will gather with Israel, all shall come to Zion, all shall dwell in the cities of holiness, all shall see the face of the Lord for they are pure in heart.

Armageddon: The Abomination of Desolation

Daniel speaks of something called "the abomination that maketh desolate" (Dan. 12:11), and specifies that it shall take place when "the sanctuary," which is the temple in Jerusalem, is "trodden under foot" (Dan. 8:13). Speaking of "the buildings of the temple," Jesus said, "They shall be thrown down, and left unto you desolate." Also: "There shall not be left here, upon this temple, one stone upon another that shall not be thrown down."

Then, on Olivet, the disciples asked: "Tell us when shall these things be which thou hast said concerning the destruction of the temple." Our Lord recited various

471

events destined to occur and then said: "When you, therefore, shall see the abomination of desolation, spoken of by
Daniel the prophet, concerning the destruction of Jerusalem, then you shall stand in the holy place."

For the saints in that dread and evil day, Jesus counseled: "Then let them who are in Judea flee into the mountains." They are to leave the city and the land and go to a
place of safety. "Let him who is on the housetop flee, and
not return to take anything out of his house; Neither let him
who is in the field return back to take his clothes." Their
flight must be in haste. Roman steel will take the life of any
who linger. Houses and crops and property are of no moment. If their lives are to be spared, they must forsake the
things of this world and assemble with the fleeing saints in
holy places, there to prepare themselves for a better world
where the riches of eternity are found.

"And wo unto them that are with child, and unto them
that give suck in those days." Anything that delays their
flight or hinders their escape will seem as burdensome as a
great millstone round their necks. "Therefore, pray ye the
Lord that your flight be not in the winter, neither on the
Sabbath day." The fewer the restrictions and burdens surrounding their flight to freedom, the better. "For then, in
those days, shall be great tribulation on the Jews, and upon
the inhabitants of Jerusalem, such as was not before sent
upon Israel, of God, since the beginning of their kingdom
until this time; no, nor ever shall be sent again upon
Israel."

Guided by inspiration, the primitive saints withdrew
from Jerusalem and Judea before the desolating scourges
fell upon the city and the people. The saints left the unholy
city and went to a place of safety, a holy place, a place
made holy by their presence, for it is not places but people
that are holy. Then Titus came with his legions; a spirit of
blind fanaticism swept over the whole Jewish nation; and in
the war that followed, more than a million Jews in

Jerusalem were slain, every stone in the temple was torn from its place, and the balance of the people were carried away as captives and slaves. And it all came to pass because of sin and iniquity, because the Jewish nation rejected, scourged, and crucified their King. It came to pass because of abominations in the hearts of men, and it was a scourge and an abomination to them.

Then, in the Olivet discourse, when Jesus came to a consideration of the events of the last days, he said: "And again shall the abomination of desolation, spoken of by Daniel the prophet, be fulfilled." That which once happened to Jerusalem and its inhabitants shall happen again. "And immediately after the tribulation of those days, the sun shall be darkened, and the moon shall not give her light, and the stars shall fall from heaven, and the powers of heaven shall be shaken." (JS-M 1:2-33.) Such shall come to pass when the Lord Jesus comes again, when he puts his foot once more upon the Mount of Olives, when the earth reels to and fro.

In Luke's account of the abomination of desolation that took place in A.D. 70, we find these words of the Lord Jesus: "And when ye shall see Jerusalem compassed with armies, then know that the desolation thereof is nigh." So shall it be again; so shall it be shortly after the opening of the seventh seal when all the nations of the earth are gathered at Jerusalem. "Then let them which are in Judea flee to the mountains; and let them which are in the midst of it depart out; and let not them that are in the countries enter thereinto." Is this the way the saints shall be saved in the last days when two-thirds of the inhabitants shall be cut off and die and only one-third be left? If more than a million were put to the sword in A.D. 70, how great shall be the slaughter when atomic bombs are used? "For these be the days of vengeance, that all things which are written may be fulfilled." And again, in another day of vengeance, with even more of the prophetic word to be fulfilled, how great shall be the overflowing of abomination. "But woe unto them that are with child, and to them that give suck, in those days! for there shall be great distress in the land, and wrath upon this people." As it was once, so shall it be again. "And they shall fall by the edge of the sword, and shall be led away captive into all nations: and Jerusalem shall be trodden down of the Gentiles, until the times of the Gentiles be fulfilled." Will the temple be destroyed as it once was? How long shall the forces of evil control the city before the God of Battles comes down in fury and vengeance? These things we do not know. Of this only are we certain: At that day "there shall be signs in the sun, and in the moon, and in the stars; and upon the earth distress of nations, with perplexity." (Luke 21:20-25.) And then the Lord our God shall come in glory.

Pending that day, we are reminded that the Lord has said to us in our day: "A desolating scourge shall go forth among the inhabitants of the earth, and shall continue to be poured out from time to time, if they repent not"—and they will not repent—"until the earth is empty, and the inhabitants thereof are consumed away and utterly destroyed by the brightness of my coming. Behold, I tell you these things, even as I also told the people of the destruction of Jerusalem; and my word shall be verified at this time as it hath hitherto been verified." (D&C 5:19-20.)

And also: "In that generation" when "the times of the Gentiles" is fulfilled, "there shall be men standing in that generation, that shall not pass until they shall see an overflowing scourge; for a desolating sickness shall cover the land. But my disciples shall stand in holy places"—as did the primitive saints—"and shall not be moved; but among the wicked, men shall lift up their voices and curse God and die." (D&C 45:30-32.)

It is for these very reasons, among others, that we are commanded to "go forth among the Gentiles for the last time, as many as the mouth of the Lord shall name, to bind up the law and seal up the testimony, and to prepare the saints for the hour of judgment which is to come; That their souls may escape the wrath of God, the desolation of abomination which awaits the wicked, both in this world and in the world to come.'' (D&C 88:84-85.) And thus it is.

Chapter 40

ARMAGEDDON: GOG AND MAGOG

Armageddon: A Religious War

In the coming day—a dire, dread, damning day—woes without measure will fall upon men. Pestilence, plagues, and death will stalk the earth. The kings of the earth and of the whole world will gather to fight the battle of that great day of God Almighty. Their command center will be at Armageddon, overlooking the valley of Megiddo. All nations will be gathered against Jerusalem. Two hundred thousand thousand warriors and more—two hundred million men of arms and more—shall come forth to conquer or die on the plains of Esdraelon and in all the nations of the earth. At the height of this war, the Lord Jesus will put his foot on the Mount of Olives and save his ancient covenant people. Of all this we are aware.

Now it is our purpose to show that this war will be a religious war, a war in which the servants of Satan assail the servants of the Lord and those allied with them. The great and abominable church will wage war against everything that is decent in the world and will then be thrown down by devouring fire. The two witnesses we shall call to give extended testimony about this coming conflict with Gog and Magog are Daniel and Ezekiel. Their words we shall accept as law. Some of it will come to us in plainness; other portions of what they have to say will be hidden behind strange names and among unknown nations.

Daniel, speaking of that which shall come to pass "in the latter days" (Dan. 10:14), says a king of the south and a king of the north shall each have dominion and power over nations and peoples. Who these kings shall be and what nations shall be subject to them, no man knows. It is sufficient for our present purposes to know that the king of the north shall come with his armies and overrun the "chosen people, . . . and none shall stand before him: and he shall stand in the glorious land, which by his hand shall be consumed." The chosen people are the servants of the Lord with whom he has made the covenant of salvation; and the glorious land is Palestine, the Holy Land, the land promised of God to the seed of Abraham, with whom the covenant of salvation was made in days of old.

After this there will be wars and intrigue, with one king following another. Then again a king will come from the north. "His heart shall be against the holy covenant; and he shall do exploits, and return to his own land." It is a holy war; his armies are fighting a people because of their religion. He shall come again and be repulsed. Again Daniel says he shall "have indignation against the holy covenant." And also, he shall "have intelligence with them that forsake the holy covenant." Traitors to the cause of truth and righteousness will give their support to him.

When he comes again, it will be the occasion of "the abomination that maketh desolate," which we have heretofore seen means the fall of Jerusalem again in the final great war. We do not speculate as to what nations are involved in these wars. It is well known that the United States and Great Britain and the Anglo-Saxon peoples have traditionally been linked together in causes designed to promote freedom and guarantee the rights of man. It is also well known that there are other nations, ruled by a godless communistic power, that have traditionally fought to enslave rather than to free men. It is fruitless to try and name nations and set forth the alliances that are to be. Our purpose in alluding at all to these recitations of Daniel is to show that Armageddon will be a holy war. There will be political overtones, of course. Wars are fought by nations, which are political entities. But the underlying causes and the moving power in the hearts of men will be their views on religious issues. The grand desideratum will be whether they are for Christ and his gospel or against him and his cause.

Having these things in mind, it is instructive to ponder what Daniel has to say about these final great conflicts that usher in the day of millennial peace. After speaking of "the abomination that maketh desolate," Daniel says: "And such as do wickedly against the covenant shall be corrupt by flatteries." Those who oppose the covenant that is the everlasting gospel shall be flattered into joining the godless forces. "But the people that do know their God shall be strong, and do exploits." God is known by revelation; knowledge of him is found in the hearts of the faithful. "And they that understand among the people shall instruct many." The gospel will be taught; the mind and will of the Lord will be proclaimed; those who oppose the cause of truth and righteousness will do so with their eyes open. "Yet they shall fall by the sword, and by flame, by captivity, and by spoil, many days." These events shall go forward over a long period of time; there will be ample opportunity for all nations to choose the course they will pursue; the testing purposes of mortality will be fulfilled.

"And some of them of understanding shall fall, to try them, and to purge, and to make them white, even to the time of the end: because it is yet for a time appointed." Though they fall in this life, they shall rise in eternal glory in the next. Even the saints must be tried and tested to the full; the Lord is determining whether they will abide in his covenant even unto death, and those who do not so abide are not worthy of him.

At this point Daniel describes the anti-gospel, anti-Christ, anti-God nature of the king and his armies from the north. "He shall exalt himself, and magnify himself above every god," the scripture saith, "and shall speak marvellous things against the God of gods, and shall prosper till the indignation be accomplished: for that that is determined shall be done." Already the communistic nations exhibit this spirit. As the polarization between good and evil continues apace in the last days, we may expect to see even more resistance manifest by them toward God and his laws.

"Neither shall he regard the God of his fathers," the account continues, "nor the desire of women, nor regard any god: for he shall magnify himself above all. But in his estate shall he honour the God of forces: and a god whom his fathers knew not shall he honour with gold, and silver, and with precious stones, and pleasant things. Thus shall he do in the most strong holds with a strange god, whom he shall acknowledge and increase with glory: and he shall cause them to rule over many, and shall divide the land for gain." From the perspective of Daniel, in whose day all men worshipped one kind of a god or another, what would be more strange than to worship a god composed of spirit nothingness, or, as atheists do, to worship a philosophy that says there is no god. Clearly the great issues at Armageddon are God and religion and a way of worship. Satan will have done his work well; by then billions of earth's inhabitants (even more so then than now) will be in open rebellion against the gospel and every principle of truth and virtue found therein.

Now Daniel turns to the war itself. "And at the time of the end," he says, "shall the king of the south push at him: and the king of the north shall come against him like a whirlwind, with chariots, and with horsemen, and with many ships; and he shall enter into the countries, and shall overflow and pass over." It is a worldwide conflict. "He shall enter also into the glorious land"—Armageddon and Jerusalem are the central sites—"and many countries shall be overthrown." Some nations shall escape, and "he shall have power over the treasures of gold and of silver, and over all the precious things" of many others. "But tidings out of the east and out of the north shall trouble him: therefore he shall go forth with great fury to destroy, and utterly to make away many. And he shall plant the tabernacles of his palace between the seas in the glorious holy mountain; yet he shall come to his end, and none shall help him." (Dan. 11:15-45.)

As far as Daniel's account is concerned, the conclusion of the whole matter is summed up in these words: "And at that time"—the time of the end—"shall Michael stand up, the great prince which standeth for the children of thy people"—he shall sit at Adam-ondi-Ahman, as we shall hereafter see—"and there shall be a time of trouble, such as never was since there was a nation even to that same time: and at that time thy people shall be delivered, every one that shall be found written in the book." The full impact of Armageddon, of the abomination of desolation, of the final great war of the ages—the full impact shall fall upon the ungodly among men, and only those whose names are written in the Book of Life will find a full measure of security and joy.

Then shall be brought to pass the resurrection that attends the return of our Blessed Lord. "And many of them that sleep in the dust of the earth shall awake, some to everlasting life, and some to shame and everlasting contempt. And they that be wise shall shine as the brightness of the firmament; and they that turn many to righteousness as the stars for ever and ever."

After learning all these things, Daniel asked an angelic ministrant who ministered unto him this question: "How long shall it be to the end of these wonders?" In reply he was told: "The words are closed up and sealed till the time of the end. Many shall be purified, and made white, and tried; but the wicked shall do wickedly: and none of the wicked shall understand; but the wise shall understand." (Dan. 12:1-10.) And thus it is.

Gog and Magog Attack the Covenant People

Ezekiel gives us another view and perspective of what shall be when the armies from the north invade the glorious land. This is the religious war of which Daniel spoke. It is a holy war in which emotion rules and ways of worship are at stake. It is a war between Christ and his gospel, and Lucifer who sought to deny men their agency even before the world was. In it we shall see Christ come to champion the cause of his people, and in it we shall see the fall of the great and abominable church, which is the church of the devil. She shall fall as Babylon of old fell.

Gog and Magog are all the nations of the earth who take up the sword against Israel and Jerusalem in the day of Armageddon. Their identities remain to be revealed when the battle alliances are made. We can assume, however, that the United States, as the defender of freedom in all the world, will head one coalition, and that Russia, whose avowed aim is to destroy freedom in all nations, will head the enemies of God.

Ezekiel's prophetic utterances begin with the divine assurance that Gog and Magog and all their armies shall be defeated. It could not be otherwise. God and his purposes must and shall prevail. To all these nations, combined in one great and evil enterprise against his people, the Lord says: "I will turn thee back, and put hooks into thy jaws, and I will bring thee forth, and all thine army, horses and horsemen, all of them clothed with all sorts of armour, even a great company with bucklers and shields, all of them handling swords." Their weaponry and military prowess and massive strength shall be of no moment in that day. The Lord himself is governing the outcome of the battle. Gog and all his multitudes shall fall and fail, and shall be as when God overthrew Sodom and Gomorrah.

The destined events are these: "In the latter years," Israel shall return to her land, coming out of all the nations of the earth. Old Jerusalem shall be rebuilt and the latter-day temple shall stand within its walls. When the appointed time comes to assemble all nations to fight against Jerusalem, Gog and Magog shall come according to this promise. "Thou shalt ascend and come like a storm, thou shalt be like a cloud to cover the land, thou, and all thy bands, and many people with thee."

. Nations that go to war are engaged in either righteous or evil causes. The Lamanite assaults were evil; the Nephite defenses were righteous. Israel's attacks on the Amorites and other inhabitants of Canaan were directed by the Lord and were right. When the Philistines came against David and his people, their cause was evil. It was the will of the Lord that the American colonies free themselves from European domination in the revolutionary war, and so their cause was just. Armageddon will be a war of aggression instituted by Gog and Magog. Theirs will be an evil cause. Those nations that defend Israel and Jerusalem will be doing what the Lord wants done. To them it will be a righteous war.

And so, of Gog and Magog, Ezekiel prophesied: "Thus saith the Lord God; It shall also come to pass, that at the same time shall things come into thy mind, and thou shalt think an evil thought." Is not this also the case with all nations that seek to subjugate and enslave other peoples and nations? "And thou shalt say, I will go up to the land of unwalled villages; I will go to them that are at rest, that dwell safely, all of them dwelling without walls, and having neither bars nor gates." The destructive power of their weapons will be so great that it will be as though the cities of the earth were unwalled villages.

Thus Gog and Magog shall go forth "to take a spoil, and to take a prey; to turn thine hand upon the desolate places that are now inhabited, and upon the people that are gathered out of the nations, which have gotten cattle and goods, that dwell in the midst of the land." Conquerors steal from their victims. Nebuchadnezzar takes the golden vessels from the temple. Hitler makes bare the art galleries of France. Gog and Magog shall confiscate the wealth of Israel, and those who see it shall say, "Art thou come to take a spoil? hast thou gathered thy company to take a prey? to carry away silver and gold, to take away cattle and goods, to take a great spoil?" To the victor belong the spoils; the mere fact that Armageddon is a religious war will not deny Gog his gold.

"Therefore, son of man," the Lord says to Ezekiel, "prophesy and say unto Gog, Thus saith the Lord God; In that day when my people of Israel dwelleth safely, shalt thou not know it? And thou shalt come from thy place out of the north parts, thou, and many people with thee, all of them riding upon horses, a great company, and a mighty army: And thou shalt come up against my people of Israel, as a cloud to cover the land; it shall be in the latter days, and I will bring thee against my land, that the heathen may know me, when I shall be sanctified in thee, O Gog, before their eyes." O Gog, O Magog, how great are thy hosts; how strong is thy armor; how destructive is thy power! When thou falleth, with all thy greatness, all men will know that God alone could defeat such dread and fearsome hosts.

"Thus saith the Lord God; Art thou he of whom I have spoken in old time by my servants the prophets of Israel, which prophesied in those days many years that I would bring thee against them?" We suppose all of the prophets in Israel spoke more or less about the second coming of the King of Israel and about the wars and desolations that would precede and attend that dreadful day. The preserved words of many of them testify of that which is to be in the last days. Isaiah tells us of the fire and blood and desolation that will attend the Second Coming, and that "the slain of the Lord shall be many" in that day. (Isa. 66:16.) Jeremiah says the Lord will "call for a sword upon all the inhabitants of the earth, . . . And the slain of the Lord shall be at that day from one end of the earth even unto the other end of the earth.'' (Jer. 25:29, 33.) Zechariah sets forth in extenso what shall take place when the Lord gathers ''all nations against Jerusalem.'' (Zech. 12–14.) Zephaniah devotes almost the entire three chapters of his writings to the same thing. So also does Joel. Daniel and Malachi in due course will open their mouths on the same matters. There is nothing hidden or secret about the general course of events that the Lord God shall bring to pass in his own good time, a time that is now not far distant.

''And it shall come to pass at the same time when Gog shall come against the land of Israel, saith the Lord God, that my fury shall come up in my face. For in my jealousy and in the fire of my wrath have I spoken, Surely in that day there shall be a great shaking in the land of Israel''—this is the mighty earthquake when the Mount of Olives cleaves and mountains and valleys and continents change their shapes, as we have so often noted—''So that the fishes of the sea, and the fowls of the heaven, and the beasts of the field, and all creeping things that creep upon the earth, and all the men that are upon the face of the earth, shall shake at my presence, and the mountains shall be thrown down, and the steep places shall fall, and every wall shall fall to the ground.'' This is the moment of the Lord's return. All things shall shake at his presence. The earthquakes and the tremblings and the distortions of the landmasses of our planet shall all take place when and as he comes to dwell again among men.

What of Gog and all his hosts in that dread day? What of the nations who have come to battle against the chosen people? Ezekiel's accounts are not chronological, and much that he recites will require periods of time to accomplish. But incident to the Second Coming, this word will be fulfilled: ''And I will call for a sword against him throughout all my mountains, saith the Lord God: every man's sword shall be against his brother.'' This, in truth, will be a worldwide conflict; the sword that is wielded in the mountains of Israel will be the same sword that slays men in all nations.

"And I will plead against him with pestilence and with blood; and I will rain upon him, and upon his bands, and upon the many people that are with him, an overflowing rain, and great hailstones, fire, and brimstone." It shall be, in the literal and full sense of the word, as it was with Sodom and Gomorrah. Fire and brimstone will fall upon the armies of the wicked in all nations. That which is going forward in Palestine is but a type and a shadow of that which shall be in all nations and among all peoples. We must remind ourselves that this is a worldwide conflict and that all nations are involved. "Thus will I magnify myself, and sanctify myself; and I will be known in the eyes of many nations, and they shall know that I am the Lord." (Ezek. 38:1-23.) All men will know that no power save the power of God can bring to pass that which has thus been brought to pass.

Gog and Magog: Their Fall and Destruction

We now come to the prophetic word about the destruction of Gog and Magog, and all the nations that have forsaken the Lord, and all the wicked in all the earth. "I am against thee, O Gog," saith the Lord. "And I will turn thee back, and leave but the sixth part of thee." Gog, who came from the "north parts" to do battle "upon the mountains of Israel," shall return to the lands whence she came. But she will leave five dead bodies behind for every one live man who returns. She came, a mighty host, like a storm and like a cloud covering the land; she shall return, few in number, bowed and beaten by the rains of the Almighty.

"And I will smite thy bow out of thy left hand, and will cause thine arrows to fall out of thy right hand." Her weapons of war will not serve their purpose; she will be without oil for her war machines, and her bullets will be defective and not find their marks. "Thou shalt fall upon the mountains of Israel, thou, and all thy bands, and the people that is with thee.'' Death and destruction shall leave the slain of the Lord in all the earth.

"I will give thee unto the ravenous birds of every sort, and to the beasts of the field to be devoured. Thou shalt fall upon the open field: for I have spoken it, saith the Lord God.'' Pestilence, plagues, disease shall sweep as a desolating scourge through the ranks of the armed ones. And the weapons of war in the hands of the defenders of Israel shall take their toll. Dead bodies, unburied, will litter the land.

"And I will send a fire on Magog, and among them that dwell carelessly in the isles''—it is the great day of burning—"and they shall know that I am the Lord.'' None but the Lord himself can cause the elements to melt with fervent heat so that every corruptible thing is consumed. "So will I make my holy name known in the midst of my people Israel; and I will not let them pollute my holy name any more: and the heathen shall know that I am the Lord, the Holy One in Israel.'' How could it be otherwise? The wicked are destroyed, and the heathen nations—yet to hear the gospel and be converted—shall have all these great wondrous signs before them.

"Behold, it is come, and it is done, saith the Lord God; this is the day whereof I have spoken.'' This is the day! Oh, blessed day! The Lord reigns; the year of his redeemed has come; this is the day!

At this point in his prophetic utterances—which are not and were not intended to be chronological—Ezekiel tells in graphic language of the aftermath of the defeat of Gog and Magog by the sword. We would be derelict if we did not quote his very words, words written by the power of the Spirit. They are indeed the words of the Lord himself.

"And they that dwell in the cities of Israel shall go forth, and shall set on fire and burn the weapons, both the shields and the bucklers, the bows and the arrows, and the handstaves, and the spears, and they shall burn them with fire seven years: So that they shall take no wood out of the field, neither cut down any out of the forests; for they shall burn the weapons with fire.'' It seems to us as we consider this coming eventuality that almost all of the wealth of the world will have been spent for weapons of war. It is indeed Lucifer's last chance to destroy the souls of men on the field of battle before he is bound and has no power for the space of a thousand years.

''And they shall spoil those that spoiled them, and rob those that robbed them, saith the Lord God.'' From the standpoint of time all this must take place before the cleansing fires prepare the earth for the abode of the Clean One.

''And it shall come to pass in that day, that I will give unto Gog a place there of graves in Israel, the valley of the passengers on the east of the sea: and it shall stop the noses of the passengers: and there shall they bury Gog and all his multitude: and they shall call it The valley of Hamon-gog. And seven months shall the house of Israel be burying of them, that they may cleanse the land.'' Has there ever been such an enterprise as this? Will there ever be such a graveyard as Palestine? There the embalmed bodies of the righteous rest in sacred tombs, awaiting the sound of the trump of God that shall call them forth in the resurrection of life; and there the mangled carcasses of the wicked shall lie in unmarked graves, awaiting the sound of a later trump that will call them forth in the resurrection of damnation.

''Yea, all the people of the land shall bury them,'' the divine word continues, ''and it shall be to them a renown the day that I shall be glorified, saith the Lord God. And they shall sever out men of continual employment, passing through the land to bury with the passengers those that remain upon the face of the earth, to cleanse it: after the end of seven months shall they search. And the passengers that pass through the land, when any seeth a man's bone, then shall he set up a sign by it, till the buriers have buried it in the valley of Hamon-gog. And also the name of the city shall be Hamonah. Thus shall they cleanse the land." (Ezek. 39:1-16.)

As we close this portion of our analysis, we must note that the great war involving Gog and Magog is both premillennial, as we have here set forth, and also postmillennial in the sense that there will be another great conflict with wicked nations just before this globe becomes a celestial sphere. We shall speak of this hereafter. The similarities between the two great conflicts justify calling them by the same name. This John does in these words: "And when the thousand years are expired, Satan shall be loosed out of his prison, And shall go out to deceive the nations which are in the four quarters of the earth, Gog and Magog, to gather them together to battle: the number of whom is as the sand of the sea. And they went up on the breadth of the earth, and compassed the camp of the saints about, and the beloved city: and fire came down from God out of heaven, and devoured them." (Rev. 20:7-9.)

As with some Messianic prophecies that speak of both the first and the second advents of our Lord in the same language, it may be that portions of Ezekiel's great prophecy are subject to dual fulfillment. Our concern is with what lies ahead for us. Postmillennial events will be revealed in full to those who live during the Millennium. The knowledge then given will stand as a warning for those of future generations, even as the words of Ezekiel warn us to live as becometh saints. We speculate that much the same thing that happens in the first war with Gog and Magog will be repeated in the second.

The Supper of the Great God

After the defeat by the sword of the armies of Gog and Magog, and in the day when the slain of the Lord cover the earth and are as dung upon its face, then the fowls and the beasts shall gorge themselves upon the flesh and blood of the dead. This awful happening, attended by all the stench and stink of the rotting corpses, is set forth in both the Old Testament and the New and in latter-day revelation. It will indeed be something to behold.

This word came from the Lord to Ezekiel, saying: "Speak unto every feathered fowl, and to every beast of the field, Assemble yourselves, and come; gather yourselves on every side to my sacrifice upon the mountains of Israel, that ye may eat flesh, and drink blood." The mountains of Israel are but the illustration; the same event will occur in all nations and among all peoples, for Armageddon knows no bounds. "Ye shall eat the flesh of the mighty, and drink the blood of the princes of the earth, of rams, of lambs, and of goats, of bullocks, all of them fatlings of Bashan." In that day the flesh and blood of the great and mighty of the earth shall be of no more worth than that of the animals of the fields. "And ye shall eat fat till ye be full, and drink blood till ye be drunken, of my sacrifice which I have sacrificed for you. Thus ye shall be filled at my table with horses and chariots, with mighty men, and with all men of war, saith the Lord God." There neither has been nor will be any feast like unto this feast. What a blessing it will be for the earth to burn and be cleansed of its corruption and its filth. "And I will set my glory among the heathen, and all the heathen shall see my judgment that I have executed, and my hand that I have laid upon them." (Ezek. 39:17-21.)

John, in his visions of what was to be in the last days, saw "an angel standing in the sun" and heard him cry "to all the fowls that fly in the midst of heaven, Come and gather yourselves together unto the supper of the great God; That ye may eat the flesh of kings, and the flesh of captains, and the flesh of mighty men, and the flesh of horses, and of them that sit on them, and the flesh of all men, both free and bond, both small and great." (Rev. 19:17-18.) And our latter-day revelation, speaking of those who have fallen by the plagues and by the sword in Armageddon, says: "And it shall come to pass that the beasts of the forest and the fowls of the air shall devour them up.'' (D&C 29:20.)

We have set forth, thus, what the inspired writers say about the blood-soaked scene of gore and corruption that is yet to be. It makes us wonder why it has been revealed in such detail in at least three dispensations. Certainly it will be a literal event in the coming day. But more than this, it surely bears witness of other truths that men should know. It testifies that wickedness shall cover the earth in the last days; that all nations shall take up the sword in the final war of the ages; that men in uncounted numbers will die of plagues and pestilence and by the edge of the sword; and that the dead bodies of all, kings and rulers included, heaped as dung upon the ground, shall, in death, have no more worth than the carcasses of the beasts of the field. Perhaps, above all else, the horror of it all stands as a call to wayward men to repent, to cease their warfare against God, and to seek an inheritance with his people, many of whom will be preserved in that dread day.

Armageddon Ushers in the Millennium

There are three great things that will grow out of and come because of Armageddon. They are:

1. *In the course of this final great conflict the Lord himself shall return, the vineyard shall be burned, and the millennial day will dawn.*

2. *Out of the defeat of Gog and Magog comes the end of all the nations of the earth and the final triumph of Israel as a people and as a nation.*

3. *Out of Armageddon comes the destruction of the political kingdom on earth of Lucifer and the fall of the great and abominable church.*

As to the Second Coming and the millennial day thus commenced, we have heretofore made frequent allusion to these and shall deal more particularly with them hereafter.

As to the coming end of all nations and the final triumph of Israel, we should make a brief comment. Many of the present nations of the earth will be here, flourishing, fighting, struggling for a place in the sun, when the Lord comes. It is our firm conviction as a people that the stars and stripes will be waving triumphantly in the breeze, as a symbol of the greatness and stability of the United States of America, when the Lord comes. This nation was established to be the Lord's base of operations in this final gospel dispensation. From it the gospel is to go to every other nation and people. The greater its influence among the nations of the world, the more rapidly the gospel spreads. But the Lord has told us that all nations, the United States included, shall cease to be when he comes. These are his words: "With the sword and by bloodshed the inhabitants of the earth shall mourn; and with famine, and plague, and earthquake, and the thunder of heaven, and the fierce and vivid lightning also, shall the inhabitants of the earth be made to feel the wrath, and indignation, and chastening hand of an Almighty God, until the consumption decreed hath made a full end of all nations." (D&C 87:6.)

There will be no law but the Lord's law when he comes, and that law will be administered by the nation then set up to rule the world. That nation is Israel. They will possess the political kingdom. Thus the Lord said through Jeremiah: "Fear not thou, O my servant Jacob, and be not dismayed, O Israel: for, behold, I will save thee from afar off, and thy seed from the land of their captivity; and Jacob shall return, and be in rest and at ease, and none shall make him afraid. Fear thou not, O Jacob my servant, saith the Lord: for I am with thee; for I will make a full end of all the nations whither I have driven thee: but I will not make a full end of thee, but correct thee in measure; yet will I not leave thee wholly unpunished." (Jer. 46:27-28.) Also: "Thou art my battle axe and weapons of war," the Lord said to Israel, "for with thee will I break in pieces the nations, and with thee will I destroy kingdoms." (Jer. 51:20.) This we have seen shall be the case at Armageddon.

Now let us return to Ezekiel's prophetic word relative

to Gog and Magog and the Lord's chosen Israel. Based on all that is set forth with reference to this final series of wars, the Lord says: "So the house of Israel shall know that I am the Lord their God from that day and forward." Those who remain will believe in him and recognize his hand in all that has happened to them as individuals and as a nation. "And the heathen shall know that the house of Israel went into captivity for their iniquity: because they trespassed against me, therefore hid I my face from them, and gave them into the hand of their enemies: so fell they all by the sword. According to their uncleanness and according to their transgressions have I done unto them, and hid my face from them." It is the age-old testimony borne by all the prophets of Israel. That people was scattered because they forsook the Lord and his laws and chose to worship other gods. They will be gathered when they come unto Christ, believe his gospel, and worship the Father in his name, as did their fathers.

"Therefore thus saith the Lord God; Now will I bring again the captivity of Jacob, and have mercy upon the whole house of Israel, and will be jealous for my holy name; After that they have borne their shame, and all their trespasses whereby they have trespassed against me, when they dwelt safely in their land, and none made them afraid. When I have brought them again from the people, and gathered them out of their enemies' lands, and am sanctified in them in the sight of many nations; Then shall they know that I am the Lord their God, which caused them to be led into captivity among the heathen: but I have gathered them unto their own land, and have left none of them any more there." Such also is the age-old testimony of all the prophets. Israel, blessed Israel, shall return to her ancient lands and believe again those saving truths which brought joy and peace and eternal reward to her fathers.

Then comes the glorious promise: "Neither will I hide my face any more from them: for I have poured out my spirit upon the house of Israel, saith the Lord God." (Ezek.

39:22-29.) Israel shall remain and rule and be established forever. Hers is the one kingdom that shall prevail, because it is the Lord's kingdom. The Lord will restore again the kingdom to Israel, according to the promises.

As to the destruction of the political kingdom of Lucifer on earth and the fall of the great and abominable church, there are a few additional things that must be said. After reciting some of the plagues and desolations of the last days, and after speaking of the Supper of the Great God as set forth by Ezekiel, our latter-day revelation says: "And the great and abominable church, which is the whore of all the earth, shall be cast down by devouring fire, according as it is spoken by the mouth of Ezekiel the prophet, who spoke of these things, which have not come to pass but surely must, as I live, for abominations shall not reign." (D&C 29:21.)

Now, Ezekiel spoke only of devouring fire—of fire and brimstone—being rained upon Gog and Magog and all the nations that fought against Israel. He made no mention of a great and abominable church being involved, but the Lord here tells us that it was, in fact, the great whore of all the earth who was being destroyed by the fire. That is to say, there is both a political and an ecclesiastical kingdom of Lucifer on earth. It is with his kingdom as it is with the Lord's. There is an ecclesiastical kingdom of God on earth that is The Church of Jesus Christ of Latter-day Saints, and there shall be a political kingdom of God on earth in that day when the kingdom is restored to Israel and the Lord himself reigns. Satan's kingdom is composed of all that is evil and corrupt and carnal and wicked no matter where it is found. He operates through what we call churches, and he operates through what we call governments. Both are part of his kingdom. And in the final great day that lies ahead, the fall of one will be the fall of the other. When Babylon falls, she will take with her the churches of the world and the nations of the world. As the Lord makes a full end of all nations, so he will make a full end of all evil

493

churches. Men will be free to believe as they choose during the Millennium, but the great and abominable church, the whore of all the earth, will no longer be among men, because the wicked portion of mankind will have been burned as stubble.

At Armageddon that great political power which "seeketh to overthrow the freedom of all lands, nations, and countries," and which "bringeth to pass the destruction of all people," and which is itself "built up by the devil" (Ether 8:25)—that very political kingdom, in all its parts, shall be burned with fire. It is the great and abominable church.

And thus out of Armageddon and the burning of the vineyard will come the great millennial blessings for all those who abide the day, the great and dreadful day of the Lord, to which we shall now turn our attention.

Chapter 41

THE GREAT AND DREADFUL DAY OF THE LORD

The Great Day of His Wrath

The great and dreadful day of the Lord! What is it, and when will it come? Is it a day of sorrow or of joy? Is it our desire to live when that dread hour arrives, or will we plead for a merciful death lest the devastations and suffering be greater than we can bear? Will it be a day of vengeance and suffering or a day of redemption and peace?

Having spoken of the plagues and pestilence of the last days; having seen men's flesh fall from off their bones and their eyes drop from their sockets as incurable diseases cursed whole nations of men; having viewed with wonder and awe the fall and burning of the great whore of all the earth with whom the masses of men wallowed in evil debauchery; having seen all nations besiege Jerusalem, and having gasped in horror as the two-edged swords made bare the bowels of millions of the wicked wretches of the world, to say nothing of the kings and mighty ones who ruled over them—being aware of all these things, and all that attends them, what more can we possibly say about a day that bears the name "the great and dreadful day of the Lord"?

And yet there is more—much, much more—that

makes us wonder. Is the coming day one for whose coming we should yearn? Or is it a day to be shunned, one we hope will be reserved for some future age? The answers to be given depend upon whose lips phrase the questions. For the faithful saints, the divine word is: Let the day come. The universal plea on every righteous tongue is: "Thy kingdom come. Thy will be done in earth, as it is in heaven." (Matt. 6:10.) In the heart of every true believer is the plea: Come, O thou King of Kings; save us, O our God. We have waited long for thee. Oh, that thou mightest rend the heavens and come down in glory in our day.

But among the wicked it is not and it ought not so to be. To them the divine word acclaims: "Woe unto you that desire the day of the Lord! to what end is it for you? the day of the Lord is darkness, and not light. As if a man did flee from a lion, and a bear met him; or went into the house, and leaned his hand on the wall, and a serpent bit him. Shall not the day of the Lord be darkness, and not light? even very dark, and no brightness in it?" (Amos 5:18-20.) In truth and in reality, except for faithful members of The Church of Jesus Christ of Latter-day Saints; except for other decent and upright people who are living clean and proper lives in spite of the allurements and enticings of the world; except for those who are living either a celestial or a terrestrial law—except for these, the Second Coming will be a day of vengeance and of wrath. As a warning to ourselves and to all men, we shall now turn our attention to the revealed word that identifies that great and dreadful day as a day of wrath and sorrow.

Many revelations speak of the wrath of a just God that shall be poured out upon men and nations in the day of his coming. Some of these we have quoted or shall quote in other connections; let us, however, make brief references or allusions at this point to a few of the more important passages that have bearing on the points involved. "I will punish the world for their evil, and the wicked for their iniquity," the Lord told Isaiah, with reference to his second coming, "and I will cause the arrogancy of the proud to cease, and will lay low the haughtiness of the terrible." Will the Lord be angry with the wicked and manifest his wrath upon men in so doing? He says: "I will shake the heavens, and the earth shall remove out of her place, in the wrath of the Lord of hosts, and in the day of his fierce anger." (Isa. 13:11, 13.) And again: "Behold, the Lord cometh out of his place to punish the inhabitants of the earth for their iniquity." (Isa. 26:21.)

What comfort is there for the wicked in such prophetic words as these preserved for us by Zephaniah? "The great day of the Lord is near, it is near, and hasteth greatly, even the voice of the day of the Lord." He is speaking of our day. We live in the last days, when the day of the Lord is near. "The mighty man shall cry there bitterly." How could it be otherwise as men fall in Armageddon and the other wars that are ordained? "That day is a day of wrath, a day of trouble and distress, a day of wasteness and desolation, a day of darkness and gloominess, a day of clouds and thick darkness, a day of the trumpet and alarm against the fenced cities, and against the high towers." These next words bear an added witness of the fate of unnumbered millions in the final premillennial wars: "And I will bring distress upon men, that they shall walk like blind men, because they have sinned against the Lord: and their blood shall be poured out as dust, and their flesh as the dung." And what of their money and the power it brings—will it save them? "Neither their silver nor their gold shall be able to deliver them in the day of the Lord's wrath; but the whole land"—or, better, the whole earth—"shall be devoured by the fire of his jealousy: for he shall make even a speedy riddance of all them that dwell in the land." (Zeph. 1:14-18.)

By way of counsel to his people who shall live in this day of anger and wrath, the Lord says: "Wait ye upon me, saith the Lord, until the day that I rise up to the prey: for my determination is to gather the nations, that I may as-

semble the kingdoms"—this, of course, is at Armageddon—"to pour upon them mine indignation, even all my
fierce anger: for all the earth shall be devoured with the fire
of my jealousy." (Zeph. 3:8.)

Nahum also has somewhat to say about these matters.
His words are an added testimony and another view of
what is to be in the great and dreadful day. "God is jealous,
and the Lord revengeth," he says; "the Lord revengeth,
and is furious; the Lord will take vengeance on his adversaries, and he reserveth wrath for his enemies." However
much it may be supposed, by those who are wise in their
own conceits, that God is a God of mercy and peace and
love, in whom no harshness or stern judgment is to be
found, the fact is that he is a God of wrath, and anger, and
vengeance, and destruction, where the wicked are concerned. Mercy and love and kindness are for the God-
fearing and the righteous among men. "The Lord is slow to
anger, and great in power, and will not at all acquit the
wicked: the Lord hath his way in the whirlwind and in the
storm, and the clouds are the dust of his feet. He rebuketh
the sea, and maketh it dry, and drieth up all the rivers. . . .
The mountains quake at him, and the hills melt, and the
earth is burned at his presence, yea, the world, and all that
dwell therein." This is Nahum's unique way of foretelling
the great day of burning.

Then he asks: "Who can stand before his indignation?
and who can abide in the fierceness of his anger? his fury is
poured out like fire, and the rocks are thrown down by
him." (Nah. 1:2-6.) And to these questions we answer:
Those who love and serve him with all their hearts shall
never be called upon to stand before his indignation or to
abide in the presence of his fierce anger.

Do these utterances of the ancient prophets seem brutal
and punitive? Do they project the image of an austere and
stern Deity who deals with men in a harsh and iron-fisted
way? Does it seem from them that his purpose is to crush
and condemn rather than save and exalt? It would seem

that the answer in each instance is yes; and if this is so, so be it. That is, the answers are yes, where the wicked and ungodly are concerned. In his love and in his mercy, a gracious God seeks the salvation of all his children. But he cannot save the righteous without damning the wicked; he cannot reward the obedient without condemning the rebellious; he cannot fill the hearts of the righteous with unmeasured blessings without pouring out his wrath upon the wicked. Indeed, how could a just and holy Being who cannot look upon sin with the least degree of allowance do other than send wrath and vengeance upon those who worship Satan and rebel against Him?

And so we find in our latter-day revelations a complete endorsement and approval of all that he said to the ancient prophets about the day of his wrath. These revelations speak of "the day when the wrath of God shall be poured out upon the wicked without measure." (D&C 1:9.) In them he says: "Hear the word of him whose anger is kindled against the wicked and rebellious. . . . Let the wicked take heed, and let the rebellious fear and tremble; and let the unbelieving hold their lips, for the day of wrath shall come upon them as a whirlwind, and all flesh shall know that I am God." (D&C 63:2, 6.) "Behold, the day has come, when the cup of the wrath of mine indignation is full," saith the Lord. (D&C 43:26.) "For behold, mine anger is kindled against the rebellious, and they shall know mine arm and mine indignation, in the day of visitation and of wrath upon the nations." (D&C 56:1.)

It is not a pleasant thing to think of that which lies ahead for worldly people, for those in all nations who walk in carnal paths, for those in the Church who do not keep the commandments. "The time is soon at hand that I shall come in a cloud with power and great glory," saith the Lord. "And it shall be a great day at the time of my coming, for all nations shall tremble." (D&C 34:7-8.) "For when the Lord shall appear he shall be terrible unto them, that fear may seize upon them, and they shall stand afar off and tremble. And all nations shall be afraid because of the terror of the Lord, and the power of his might." (D&C 45:74-75.)

Is it any wonder that men in that day, as Jesus promised, shall say "to the mountains, Fall on us; and to the hills, Cover us"? (Luke 23:30.) Yea, in that day shall be fulfilled that which is written: "And the kings of the earth, and the great men, and the rich men, and the chief captains, and the mighty men, and every bondman, and every free man, hid themselves in the dens and in the rocks of the mountains; and said to the mountains and rocks, Fall on us, and hide us from the face of him that sitteth on the throne, and from the wrath of the Lamb: For the great day of his wrath is come; and who shall be able to stand?" (Rev. 6:15-17.)

The Day of Vengeance

Does it seem strange that the meek and lowly Nazarene is also a God of vengeance? Are modern religionists in the cults of Christendom so imbued with the idea that he is a God of mercy that they forget completely that he is also a God of justice? Can he be a God of rewards without being a God of punishments?

Truly, wrath and vengeance are bedfellows. When the Lord pours out his wrath without measure, the wicked suffer the vengeance of a just God in exactly the same proportion. It is their day of reckoning; they are given measure for measure as their deeds warrant; it is a day of retribution and avengement. It is "the day when the Lord shall come to recompense unto every man according to his work, and measure to every man according to the measure which he has measured to his fellow man." (D&C 1:10.)

What says the holy word as to the vengeance of God in that great and dreadful day of his coming? To Enoch the Lord said: "As I live"—these are the words of an oath, an oath sworn in his own name—"even so will I come in the

last days, in the days of wickedness and vengeance."
(Moses 7:60.) Through Isaiah this word came to Israel: "Be
strong, fear not: behold, your God will come with vengeance, even God with a recompence; he will come and
save you." (Isa. 35:4.) "For it is the day of the Lord's
vengeance, and the year of recompences for the controversy of Zion." (Isa. 34:8.) Of that day the Lord said
to Micah: "And I will execute vengeance in anger and
fury upon the heathen, such as they have not heard."
(Micah 5:15.)

Paul said to certain of the saints in his day: "It is a
righteous thing with God to recompense tribulation to them
that trouble you." Vengeance is poured out in righteousness; it comes as a just and proper reward for the deeds
done in the flesh; it is the Lord's way of recompensing the
wicked for their rejection of his truths and the persecutions
they have heaped upon his people. "To you who are troubled," Paul continues, "rest with us, when the Lord Jesus
shall be revealed from heaven with his mighty angels, In
flaming fire taking vengeance on them that know not God,
and that obey not the gospel of our Lord Jesus Christ: Who
shall be punished with everlasting destruction from the
presence of the Lord, and from the glory of his power;
When he shall come to be glorified in his saints, and to be
admired in all them that believe . . . in that day." (2 Thes.
1:6-10.) This is not Paul's idea, nor is it ours. He did not
originate the concept, nor did we. The law of vengeance
comes from God, and what can man do to change it?
"Vengeance is mine; I will repay, saith the Lord."
(Rom. 12:19.)

In like manner our modern revelations bear a confirming witness of the vengeance that shall come upon the
wicked in the last days. "And it shall come to pass, because of the wickedness of the world," the Lord said to
Joseph Smith, "that I will take vengeance upon the wicked,
for they will not repent; for the cup of mine indignation is

full; for behold, my blood shall not cleanse them if they hear me not." (D&C 29:17.) *They will not repent.* It is in their power to do so; all men have it in their power to believe and obey and be saved; all are able to obtain a celestial inheritance by obedience to the laws and ordinances of the gospel. But the reality is, *they will not repent.* Hence, vengeance is their just recompense.

"Behold, vengeance cometh speedily upon the inhabitants of the earth, a day of wrath, a day of burning, a day of desolation, of weeping, of mourning, and of lamentation; and as a whirlwind it shall come upon all the face of the earth, saith the Lord." There is a certain smugness in the Church, a feeling that all these things are for others, not for us. But do not the same hurricanes often destroy the homes of the righteous as well as the wicked? And do not the same drouths often burn the crops of the saints along with those of the Gentiles? Do not the righteous and the wicked often fight side by side in the same wars? And do not atomic bombs fall on all the inhabitants of doomed cities? Where, then, shall the vengeance of the last days be found? The Lord says: "And upon my house shall it begin, and from my house shall it go forth, saith the Lord; First among those among you, saith the Lord, who have professed to know my name and have not known me, and have blasphemed against me in the midst of my house, saith the Lord." (D&C 112:24-26.) Vengeance is for the wicked, in and out of the Church, and only the faithful shall be spared, and many of them only in the eternal perspective of things.

Thus the Lord says to his saints: "Hearken, O ye people of my church, saith the Lord your God, and hear the word of the Lord concerning you—The Lord who shall suddenly come to his temple; the Lord who shall come down upon the world with a curse to judgment; yea, upon all the nations that forget God, and upon all the ungodly among you." (D&C 133:1-2.) The saints in the Church and the Gentiles in the world will both be judged by the same standard—the standard of Christ. How can anyone be judged by any other measuring rod? He hath given a law unto all things, and all things are subject to him.

Isaiah and Joseph Smith join hands to paint a dramatic picture of the vengeance and the love of the Lord at his second coming. To each of them the Lord revealed the same truths, which each recorded in language suited to the understandings of people in his day. Isaiah asked these questions: "Who is this that cometh from Edom, with dyed garments from Bozrah? this that is glorious in his apparel, travelling in the greatness of his strength?" Perhaps there was some such event known to ancient Israel that their prophet chose to use in teaching them of the Second Coming. In any event the revealed answer came: "I that speak in righteousness, mighty to save." The answer comes from their Savior. The next question was: "Wherefore art thou red in thine apparel, and thy garments like him that treadeth in the winefat?" In answer the Lord said: "I have trodden the winepress alone; and of the people there was none with me: for I will tread them in mine anger, and trample them in my fury; and their blood shall be sprinkled upon my garments, and I will stain my raiment."

This picture is a familiar one in Israel. The wine is trampled from the grapes in great vats, staining the garments of the laborers as though with blood. But in this case the second coming of Christ is involved, the one harvesting the crop is the Lord himself, and the winepress is full of the wrath of God. Thus John heard a command given to one of the angels of God in heaven. It was: "Thrust in thy sharp sickle, and gather the clusters of the vine of the earth; for her grapes are fully ripe." It is the day of harvest. "And the angel thrust in his sickle into the earth, and gathered the vine of the earth, and cast it into the great winepress of the wrath of God. And the winepress was trodden without the city, and blood came out of the winepress." (Rev. 14:18-20.)

With this in mind, we hear the rest of the answer as to why the Lord was red in his apparel: "For the day of vengeance is in mine heart, and the year of my redeemed is come." The Lord, coming in the day of vengeance, is pouring out the wrath of God upon the wicked, which is symbolized by the great winepress filled with the red juice of grapes. "And I looked, and there was none to help," the Lord continued, "and I wondered that there was none to uphold: therefore mine own arm brought salvation unto me; and my fury, it upheld me." Christ alone hath brought salvation to Israel and to all men. "And I will tread down the people in mine anger, and make them drunk in my fury, and I will bring down their strength to the earth." (Isa. 63:1-6.) As the grapes are trodden in the winepress of wrath, so shall the wicked be trodden down at the last days.

Joseph Smith's comparable and clarifying revelation says: "And it shall be said: Who is this that cometh down from God in heaven with dyed garments; yea, from the regions which are not known, clothed in his glorious apparel, traveling in the greatness of his strength? And he shall say: I am he who spake in righteousness, mighty to save." All through their ancient history, it was this Lord Jehovah who called upon his people, inviting them to come unto him and live his laws and be saved.

"And the Lord shall be red in his apparel, and his garments like him that treadeth in the wine-vat. . . . And his voice shall be heard: I have trodden the winepress alone, and have brought judgment upon all people; and none were with me; And I have trampled them in my fury, and I did tread upon them in mine anger, and their blood have I sprinkled upon my garments, and stained all my raiment; for this was the day of vengeance which was in my heart." (D&C 133:46-51.) How awful is the scene in this day of vengeance. The blood of the slain at the coming of the Lord will stain his garments as the red wine stains the raiment of those who tread on the grapes. He will tread on them as men trample on the fruit of the vine. Thus it shall be when the Son of Man harvests the earth, and when "he treadeth the winepress of the fierceness and wrath of Almighty God." (Rev. 19:15.)

The Year of the Lord's Redeemed

Is there no hope for anyone in the dreadful day? There is for those who are true and faithful in all things. For them, whether in life or in death, it will be a time of glory and renown. Will they escape the outpouring of divine wrath and avoid the vengeance with which the wicked will be smitten? They will. They are the true Israel who yearn for the restoration to them of the ancient kingdom. They are the ones who shall abide the day and who shall live and reign on earth with their Lord for the space of a thousand years. And blessed are they, for they shall inherit the earth.

Isaiah and Joseph Smith now turn to a consideration of the love and mercy and goodness that shall be showered upon the faithful in Israel in the day of their Lord's return. It shall fall as the gentle rain from heaven upon those who know the Lord and believe his gospel and seek his face. "Oh that thou wouldest rend the heavens," they pray, "that thou wouldest come down, that the mountains might flow down at thy presence, As when the melting fire burneth, [and] the fire causeth the waters to boil." All this is descriptive of what shall be when the elements melt with fervent heat and the valleys and mountains are no more. Why do the faithful yearn for such a day? It is the one in which the yoke of the world will be removed from their shoulders. How proper it is for them to plead with their Lord to come down, "to make thy name known to thine adversaries, that the nations may tremble at thy presence!" Let Israel be free; let the wicked and ungodly be removed. When shall it be? "When thou didst terrible things which we looked not for, thou camest down, the mountains flowed down at thy presence."

Then comes one of the most glorious promises in all holy writ. "For since the beginning of the world men have not heard," the holy account continues, "nor perceived by the ear, neither hath the eye seen, O God, beside thee, what he hath prepared for him that waiteth for him." Then and in that day, for one thing, they will be with their Lord; he will be among them as he was in Enoch's ancient city. Hence they say: "Thou meetest him that rejoiceth and worketh righteousness, those that remember thee in thy ways." (Isa. 64:1-5.)

When shall all these things come to pass? When will the importuning cries ascend to the throne of grace? When, oh when, will there be righteous men on earth who know enough about the Lord and his purposes and plans to plead with him to come down in all the glory of his strength? It should be done in our day. We are the ones who are appointed to make the petitions. Thus our revelation recites that an angel shall fly through the midst of heaven bringing anew the fulness of the everlasting gospel. "And this gospel"—the restored gospel—"shall be preached unto every nation, and kindred, and tongue, and people."

How shall it be preached? "The servants of God shall go forth, saying with a loud voice: Fear God and give glory to him, for the hour of his judgment is come; and worship him that made heaven, and earth, and the sea, and the fountains of waters—Calling upon the name of the Lord day and night, saying: O that thou wouldst rend the heavens, that thou wouldst come down, that the mountains might flow down at thy presence." That is our message. We call upon the world to worship the true God who created all things and to plead with him for the return of his Son that the blessings promised the faithful may be realized.

"And it shall be answered upon their heads"—the Lord will hear their prayers and come down as they have petitioned—"for the presence of the Lord shall be as the melting fire that burneth, and as the fire which causeth the waters to boil." All that is destined to attend his coming shall surely come to pass as the holy word asserts.

Then shall his saints say: "O Lord, thou shalt come

down to make thy name known to thine adversaries, and all nations shall tremble at thy presence—When thou doest terrible things, things they look not for." Who among the wicked and ungodly look for the Lord to pour out plagues, to spread pestilence, to decree wars, to come in burning fire and consume every corruptible thing, to cause such upheavals that mountains and valleys and continents and oceans shall all be rearranged? "Yea, when thou comest down, and the mountains flow down at thy presence, thou shalt meet him who rejoiceth and worketh righteousness, who remembereth thee in thy ways." Truly, it is the true saints, the faithful members of the kingdom, those who have kept themselves unspotted from the world—they are the ones the Lord shall meet and reward and save when he comes. They are the ones who shall receive a fulfillment of the promise: "For since the beginning of the world have not men heard nor perceived by the ear, neither hath any eye seen, O God, besides thee, how great things thou hast prepared for him that waiteth for thee." (D&C 133:37-45.)

For the wicked and ungodly, the Second Coming is a day of vengeance; for the saints of the Most High, it ushers in an era of righteousness and joy and peace. They are then redeemed and freed from all oppression. "Let the wicked perish at the presence of God," saith the scripture. "But let the righteous be glad; let them rejoice before God: yea, let them exceedingly rejoice." (Ps. 68:2-3.)

In that day, as Isaiah expresses it, the righteous shall say: "I will mention the loving kindnesses of the Lord, and the praises of the Lord, according to all that the Lord hath bestowed on us, and the great goodness toward the house of Israel, which he hath bestowed on them according to his mercies, and according to the multitude of his loving kindnesses. For he said, Surely they are my people, children that will not lie: so he was their Saviour." And how sweet and tender this expression is: "In all their affliction he was afflicted." Their sorrows were his; their pains also; he himself bore their afflictions. "And the angel of his presence saved them''—oh, how often it was so—and ''in his love and in his pity he redeemed them; and he bare them, and carried them all the days of old.'' (Isa. 63:7-9.)

And lest we forget, lest we fail to see the full and true meaning of his ancient word given through Isaiah, we find the same Lord saying to Joseph Smith: ''And now the year of my redeemed is come''—having reference to his return and the ushering in of the millennial era—''and they shall mention the loving kindness of their Lord, and all that he has bestowed upon them according to his goodness, and according to his loving kindness, forever and ever.'' Truly he spoke thus in olden times, and truly he spoke in like words in our day. ''In all their afflictions he was afflicted. And the angel of his presence saved them; and in his love, and in his pity, he redeemed them, and bore them, and carried them all the days of old.'' (D&C 133:52-53.)

How comforting it is to know that for the saints the great and dreadful day of the Lord shall be one of loving-kindness and goodness! Thanks be to God for his tender mercies and saving grace!

Chapter 42

THE DAY
OF JUDGMENT

The Psalmic Prophecies of the Judgment

Cleopas and Luke, valiant and faithful disciples of the Lord Jesus in their day and generation, walked and conversed with the Risen Lord on the Emmaus Road for some two or three hours. It was the day of the first Easter. Jesus withheld his identity from them; they manifest doubts and anxieties about the reports of his resurrection and triumphal status as the King of Israel. Jesus said to them: "O fools, and slow of heart to believe all that the prophets have spoken: Ought not Christ to have suffered these things, and to enter into his glory? And beginning at Moses and all the prophets, he expounded unto them in all the scriptures the things concerning himself."

That evening in the upper room where many of disciples were eating together and bearing testimony of what various of their number had that day seen and heard and learned about the Risen One, and as Cleopas and Luke told of their conversations on the Emmaus Road, and how the identity of Jesus was made known unto them in the breaking of bread in Emmaus, the Lord Jesus himself stood in their midst. He spoke; he ate; and they felt the nail marks in his hands and feet and thrust their hands into the gaping spear wound in his riven side. Then Jesus said: "These are the words which I spake unto you, while I was yet with you,

509

that all things must be fulfilled, which were written in the law of Moses, and in the prophets, and in the psalms, concerning me." Having so said, "Then opened he their understanding," Luke tells us, "that they might understand the scriptures." (Luke 24:25-27, 44-45.)

The great message coming from the Emmaus Road and the upper room is, of course, that their Lord—Jesus of Nazareth of Galilee, the carpenter's son, the one with whom they had lived and labored for the three years of his mortal ministry—had now risen from the dead; that he had come forth in glorious immortality as the first fruits of them that slept; and that, therefore, he was the Son of God as he had so often testified in the days of his flesh. There are no more glorious truths than these. But another message delivered on these two occasions is that all things pertaining to his birth and ministry and death and glorification—and, we hasten to add, all things pertaining to his return in judgment in the last days—were before taught in the law of Moses and in the Psalms and in the Prophets.

And all things recorded in these holy scriptures must and shall be fulfilled, as pertaining to both his first and his second advents. It is our responsibility to search the holy word, uncover the prophetic utterances, and learn how and when and in what way they shall be fulfilled, lest he say to us, "O fools, and slow of heart to believe all that the prophets have spoken."

With reference to the coming day of judgment, let us turn first to the Psalms, to those inspired poetic gems of rhythmic beauty, which speak in grand words of the return of the Lord Jesus to judge the world. They speak as plainly of this coming day as they do with reference to his first coming, and to his ministry, atoning sacrifice, death, and resurrection. Indeed, it is the divine purpose to set forth in prose, poetry, and song repeated allusions to and truths about the Lord Jesus and all that he has done and yet will do in the eternal scheme of things. It is the divine purpose to keep the hearts of men turned everlastingly to Him by whom all things are, by whom salvation comes, by whom men are resurrected, judged, and awarded their places in the mansions that are prepared.

What then say the Psalms about the coming day of judgment? They say: "The Lord shall endure for ever [or, better, sitteth (as king) for ever]: he hath prepared his throne for judgment. And he shall judge the world in righteousness, he shall minister judgment to the people in uprightness." Jehovah is the Judge; the Lord Jehovah judgeth all men; the Father hath committed all judgment unto the Son. "The Lord is known by the judgment which he executeth: the wicked is snared in the work of his own hands. . . . The wicked shall be turned into hell, and all the nations that forget God." How can a just God do other than send the wicked to hell? If he saves the righteous, he must damn the wicked. He shall make a full end of all nations at his coming, and the wicked among them shall be burned, with their eternal spirits, as a consequence, going to hell. "Arise, O Lord; let not man prevail: let the heathen be judged in thy sight." (Ps. 9:7-8, 16-17, 19.) Such are the inspired words of David the king.

From Asaph the seer, who wrote in words of psalmic rhythm and beauty, we have received this prophetic word: "Our God shall come, and shall not keep silence: a fire shall devour before him, and it shall be very tempestuous round about him. He shall call to the heavens from above, and to the earth, that he may judge his people. Gather my saints together unto me; those that have made a covenant with me by sacrifice. And the heavens shall declare his righteousness: for God is judge himself." (Ps. 50:3-6.) Amid devouring fire, with angelic trumpets heralding the word from one end of heaven to the other, the Great God will come to his saints, to the people prepared to receive him. Angelic choirs—and, be it noted, Asaph, who gave us this word, was the leader of David's choir—shall rend the heavens with songs of praise and adoration. And it is pleasant to suppose that Asaph and other like-seeric musicians

511

shall lead the heavenly choirs that shall sing in that day.

These words also come to us from Asaph: "Thou didst cause judgment to be heard from heaven; the earth feared, and was still, when God arose to judgment, to save all the meek of the earth." (Ps. 76:8-9.) Truly the meek shall inherit the earth in the day of judgment. And yet again: "Arise, O God, judge the earth: for thou shalt inherit all nations." (Ps. 82:8.)

In two other Psalms, whose authors are unknown and who well may have been either Asaph or David, we find these expressions: "Say among the heathen that the Lord reigneth: the world also shall be established that it shall not be moved: he shall judge the people righteously. . . . For he cometh, for he cometh to judge the earth: he shall judge the world with righteousness, and the people with his truth." (Ps. 96:10, 13.) When the Lord comes to reign, all men will be judged "with his truth," which is his gospel. "Let the floods clap their hands: let the hills be joyful together before the Lord; for he cometh to judge the earth: with righteousness shall he judge the world, and the people with equity." (Ps. 98:8-9.)

Isaiahanic Prophecies of the Judgment

Our friend Isaiah—than whom few prophets have been greater—is known in all Christendom as the Messianic prophet. And truly he spake many wondrous things about the coming of the Messiah in the meridian of time. But those of us who hold the key that opens the full and true meaning of his many prophetic utterances know that the burden of his message pertained to the last days. Included in this greater portion of his Spirit-guided sayings, he had much to say about the day of judgment incident to the second coming of the Son of Man. Much that he wrote about the day of vengeance, the fall of Babylon, and the awful Armageddon that lies ahead, we have already considered. Let us now set forth some of that which he recorded relative to the Lord Jesus sitting in judgment when he comes again in all the glory of his Father's kingdom.

In his great prophecy about the gathering of Israel and the building of the temple in the tops of the mountains in the last days, Isaiah says: "And he [Christ] shall judge among the nations, and shall rebuke many people: and they shall beat their swords into plowshares, and their spears into pruninghooks: nation shall not lift up sword against nation, neither shall they learn war any more." (Isa. 2:4.) The setting here is one of judgment followed by millennial peace. The nations are judged, the wicked are rebuked, and the social order destined to prevail on the new heaven and the new earth is ushered in. Micah, in the same prophecy, has him judging "among many people" and rebuking "strong nations afar off" (Micah 4:3), but the thought and intent are the same. The Lord Jesus sits in judgment at his coming.

Then in his insightful prophetic utterance about the Stem of Jesse (who is Christ), Isaiah intones: "He shall not judge after the sight of his eyes, neither reprove after the hearing of his ears." There is more to judgment than seeing and hearing, more than heeding the words of witnesses, more than appears on the surface. There is, in addition, that which is in the heart of those who are judged. And so, "With righteousness shall he judge the poor, and reprove with equity for the meek of the earth." How favored are the faithful poor—poor as pertaining to the things of this world, rich as pertaining to eternity—and how blessed are the meek, for they shall inherit the earth. "And he shall smite the earth with the rod of his mouth, and with the breath of his lips shall he slay the wicked." The vineyard shall be burned and every corruptible thing shall be consumed. "And righteousness shall be the girdle of his loins, and faithfulness the girdle of his reins." (Isa. 11:3-5.) All that he does, both for the righteous and the wicked, shall be just and right. Then the account speaks of the wolf and the lamb dwelling together and various other things that will prevail during the Millennium and after the judgment that precedes it.

Of these same events, in another context, Isaiah says: "And in mercy shall the throne be established: and he [Christ] shall sit upon it in truth in the tabernacle of David, judging, and seeking judgment, and hasting righteousness." (Isa. 16:5.) We hear again the counsel: "Be strong, fear not: behold, your God will come with vengeance, even God with a recompence; he will come and save you" (Isa. 35:4)—meaning he will pour out vengeance upon the enemies of Israel; he will reward them for all their evil deeds and opposition to his covenant people; and he will save Israel with an everlasting salvation.

Speaking of the day when "every valley shall be exalted, and every mountain and hill shall be made low," and the various other things that will accompany the Second Coming, Isaiah says: "Behold, the Lord God will come with strong hand, and his arm shall rule for him: behold, his reward is with him, and his work before him." (Isa. 40:1-10.) Then, speaking of the day when the "standard" of salvation is lifted in the last days, Isaiah gives the Lord's decree to Zion in these words: "Behold, thy salvation cometh; behold, his reward is with him, and his work before him." (Isa. 62:10-11.) He rewards the faithful at his coming; they are judged and found worthy; they abide the day. And then, at long last, after six thousand years during which sin and war and evil have hindered and defeated his eternal purposes, then, in the promised millennial day, the Lord's work will prosper perfectly. So glorious shall be the state of so many for the space of a thousand years that, for the first time, as it were, the Lord's work of bringing to pass the eternal life of man will truly be before him.

Knowing and believing all these things, we are prepared to exult in our hearts and praise the Lord with our lips for his goodness, as we hear a divine voice acclaim: "Hearken unto me, my people," and the Latter-day Saints are the

Lord's people, "and give ear unto me, O my nation: for a law shall proceed from me, and I will make my judgment to rest for a light of the people." Thanks be to God, that law now has come; it is the fulness of his everlasting gospel; by it he will judge the world, and it now stands as a light for all men. "My righteousness is near." The millennial day is almost upon us. "My salvation is gone forth." The gospel is being preached to prepare a people for the coming day. "And mine arms shall judge the people; the isles shall wait upon me, and on mine arm shall they trust." The Lord shall soon come to judge the people. Hence, "Lift up your eyes to the heavens," O ye saints of the Most High, "and look upon the earth beneath." Read the signs of the times, the signs now being shown forth in the heavens above and in the earth beneath. "For the heavens shall vanish away like smoke, and the earth shall wax old like a garment, and they that dwell therein shall die in like manner." This old world shall die; there shall be a new heaven and a new earth; it will be a millennial earth. And "my salvation shall be for ever, and my righteousness shall not be abolished," saith the Lord. (Isa. 51:4-6.)

The New Testament Doctrine of the Judgment

In all ages, from Adam to this hour, the holy prophets have taught the true doctrine of the judgment. They have always set forth those concepts and verities that would encourage men to live in such a manner as to gain the glorious reward of eternal life when their day and time came to stand before the Eternal Bar. The hour of judgment is not the same for every man. Some are judged at one time and others at a different hour. There are, in fact, many days of judgment available, but always the same Judge sits at the same judgment bar, always the same laws govern the procedures, and always a just and right judgment is imposed.

Our birth into mortality is a day of judgment in that it signalizes we were found worthy while in the premortal life to undergo a mortal probation and thus to continue on the

515

course leading to eternal life. There are those who press forward along this course during this mortal probation—with a steadfastness in Christ, having a perfect love of God and of all men, keeping the commandments, and doing only those things that please their Lord—until they are translated and taken up into heaven, or until their calling and election is made sure. Either of these glorious eventualities is in itself a day of judgment. Their celestial inheritance is thus assured, though they have not yet gained bodies of immortal glory. Death also is a day of judgment when the spirits of men go to either paradise or hell as their deeds warrant.

The second coming of Christ is the great day of judgment for all men, both the living and the dead. In it those who qualify come forth in the resurrection of the just and obtain their rewards in the kingdoms established for them. At that time the decree goes forth that the rest of the dead shall remain in their graves to await the resurrection of the unjust and their consequent telestial inheritance. At that time the wicked among men are consumed as stubble, their bodies become dust again, and their spirits are consigned to an eternal hell to await the day of the resurrection of damnation. At that time those mortals who are worthy escape the burning, abide the day, and remain on the new earth with its new heavens in the presence of earth's new King.

Then, in the final day, when all is done and accomplished according to the divine purpose—after all men, the sons of perdition included, have risen from death to life and have become immortal—all men will stand before the bar of God in a final day of judgment. The eventual destiny of all men will have been determined before that day, but then the final and irrevocable decrees will be issued as pertaining to every living soul.

With this perspective before us, it is now our purpose to summarize the New Testament doctrine of the day of judgment as it pertains particularly to the second coming of the great and eternal Judge of quick and dead. We will do so under the following headings:

1. *Christ the Lord Is the Judge of All.*

That Lord—the Lord Jehovah—whom all the ancient prophets identified as the one who should judge the world is the Lord Jesus Christ. The spirit Jehovah became the mortal Christ, and the Lord Jesus, rising in glorious immortality, became the incarnate Jehovah who now sits on the right hand of the Majesty on High. Thus Jesus said: "The Father judgeth no man, but hath committed all judgment unto the Son: That all men should honour the Son, even as they honour the Father." And further: The Father "hath given him authority to execute judgment also, because he is the Son of man." He is the Son of Man of Holiness who is God. "I can of mine own self do nothing," Jesus continued, "as I hear, I judge: and my judgment is just; because I seek not mine own will, but the will of the Father which hath sent me." (John 5:22-23, 27, 30.) Christ is the Eternal Judge, and he does and shall operate in strict conformity to those eternal laws which he and his Father ordained from before the foundations of the world.

In harmony with this concept Jesus said: "For the Son of man shall come in the glory of his Father with his angels; and then he shall reward every man according to his works." (Matt. 16:27.) "Whosoever therefore shall be ashamed of me and of my words in this adulterous and sinful generation; of him also shall the Son of man be ashamed, when he cometh in the glory of his Father with the holy angels." (Mark 8:38.) And speaking of this day, Paul said that God "hath appointed a day, in the which he will judge the world in righteousness by that man [Christ] whom he hath ordained; whereof he hath given assurance unto all men, in that he hath raised him from the dead." (Acts 17:31.)

2. *The Second Coming Is the Day of Judgment.*

On this point Jude tells us: "And Enoch also, the seventh from Adam, prophesied of these, saying, Behold, the

Lord cometh with ten thousands of his saints, To execute judgment upon all, and to convince all that are ungodly among them of all their ungodly deeds which they have ungodly committed, and of all their hard speeches which ungodly sinners have spoken against him." (Jude 1:14-15.) Their words and their deeds, and, we may add, their thoughts, will condemn the ungodly in that dread day.

John describes that day, when the kingdoms of men are destroyed and the Lord comes to reign, in this way: "And the nations were angry, and thy wrath is come, and the time of the dead, that they should be judged, and that thou shouldest give reward unto thy servants the prophets, and to the saints, and them that fear thy name, small and great; and shouldest destroy them which destroy the earth." (Rev. 11:18.) John also records that in the day when "the hour of his judgment is come," Babylon shall fall and the wrath of God shall be "poured out without mixture" upon the wicked. (Rev. 14:7-10.)

3. *All Men Are Judged by Gospel Law.*

How and by what law will men be judged at the Second Coming? They will be judged by Christ and by his law, which is the gospel. Indeed, there is no other law by which they could be judged. He hath given a law unto all things. Those who abide the law are justified; those who break the law are condemned. Murder is murder in and out of the Church; sin is sin by whomsoever it is committed; evil is evil no matter where it is found. The standard and rule of judgment is the gospel; there is no other.

Let us hear what Paul has to say about this. He speaks of "the day of wrath and revelation." He addresses himself to Jew and Gentile, member and nonmember, believer and nonbeliever alike. His subject is "the righteous judgment of God." And he says that God "will render to every man according to his deeds." It matters not who they are, whether they are numbered with the saints or have cast their lot with the wicked and ungodly. Christ will judge all men according to his law, which is his gospel.

To the faithful saints, whom Paul describes as those "who by patient continuance in well doing seek for glory and honour and immortality," the promised reward is "eternal life." But for the wicked and ungodly, whom he describes as those "that are contentious, and do not obey the truth, but obey unrighteousness," there is no promise of eternal life. Instead they receive "indignation and wrath, tribulation and anguish." These are the heritage of "every soul of man that doeth evil." On the other hand, "glory, honour, and peace" are reserved for "every man that worketh good." "For as many as have sinned without law shall also perish without law," Paul says, "and as many as have sinned in the law shall be judged by the law." God, he says, is no respecter of persons, and "in the day when God shall judge the secrets of men by Jesus Christ"—note it—the judgment shall be "according to my gospel." (Rom. 2:5-16.)

Peter promises the faithful who stand fast in the fiery trials of life and who are "partakers of Christ's sufferings; that, when his glory shall be revealed," at His second coming, they shall "be glad also with exceeding joy." (1 Pet. 4:12-13.) And John records of that day: "He that is unjust, let him be unjust still: and he which is filthy, let him be filthy still: and he that is righteous, let him be righteous still: and he that is holy, let him be holy still. And, behold, I come quickly; and my reward is with me, to give every man according as his work shall be." (Rev. 22:11-12.)

One of the grandest expressions in all literature is the sweet yet awesome account Jesus gives of himself, seated on his glorious throne, in the coming day of judgment. He says: "When the Son of man shall come in his glory, and all the holy angels with him"—it is the day of his glorious return attended by legions of exalted beings from ages past—"then shall he sit upon the throne of his glory." The judgment is set and the books are opened, as it were. "And before him shall be gathered all nations: and he shall separate them one from another, as a shepherd divideth his sheep from the goats: And he shall set the sheep on his right hand, but the goats on the left." (Matt. 25:31-33.) The standard by which the assembled hosts will then be judged is whether they have lived Christian lives; whether they have ministered to the needs of their fellowmen; whether they have fed the hungry, clothed the naked, and visited the sick and imprisoned. It will be whether they have lived the laws revealed by him who is the Judge.

4. *The Apostles Shall Sit as Judges at the Second Coming.*

Jesus said to the Twelve who were with him in Jerusalem: "In the regeneration when the Son of man shall sit in the throne of his glory, ye also shall sit upon twelve thrones, judging the twelve tribes of Israel." (Matt. 19:28.) John said: "And I saw thrones, and they sat upon them, and judgment was given unto them: and I saw the souls of them that were beheaded for the witness of Jesus, and for the word of God, and which had not worshipped the beast, neither his image, neither had received his mark upon their foreheads, or in their hands; and they lived and reigned with Christ a thousand years." (Rev. 20:4.) The reality is that there will be a whole hierarchy of judges who, under Christ, shall judge the righteous. He alone shall issue the decrees of damnation for the wicked.

5. *The Final Day of Judgment Comes After the Millennium.*

Life continues during and after the Millennium. The resurrection of the unjust takes place after the Millennium. And the final great day of judgment will take place at the end of the earth. Hence John said: "And I saw a great white throne, and him that sat on it, from whose face the earth and the heaven fled away; and there was found no place for them." Christ sitteth upon the throne in the final day of judgment. "And I saw the dead, small and great, stand before God; and the books were opened: and another book was opened, which is the book of life: and the dead were judged out of those things which were written in the books, according to their works." (Rev. 20:11-12.)

The Day of Judgment Is Near

We have now seen what the ancient prophets and seers had to say about the day of judgment that is to accompany the Second Coming. As far as their prophetic writings reveal, some of the biblical prophets seem to have been concerned with almost nothing else. Their interest in these matters sets a pattern for us. Indeed, of all the people who have ever lived, we are the ones who should have greater anxiety and concern about what is to be in the great and dreadful day than any others. We are the ones who live when the dread events are dawning and when they may come to full fruition.

Providentially, our modern revelations about the day of judgment are often couched in the same language and abound in the same phrases as those used by the ancient prophets. These latter-day renditions of what is in the mind of Deity often amplify, clarify, and put a divine stamp of approval upon what was said anciently. We have, for instance, quoted from Isaiah 11 about the Lord coming to judge the world and usher in the Millennium. Nephi, with these same words before him on the brass plates, paraphrases, interprets, and expands them as follows: "And it shall come to pass that the Lord God shall commence his work among all nations, kindreds, tongues, and people, to bring about the restoration of his people upon the earth." These introductory words name the time in which the day of judgment shall come. It shall be after the restoration of the Lord's people has its beginning, but before it is all accomplished. In this setting Nephi picks up the thought content of Isaiah's inspired writing. "And with righteousness shall the Lord God judge the poor, and reprove with equity for the meek of the earth." The Great Judge shall sit in judgment. "And he shall smite the earth with the rod of his mouth; and with the breath of his lips shall he slay the wicked." So shall it be in the day of burning. "For the time speedily cometh that the Lord God shall cause a great division among the people, and the wicked will he destroy; and he will spare his people, yea, even if it so be that he must destroy the wicked by fire." The polarization that will gather the righteous into one camp and the wicked into another has already commenced, and these processes shall continue until the Lord comes. In that day, "Righteousness shall be the girdle of his loins, and faithfulness the girdle of his reins." (2 Ne. 30:8-11.) His judgments in that day shall be just. Nephi's language, quoted and paraphrased from Isaiah, then goes on to describe millennial conditions.

Similarly, referring repeatedly to various ancient scriptures, the Lord tells us that he "shall come to recompense unto every man according to his work, and measure to every man according to the measure which he has measured to his fellow man"; that "his sword is bathed in heaven, and it shall fall upon the inhabitants of the earth"; and that he "shall come down in judgment upon Idumea, or the world." (D&C 1:10, 13, 36.) In like manner, also to Joseph Smith the Lord said: "Mine apostles, the Twelve which were with me in my ministry at Jerusalem, shall stand at my right hand at the day of my coming in a pillar of fire, being clothed with robes of righteousness, with crowns upon their heads, in glory even as I am, to judge the whole house of Israel, even as many as have loved me and kept my commandments, and none else." (D&C 29:12.)

So also we read: "Be patient in tribulation until I come; and, behold, I come quickly, and my reward is with me, and they who have sought me early shall find rest to their souls." (D&C 54:10.) And also: "Wo unto you rich men, that will not give your substance to the poor, for your riches will canker your souls; and this shall be your lamentation in the day of visitation, and of judgment, and of indignation: The harvest is past, the summer is ended, and my soul is not saved! . . . For behold, the Lord shall come, and his recompense shall be with him, and he shall reward every man, and the poor shall rejoice." (D&C 56:16, 19.)

Need we say that the day of judgment is near, even at our doors? Truly, as the Lord measures time, the coming of the Great Judge is at hand. Elijah the prophet, whose return must be "before the coming of the great and dreadful day of the Lord" (Mal. 4:5), has already come. He appeared to Joseph Smith and Oliver Cowdery in the Kirtland Temple on April 3, 1836. Among other things, he then said: "By this ye may know that the great and dreadful day of the Lord is near, even at the doors." (D&C 110:16.) If such was the case in 1836, how much more so is it today?

Further, the signs of the times, in profuse abundance, all as promised by the prophets of old, are being manifest on every hand. The tender branches of the fig-tree are already covered with leaves. We know that "summer is nigh at hand." And as Jesus said on Olivet, "So likewise, mine elect, when they shall see all these things, they shall know that he is near, even at the doors." (JS-M 1:38-39.) Gospel light has pierced the long night of darkness that covered the earth; the gospel in all its glory, beauty, and perfection now shines forth in celestial splendor; a people once again is being prepared to meet their God. Israel is gathering into the appointed stakes; the walls of Zion are rising in holy places; and the promises made to the fathers have been planted in the hearts of the children. Wars and rumors of wars cover the earth; famines and diseases and an upheaval of the elements are increasing; and we have had a beginning taste of the plagues and pestilences and death and destruction. Armageddon is just around the corner. The hour is near, and the day is at hand.

Chapter 43

THE DAY
OF BURNING

He Comes — in Flaming Fire

Our Lord—the blessed Jesus, who came once as
Mary's son and lived as a mortal among men—shall come
again in all the glory of his Father's kingdom. He came
once, born as a baby among babies in Bethlehem; he grew
up as a child among children in Galilee; and he walked as a
man among men, preaching and ministering throughout all
Palestine.

Jesus of Nazareth came into this life alone, a single
spirit entering mortality at the appointed time. Though
angels heralded his presence and heavenly choirs sang of
his birth, the earth did not shake, the heavens did not roll
together as a scroll, fires and tempests did not testify of his
coming. The earth did not reel to and fro as a drunken man,
and the mountains and valleys remained as they had been
in ages past.

But it shall be otherwise when he comes again. He shall
not come in secret. His advent will not be in a caravanserai,
near a little village in Judea, among tethered beasts of
burden. "The Son of Man cometh not in the form of a
woman," as the sect of Shakers supposed, "neither of a
man traveling on the earth." (D&C 49:22.) This time all the
thunders of heaven will herald his approach and that of
those who are with him. "Behold, the Lord cometh with

ten thousands of his saints, to execute judgment upon all,'' as promised by Enoch of old. (Jude 1:14-15.)

This time he shall come in flaming fire, the vineyard shall be burned, and every living soul on earth shall know that a new order, of worldwide dimensions, has been ushered in. Thus saith the holy word: "The Lord Jesus shall be revealed from heaven with his mighty angels, in flaming fire taking vengeance on them that know not God, and that obey not the gospel of our Lord Jesus Christ." (2 Thes. 1:7-8.)

In flaming fire! What kind of fire? Flaming fire is flaming fire. It is actual, literal fire, fire that burns trees, melts ore, and consumes corruption. It is the same kind of fire that burned in the furnace of Nebuchadnezzar when Shadrach, Meshach, and Abednego were cast into its blazing flames. And though the heat and flames of fire "slew those men" whose lot it was to cast the three Hebrews into its flames, yet, miraculously, upon the bodies of these three "the fire had no power, nor was an hair of their head singed, neither were their coats changed, nor the smell of fire had passed on them." (Dan. 3:16-27.) And so shall it be at the Second Coming when the same literal fire burns over all the earth. The wicked shall be consumed and the righteous shall be as though they walked in the furnace of Nebuchadnezzar.

Graphic accounts of the fire and burning that will attend the Second Coming are found in the ancient word. "Our God shall come, and shall not keep silence," acclaims the Psalmist; "a fire shall devour before him, and it shall be very tempestuous round about him." (Ps. 50:3.) And also: "The Lord reigneth. . . . A fire goeth before him, and burneth up his enemies round about. His lightnings enlightened the world: the earth saw, and trembled. The hills melted like wax at the presence of the Lord, at the presence of the Lord of the whole earth." (Ps. 97:1-5.)

None of the prophets excel Isaiah in literary craftsmanship and in the use of grand imagery to teach and testify about the God of Israel and his laws. "The Lord cometh," Isaiah says, "burning with his anger, and . . . his lips are full of indignation, and his tongue as a devouring fire. . . . And the Lord shall cause his glorious voice to be heard, and shall shew the lighting down of his arm, with the indignation of his anger, and with the flame of a devouring fire, with scattering [i.e., with a blast], and tempest, and hailstones." And "the breath of the Lord, like a stream of brimstone," shall kindle the fires that destroy false worship. (Isa. 30:27-33.) "For, behold, the Lord will come with fire, and with his chariots like a whirlwind, to render his anger with fury, and his rebuke with flames of fire. For by fire and by his sword will the Lord plead with all flesh: and the slain of the Lord shall be many." (Isa. 66:15-16.)

And, rising to Isaiahanic heights, Habakkuk tells of a vision he saw of the Second Coming. "God came," he says, even "the Holy One. . . . His glory covered the heavens, and the earth was full of his praise. And his brightness was as the light. . . . Before him went the pestilence, and burning coals [fiery bolts] went forth at his feet. He stood, and measured [shook] the earth: he beheld, and drove asunder the nations; and the everlasting mountains were scattered, the perpetual hills did bow." (Hab. 3:3-6.) We shall speak more particularly of the coming of the Lord in flaming fire, as the scriptures do, in connection with the cleansing and burning of the vineyard.

He Comes—and the Elements Melt

When the Lord comes in his glory, in flaming fire, that fire will both cleanse the vineyard and burn the earth. In that day, so intense shall be the heat and so universal the burning, the very elements of which this earth is composed shall melt. The mountains, high and glorious and made of solid rock, shall melt like wax. They shall become molten and flow down into the valleys below. The very earth itself, as now constituted, shall be dissolved. All things shall burn with fervent heat. And out of it all shall come new heavens and a new earth whereon dwelleth righteousness. It is of these things—and they, above all else, show the literal nature of the burning fires that shall attend that dreadful day—it is of them that we must now make mention.

Peter, along with James and John, the other two members of the First Presidency in their day, saw in vision the transfiguration of the earth. These three were then with Jesus on Mount Hermon. It was the occasion when he himself was also transfigured before them. Speaking of this day of transfiguration, this millennial day—ushered in, as it will be, by the day of burning—our revelation says: "The earth shall be transfigured, even according to the pattern which was shown unto mine apostles upon the mount; of which account the fulness ye have not yet received." (D&C 63:20-21.) Thus these holy apostles saw the pattern, the way, and the manner in which the transfiguration of the earth occurred. A part, but not all, of what they saw, we know.

Knowing how this transfiguration was to take place, having seen it all in vision, Peter has left us these graphic words: "The heavens and the earth, which are now," he says, meaning our present earth and the aerial heavens that surround it, are "reserved unto fire against the day of judgment and perdition of ungodly men." Then, recording what he and his brethren had seen on the Mount of Transfiguration, Peter said: "But the day of the Lord will come as a thief in the night; in the which the heavens shall pass away with a great noise, and the elements shall melt with fervent heat, the earth also and the works that are therein shall be burned up."

Fervent heat—what is it? It is hot, glowing heat. The word itself comes from the Latin verb *fervere*, meaning to boil or to glow. It is the heat of which our revelation, alluding to a prophecy of Isaiah (Isa. 64:1-3), says: "The presence of the Lord shall be as the melting fire that burneth, and as the fire which causeth the waters to boil."

527

(D&C 133:41.) There has as yet been no heat on earth of such extent and intensity that it could melt the very planet itself. Such is reserved for the day of burning.

"Seeing then that all these things shall be dissolved," Peter continues, "what manner of persons ought ye to be in all holy conversation and godliness, looking for and hasting unto the coming of the day of God, wherein the heavens being on fire shall be dissolved, and the elements shall melt with fervent heat?" Work righteousness or be burned! How persuasive is this exhortation to walk uprightly before the Lord! "Nevertheless we, according to his promise, look for new heavens and a new earth, wherein dwelleth righteousness." The transfiguration shall truly come to pass; the wicked shall be burned as stubble, and the Lord will reign in millennial splendor among those that remain. "Wherefore, beloved, seeing that ye look for such things, be diligent that ye may be found of him in peace, without spot, and blameless." (2 Pet. 3:7-14.)

These same things were known to the ancient prophets, and some allusions to them have been preserved for us in their writings. Speaking of the Second Coming, Isaiah says: "The earth is utterly broken down, the earth is clean dissolved, the earth is moved exceedingly." (Isa. 24:19.) Amos says: "And the Lord God of hosts is he that toucheth the land, and it shall melt, and all that dwell therein shall mourn. . . . And all the hills shall melt." (Amos 9:5, 13.) Then he speaks of that portion of the gathering of Israel which is to take place during the Millennium.

Micah leaves us his witness in these words: "The Lord cometh forth out of his place, and will come down, and tread upon the high places of the earth. And the mountains shall be molten under him, and the valleys shall be cleft, as wax before the fire, and as the waters that are poured down a steep place." (Micah 1:3-4.)

And how pointed and express are the words of Nahum: "God is jealous, and the Lord revengeth; the Lord revengeth, and is furious; the Lord will take vengeance on his adversaries, and he reserveth wrath for his enemies." This is the great and dreadful day of the Lord, the day of vengeance that was in his heart, the day of burning in which every corruptible thing shall be consumed. "The Lord is slow to anger, and great in power, and will not at all acquit the wicked: the Lord hath his way in the whirlwind and in the storm, and the clouds are the dust of his feet." Nahum is seeing the desolations of the last days. "The mountains quake at him, and the hills melt, and the earth is burned at his presence, yea, the world, and all that dwell therein." (Nahum 1:2-5.)

Upon all this—all that Peter and the prophets have said about the flaming fires and burning heat that shall attend his coming—the Lord has put his stamp of approval. After saying that every corruptible thing shall be consumed at that dread day, he adds: "And also that of element shall melt with fervent heat; and all things shall become new, that my knowledge and glory may dwell upon all the earth." (D&C 101:25.)

He Comes—to Cleanse His Vineyard

In the full sense of the word, the whole earth is the vineyard of the Lord. In it, from time to time, in one place or another, all according to his good will and pleasure, the Lord of the vineyard plants peoples and nations and kindreds and tongues. Always he gives them such nourishment as they can bear, and some bring forth good fruit, others evil. He plants tame olive trees in choice spots and lets wild trees grow where they will. Branches are grafted back and forth in the hopes of turning the balance in favor of the good so the Lord of the vineyard may reap a rich harvest. "For behold, the field is white already to harvest; and it is the eleventh hour, and the last time that I shall call laborers into my vineyard," he says. "And my vineyard has become corrupted every whit; and there is none which doeth good save it be a few; and they err in many instances because of priestcrafts, all having corrupt minds." (D&C

33:3-4.) Even the good fruit is not as good as it ought to be.

In a more particular and limited sense, "the vineyard of the Lord of hosts is the house of Israel" (Isa. 5:7), and they of Israel are the trees of his planting. They were planted as tame olive trees in Palestine and were given every opportunity to bring forth good fruit. Fruitless branches were cut off and grafted into wild trees in the nethermost part of the vineyard of the world. And even now some of these branches are being brought back from their wild and Gentile state and once again are being given life and sustenance from the roots of the original tame trees.

Laborers are again called to labor in the Church and in the world for the salvation of men. They are going out to prune the vineyard for the last time. And the branches that bear no fruit—whether in the Church or in the world— shall soon be burned. The burning of the earth both is and includes the burning of the vineyard, depending upon what is meant by vineyard. The wicked and ungodly, in and out of the Church, shall be consumed in the fires. And "if the fire can scathe a green tree for the glory of God," our scripture says with reference to that which befalls even the righteous, "how easy it will burn up the dry trees to purify the vineyard of corruption." (D&C 135:6.)

In the allegory of the tame and wild olive trees, the Prophet Zenos, speaking of the final pruning of the vineyard in our day, records these words of the Lord of the vineyard: "And for the last time have I nourished my vineyard, and pruned it, and dug about it, and dunged it"—all of which is now going forward—"wherefore I will lay up unto mine own self of the fruit, for a long time, according to that which I have spoken. And when the time cometh that evil fruit shall again come into my vineyard"—when corruption begins to enter the only true Church and kingdom of God—"then will I cause the good and the bad to be gathered; and the good will I preserve unto myself, and the bad will I cast away into its own place.

And then cometh the season and the end; and my vineyard will I cause to be burned with fire." (Jacob 5:76-77.)

Then, as Isaiah says, "the light of Israel shall be for a fire, and his Holy One for a flame." Then shall the flame "burn and devour his thorns and his briers in one day." Then shall it "consume the glory of his forest, and of his fruitful field, both soul and body. . . . And the rest of the trees of his forest shall be few, that a child may write them." (Isa. 10:17-19.) And what follows speaks of the glory of that portion of Israel destined to gather in the millennial day.

It is of these last days of darkness and delusion that the holy word says: "Behold, the Lord maketh the earth empty, and maketh it waste, and turneth it upside down, and scattereth abroad the inhabitants thereof." Because the fruit is evil and few men stay on the Lord, the earth shall be emptied of its inhabitants—almost. "And it shall be, as with the people, so with the priest; as with the servant, so with his master; as with the maid, so with her mistress; as with the buyer, so with the seller; as with the lender, so with the borrower; as with the taker of usury, so with the giver of usury to him." The evil fruit that grows on the trees of the world will cover the earth. Those in all levels of society, high and low, will bring forth works fit only for the burning.

"The land shall be utterly emptied, and utterly spoiled: for the Lord hath spoken this word. The earth mourneth and fadeth away, the world languisheth and fadeth away, the haughty people of the earth do languish." The time of the end of the world is at hand. "The earth also is defiled under the inhabitants thereof." Why has all this evil come upon the trees of his forest? "Because they have transgressed the laws, changed the ordinance, broken the everlasting covenant." Apostasy reigns supreme; an evil tree cannot bring forth good fruit. Do men gather grapes of thorns or figs of thistles? "Therefore hath the curse devoured the earth, and they that dwell therein are desolate: therefore the inhabitants of the earth are burned, and few men left." (Isa. 24:1-6.) Truly, the vineyard shall be burned of corruption in the coming day!

He Comes—It Is the End of the World

The end of the world—what is it, and when shall it be? It is not the end of the earth. By the world we mean the customs, practices, and interests of men as social beings. We mean the social order that prevails among those who live on the earth. We mean the carnality, sensuality, and devilishness that rules in the lives of the wicked and ungodly. We mean the way of life followed by those who love Satan more than God because their deeds are evil.

Worldly people lie and steal and cheat; they take advantage of their neighbor for a word; and they bear false witness, both with the voice of gossip and on the witness stand when they have sworn to speak only the truth. Worldly people rob and plunder and murder. They accept war as a matter of national policy. They are lewd and lascivious. Sex sin is their friend; pornography walks with them; their conversation is profane and vulgar. They include adulterers and homosexuals and those whose thoughts dwell on low and base and sex-oriented things.

The world is evil, carnal, base. It fights the truth, kills the prophets, slays the saints. Worldly people oppose and fight The Church of Jesus Christ of Latter-day Saints because they belong to another kingdom, the kingdom of the devil. The end of the world is the end of all this: it is the end of wickedness; it is the ushering in of a new world, a new age, a new social order—the order of peace and righteousness.

Jesus said: "I am not of the world." (John 17:16.) "I have overcome the world." (John 16:33.) To his apostles he explained: "If ye were of the world, the world would love his own: but because ye are not of the world, but I have chosen you out of the world, therefore the world hateth you." (John 15:19.) And it was the beloved John who counseled: "Love not the world, neither the things that are in the world. If any man love the world, the love of the Father is not in him. For all that is in the world, the lust of the flesh, and the lust of the eyes, and the pride of life, is not of the Father, but is of the world." And having so taught, he added these words of wondrous comfort: "And the world passeth away, and the lust thereof: but he that doeth the will of God abideth for ever." (1 Jn. 2:15-17.)

One of the questions that the disciples asked Jesus on Olivet was: "What is the sign of thy coming, and of the end of the world, or the destruction of the wicked, which is the end of the world?" His answer included the whole Olivet Discourse. He spoke of the things that must occur before he came again, including the restoration of the gospel in the last days, which restored gospel, he said, "shall be preached in all the world, for a witness unto all nations, and then shall the end come, or the destruction of the wicked."

We are now in process of preaching the gospel to the world. It has not yet been offered to those in every nation in the full and true sense of the word. And the Lord will not return until we have accomplished the work he has given us to do. Up to this point in time we have received the gospel, the kingdom has been established, and the word is going forth as rapidly as our strength and means allow. Many of the Lord's latter-day servants are faithful and true in their attempts to spread the saving truths; others are slothful, seem to care little for the great commission given them, and partake more or less of the spirit of the world. Knowing that such would be the case in our day, Jesus climaxed his Olivet Discourse by telling about the faithful and the unfaithful members of the Church in the last days.

"Who, then, is a faithful and wise servant," he asked, "whom his lord hath made ruler over his household, to give them meat in due season? Blessed is that servant whom his lord, when he cometh, shall find so doing; and verily I say unto you, he shall make him ruler over all his goods." Exaltation consists in receiving, inheriting, and possessing all that the Father hath. Those who so obtain shall rule and reign forever. To say they shall be rulers over all their Lord's goods is but the beginning description of their eventual status.

"But if that evil servant shall say in his heart"—he is speaking now of rebellious church officers in the last days; he is speaking of those who have rulership in his church in the dispensation of the fulness of times; he is speaking of those who live just before the Second Coming—if any such shall say in his heart, "My lord delayeth his coming, and shall begin to smite his fellow-servants, and to eat and drink with the drunken, the lord of that servant shall come in a day when he looketh not for him, and in an hour that he is not aware of, and shall cut him asunder, and shall appoint him his portion with the hypocrites; there shall be weeping and gnashing of teeth. And thus cometh the end of the wicked, according to the prophecy of Moses, saying: They shall be cut off from among the people; but the end of the earth is not yet, but by and by." (JS-M 1:4, 31, 49-55.)

The end of the world is near; it shall soon come; it shall come suddenly, with violence, and amidst burning and desolation. The warning voice, sent forth from God in our day, pleads with all men to prepare themselves so they can abide the day and not be cut off from among the people. "Ye say that ye know that the end of the world cometh," Jesus said to his disciples, and "ye say also that ye know that the heavens and the earth shall pass away," he continued; "and in this ye say truly, for so it is." The end of the world shall come when the heavens and the earth, as now constituted, pass away. It shall come when there are new heavens and a new earth, millennial heavens and a millennial earth. "But these things which I have told you shall not pass away until all shall be fulfilled." That is, the ancient disciples were not to suppose that the end would come in their day. There was to be an apostasy, and a scattering of Israel, and a restoration of the gospel, and a gathering of the elect, and the establishment of Zion anew—all before the end of the world. After all this—"in that day," Jesus continued, there "shall be heard of wars and rumors of wars, and the whole earth shall be in commotion, and men's hearts shall fail them, and they shall say that Christ delayeth his coming until the end of the earth"—then, in that day, the end of the world will come. (D&C 45:22-26.) And we now live in the beginning days of sorrow and war and commotion and disbelief that will usher in the day of burning. World conditions are evil and corrupt. They will continue to degenerate and get worse. Then suddenly, in a not distant day, when all the prophecies have been fulfilled to the uttermost, the end will come and the wicked will be destroyed.

The Second Day of Burning

The end of the world ushers in the millennial era. The end of wickedness brings in the new day of righteousness. This old earth and this old heaven, with all their evil and corruption and worldliness, shall come to an end; and there will be new heavens and a new earth whereon dwelleth righteousness. All this shall come to pass in the great day of burning that is soon to be.

This earth, the very planet on which we live, is being prepared for eternal salvation. As with all things, it was created first as a spirit sphere. Then came the physical creation in which it was made and organized as a terrestrial or paradisiacal planet. In that day there was no death. Then Adam fell and brought death into the world, and the effects of his fall passed upon himself, upon Eve, and upon all forms of life, and upon the earth itself.

This earth, this orb, this planet, fell and became a telestial earth, which it now is. In this fallen state, as with those fallen men who become heirs of salvation, the earth was baptized by immersion; the waters of Noah covered its entire surface, and the corruption on its face was buried in them. When the Lord comes again, our earth will be baptized with fire so that dross and evil will be consumed with fervent heat, even as these are burned out of a human soul through the baptism of the Spirit.

In this day of burning there will be the new heavens and the new earth of which the revelations speak. The earth will become again a paradisiacal or terrestrial sphere. It will be renewed and be as it originally was in the day of the Garden of Eden. Death as we know it, meaning physical death, will cease. Men, for instance, will then live to the age of a hundred years and be changed from their terrestrial mortality to a state of eternal immortality in the twinkling of an eye. Then after the Millennium, plus a little season, which we assume will be a thousand years, the earth will again be burned; it will again be changed; there will again be new heavens and a new earth, but this time it will be a celestial earth. This is also spoken of as the resurrection of our planet.

Speaking of the death of the earth, and in acclaiming the glory of God, the Psalmist says: "Thou laid the foundation of the earth: and the heavens are the work of thy hands. They shall perish, but thou shalt endure: yea, all of them shall wax old like a garment; as a vesture shalt thou change them, and they shall be changed." (Ps. 102:25-26.) To Isaiah the Lord speaks in a like vein: "Lift up your eyes to the heavens, and look upon the earth beneath," the divine voice acclaims, "for the heavens shall vanish away like smoke, and the earth shall wax old like a garment, and they that dwell therein shall die in like manner: but my salvation shall be for ever, and my righteousness shall not be abolished." (Isa. 51:6.) As with men, so with the earth; both shall die and both shall be resurrected.

By revelation in our day the Lord says: "The great Millennium, of which I have spoken by the mouth of my servants, shall come. For Satan shall be bound, and when he is loosed again he shall only reign for a little season, and then cometh the end of the earth." It will, of course, be the end of the world of wickedness that then exists, but it will also be the end of the earth. "And he that liveth in righteousness shall be changed in the twinkling of an eye, and the earth shall pass away so as by fire." (D&C 43:30-32.) This is the second day of burning, the day when planet earth becomes a celestial sphere, an abiding place for the Lord God and the holy men of all ages as their time and circumstances permit. This will complete the salvation of the earth; it will then have become an eternal heaven whereon those who gain eternal life may live forever.

Chapter 44

ABIDING THE DAY

"Who May Abide the Day of His Coming?"

A gracious God, who does all things well and is himself all powerful, all wise, and all knowing, reveals his mind and will to men so they can advance and progress and become like him. He gives his doctrines to men so they will know what to believe and what to do to gain eternal life. All doctrine—all gospel concepts of every sort and nature—all are revealed and preached to prepare men for celestial rest. And we have no better illustration of this than the doctrine of the second coming of the Son of Man. One of the chief reasons this doctrine is revealed is to teach us what we must do, whether in life or in death, to abide the day.

Our prophetic friends in days of old were wont to counsel the saints on the doctrine of abiding the day of the coming of the Lord. Their words have greater import for us, as the day itself draws near, than they did for those in ancient times. We shall note, for our own guidance, what some of our brethren of old had to say about this doctrine. As we do so, it will be impressed upon us anew, with great force and power, that the righteous shall abide the day of his coming and the wicked shall be burned as stubble. It is hoped that this will guide us in choosing which group to join and where we should pledge our personal allegiance.

Let us turn first to some of the pointed and poetic words of Isaiah. "The sinners in Zion are afraid," he said, as he viewed with seeric vision the Zion of God in the last days. "Fearfulness hath surprised the hypocrites," he intoned, as he foresaw that even in the Church and kingdom of God in our dispensation there would be those who did not keep their covenants and walk uprightly before the Lord. Then, speaking of the elect of God in the day of their Lord's return, he cried out: "Who among us"—among the saints of the living God, among the true believers, among those who have forsaken the world and know the course leading to eternal life—"shall dwell with the devouring fire? who among us shall dwell with everlasting burnings?" When the vineyard is burned, who among us shall withstand the flaming fires? When the elements melt with fervent heat and all things become new, who among us shall withstand the searing heat? And, finally, when this earth becomes a celestial sphere—a sphere of everlasting burnings—who among us shall find place thereon?

His answer comes with all the surety that attends pure and perfect prophetic knowledge. "He that walketh righteously, and speaketh uprightly," he says; "he that despiseth the gain of oppressions, that shaketh his hands from holding of bribes, that stoppeth his ears from hearing of blood, and shutteth his eyes from seeing evil." How deep is the meaning of the prophetic word. In the world men amass fortunes by oppressing the poor; their hands are ever grasping after bribes and ill-gotten gain; their spoken words concern blood and war and how they will profit thereby; and they see and rejoice in evil on every hand. With him that is righteous, it is not so. His heart is on the riches of eternity that it is the good pleasure of the Father to give to his saints. And as a result, "He shall dwell on high."

With reference to all those who are able to pass through the devouring fires of the Second Coming, the promise is: "Thine eyes shall see the king in his beauty." Christ shall live and reign among them. "They shall behold the land that is very far off." Theirs shall be a millennial inheritance on the new heavens and the new earth that are to be. (Isa. 33:14-17.)

Joel, one of our ancient friends in whose prophetic renown we rejoice, one who wrote with power and insight of our day and of the second coming of that Lord in whom the saints of all dispensations delight, the prophet Joel said: "And the Lord shall utter his voice before his army: for his camp is very great"—he speaks of the day of Armageddon—"for he is strong that executeth his word: for the day of the Lord is great and very terrible." Of all this we have made ourselves somewhat aware. The great and dreadful day of the Lord is all that the prophets have said and more; mere words cannot describe the horror of the coming holocaust nor the terror that will take hold of the wicked in that day. Having so reminded us, Joel asks: "And who can abide it?"

Who indeed? Who among us shall qualify to remain in the flesh and enjoy the blessings of the new heavens and the new earth that are to be? As all those with sense and knowledge and discernment know, it will be those who believe and obey. "Therefore also now, saith the Lord, turn ye even to me with all your heart, and with fasting, and with weeping, and with mourning." Come, worship the Lord in Spirit and in truth. "And rend your heart, and not your garments." Let the substance be more than ritual. "And turn unto the Lord your God: for he is gracious and merciful, slow to anger, and of great kindness, and repenteth him of the evil." (Joel 2:11-13.) These words are addressed to Israel, to gathered Israel, to Israel of the last days. We are they.

Though "the Lord is slow to anger, and great in power," Nahum tells us, he "will not at all acquit the wicked." When is it that the wicked shall be rewarded for their evil deeds? It is in the day of his coming, for "the mountains quake at him, and the hills melt, and the earth is burned at his presence, yea, the world, and all that dwell therein." It is the end of the world; every corruptible thing is consumed in the fire; the wicked are cut off from among the people.

Then Nahum asks the age-old questions: "Who can stand before his indignation? and who can abide in the fierceness of his anger?" As to the righteous, the answer comes: "The Lord is good, a strong hold in the day of trouble; and he knoweth them that trust in him." As to the wicked, the divine word says: "His fury is poured out like fire, and the rocks are thrown down by him. . . . For while they [the wicked] be folden together as thorns, and while they are drunken as drunkards, they shall be devoured as stubble fully dry." (Nahum 1:3-10.)

"Every Corruptible Thing . . . Shall Be Consumed"

Our revelations tells us that when the Lord comes, "every corruptible thing, both of man, or of the beasts of the field, or of the fowls of the heavens, or of the fish of the sea, that dwells upon all the face of the earth, shall be consumed; and also that of element shall melt with fervent heat." (D&C 101:24-25.) With this concept before us, we are able to envision what Zephaniah meant in the emphatic pronouncements he made along this same line. We shall now digest and quote a few of his words.

"I will utterly consume all things from off the land, saith the Lord." He is speaking of the day of burning that shall attend the Second Coming. "I will consume man and beast; I will consume the fowls of the heaven, and the fishes of the sea, and the stumblingblocks with the wicked; and I will cut off man from off the land, saith the Lord." Nothing that is evil and wicked shall abide the day; all that falls short of the required standard shall be burned in the fires of fervent heat; it shall be as with man, so with the beast. Nothing that is corruptible shall remain.

False worship shall cease. The great and abominable church shall tumble to the dust; Babylon shall fall; the church of the devil, composed of the tares of the earth, shall be burned. "I will cut off the remnant of Baal," the Lord says. It shall be with them as it was with the priests of Baal in the days of Elijah. False priests, "and them that worship the host of heaven upon the housetops; and them that worship . . . and that swear by Malcham [the god of the Ammonites]; and them that are turned back from the Lord [apostates]; and those that have not sought the Lord, nor enquired for him [lukewarm members of the Church, among others]"—all these shall be consumed.

Zephaniah speaks of punishment for those who deal in "violence and deceit," for the drunken who are "settled on their lees," and for those who think the Lord will pour no "evil" upon them in the day of his coming. "That day is a day of wrath," saith the Lord, "a day of trouble and distress, a day of wasteness and desolation, a day of darkness and gloominess, a day of clouds and thick darkness." Can anything but evil befall the wicked in the great and dreadful day? "And I will bring distress upon men, that they shall walk like blind men, because they have sinned against the Lord." Is not this the case today with men and their leaders? "And their blood shall be poured out as dust, and their flesh as the dung." And shall this not come to pass in the great wars of the last days? "Neither their silver nor their gold shall be able to deliver them in the day of the Lord's wrath; but the whole land shall be devoured by the fire of his jealousy: for he shall make even a speedy riddance of all them that dwell in the land." (Zeph. 1:2-18.)

The prophetic word would be incomplete if it did not tell men what they must do to avoid being consumed in the dread day of burning that will attend our Lord's glorious return. "Gather yourselves together" is the divine call to Israel. "Seek ye the Lord, all ye meek of the earth, which have wrought his judgment; seek righteousness, seek meekness: it may be ye shall be hid in the day of the Lord's anger." (Zeph. 2:1-3.) Believe the gospel; join the only true and living Church; keep the commandments—this is the voice of the Lord to all men everywhere. "Therefore wait ye upon me, saith the Lord, until the day that I rise up to the prey: for my determination is to gather the nations, that I may assemble the kingdoms, to pour upon them mine indignation, even all my fierce anger: for all the earth shall be devoured with the fire of my jealousy." (Zeph. 3:8.) He speaks of Armageddon, which in part shall consume the wicked.

Men's Works Tried by Fire

The fierce flames, the fervent heat, the burning fires of the Second Coming that destroy the wicked shall also cleanse the righteous. When we say that the wicked and ungodly shall be consumed; when we say that only the righteous shall abide the day; when we say that there shall be an entire separation between the righteous and the wicked in that day—we must take into account the fact that there are no perfect men. All men fall short of divine standards; none attain the high state of excellence manifest in the life of the Lord Jesus; even the most faithful saints commit sin and live in some degree after the manner of the world. But such worldly works as remain with the righteous shall be burned so that the saints themselves may be saved. Let us take this comforting assurance from the inspired writings of one of our apostolic colleagues of old.

Paul said: "Other foundation can no man lay than that is laid, which is Jesus Christ." Our house of salvation must be built on Christ. He is our Savior. our Redeemer, our Advocate, our Mediator. He brought life and immortality to light through his gospel. He alone makes salvation possible; we are saved by his goodness and grace, provided we keep his commandments.

But not all men build on this one secure foundation, and some who do may yet remain entangled in worldly pursuits that keep them from living as near perfection as the gospel cause enables them to do. And so Paul continued: "Now if any man build upon this foundation"—that is, upon the foundation of Christ—with "gold, silver, precious stones, wood, hay, stubble"—that is, if their hearts are still set somewhat upon the things of this world—yet "every man's work shall be made manifest: for the day shall declare it, because it shall be revealed by fire; and the fire shall try every man's work of what sort it is." In the day of burning, all evil and corruptible works shall be consumed; only good works will remain. "If any man's work abide which he hath built thereupon"—that is, which he has built upon Christ—"he shall receive a reward." Then comes the comforting assurance: "If any man's work shall be burned," because some things in his life are yet worldly, "he shall suffer loss." No one ever gets an unearned blessing. "But he himself shall be saved; yet so as by fire." (1 Cor. 3:11-15.) The Prophet Joseph Smith changed this last sentence to read: "But he himself may be saved; yet so as by fire." (JST, 1 Cor. 3:15.) Thus the burning that destroys every corruptible thing is the same burning that cleanses the righteous. Evil and sin and dross will be burned out of their souls because they qualify to abide the day, even though all their works have not been as those of Enoch and Elijah. If only perfect people were saved, there would be only one saved soul—the Lord Jesus.

We have in holy writ many illustrations of the people and the works that will abide the day, and what works, and of whom, will be burned at His coming. Perhaps no prophet has surpassed Malachi in discoursing on these matters. He announces that the Lord will come in the last days and then asks: "But who may abide the day of his coming? and who shall stand when he appeareth?" The reason some will not abide the day is given in these words: "He is like a refiner's fire, and like fullers' soap: and he shall sit as a refiner and purifier of silver; and he shall purify the sons of Levi, and purge them as gold and silver." Their evil works shall be burned, and they themselves shall be cleansed and saved, as Paul's exposition assures us.

Then Malachi sets forth the words of the Lord Jehovah,

who is the Lord Jesus, as he speaks in the first person. "And I will come near to you to judgment," he says. The Second Coming is the day of judgment. "And I will be a swift witness against the sorcerers, and against the adulterers, and against false swearers, and against those that oppress the hireling in his wages, the widow, and the fatherless, and that turn aside the stranger from his right, and fear not me, saith the Lord of hosts." The works here named, together with those who do them, shall be burned at his coming. None who live in this worldly way shall abide the day. Then comes the promise that the faithful in Israel shall be saved. "Ye sons of Jacob are not consumed," saith the Lord. Those who are not consumed abide the day.

But the unfaithful in gathered Israel have no such promise. They are told: "even from the days of your fathers ye are gone away from mine ordinances, and have not kept them." The Lord's ordinances are his laws and commandments. There are those in the Church who have not walked in the light and kept the covenant made in the waters of baptism. "Return unto me, and I will return unto you, saith the Lord of hosts." There is yet time; the day is not at hand, and the hour has not arrived. There is yet a little season in which men may repent. But the lukewarm members of the Church, assuming in their minds that they have done no great evil, ask: "Wherein shall we return?" What have we done that is so grossly amiss? Have we not shown some measure of devotion? Surely we do not walk in a wicked way; what is our offense?

Then, as though the answer came from the fires and thunders of Sinai, the Lord of Hosts asked: "Will a man rob God?" Some might sink to such a depth as to rob their fellowmen. But who would be so vile, so devoid of all decency and right, so defiantly rebellious as to rob the Great God who created all things and who has poured out his bounties without measure upon men in all nations? Who would rob God? "Yet ye have robbed me," saith the Lord. In seeming unbelief that they could be accused of so gross a crime, even the most rebellious in Israel ask, "Wherein have we robbed thee?" The answer is forthcoming. He whose judgments are just and who does all things well replies: "In tithes and offerings." All Israel has covenanted in the waters of baptism to pay one-tenth of their increase annually into the tithing funds of the Church. That tenth is the Lord's tenth. It no longer belongs to the steward in whose hands it rests for the moment. It is the Lord's. To misappropriate the Lord's property is dishonest. In his sight it is robbery. Hence he says: "Ye are cursed with a curse; for ye have robbed me, even this whole nation." (Mal. 3:1-9.)

What is it that we thus learn from the Lord with reference to those who shall abide the day of his coming? We learn that those in Israel who are refined and purified shall walk unharmed in the furnace of Nebuchadnezzar, as it were, and upon their bodies the millennial fires have no power. Not a hair of their heads shall be singed, and the smell of fire shall not cling to their garments. But as for the sorcerers, the adulterers, the false swearers, those who oppress the poor, and those who rob God—none of these shall abide the day. And as to his own covenant people who choose to rob him of that which is his, the Lord in our day has issued this warning: "Behold, now it is called today until the coming of the Son of Man, and verily it is a day of sacrifice, and a day for the tithing of my people; for he that is tithed shall not be burned at his coming." (D&C 64:23.)

The Wicked Shall Be Burned at His Coming

Sometimes even the saints of the Most High become discouraged in their warfare with the world. Some among them forget for a moment that there will be a day of burning in which the wicked shall be consumed; some wonder if all their service and selflessness and sacrifice are worth the price. Knowing their thoughts and hearing their words, the Lord rebukes them by saying: "Your words have been stout against me." 'You have complained about the hardships of life and forgotten that I have ordained all these things for your ultimate glory and blessing.' To this the Lord's people reply: "What have we spoken so much against thee?" The Lord responds: "Ye have said, It is vain to serve God: and what profit is it that we have kept his ordinance, and that we have walked mournfully before the Lord of hosts?" 'Is it worth it to keep the commandments of God and deny ourselves all these pleasant delicacies and diversions that abound in the lives of other people?' Then the Lord explains: "Now"—in this present world of wickedness; in this day of carnality and evil; in this day when the wicked and ungodly do whatever is right in their own eyes—"Now we call the proud happy; yea, they that work wickedness are set up; yea, they that tempt God are even delivered." It is their world; it is their day; it is the hour of their delight. But soon their world will end; their day will pass away; and what they suppose are the delights of life will turn to ashes in their hands.

But for those who fear the Lord and keep his commandments, it shall be otherwise. They shall abide the coming day. "And they shall be mine, saith the Lord of hosts, in that day when I make up my jewels; and I will spare them, as a man spareth his own son that serveth him." They shall not be burned. "Then shall ye return, and discern between the righteous and the wicked, between him that serveth God and him that serveth him not." (Mal. 3:13-18.) However much the wicked may prevail in their own world; however eminent and great they now are in the eyes of their ilk; however much they may suppose their carnal course is one of happiness—yet in the day of burning (when there shall be a complete separation of the righteous and the wicked), those who serve God shall triumph. The new world will be their world.

"For, behold, the day cometh, that shall burn as an oven; and all the proud, yea, and all that do wickedly, shall be stubble: and the day that cometh shall burn them up, saith the Lord of hosts, that it shall leave them neither root nor branch.'' (Mal. 4:1.) Moroni's rendition of this statement as given to the Prophet on that September night in 1823 changed a portion of it to say: "For they that come shall burn them, saith the Lord of Hosts." (JS-H 1:37.) And, alluding to and paraphrasing Malachi's words, the Lord said in our day: "For after today cometh the burning—this is, speaking after the manner of the Lord—for verily I say, tomorrow all the proud and they that do wickedly shall be as stubble; and I will burn them up, for I am the Lord of Hosts; and I will not spare any that remain in Babylon. Wherefore, if ye believe me, ye will labor while it is called today." (D&C 64:24-25.)

Let us, then, labor while it is called today. Let us put our hands to the plow and look not back, lest we, like Lot's wife, become entangled again in the web of worldliness and lose our souls. Let us gather to Zion and within her walls rejoice. And thanks be to God for the restoration of the everlasting gospel; thanks be to him for the gathering of Israel and for the standard of righteousness that now waves in the mountains of Israel. Thanks be to his holy name for revealing anew what men must do "to prepare their hearts and be prepared in all things against the day when tribulation and desolation are sent forth upon the wicked."

For thus saith the Lord: "The hour is nigh and the day soon at hand when the earth is ripe; and all the proud and they that do wickedly shall be as stubble; and I will burn them up, saith the Lord of Hosts, that wickedness shall not be upon the earth; For the hour is nigh, and that which was spoken by mine apostles must be fulfilled; for as they spoke so shall it come to pass; For I will reveal myself from heaven with power and great glory, with all the hosts thereof, and dwell in righteousness with men on earth a thousand years, and the wicked shall not stand." (D&C 29:8-11.)

Chapter 45

THE DAY
OF SEPARATION

This Evil Day

This is an evil day, a day of disease and darkness and death. Our society is sick; our governments lack vision; our educational system takes an amoral and neutral position on the great Christian verities. Even the churches of Christendom, so-called, to say nothing of the non-Christian and pagan ways of worship, are decadent, sin-ridden, and incapable of raising the warning voice. Even in the one true Church, sad and unfortunate as it may be, the wheat and tares together grow.

Crime of every sort is increasing. Murder and rape and robbery are as much a way of life as they were in the days of Noah. Sexual perversions are lauded as an acceptable life-style for a growing portion of the people of our planet. Satan is abroad in the land. He and his fellow demons rage in the hearts of men. He sits in high places and rules in organizations of all sorts. It is his world; he knows it, and he is in command. There is rejoicing in the courts of hell and laughter on the lips of its courtiers as they survey the shambles they have made of our modern social structure.

In this present world of carnality and evil, the righteous and the wicked mingle in the same congregations. And as far as the arm of flesh is concerned, there is no way to stay the surging flood of evil that has been unloosed. The divine purpose allows iniquity to abound and sin to increase. The saints of God do and shall continue to strive with all their power to build dikes of righteousness that will contain the tides of evil that are sweeping over all the earth. But it will be a losing affray; at least it will be a war they will not win until the Man of War who is the God of Battles comes to champion their cause—which is his cause—and to fight their battles and to destroy their enemies.

This is a day in which—ere long!—"the wrath of God shall be poured out upon the wicked without measure." (D&C 1:9.) This is a day, saith the Lord, in which "a desolating scourge shall go forth among the inhabitants of the earth, and shall continue to be poured out from time to time, if they repent not, until the earth is empty, and the inhabitants thereof are consumed away and utterly destroyed by the brightness of my coming." (D&C 5:19.) "For I, the Almighty, have laid my hands upon the nations, to scourge them for their wickedness. And plagues shall go forth, and they shall not be taken from the earth until I have completed my work, which shall be cut short in righteousness—until all shall know me, who remain." (D&C 84:96-98.)

This is a day of which the Lord says: "I, the Lord, am angry with the wicked; I am holding my Spirit from the inhabitants of the earth. I have sworn in my wrath, and decreed wars upon the face of the earth, and the wicked shall slay the wicked, and fear shall come upon every man; and the saints also shall hardly escape; nevertheless, I, the Lord, am with them, and will come down in heaven from the presence of my Father and consume the wicked with unquenchable fire." (D&C 63:32-34.)

As we are acutely aware: "They that are wise and have received the truth, and have taken the Holy Spirit for their guide, and have not been deceived . . . they shall not be hewn down and cast into the fire, but shall abide the day." And conversely: "Calamity shall cover the mocker, and the scorner shall be consumed; and they that have watched

for iniquity shall be hewn down and cast into the fire.''
(D&C 45:50, 57.) Truly, ''he that is not purified shall not
abide the day.'' (D&C 38:8.)

The Burning of the Tares

We have made repeated references to the burning of the
vineyard, which is the earth, and to the fact that every
corruptible thing of every sort, including those portions of
all forms of life that do not meet the divine standard, shall
be consumed at the Second Coming. This is the cleansing
of the earth and its atmospheric heavens that will change it
into a new heaven and a new earth. This is also the occasion when the tares shall be burned, and the burning of the
tares is the destruction of the wicked at our Lord's return.

As faith precedes the miracle, so wickedness precedes
the burning. It was so in Sodom, and so it shall be in the
coming day. The law is the Lord's; it is that the wicked of
all ages shall burn in hell, and those who live in the day of
his coming shall be as stubble. The fires of a just God shall
leave them neither root nor branch. And so, as the day of
burning nears, we are more deeply concerned than men
have ever been as to what is involved in the soon-to-be
burning of the tares.

In the parable of the wheat and the tares the kingdom of
heaven, meaning the true Church and kingdom of God on
earth, was likened unto a man who sowed good seed in his
field. The one who sowed the seed was the Lord Jesus; the
field was the world; the good seed was the children of the
kingdom, the true saints, the believing and obedient souls
who accepted the gospel and forsook the world to serve
Christ. But while men slept, the Lord's enemy, who is
Satan, the devil, the evil one, came and sowed tares among
the wheat and went his way. Tares, in the literal sense of
the word, are a noxious weed that resembles wheat; they
are a ''bastard wheat'' that is so much like the true wheat
that the plants cannot be distinguished from it until the
grain begins to ripen. In the parable the tares are the chil-

dren of the wicked one; they are those in the Church and in the world who live wicked and ungodly lives, who are carnal, sensual, and devilish, and who live after the manner of the world.

"But when the blade was sprung up, and brought forth fruit," the parable continues, "then appeared the tares also." Seeing this, the Lord's servants asked if they should gather up the tares. The answer: "Nay; lest while ye gather up the tares, ye root up also the wheat with them. Let both grow together until the harvest, and in the time of harvest, I will say to the reapers, Gather ye together first the wheat into my barn; and the tares are bound in bundles to be burned."

What then, is the meaning of the parable, and how shall we interpret it? Jesus answers: "The harvest is the end of the world, or the destruction of the wicked." The fulfillment is yet future; the end of the world is not yet, but by and by. "The reapers are the angels, or the messengers sent of heaven." They are the servants of the Lord who go forth to harvest the earth, and to gather the wheat into barns. "As, therefore, the tares are gathered and burned in the fire, so shall it be in the end of this world, or the destruction of the wicked." After a farmer harvests his wheat, he burns the field to destroy the weeds, lest they reseed the field and his land be ruined. "For in that day, before the Son of man shall come, he shall send forth his angels and messengers of heaven." Moroni and the other angels have come and the messengers chosen of heaven are now going forth. "And they shall gather out of his kingdom all things that offend, and them which do iniquity, and shall cast them out among the wicked; and there shall be wailing and gnashing of teeth." The Church must be cleansed before the Lord comes; the tares must be cast out with their like kinds in the world, there to be burned. "For the world shall be burned with fire." (Matt. 13:24-30, 36-43; JST, Matt. 13:29, 39-44.)

That we might catch the full vision and import of this

parable, the Lord gave to it a new and enlarged meaning in our day. He said that "the field was the world, and the apostles were the sowers of the seed," and that Satan, operating through the Babylonish whore, which is the great and abominable church, sowed the tares, which then grew and choked the wheat, and drove the true Church into the wilderness. This is descriptive of the great apostasy. Finally, in the last days, comes the restoration. Good seed is again sown in the field of the Lord; again the blade springs forth in a tender and delicate form. Again it grows among the tares sown by the evil one, and again the angels plead with the Lord of the harvest for permission to go forth and reap down the fields. "But the Lord saith unto them, pluck not up the tares while the blade is yet tender (for verily your faith is weak), lest you destroy the wheat also. Therefore, let the wheat and the tares grow together until the harvest is fully ripe; then ye shall first gather out the wheat from among the tares, and after the gathering of the wheat, behold and lo, the tares are bound in bundles, and the field remaineth to be burned." (D&C 86:1-7.)

Speaking of this parable, the Prophet Joseph Smith, with a wondrous flow of inspired words, tells us: "The harvest and the end of the world have an allusion directly to the human family in the last days." The message of the parable is for us in this day. "As, therefore, the tares are gathered and burned in the fire, so shall it be in the end of the world; that is, as the servants of God go forth warning the nations, both priests and people, and as they [the priests and people] harden their hearts and reject the light of truth, these first being delivered over to the buffetings of Satan, and the law and the testimony being closed up, as it was in the case of the Jews, they are left in darkness, and delivered over unto the day of burning; thus being bound up by their creeds, and their bands being made strong by their priests, [they] are prepared for the fulfilment of the saying of the Savior—'The Son of Man shall send forth His angels, and gather out of His Kingdom all things that offend, and them which do iniquity, and shall cast them into a furnace of fire, there shall be wailing and gnashing of teeth.'

"We understand that the work of gathering of the wheat into barns, or garners, is to take place while the tares are being bound over, and [incident to the] preparing for the day of burning; that after the day of burnings, the righteous shall shine forth like the sun, in the Kingdom of their Father." (*Teachings*, pp. 97-98, 101.)

And so it is that we hear the voice of the Lord saying in our day: "All flesh is corrupted before me; and the powers of darkness prevail upon the earth, among the children of men, in the presence of all the hosts of heaven—Which causeth silence to reign, and all eternity is pained, and the angels are waiting the great command to reap down the earth, to gather the tares that they may be burned; and, behold, the enemy is combined." (D&C 38:11-12.)

And also: "I must gather together my people, according to the parable of the wheat and the tares, that the wheat may be secured in the garners to possess eternal life, and be crowned with celestial glory, when I shall come in the kingdom of my Father to reward every man according as his work shall be; While the tares shall be bound in bundles, and their bands made strong, that they may be burned with unquenchable fire." (D&C 101:65-66.)

"Cut Off from Among the People"

We live in a day when the whole social structure is dividing itself into two camps. This is a day of the polarization of all people. In the Church the faithful members are perfecting their lives and drawing nearer to the Lord and his way of life. In the world wickedness is increasing and the rebellious and carnal among men are sinking to lower levels of evil and depravity than has been the case in any past days. These trends will continue unabated until the Lord comes. When he arrives there will be, on the one hand, a people prepared to meet him, and, on the other hand, there will be greater wickedness and carnality than has ever before been known. As time goes on, fewer and fewer among men will remain aloof from one or the other of these camps.

Then when the Lord comes, he himself will both cause and complete the division among the people. Then there will be a great day of separation in which the wicked will be consumed and the righteous will be rewarded. In discoursing upon the great day of restoration and the millennial conditions that will then be ushered in, Nephi says: "For the time speedily cometh that the Lord God shall cause a great division among the people, and the wicked will he destroy; and he will spare his people, yea, even if it so be that he must destroy the wicked by fire." (2 Ne. 30:10.) This, of course, has reference to the day of burning that will attend the Lord's return. This is the same day of which the Lord said to Zechariah, "I will remove the iniquity of that land in one day." The wicked shall cease to be on earth. But as to the righteous: "In that day, saith the Lord of hosts, shall ye call every man his neighbour under the vine and under the fig tree." (Zech. 3:9-10.) The saints will continue to inherit the earth during the Millennium.

Our latter-day revelations speak with great particularity about what is to transpire with reference to the righteous and the wicked when the Lord comes. "And he that liveth when the Lord shall come, and hath kept the faith, blessed is he; nevertheless, it is appointed to him to die at the age of man. Wherefore, children shall grow up until they become old; old men shall die; but they shall not sleep in the dust, but they shall be changed in the twinkling of an eye. . . . These things are the things that ye must look for; and, speaking after the manner of the Lord, they are now nigh at hand, and in a time to come, even in the day of the coming of the Son of Man. And until that hour there will be foolish virgins among the wise; and at that hour cometh an entire separation of the righteous and the wicked; and in that day will I send mine angels to pluck out the wicked and cast them into unquenchable fire." (D&C 63:50-54.)

This division among the people, this entire separation of the righteous and the wicked, this destruction of the ungodly and the saving of the righteous by fire—all of this was taught in ancient Israel by reference to one of Moses' greatest Messianic prophecies. Moses, the mediator of the old covenant (the law), which prepared men to receive the new covenant (the gospel), of which Christ was the Mediator—Moses proclaimed to Israel of old: "The Lord thy God will raise up unto thee a Prophet from the midst of thee, of thy brethren, like unto me; unto him ye shall hearken." So spake the ancient lawgiver with reference to the Lord Jesus Christ, their Promised Messiah. "And the Lord said unto me," Moses continued, "I will raise them up a Prophet from among their brethren, like unto thee, and will put my words in his mouth; and he shall speak unto them all that I shall command him. And it shall come to pass, that whosoever will not hearken unto my words which he shall speak in my name, I will require it of him." (Deut. 18:15, 17-19.)

There well may have been more to these ancient words than is recorded in Deuteronomy. At least Jesus and all the prophets gave them a more express and expanded meaning than they seem to have in their Old Testament context. Jesus, on Olivet, after speaking of unfaithful servants who ate and drank with the drunken, who forsook the labors of their ministry, and who, accordingly, were cut asunder and appointed their portion with the hypocrites, where there was weeping and gnashing of teeth—Jesus said: "And thus cometh the end of the wicked, according to the prophecy of Moses, saying: They shall be cut off from among the people." To this Jesus added, "But the end of the earth is not yet, but by and by," meaning that the destruction of the wicked is the end of the world but not the end of the earth. (JS-M 1:55.)

Peter quoted Moses' Messianic words, rendering in this way the portion about the Lord requiring men to heed the

Messianic message: "And it shall come to pass, that every soul, which will not hear that prophet, shall be destroyed from among the people." (Acts 3:22-23.) When Moroni came to Joseph Smith, he quoted Peter's words "precisely as they stand in our New Testament. He said that that prophet was Christ; but the day had not yet come when"—and at this point he targums or interprets Peter's words—"when 'they who would not hear his voice should be cut off from among the people,' but soon would come." (JS-H 1:40.)

Our blessed Lord, ministering in glorious immortality among the Nephite Hebrews, testified: "I am he of whom Moses spake, saying: A prophet shall the Lord your God raise up unto you of your brethren, like unto me; him shall ye hear in all things whatsoever he shall say unto you. And it shall come to pass that every soul who will not hear that prophet shall be cut off from among the people." (3 Ne. 20:23.) And further, after having spoken of the restoration of the gospel in our day by one of his appointed servants, the Risen Lord said: "Therefore it shall come to pass that whosoever will not believe in my words, who am Jesus Christ, which the Father shall cause him [the restorer of eternal truth in the last days] to bring forth unto the Gentiles, and shall give unto him power that he shall bring forth unto the Gentiles, (it shall be done even as Moses said) they shall be cut off from among my people who are of the covenant." (3 Ne. 21:10-11.)

In his revealed preface to his book of commandments the Lord says: "And the arm of the Lord shall be revealed; and the day cometh that they who will not hear the voice of the Lord, neither the voice of his servants, neither give heed to the words of the prophets and apostles, shall be cut off from among the people." Why? Because of apostasy; because they do not keep the commandments; because "they have strayed from mine ordinances, and have broken mine everlasting covenant"; because "they seek not the

557

Lord to establish his righteousness, but every man walketh in his own way''—these are the reasons they shall be cut off from among the people. (D&C 1:14-16.)

How and in what manner will the wicked be cut off in the last days? In two ways: first, by the plagues and desolations that have already commenced and that are yet to be poured out upon the wicked, and then by the burning fires of vengeance that shall attend the Second Coming. Thus Jacob says that the Lord will gather his people again into his holy sheepfold, and that "the Messiah will . . . manifest himself unto them in power and great glory, unto the destruction of their enemies, when that day cometh when they shall believe in him; and none will he destroy that believe in him. And they that believe not in him shall be destroyed, both by fire, and by tempest, and by earthquakes, and by bloodsheds, and by pestilence, and by famine." (2 Ne. 6:13-15.)

Jacob's brother Nephi gives what is perhaps the best analysis in all the scriptures relative to those events which will be consummated by the cutting off of the wicked from among the people. He speaks of the day of gathering in which Israel "shall be brought out of obscurity and out of darkness," a day that has now commenced. Israel is no longer hidden and obscure; her whereabouts are known. She is scattered in all nations, and she is now coming out of the darkness of the ages. The light of heaven is beginning to dwell in her heart. Her children are joining the true Church. It is the day when "they shall know that the Lord is their Savior and their Redeemer, the Mighty One of Israel." It is the day in which "the blood of that great and abominable church, which is the whore of all the earth, shall turn upon their own heads; for they shall war among themselves, and the sword of their own hands shall fall upon their own heads, and they shall be drunken with their own blood." Even now the nations and kingdoms that comprise the great and abominable church are at each other's throats from time to time, and this shall increase until the great day of Armageddon when that evil church shall be utterly destroyed. "And every nation which shall war against thee, O house of Israel, shall be turned one against another, and they shall fall into the pit which they digged to ensnare the people of the Lord." Israel shall come off triumphant; truth will prevail; the Lord's cause shall conquer all. "And all that fight against Zion shall be destroyed, and that great whore, who hath perverted the right ways of the Lord, yea, that great and abominable church, shall tumble to the dust and great shall be the fall of it."

When the church of the devil is destroyed at our Lord's return, who will remain on earth over whom Satan can rule? When his kingdom is destroyed and its municipals are burned, who will be left on earth to do his bidding? Clearly, if Satan has neither a kingdom on earth among mortals nor servants among men who will do his bidding, his reign of blood and horror on earth must cease. And so Nephi says: "The time cometh speedily that Satan shall have no more power over the hearts of the children of men; for the day soon cometh that all the proud and they who do wickedly shall be as stubble; and the day cometh that they must be burned." It is clear from the context that Nephi gained these views from someone whom he identifies simply as "the prophet," and that they are the same views Malachi had before him when he wrote the words of his prophecy.

"For the time soon cometh that the fulness of the wrath of God shall be poured out upon all the children of men; for he will not suffer that the wicked shall destroy the righteous. Wherefore, he will preserve the righteous by his power, even if it so be that the fulness of his wrath must come, and the righteous be preserved, even unto the destruction of their enemies by fire. Wherefore, the righteous need not fear; for thus saith the prophet, they shall be saved, even if it so be as by fire." Whatever desolations and destructions may befall all men, both the righteous and

559

the wicked, prior to the coming of the Lord, in that day the final triumph of the God-fearing and the upright shall be brought to pass.

"Behold, my brethren, I say unto you, that these things must shortly come; yea, even blood, and fire, and vapor of smoke must come; and it must needs be upon the face of this earth; and it cometh unto men according to the flesh if it so be that they will harden their hearts against the Holy One of Israel." Men would be spared the desolations of the last days if they would repent and live the gospel. The Lord does not delight in the destruction of the wicked. His bounteous mercy and grace and goodness are available for all men in all ages, but they are poured out only upon those whose works merit the receipt of such a wondrous boon. "For behold, the righteous shall not perish; for the time surely must come that all they who fight against Zion shall be cut off."

In this setting Nephi comes to the words of Moses that we are considering. "And the Lord will surely prepare a way for his people, unto the fulfilling of the words of Moses, which he spake, saying: A prophet shall the Lord your God raise up unto you, like unto me; him shall ye hear in all things whatsoever he shall say unto you. And it shall come to pass that all those who will not hear that prophet shall be cut off from among the people. And now I, Nephi, declare unto you, that this prophet of whom Moses spake was the Holy One of Israel; wherefore, he shall execute judgment in righteousness. And the righteous need not fear, for they are those who shall not be confounded." (1 Ne. 22:12-22.)

Truly, as Isaiah saith, in the day of his coming "he shall smite the earth with the rod of his mouth, and with the breath of his lips shall he slay the wicked." (Isa. 11:4.) "Then shall be fulfilled that which is written, that in the last days, two shall be in the field, the one shall be taken, and the other left; Two shall be grinding at the mill, the one shall be taken, and the other left." (JS-M 1:44-45.) And as

Jesus also said: "I tell you, in that night there shall be two men in one bed; the one shall be taken, and the other shall be left. Two women shall be grinding together; the one shall be taken, and the other left. Two men shall be in the field; the one shall be taken, and the other left." (Luke 17:34-36.) Truly, there shall be a complete separation of the righteous and the wicked in the day of his coming. What manner of men ought we, therefore, to be?

Chapter 46

HE COMETH IN GLORY

"Prepare to Meet Thy God"

We have woven the doctrine of the Second Coming, including much of the prophetic word relative to that glorious day of promise, into one great tapestry that is as broad as eternity and as beautiful as any of the paintings that hang in celestial galleries. Or, rather, we have pierced the veil as best we could, to let those who seek the face of the Lord gain glimpses of what the Master Weaver has himself woven on the tapestries of eternity.

We have seen threads of ten thousand kinds; we have viewed scenes of every hue and nature; our souls have been thrilled with the divine artistry of it all. And in the center of this glorious work of heavenly art we see the Son of God coming in glory and splendor to be with men again; we see him conferring renown and honor upon his saints; we see him living and reigning in the midst of his beloved Israel for the space of a thousand years. It is this grand consummation, this wondrous and blessed day, toward which all things point.

And how could it be otherwise? The whole purpose of the Father is to save his people. He created the earth, peopled it with his children, and gave them the holy gospel—all to the end that they might believe and obey and be saved. He sent Adam to be the common parent of all men and to bring mortality and procreation and death into being. He sent his Son to ransom men from the fall and to bring to pass the immortality and eternal life of man. And he promised that he would destroy the wicked and bring peace and glory and triumph to his people in the great millennial day.

All things through the ages have pointed to this final day of rest and peace. And throughout this whole work, with inept and faltering fingers, we have sought to weave, page by page, those threads which belong in the Lord's eternal tapestry, and chapter by chapter we have attempted to describe the scenes the Lord has envisioned from the beginning—all to the end that those now living might know what to expect and how to prepare for the coming day.

Now let us gaze in rapture upon this glorious tapestry, which depicts the most majestic event since the very creation of the earth itself. No one prophet has told us all that is to be in that day of glory and wonder. Each has woven a few threads into the grand design; each has added a hue and a dimension to give depth and perspective to the scene; each has borne his appointed witness relative to the coming of the one who is Lord of them all.

As we gaze in awe at the grand picture, we see the Lord Jesus ascending from Olivet as angelic witnesses testify that he shall come again in like manner at that place. From this splendid scene our eyes turn to the dark and dire and devilish days when Satan has dominion over his own. We see false churches, false worship, and false prophets. Iniquity abounds and evil is everywhere. There is universal apostasy; darkness covers the earth and gross darkness the minds of the people; it is the evil night that must precede the dawn of the restoration.

Then—praise God!—the age of restoration arrives. Light shines in the eastern sky. The glorious gospel is restored; the dispensation of the fulness of times is ushered in; and the Church of the living God is given again to the saints of the Most High. The everlasting word goes forth;

the Book of Mormon bears witness of our Lord and his gospel; the name of Joseph Smith is spoken from the house-tops in reverential tones. Ancient prophets confer power and authority upon their mortal fellow servants. And Israel begins to gather again. The Lamanites, the Jews, and the Gentiles all play their appointed roles. Temples rise in the tops of the mountains of Israel, the holy Zion of God is built up again, and two world capitals rise in splendor so the law can go forth from Zion and the word of the Lord from Jerusalem.

From these pleasant scenes our eyes are diverted to the world of wickedness of the last days. We are sickened at the sight of sin; we tremble as we see the plagues and pestilence and disasters and wars. In the background, woven with threads of fire, we see Armageddon and burning and destruction. It is with relief that we see the whorish Babylon, with all her evil and sensuality, burned with everlasting fire. Lo, this is the great and dreadful day of the Lord. It is a day of judgment and of fire and of the entire separation of the righteous and the wicked. Also in the background we see the return of the Ten Tribes, the perfecting of Zion, and the descent from heavenly heights of the City of Holiness.

And in the center of all things standeth Christ. Lo, he comes, as it is written of him. Angelic hosts attend; tens of thousands of his saints make up his train; the holy apostles and the prophets of all ages are on his right hand and on his left, having crowns of gold upon their heads. And the tapestry stretches on into eternity. No man can view it all, and we marvel at what we have seen and prepare ourselves to see more. We know that what we have seen is hidden from the world; the view is reserved for those whose spiritual eyes are open. In the world, as Jeremiah foresaw, "both prophet and priest are profane"; the ministers of religion do not take counsel from the Lord; there is darkness and apostasy. But the saints have this prophetic word: "In the latter days ye shall consider it perfectly." (Jer.

23:11, 20.) And so, as we gaze in worshipful wonder at the transcendent tapestry of Him whose servants we are, we cry aloud: "Prepare to meet thy God, O Israel." (Amos 4:12.)

Those who are preparing to meet their God are the Lord's people; all others hearken to the voice of a different shepherd. The true saints can read the signs of the times. They know that the apostasy, the restoration, the gathering of Israel, and the building up of Zion in the last days are all necessary preludes to the glorious return of the Lord Jesus. Their constant prayers ascend to heaven, saying: "Thy kingdom come. Thy will be done in earth, as it is in heaven." (Matt. 6:10.) 'Let the millennial day dawn; let peace and righteousness dwell on earth; let thy people be saved with an everlasting salvation.' "Oh that thou wouldest rend the heavens, that thou wouldest come down, that the mountains might flow down at thy presence." (Isa. 64:1.) They say: "I will wait upon the Lord, that hideth his face from the house of Jacob, and I will look for him." (Isa. 8:17.) Truly, "the people of the Lord are they who wait for him; for they still wait for the coming of the Messiah," and "he will manifest himself unto them in power and great glory, unto the destruction of their enemies." (2 Ne. 6:13-14.)

The Blessed One Cometh

Almost all of the prophets speak of the glory and grandeur of the Second Coming. It is to be a day of wondrous renown in which all Israel and all the saints shall come off triumphant. We have spoken somewhat about this in various places throughout this work. And we shall now sample the prophetic word with a view to gaining a feeling relative to what is to be. So voluminous are the accounts in this field that we shall scarcely allude to a hundredth part of them. By themselves they would constitute a book on the Second Coming, and even then their meaning would be known and their import felt only by those enlightened by the power of the Spirit. Truly, this is a realm in which the things of God can be known only by the power of the Holy Ghost. How can the finite mind, unquickened by a higher power, even conceive how resurrected beings can return and live among men; how mortals can be freed from disease and sorrow; and how they can live, without death, until they are the age of a tree? How can the mortal man envision the return in glorious immortality of one who died upon a cross and was buried in a tomb? How can we comprehend how earthly bodies can stand unharmed in flaming fire as the very elements melt with fervent heat? How can we understand the innate glory of ten thousand times ten thousand things that will attend and follow the return of the Son of Man? As we turn our attention to these things, it will be well worth our while to ponder some portions at least of the prophetic word.

Jesus himself said that at his coming his people would say of him: "Blessed is he who cometh in the name of the Lord, in the clouds of heaven, and all the holy angels with him." Since that primeval day when the Lord "laid the foundations of the earth," and in which "the morning stars sang together, and all the sons of God shouted for joy" (Job 38:4-7), since the day of creation's dawn, has there ever been another time when all the angels of God in heaven have participated in one single event? Of the day of his return, Jesus also said: "They shall see the Son of Man coming in the clouds of heaven, with power and great glory; and whoso treasureth up my word, shall not be deceived, for the Son of Man shall come, and he shall send his angels before him with the great sound of a trumpet, and they shall gather together the remainder of his elect from the four winds, from one end of heaven to the other." (JS-M 1:1, 36-37.) Who else will ever come in the Father's name in the clouds of heaven with great glory shining forth on every hand? Who else will command legions of angels to do his bidding in all parts of the earth?

Hear also these words from Jesus: "When the Son of

man shall come in his glory, and all the holy angels with
him"—there is no doubt as to who shall be in atten-
dance—"then shall he sit upon the throne of his glory: And
before him shall be gathered all nations: and he shall separate them one from another, as a shepherd divideth his
sheep from the goats." (Matt. 25:31-32.) All the holy
angels, all the nations of men, one throne, one Supreme
Judge, one day of millennial judgment—has there ever
been such a scene as this? How aptly Jesus chooses his
words to show the incomparable glory of the coming day!

Jude and Enoch, though separated by three thousand
years, unite their voices in testifying of the glory and judgment that will attend the Second Coming. In speaking of
the condemnation that will befall "ungodly men" in that
great day, Jude says: "And Enoch also, the seventh from
Adam, prophesied of these, saying, Behold, the Lord cometh with ten thousands of his saints, To execute judgment
upon all, and to convince all that are ungodly among them
of all their ungodly deeds which they have ungodly committed, and of all their hard speeches which ungodly sinners
have spoken against him." (Jude 1:4, 14-15.) The ten thousands of his saints are the holy angels; they are the righteous of ages past who are already resurrected. They shall
attend their Lord and shall, by assignment from him, "execute judgment." They are the ones of whom Malachi
wrote: "They that come shall burn them, saith the Lord of
Hosts, that it shall leave them neither root nor branch."
(JS-H 1:37.) The day of judgment, the day of burning, ten
thousands of judges—"Do ye not know that the saints shall
judge the world?" Paul asked (1 Cor. 6:2)—how majestic
and awesome shall this day be!

What saith Isaiah, the Messianic prophet, about the
glory and power of that great day when the Lord shall come
again? His message is one of fear and dread for the wicked,
one of peace and security for the righteous. "O ye wicked
ones," he cries, "enter into the rock, and hide thee in the
dust, for the fear of the Lord and the glory of his majesty

shall smite thee.'' None can hide from the Lord of Hosts; none can avoid the piercing gaze of the all-seeing eye; none can flee to a place beyond Jehovah's jurisdiction. In that great day the wicked will wish they could become part of the rocks—hidden, obscure, overlooked. They will seek to hide in and be as the dust of the earth, lest they be called before the Eternal Bar to face Him who is judge of all. ''And it shall come to pass that the lofty looks of man shall be humbled, and the haughtiness of men shall be bowed down, and the Lord alone shall be exalted in that day.'' Kings and rulers, the mighty and great, the rich and the proud—all that walk in wickedness—shall be abased. The Lord alone—together with those who have become like him!—shall be exalted in that day.

''For the day of the Lord of Hosts soon cometh upon all nations, yea, upon every one''—none shall escape—''yea, upon the proud and lofty, and upon every one who is lifted up, and he shall be brought low.'' Both nations and people will be humbled. He will make a full end of all nations, and the wicked who comprise them shall be burned as stubble. Then, using that type of poetic imagery for which he has such great renown, Isaiah continues: ''Yea, and the day of the Lord shall come upon all the cedars of Lebanon, for they are high and lifted up; and upon all the oaks of Bashan; and upon all the high mountains, and upon all the hills, and upon all the nations which are lifted up, and upon every people; and upon every high tower, and upon every fenced wall; and upon all the ships of the sea, and upon all the ships of Tarshish, and upon all pleasant pictures.'' The earth itself and the vegetation that grows from the ground shall be affected. The mountains and hills shall be made low. Every nation and people shall feel the arm of the Almighty. Their defenses, their armaments, their weapons of war shall avail them nothing. Their commerce and wealth shall vanish away, and even the pleasant scenes of this mortal earth shall be no more. When else shall such earthshaking wonders as these even come into mind?

And then, by way of poetic reprise, and with a divine and thunderous emphasis, Israel's poetic prophet acclaims again: "And the loftiness of man shall be bowed down, and the haughtiness of men shall be made low; and the Lord alone shall be exalted in that day." Then he says that "the fear of the Lord shall come upon them, and the glory of his majesty shall smite them, when he ariseth to shake terribly the earth." (2 Ne. 12:10-19.) The earth shall reel to and fro; it shall shake; all things shall change in that day when it becomes a new heaven and a new earth. How glorious and wondrous shall that day be!

Latter-day Israel has these promises, relayed to them by the mouth of Isaiah: "Your God will come with vengeance, even God with a recompence; he will come and save you." (Isa. 35:4.) "And the Redeemer shall come to Zion, and unto them that turn from transgression in Jacob, saith the Lord." (Isa. 59:20.) "He shall appear to your joy. . . . For, behold, the Lord will come with fire, and with his chariots like a whirlwind, to render his anger with fury, and his rebuke with flames of fire." (Isa. 66:5, 15.) Truly, great are the words of Isaiah.

Others of the prophets speak similarly. By the mouth of Zechariah, the Lord promises to be "the glory in the midst" of Jerusalem in the latter days. "Sing and rejoice, O daughter of Zion," he says, "for, lo, I come, and I will dwell in the midst of thee, saith the Lord. And many nations shall be joined to the Lord in that day, and shall be my people: and I will dwell in the midst of thee, and thou shalt know that the Lord of hosts hath sent me unto thee. And the Lord shall inherit Judah his portion in the holy land, and shall choose Jerusalem again." (Zech. 2:4-5, 10-12.) Once again this time in the latter days, the Lord Jesus shall dwell among his people; Jerusalem shall be his abode as it once was.

Haggai records this word from on high: "Thus saith the Lord of hosts: Yet once, it is a little while, and I will shake the heavens, and the earth, and the sea, and the dry land;

and I will shake all nations, and the desire of all nations shall come." (Hag. 2:6-7.) Of the Second Coming Habakkuk testified: "God came. . . . His glory covered the heavens, and the earth was full of his praise. And his brightness was as the light. . . . Before him went the pestilence, and burning coals went forth at his feet. He stood, and measured the earth: he beheld, and drove asunder the nations; and the everlasting mountains were scattered, the perpetual hills did bow: his ways are everlasting." (Hab. 3:3-6.) And of the millennial day, he said: "The Lord is in his holy temple: let all the earth keep silence before him." (Hab. 2:20.) Hosea speaks of "the Holy One in the midst of thee." (Hosea 11:9.) Joel records these words of the Lord: "Ye shall know that I am in the midst of Israel, and that I am the Lord your God, and none else: and my people shall never be ashamed." (Joel 2:27.) "I am the Lord your God dwelling in Zion, my holy mountain: then shall Jerusalem be holy, and there shall be no strangers pass through her any more. . . . For the Lord dwelleth in Zion." (Joel 3:17, 21.) And Zephaniah records this joyful word: "Sing, O daughter of Zion; shout, O Israel; be glad and rejoice with all the heart, O daughter of Jerusalem. The Lord hath taken away thy judgments, he hath cast out thine enemy: the king of Israel, even the Lord, is in the midst of thee: thou shalt not see evil any more. In that day it shall be said to Jerusalem, Fear thou not: and to Zion, let not thine hands be slack. The Lord thy God in the midst of thee is mighty; he will save, he will rejoice over thee with joy; he will rest in his love, he will joy over thee with singing." (Zeph. 3:14-17.) And in the Psalmic word we read: "When the Lord shall build up Zion, he shall appear in his glory." (Ps. 102:16.) The intent and meaning of these and many other passages are evident. We need not say more on this point.

"Prepare Ye the Way of the Lord"

These are the last days; the signs of the times are now being shown forth on every hand; and the coming of the

Lord is not far distant. In the early days of this final gospel dispensation, when his servants were just beginning to lay the foundations of his earthly kingdom, the Lord said: "The voice of the Lord is unto the ends of the earth, that all that will hear may hear: Prepare ye, prepare ye for that which is to come, for the Lord is nigh." (D&C 1:11-12.) Prepare for the pestilence and plagues and sorrows of the last days. Prepare for the second coming of the Son of Man. Prepare to abide the day, to stand when he appeareth, and to live and reign with him on earth for a thousand years. Prepare for the new heaven and the new earth whereon dwelleth righteousness. Prepare to meet thy God.

Speaking of our day, Isaiah said that a voice would cry in the wilderness—that a sweet voice of sound doctrine and true testimony would be heard in the wilderness of sin—and that the voice would say: "Prepare ye the way of the Lord, make straight in the desert a highway for our God. Every valley shall be exalted, and every mountain and hill shall be made low: and the crooked shall be made straight, and the rough places plain: And the glory of the Lord shall be revealed, and all flesh shall see it together: for the mouth of the Lord hath spoken it." The great day of his coming is at hand. The Lord's people must be ready. They must do the things he has commanded, as a people and as individuals, to stand in his presence and receive his approval when he comes.

"O Zion, that bringest good tidings," Isaiah exhorts, "get thee up into the high mountain; O Jerusalem, that bringest good tidings, lift up thy voice with strength; lift it up, be not afraid; say unto the cities of Judah, Behold your God!" Be ready; prepare; believe his word; live his law; do the assigned labors; qualify as his people; send forth the glad tidings that he is near. "Behold, the Lord God will come with strong hand, and his arm shall rule for him: behold, his reward is with him, and his work before him." In that glorious day, far more than when he came before, "He shall feed his flock like a shepherd: he shall gather the lambs with his arm, and carry them in his bosom, and shall gently lead those that are with young." (Isa. 40:3-11.) Then shall be fulfilled that which is written, "The Lord is my shepherd; . . . and I will dwell in the house of the Lord for ever." (Ps. 23:1, 6.)

Prepare ye the way of the Lord! How is it done, and what arrangements must be made? How do we prepare for the coming of him whose we are, him who redeemed us and in whose pastures we feed? What must be done to prepare the way before him? Even as he will not come unattended, so all things must be in readiness when he arrives. And the preparation he requires is specific and personal for individuals; it is general and of universal application for his congregations; and it is fearsome and dreadful where the masses of men are concerned.

As individuals, we prepare to meet our God by keeping his commandments and living his laws. He will receive into his own bosom those only who abide the day of his coming. We prepare the way before his face by being born again, by cleansing and perfecting our souls, by gaining the companionship and sanctifying power of the Holy Spirit in our lives. The gospel in its everlasting fulness, restored as it has been in these last days, is here to prepare a people for the second coming of the Son of Man.

As congregations and as a people, we prepare the way before him by doing the worldwide work he requires at our hands. Before he comes, the gospel must be preached in every nation, to every people, with signs following those who believe. Before he comes, the name of Joseph Smith and the message of the Book of Mormon must be proclaimed from the housetops. Before he comes, many of the lost sheep of Israel must be gathered out of Babylon into the stakes of Zion, stakes now organized and yet to be organized in all nations. Before he comes, Zion must be built up, temples must rise wherever there are stakes, and the promises made to the fathers must be planted in the hearts of the children. Before he comes, his people must forsake the world; they must gather around the ensign raised in these latter days; they must be tried, so as by fire, to see if they will abide in his covenant, even unto death.

And as to the masses of men, as to the wicked and ungodly in general, as to those who esteem the things of this world of greater worth than the riches of Christ—all these are preparing, not to receive the joy of his countenance, but for the great day of burning. For them the Second Coming will be the day of vengeance that has been in the heart of the one to whom every knee shall bow and every tongue confess that he is Lord of all.

How can any people prepare to meet their God, how can any person know what to do in his individual case to prepare the way before his Lord, how can any and all know the course they should pursue except such is revealed to them from on high? The Second Coming is the Lord's doing, not man's. He will bring it to pass with power. He will do all that he has said. And he will require all others to meet his needs and conform to his standards. There must be general revelation to his people directing them in their course; and there must be personal revelation, coming by the power of the Holy Ghost, to each individual saint, directing him in the course he should pursue. The ancient scriptures and the modern scriptures contain much that has been revealed relative to this glorious and dread day. One of the great secrets of understanding what was revealed anciently, which is often hidden in a recitation of local historical circumstances unfamiliar to us, is to learn the same concepts from latter-day revelation. What the Lord has revealed to us ties together and interprets what he revealed to our ancient counterparts. It is appropriate at this point to sample what he has said in our day.

"Be faithful until I come, and ye shall be caught up, that where I am ye shall be also." (D&C 27:18.) "For I will reveal myself from heaven with power and great glory, with all the hosts thereof, and dwell in righteousness with men on earth a thousand years, and the wicked shall not stand."

573

(D&C 29:11.) "Wherefore, be faithful, praying always, having your lamps trimmed and burning, and oil with you, that you may be ready at the coming of the Bridegroom— For behold, verily, verily, I say unto you, that I come quickly." (D&C 33:17-18.)

To each of his servants in this day, the Lord sends this word: "Lift up your voice as with the sound of a trump, both long and loud, and cry repentance unto a crooked and perverse generation, preparing the way of the Lord for his second coming." And then, that all may understand what lies ahead, he says: "For behold, verily, verily, I say unto you, the time is soon at hand that I shall come in a cloud with power and great glory. And it shall be a great day at the time of my coming, for all nations shall tremble. But before that great day shall come, the sun shall be darkened, and the moon be turned into blood; and the stars shall refuse their shining, and some shall fall, and great destructions await the wicked." The very reason for preaching the gospel to the world is so believing souls may escape the sorrows and desolations that lie ahead. "Wherefore, lift up your voice and spare not, for the Lord God hath spoken; therefore prophesy, and it shall be given by the power of the Holy Ghost. And if you are faithful, behold, I am with you until I come—And verily, verily, I say unto you, I come quickly." (D&C 34:6-12.)

"They shall look for me, and, behold, I will come; and they shall see me in the clouds of heaven, clothed with power and great glory; with all the holy angels; and he that watches not for me shall be cut off." (D&C 45:44.)

"Prepare ye the way of the Lord, prepare ye the supper of the Lamb, make ready for the Bridegroom." (D&C 65:3.)

"Prepare ye, prepare ye, O inhabitants of the earth; for the judgment of our God is come. Behold, and lo, the Bridegroom cometh; go ye out to meet him." (D&C 88:92.)

Chapter 47

THE PRIVATE AND PUBLIC APPEARANCES

Our Lord's Many Appearances

The second coming of the Son of Man consists not of one but of many appearances. Our blessed Lord will come—attended by all the hosts of heaven, and in all the glory of his Father's kingdom—not to one but to many places. He will stand on one continent after another, speak to one great assemblage after another, and work his will among succeeding groups of mortals. Allusions to and some explanations concerning these various appearances are found in the ancient word. These, however, might well go unnoticed or remain without proper interpretation if it were not for the clarifying views found in latter-day revelation.

For instance, one of David's psalms calls upon us to "give unto the Lord the glory due unto his name," and then, rather enigmatically, the inspired psalmic word acclaims: "The voice of the Lord is upon the waters: the God of glory thundereth: the Lord is upon many waters. The voice of the Lord is powerful; the voice of the Lord is full of majesty," and a number of similar expressions. Then the millennial setting is shown by prophetic assurance, "The Lord sitteth King for ever. The Lord will give strength unto his people; the Lord will bless his people with peace." (Ps. 29:1-11.) Joel also, in the midst of an extended prophecy about the Second Coming, has this to say about the voice of the Lord in that day: "The Lord also shall roar out of Zion, and utter his voice from Jerusalem; and the heavens and the earth shall shake: but the Lord will be the hope of his people, and the strength of the children of Israel." (Joel 3:16.) Note the two places, Zion and Jerusalem, from which the voice will go forth. We shall set forth shortly how the voice of the Lord will be involved in his coming.

John the Beloved Revelator saw in vision a Lamb standing "on the mount Sion, and with him an hundred and forty and four thousand, having his Father's name written in their foreheads." Thereupon, as he records it, "I heard a voice from heaven, as the voice of many waters, and as the voice of a great thunder." (Rev. 14:1-2.) And Malachi prophesies: "The Lord, whom ye seek, shall suddenly come to his temple, even the messenger of the covenant, whom ye delight in: behold, he shall come, saith the Lord of hosts. But who may abide the day of his coming?" (Mal. 3:1-2.)

Jesus ascended from the Mount of Olives as an angelic voice acclaimed: "This same Jesus, which is taken up from you into heaven, shall so come in like manner as ye have seen him go into heaven" (Acts 1:11), leaving us to suppose that he will return to the same holy spot on that beloved mountain, to the same mountain where the great Olivet Discourse relative to his coming was delivered. And this, as we learn from Zechariah, shall come to pass in the full and literal sense of the word. Speaking of the final great day of Armageddon, the prophetic word recites: "Then shall the Lord go forth, and fight against those nations, as when he fought in the day of battle. And his feet shall stand in that day upon the mount of Olives, which is before Jerusalem on the east. . . . And the Lord my God shall come, and all the saints with thee." (Zech. 14:3-5.)

In revealing to us some of the things he taught his disciples on Olivet, the Lord included these words: "Then shall the arm of the Lord fall upon the nations. And then shall the Lord set his foot upon this mount [the Mount of Olives], and it shall cleave in twain, and the earth shall tremble, and reel to and fro, and the heavens also shall shake. And the Lord shall utter his voice, and all the ends of the earth shall hear it.'' (D&C 45:47-49.)

And in a divine proclamation also given in our day we are told: ''Hearken and hear, O ye inhabitants of the earth. Listen, ye elders of my church together, and hear the voice of the Lord; for he calleth upon all men, and he commandeth all men everywhere to repent. For behold, the Lord God hath sent forth the angel crying through the midst of heaven, saying: Prepare ye the way of the Lord, and make his paths straight, for the hour of his coming is nigh— When the Lamb shall stand upon Mount Zion, and with him a hundred and forty-four thousand, having his Father's name written on their foreheads. Wherefore, prepare ye for the coming of the Bridegroom; go ye, go ye out to meet him. For behold, he shall stand upon the mount of Olivet, and upon the mighty ocean, even the great deep, and upon the islands of the sea, and upon the land of Zion. And he shall utter his voice out of Zion, and he shall speak from Jerusalem, and his voice shall be heard among all people; and it shall be a voice as the voice of many waters, and as the voice of a great thunder, which shall break down the mountains, and the valleys shall not be found.'' (D&C 133:16-22.)

Where, then, will the Lord come, in what places will he stand, and whence shall his voice be heard? The Lord, whom we seek, shall suddenly come to his temple, meaning that he will come to the earth, which is his temple, and also that he will come to those holy houses which he has commanded us to build unto his blessed name. Indeed, he came suddenly to the Kirtland Temple on the 3rd day of April in 1836; he has also appeared in others of his holy houses; and he will come in due course to the temples in Jackson County and in Jerusalem. And he will come to his American Zion and his Jewish Jerusalem. His voice will roar forth from both world capitals. He will speak personally, angelic ministrants will proclaim his word, and his mortal servants will speak with his voice. His feet will stand on Olivet on the east of Jerusalem, and he will come with the 144,000 high priests to Mount Zion in America. And where else? Upon the oceans and the islands and the continents, in the land of Zion and elsewhere. The clear meaning is that there will be many appearances, in many places, to many people. And when the day is at hand and the hour has arrived, he will come quickly, as the prophetic word, both ancient and modern, so repetitiously attests. "Surely I come quickly," saith the Lord, to which John replies: "Even so, come, Lord Jesus." (Rev. 22:20.) And we echo John's plea.

He Cometh to Adam-ondi-Ahman

We now come to the least known and least understood thing connected with the Second Coming. It might well be termed the best-kept secret set forth in the revealed word. It is something about which the world knows nothing; it is a doctrine that has scarcely dawned on most of the Latter-day Saints themselves; and yet it is set forth in holy writ and in the teachings of the Prophet Joseph Smith with substantially the same clarity as any of the doctrines of the kingdom. It behooves us to make a needed brief commentary about it.

Before the Lord Jesus descends openly and publicly in the clouds of glory, attended by all the hosts of heaven; before the great and dreadful day of the Lord sends terror and destruction from one end of the earth to the other; before he stands on Mount Zion, or sets his feet on Olivet, or utters his voice from an American Zion or a Jewish Jerusalem; before all flesh shall see him together; before any of his appearances, which taken together comprise the second coming of the Son of God—before all these, there is to be a secret appearance to selected members of his Church. He will come in private to his prophet and to the apostles then living. Those who have held keys and powers and authorities in all ages from Adam to the present will also be present. And further, all the faithful members of the Church then living and all the faithful saints of all the ages past will be present. It will be the greatest congregation of faithful saints ever assembled on planet earth. It will be a sacrament meeting. It will be a day of judgment for the faithful of all the ages. And it will take place in Daviess County, Missouri, at a place called Adam-ondi-Ahman.

Adam-ondi-Ahman, of eternal fame, first comes to our attention because of a great conference held there by Father Adam in his day. "Three years previous to the death of Adam, he called Seth, Enos, Cainan, Mahalaleel, Jared, Enoch, and Methuselah, who were all high priests, with the residue of his posterity who were righteous, into the valley of Adam-ondi-Ahman, and there bestowed upon them his last blessing." Nearly a thousand years had then passed since the first man and the first woman had stepped from Eden's garden into the lone and dreary world, there to begin the procreative processes that peopled a planet. We do not know how many million mortals made this earth their home in that day, or how many of them were true and faithful to that Lord whom Adam served. Disease and plagues were not then as common and horrendous as they are now. The physical bodies of earth's inhabitants had not yet degenerated to the disease-ridden, germ-governed shells of their former glory that is now the norm. We can suppose the population of the earth far exceeded that of later ages when the ills of the flesh and a rising infant mortality set a sin-inflicted limit on the numbers of men. And it is not unreasonable to suppose that many righteous spirits were born in that blessed day and that the numbers of the righteous were exceedingly great. We may not be amiss in supposing that many millions responded to the call to come to a general conference in Adam-ondi-Ahman.

This we do know, however: "The Lord appeared unto them"—Jesus Christ their King stood in their midst—"and they rose up and blessed Adam, and called him Michael, the prince, the archangel." How great and glorious is the eternal stature of the first man! "And the Lord administered comfort unto Adam, and said unto him: I have set thee to be at the head; a multitude of nations shall come of thee, and thou art a prince over them forever. And Adam stood up in the midst of the congregation; and, notwithstanding he was bowed down with age, being full of the Holy Ghost, predicted whatsoever should befall his posterity unto the latest generation." Such is an abbreviated account of what happened at Adam-ondi-Ahman in that pristine day. Our revelation that recites these words closes with the statement: "These things were all written in the book of Enoch, and are to be testified of in due time." (D&C 107:53-57.)

When the full account comes to us, we suppose we shall read of the offering of sacrifices in similitude of the sacrifice of the Only Begotten; of the testimonies borne by both men and women; of great doctrinal sermons delivered by the preachers of righteousness who then ministered among them; and of the outpouring of spiritual gifts upon the faithful then assembled. What visions they must have seen; what revelations they must have received; what feelings of rapture must have filled their bosoms as they feasted upon the things of eternity! Did Adam speak of the great latter-day gathering at Adam-ondi-Ahman, and did the faithful see with their spirit eyes what was then to be? These and a thousand other things "are to be testified of in due time." But this we do know: All that happened at Adam-ondi-Ahman in those early days was but a type and a shadow—a similitude, if you will—of what shall happen at the same blessed place in the last days when Adam and Christ and the residue of men who are righteous assemble again in solemn worship.

If we are to understand what shall transpire at Adam-ondi-Ahman in the near future, we must first envision the relationship between the Lord Jehovah, who is Christ our

Savior, and the man Adam. Christ is the Firstborn of the Father, the Only Begotten in the flesh, and the Lamb slain from the foundation of the world. He is the Redeemer of the world and the Savior of men. He is the Son of God and is one with the Father in power, might, and dominion. Adam is the foremost spirit next to the Lord Jehovah. He is the archangel, the captain of the Lord's hosts who led the armies of heaven when Lucifer rebelled; he is Michael, the mightiest of all the spirit host save only the Lord Jesus; and he came to earth as Adam, the first man. His relationship with the God of Israel is set forth in the revelation which says that "the Lord God, the Holy One of Zion, . . . hath established the foundations of Adam-ondi-Ahman," and "hath appointed Michael your prince, and established his feet, and set him upon high, and given unto him the keys of salvation under the counsel and direction of the Holy One, who is without beginning of days or end of life." (D&C 78:15-16.) Thus Adam stands next to the Holy Messiah, receives counsel and direction and power from him, and (under Christ) administers salvation to all men.

The Prophet Joseph Smith instructed the early brethren at great length on these matters. "The Priesthood was first given to Adam," he said; "he obtained the First Presidency, and held the keys of it from generation to generation. He obtained it in the Creation, before the world was formed." Priesthood is the power and authority of God. By it the worlds were made; by it the Lord's agents do everything that is needed for the salvation of men. The keys are the right of presidency; they empower their holders to direct the manner in which others use their priesthood. Presiding officers hold keys and perform whatever labors they are authorized by the Lord to perform. Adam held the priesthood and the keys. "He had dominion given him over every living creature. He is Michael the Archangel, spoken of in the Scriptures. Then to Noah, who is Gabriel: he stands next in authority to Adam in the Priesthood; he was called of God to this office, and was the father of all living in this day, and to him was given the dominion. These men held keys first on earth, and then in heaven." Thus Adam is first and Noah is second, among all the inhabitants of the earth, save Jesus only, where both priesthood and keys are concerned.

"The Priesthood is an everlasting principle," the Prophet continued, "and existed with God from eternity, and will to eternity, without beginning of days or end of years. The keys have to be brought from heaven whenever the Gospel is sent. When they are revealed from heaven, it is by Adam's authority." Adam, under the direction of the Holy One, holds the keys of salvation for all men. He presides over all dispensations; all the dispensation heads and all the prophets receive direction from him; all report their labors to him. He is the chief person in the hierarchy of God, and he directs all of the affairs of the Lord on earth.

"Daniel in his seventh chapter speaks of the Ancient of Days; he means the oldest man, our Father Adam, Michael, he will call his children together and hold a council with them to prepare them for the coming of the Son of Man." By his children is meant the residue of his posterity that are righteous; all of his posterity will not be involved, only those—as it was in the days of the original gathering at Adam-ondi-Ahman—who are worthy. "He (Adam) is the father of the human family, and presides over the spirits of all men, and all that have had the keys must stand before him in this grand council." Every prophet, apostle, president, bishop, elder, or church officer of whatever degree—all who have held keys shall stand before him who holds all of the keys. They will then be called upon to give an account of their stewardships and to report how and in what manner they have used their priesthood and their keys for the salvation of men within the sphere of their appointments.

"This," the grand council of Adam-ondi-Ahman, "may take place before some of us leave this stage of action. The Son of Man stands before him, and there is given him glory and dominion. Adam delivers up his stewardship to Christ, that which was delivered to him as holding the keys of the universe, but retains his standing as head of the human family." This explanation is descriptive of the priesthood order of things. Every man is honored in his position; every man is accountable for the manner in which he performs under his divine commission. Adam is at the head, and he supervises all others.

"The Father called all spirits before Him at the creation of man, and organized them." This was the grand council in heaven of which we so often speak. "He (Adam) is the head, and was told to multiply." He, under Christ, was at the head in preexistence; and he, under Christ, is at the head so far as all things pertaining to this earth are concerned. "The keys were first given to him, and by him to others. He will have to give an account of his stewardship, and they to him." And as all the spirits of men attended the grand council in preexistence, so all the righteous shall attend a like council at Adam-ondi-Ahman before the winding-up scenes.

"Christ is the Great High Priest; Adam next. Paul speaks of the Church coming to an innumerable company of angels—to God the Judge of all—the spirits of just men made perfect; to Jesus the Mediator of the new covenant. (Hebrews 12:22-24.)" In this setting, as he speaks of an innumerable company of angels and of the just and great of all ages who have gained membership in the Church of the Firstborn, which is the Church among exalted beings, the Prophet then says: "I saw Adam in the valley of Adam-ondi-Ahman. He called together his children and blessed them with a patriarchal blessing. The Lord appeared in their midst, and he (Adam) blessed them all, and foretold what should befall them to the latest generation. This is why Adam blessed his posterity; he wanted to bring them into the presence of God." (*Teachings*, pp. 157-59.) Thus, we are left to conclude that the ancient gathering of the righteous at Adam-ondi-Ahman involved a great host of

583

people, even as will be the case with the like gathering that is soon to be in the last days.

Daniel's account of the great latter-day council at Adam-ondi-Ahman includes these words: "I beheld till the thrones were cast down, and the Ancient of days did sit, whose garment was white as snow, and the hair of his head like the pure wool: his throne was like the fiery flame, and his wheels as burning fire. A fiery stream issued and came forth from before him: thousand thousands ministered unto him, and ten thousand times ten thousand stood before him: the judgment was set, and the books were opened." (Dan. 7:9-10.) Thrones are cast down: the kingdoms of this world cease; it is the day when the Lord makes a full end of all nations. He alone shall be exalted in that day. The Ancient of Days, the oldest and most ancient of men, Adam our father, sits in judgment over the righteous of his race. Be it remembered that the Twelve Apostles of the Lamb, who were with the Lord in his ministry in Jerusalem, shall judge the whole house of Israel, meaning that portion of Israel who have kept the commandments, "and none else." (D&C 29:12.) There will be a great hierarchy of judges in that great day, of whom Adam, under Christ, will be the chief of all. Those judges will judge the righteous ones under their jurisdiction, but Christ himself, he alone, will judge the wicked. All this we have heretofore set forth; now we are seeing Adam sitting in his judicial capacity. And the scene is glorious indeed.

Who are the "thousand thousands" who "ministered unto him"? Are not these the millions who have held keys and powers and authorities in all dispensations? Are they not the ones who are called to report their stewardships and to give an accounting of how and in what manner they have exercised the keys of the kingdom in their days? Will not every steward be called upon to tell what he has done with the talents with which he was endowed? Truly, it shall be so; and those who minister unto the Ancient of Days are indeed the ministers of Christ reporting their labors to their immediate superiors, even back to Adam, who holds the keys of salvation over all the earth for all ages.

And who are the "ten thousand times ten thousand" who stand before him? Are not these the one hundred million and more who have been faithful and true in the days of their mortal probations? Are they not the same "ten thousand times ten thousand" who are "kings and priests," and who will live and reign with Christ a thousand years? Are they not the ones who shall sing in that great day the song of the redeemed, saying, "Worthy is the Lamb that was slain to receive power, and riches, and wisdom, and strength, and honour, and glory, and blessing . . . Blessing, and honour, and glory, and power, be unto him that sitteth upon the throne, and unto the Lamb for ever and ever"? (Rev. 5:10-13.) Truly, it is so; this is a part of that great day for which all the righteous have yearned, and the Lord Jesus, in its course, is using and honoring his ministers. Each one is operating within the sphere of his assignment; each is serving in his appointed way. The judgment is set and the books are opened, and the Lord God, who is judge of all, is judging all by the hands of his servants whom he hath appointed. This is that of which John wrote: "And I saw thrones, and they sat upon them, and judgment was given unto them. . . . And they lived and reigned with Christ a thousand years." (Rev. 20:4.)

But Daniel has yet more to say about the great events soon to transpire at Adam-ondi-Ahman. And we need not suppose that all these things shall happen in one single meeting or at one single hour in time. It is proper to hold numerous meetings at a general conference, some for the instruction of leaders, others for edification of all the saints. In some, business is transacted; others are for worship and spiritual refreshment. And so Daniel says: "I saw in the night visions, and, behold, one like the Son of man came with the clouds of heaven, and came to the Ancient of days, and they brought him near before him." Christ comes to Adam, who is sitting in glory. He comes to conform to his own priestal order. He comes to hear the report of Adam for his stewardship. He comes to take back the keys of the earthly kingdom. He comes to be invested with glory and dominion so that he can reign personally upon the earth. As President Joseph Fielding Smith expresses it: "Our Lord will then assume the reigns of government; directions will be given to the Priesthood; and He, whose right it is to rule, will be installed officially by the voice of the Priesthood there assembled." (*The Way to Perfection*, p. 291.) Thus Daniel says: "And there was given him dominion, and glory, and a kingdom, that all people, nations, and languages, should serve him: his dominion is an everlasting dominion, which shall not pass away, and his kingdom that which shall not be destroyed."

Daniel also tells us of the conflict between the kingdoms of this world and the kingdom of God. In spite of the opposition of the world, he says, "the saints of the most High shall take the kingdom, and possess the kingdom for ever, even for ever and ever." And also: "I beheld, and the same horn made war with the saints, and prevailed against them; until the ancient of days came, and judgment was given to the saints of the most High; and the time came that the saints possessed the kingdom." In this present world Lucifer reigns. This is the great day of his power. The kingdoms of men prevail in many ways over the Church and kingdom of God. Evil forces "devour the whole earth, and shall tread it down, and break it in pieces." But Lucifer's day is limited; he shall soon be bound. "The judgment shall sit, and they shall take away his dominion, to consume and to destroy" the Lord's work and his kingdom. "And the kingdom and dominion, and the greatness of the kingdom under the whole heaven, shall be given to the people of the saints of the most High, whose kingdom is an everlasting kingdom, and all dominions shall serve and obey him." (Dan. 7:13-27.)

The worshipful nature of the final gatherings at Adam-ondi-Ahman—and surely such will be patterned after what happened there anciently—the worshipful wonder of it all is seen in the administration of the sacramental emblems that will then take place. These are the emblems that testify of the spilt blood and broken flesh of our Redeeming Lord, even as the shed blood and broken flesh of sacrificial animals bore a like witness in days of old. In the upper room, as he and his disciples kept the Feast of the Passover, Jesus instituted the ordinance of the sacrament. After doing so he said: "But I say unto you, I will not drink henceforth of this fruit of the vine, until that day when I drink it new with you in my Father's kingdom." (Matt. 26:29.)

With reference to the use of sacramental wine in our day, the Lord said to Joseph Smith: "You shall partake of none except it is made new among you; yea, in this my Father's kingdom which shall be built up on the earth." In so stating, he is picking up the language he used in the upper room. Then he says: "The hour cometh that I will drink of the fruit of the vine with you on the earth." Jesus is going to partake of the sacrament again with his mortal disciples on earth. But it will not be with mortals only. He names others who will be present and who will participate in the sacred ordinance. These include Moroni, Elias, John the Baptist, Elijah, Abraham, Isaac, Jacob, Joseph (who was sold into Egypt), Peter, James, and John, "and also with Michael, or Adam, the father of all, the prince of all, the ancient of days." Each of these is named simply by way of illustration. The grand summation of the whole matter comes in these words: "And also with all those whom my Father hath given me out of the world." (D&C 27:4-14.) The sacrament is to be administered in a future day, on this earth, when the Lord Jesus is present, and when all the righteous of all ages are present. This, of course, will be a part of the grand council at Adam-ondi-Ahman.

Adam-ondi-Ahman—meaning the place or land of God where Adam dwelt—is at a place called Spring Hill, Daviess County, Missouri. This site is named by the Lord "Adam-ondi-Ahman, because, said he, it is the place where Adam shall come to visit his people, or the Ancient of Days shall sit, as spoken of by Daniel the prophet." (D&C 116.) There is a great valley there in which the righteous will assemble; and where there are valleys, the surrounding elevations are called mountains. Thus our revelations speak of "the mountains of Adam-ondi-Ahman" and of "the plains of Olaha Shinehah, or the land where Adam dwelt." (D&C 117:8.) Sacred indeed is the whole region for what has taken place and what will take place in its environs.

Adam-ondi-Ahman, the land of God, the dwelling place of Adam—surely it is a blessed and holy place! There Adam our Prince will give an accounting to Christ our King. The Prince serves the King! The King always is supreme, though he honors the Prince by giving him power and dominion over his realms for an appointed season. But when the King returns, the Prince steps aside, and the Supreme Lord of all rules and reigns on earth. And thus, as the Lord lives, has it been and will it be.

Chapter 48

THE SON OF DAVID REIGNETH

The Lord Reigns on Earth

How little the world knows of the coming day when Christ, as our tenth Article of Faith says, "will reign personally upon the earth," meaning, as the Prophet tells us, that he will "visit it," from time to time, "when it is necessary to govern it." (*Teachings*, p. 268.) And how little even the saints know of the government that is to be, meaning that their King will reign over Israel, on the throne of David, being himself the Second David, and that, as a prelude thereto, the "Gentiles" will "lick up the dust" of the feet of the chosen people. (Isa. 49:23.) And yet these are profound truths that are spread forth *in extenso* in the revealed word. To understand the Second Coming, we must consider them in their proper relationship to all the events of the latter days.

The holy word, given of old, abounds in such prophetic promises as these: "And the Lord shall be king over all the earth: in that [millennial] day shall there be one Lord, and his name one." (Zech. 14:9.) The promise to Israel in that day is: "The king of Israel, even the Lord, is in the midst of thee: thou shalt not see evil any more. . . . The Lord thy God in the midst of thee is mighty; he will save, he will rejoice over thee with joy. . . . At that time will I bring you again, even in the time that I gather you." This is the

589

millennial gathering! "For I will make you a name and a praise among all people of the earth, when I turn back your captivity before your eyes, saith the Lord." (Zeph. 3:15-20.) "I am the Lord thy God, . . . for there is no saviour beside me. . . . I will be thy king: where is any other that may save thee in all thy cities?" (Hosea 13:4, 10.) And of the sanctuary from which the divine law shall go forth, the prophetic word is: "And the name of the city from that day shall be" Jehovah-shammah, "The Lord is there." (Ezek. 48:35.)

Matthew includes in the interpretation of the parable of the wicked husbandmen the statement that the disciples of that day "understood . . . that the Gentiles should be destroyed also, when the Lord should descend out of heaven to reign in his vineyard, which is the earth and the inhabitants thereof." (JST, Matt. 21:56.) In our dispensation the divine word says: "The Lord shall have power over his saints, and shall reign in their midst, and shall come down in judgment upon Idumea, or the world." (D&C 1:36.) "For I will reveal myself from heaven with power and great glory, with all the hosts thereof, and dwell in righteousness with men on earth a thousand years, and the wicked shall not stand." (D&C 29:11.) "And the Lord, even the Savior, shall stand in the midst of his people, and shall reign over all flesh." (D&C 133:25.) And our friend John, in the visions vouchsafed to him, "heard as it were the voice of a great multitude, and as the voice of many waters, and as the voice of mighty thunderings, saying, Alleluia: for the Lord God omnipotent reigneth." (Rev. 19:6.) The Lord reigneth! How glorious is the day! Hallelujah (praise Jehovah), for Jehovah reigneth! Alleluia (praise Christ), for Christ reigneth! And the Lord Jehovah is the Lord Jesus; they are one and the same.

When the Lord reigns, how will he do it? John says: "He shall rule them with a rod of iron." (Rev. 19:15.) What is the rod of iron? Nephi says: "I beheld that the rod of iron . . . was the word of God, which led to the fountain of living waters, or to the tree of life." (1 Ne. 11:25.) Thus, Christ reigneth in and through and by means of the gospel. There is no other way. Men will be subject to him because they believe the gospel. The gospel is his law. He has no other. And so we read relative to his coming: "And another trump shall sound, which is the fifth trump, which is the fifth angel who committeth the everlasting gospel—flying through the midst of heaven, unto all nations, kindreds, tongues, and people; and this shall be the sound of his trump, saying to all people, both in heaven and in earth, and that are under the earth—for every ear shall hear it, and every knee shall bow, and every tongue shall confess, while they hear the sound of the trump, saying: Fear God, and give glory to him who sitteth upon the throne, forever and ever; for the hour of his judgment is come." (D&C 88:103-104.) Every knee shall bow! The Lord reigneth! He is King over all the earth!

David Prophesies of Christ's Reign

In the days of David, Israel's kingdom was glorious indeed. The Twelve Tribes—"instantly serving God day and night" (Acts 26:7), as Paul expressed it—were united; they were independent of any other earthly power; freedom and power and prestige welled up in the hearts of the chosen seed. A thousand years later, when the Son of David walked among them, Israel had no kingdom. Her municipals were scattered among the nations where most of them served other gods and no longer knew the Lord Jehovah whose people they once were. The remnant in Palestine bowed beneath the Gentile rod and served the Herods and the Caesars whose swords were sharp and whose arms were as iron. Up to that time the prophetic word relative to the glorious restoration of the chosen people in might and power and dominion seemed as distant as it had when Nebuchadnezzar took their fathers into Babylon. The prophetic pronouncements of what was to be in the Messianic day were yet to be fulfilled. Hence we hear the ancient Twelve on Olivet, when the hour for the ascension had arrived, asking Jesus: "Lord, wilt thou at this time restore again the kingdom to Israel?" (Acts 1:6.)

Restore again the kingdom to Israel! When will the Lord's kingdom come? When will it be set up again on earth as it once was—with a king and a court, with laws and judges, with power and magnificence? Such was not for the day of Peter and Paul; it was reserved for our day, and the promised consummation is not far distant. What is more appropriate, then, than to have David himself prophesy of his even greater Son who will one day sit on his father's throne and reign over the house of Israel forever? It is to the words of the sweet singer of Israel that we shall turn first as we consider the coming reign of the Second David. His words relative to the millennial day are comparable to those he spoke about the meridian day. The Spirit revealed to David wondrous truths relative to the two comings of his incomparable Son.

"The Lord most high is terrible," the psalmic word recites; "he is a great King over all the earth. He shall subdue the people under us, and the nations under our feet." All nations shall be subject to Israel in that great day. The Gentiles shall bow beneath the gospel rod. "He shall choose our inheritance for us." The meek shall inherit the earth. "For God is the King of all the earth: sing ye praises with understanding. God reigneth over the heathen: God sitteth upon the throne of his holiness. . . . He is greatly exalted." (Ps. 47:2-9.) "O let the nations be glad and sing for joy: for thou shalt judge the people righteously, and govern the nations upon earth." This is the millennial day. "Then shall the earth yield her increase; and God, even our own God, shall bless us." (Ps. 67:4-6.)

From a prayer of David we extract these words which are clearly Messianic, though some of them, as originally given, applied to contemporary events. It was the prophetic practice among the Hebrews to use local circumstances as similitudes to teach the glories and wonders of the gospel

592

and of the Messiah who would come to save his people. "He shall judge thy people with righteousness, and thy poor with judgment," David said. "He shall judge the poor of the people, he shall save the children of the needy, and shall break in pieces the oppressor. They shall fear thee as long as the sun and moon endure, throughout all generations." The Lord's reign shall be eternal; the saints shall possess the kingdom forever and ever. "He shall come down like rain upon the mown grass: as showers that water the earth." As the dews of heaven, so shall the knowledge of God descend upon those who seek his face. "In his day shall the righteous flourish; and abundance of peace so long as the moon endureth." How glorious shall be that blessed day of righteousness and peace. "He shall have dominion also from sea to sea, and from the river unto the ends of the earth. They that dwell in the wilderness shall bow before him; and his enemies shall lick the dust." Israel truly shall stand triumphant in that day.

"Yea, all kings shall fall down before him: all nations shall serve him." Christ is King of all. "For he shall deliver the needy when he crieth; the poor also, and him that hath no helper. He shall spare the poor and the needy, and shall save the souls of the needy. He shall redeem their soul from deceit and violence: and precious shall their blood be in his sight. . . . His name shall endure for ever: his name shall be continued as long as the sun: and men shall be blessed in him: all nations shall call him blessed. Blessed be the Lord God, the God of Israel, who only doeth wondrous things. And blessed be his glorious name for ever: and let the whole earth be filled with his glory." (Ps. 72:2-19.) Granted that some of the language is figurative and will not find literal fulfillment in the millennial day, yet the concepts taught are truly glorious. In substance and in thought content they all shall surely come to pass.

Other psalmic pronouncements that will find total fulfillment only in the millennial day include: "Arise, O God, judge the earth: for thou shalt inherit all nations."

(Ps. 82:8.) "O worship the Lord in the beauty of holiness: fear before him, all the earth. Say among the heathen that the Lord reigneth. . . . He shall judge the people righteously. . . . He cometh to judge the earth: he shall judge the world with righteousness, and the people with his truth." (Ps. 96:9-13.) "The Lord reigneth; let the earth rejoice. . . . Clouds and darkness are round about him: righteousness and judgment are the habitation of his throne. A fire goeth before him, and burneth up his enemies round about. His lightnings enlightened the world: the earth saw, and trembled. The hills melted like wax at the presence of the Lord, at the presence of the Lord of the whole earth." (Ps. 97:1-5.) "The Lord reigneth; let the people tremble. . . . The Lord is great in Zion." (Ps. 99:1-2.) "All thy works shall praise thee, O Lord; and thy saints shall bless thee. They shall speak of the glory of thy kingdom, and talk of thy power; To make known to the sons of men his mighty acts, and the glorious majesty of his kingdom. Thy kingdom is an everlasting kingdom, and thy dominion endureth throughout all generations." (Ps. 145:10-13.) "The Lord shall reign for ever, even thy God, O Zion, unto all generations. Praise ye the Lord." (Ps. 146:10.) Those with spiritual insight find in the Psalms priceless pearls of wisdom and revelation. Truly, their pleasant words and sweet similitudes open the eyes of our understanding with reference to the coming reign of the Son of David.

Christ Reigns on David's Throne

The Lord Jesus Christ—the King of heaven and the rightful ruler of the earth—set up his earthly kingdom among men on the 6th day of April in 1830. That kingdom, now named The Church of Jesus Christ of Latter-day Saints, is an ecclesiastical kingdom. It is ruled and governed by the priesthood; it administers the gospel; it holds the keys of salvation for all men. It is the only true and living church upon the face of the whole earth and is the one place where salvation may be found. It is, in the true and literal sense of the word, the kingdom of God on earth, and as such it is preparing men to go to the kingdom of God in heaven, which is the celestial kingdom.

When the Lord, in the first instance, in the days of Adam set up his kingdom on earth, it was both an ecclesiastical and a political kingdom. From the day of the first man down to the flood, all of the righteous people in earth were governed, both ecclesiastically and politically, by the same leaders and with the same power—the power and authority of the holy priesthood. Apostate peoples who broke off from the true church, as then officered and organized, created both churches and governments of their own. Often these were united as one, patterning themselves after the true Adamic system; sometimes the two ways of life were separately administered. Such peoples had false religions and, from the true theocratic perspective, false governments also. There is only one true religion, the religion in which God rules by revelation. And, in the full and divine sense, there is only one true government, the government in which God rules. All things are spiritual unto the Lord; from his standpoint there is no such thing as a temporal commandment, and it is his right to rule in all things both temporal and spiritual.

For the time being, however, because men are not prepared and are unwilling to take direction from the Lord; because they love darkness rather than light, their deeds being evil; because they choose to believe false religions and to be governed by political powers that fall short of the perfect and divine standard—because of these conditions, the Lord has ordained a system under which church and state should be separated. In the full and true sense this system of separation of church and state is in active operation only in the United States of America. Some other nations make reasonable attempts to allow freedom of worship, but most of the population of the earth is ruled by governments that also tell them what they must believe, how and what they must worship, and what they must do, as they falsely suppose, to gain salvation. These are corrupt, evil, and apostate systems. As the union of church and state under God is the most perfect form of worship and government, so the union of church and state under man leads to false worship and denies men a hope of full salvation. Whenever in our day the power of the state, with its armies and jails, usurps the prerogatives of the church and proceeds to govern in religious matters, the church of the evil one flourishes. Men are hailed before a Spanish inquisition; they are put to death for forsaking Islam and becoming Christians; they are driven into ghettos and murdered in concentration camps; or they are scourged in synagogues and crucified on crosses. There is nothing more evil, more cruel, more wicked than false religion that can survive only by the sword of Cortez, or the armies of Mohammed, or the gestapo of Hitler.

Both church and state, as the world knows them, will soon cease to be. When the Lord comes again, he will set up anew the political kingdom of God on earth. It will be joined with the ecclesiastical kingdom; church and state will unite; and God will govern in all things. But even then, as we suppose, administrative affairs will be departmentalized, for the law will go forth from Zion (in Jackson County), and the word of the Lord from Jerusalem (in Palestine). But, nonetheless, once again the government of the earth will be theocratic. God will govern. This time he will do it personally as he reigns over all the earth. And all of this presupposes the fall of Babylon, and the death of false religions, and the fall of all earthly governments and nations. And these things, as we are aware, shall surely come to pass.

Thus, when we speak of the Lord returning to reign personally upon the earth, we are talking about a literal return. We have in mind a King ruling on a throne. We mean that laws will come forth from a Lawgiver; that judges will be restored as of old; that there will be a full end of all nations as these now exist; that earth's new King will have dominion and power over all the earth; and that Israel, the chosen people, will possess the kingdom and have everlasting dominion. It is to these things that we shall now turn our attention.

Isaiah, in one of his greatest Messianic utterances, acclaims: "And the government shall be upon [Messiah's] shoulder. . . . Of the increase of his government and peace there shall be no end, upon the throne of David, and upon his kingdom, to order it, and to establish it with judgment and with justice from henceforth even for ever." (Isa. 9:6-7.) Isaiah's words, thus given, are but the foundation for the angelic proclamation of Gabriel to the Virgin of Nazareth of Galilee. Of the child Jesus whom she should bear, the angelic word promised: "He shall be great, and shall be called the Son of the Highest: and the Lord God shall give unto him the throne of his father David: And he shall reign over the house of Jacob for ever; and of his kingdom there shall be no end." (Luke 1:31-33.) Thus, Christ shall provide the government. He shall reign on the throne of David forever. Peace shall prevail, and justice and judgment shall be the order of the day. And it is Israel, the chosen ones, over whom he shall reign in a kingdom that shall never cease. There is nothing figurative about this; it is not something that can be spiritualized away. It is the coming reality; it shall surely come to pass.

Isaiah, speaking of the Second Coming, also says: "Then the moon shall be confounded, and the sun ashamed, when the Lord of hosts"—for such he is!— "shall reign in mount Zion, and in Jerusalem, and before his ancients gloriously." (Isa. 24:23.) His ancients are the prophets and patriarchs of olden times who, as we shall hereafter see, shall reign with him on earth. Isaiah also promises: "Behold, a king shall reign in righteousness, and princes shall rule in judgment." (Isa. 32:1.) And also, speaking of the millennial day when men "shall see the king in his beauty," Isaiah says: "For the Lord is our judge, the

Lord is our lawgiver, the Lord is our king; he will save us.'' (Isa. 33:17, 22.) In the full and true sense, the Lord will not stand as Judge, or Lawgiver, or King, and will not save men to the full, until the Millennium.

Our latter-day revelations bear a like testimony. "In time ye shall have no king nor ruler, for I will be your king and watch over you,'' the Lord tells us. "Wherefore, hear my voice and follow me, and you shall be a free people, and ye shall have no laws but my laws when I come, for I am your lawgiver, and what can stay my hand?'' (D&C 38:21-22.) And also: "For the Lord shall be in their midst, and his glory shall be upon them, and he will be their king and their lawgiver.'' (D&C 45:59.) And yet again: "Be subject to the powers that be''—to the governments that now exist—"until he reigns whose right it is to reign, and subdues all enemies under his feet. Behold, the laws which ye have received from my hand are the laws of the church, and in this light ye shall hold them forth.'' (D&C 58:22-23.) For the present we are subject to the laws of the land; when the true and perfect millennial order prevails, all rule and government, both civil and ecclesiastical, will come from our Eternal Head.

Others of the prophets also have somewhat to say about these things. In a rather remarkable passage Zechariah ties the gathering of Israel and the millennial reign together in these words: "Ho, ho, come forth, and flee from the land of the north, saith the Lord.'' This is his call to Israel and to Judah, his ancient covenant people, scattered as they are in the lands northward from Palestine. This is the call that has now commenced and will yet go forth with increased sound. "For I have spread you abroad as the four winds of the heaven, saith the Lord.'' Israel is scattered, and Israel must be gathered. "Deliver thyself, O Zion, that dwellest with the daughter of Babylon.'' Go ye out from Babylon; flee from the world; turn from your apostate and fallen ways; return unto the God of Israel. And as to those nations and this Babylon (the world) that have wrought so great a havoc upon the chosen seed, the divine word says: "For thus saith the Lord of hosts; After the glory hath he sent me unto the nations which spoiled you: for he that toucheth you toucheth the apple of his eye. For, behold, I will shake mine hand upon them [the nations], and they shall be a spoil to their servants: and ye shall know that the Lord of hosts hath sent me." Israel shall finally prevail over the Gentile nations. Her eternal triumph is assured.

"Sing and rejoice, O daughter of Zion: for, lo, I come, and I will dwell in the midst of thee, saith the Lord." The Lord Jesus Christ shall reign personally upon the earth. "And many nations shall be joined to the Lord in that day, and shall be my people." Gentile nations shall be converted; the blacks shall receive the priesthood; nations long outside the pale of saving grace shall come into the fold and shall rise up and bless Abraham as their father. "And I will dwell in the midst of thee, and thou shalt know that the Lord of hosts hath sent me unto thee. And the Lord shall inherit Judah his portion in the holy land, and shall choose Jerusalem again." How wondrous it shall be. "Be silent, O all flesh, before the Lord: for he is raised up out of his holy habitation." (Zech. 2:6-13.) So shall it be in the coming day.

Zechariah also says: "He shall speak peace unto the heathen: and his dominion shall be from sea even to sea, and from the river even to the ends of the earth." (Zech. 9:10.) Ezekiel saw in vision "the glory of the God of Israel," and "his voice was like a noise of many waters: and the earth shined with his glory." With reference to the Lord's holy sanctuary, the voice said: "Son of man, the place of my throne, and the place of the soles of my feet, where I will dwell in the midst of the children of Israel for ever, and my holy name, shall the house of Israel no more defile. . . . And I will dwell in the midst of them for ever." (Ezek. 43:2-9.) His throne shall be in his holy house; his reign shall be a personal one, even the very soles of his feet again treading the dust of the earth; and Israel shall honor and serve him. Of that day Micah says: "And the Lord shall reign over them in Mount Zion from henceforth, even for ever." (Micah 4:7.) And because the law is to go forth in that day from an American Zion, he himself said to Nephite Israel: "This people will I establish in this land [the Americas], unto the fulfilling of the covenant which I made with your father Jacob; and it shall be a New Jerusalem. And the powers of heaven shall be in the midst of this people; yea, even I will be in the midst of you." (3 Ne. 20:22.)

Nephi speaks of the destruction of the kingdom of the devil in the last days, of the wicked being brought low in the dust, and of their being consumed as stubble. "And the time cometh speedily," when all this is brought to pass, he says, "that the righteous must be led up as calves of the stall, and the Holy One of Israel must reign in dominion, and might, and power, and great glory." (1 Ne. 22:23-24.) Truly, he shall reign whose right it is; he shall make "a full end of all nations" (D&C 87:6), and with his saints he shall possess the kingdom forever and ever. In that day a great voice in heaven shall say: "The kingdoms of this world are become the kingdoms of our Lord, and of his Christ; and he shall reign for ever and ever." (Rev. 11:15.)

The eventual triumph of the Lord's people is assured; there is to be a millennial day of glory and honor and peace; the fulness of the earth shall be theirs in that day, and all nations and kingdoms shall serve and obey them. But all the promised rewards need not be deferred until that day. Even now the saints can begin the process of inheriting the kingdom. They have power to begin to reap some of the millennial rewards. "I have decreed a decree which my people shall realize," the Lord said in the early days of this dispensation, "inasmuch as they hearken from this very hour unto the counsel which I, the Lord their God, shall give unto them. Behold they shall, for I have decreed it, begin to prevail against mine enemies from this very hour. And by hearkening to observe all the words which I, the Lord their God, shall speak unto them, they shall never

cease to prevail until the kingdoms of the world are subdued under my feet, and the earth is given unto the saints,
to possess it forever and ever.'' (D&C 103:5-7.)

Chapter 49

THE SECOND DAVID REIGNETH

The Branch of David Reigneth

David, who slew Goliath, mighty, mighty David, the one king above all others to whom ancient Israel for a thousand long years looked as a symbol of Israelite triumph and glory—mighty David became the similitude for the very Messiah himself. As David slew Goliath and saved Israel from the Philistines, so the Messiah would break the Gentile bands and remove from his people the alien yoke. As David united and ruled over the Twelve Tribes of Israel, so the Messiah would unite the two kingdoms, Judah and Israel, and reign over one people in peace and glory forever. It is a grand and comforting feeling to know that the house of which you are a part—your own kindred and people—shall one day destroy their enemies and rule the world. Blessed Israel had this hope; King David was its symbol, a type and a shadow of what was to be, and the Messiah, Israel's Eternal King, would bring it to full fruition. Thus David the Son of Jesse became the type and figure for yet another, for David the Son of God, for the Messiah who, according to the flesh, would come as the Son of David. Let us, then, hear the prophetic word relative to these things.

Messiah's latter-day reign over the chosen people, his triumphant rule over the Twelve Tribes of Israel, his exercise of kingly power like his father David—all this presupposes the gathering together of scattered Judah and lost Israel. Let Israel gather first and then let Messiah reign. And so we read in holy writ: "I will gather the remnant of my flock out of all countries whither I have driven them, and will bring them again to their folds; and they shall be fruitful and increase." They shall come into the fold of Judah in Jerusalem, into the fold of Joseph in America, into the folds established in the stakes of Zion in all nations. "And I will set up shepherds over them which shall feed them." Once again they shall hear the good word of God; they shall bask in the light of the gospel; they shall rejoice in Jehovah as their Shepherd. "And they shall fear no more, nor be dismayed, neither shall they be lacking, saith the Lord." All their needs will be supplied by the Shepherd of Israel.

Then a glorious thing will happen. The kingdom will be restored to Israel, and they shall gain the political power as well as the ecclesiastical. "Behold, the days come, saith the Lord, that I will raise unto David a righteous Branch, and a King shall reign and prosper, and shall execute judgment and justice in the earth." Jehovah reigneth; Christ reigneth; the Son of David sits on the throne of his father. "In his days Judah shall be saved, and Israel shall dwell safely"—the two ancient kingdoms shall be one again— "and this is his name whereby he shall be called, THE LORD OUR RIGHTEOUSNESS." The King who reigns on David's throne is the Lord.

With Israel gathered again, with the scattered remnants of Jacob rejoicing anew in the very things their fathers possessed, with the Appointed One reigning on the throne of David forever, is it any wonder that the glories of their ancient history shall fade into a comparative insignificance? "Therefore, behold, the days come, saith the Lord, that they shall no more say, The Lord liveth, which brought up the children of Israel out of the land of Egypt; But, The Lord liveth, which brought up and which led the seed of the house of Israel out of the north country, and from all countries whither I had driven them; and they shall dwell in their own land." (Jer. 23:3-8.) What was the deliverance from Egypt, with the plagues and miracles and parting of the Red Sea, in comparison with the assembling of Israel from the ends of the earth to bow before the throne of the Lord Our Righteousness? The Lord Our Righteousness, he who is our Lord when we are righteous—what can compare with his personal reign? The seed of Israel will be more blessed than were their fathers of old; the latter-day glory will exceed that of Sinai and Horeb and Carmel.

Also in the writings of Jeremiah we find the Lord's promise to reveal unto his people in the latter days "the abundance of peace and truth," meaning the gospel, and to gather them "as at the first." Then again he makes the great promise concerning the Seed of David. "In those days, and at that time, will I cause the Branch of righteousness to grow up unto David; and he shall execute judgment and righteousness in the land." Jeremiah's other promise was that the Lord would raise up unto David a righteous branch, a branch that would be the Seed of David. This time the promise is that he will raise up the Branch of righteousness, a Branch that is the Son of Righteousness, meaning the Son of God. In this connection be it remembered that the Book of Mormon uses the name Son of Righteousness as one of the names of Christ. Thus the Branch is to be both the Son of David, after the flesh, and the Son of God, in the eternal sense. Of the days of his reign the account continues: "In those days shall Judah be saved, and Jerusalem shall dwell safely: and this is the name wherewith she shall be called, The Lord our righteousness." That is to say, the Holy City also shall bear the name of the great King who reigns there. "For thus saith the Lord; David shall never want a man to sit upon the throne of the house of Israel." (Jer. 33:6-7, 15-17.) Manifestly this promise to David that he shall have posterity reigning on his throne forever can be fulfilled only in and through Christ, the Eternal King.

Additional knowledge about the Branch of David, who is also the Branch of God, is recorded in Zechariah. "Thus speaketh the Lord of hosts," says Zechariah, "Behold the man whose name is The BRANCH; and he shall grow up out of his place, and he shall build the temple of the Lord: Even he shall build the temple of the Lord; and he shall bear the glory, and shall sit and rule upon his throne; and he shall be a priest upon his throne." (Zech. 6:12-13.) The Reigning One, at whose direction the temples in Jerusalem and elsewhere shall be built in the last days, shall be both a king and a priest. Indeed, he is the Great High Priest, and in the eternal sense, those who rule and reign everlastingly are all both kings and priests. It could not be otherwise, for the power by which they reign is the priestly power of the Almighty.

These words, also in Zechariah, place the reign of the Branch in its true millennial setting. "I will bring forth my servant the BRANCH," saith the Lord, "and I will remove the iniquity of that land in one day," the day of burning in which every corruptible thing shall be consumed. "In that day, saith the Lord of hosts, shall ye call every man his neighbour under the vine and under the fig tree." (Zech. 3:8-10.) These last words contain the prophetic figure of speech that describes life during the Millennium. Micah, for instance, says that during that blessed era of peace, "They shall sit every man under his vine and under his fig tree; and none shall make them afraid." (Micah 4:4.)

David—Our Eternal King

Even as the Book of Mormon (the Stick of Joseph in the hands of Ephraim), and the Bible (the Stick of Judah) become one in the Lord's hands; even as they both contain the fulness of the everlasting gospel; even as men in our day must accept and believe both volumes of holy scripture to be saved—so shall perfect unity return to the divided houses of Israel in the last days. The kingdom of Judah (whence the Bible comes) and the kingdom of Israel (whence, through Joseph, the Book of Mormon comes)— these two kingdoms shall become one in the Lord's hands. Such is the word that the Lord gave to Ezekiel. The Bible and the Book of Mormon, companion volumes of holy scripture, are now one in the Lord's hands; both are published to the world; both contain the mind and will and voice of the Lord to all men. And both are the tools used by the elders of Israel to gather in the long dispersed and widely scattered lost sheep of that ancient house. Indeed, the Book of Mormon, proving as it does the truth and divinity of the Lord's latter-day work, is the message sent to Israel that causes them to gather again into the sheep-fold of their fathers.

It is in this setting, then, the setting showing forth the power and influence of the Bible and the Book of Mormon, that the Lord tells Ezekiel of the gathering of Israel and the reign of David over them. "I will take the children of Israel from among the heathen, whither they be gone," saith the Lord, "and will gather them on every side, and bring them into their own land." This gathering is now in process and will continue until the two ancient kingdoms are fully established again. "And I will make them one nation in the land upon the mountains of Israel; and one king shall be king to them all: and they shall be no more two nations, neither shall they be divided into two kingdoms any more at all." The illustration used to teach the unity and oneness of this gathering is perfect. The two nations shall be one as the Bible and the Book of Mormon are one. No one who truly believes the Bible can reject the Book of Mormon, and every person who believes the Book of Mormon believes also the Bible. They speak with one voice. And so shall it be with the two kingdoms of Israel. They will be perfectly united in the last days, believing the same truths, walking in the same paths, worshipping the same Lord, and glorying in the same eternal covenants. "Neither shall they defile themselves any more with their idols, nor with their detestable things, nor with any of their transgressions." False worship shall cease where they are concerned. As their fathers rejected Baal, so they shall forsake the creeds of Christendom that exhort men to worship an incomprehensible spirit nothingness to which the names of Deity have been given. No more will they walk in the ways of the world; no more will they wallow in the mire of Babylon; no more will they delight in the passions and lusts of carnal men. "But I will save them out of all their dwellingplaces, wherein they have sinned," saith the Lord, "and will cleanse them: so shall they be my people, and I will be their God." Their sins will be washed away in the waters of baptism; they will be born again; and they will become the children of Christ, his sons and his daughters.

It is in this setting—a setting of faith and conversion and gathering; a setting of unity and oneness and righteousness; a setting of worthiness and obedience—it is in this setting that the Lord says: "And David my servant shall be king over them." What David? The Eternal David, the Lord Our Righteousness, who shall dwell among his people and reign in power and glory over all the earth. "And they all shall have one shepherd." What Shepherd? The Good Shepherd, the Lord Jehovah, who led their fathers anciently and will now lead them in the same paths. "For there is one God and one Shepherd over all the earth." (1 Ne. 13:41.) And "they shall also walk in my judgments, and observe my statutes, and do them." They shall keep the commandments, even as the people did in the Zion of old, when once before the Lord came and dwelt with his people and they dwelt in righteousness.

"And they shall dwell in the land that I have given unto Jacob my servant, wherein your fathers have dwelt; and they shall dwell therein, even they, and their children, and their children's children for ever." Of course, as we have seen, the ancient tribes shall be established, at least on a representative basis, in the very lands where their forebears dwelt. There was no better or more explicit way for the Lord to teach the glory and beauty and wonder of the gathering and the triumphal reign. But they shall also dwell in all the earth, for the whole world will become one great Zion, one bounteous Garden of Eden. "And my servant David shall be their prince for ever." David reigns forever! He is Christ the Lord, the Son of David, after the manner of the flesh, David's Lord, speaking from the perspective of eternity.

"Moreover I will make a covenant of peace with them," saith the Lord; "it shall be an everlasting covenant with them." The gospel is the new and everlasting covenant. It bringeth peace, and peace will prevail on earth for the space of a thousand years because men live in harmony with its eternal principles. "And I will place them, and multiply them, and will set my sanctuary in the midst of them for evermore." The temples of the Lord will dot the earth during the Millennium. In them the living will receive the ordinances of exaltation, and the work will be wound up for the worthy dead of all ages. "My tabernacle also shall be with them: yea, I will be their God, and they shall be my people." How sweet and lovely is this thought! When the Lord's true tabernacle is with men; when they assemble therein to worship the Father, in the name of the Son, by the power of the Holy Spirit; when their lives at long last conform to the divine will and pattern—then they are his people and he is their God. "And the heathen shall know that I the Lord do sanctify Israel, when my sanctuary shall be in the midst of them for evermore." (Ezek. 37:15-28.) David reigns; how glorious is the day!

The same God who revealed his mind and will concerning Israel and her King to Ezekiel gave a similar message to Jeremiah. That word, as it pertained to the gathering of his people, included these promises: "I will break [the Gentile] yoke from off thy neck, and will burst thy bonds," saith the Lord. "Therefore fear thou not, O my servant Jacob, saith the Lord; neither be dismayed, O Israel: for, lo, I will save thee from afar, and thy seed from the land of their captivity; and Jacob shall return, and shall be in rest, and be quiet, and none shall make him afraid." Truly this is his millennial destiny. "For I am with thee, saith the Lord, to save thee; though I make a full end of all nations whither I have scattered thee, yet will I not make a full end of thee: but I will correct thee in measure, and will not leave thee altogether unpunished." The one nation that shall survive the great and dreadful day is the nation of Israel. And as to them and their nation, the divine word is: "They shall serve the Lord their God, and David their king, whom I will raise up unto them." (Jer. 30:8-11.)

Hosea records his views in these words: "For the children of Israel shall abide many days without a king, and without a prince, and without a sacrifice, and without an image, and without an ephod, and without teraphim." Their heaven-directed government and their God-given religion shall cease. They shall be subject to the powers that be and shall serve other gods than the Lord. Such is the state of most of them at this time. But, "Afterward shall the children of Israel return, and seek the Lord their God, and David their king; and shall fear the Lord and his goodness in the latter days." (Hosea 3:4-5.) They shall respond to the call of the elders of the restoration, who themselves are of Israel, and who send forth the message to their fellows to worship that God who made heaven and earth and the sea and the fountains of waters and, worshipping him, to return thereby to the kingdom of the great King who is the Second David.

To Amos the divine word came, saying: "Behold, the eyes of the Lord God are upon the sinful kingdom"—ancient Israel and her kingdom—"and I will destroy it from off the face of the earth; saving that I will not utterly destroy the house of Jacob, saith the Lord." Their kingdom went the way of the other evil kingdoms of old; their nation became but a memory; and because they sinned, they became subject to other sinners whose arms were stronger and whose swords were sharper. But they remained as individuals; the house of Jacob, as a people, yet had an eternal destiny. "For, lo, I will command, and I will sift the house of Israel among all nations, like as corn is sifted in a sieve, yet shall not the least grain fall upon the earth." Israel shall be scattered, and not one grain shall bring forth fruit unto eternal life until the day of gathering when they repent of their sins and return to the Lord. "All the sinners of my people shall die by the sword," and in plagues and in other ways; they shall be as other men in the world.

But it will not ever be thus. "In that day"—the latter days—"will I raise up the tabernacle of David that is fallen, and close up the breaches thereof; and I will raise up his ruins, and I will build it as in the days of old." Israel shall assemble and worship the true God, and the old kingdom shall then be established anew. Bounteous harvests will grace the earth, and Israel and the Gentiles who join with her "shall build the waste cities, and inhabit them; and they shall plant vineyards, and drink the wine thereof; they shall also make gardens, and eat the fruit of them." Peace will prevail. "And I will plant them upon their land, and they shall no more be pulled up out of their land which I have given them, saith the Lord thy God." (Amos 9:8-15.)

In the day of gathering the Lord promises to save his flock. "And I will set up one shepherd over them," he says, "and he shall feed them, even my servant David; he shall feed them, and he shall be their shepherd. And I the Lord will be their God, and my servant David a prince among them; I the Lord have spoken it." (Ezek. 34:22-24.)

There is, of course, much more. Whole volumes might be written about Israel—her scattering, gathering, and final triumph—but we have confined ourselves here to passages that speak of the King and the Shepherd who is destined to rule and reign on the throne of David in the millennial day. How beauteous the holy word is! How better could the ancient prophets have taught the glory and power of

Christ's millennial reign than to equate it with the image David had in the eyes of the people? And David's greater Son shall soon come as the Second David to rule and reign over Israel and the world forever. Thanks be to God for the hope and joy that come to us because of this assured verity.

Chapter 50

THE NEW HEAVEN
AND NEW EARTH

The Salvation of the Earth

We are approaching the day when there will be a new heaven and a new earth. By earth we mean this planet, this orb, this abiding place for mortal men; we mean the lands and the seas, the ground whereon we walk, and the pleasant valleys and towering mountains; we mean the great rivers and small streams, the Edenic gardens and the desert waste lands; we mean all of the places where the soles of our feet have trod. By heaven we mean the atmospheric heavens, the layers of air and moisture that surround the earth, the clouds of heaven and the free-moving breezes; we mean the life-giving breath that is breathed into the nostrils of living creatures; we mean the blue skies and the rainbow-hued panoramas of color that attend the rising and setting sun. And when we say the heavens and the earth shall be made new, we have in mind changes so dramatic and alterations of such giant proportion that things as they are now will scarcely be remembered or brought to mind.

In order to understand the doctrine of a new heaven and a new earth, we must have an awareness of the old heaven and the old earth. We must know that they were not always in their present state and that their eventual destiny is to be the home and abiding place of exalted beings. We must know that the earth itself is subject to eternal law and is in process of gaining its salvation. Truly is it written that the earth "must needs be sanctified from all unrighteousness, that it may be prepared for the celestial glory; For after it hath filled the measure of its creation, it shall be crowned with glory, even with the presence of God the Father." And also: "The earth abideth the law of a celestial kingdom, for it filleth the measure of its creation, and transgresseth not the law—Wherefore, it shall be sanctified; yea, notwithstanding it shall die, it shall be quickened again, and shall abide the power by which it is quickened, and the righteous shall inherit it." (D&C 88:18-19, 25-26.)

As to the plan of salvation for men, it includes successive phases of existence and requires certain acts on the part of the candidates for salvation. Men were born as the spirit children of God. The first man, Adam, was placed on earth in an Edenic or paradisiacal or terrestrial state, in which there was neither procreation nor death. Then came the fall, which brought mortality with its consequent procreation and death, and all men are now in a mortal, a fallen, or a telestial state. Those who live on earth during the Millennium will gain a terrestrial state in which there will be no death, in the sense of separation of body and spirit, although they will continue to have children. To gain salvation, men must be baptized in water and of the Spirit; they must obey a celestial law; and they must die and rise again in immortality. The ultimate destiny of saved beings is to dwell in the celestial kingdom.

As to the plan of salvation for the earth, it also calls for successive phases of existence and for whatever else is involved for the earth to abide the law and fill the full measure of its creation. This earth was first created as a spirit planet. Then came the Edenic or paradisiacal or terrestrial creation, during which period all forms of life were placed on its surface, in its waters, or in the atmospheric heavens that surround it. Next came the fall—the fall of man, the fall of all forms of life, and the fall of the earth. The fallen earth became a telestial sphere, which it now is.

In the coming millennial day it will be renewed and receive again its paradisiacal glory and will thus return to its terrestrial or Edenic state. And its final destiny is to become a celestial globe and shine like the sun in the firmament. In the process of abiding a celestial law, the earth was baptized by immersion in the days of Noah; and it will be baptized by fire at the Second Coming. This old earth is also destined to die and to be resurrected in the day of quickening. During the Millennium it will, in effect, be in a translated state, which, as pertaining to men, is the state Enoch and his people and some others attained. Thus, the earth was first a spirit planet and then a terrestrial globe. It is now a telestial earth; during the Millennium it will become terrestrial again; and finally, it will become a celestial earth. With an awareness of all this, we are ready to consider the new heaven and new earth that is soon to be.

The Paradisiacal Earth

"We believe"—it is an official, a formal, a canonized pronouncement—"that the earth will be renewed and receive its paradisiacal glory." (A of F 10.) All things when first created—the earth and all forms of life—were paradisiacal in nature and were pronounced by their Creator as "very good." (Moses 2:31.) There was no sin, no sorrow, and no death in that day. And the Great Creator blessed the earth and all things on its face. Then came the fall, and the earth which God had blessed was cursed. "Cursed shall be the ground for thy sake," he said to Adam; "in sorrow shalt thou eat of it all the days of thy life. Thorns also, and thistles shall it bring forth to thee, and thou shalt eat the herb of the field." (Moses 4:23-24.) To Cain the Lord said: "When thou tillest the ground it shall not henceforth yield unto thee her strength." (Moses 5:37.) And later, with reference to all men, the divine account says: "And God cursed the earth with a sore curse, and was angry with the wicked, with all the sons of men whom he had made." (Moses 5:56.) That curse now prevails; it is in full operation, and it will continue so to be until the millennial day. Then the earth and all things that remain after the day of burning will return to a paradisiacal state, a state in which all things will be blessed and prospered as they were in the primeval day. A thing cannot be renewed unless it was new in the first instance. The earth was paradisiacal once, and it will become so again.

Enoch sought to learn from the Lord when the curse would be removed and when the earth would be blessed again. After he and his city had been translated, "Enoch looked upon the earth; and he heard a voice from the bowels thereof, saying: Wo, wo is me, the mother of men; I am pained, I am weary, because of the wickedness of my children. When shall I rest, and be cleansed from the filthiness which is gone forth out of me? When will my Creator sanctify me, that I may rest, and righteousness for a season abide upon my face?" How graphic and wondrous is this way of teaching—to let the very earth itself cry out for rest and blessings! "And when Enoch heard the earth mourn, he wept, and cried unto the Lord, saying: O Lord, wilt thou not have compassion upon the earth? Wilt thou not bless the children of Noah?" And the Lord did then bless the earth to this extent: he decreed that life on its face should never again be destroyed by a flood. But the basic questions remained unanswered, and so Enoch yet "cried unto the Lord, saying: When the Son of Man cometh in the flesh, shall the earth rest? I pray thee, show me these things." He then saw the crucifixion, the convulsions of nature that attended it, the opening of the prison doors, and the reserving of the wicked "in chains of darkness until the judgment of the great day. And again Enoch wept and cried unto the Lord, saying: When shall the earth rest? And Enoch beheld the Son of Man ascend up unto the Father; and he called unto the Lord, saying: Wilt thou not come again upon the earth? . . . I ask thee if thou wilt not come again on the earth." How great were the pleadings of this holy prophet to know what would be in the last days!

"And the Lord said unto Enoch: As I live, so will I come in the last days, in the days of wickedness and vengeance. . . . And the day shall come that the earth shall rest, but before that day the heavens shall be darkened, and a veil of darkness shall cover the earth; and the heavens shall shake, and also the earth; and great tribulations shall be among the children of men, but my people will I preserve." Then the Lord told Enoch of the restoration of the gospel, the coming forth of the Book of Mormon, the building of the New Jerusalem, and the return of the original Zion, and gave him the promise that "for the space of a thousand years the earth shall rest. And it came to pass that Enoch saw the day of the coming of the Son of Man, in the last days, to dwell on the earth in righteousness for the space of a thousand years." (Moses 7:48-65.)

Isaiah speaks of the latter-day glory and triumph of Israel as a people, of their return from captivity, of the dominion they will have over the nations that oppressed them, and of the fall of Babylon. Then, using the same concept—that of the earth resting in the day of its paradisiacal glory—he says in majestic simplicity: "The whole earth is at rest, and is quiet: they break forth into singing." (Isa. 14:1-8.) How pleasing that day will be! As the Lord worked six days in the creation and rested the seventh, as man is commanded to labor for six days and then rest and worship on the seventh, so the earth itself, after being cursed with the wickedness of her children during six long millenniums, shall soon enjoy a Sabbath of rest for the promised thousand years.

The Day of Transfiguration

This earth as it is now constituted, and the atmospheric heavens as they now are, both of them in their fallen and telestial state shall soon cease to be. They shall die. As with men, so with the earth; death is essential to salvation. A change must take place in the earth; it must go from a lower to a higher state. It is now in a telestial state and must be transformed into one that is terrestrial before it eventually receives its final celestial glory. All this is set forth in the holy word. The inspired Psalmist, for instance, in extolling the greatness of God says: "O my God, . . . thy years are throughout all generations. Of old hast thou laid the foundation of the earth: and the heavens are the work of thy hands. They shall perish, but thou shalt endure: yea, all of them shall wax old like a garment; as a vesture shalt thou change them, and they shall be changed: But thou art the same, and thy years shall have no end." (Ps. 102:24-27.) The earth shall wax old; it shall perish; it shall be changed!

As with so many of the mysteries of the kingdom, Isaiah leaves us a plain and precious witness of the change that is to be in the earth. To him the Lord said: "Lift up your eyes to the heavens, and look upon the earth beneath: for the heavens shall vanish away like smoke, and the earth shall wax old like a garment, and they that dwell therein shall die in like manner: but my salvation shall be for ever, and my righteousness shall not be abolished." (Isa. 51:6.) It is the same message as that delivered by the Psalmist. The heavens and the earth, being old and having served their purpose where men are concerned, shall die. The atmospheric heavens as they now are shall cease to be, and so also will it be with the earth. They shall be changed. "The windows from on high are open, and the foundations of the earth do shake. The earth is utterly broken down, the earth is clean dissolved, the earth is moved exceedingly." Prophets always use the best language at their command to describe what the Lord wants them to say. These words of Isaiah are to be interpreted as meaning exactly what they say. "The earth shall reel to and fro like a drunkard, and shall be removed like a cottage; and the transgression thereof shall be heavy upon it; and it shall fall, and not rise again." (Isa. 24:18-20.) When the Lord comes and the telestial earth ceases to be, when it dies its appointed death, it will not rise again in its old fallen and degenerate state. The day will then have arrived that is referred to in the writings of Isaiah in these words: "For, behold, I create new heavens and a new earth," saith the Lord, "and the former shall not be remembered, nor come into mind." (Isa. 65:17.) So glorious shall the new earth be that men will no longer concern themselves with what once was.

Moroni inserted into his digest of the writings of Ether these words: "The earth shall pass away. And there shall be a new heaven and a new earth; and they shall be like unto the old save the old have passed away, and all things have become new." (Ether 13:8-9.) Life will go on during the Millennium. The earth as a sphere will still be here. And the new earth will be patterned after the old one in the same sense that translated beings are patterned after the mortal men they once were. They are the same persons, but their nature and powers and faculties are so changed that their whole way of life is new. So shall it be as between our present earth and the new earth that is to be.

Peter calls this day when there will be a new heaven and a new earth; this day when the earth shall wax old and die and in which the heavens shall vanish away like smoke; this day in which things on earth will be changed as men change the vestures that clothe them; this day in which the earth will be broken down and dissolved and moved exceedingly; this day in which the earth will be renewed and receive its paradisiacal glory and become again as it originally was in the day of the Garden of Eden—Peter calls this day "the times of refreshing" that "shall come from the presence of the Lord" when "he shall send Jesus Christ, which before was preached" unto the Jews. (Acts 3:19-20.) It will be the day of change needed to make the earth a fit habitation for its true King and the other resurrected beings who will live and reign with him for the appointed thousand years. And well might Peter so speak. He was one of three in the meridian of time, the other two being James and John, who saw in vision the whole glorious renewal of the earth. Alluding to what they saw on the Mount of Transfiguration, our revealed word says: "He that endureth in faith and doeth my will, the same shall overcome, and shall receive an inheritance upon the earth when the day of transfiguration shall come; When the earth shall be transfigured, even according to the pattern which was shown unto mine apostles upon the mount; of which account the fulness ye have not yet received." (D&C 63:20-21.) The new heaven and new earth, the paradisiacal earth, the renewed earth, the refreshed earth, the transfigured earth, the millennial earth—all these are one and the same. How blessed the earth will be in that day!

The Transfigured Earth

What will the transfigured earth be like? Unto what shall we compare it? And how shall we find words to describe the glory and beauty of all things in that day? Providentially the prophetic word gives us glimpses of the future. Using the best language at their command, our inspired forerunners have recorded some of the visions vouchsafed to them relative to the new heaven and the new earth, and they have written down some of the revelations they received about the wonders of the Millennium. In their accounts we read of mountains becoming plains, of valleys ceasing to be, and of the very landmasses of the earth uniting into one grand continent. We read of deserts becoming gardens and of the whole earth yielding her fruit as in Eden of old. The prophetic word, designed as it is to encourage us to prepare to abide the day, is fascinating to the extreme. And it is to this word that we now turn as we seek to weave into the eternal tapestry of the Second Coming those threads which will picture the new heaven and the new earth that are to be. Then, in later chapters, we shall speak of the kind of life men, and all created things, shall live on their newly made paradisiacal planet.

Our course is charted for us with reference to these coming events by this divine word: "Be not deceived, but continue in steadfastness, looking forth for the heavens to be shaken, and the earth to tremble and to reel to and fro as a drunken man, and for the valleys to be exalted, and for the mountains to be made low, and for the rough places to become smooth—and all this when the angel shall sound his trumpet." (D&C 49:23.) And, be it noted, this divine exhortation has the effect of endorsing and approving what the ancient prophets have said about the changes in the earth that will occur as the millennial day dawns.

One of the plainest and most-oft-repeated statements about the ushering in of the Millennium is the promise of a great shaking of the earth, of earthquakes that are everywhere at one and the same time, and of mountains and valleys and seas and landmasses that move. "Yet once, it is a little while," saith the Lord, "and I will shake the heavens, and the earth, and the sea, and the dry land; and I will shake all nations, and the desire of all nations shall come." (Hag. 2:6-7.) Christ, the Desire of all nations, shall come amid the greatest shaking of the earth and of all things that there has ever been or ever will be in the entire history of this planet.

Everything on earth—the historical events then in progress, the beasts and all forms of life, and the inanimate objects that do not act for themselves—everything on earth will be affected by the great shaking. For instance, John tells us that in the midst of Armageddon, there will be "a great earthquake, such as was not since men were upon the earth, so mighty an earthquake, and so great." (Rev. 16:18.) Through Ezekiel the Lord said of that same day: "Surely in that day there shall be a great shaking in the land of Israel; so that the fishes of the sea, and the fowls of the heaven, and the beasts of the field, and all creeping things that creep upon the earth, and all the men that are upon the face of the earth, shall shake at my presence, and the mountains shall be thrown down, and the steep places shall fall, and every wall shall fall to the ground." (Ezek. 38:19-20.) And the Lord shall come. "And his feet shall stand in that day upon the mount of Olives, which is before Jerusalem on the east, and the mount of Olives shall cleave in the midst thereof toward the east and toward the west, and there shall be a very great valley; and half of the mountain shall remove toward the north, and half of it toward the south. And ye shall flee to the valley of the mountains; . . . yea, ye shall flee, like as ye fled from before the earthquake in the days of Uzziah king of Judah: and the Lord my God shall come, and all the saints with thee." (Zech. 14:4-5.) The prophetic word in Joel attests that at the Second Coming "the heavens and the earth shall shake" (Joel 3:16), and our latter-day revelation says "the everlasting hills shall tremble" (D&C 133:31).

We have already quoted the words in Isaiah that say the earth will be dissolved. The Psalmist says the same thing: "The earth and all the inhabitants thereof are dissolved." (Ps. 75:3.) Peter picks up this same theme and explains how it shall come to pass. "The day of the Lord will come," he says, "in the which the heavens shall pass away with a great noise, and the elements shall melt with fervent heat, the earth also and the works that are therein shall be burned up." This we have heretofore considered in other connections. But now note particularly what will happen to the earth. "Seeing then that all these things shall be dissolved," Peter continues, "what manner of persons ought ye to be in all holy conversation and godliness, looking for and hasting unto the coming of the day of God, wherein the heavens being on fire shall be dissolved, and the elements shall melt with fervent heat?" These things, he says, shall come to pass in the day when there are "new heavens and a new earth." (2 Pet. 3:10-13.)

Being aware, thus, that the heavens and the earth, as they now are, shall be dissolved and that the very elements shall melt with fervent heat, we catch a new vision of what is meant by the prophetic word that the mountains shall melt at the Second Coming. Nahum says: "The mountains quake at him, and the hills melt, and the earth is burned at his presence, yea, the world, and all that dwell therein." (Nahum 1:5.) "For, behold, the Lord cometh forth out of his place, and will come down, and tread upon the high places of the earth. And the mountains shall be molten under him, and the valleys shall be cleft, as wax before the fire, and as the waters that are poured down a steep place." (Micah 1:3-4.) Our revelation, echoing the prayer found in chapter 64 of Isaiah, says that the servants of God in the last days will call upon the name of the Lord day and night in these words: "O that thou wouldst rend the heavens, that thou wouldst come down, that the mountains might flow down at thy presence." They are answered that "the presence of the Lord shall be as the melting fire that burneth, and as the fire which causeth the waters to boil." In their prayers the saints will say: "Yea, when thou comest down, and the mountains flow down at thy presence, thou shalt meet him who rejoiceth and worketh righteousness, who remembereth thee in thy ways." (D&C 133:40-44.) And so Isaiah says: "Prepare ye the way of the Lord. . . . Every valley shall be exalted, and every mountain and hill shall be made low: and the crooked shall be made straight, and the rough places plain: And the glory of the Lord shall be revealed, and all flesh shall see it together." (Isa. 40: 3-5.) And so Zechariah says: "And the Lord shall be king over all the earth. . . . All the land shall be turned as a plain. . . . And men shall dwell in it, and there shall be no more utter destruction." (Zech. 14:9-11.)

When the Lord first created this earth, as appears from the revealed account, all of the landmasses were in one place and all of the great waters in another. Continents and islands as we now know them did not exist. "And I, God, said: Let the waters under the heaven be gathered together unto one place, and it was so; and I, God, said: Let there be dry land; and it was so. And I, God, called the dry land Earth; and the gathering together of the waters, called I the Sea; and I, God, saw that all things which I had made were good." (Moses 2:9-10.) Continents and islands, each in their several positions, came into being later, we suppose in large measure as part of the universal flood and the changes then wrought upon the earth. The account in Genesis says the earth was divided in the days of Peleg (Gen. 10:25), meaning, as we suppose, that the division into continents and islands was completed in his day. Peleg was, in fact, the fifth generation from Noah, and his name means division. In any event, there now are continents and islands, which was not always the case.

Now, when the Lord stands upon Olivet and when he utters his voice from Zion and from Jerusalem, it shall be heard among all people. "And it shall be a voice as the voice of many waters, and as the voice of a great thunder, which shall break down the mountains, and the valleys shall not be found. He shall command the great deep, and it shall be driven back into the north countries, and the islands shall become one land; And the land of Jerusalem [the Holy Land] and the land of Zion [America] shall be turned back into their own place, and the earth shall be like as it was in the days before it was divided. And the Lord, even the Savior, shall stand in the midst of his people, and shall reign over all flesh." (D&C 133:20-25.) It is an interesting speculative enterprise to look at a map or a globe of the world and to wonder how, with modest adjustments involving the rising and sinking of various areas of the earth, the continents and islands might fit back together again. There is much to indicate they once were joined and would easily fit back in their former positions.

Knowing as we do from latter-day revelation that the islands and continents were once joined in one landmass and will yet again be joined, we find new meaning in allusions and comments found in the ancient scriptures. As part of a description of the Second Coming, John tells us: "And the heaven departed as a scroll when it is rolled together; and every mountain and island were moved out of their places." (Rev. 6:14.) In connection with the greatest earthquake of the ages, John says: "And every island fled away, and the mountains were not found." (Rev. 16:20.) Also in a Second Coming setting John speaks of the voice of the Lord "as the voice of many waters, and as the voice of a great thunder." (Rev. 14:2.) This is the identical language used by the Lord in telling Joseph Smith that the mountains and valleys shall not be found, that the great deep (apparently the Atlantic Ocean) will be driven back into the north countries, "and the islands shall become one land." (D&C 133:22-23.) The voice of many waters and of a great thunder could well be the thunderous surging of a whole ocean moving half an earth's distance from where it now is. And all of this gives deep meaning to John's account, which says: "And I saw a new heaven and a new earth: for the first heaven and the first earth were passed away; and there was no more sea." (Rev. 21:1.) The apparent meaning of this is that the sea, or ocean, that separates the continents will cease to be, for their great landmasses will be joined together again.

Isaiah, speaking of Zion and Jerusalem in a Second Coming setting, in an apparent reference to the joining of the continents, and using that prophetic imagery for which he has such great renown, says: "Thy land shall be married." (Isa. 62:4.) Also in a setting relative to the Millennium and the gathering of Israel, Isaiah says, "There shall be an highway for the remnant of his people, which shall be left." That is, those who are left because they have abided the day of our Lord's coming shall find a highway to lead them to their appointed gathering places. It shall then be, Isaiah says, "like as it was to Israel in the day that he came up out of the land of Egypt." (Isa. 11:16.) As the Lord provided a highway through the Red Sea for his people anciently, as they traveled to their promised land, so will he provide a way for them to travel in the latter days. Our latter-day revelation, after stating that the great deep shall be driven back into the north countries and that the continents shall become one land, states that "they who are in the north countries," meaning the Ten Tribes, shall return. "And an highway shall be cast up in the midst of the great deep" for them. (D&C 133:23-27.) Would we go too far astray if we were to suggest that the highway is created by the joined landmasses, and that as ancient Israel found a dry path through the Red Sea, so latter-day Israel will find a dry path where the Atlantic Ocean once was? It is at least a thought to ponder, for surely we are expected to seek for interpretations relative to all that has been revealed concerning the Lord and his coming.

After our Lord comes and the new heaven and the new earth are a reality, then the earth will bring forth bounteously to support the billions of our Father's children who shall soon find lodgment on its surface. We do not know what changes will cause this to be. Our knowledge is limited to a few slivers of revealed truth here and there throughout the canonized word. Our revealed description of the millennial return of Israel says: "They shall smite the rocks, and the ice shall flow down at their presence. . . . And in the barren deserts there shall come forth pools of living water; and the parched ground shall no longer be a thirsty land." (D&C 133:26-29.) If the great ice masses shall flow down before them, it presupposes worldwide climatic changes. And if the deserts are freely watered, conditions will be far from what they now are. It could be—we do not know, we can only speculate—it could be that the axis of the earth will become upright and no longer have the twenty-three-and-a-half-degree tilt that causes seasons. It could be—we do not know—that such was the case in the beginning, which might account for the great glacial ages about which scientists speculate. The first mention in the scriptures of "seedtime and harvest, and cold and heat, and summer and winter," as we know them, is found after the flood of Noah. (Gen. 8:22.) At this point, it is wise to state that there is much more that we do not know than that which is known about many things that were anciently and that will be again.

The change in the earth itself is described in Isaiah on this wise: "Thorns and briers" shall prevail in the land, "Until the spirit be poured upon us from on high, and the wilderness be a fruitful field, and the fruitful field be counted for a forest." Then righteousness will prevail, "And my people shall dwell in a peaceable habitation, and in sure dwellings, and in quiet resting places," saith the Lord. (Isa. 32:13-18.) "The wilderness and the solitary place shall be glad for them; and the desert shall rejoice, and blossom as the rose. It shall blossom abundantly, and rejoice even with joy and singing. . . . For in the wilderness shall waters break out, and streams in the desert. And the parched ground shall become a pool, and the thirsty land springs of water." (Isa. 35:1-7.) "I will even make a way in the wilderness, and rivers in the desert," saith the Lord. (Isa. 43:19.) "For the Lord shall comfort Zion: he will comfort all her waste places; and he will make her wilderness like Eden, and her desert like the garden of the Lord; joy and gladness shall be found therein, thanksgiving, and the voice of melody." (Isa. 51:3.)

And to Isaiah's witness, let us add this one prophetic promise from Joel: "And it shall come to pass in that day, that the mountains shall drop down new wine, and the hills shall flow with milk, and all the rivers of Judah shall flow with waters. . . . Judah shall dwell for ever, and Jerusalem from generation to generation. For I will cleanse their blood that I have not cleansed: for the Lord dwelleth in Zion." (Joel 3:18-21.)

So shall it be on the transfigured earth. .

Chapter 51

THE SECOND COMING AND THE RESURRECTION

The Dead: Their Glorious Rising

Of all the resurrections that ever have been or ever will be upon this earth, the most glorious—the one that transcends all others in power, grandeur, and might—will be the resurrection that attends the return of the Lord Jesus. He will come with ten thousands of his saints, all of them resurrected persons from ages past. He will call forth from their graves and from the watery deep ten thousands of his other saints, all of them righteous persons who have lived since his mortal ministry. Those among his saints on earth who are faithful will be caught up to meet him in the clouds of glory, and they will then return to earth with him to live out their appointed days on the new earth with its new heavens.

Job's ever-recurring question—"If a man die, shall he live again?'' (Job 14:14)—has been answered, long since, with all the finality of a divine *ipse dixit*. Man shall live again; nay, man does live again, for the Lord Jesus burst the bands of death and gained the victory over the grave. And with him in his resurrection were all the righteous dead from the day of righteous Abel to that of Zacharias the son of Barachias, as it were, whom they slew between the temple and the altar. In that mighty host was Job himself. Indeed, with Christ in his resurrection were Adam and

Noah and Job; with him were Abraham, Isaac, and Jacob, and all the holy prophets; with him were Enoch and Moses and Elijah and all other translated persons; and with him were all the saints of all prior ages who had been true and faithful in all things—all came forth in glorious immortality when the Lord Jesus turned the key. (D&C 133:54-56.)

And all those who were with Christ in his resurrection, and all others who have since been resurrected, they are the ones who shall return with him in the day of his coming; they are the ones who shall be with him when he calls the sleeping saints to awake and rise from their graves. Thus Job testifies: "I know that my redeemer liveth, and that he shall stand at the latter day upon the earth: And though after my skin worms destroy this body, yet in my flesh shall I see God: Whom I shall see for myself, and mine eyes shall behold, and not another; though my reins be consumed within me." (Job 19:25-27.) And as it is with Job, so shall it be with all the faithful: all shall stand in the latter days upon the earth; all, in their flesh, shall see their God; all shall be with their Risen Lord by whom the resurrection comes.

Those in days past who did not believe and obey the truths of heaven, so as to cleanse and perfect their own souls, shall not be found in the clouds of heaven with the Returning One. And those who do not live the laws of the holy gospel shall not have part in that glorious resurrection which attends his return. Thus we hear Jesus say: "Whosoever shall be ashamed of me, and of my words, in this adulterous and sinful generation, of him also shall the Son of Man be ashamed, when he cometh in the glory of his Father with the holy angels." And what applied in that day applies also in this. Those who do not flee from this present evil world and find gospel refuge and gospel peace with the true saints, of them shall the Lord, whose gospel it is, be ashamed in the dreadful day ahead. "And they shall not have part in that resurrection when he cometh. For verily I say unto you, That he shall come; and he that layeth down his life for my sake and the gospel's, shall come with him, and shall be clothed with his glory in the cloud, on the right hand of the Son of man.'' (JST, Mark 8:41-43.)

Speaking of all who have died in the faith since the resurrection of Christ, and of all who are true and faithful in the day of his return, Paul gives us these consoling words: ''I would not have you to be ignorant, brethren, concerning them which are asleep, that ye sorrow not, even as others which have no hope.'' Truly, those who believe and obey find peace in this world and have a hope of eternal life in the world to come. ''For if we believe that Jesus died and rose again, even so them also which sleep in Jesus will God bring with him.'' All the dead of all the ages, having risen in glorious immortality, will come with the Lord Jesus to the millennial earth. ''For this we say unto you by the word of the Lord, that we which are alive and remain unto the coming of the Lord shall not prevent them which are asleep. For the Lord himself shall descend from heaven with a shout, with the voice of the archangel, and with the trump of God: and the dead in Christ shall rise first.'' The saints shall come forth from their graves, even before he sets foot on earth. ''Then we which are alive and remain shall be caught up together with them in the clouds, to meet the Lord in the air: and so shall we ever be with the Lord.'' He shall return; the immortal saints will return with him; and those who are yet mortal shall return to continue their lives in his presence on the earth. ''Wherefore comfort one another with these words.'' (1 Thes. 4:13-18.)

Thus Paul says: ''Behold, I shew you a mystery''—and how mysterious and strange it is to worldly people, particularly those who have pledged their allegiance to the evolutionary fantasies of Darwinism. ''We shall not all sleep, but we shall all be changed, In a moment, in the twinkling of an eye, at the last trump: for the trumpet shall sound, and the dead shall be raised incorruptible, and we shall be changed.'' (1 Cor. 15:51-52.) Those who abide the day of the Lord's coming will be changed so as to stand the fire and the glory of that dread time; they will be changed when

629

they are caught up to meet the Lord in the air, and they will be changed again when they attain their prescribed age and gain their immortal glory.

Thus also we read in our revelations: "He that endureth in faith and doeth my will, the same shall overcome, and shall receive an inheritance upon the earth when the day of transfiguration shall come. . . . Yea, and blessed are the dead that die in the Lord, from henceforth, when the Lord shall come, and old things shall pass away, and all things become new, they shall rise from the dead and shall not die after, and shall receive an inheritance before the Lord, in the holy city." Both the living and the dead shall be blessed with a millennial inheritance. "And he that liveth when the Lord shall come, and hath kept the faith, blessed is he; nevertheless, it is appointed to him to die at the age of man. Wherefore, children shall grow up until they become old; old men shall die; but they shall not sleep in the dust, but they shall be changed in the twinkling of an eye." Such is the doctrine Paul taught, as did all the prophets and apostles of old. "Wherefore, for this cause preached the apostles unto the world the resurrection of the dead." When shall all these things be? The divine answer affirms: "These things are the things that ye must look for; and, speaking after the manner of the Lord, they are now nigh at hand, and in a time to come, even in the day of the coming of the Son of Man." (D&C 63:20, 49-53.) "And all they who suffer persecution for my name, and endure in faith, though they are called to lay down their lives for my sake yet shall they partake of all this glory." (D&C 101:35.)

When Shall the Dead Rise?

"To every thing there is a season, and a time to every purpose under the heaven." (Eccl. 3:1.) So saith the Preacher. And true it is. There is a time to be born and a time to live, and a time to die and a time to live again. There is a time to put on this mortal clay and gain these mortal experiences and a time to shuffle off this mortal coil with all its troubles and sorrows. There is a time to face the sorrow of death and a time to rise in immortality and lay hold on everlasting life.

And so we ask: When shall the dead rise? When shall the prisoners be freed from their prison house? When shall their bodies and spirits join together inseparably to form immortal souls? We hear the Lord Jehovah, in whom is "everlasting strength," say to the faithful of Israel: "Thy dead men shall live." If a man dies, he shall rise again. But when shall it be ? The Lord Jehovah answers: "Together with my dead body shall they arise." The time shall come for a God to be born, for a God to live among men, for a God to die, and for a God to rise again. Then there shall be a resurrection of the righteous; then they shall come forth; then the cry will go forth: "Awake and sing, ye that dwell in dust." Then "the earth shall cast out the dead." (Isa. 26:4, 19.) Such was the Messianic promise, and as Isaiah testified, so it came to pass. Christ gained the victory over death and hell for himself and for all those who believed in his holy name and who walked as becometh saints. That was the first resurrection.

How resurrections are numbered or how many there are is of no special moment. What matters is the kinds and types of resurrections and who shall come forth in them. Abinadi, who ministered among his American Hebrew brethren a century and a half before the birth of that Lord whose servant he was, prophesied: "The bands of death shall be broken, and the Son reigneth, and hath power over the dead; therefore, he bringeth to pass the resurrection of the dead." The Son is the Lord Jehovah of whom Isaiah spoke. He is the firstfruits of them that slept, and in some way incomprehensible to us, the power of his resurrection passes upon all men so that all shall rise from the dead. The miracle in all this is like the miracle of creation itself.

"And there cometh a resurrection," Abinadi continues, "even a first resurrection." It could not have been other than a first resurrection, for it involved Christ, the firstfruits, and those who came forth along with his dead body. It would be, Abinadi prophesied, "even a resurrection of those that have been, and who are, and who shall be, even until [the time of] the resurrection of Christ—for so shall he be called." To be with Christ in his resurrection—such was the glorious hope of all the saints who lived from the day of the first Adam, by whom mortality came, to the day of the Second Adam, by whom immortality came. Thus, Abinadi continues, "the resurrection of all the prophets, and all those that have believed in their words, or all those that have kept the commandments of God, shall come forth in the first resurrection; therefore, they are the first resurrection."

What is the reward and status of those who were with Christ in his resurrection? "They are raised to dwell with God who has redeemed them; thus they have eternal life through Christ, who has broken the bands of death." (Mosiah 15:20-23.) Theirs is a state of glory and exaltation. Three of them—Abraham, Isaac, and Jacob—are singled out by name and made patterns for all the rest. Of these three the Lord says: "They have entered into their exaltation, according to the promises, and sit upon thrones, and are not angels but are gods." (D&C 132:29, 37.) These are they who were with Christ in his resurrection, who, as Matthew says, "came out of the graves after his resurrection, and went into the holy city, and appeared unto many." (Matt. 27:53.) These are they whom the Lord Jesus will bring with him in the clouds of glory when he comes to rule and reign among men for a thousand years.

The first resurrection that concerned Abinadi, and all the prophets and saints who lived and died before the day of atonement, occurred in the meridian of time. Some others have been resurrected since then. We know of Moroni, John the Baptist, and Peter and James, all of whom had ministerial assignments to be performed among mortals that required angelic messengers who had bodies of flesh and bones. It may be that many others have also burst the bands of death and risen from their graves. But for the generality of the saints, the first resurrection is the one that will attend our Lord's return. All we know with surety as to the time of any individual's resurrection is that "every man" will come forth "in his own order," that "celestial bodies, and bodies terrestrial," and bodies telestial will all come forth, successively, to find their places in kingdoms having the same names. (1 Cor. 15:23-44.)

Those who "keep the commandments of God, and the faith of Jesus," shall come forth in the first resurrection, which is also called the resurrection of life, or the resurrection of the just. It is of them that John wrote: "Blessed are the dead which die in the Lord from henceforth: Yea, saith the Spirit, that they may rest from their labours; and their works do follow them." (Rev. 14:12-13.) It is of them that Jesus says: "At the day of my coming in a pillar of fire, . . . a trump shall sound both long and loud, even as upon Mount Sinai, and all the earth shall quake, and they shall come forth—yea, even the dead which died in me, to receive a crown of righteousness, and to be clothed upon, even as I am, to be with me, that we may be one." (D&C 29:12-13.) And also: "Hearken ye, for, behold, the great day of the Lord is nigh at hand. For the day cometh that the Lord shall utter his voice out of heaven; the heavens shall shake and the earth shall tremble, and the trump of God shall sound both long and loud, and shall say to the sleeping nations: Ye saints arise and live; ye sinners stay and sleep until I shall call again." (D&C 43:17-18.)

In the great Olivet Discourse, Jesus spoke of the signs of his coming, of the redemption of his saints, and of the restoration of scattered Israel. He held up the hope of a glorious resurrection as the greatest triumph any of his saints could achieve in the day of redemption. "For as ye have looked upon the long absence of your spirits from your bodies to be a bondage, I will show unto you how the day of redemption shall come, and also the restoration of the scattered Israel," he said. (And may we here insert that all of the faithful of all of the ages have striven or are now striving so to live that they will come forth from their graves and enter into their immortal rest at the earliest possible time.) And so Jesus told of the signs and wonders that would precede and attend his glorious return, and of the plagues and desolations to be poured out upon the world, and then, by way of promise, said: "But before the arm of the Lord shall fall, an angel shall sound his trump, and the saints that have slept shall come forth to meet me in the cloud." The first resurrection will precede the desolations and horrors to be poured out upon the wicked without measure in the day of our Lord's return. "Wherefore, if ye have slept in peace blessed are you," he continues, "for as you now behold me and know that I am, even so shall ye come unto me and your souls shall live, and your redemption shall be perfected; and the saints shall come forth from the four quarters of the earth." That is to say, the saints who are alive and who are worthy shall be caught up to meet the Lord and the heavenly hosts that accompany him.

Now note the chronology. Jesus' next words are: "Then"—that is, after the saints that sleep have been resurrected, and after the living saints have come forth from the four quarters of the earth—"Then shall the arm of the Lord fall upon the nations. And then shall the Lord set his foot upon this mount, and it shall cleave in twain, and the earth shall tremble, and reel to and fro, and the heavens also shall shake." (D&C 45:16-48.) And then he speaks of the calamities and the burning of the iniquitous and of his appearance to the Jews who remain. Truly the righteous need not fear, for either in life or in death their redemption is assured.

Jesus Comes and the Dead Rise

No matter when they lived, the righteous dead, those destined to gain eternal life in our Father's kingdom, always come forth in the next available resurrection. That resurrection to them is the first resurrection. For us the first resurrection will take place when our Lord returns attended by those who came forth in a previous first resurrection. Then all the righteous dead, all having risen in glorious immortality, will live and reign with him on earth. Let us now see how and in what way all the resurrections that lie ahead relate to the great and dreadful day of his coming.

It is not possible for us, in our present relatively low state of spiritual understanding, to specify the exact chronology of all the events that shall attend the Second Coming. Nearly all of the prophetic word relative to our Lord's return links various events together without reference to the order of their occurrence. Indeed, the same scriptural language is often used to describe similar events that will take place at different times. Thus, in the midst of prophetic pronouncements relative to "the day of the Lord's vengeance," when "the indignation of the Lord" shall fall "upon all nations, and his fury upon all their armies," Isaiah says: "And all the host of heaven shall be dissolved, and the heavens shall be rolled together as a scroll." (Isa. 34:2-8.) In speaking of that which shall transpire during "the sixth seal"—that is, during the sixth one-thousand-year period of the earth's temporal continuance, which is the era in which we now live—John tells us of an earthquake, of the sun and moon being darkened, and of the stars falling upon the earth. Then he says: "And the heaven departed as a scroll when it is rolled together; and every mountain and island were moved out of their places." It is "the great day of his wrath." (Rev. 6:12-17.) Later John says that during "the seventh seal," and thus in a day yet to be, "there was silence in heaven about the space of half an hour." (Rev. 8:1.)

All these things, particularly the hidden and undefined period of silence, are somewhat enigmatic. The Lord has not yet seen fit to tell us their full and complete meanings. But, having them before us, let us see what the Lord has said about them in latter-day revelation, with particular reference to the resurrection. After saying that the great and abominable church "is the tares of the earth," and that "she is ready to be burned," the revealed word affirms: "And there shall be silence in heaven for the space of half an hour; and immediately after shall the curtain of heaven be unfolded, as a scroll is unfolded after it is rolled up, and the face of the Lord shall be unveiled." Then—and these events, of necessity, are chronological—then "the saints that are upon the earth, who are alive, shall be quickened and be caught up to meet him." These are they of whom Paul and others have spoken, as we have heretofore seen. They all shall abide the day and receive an inheritance in the holy city.

"And they"—it is his saints of whom the Lord is speaking—"who have slept in their graves shall come forth, for their graves shall be opened; and they also shall be caught up to meet him in the midst of the pillar of heaven—They are Christ's, the first fruits, they who shall descend with him first, and they who are on the earth and in their graves, who are first caught up to meet him; and all this by the voice of the sounding of the trump of the angel of God." (D&C 88:94-98.)

Christ's, the first fruits—who are they? They are all those who were with him in his resurrection. They are all those of Enoch's city, a righteous people who first were translated and who then gained full immortality when Christ rose from his tomb. They are all those of ages past who have burst the bands of death. They are the living saints who are quickened by the power of God and are caught up to meet their Lord in the air. They are the righteous dead who shall come forth in this, the morning of the first resurrection, to receive an inheritance of eternal life and to be one with their glorious Lord. All these shall have an inheritance of exaltation in the highest heaven of the celestial world. All these shall "behold" their Lord's "face in righteousness," for they shall "awake" with his "likeness." (Ps. 17:15.)

"And after this another angel shall sound, which is the

second trump; and then cometh the redemption of those who are Christ's at his coming''—meaning after his coming—''who have received their part in that prison which is prepared for them, that they might receive the gospel, and be judged according to men in the flesh.'' These are they who come forth with bodies terrestrial and who shall go to the terrestrial kingdom. ''And again, another trump shall sound, which is the third trump; and then come the spirits of men who are to be judged, and are found under condemnation; and these are the rest of the dead; and they live not again until the thousand years are ended, neither again, until the end of the earth.'' Theirs shall be a telestial inheritance. ''And another trump shall sound, which is the fourth trump, saying: There are found among those who are to remain until that great and last day, even the end, who shall remain filthy still.'' (D&C 88:99-102.) These, of course, are the sons of perdition.

Thus all shall rise from death to life, all shall come forth from the grave, all shall live forever in immortality. But oh, what a difference it makes whether we come forth in the resurrection of the just or that of the unjust, whether we are caught up to meet the Lord in the air or whether we are told to remain asleep in the dust of the earth until he calls again. How expressive are the words of Abinadi: ''There is a resurrection, therefore the grave hath no victory, and the sting of death is swallowed up in Christ. . . . Even this mortal shall put on immortality, and this corruption shall put on incorruption, and shall be brought to stand before the bar of God, to be judged of him according to their works whether they be good or whether they be evil—If they be good, to the resurrection of endless life and happiness; and if they be evil, to the resurrection of endless damnation, being delivered up to the devil, who hath subjected them, which is damnation—Having gone according to their own carnal wills and desires; having never called upon the Lord while the arms of mercy were extended towards them; for the arms of mercy were extended towards them, and they would not; they being warned of their iniquities and yet they would not depart from them; and they were commanded to repent and yet they would not repent. And now, ought ye not to tremble and repent of your sins, and remember that only in and through Christ ye can be saved?'' (Mosiah 16:8-13.)

Israel: Her Resurrected Glory

Ancient Israel knew that their destiny was to inherit the earth, to receive their promised land again in eternity, and to live and reign forever in the presence of their King. Yea, and not only Israel, but all the righteous saints who preceded them knew also that their final glory and triumph would be in the day of resurrection. Hence the great need so to live as to come forth in the resurrection of life and endless happiness rather than in the resurrection of endless damnation. Thus, ''Enoch saw the day of the coming of the Son of Man, in the last days, to dwell on the earth in righteousness for the space of a thousand years; . . . and he saw the day of the righteous, [and] the hour of their redemption.'' (Moses 7:65-67.) And thus our revelations, paraphrasing Isaiah, say: ''And now the year of my redeemed is come; . . . And the graves of the saints shall be opened; and they shall come forth and stand on the right hand of the Lamb, when he shall stand upon Mount Zion, and upon the holy city, the New Jerusalem; and they shall sing the song of the Lamb, day and night forever and ever.'' (D&C 133:52, 56. See also Isa. 63:4-9.)

In the last days, when all things are in readiness for our Lord's return, ''there shall be a time of trouble, such as never was since there was a nation [of Israel] even to that same time: and at that time thy people shall be delivered, every one that shall be found written in the book [meaning in the Lamb's Book of Life]. And many of them that sleep in the dust shall awake, some to everlasting life, and some to shame and everlasting contempt.'' (Dan. 12:1-2.) So spoke Daniel. Hosea's like witness to that same people acclaimed: "O Israel, thou hast destroyed thyself; but in me is thine help." No matter that you have apostatized and been cursed and peeled and driven, lo, these many years. In the last days thy seed shall return to the ancient sheepfold. And even the worthy dead, of them it is written: "I will ransom them from the power of the grave," saith the Lord. "I will redeem them from death: O death, I will be thy plagues; O grave, I will be thy destruction." (Hosea 13:9-14.)

Ezekiel's grand vision of the valley of dry bones contains in many respects the most insightful description of the resurrection ever to find its way into the canonized accounts. "Can these bones live?" the Lord asked. His answer: "Behold, I will cause breath [spirit] to enter into you, and ye shall live: And I will lay sinews upon you, and will bring up flesh upon you, and cover you with skin." Flesh and bones and sinews and skin and all the organs of the human body are perfected and placed in their glorified state in the resurrected body. That body walks and talks as Jesus did on the Emmaus road; it eats and digests food as he did in the upper room; it is real and literal and tangible. And so the Lord said to Ezekiel: "These bones are the whole house of Israel. . . . Behold, O my people, I will open your graves, and cause you to come up out of your graves, and bring you into the land of Israel. And ye shall know that I am the Lord, when I have opened your graves, O my people, and brought you up out of your graves, And shall put my spirit in you, and ye shall live, and I shall place you in your own land." (Ezek. 37:1-14.)

Knowing thus that immortal men shall dwell on the same earth that once was theirs; knowing that Israel shall inherit even the very parcels of land promised their fathers; and knowing that Christ our King shall reign personally upon the earth during the Millennium—this knowledge puts us in a position to understand the promises that exalted beings shall live and reign with their Lord during the coming blessed period of peace. "In mine own due time will I come upon the earth in judgment," the Lord says, "and my people shall be redeemed and shall reign with me on earth. For the great Millennium, of which I have spoken by the mouth of my servants, shall come." (D&C 43:29-30.) The Beloved John tells us that "Jesus Christ . . . hath made us [the faithful elders of his kingdom] kings and priests unto God and his Father." (Rev. 1:5-6.) And we might add, he hath made the faithful sisters of his kingdom queens and priestesses. And further: He hath "made us unto our God kings and priests: and we shall reign on the earth." (Rev. 5:10.) What is a king without a kingdom? Unless they are given dominion and power over an appointed kingdom, their reign will be shallow and powerless.

If righteous men come up in the resurrection to reign as kings, and if Christ our Lord is their King, then he, as the scriptures say, is a King of kings. In the same sense he becomes a Lord of lords, a Ruler of rulers, and a God of gods. (Rev. 19:16.) Truly, blessed is the Lord, and blessed also are all they who become one with him and who receive all that his Father hath. "And I saw thrones, and they sat upon them," our apocalyptic friend says of exalted men, "and judgment was given unto them: and I saw the souls of them that were beheaded for the witness of Jesus, and for the word of God, . . . and they lived and reigned with Christ a thousand years. . . . Blessed and holy is he that hath part in the first resurrection: on such the second death hath no power, but they shall be priests of God and of Christ, and shall reign with him a thousand years." (Rev. 20:4-6.) Of these things the Prophet Joseph Smith said: "Christ and the resurrected Saints will reign over the earth during the thousand years. They will not probably dwell upon the earth [in the sense of having a permanent residence here], but will visit it when they please, or when it is necessary to govern it." (*Teachings*, p. 268.) Earth's main inhabitants, as we are about to see, will be those who continue to come here from celestial realms to gain their bodies and to prepare themselves for immortal glory.

Chapter 52

MORTAL MAN AFTER THE SECOND COMING

Man: In What Form Is He Found?

What will be the nature of life in all its forms and varieties during the Millennium? Will man and all living things, in their infinite variety, remain as they are now? Are there changes that must take place in man, and in beasts, fowls, fishes, and creeping things, to enable them to dwell on the new earth and to breathe the air of the new heavens that will surround it? And with reference to man in particular, what kind of life will he live when Satan is bound and death and disease and sorrow as we know them are no more?

Our mortal experiences and our finite logic—devoid of divine guidance, and without revelation from on high—would lead us to assume that life has always been as it now is, and that all things will continue everlastingly as they now are. But such is as far from the fact as heaven is from hell. Neither the earth, nor man, nor life of all sorts and kinds, has always been as it now is. Mortality is but a slight and passing phase of existence, a shimmering moonbeam that shines for a moment in the darkness of our earthbound life; it is but a day in an endless eternity; something else came before, and an entirely different way of life will follow after.

Before we can even glimpse the nature of things millennial, we must know something about the great and eternal stages through which our planet has passed and will pass. This earth has not always been as it now is, and it will not long remain in its present state. It has changed in the past, and it will take on a new form in the future. Before we can understand the nature of man and his life on the new earth that is to be, we must know something about the phases of existence through which he may or can pass. He has not always been a benighted, corruptible mortal, subject to disease and death, nor will he always so remain.

We need not suppose, in our smug self-sufficiency, that we know all things about the human race or about the creation and stages of existence of the planet given of God as a home for his children. We can no more understand ourselves than we can comprehend that God who made us. We can no more envision how and in what manner the Lord created the earth, and how he changes it from one type and kind of sphere to another, than we can step forth and duplicate his omnipotent enterprises. But we do possess some slivers of eternal truth, and we have received certain basic truths about ourselves and the earth that enable us to understand the over-all scheme of things. It is this revealed knowledge that enables us to view millennial life in its proper perspective and relationship to all things.

This earth was created first spiritually. It was a spirit earth. Nothing then lived on its face, nor was it designed that anything should. Then came the physical creation, the paradisiacal creation, the creation of the earth in the Edenic day and before the fall of man. After the fall, the earth became telestial in nature; it fell from a terrestrial to a telestial state; it became a fit abode for mortal life. Such is the state in which it now is. When the millennial day dawns, the earth will be renewed and receive its paradisiacal glory; it will return to its Edenic state; it will be (as contrasted with its present state) a new heaven and a new earth. In the process of change the earth will be burned; it will dissolve; the elements will melt with fervent heat, and all things will become new. There will also be a short postmillennial period of which we know very little, and finally the earth will become a celestial sphere and will shine like the sun in the firmament.

In its present telestial state, wickedness prevails on its face and anyone can live here no matter what his life-style. When the earth returns to its terrestrial state, none will be able to live on its surface unless they abide at least a terrestrial law. Hence, every corruptible thing will be consumed when the earth is cleansed at the beginning of the Millennium. That is, all who are worldly, all who are carnal, sensual, and devilish, all who are living a telestial law will be destroyed. Finally, when the earth becomes a celestial sphere, none shall remain on its face except those who are living a celestial law. This earth will then become a celestial kingdom.

Man and all forms of life existed as spirit beings and entities before the foundations of this earth were laid. There were spirit men and spirit beasts, spirit fowls and spirit fishes, spirit plants and spirit trees. Every creeping thing, every herb and shrub, every amoeba and tadpole, every elephant and dinosaur—all things—existed as spirits, as spirit beings, before they were placed naturally upon the earth. Then natural, or earthly, or paradisiacal bodies were provided for spirit men and all forms of life. Our first parents and the original forms of life of every kind and specie were placed on earth in a paradisiacal state. In that state there was no procreation, no death, no mortality (as we know it), and no blood flowing in the veins of man or of the animal kingdom. Then came the fall, the effects of which passed upon all mankind and upon every form of life. Sorrow and disease and death entered the world. Man and all created things were able to procreate and reproduce their kind. Blood began to flow in the veins of man and beast. Their bodies underwent a change and they became mortal. Mortality is the state in which procreation abounds and death prevails. When mortals die, they live again as spirits, except that they do not return to the presence of God, but abide in a place appointed, where they await the day of their resurrection.

Some mortals have been translated. In this state they are not subject to sorrow or to disease or to death. No longer does blood (the life-giving element of our present mortality) flow in their veins. Procreation ceases. If they then had children, their offspring would be denied a mortal probation, which all worthy spirits must receive in due course. They have power to move and live in both a mortal and an unseen sphere. All translated beings undergo another change in their bodies when they gain full immortality. This change is the equivalent of a resurrection. All mortals, after death, are also resurrected. In the resurrected state they are immortal and eternal in nature, and those among them who are privileged to live in the family unit have spirit children. Millennial man will live in a state akin to translation. His body will be changed so that it is no longer subject to disease or death as we know it, although he will be changed in the twinkling of an eye to full immortality when he is a hundred years of age. He will, however, have children, and mortal life of a millennial kind will continue. We shall speak more particularly of all this shortly.

During the Millennium there will, of course, be two kinds of people on earth. There will be those who are mortal, and those who are immortal. There will be those who have been changed or quickened or transfigured or translated (words fail us to describe their state), and those who have gone through a second change, in the twinkling of an eye, so as to become eternal in nature. There will be those who are on probation, for whom earth life is a probationary estate, and who are thus working out their own salvation, and those who have already overcome the world and have entered into a fulness of eternal joy. There will be those who will yet die in the sense of being changed from their quickened state to a state of immortality, and those who, having previously died, are then living in a resurrected state. There will be those who are subject to the kings and priests who rule forever in the house of Israel, and those who, as kings and priests, exercise power and dominion in the everlasting kingdom of Him whose we are. There will be those who, as mortals, provide bodies for the spirit children of the Father, for the spirits whose right it is to come to earth and gain houses for their eternal spirits, and those who, as immortals (Abraham is one), are already begetting spirit children of their own. There will be those for whom the fulness of eternal glory is ahead, and those who, again like Abraham, have already entered into their exaltation and sit upon their thrones and are not angels but are gods forever and ever. We have heretofore summarized such things as we know about the immortal beings who shall dwell, from time to time, on earth during the Millennium. We shall now consider such things as have been revealed with reference to those who are born and who live here during the thousand years of plenty and peace.

Man: His Millennial State

We shall use the word *mortal* to describe those who live on earth during the Millennium and who are not resurrected. They will be mortal in the sense that they have the power of procreation and will beget children. "And the earth shall be given unto them for an inheritance," saith the Lord, "and they shall multiply and wax strong, and their children shall grow up without sin unto salvation." (D&C 45:58.) They are the ones of whom the Lord said: "They shall see the kingdom of God coming in power and great glory; . . . For behold, the Lord shall come, and his recompense shall be with him, and he shall reward every man, and the poor shall rejoice; And their generations"—their posterity, the seed of their bodies, the lives that come into being because of them, their children—"shall inherit the earth from generation to generation, forever and ever." (D&C 56:18-20.)

Men during the Millennium will be mortal because they will die—not as men die now, with the spirit leaving the body and the body returning to the dust whence it came, but they will die according to the pattern and system ordained to occur during that blessed period of the earth's temporal continuance. There will be no graves during the Millennium. Men's bodies will not see corruption, and their spirits will not go to a spirit world, there to await a future resurrection. Rather, "children shall grow up until they become old; old men shall die; but they shall not sleep in the dust, but they shall be changed in the twinkling of an eye." (D&C 63:51.) "In that day an infant shall not die until he is old; and his life shall be as the age of a tree; and when he dies he shall not sleep, that is to say in the earth, but shall be changed in the twinkling of an eye, and shall be caught up, and his rest shall be glorious." (D&C 101:30-31.) Such is the revealed word as it came to Joseph Smith. The same truths, as given to Isaiah, announce: "There shall be no more thence an infant of days, nor an old man that hath not filled his days: for the child shall die an hundred years old; but the sinner being an hundred years old shall be accursed." (Isa. 65:20.) Isaiah's description of life and death during the Millennium seems to preserve the concept that even then—even in that blessed day when Satan is bound and righteousness overflows—even then men are free to come out in open rebellion and, as sinners, suffer the fate reserved for the sons of perdition. Manifestly they, being accursed, would die the death with which we are familiar, for their resurrection is destined to be in that final day when those shall come forth "who shall remain filthy still." (D&C 88:102.)

There are no words in our language that accurately convey to our minds either the nature of man or the type of life he is destined to live during the Millennium. In that day, in process of time at least, the Lord has promised to restore "a pure language," so that all men may "call upon the name of the Lord, to serve him with one consent." (Zeph.

3:9.) For the present, however, conditions in that blessed day are so far outside the realm of our experience that we do not have the language at our command to describe them. Perhaps the best thing we can do is to describe the life and status of translated beings and to say that their life is closely akin to that of millennial man.

Enoch and his city were all translated and taken up into heaven without tasting death. So also were Moses and Elijah and Alma and many others of whom we have no record. Indeed the whole focus of life among the worthy saints from the day of Enoch to the day of Abraham was so to live that they would be caught up and receive an inheritance in that city whose builder and maker was God. All these were with Christ in his resurrection; that is, they received their resurrected and immortal bodies at that time. John the Revelator and the Three Nephites and others whose identity is unknown have been translated since the day of Christ. They are all carrying on their ministries of preaching and prophesying and will do so until the Second Coming, when they will receive their resurrected and immortal bodies. The Lord, for instance, promised John: "Thou shalt tarry until I come in my glory, and shalt prophesy before nations, kindreds, tongues and people." This ministry is among mortals on earth, but John has great powers that mortals do not possess. "I will make him as flaming fire and a ministering angel," the Lord promised, and "he shall minister for those who shall be heirs of salvation who dwell on the earth." (D&C 7:3-6.)

It is from the Book of Mormon account relative to the Three Nephites that we gain our greatest scriptural knowledge about translated beings. Jesus told them: "Ye shall never taste of death; but ye shall live to behold all the doings of the Father unto the children of men, even until all things shall be fulfilled according to the will of the Father, when I shall come in my glory with the powers of heaven. And ye shall never endure the pains of death; but when I shall come in my glory ye shall be changed in the twinkling

647

of an eye from mortality to immortality; and then shall ye be blessed in the kingdom of my Father.'' Similarly, the faithful saints who are alive when the Lord comes, and who are caught up to meet him in the midst of the pillar of heaven, shall be quickened. Their bodies shall be changed from mortality as we know it to a millennial-type mortality, to the type of mortality possessed by translated beings. Those who are born during the Millennium will enjoy this same quickened state, and all of them, each in his order, will be changed in the twinkling of an eye to his resurrected and immortal state when he becomes one hundred years of age.

"And again, ye shall not have pain while ye shall dwell in the flesh,'' the Lord Jesus promised them, "neither sorrow save it be for the sins of the world.'' (3 Ne. 28:7-9.) Similarly, pain and sorrow, tears and weeping, and the anguish and sadness of our day—all these shall cease in the millennial day. Our revelation says simply: "And there shall be no sorrow because there is no death.'' (D&C 101:29.) Isaiah promised: "He will swallow up death in victory; and the Lord God will wipe away tears from off all faces.'' (Isa. 25:8.) And to Isaiah the Lord said: "Be ye glad and rejoice for ever in that which I create: for, behold, I create Jerusalem a rejoicing, and her people a joy. And I will rejoice in Jerusalem, and joy in my people: and the voice of weeping shall be no more heard in her, nor the voice of crying.'' (Isa. 65:18-19.) And from the pen of the Revelator we learn: "And God shall wipe away all tears from their eyes; and there shall be no more death, neither sorrow, nor crying, neither shall there be any more pain: for the former things are passed away.'' (Rev. 21:4.)

After summarizing many things that happened to the Three Nephites in the course of their ministry among the descendants of Lehi, Mormon said: "And they are as the angels of God, and if they shall pray unto the Father in the name of Jesus they can show themselves unto whatsoever man it seemeth them good.'' Then, in discussing whether they were mortal or immortal, Mormon gave this exposition: "I have inquired of the Lord, and he hath made it manifest unto me that there must needs be a change wrought upon their bodies, or else it needs be that they must taste of death." It is one thing to die and another to taste of death. All men shall die, but those who receive an instantaneous change from mortality to immortality do not taste of death. And so Mormon continues: "Therefore, that they might not taste of death there was a change wrought upon their bodies, that they might not suffer pain nor sorrow save it were for the sins of the world. Now this change was not equal to that which shall take place at the last day; but there was a change wrought upon them, insomuch that Satan could have no power over them, that he could not tempt them"—and surely this will be the case with men during the Millennium—"and they were sanctified in the flesh, that they were holy, and that the powers of the earth could not hold them. And in this state they were to remain until the judgment day of Christ; and at that day they were to receive a greater change, and to be received into the kingdom of the Father to go no more out, but to dwell with God eternally in the heavens." (3 Ne. 28:30-40.)

The Growing Glory of the Millennium

Our Blessed Lord will come at the appointed time. The great conference at Adam-ondi-Ahman will assemble to worship the King on schedule. There will be an exact moment when his foot first touches the Mount of Olives. He will stand on Mount Zion with the 144,000 high priests at a given point in time. Armageddon will spread its fire and horror and death when and as decreed in the divine timetable. The tares will be burned and the vineyard cleansed of corruption when the Lord Jesus returns. And there will be a day and an hour and a split second that marks the beginning of the Millennium. The seventh of the thousand-year periods can only commence at one single instant in time. As we have seen, many of the events incident to the Second Coming will take place during the close of the sixth seal and others after the opening of the seventh seal. And yet the formal beginning of the Millennium will take place at a fixed and determined and set moment. It cannot be hastened by righteousness nor delayed by wickedness. The old earth will die, and the new heaven and the new earth will be born at as exact an instant as is the case with the birth or death of any form of life. We speak thus so there will be no confusion or misunderstanding when we also say that the full glory and wonder of the millennial day will unfold gradually; that there will be wicked men on earth after the Millennium has commenced; and that the final glory and triumph of Israel will take place gradually after the Millennium itself has been ushered in. Let us now see what the holy word has to say relative to these things.

First, the cleansing of the vineyard, the burning of the earth, and the destruction of the wicked by fire shall all come to pass in a short time, in a single day, as it were. And then there will be but few men left on earth. "I will remove the iniquity of that land in one day," the Lord told Zechariah. (Zech. 3:9.) And in Isaiah we find numerous prophetic expressions phrased in that imagery in which he so excelled. "Many houses shall be desolate, even great and fair, without inhabitant." (Isa. 5:9.) Those sent to raise the warning voice to the world are to do so "until the cities be wasted without inhabitant, and the houses without man, and the land be utterly desolate, and the Lord have removed men far away." (Isa. 6:11-12.) In the day of the Lord's coming, "the light of Israel shall be for a fire, and his Holy One for a flame: and it shall burn and devour his thorns and his briers in one day; and shall consume the glory of his forest, and of his fruitful field, both soul and body: and they shall be as when a standardbearer fainteth. And the rest of the trees of his forest shall be few, that a child may write them." (Isa. 10:17-19.) "Behold, the Lord maketh the earth empty, and maketh it waste, and turneth it upside down, and scattereth abroad the inhabitants thereof. . . . The land shall be utterly emptied, and utterly spoiled. . . . Therefore hath the curse devoured the earth, and they that dwell therein are desolate: therefore the inhabitants of the earth are burned, and few men left.'' (Isa. 24:1-6.) Who can doubt that there will be but few men left at the beginning of the Millennium?

The prophetic word that sets forth what is to be during the Millennium speaks of ''new heavens and a new earth, wherein dwelleth righteousness.'' (2 Pet. 3:13.) It says that every corruptible thing shall be consumed when the vineyard is burned. And yet the Prophet Joseph Smith said: ''There will be wicked men on the earth during the thousand years. The heathen nations who will not come up to worship will be visited with the judgments of God, and must eventually be destroyed from the earth.'' (*Teachings*, pp. 268-69.) Taken together, these concepts mean that wickedness that is telestial in nature, wickedness that consists of living after the manner of the world, that wickedness which is carnal, sensual, and devilish by nature—all such shall cease. Those who so live will be destroyed. They are the tares of the earth.

But wickedness is a matter of degree, and even those who are upright and decent by worldly standards but who reject the gospel and do not worship the true God are considered to be wicked by gospel standards. They are ''under the bondage of sin.'' They do not accept the message of the restoration and gain a remission of their sins in the waters of baptism. ''And by this you may know the righteous from the wicked, and that the whole world groaneth under sin and darkness even now.'' (D&C 84:49-53.) Thus the divine word, as given by Zechariah, says that ''it shall come to pass''—in the millennial day—''that every one that is left [after Armageddon] of all the nations which came against Jerusalem shall even go up from year to year to worship the King, the Lord of hosts, and to keep the feast of tabernacles. And it shall be, that whoso will not come up of all the families of the earth unto Jerusalem to worship the King, the Lord of hosts, even upon them shall be no rain. And if the family of Egypt go not up, and come not, that have no rain; there shall be the plague, wherewith the Lord will smite the heathen that come not to keep the feast of tabernacles. This shall be the punishment of Egypt, and the punishment of all nations that come not up to keep the feast of tabernacles." (Zech. 14:16-19.) Thus there will be many churches on earth when the Millennium begins. False worship will continue among those whose desires are good, "who are honorable men of the earth," but who have been "blinded by the craftiness of men." (D&C 76:75.) Plagues will rest upon them until they repent and believe the gospel or are destroyed, as the Prophet said. It follows that missionary work will continue into the Millennium until all who remain are converted. Then "the earth shall be full of the knowledge of the Lord, as the waters cover the sea." (Isa. 11:9.) Then every living soul on earth will belong to The Church of Jesus Christ of Latter-day Saints.

The Millennial Way of Life

With the concept before us of a growing and glorious Millennium in which every living soul will be converted and come into the sheepfold of Israel, we are ready to view with rejoicing the way of life that will prevail on the new earth. Thanks to our friend Isaiah, we have many pen pictures, inscribed with spiritual insight and poetic genius, that tell us of what is to be in that great day. We cannot do better than to pick from his seeric sayings a few of the highlights, adding a word here and there that has fallen from other prophetic lips.

As we have heretofore seen, the millennial day is one in which the Lord himself will dwell with men. This is a boon of inestimable worth. We can scarcely conceive of the glory and wonder of it all. The Lord Jesus Christ, the King of heaven, our Savior and Redeemer, the Lord God Omnipotent dwelling among men! In our day righteous men strive all their days to see a glimpse of his face and to hear a word from his lips, and few there be with faith sufficient to part the veil and see and hear for themselves. Isaiah himself was one of these. "In the year that king Uzziah died," Isaiah tells us, "I saw also the Lord sitting upon a throne, high and lifted up, and his train filled the temple. . . . Then said I, Woe is me! for I am undone; because I am a man of unclean lips, and I dwell in the midst of a people of unclean lips: for mine eyes have seen the King, the Lord of hosts." (Isa. 6:1, 5.) But in the millennial day the righteous shall see his face and hear his voice; they shall receive light and truth and wisdom as such fall from his lips. His throne shall be set up among them, and they shall hear him preach in their conferences. His voice shall again be heard on a mountain in Galilee as the Sermon on the Mount takes on a new and expanded meaning that none of us ever thought that it had. We shall hear again, in an upper room, as it were, the sermon on love and on the Second Comforter, and feel anew the power and spirit of the Intercessory Prayer. And to these will be added such other sermons as have never entered the heart of man as Jesus expounds the mysteries of eternity. Truly, truly did Isaiah promise: "For since the beginning of the world men have not heard, nor perceived by the ear, neither hath the eye seen, O God, beside thee, what he hath prepared for him that waiteth for him." (Isa. 64:4.)

In that day the Lord Jesus will hear the pleas of his people and answer them with blessings upon their heads. "And it shall come to pass, that before they call, I will answer; and while they are yet speaking, I will hear." (Isa. 65:24.) "And in that day whatsoever any man shall ask, it shall be given unto him." (D&C 101:27.) And "with righteousness" shall the Lord "judge the poor, and reprove with equity for the meek of the earth." Unjust judgments shall cease. That God who is no respecter of persons will weigh every man in the same balance, and all will be judged fairly and equitably. "And righteousness shall be the girdle of his loins, and faithfulness the girdle of his reins." (Isa.

11:4-5.) He shall be clothed in the robes of righteousness! He shall wear the garments of faithfulness! Even the girdles and robes and sandals and garments which cover his body and adorn his feet shall bear witness of his goodness and grace. "In that day shall there be [even] upon the bells of the horses, HOLINESS UNTO THE LORD; and the pots in the Lord's house shall be like the bowls before the altar. Yea, every pot in Jerusalem and in Judah shall be holiness unto the Lord of hosts." (Zech. 14:20-21.) What a glorious day it will be when Christ the Lord reigns and judges his people! How, oh how all the things shall be centered in the Lord and shall bear record of his goodness in that day!

In that day there will be peace on earth; wars will be unknown and unheard of; crime and evil and carnality will vanish away; and the Son of Righteousness shall replace evil with good, for he, as "The Prince of Peace," and the Creator of Righteousness, shall reign "upon the throne of David." (Isa. 9:6-7.) There will be no murders; even if an evil Cain should seek the life of a righteous Abel, he could not slay him. During the Millennium there will be no death because, for one reason, there will be no blood to spill upon the ground. There will be no robbings, nor stealing, nor kidnapping, nor treachery, nor immorality, nor lasciviousness, nor any manner of evil. What would our society be like if these sins and all their ilk were abolished, if there were no prisons for the criminals, no reformatories for the recalcitrant, no lands of banishment for the treasonous? Where there is peace, there is neither crime nor war. And in that day men "shall beat their swords into plowshares, and their spears into pruninghooks: nation shall not lift up sword against nation, neither shall they learn war any more." (Isa. 2:4.) "He maketh wars to cease unto the end of the earth." (Ps. 46:9.) "The whole earth is at rest, and is quiet: they break forth into singing." (Isa. 14:7.) "And the work of righteousness shall be peace; and the effect of righteousness quietness and assurance for ever. And my people," saith the Lord, "shall dwell in a peaceable habitation, and in sure dwellings, and in quiet resting places." (Isa. 32:17-18.)

In that day family units will be perfected according to the plans made in the heavens before the peopling of the earth. Celestial marriage in its highest and most glorious form will bind men and women together in eternal unions, and the resultant families will truly continue forever. One of the most provocative millennial passages forecasts the order of matrimony that will then prevail, saying: "And in that day"—the millennial day—"seven women shall take hold of one man, saying, We will eat our own bread, and wear our own apparel: only let us be called by thy name, to take away our reproach," the reproach of being without a husband, without children, without a family of their own. This shall come to pass after the destruction of the wicked, and it is one of many scriptural intimations that the generality of women are more spiritual than are most men. The inference is that far more women will abide the day of his coming than will be the case with men. And they, being clean and upright, and desiring family units and children and the exaltation that grows out of all these things, will turn to the marriage discipline of Abraham their father so they may be blessed like Sarah of old.

"In that day"—the millennial day, the day in which seven women shall cleave unto one man—"shall the branch of the Lord be beautiful and glorious." He is speaking of those who are left on the olive tree that is Israel. "And the fruit of the earth shall be excellent and comely for them that are escaped of Israel." Only those in Israel who abide the day and escape its burning desolations shall partake of the millennial glory. "And it shall come to pass, that he that is left in Zion, and he that remaineth in Jerusalem, shall be called holy, even every one that is written among the living in Jerusalem: When the Lord shall have washed away the filth of the daughters of Zion, and shall have purged the blood of Jerusalem from the midst thereof by the spirit of judgment, and by the spirit of burning." Only the righteous in Israel shall remain. They shall be holy, for they have not been consumed in the day of burning. "And the Lord will create upon every dwelling place of mount Zion, and upon her assemblies, a cloud and smoke by day, and the shining of a flaming fire by night: for upon all the glory shall be a defence. And there shall be a tabernacle for a shadow in the daytime from the heat, and for a place of refuge, and for a covert from storm and from rain." (Isa. 4:1-6.)

In that day "the eyes of the blind shall be opened, and the ears of the deaf shall be unstopped. Then shall the lame man leap as an hart, and the tongue of the dumb sing." (Isa. 35:5-6.) The miracles of Jesus when he once dwelt among men are but a pattern and a sample of what shall be when he comes again. "He shall feed his flock like a shepherd: he shall gather the lambs with his arm, and carry them in his bosom, and shall gently lead those that are with young." (Isa. 40:11.) The abundance of our Lord's teachings and of his tender care when he was once among us are but a small part of what shall be when he comes again to be with his people.

In that day Israel "shall build the old wastes, they shall raise up the former desolations, and they shall repair the waste cities, the desolations of many generations." (Isa. 61:4.) "And they shall build houses, and inhabit them; and they shall plant vineyards, and eat the fruit of them. They shall not build, and another inhabit; they shall not plant, and another eat: for as the days of a tree are the days of my people, and mine elect shall long enjoy the work of their hands," saith the Lord. "They shall not labour in vain, nor bring forth for trouble; for they are the seed of the blessed of the Lord, and their offspring with them." (Isa. 65:21-23.) Yea, thus saith the Lord unto his people Israel: "In that day shalt thou not be ashamed for all thy doings, wherein thou hast transgressed against me: for then I will take away out of the midst of thee them that rejoice in thy pride, and thou shalt no more be haughty because of my holy mountain.'' What a change it will be even for the chosen people when only the righteous among them remain in the millennial day. ''I will also leave in the midst of thee an afflicted and poor people, and they shall trust in the name of the Lord.'' These are the poor of this world who are rich in faith. ''The remnant of Israel''—those who abide the day—''shall not do iniquity, nor speak lies; neither shall a deceitful tongue be found in their mouth: for they shall feed and lie down, and none shall make them afraid.'' Their new state shall be far removed from what once prevailed among them.

''Sing, O daughter of Zion; shout, O Israel; be glad and rejoice with all the heart, O daughter of Jerusalem. The Lord hath taken away thy judgments, he hath cast out thine enemy: the king of Israel, even the Lord, is in the midst of thee: thou shalt not see evil any more. In that day it shall be said to Jerusalem, Fear thou not: and to Zion, let not thine hands be slack. The Lord thy God in the midst of thee is mighty; he will save, he will rejoice over thee with joy; he will rest in his love, he will joy over thee with singing.'' (Zeph. 3:11-17.) Such shall be the promised day, the day of the triumphant gathering of Israel, the day in which the Lord will make his people rulers over all the earth. This is the day in which ''their enemies shall become a prey unto them.'' (D&C 133:28.) This is the day when the Lord will fulfill his promise: ''For as the new heavens and the new earth, which I will make, shall remain before me, saith the Lord, so shall your seed and your name remain.'' (Isa. 66:22.)

We have spoken thus about mankind in general and Israel in particular in setting forth, briefly, their millennial states. But what about other forms of life? Will their life and birth and death be as it now is? Or will they too be changed when the new heavens and the new earth replace this old mortal sphere? It is written: ''And he that sat upon the throne said, Behold, I make all things new.'' (Rev. 21:5.) All things includes all things, and although the scriptures do not speak with particularity about the millennial status of plants and herbs and trees and the vegetable kingdom, we do know that they will go back to that state of existence which was theirs in the Edenic day. But the revealed word does have somewhat to say about the animal kingdom. "In that day," for one thing, "the enmity of man, and the enmity of beasts, yea, the enmity of all flesh, shall cease from before my face," the Lord says. (D&C 101:26.) There will be no wild animals. The coyote will not stalk the deer, and the wolf will not kill the sheep, and all forms of life will be the friends and servants of men.

Isaiah gives us these poetically phrased particulars about animal life during the Millennium. "The wolf and the lamb shall feed together," he says, "and the lion shall eat straw like the bullock." Implicit in this pronouncement is the fact that man and all forms of life will be vegetarians in the coming day; the eating of meat will cease, because, for one thing, death as we know it ceases. There will be no shedding of blood, because man and beast are changed (quickened) and blood no longer flows in their veins. "And dust shall be the serpent's meat," meaning, as we suppose, that they shall no longer eat mice and vermin and animal life. "They shall not hurt nor destroy in all my holy mountain, saith the Lord." (Isa. 65:25.) And further: "The wolf also shall dwell with the lamb, and the leopard shall lie down with the kid; and the calf and the young lion and the fatling together; and a little child shall lead them. And the cow and the bear shall feed; their young ones shall lie down together: and the lion shall eat straw like the ox. And the suckling child shall play on the hole of the asp, and the weaned child shall put his hand on the cockatrice' den [adders' den]. They shall not hurt nor destroy in all my holy mountain." (Isa. 11:6-9.)

Having spoken thus about the millennial state of man and all forms of life, we are ready to consider the great and eternal purpose of the Millennium itself, which is to provide an atmosphere for a way of worship that will lead worthy spirits to eternal life in our Father's kingdom. We shall now turn to the glorious matter of that true and perfect worship destined to cover the earth after it has become a new earth and the wicked have been consumed.

Chapter 53

MILLENNIAL WORSHIP

Why There Is a Millennium

The purpose of the Millennium is to save souls. There can be no doubt about this. It is the Lord's work and his glory to bring to pass the immortality and eternal life of man. This is axiomatic among us. All that he does during all the endless ages of his everlasting existence is designed to save souls. There is no aim or end or purpose in anything that comes from God, except to further the salvation of his children.

The Almighty Elohim is the father of billions of spirit children, all of whom lived for millions (perhaps billions) of years in his eternal presence. He ordained and established the plan and system whereby they might advance and progress and become like him. That plan is the gospel of God, known to us as the gospel of Jesus Christ because he is the one chosen to put all of its terms and conditions into operation.

Our Eternal Father knows all of his spirit children, and in his infinite wisdom, he chooses the very time that each comes to earth to gain a mortal body and undergo a probationary experience. Everything the Lord does is for the benefit and blessing of his children. And each of those children is subjected to the very trials and experiences that Omniscient Wisdom knows he should have. Those who were entitled to an inheritance in Enoch's Zion came to earth in that day. Those whose spiritual stature qualified them for life among the Nephites during that nation's golden era found their inheritance with that people in ancient America. Apostles and prophets are sent to earth to do the work of apostles and prophets at the time and season when their particular talents are needed. All of the elders of Israel were foreordained and sent to earth in the house of Jacob to minister to their kinsmen and to the Gentiles. Indeed, spiritually endowed souls, in large measure, have been born in the house of Israel ever since the day of Father Jacob. We are here now in latter-day Israel, scattered in all the nations of the earth, because that is where the Lord wants us to be, and that is where we need to be for our own development, advancement, and salvation.

Millions of children, from Adamic times to our day, have died before they arrived at the age of accountability, and, because they were alive in Christ and had never died spiritually, they shall have eternal life. It will come to them through the atonement of Christ. They never were called upon to undergo and overcome the trials and temptations that almost overpower us. Billions of spirits will come to earth during the Millennium, when Satan is bound, when there is peace on earth, when there is no sorrow because there is no death, when they will not be confronted with the evil and carnality that face us. They will grow up without sin unto salvation. Thus saith the holy word.

Knowing this, we are obliged to conclude that a millennial inheritance is the kind and type of mortal life that billions of spirits are entitled to receive. Whatever the Lord does is right whether we understand his purposes or not. Without question there are many valiant souls now living who are worthy to receive a millennial birth, but who were sent to earth in this day of wickedness to be lights and guides to other men and to lead many of our Father's children to eternal life. But nonetheless, there will be billions of millennial mortals who will never be tested, as fully as we are, and who will go on to eternal life, as do little children, because an Almighty God in his infinite wisdom arranges that kind of a life for them. The Lord gives each of us what we need. And, we repeat, the whole millennial system has been ordained and established to save souls. There is no other reason for any of the Lord's dealings with his children. He wants them to gain salvation, and he does for them what he knows they need done, in each instance, to hasten them along the way to perfection. We must understand and believe these concepts if we are to envision properly the worship that will prevail on earth during the soon-to-be thousand years of peace and righteousness.

Why False Worship Shall Cease

Because the Millennium is designed to save souls, the whole system of worldly worship that now prevails on earth—in which there is no salvation—will come to an end. The worship of the beast and of his image and of every false god will cease. Because salvation comes only to those who worship the Father, in the name of the Son, by the power of the Holy Ghost, such is the sole and only kind of worship that will be found on earth when full millennial conditions prevail. The worship of other gods than the Lord will fade into the shadows of the past. No longer will men heap adoration upon idols, or pay homage to a spirit essence that fills the immensity of space, or reverence the laws and powers of nature as though they were God himself. No longer will they pray to supposed saints, pleading with them to mediate between them and the Lord.

Because salvation results from rigid adherence to principles of true religion, all forms of false religion will come to an end. False religions will die; heresies will cease; false doctrines will no longer be taught. Because there is and can be only one true Church and kingdom of God on earth, all the churches of men and of devils will go out of existence. The great and abominable church, whose founder and preserver is Lucifer, will be no more. Communism and its system of force and anarchy and compulsion will be overthrown. There is an eternal principle, as eternal and everlasting as God himself, that truth will prevail. And the millennial era is the time appointed for right to prevail and for truth to triumph.

Why, why will all this come to pass? Because neither the world, nor worldliness, nor false churches, nor false religions can lead men to salvation. And the Millennium is designed to save souls. And how, how will it be brought to pass? In two ways: by the destruction of the wicked as the Millennium dawns, and by the labors of the Lord's witnesses during the early years of that blessed era of peace. We have already spoken of both of these eventualities. The vineyard is to be burned; every corruptible thing will be consumed; the proud and all they that do wickedly shall be burned as stubble. The tares, even now, are being bound in bundles preparatory to the great day of burning. The great and abominable church shall soon fall, and its zealots will be destroyed by devouring fire. Then those who remain, of all sects, parties, and denominations, being the upright among men, will be converted to the gospel so that the prophetic word may be fulfilled which says: "For the earth shall be filled with the knowledge of the glory of the Lord, as the waters cover the sea." (Hab. 2:14.)

Looking forward to this great day, the scriptures speak of the blessings to be bestowed upon the saints and the curses that will come upon those who practice false religion and who worship gods other than the Lord. "The Lord reigneth"—it is the millennial day—"let the earth rejoice," saith the Psalmist. "A fire goeth before him, and burneth up his enemies round about." It is the promised day of burning. "The hills melted like wax at the presence of the Lord, at the presence of the Lord of the whole earth." This we have considered in connection with the new earth and the new heavens that are to be. "The heavens declare his righteousness, and all the people see his glory." Blessed be the righteous in that day. And: "Con-

663

founded be all they that serve graven images, that boast themselves of idols." (Ps. 97:1-7.) Graven images and idols—these are the signs and symbols of false religions. They identified false worship anciently in the literal sense, and they identify it today in either a literal or a figurative sense, as the case may be.

Isaiah uses a similar approach to the destruction of false worship both at the dawn of and during the Millennium. After speaking of the era of peace in which "nation shall not lift up sword against nation, neither shall they learn war any more," he says: "Their land is also full of idols; they worship the work of their own hands, that which their own fingers have made." Such shall be the state of the masses of men when the Lord comes. Isaiah says that "the fear of the Lord and the glory of his majesty shall smite" the wicked. "For the day of the Lord of Hosts soon cometh upon all nations, yea, upon every one; yea, upon the proud and lofty, and upon every one who is lifted up, and he shall be brought low. . . . And the loftiness of man shall be bowed down, and the haughtiness of men shall be made low; and the Lord alone shall be exalted in that day." All this, in principle, we have heretofore set forth. Now note: "And the idols he shall utterly abolish." False worship shall cease. It will happen in a day, as it were, where Babylon is concerned, but it will take a little longer where those religious systems of lesser evil are concerned.

And what of those who have believed in false systems of salvation? "They shall go into the holes of the rocks, and into the caves of the earth," saith Isaiah, "for the fear of the Lord shall come upon them and the glory of his majesty shall smite them, when he ariseth to shake terribly the earth." But back to the false systems of religion themselves: "In that day a man shall cast his idols of silver, and his idols of gold, which he hath made for himself to worship, to the moles and to the bats." (2 Ne. 12:8-20; Isa. 2:4-20.) Men shall no longer worship gods they themselves have made. It matters not whether they are carved from stone or cast in molds. It matters not whether they are graven with an artificer's tools or described in the creeds of an apostate Christendom. Truly this is what Jeremiah foresaw when he recorded that the converts to the restored gospel in the latter days would say: "Surely our fathers have inherited lies, vanity, and things wherein there is no profit. Shall a man make gods unto himself, and they are no gods?" (Jer. 16:19-20.)

Micah received virtually the same vision of the millennial era that came to Isaiah. After bearing record of the peace that will prevail when nations no longer learn war, Micah tells us of the worship that will then prevail on earth. "For all people will walk every one in the name of his god," he says, "and we will walk in the name of the Lord our God for ever and ever. In that day . . . the Lord shall reign over them in mount Zion from henceforth, even for ever." (Micah 4:5-7.) The Lord then told Micah what would happen to the religions of the world when the Millennium was ushered in. The word so revealed is of such import that Jesus quoted it to the Nephites with a few additional expressions. These are the words of Deity to Israel: "And I will cut off witchcrafts out of thy land, and thou shalt have no more soothsayers; thy graven images I will also cut off, and thy standing images out of the midst of thee, and thou shalt no more worship the works of thy hands; and I will pluck up thy groves out of the midst of thee; so will I destroy thy cities." False worship shall cease; false gods shall be no more; and even the places of false worship, be they groves or cathedrals, shall be plucked up. Religions that are not of God will find no adherents.

And what happens when men reject false worship and turn to the Lord? The Lord gives this answer: "And it shall come to pass that all lyings, and deceivings, and envyings, and strifes, and priestcrafts, and whoredoms, shall be done away." True religion always has caused and always will cause men to forsake all evil and cleave unto the good. But

665

of those, even in the Millennium, who do not turn unto the Lord, Jesus says: "For it shall come to pass, saith the Father, that at that day whosoever will not repent and come unto my Beloved Son, them will I cut off from among my people, O house of Israel; and I will execute vengeance and fury upon them, even as upon the heathen, such as they have not heard." (3 Ne. 21:16-21; Micah 5:12-15.)

Why Satan Shall Be Bound

There is nothing that dramatizes better the difference between us men in this day, and our seed who will live in the millennial day, than the simple fact that then, in that day, Satan will be bound. Today he rages in the hearts of men; today he is the father of lies and the master of sin; today he fosters crime, promotes evil, and stirs up wars. His works, those in which his soul rejoices, are the works of the flesh. And "the works of the flesh," Paul tells us, are these: "Adultery, fornication, uncleanness, lasciviousness, idolatry, witchcraft, hatred, variance, emulations, wrath, strife, seditions, heresies, envyings, murders, drunkenness, revellings, and such like." (Gal. 5:19-21.) But in the coming day all this will cease. The Millennium will be a day of peace and righteousness. "And Satan shall be bound, that he shall have no place in the hearts of the children of men." (D&C 45:55.) Yea, "Satan shall be bound, [even] that old serpent, who is called the devil, and [he] shall not be loosed for the space of a thousand years." (D&C 88:110.)

When the Eternal Father announced his plan of salvation—a plan that called for a mortal probation for all his spirit children; a plan that required a Redeemer to ransom men from the coming fall; a plan that could only operate if mortal men had agency—when the Father announced his plan, when he chose Christ as the Redeemer and rejected Lucifer, then there was war in heaven. That war was a war of words; it was a conflict of ideologies; it was a rebellion against God and his laws. Lucifer sought to dethrone God, to sit himself on the divine throne, and to save all men without reference to their works. He sought to deny men their agency so they could not sin. He offered a mortal life of carnality and sensuality, of evil and crime and murder, following which all men would be saved. His offer was a philosophical impossibility. There must needs be an opposition in all things. Unless there are opposites, there is nothing. There can be no light without darkness, no heat without cold, no virtue without vice, no good without evil, no salvation without damnation.

And so, in the courts of heaven, the war of wars was waged. Christ and Michael and a mighty host of noble and great spirits preached the gospel of God and exhorted their brethren to follow the Father. Lucifer and his lieutenants preached another gospel, a gospel of fear and hate and lasciviousness and compulsion. They sought salvation without keeping the commandments, without overcoming the world, without choosing between opposites. And they "prevailed not; neither was their place found any more in heaven. And the great dragon was cast out, that old serpent, called the Devil, and Satan, which deceiveth the whole world: he was cast out into the earth, and his angels were cast out with him." And his legions, the legions of hell, are everywhere. They are "the third part of the stars of heaven," the one-third of the spirit children of the Father; and they were cast out of their heavenly home because of rebellion. And so the holy word says: "Woe to the inhabiters of the earth and of the sea! for the devil is come down unto you, having great wrath." And he goes forth "to make war" with all men and particularly with those who "keep the commandments of God, and have the testimony of Jesus Christ." (Rev. 12:4-17.) And the war that is now going on among men, the war between good and evil, is but a continuation of the war that began in heaven.

But wickedness shall soon be driven from the face of the earth. "For the great Millennium, of which I have spoken by the mouth of my servants, shall come. For Satan shall be bound, and when he is loosed again he shall only reign for a little season, and then cometh the end of the earth." (D&C 43:30-31.) John's graphic account of the binding of Satan comes to us in these words: "And I saw an angel come down from heaven, having the key of the bottomless pit and a great chain in his hand. And he laid hold on the dragon, that old serpent, which is the Devil, and Satan, and bound him a thousand years, and cast him into the bottomless pit, and shut him up, and set a seal upon him, that he should deceive the nations no more, till the thousand years should be fulfilled: and after that he must be loosed a little season." (Rev. 20:1-3.)

What does it mean to bind Satan? How is he bound? Our revelation says: "And in that day Satan shall not have power to tempt any man." (D&C 101:28.) Does this mean that power is withdrawn from Satan so that he can no longer entice men to do evil? Or does it mean that men no longer succumb to his enticements because their hearts are so set on righteousness that they refuse to forsake that which is good to follow him who is evil? Clearly it means the latter. Satan was not bound in heaven, in the very presence of God, in the sense that he was denied the right and power to preach false doctrine and to invite men to walk away from that God whose children they were; nay, in this sense, he could not have been bound in heaven, for even he must have his agency.

How, then, will Satan be bound during the Millennium? It will be by the righteousness of the people. Thus Nephi says: "The time cometh speedily that Satan shall have no more power over the hearts of the children of men; for the day soon cometh that all the proud and they who do wickedly shall be as stubble; and the day cometh that they must be burned." The destruction of the wicked sets the stage for millennial righteousness. When the wicked are burned, those who are left will not be susceptible to the promptings from beneath. "And the time cometh speedily that the righteous must be led up as calves of the stall, and the Holy

One of Israel must reign in dominion, and might, and power, and great glory.'' During the Millennium, when the Lord reigns, children will grow up in an environment of righteousness. No longer will the calves of Abraham's herds and the lambs of Jacob's flocks be lost in the deserts of sin; no longer will they forage for food by the wayside and drink water from stagnant pools; no longer will they be pulled down by the evils and designs of conspiring men. In the millennial day, in the household of faith, children will be brought up in the nurture and admonition of the Lord, as calves in the stall, as lambs in the sheepcote.

And in that day, the Holy One of Israel "gathereth his children from the four quarters of the earth; and he numbereth his sheep, and they know him; and there shall be one fold and one shepherd; and he shall feed his sheep, and in him they shall find pasture.'' It is, then, in this blessed millennial setting that the great proclamation about the binding of Satan is made. "And because of the righteousness of his people, Satan has no power; wherefore, he cannot be loosed for the space of many years; for he hath no power over the hearts of the people, for they dwell in righteousness, and the Holy One of Israel reigneth.'' (1 Ne. 22:15, 24-26.) Thus Satan is bound because he "shall have power over the hearts of the children of men no more, for a long time.'' (2 Ne. 30:18.) Thus the probationary nature of man's second estate is preserved even during the Millennium. It is not that men cannot sin, for the power is in them to do so—they have their agency—but it is that they do not sin because Satan is subject to them, and they are not enticed by his evil whisperings.

Come: Worship and Be Saved

The whole purpose of our mortal life is to gain salvation; it is to return to our Father as members of his family; it is to gain an inheritance of eternal life in his everlasting kingdom. Eternal life is made available through the atonement of Christ and comes to those who believe and obey. It

669

is reserved for the faithful who accept the gospel and live its laws. It comes to those who worship the Father in spirit and in truth. Thus all the purposes of life either do or should center in the glorious gospel.

We rejoice in the gospel, which is the plan of salvation, as have our forebears in all past dispensations. We seek to believe the Lord's law in spite of the philosophies of men, as did the faithful before us. We strive to live in harmony with the divine will notwithstanding the enticements of the flesh, as did they of old. And both we and they have looked forward and do look forward to the glorious promised day when the philosophies of men and the enticements of the flesh will no longer lead men away from the truths of salvation. The blessings of the millennial day of peace and righteousness and perfect worship—out of which full salvation comes—have always been known to true believers. Let us dip into the scriptural treasure house and see how those of old felt about the day of millennial worship.

In the day when only a handful of men, the few that were called Israel, worshipped the true God, and when with a mortal eye no man could foresee that the heathen nations would become one with the chosen people, the Spirit caused the Psalmist to acclaim unto the Lord: "All the earth shall worship thee, and shall sing unto thee; they shall sing to thy name." (Ps. 66:4.) "All nations whom thou hast made shall come and worship before thee, O Lord; and shall glorify thy name." (Ps. 86:9.) "O sing unto the Lord a new song," cried the Psalmist, "sing unto the Lord, all the earth. . . . For he cometh to judge the earth: he shall judge the world with righteousness, and the people with his truth." (Ps. 96:1, 13.)

Isaiah looked forward to the day when "the earth shall be full of the knowledge of the Lord, as the waters cover the sea." (Isa. 11:9.) "And in that day"—the millennial day in which all men worship the Father in spirit and in truth—his people shall say: "Behold, God is my salvation; I will trust, and not be afraid: for the Lord JEHOVAH is my strength and my song; he also is become my salvation." How few there were who worshipped at Jehovah's altars in Isaiah's day! How glorious it will be when all men in all nations turn unto him! When they do, this shall be their promise: "With joy shall ye draw water out of the wells of salvation." They shall all drink the living waters. "And in that day shall ye say, Praise the Lord, call upon his name, declare his doings among the people, make mention that his name is exalted. Sing unto the Lord; for he hath done excellent things: this is known in all the earth. Cry out and shout, thou inhabitant of Zion: for great is the Holy One of Israel in the midst of thee." (Isa. 12:1-6.) In that day, the day when "the Lord God will cause righteousness and praise to spring forth before all the nations," each of those who drinks water from the wells of salvation will say: "I will greatly rejoice in the Lord, my soul shall be joyful in my God; for he hath clothed me with the garments of salvation, he hath covered me with the robe of righteousness, as a bridegroom decketh himself with ornaments, and as a bride adorneth herself with her jewels." (Isa. 61:10-11.)

Truly the millennial era is the age of salvation. It has been established by the Lord to save souls. Truly he shall send to earth during that blessed period those who earned the right, by faith and devotion in the premortal life, to receive their mortal probation in a day of peace and righteousness. It is not unreasonable to suppose that more people will live on earth during the millennial era than in all the six millenniums that preceded it combined. And all those who live on the new earth with its new heavens shall be saved. The Lord be praised for his goodness and grace.

Chapter 54

THE NATURE OF MILLENNIAL WORSHIP

Worship in the Gospel Way

We say again—the concept must be engraved in our hearts with a pen of iron—we say again: The Millennium is designed to save souls. It has no other purpose. Accordingly, if salvation is gained by those who believe the gospel and obey its laws, and it is, then the gospel must continue during the Millennium. If the Church administers the gospel so as to make salvation possible, and it does, then the Church must endure through the Millennium. If the holy priesthood is the power to seal men up into eternal life, and it is, then this very delegation of power and authority from the Almighty must continue to bestow its beneficent blessings during the Millennium. The gospel in its everlasting fulness, including all of its saving powers, truths, and ordinances; The Church of Jesus Christ of Latter-day Saints, "the only true and living church upon the face of the whole earth" (D&C 1:30), the one place where salvation may be found; the Melchizedek Priesthood, which is "the power of an endless life" (Heb. 7:16), the power to create, to redeem, to save, and to exalt—these three (the gospel, the Church, and the priesthood) must and shall continue during the Millennium.

It may be that the name of the Church will change. Only in our dispensation has it borne its present name. It may become The Church of Jesus Christ of Millennial Saints. No matter, it will always be his church and his kingdom; it will always carry his name. It may be that we shall cease speaking of the Melchizedek Priesthood and call the Holy Order by its ancient name, ''the Holy Priesthood, after the Order of the Son of God.'' (D&C 107:3.) No matter, it will be the same power and the same authority, and it will serve the same purpose. We see no reason why the name of the gospel should change. It was called the gospel of God in the preexistent eternities, meaning it was the plan of salvation ordained and established by God the Father to save his children. It is known to us as the gospel of Jesus Christ because our Lord put all of its terms and conditions into full operation when he bore the sins of men in Gethsemane and laid down his life on the Golgothan cross. No doubt the new dispensation will be called the millennial dispensation rather than the dispensation of the fullness of times, as at present. Again, no matter, for all dispensations have their own names, each indicative of the age of the earth involved, but all are dispensations of the same eternal gospel, given from God in heaven and received by man on earth. As the Adamic dispensation merged into the Enochian, so shall our dispensation grow into the great millennial outpouring of divine grace.

Gospel laws and gospel ordinances are eternal. They are the same in all ages and on all worlds. During the Millennium children will be named and blessed by the elders of the kingdom. When those of the rising generation arrive at the years of accountability, they will be baptized in water and of the Spirit by legal administrators appointed so to act. Priesthood will be conferred upon young and old, and they will be ordained to offices therein as the needs of the ministry and their own salvation require. At the appropriate time each person will receive his patriarchal blessing, we suppose from the natural patriarch who presides in his family, as it was in Adamic days and as it was when Jacob blessed his sons. The saints will receive their endowments in the temples of the Lord, and they will receive the blessings of celestial marriage at their holy altars. And all of the faithful will have their callings and elections made sure and will be sealed up unto that eternal life which will come to them when they reach the age of a tree. We see no reasons why the ordinances of administering to the sick or the dedication of graves should continue, for disease and death shall be no more.

Gospel doctrines also are eternal. The saving truths never vary. They too are the same in all ages and on all earths. And they center in and bear testimony of the Lord Jesus Christ and his infinite and eternal atonement. During the Millennium the sweetness of song and the voice of sermon will unite to testify of all things pertaining to Christ and his goodness and grace. Thus our revelations say that when the year of Christ's redeemed is come, when the millennial era dawns, his saints "shall mention the loving kindness of their Lord, and all that he has bestowed upon them according to his goodness, and according to his loving kindness, forever and ever." And when the graves are opened and the saints "come forth and stand on the right hand of the Lamb, when he shall stand upon Mount Zion, and upon the holy city, the New Jerusalem," then, saith the holy word, "they shall sing the song of the Lamb, day and night forever and ever." (D&C 133:52, 56.)

In song and in sermon, the glad tidings of salvation will be stated and restated. The sermons will be the mind and will and voice of the Lord, and the very power of God unto salvation itself, for they will be spoken by the power of the Holy Ghost. And as to the song of the Lamb, the Lord has revealed to us some at least of the words it contains, words of worship and wonder and beauty. John's account tells us the saints sang "a new song." In praising Christ it acclaims: "For thou wast slain, and hast redeemed us to God by thy blood out of every kindred, and tongue, and people, and nation; and hast made us unto our God kings and priests: and we shall reign on the earth." Then John "heard the voice of many angels, . . . and the number of them was ten thousand times ten thousand, and thousands of thousands; saying with a loud voice, Worthy is the Lamb that was slain to receive power, and riches, and wisdom, and strength, and honour, and glory, and blessing." After this the ancient apostle says: "And every creature which is in heaven, and on the earth, and under the earth, and such as are in the sea, and all that are in them, heard I saying, Blessing, and honour, and glory, and power, be unto him that sitteth upon the throne, and unto the Lamb for ever and ever." (Rev. 5:9-13.) Truly, in our present state we have no way to comprehend or feel the glory and majesty of the worship that will prevail during the Millennium.

The Day of Millennial Revelation

We have the fulness of the everlasting gospel, meaning that we have all that is needed to gain the fulness of salvation. We have every truth, doctrine, and principle, every rite, power, and ordinance—all that is needed—to gain exaltation in the highest heaven of the celestial world. But we do not know all things; there are doctrines in endless array of which we know next to nothing; indeed, there are more things in the darkness of the unknown than there are in the light of the known. We do not even know what the faithful knew in Enoch's Zion, nor among the Nephites when they dwelt in righteousness for generations. We do not know what is on the sealed portion of the plates from which the Book of Mormon came. Ours is a day for drinking milk; the day when we, as a people at least, can partake of the meat of the word is in the future.

That future is millennial. In that day, "all things shall become new," saith the Lord, "that my knowledge and glory may dwell upon all the earth. . . . Yea, verily I say unto you, in that day when the Lord shall come, he shall reveal all things—Things which have passed, and hidden things which no man knew, things of the earth, by which it was made, and the purpose and the end thereof—Things most precious, things that are above, and things that are beneath, things that are in the earth, and upon the earth, and in heaven." (D&C 101:25, 32-34.) As we ponder these heaven-sent words, we are led to exclaim: Thanks be to him who is the Way, the Truth, and the Life, who knows all things and who seeks to pour out his revelations, and all the knowledge of eternity, upon all who will receive them. Ere long the dark veil of ignorance and unbelief that covers the earth and blinds the minds of men shall be pierced. Light and truth will fall from heaven as does rain from the clouds above.

The knowledge of God, the knowledge of those Gods whom it is life eternal to know, shall be in every heart. No longer will theologians suppose that God is a spirit essence that fills immensity while he dwells in the human heart. No longer will philosophers pontificate about some great first cause that inexplicably brought order into a chaotic universe. No longer will Babylonish churches place crucifixes in the hands, or the images of Diana of the Ephesians, as it were, and no longer will they worship the works of their own hands in the great cathedrals of Christendom. The knowledge of God, the truth about God, the fact that he is a Holy Man, will come by revelation into every human heart. The knowledge of God will cover the earth.

All things are to be revealed in the millennial day. The sealed part of the Book of Mormon will come forth; the brass plates will be translated; the writings of Adam and Enoch and Noah and Abraham and prophets without number will be revealed. We shall learn a thousand times more about the earthly ministry of the Lord Jesus than we now know. We shall learn great mysteries of the kingdom that were not even known to those of old who walked and talked with the Eternal One. We shall learn the details of the creation and the origin of man and what fools mortals are to follow the fads of the evolving evolutionary nonsense that litters the textbooks of academia. Nothing in or on or over the earth will be withheld from human ken, for eventually man, if he is to be as his Maker, must know all things.

Hear in this connection these words of Nephi: In that day, "the earth shall be full of the knowledge of the Lord as the waters cover the sea. Wherefore, the things of all nations shall be made known; yea, all things shall be made known unto the children of men. There is nothing which is secret save it shall be revealed; there is no work of darkness save it shall be made manifest in the light; and there is nothing which is sealed upon the earth save it shall be loosed. Wherefore, all things which have been revealed unto the children of men shall at that day be revealed." (2 Ne. 30:15-18.) Surely man could not ask for more than this in the way of light and truth and knowledge, and yet expect to remain in the flesh as a mortal and be in process of working out his salvation. Surely this is the day in which the Lord shall fulfill the promise of holy writ that says: "God shall give unto you knowledge by his Holy Spirit, yea, by the unspeakable gift of the Holy Ghost, [knowledge] that has not been revealed since the world was until now; which our forefathers have awaited with anxious expectation to be revealed in the last times, which their minds were pointed to by the angels, as held in reserve for the fulness of their glory; a time to come in the which nothing shall be withheld, whether there be one God or many gods, they shall be manifest." (D&C 121:26-28.) That this outpouring of divine goodness has already commenced is not open to question. That it will continue, in far greater measure, after our Lord comes again, who can doubt?

The Day of the Second Comforter

There is a divine outpouring of heavenly grace and power that exceeds anything else known to men or angels. There is a Spirit-conferred gift that is greater than anything else of which the human mind can conceive. There is a spiritual endowment so wondrous and great, so beyond comprehension and understanding, so divine and godlike in its nature, that it cannot be described in words. It can only be felt by the power of the Spirit. Those only who are the peers of the prophets and who mingle with seers on equal terms; those only who like Isaiah and Ezekiel and John and Paul have laid their all on the altar and have risen above every carnal desire; those only who are in harmony with the Lord and his Spirit and who keep his commandments as they are kept by the angels of God in heaven—they alone can receive this gift. It is called the Second Comforter.

Our blessed Lord—alone with the Twelve in the upper room a few hours before he went to Gethsemane, where great gouts of blood would drop from every pore as he bore the sins of all men; and a few hours before, on the cross of Calvary, he would cry, "It is finished," and permit his spirit to leave the body—our blessed Lord gave his beloved friends this promise: "I will not leave you comfortless: I will come to you. Yet a little while, and the world seeth me no more; but ye see me: because I live, ye shall live also." Christ after his death will come to them. They will see him, and he will comfort them. Yea, they will both see him and feel the nail marks in his hands and in his feet and thrust their hands into his riven side. He will eat before them, and their sorrow will be turned into joy. And because of his glorious rising from the Arimathean's tomb, they too shall conquer death and break the shackles of the grave.

"At that day ye shall know that I am in my Father, and ye in me, and I in you." They will be one with him as he is one with his Father. "He that hath my commandments, and keepeth them, he it is that loveth me: and he that loveth me shall be loved of my Father, and I will love him, and will manifest myself to him." The promise is not theirs alone—the Twelve are but the pattern; all that they receive will come also to every faithful person who abides the law that entitles him to receive the same gifts and blessings. Jesus, after his death and resurrection, will manifest himself to all who have faith enough to rend the veil and see their Lord.

Jesus was then asked: "Lord, how is it that thou wilt

manifest thyself unto us, and not unto the world?'' His reply: ''If a man love me, he will keep my words: and my Father will love him, and we will come unto him, and make our abode with him.'' (John 14:18-23.) Not only will the Lord Jesus appear to the faithful, but he, in his goodness and grace, will also manifest the Father. Mortal man will see the Father and the Son. And that there will be no doubt as to the meaning of our Lord's words, it is written in our revelations: ''John 14:23—The appearing of the Father and the Son, in that verse, is a personal appearance; and the idea that the Father and the Son dwell in a man's heart is an old sectarian notion, and is false.'' (D&C 130:3.)

There are, of course, two Comforters. The Holy Ghost is the Comforter offered the saints in connection with baptism. He is a revelator and a sanctifier; he is the Holy Spirit. The gift of the Holy Ghost is the right to the constant companionship of this member of the Godhead based on faithfulness. ''Now what is this other Comforter?'' the Prophet Joseph Smith asked. His answer: ''It is no more nor less than the Lord Jesus Christ Himself; and this is the sum and substance of the whole matter; that when any man obtains this last Comforter, he will have the personage of Jesus Christ to attend him, or appear unto him from time to time, and even He will manifest the Father unto him, and they will take up their abode with him, and the visions of the heavens will be opened unto him, and the Lord will teach him face to face, and he may have a perfect knowledge of the mysteries of the Kingdom of God; and this is the state and place the ancient Saints arrived at when they had such glorious visions—Isaiah, Ezekiel, John upon the Isle of Patmos, St. Paul in the three heavens, and all the Saints who held communion with the general assembly and Church of the Firstborn.'' (*Teachings*, pp. 150-51.)

Those who receive the Second Comforter shall see the Lord. He will attend them, appear to them from time to time, and teach them face to face. It was so with the ancient Twelve after Jesus rose from the dead; it will be so with all who attain like spiritual heights, for God is no respecter of persons. Obedience to the same laws always brings the same blessings. Thus the divine word acclaims: "Verily, thus saith the Lord: It shall come to pass that every soul who forsaketh his sins and cometh unto me, and calleth on my name, and obeyeth my voice, and keepeth my commandments, shall see my face and know that I am." (D&C 93:1.)

Those who receive the Second Comforter see the visions of eternity and have a perfect knowledge of the mysteries of the kingdom. "And to them will I reveal all mysteries, yea, all the hidden mysteries of my kingdom from days of old," saith the Lord, "and for ages to come, will I make known unto them the good pleasure of my will concerning all things pertaining to my kingdom. Yea, even the wonders of eternity shall they know, and things to come will I show them, even the things of many generations. And their wisdom shall be great, and their understanding reach to heaven; and before them the wisdom of the wise shall perish, and the understanding of the prudent shall come to naught. For by my Spirit will I enlighten them, and by my power will I make known unto them the secrets of my will—yea, even those things which eye has not seen, nor ear heard, nor yet entered into the heart of man." (D&C 76:7-10.)

Among those who received the Second Comforter are the three Nephites, whom we have been using as a pattern and type of what men will be like in the Millennium. These three American apostles "were caught up into heaven, and saw and heard unspeakable things. And it was forbidden them that they should utter; neither was it given unto them power that they could utter the things which they saw and heard; and whether they were in the body or out of the body, they could not tell; for it did seem unto them like a transfiguration of them, that they were changed from this body of flesh into an immortal state, that they could behold the things of God." (3 Ne. 28:13-15.)

Now, having in mind these concepts about the Second Comforter, and knowing that all those who so obtain have their callings and elections made sure, let us catch the vision, if we can, of one of the great prophetic utterances of Jeremiah. "Behold, the days come, saith the Lord"—and we shall soon show that the days involved are millennial—"that I will make a new covenant with the house of Israel, and with the house of Judah." Hear it and mark it well: it will be a new covenant, a new and an everlasting covenant; it will be the fulness of the everlasting gospel, not in name only, but in fact and in deed, in active operation in the lives of men. It will be "not according to the covenant that I made with their fathers in the day that I took them by the hand to bring them out of the land of Egypt; which my covenant they brake, although I was an husband unto them, saith the Lord." When the Lord brought Israel out of Egypt he offered them the fulness of the gospel. Moses held the Melchizedek Priesthood, and his people could have lived the higher gospel law had they chosen to do so. But they broke not only the gospel covenant but also the Mosaic or lesser covenant, at least in large measure.

"But this shall be the covenant that I will make with the house of Israel; after those days, saith the Lord, I will put my law in their inward parts, and write it in their hearts; and will be their God, and they shall be my people." There will be a day when latter-day Israel will serve the Lord with all their hearts and make themselves worthy of the fulness of his glory. "And they shall teach no more every man his neighbour, and every man his brother, saying, Know the Lord: for they shall all know me, from the least of them unto the greatest of them, saith the Lord: for I will forgive their iniquity, and I will remember their sin no more." (Jer. 31:31-34.)

Joseph Smith tells us that Jeremiah's prophecy will be fulfilled during the Millennium. The Prophet speaks of making one's calling and election sure and of the sealing power whereby "we may be sealed up unto the day of redemption." Then he says: "This principle ought (in its proper place) to be taught, for God hath not revealed anything to Joseph, but what He will make known unto the Twelve, and even the least Saint may know all things as fast as he is able to bear them, for the day must come when no man need say to his neighbor, Know ye the Lord; for all shall know Him (who remain) from the least to the greatest." These are the very words of Jeremiah's prophecy; and they will find their complete fulfillment among those "who remain," those who abide the day, those who gain an inheritance on the new earth when it receives its paradisiacal glory again. "How is this to be done?" the Prophet asks. How shall men come to know the Lord and understand all the hidden mysteries of his kingdom without a teacher? His answer: "It is to be done by this sealing power, and the other Comforter spoken of, which will be manifest by revelation." (*Teachings*, p. 149.)

Men will know God in the millennial day because they see him. He will teach them face to face. They will know the mysteries of his kingdom because they are caught up to the third heaven, as was Paul. They will receive the Second Comforter. The millennial day is the day of the Second Comforter, and whereas but few have been blessed with this divine association in times past, great hosts will be so blessed in times to come.

What, then, will be the nature of worship during the Millennium? It will be pure and perfect, and through it men will become inheritors of eternal life. And in this connection, be it known that it is the privilege of the saints today to separate themselves from the world and to receive millennial blessings in their lives. And any person who today abides the laws that will be kept during the Millennium will receive, here and now, the spirit and blessings of the Millennium in his life, even though he is surrounded by a world of sin and evil. And so we say, in the language of Joseph Smith as he finished the record of the vision of the three degrees of glory: "Great and marvelous are the works of the Lord, and the mysteries of his kingdom which he showed unto us, which surpass all understanding in glory, and in might, and in dominion; Which he commanded us we should not write while we were yet in the Spirit, and are not lawful for man to utter; Neither is man capable to make them known, for they are only to be seen and understood by the power of the Holy Spirit, which God bestows on those who love him, and purify themselves before him; To whom he grants this privilege of seeing and knowing for themselves; That through the power and manifestation of the Spirit, while in the flesh, they may be able to bear his presence in the world of glory. And to God and the Lamb be glory, and honor, and dominion forever and ever. Amen.'' (D&C 76:114-119.)

Chapter 55

WATCH AND
BE READY

The Watchmen on Mount Ephraim

Come we now to the climax of all our stumbling and faltering words of exposition, and of exhortation, and of testimony. Come we now to the reason we have written, in weakness and in simplicity, this work. Come we now to the great object and purpose that has led us to expound so many divine doctrines, to proclaim so fervently the reality of the mighty restoration, and to testify with such unbounded zeal of the goodness and grace of that Lord who will soon descend from heaven with the shout of the archangel. That object and purpose is two-pronged:

1. It is to persuade men to believe in the Lord Jesus Christ, who when he first came worked out the infinite and eternal atonement and brought life and immortality to light through the gospel, and who shall soon come again in great glory and with wondrous power to complete the salvation of men and to live and reign on earth with the righteous for a thousand years.

2. It is to encourage those who believe so to live that, whether in life or in death, they shall abide the day of his coming and qualify to be with him forever.

And so we now say to all men everywhere, to men of all sects, parties, and denominations, but more particularly to those who believe: Hear ye the words of the watchmen, and be ye ready for that which is soon to be. "For there shall be a day"—and as the Lord lives, that day is now—"that the watchmen upon the mount Ephraim shall cry, Arise ye, and let us go up to Zion unto the Lord our God." (Jer. 31:6.) Go ye, go ye up to Zion; find refuge in one of her stakes, and be ye one with those who are pure in heart.

The Lord has prepared a feast of good things for all who come to Zion. The word has gone forth: "Prepare the table, watch in the watchtower, eat, drink." (Isa. 21:5.) The table is now loaded with meat and drink. All men are invited to come and feast on the good word of God and to drink of the waters of life, while the watchman in the watchtower stands ready to warn them of the desolations and plagues and sorrows of the last days. The time of restitution has arrived, the fulness of the everlasting gospel is once again on earth, the Book of Mormon bears its witness of Joseph Smith and of Jesus Christ and of the setting up anew of the Church and kingdom of God on earth. Angelic ministrants have conferred priesthood and keys upon men; Elijah and Elias and Moses and many prophets have restored their keys and powers; the mountain where is the Lord's house is now known in all the earth. The Church of Jesus Christ of Latter-day Saints, which administers that gospel whereby salvation comes, is now going forth, "clear as the moon, and fair as the sun, and terrible as an army with banners." (D&C 5:14.) The gospel is now being preached in one nation after another as a witness unto all people so that the end may come at the appointed time. From the spiritual standpoint, all things are in process of fulfillment so that the Lord may come at the time of his choosing.

It is in this setting that the Lord says: "Go, set a watchman, let him declare what he seeth." Let him warn the saints and the world of the wars and desolations that are to be. Let him cry repentance and invite all men to come unto Christ and be saved. Let him proclaim the everlasting gospel to the world. Let him invite men to flee from the abomination of desolation to be poured out upon the wicked in the last days. One of his cries, soon to come forth, will announce: "Babylon is fallen, is fallen."

Let every man find a watchman that he may be warned of the dangers ahead. Let him ask: "Watchman, what of the night?" And the watchman will say: "The morning cometh, and also the night: if ye will enquire, enquire ye: return, come." (Isa. 21:6, 9, 11-12.) The morning breaks, the shadows flee. Those who walk in the light of the gospel are no longer in darkness. But the night also cometh for those who turn from the light. Let all men seek light and prepare for the Second Coming. Let them inquire: Where is the word that was promised to come forth by angelic ministration when the hour of the Lord's judgment was nigh? Let them return to the ancient sheepfold; let them come to Zion, there to worship the Lord our God. Let the watchmen on Mount Ephraim raise the warning voice and let the honest in heart among all people flee to Zion, for the day of desolation is upon us.

Warnings from the Chief Watchman

Jesus himself is more pointed and express in commanding men to live righteously in order to abide the day of his Second Coming than are any of his servants. He, as the Chief Watchman on the towers of Israel, tells us in plain and powerful phrases what our fate will be if we fail to prepare for that dread day, and also of the blessings that await us if we make ourselves ready. His words abound on almost every subject throughout this work. Here we shall consider those that constitute the express commands to watch, pray, and be ready for the coming day.

On Olivet, after giving the parable of the fig tree, after saying no one would know the day or the hour of his coming, after comparing his return to the flood that swept men to a watery grave in the day of Noah, Jesus said: "Then shall be fulfilled that which is written"—he is alluding to some scripture lost to us—"that in the last days, two shall be in the field, the one shall be taken, and the other left; two shall be grinding at the mill, the one shall be taken, and the other left; and what I say unto one, I say unto all men; watch, therefore, for you know not at what hour your Lord doth come." (JS-M 1:44-46.) These words can be used in a dual way. They can be applied to the destruction of the wicked in the day of burning, when only the righteous abide the day, or they can be applied to the gathering of the remainder of the elect by the angels, when they are caught up to meet their Lord, with those who are unworthy of such a quickening being left on earth. Luke makes this latter application to words of the same meaning and then explains: "This he [Jesus] spake, signifying the gathering of his saints; and of angels descending and gathering the remainder unto them; the one from the bed, the other from the grinding, and the other from the field, whithersoever he listeth. For verily there shall be new heavens, and a new earth, wherein dwelleth righteousness. And there shall be no unclean thing; for the earth becoming old, even as a garment, having waxed in corruption, wherefore it vanisheth away, and the footstool remaineth sanctified, cleansed from all sin." (JST, Luke 17:38-40.) No matter which usage is made of the teaching involved, the conclusion is the same: watch, be ready, be worthy; there is safety in no other course.

Then Jesus, continuing the Olivet Discourse, said: "But know this, if the good man of the house had known in what watch the thief would come, he would have watched, and would not have suffered his house to have been broken up, but would have been ready. Therefore be ye also ready, for in such an hour as ye think not, the Son of Man cometh." This illustration is one of great force and power, and it takes on new and deeper meaning as wickedness, including burglary and robbery and stealing, all increase as the day of his coming nears.

Our Lord next gives another illustration with a dual application. It can refer to self-appointed servants (ministers and priests) who serve in an apostate Christendom in the last days, and it can also apply to true ministers in the day of restoration who do not walk as becometh men of Christ. "Who, then, is a faithful and wise servant," he asks, "whom his lord hath made ruler over his household, to give them meat in due season?" The Lord's ministers are appointed to feed the flock of God. "Blessed is that servant whom his lord, when he cometh, shall find so doing; and verily I say unto you, he shall make him ruler over all his goods." In the true sense this could only apply to the elders in latter-day Israel who, in fact, are the only legal administrators on earth, whose authority is traced to the Lord, and whose power and authority come in full measure from him. "But if that evil servant shall say in his heart: My lord delayeth his coming, and shall begin to smite his fellow-servants, and to eat and drink with the drunken, The lord of that servant shall come in a day when he looketh not for him, and in an hour that he is not aware of, and shall cut him asunder, and shall appoint him his portion with the hypocrites; there shall be weeping and gnashing of teeth. And thus cometh the end of the wicked, according to the prophecy of Moses, saying: They shall be cut off from among the people; but the end of the earth is not yet, but by and by." (JS-M 1:47-55.)

Mark alone of our Gospel authors preserves for us these blessed words of counsel, counsel that has double the meaning in this dispensation that it had when spoken some two thousand years ago: "Take ye heed, watch and pray: for ye know not when the time is." How true this is, even today, when we can put almost all of the signs of the times into a reasonably certain chronological order, and when we know that nearly all of them have already been shown forth. "For the Son of man is as a man taking a far journey, who left his house, and gave authority to his servants, and to every man his work, and commanded the porter to watch. Watch ye therefore: for ye know not when the master of the house cometh, at even, or at midnight, or at the cockcrowing, or in the morning: Lest coming suddenly he find you sleeping. And what I say unto you I say unto all, Watch." (Mark 13:33-37.)

As to the world, almost all who dwell therein are asleep. They know not that the promised signs are unfolding on earth and in heaven and are easily discerned by the faithful. They know not that the times of restitution have commenced that the times of refreshing may come. They know not that the Book of Mormon has come forth, according to the ancient promises, and that the everlasting gospel in all its glorious fulness is once more on earth. They know not that the Lord has sent his messenger to prepare the way before his face and that even now voices of legal administrators are crying: Behold, and lo, the Bridegroom cometh; go ye out to meet him. And as to the Church, many in it are drowsy and some sleep. The eyes of many of the saints are heavy with the sleep of the world; long hours of past vigilance have caused them to suppose that the Lord delayeth his coming, and they find it easy to eat and drink with the wicked and to live after the manner of carnal men. They are not awake and alert, watching at even, and at midnight, and at cock-crowing, and in the morning.

Luke alone of our Gospel authors records for our guidance and enlightenment these words directed to all disciples, but more especially to those of us who live at this time when the hour of our Lord's coming is nigh: "Let my disciples therefore take heed to themselves, lest at any time their hearts be overcharged with surfeiting, and drunkenness, and cares of this life, and that day come upon them unawares." Let it come upon the world unawares, as it will, but the saints of God, the children of light, those who know the signs of the times, those who have the gift of the Holy Ghost, God forbid that it take them unawares! "For as a snare shall it come on all them who dwell on the face of the whole earth." The wicked will be caught in the snare and shall not escape; the righteous will be assembled in holy places awaiting the hour when they shall be caught up to meet the Lord in the air. "And what I say unto one, I say unto all, Watch ye therefore, and pray always, and keep my commandments, that ye may be counted worthy to escape all these things which shall come to pass, and to stand before the Son of man when he shall come clothed in the glory of his Father." (JST, Luke 21:34-36.)

So speaks the Lord Jesus to the members of his Church, his Church in all ages, but particularly in these last days when the end is drawing nigh. All men are invited to forsake the world and come into the true kingdom. But the warning is to Church members, to the saints of the Most High, to the elect of God who have made covenant in the waters of baptism to serve their Lord with all their strength. To them, and in a general sense to all men, the Lord's call is: Let not drunkenness lead you to destruction. True saints are sober, reflective, in control of their faculties. Drunkenness is of the devil. Cease from surfeiting. Be not intemperate in indulging in food and drink. Avoid gluttony and winebibbing. Flee from all these things lest your hearts be set on carnal rather than spiritual things. Be not overcome by the cares of this life. It is not temporal pursuits, business dealings, civil and political positions, educational attainments, and such like things, that really matter in life. The cares of this life so often keep even the saints from preparing for the rewards of the life to come.

Watch: in Life or in Death

None of us know whether we will be alive when the Lord comes or not. Life hangs on a thread, and death is only a breath away. Nor does it matter whether we meet the Lord in life or in death if we have watched for his coming and are ready for the meeting. "I testify . . . that the coming of the Son of Man is nigh, even at your doors," the Prophet Joseph Smith said. "If our souls and our bodies are not looking forth for the coming of the Son of Man; and after we are dead, if we are not looking forth, we shall be among those who are calling for the rocks to fall upon them." (*Teachings*, p. 160.) In life or in death it is the same.

If we are prepared to meet him in life, we will be prepared to meet him in death. Hence the call of all the prophets to the saints in their days, no matter what age was involved, has been: Be ye ready now; prepare to meet thy God as though he would come in whatever dispensation is involved.

Echoing the feelings and sentiments of their Lord and writing as guided by the Holy Spirit, they of old counseled the saints in their day (and the saints in ours!) along these lines: Peter, the chief apostle, said: "Gird up the loins of your mind, be sober, and hope to the end for the grace that is to be brought unto you at the revelation of Jesus Christ." (1 Pet. 1:13.) Also: "The end of all things is at hand: be ye therefore sober, and watch unto prayer." (1 Pet. 4:7.) And yet again: "Seeing then that all these things shall be dissolved"—when the Lord comes—"what manner of persons ought ye to be in all holy conversation and godliness, looking for and hasting unto the coming of the day of God, wherein the heavens being on fire shall be dissolved, and the elements shall melt with fervent heat?" His answer: "We, according to his promise, look for new heavens and a new earth, wherein dwelleth righteousness. Wherefore, beloved, seeing that ye look for such things, be diligent that ye may be found of him in peace, without spot, and blameless." (2 Pet. 3:11-14.)

James gives us this counsel: "Be patient therefore, brethren, unto the coming of the Lord. Behold, the husbandman waiteth for the precious fruit of the earth, and hath long patience for it, until he receive the early and latter rain. Be ye also patient; stablish your hearts: for the coming of the Lord draweth nigh. Grudge not one against another, brethren, lest ye be condemned: behold, the judge standeth before the door." (James 5:7-9.) And from Paul we take these words: "Let us not sleep, as do others; but let us watch and be sober." He is speaking to the saints. "For they that sleep sleep in the night; and they that be drunken are drunken in the night. But let us, who are of the

691

day, be sober, putting on the breastplate of faith and love; and for an helmet, the hope of salvation." (1 Thes. 5:6-8.)

In all ages and as part of all dispensations the divine word is the same. In our day, as the end draws near, the Lord says: "Be faithful, praying always, having your lamps trimmed and burning, and oil with you, that you may be ready at the coming of the Bridegroom—For behold, verily, verily, I say unto you, that I come quickly." (D&C 33:17-18.) "Abide ye in the liberty wherewith ye are made free; entangle not yourselves in sin, but let your hands be clean, until the Lord comes." (D&C 88:86.) "The coming of the Lord draweth nigh, and it overtaketh the world as a thief in the night—Therefore, gird up your loins, that you may be the children of light, and that day shall not overtake you as a thief." (D&C 106:4-5.) "Go ye out from Babylon. Be ye clean that bear the vessels of the Lord. Call your solemn assemblies, and speak often one to another. And let every man call upon the name of the Lord. . . . Awake and arise and go forth to meet the Bridegroom; behold and lo, the Bridegroom cometh; go ye out to meet him. Prepare yourselves for the great day of the Lord. Watch, therefore, for ye know neither the day nor the hour." (D&C 133:5-6, 10-11.)

"Behold, I come as a thief. Blessed is he that watcheth, and keepeth his garments." (Rev. 16:15.) He that hath ears to hear, let him hear.

Chapter 56

CELESTIAL REST AND GLORY

The Celestial Earth

After the Millennium—what? Is this great day when there shall be peace on earth and goodwill in the hearts of men—is it an end in itself? Is this the day of rest and righteousness, when there is neither sorrow, disease, nor death—is it the *summum bonum* of all things? When Israel triumphs and wickedness ceases and the Lord Jehovah lives and reigns on earth—will we then reach the great end and goal toward which all things point? Or is the millennial era but a way and a means to prepare most of the spirit hosts of an Almighty Elohim for even greater heights of joy and peace, of glory and exaltation?

We have in this work, if we may borrow a concept from Isaiah, set forth "the word of the Lord . . . precept . . . upon precept, precept upon precept; line upon line, line upon line; here a little, and there a little." Step by step, point by point, doctrine by doctrine, "with stammering lips" and a faltering "tongue," we have built a house for the Millennial Messiah, as it were. In a dark and benighted world where the "tables" of doctrine "are full of vomit and filthiness, so that there is no place clean," we have sought to set forth what the Lord has revealed about his second coming and his reign in glory on the paradisiacal earth. Much that we have said is the milk of the word, but some portions have been meat and can be understood only by those "that are weaned from the milk, and drawn from the breasts." (Isa. 28:8-13.)

But all that we have said, and all that we might say if our insight were greater and our understanding more expanded, all our words are but an attempt to show the way to the eternal destiny far greater than anything millennial. The Millennium is simply a means to an end; it is that portion of the earth's temporal continuance during which billions of our Father's children will so live as to gain eternal life. Out of the millennial era will come, without question, more saved souls than will result from all the rest of the ages combined. And after the Millennium will come celestial rest and glory.

This earth is destined to be a celestial sphere. It is now in a telestial state and will return to its Edenic or terrestrial state during the Millennium. Its final destiny, in John's language, is to be "a sea of glass like unto crystal" (Rev. 4:6), which our revelation identifies as "the earth, in its sanctified, immortal, and eternal state." (D&C 77:1.) The inspired word also says: "The angels do not reside on a planet like this earth; but they reside in the presence of God, on a globe like a sea of glass and fire. . . . The place where God resides is a great Urim and Thummim. This earth, in its sanctified and immortal state, will be made like unto crystal and will be a Urim and Thummim to the inhabitants who dwell thereon." (D&C 130:6-9.)

During the Millennium, Satan is bound. Because of the righteousness of the people, he has no power over them. "And when the thousand years are expired," John tells us, "Satan shall be loosed out of his prison." (Rev. 20:7.) This means that once again men will begin to give heed to his enticements. Satan was bound among the Nephites during their golden era. None of the people were then subject to his wiles; all lived in righteousness, and all were saved. But in A.D. 201, "there began to be among them those who were lifted up in pride, such as the wearing of costly ap-

694

parel, and all manner of fine pearls, and of the fine things of the world. And from that time forth they did have their goods and their substance no more common among them. And they began to be divided into classes; and they began to build up churches unto themselves to get gain, and began to deny the true church of Christ." (4 Ne. 1:24-26.) Soon there were persecution, crime, murder, and evil of every sort. So shall it be at the end of the Millennium. Men will begin again, gradually, to partake of the things of this world; pride and carnality and crime will commence anew; true believers will be persecuted and false churches will arise. Satan will be loosed because he is no longer bound by the righteousness of the people.

"And when he [Satan] is loosed again he shall only reign for a little season, and then cometh the end of the earth." This "little season" is presumed to be another thousand years. The reasoning is that Christ came in the meridian of time, which means both the high point in time and the middle of time. The millennial era will be the seventh period of one thousand years of this earth's temporal continuance; thus an added thousand-year period is needed to place the meridian of time in the midpoint in history. But be that as it may, "he that liveth in righteousness"—at the time of the actual end of the earth—"shall be changed in the twinkling of an eye, and the earth shall pass away so as by fire." This will be a second day of burning, the day when this earth becomes a celestial globe. "And the wicked shall go away into unquenchable fire, and their end no man knoweth on earth, nor ever shall know, until they come before me in judgment." (D&C 43:31-33.)

"And again, verily, verily, I say unto you," saith the Lord, "that when the thousand years are ended, and men again begin to deny their God, then will I spare the earth but for a little season." The language here bears out the concept that apostasy and its consequent evil way of life will be the key that opens the prison in which Satan is bound. "And the end shall come, and the heaven and the earth shall be consumed and pass away, and there shall be a new heaven and a new earth." There was a new earth and new heavens when the Millennium commenced. This is a second new heaven and new earth; it is the celestial earth and its heaven. The language in each instance is similar, but the meaning is different. In one instance the new earth is the paradisiacal earth; in this case it is the celestial globe. "For all old things shall pass away, and all things shall become new, even the heaven and the earth, and all the fulness thereof, both men and beasts, the fowls of the air, and the fishes of the sea; and not one hair, neither mote, shall be lost, for it is the workmanship of mine hand." (D&C 29:22-25.) All forms of life shall then be immortal; all shall come forth from death and live in a resurrected state forever; the resurrection applies to men and animals and fowls and fishes and creeping things—all shall rise in immortality and live forever in their destined orders and spheres of existence.

The war that began in heaven and has continued on earth will reach its climax during the little season after the Millennium. John says that when Satan is loosed, he "shall go out to deceive the nations which are in the four quarters of the earth, Gog and Magog, to gather them together to battle: the number of whom is as the sand of the sea." Once again war shall cover the earth; it will be Armageddon all over again. "And they"—the armies assembled in the forces of Lucifer—"went up on the breadth of the earth, and compassed the camp of the saints about, and the beloved city: and fire came down from God out of heaven, and devoured them." (Rev. 20:8-9.) Then Satan was cast out into outer darkness forever.

In latter-day revelation the account is given thus: "And Satan shall be bound, that old serpent, who is called the devil, and shall not be loosed for the space of a thousand years. And then he shall be loosed for a little season, that he may gather together his armies." The war in heaven was a war of ideologies; it was a war to determine how men would be saved; and so it is in the warfare of the world today. Lucifer's forces advocate a plan of salvation that is contrary to the Lord's true plan. And in the process, armies assemble and wars are fought, for the devil delights in destruction. And so shall it be after the Millennium. "And Michael, the seventh angel, even the archangel, shall gather together his armies, even the hosts of heaven." The saints of God, those who are in harmony with the divine will, those who are subject to priesthood direction, those who believe in Christ and align themselves in his cause, they shall take direction from Michael, who, under Christ, holds the keys of salvation for all His children. "And the devil shall gather together his armies; even the hosts of hell, and shall come up to battle against Michael and his armies." It is a continuation of the war in heaven. "And then cometh the battle of the great God; and the devil and his armies shall be cast away into their own place, that they shall not have power over the saints any more at all. For Michael shall fight their battles, and shall overcome him who seeketh the throne of him who sitteth upon the throne, even the Lamb. This is the glory of God, and the sanctified; and they shall not any more see death." (D&C 88:110-116.)

The Meek Inherit the Earth

Who shall dwell on the celestial earth? To answer this, we need but inquire who dwells on our present earth, and who shall dwell on the paradisiacal earth that is to be? And as we are aware, any mortal can live on this present low and fallen earth who lives at least a telestial law, because this earth is in a telestial state. Those who abide the day of our Lord's return, and who thus remain to live on the new earth with its new heavens, must live at least a terrestrial law, for the earth will then return to its Edenic or terrestrial state. And in the day of burning when this earth becomes in fact a celestial globe, none will be able to live on its surface unless they live a celestial law.

Telestial law is the law of evil, carnality, and corruption. Those who so live develop telestial bodies, which can stand telestial glory, which is found in a telestial kingdom. Terrestrial law is the law of decency and uprightness from a worldly standpoint. Those who conform to this higher order thereby create for themselves terrestrial bodies, which in turn can stand terrestrial glory and go to a terrestrial kingdom. Celestial law is the law of the gospel; it is the law of Christ. It calls upon men to forsake the world and rise above every carnal and evil thing. It calls upon men to repent and be baptized and receive the sanctifying power of the Holy Spirit of God. It requires that they become new creatures of the Holy Ghost. Only those who so live acquire thereby celestial bodies; only such bodies can stand celestial glory, and this glory is found only in a celestial kingdom. Since the final destiny of this earth is to become a celestial globe, it thereby becomes the ultimate and highest heaven for all the faithful who have lived on its surface.

One of several identifying characteristics of those who live a celestial law and hence will have an eternal inheritance on this earth is to call them the meek of the earth. In the scriptural sense the meek are the God-fearing and the righteous. Jesus said of himself: "I am meek and lowly in heart." (Matt. 11:29.) The meek are those who keep the commandments and are fit persons to associate with Him in whom meekness was perfected. Hence the psalmic word, given of old, "The meek shall inherit the earth; and shall delight themselves in the abundance of peace. . . . The righteous shall inherit the land, and dwell therein for ever." (Ps. 37:11, 29.) And hence the Beatitude, spoken by Jesus in the Sermon on the Mount, "Blessed are the meek: for they shall inherit the earth." (Matt. 5:5.)

All of this brings us to the divine word, revealed in latter days to Joseph Smith, in which the Lord tells his people how to gain an inheritance on the celestial earth. "And the redemption of the soul," saith the Lord, "is through him that quickeneth all things, in whose bosom it is decreed that the poor and meek of the earth shall inherit it." This is a modern reaffirmation of the ancient doctrine that the meek shall inherit the earth. Then, of the earth itself, the revelation says: "Therefore, it must needs be sanctified from all unrighteousness, that it may be prepared for the celestial glory; for after it hath filled the measure of its creation, it shall be crowned with glory, even with the presence of God the Father; that bodies who are of the celestial kingdom may possess it forever and ever; for, for this intent was it made and created, and for this intent are they sanctified." It is common among us to say that the Lord's plan is to make of this earth a heaven and of man a God. Earth and man, both sanctified by obedience to gospel law, shall go forward everlastingly together. And whereas Christ the Son will grace the millennial earth with his presence, even God the Father will take up his abode, from time to time, on this earth in its celestial day.

"And again, verily I say unto you," the great proclamation continues, "the earth abideth the law of a celestial kingdom, for it filleth the measure of its creation, and transgresseth not the law—Wherefore, it shall be sanctified; yea, notwithstanding it shall die, it shall be quickened again, and shall abide the power by which it is quickened, and the righteous shall inherit it. For notwithstanding they die, they also shall rise again, a spiritual body." (D&C 88:17-27.) God grant that we may be among them! These are they who lived during the Millennium and were changed at the age of a tree from mortality to immortality. And also, as pertaining to men in our day, "These are they which came out of great tribulation, and have washed their robes, and made them white in the blood of the Lamb. Therefore are they before the throne of God, and serve him day and night in his temple: and he that sitteth on the throne shall dwell among them. They shall hunger no more, neither thirst anymore; neither shall the sun light on them, nor any heat. For the Lamb which is in the midst of the throne shall feed them, and shall lead them unto living fountains of waters: and God shall wipe away all tears from their eyes." (Rev. 7:14-17.)

The Celestial Jerusalem

O Jerusalem, Jerusalem, the Holy City, the City of the Great King, the symbol of Jehovah's rulership over his people, when wilt thou be sanctified and perfected? When wilt thou receive thy eternal glory and be a world capital from which the word of the Lord shall go forth to all nations? Surely it will be during the Millennium, or at least measurably so. As men measure matters of all sorts, the millennial day is the day of the triumph of Israel and of the City of David and of all the Lord's interests on earth. But there shall also be a heavenly Jerusalem, a celestial Jerusalem, a holy city in which both God and Christ will dwell, as occasion requires, and whence their word shall go forth to all the angelic hosts and to all exalted beings.

The heavenly Jerusalem is the capital city on the celestial earth. It is the place from which this celestial sphere will be governed. It is a symbol of God's eternal dominion over his own. In the extended and full sense the whole earth in that day will be a celestial Jerusalem. It was Paul, our friend of days gone by, speaking of those who would ascend the heights and receive eternal exaltation, who said: "Ye are come unto mount Sion, and unto the city of the living God, the heavenly Jerusalem, and to an innumerable company of angels, to the general assembly and church of the firstborn, which are written in heaven, and to God the Judge of all, and to the spirits of just men made perfect, and to Jesus the mediator of the new covenant." (Heb. 12:22-24.) The city of the living God, where saints and angels dwell! The Church of the Firstborn, the Church in heaven, all of whose members are exalted! Just men made perfect through Him who hath redeemed us with his blood! What greater glory can there be than to be one with those who dwell in such a city?

700

Our friend John, also an apostolic colleague of days gone by, saw in vision the Celestial City in all its glory and perfection, and it was his privilege to record for us as much of what he saw as our spiritual stature permits us to receive. He saw "that great city, the holy Jerusalem, descending out of heaven from God, having the glory of God: and her light was like unto a stone most precious, even like a jasper stone, clear as crystal; and had a wall great and high, and had twelve gates, and at the gates twelve angels, and names written thereon, which are the names of the twelve tribes of the children of Israel: on the east three gates; on the north three gates; on the south three gates; and on the west three gates."

Enoch's city shall return as the Millennium casts her silver rays o'er all the earth. It also is "the holy city, [a] new Jerusalem." But "the holy Jerusalem," the Celestial City, shall come after the Millennium, after the little season, after Michael leads the hosts of heaven against Lucifer, at whose beck the hosts of hell respond, and after the devil and his minions have been cast out into that outer darkness where they shall remain forever. And what better symbolism could the Lord have chosen to show the eternal triumph and glory of his chosen Israel than to place the names of the tribes of Jacob on the gates thereof? Surely the saved of Israel shall enter the Holy City through the gates appointed. And surely all men who are saved from the day of Abraham to the end of time shall belong to the house of Israel, for the faithful, be they Jew or Gentile, shall rise up and bless Abraham as their father. All such shall be adopted into the chosen lineage; all such shall become one with the Lord's people. Every single soul who has lived since Abraham and who gains eternal life shall rule and reign forever in his respective place in one of the tribes of those mighty patriarchs whom Jehovah himself chose to bear his name and after whom he himself has since been called. Truly he is the God of Abraham, Isaac, and Jacob.

"And the wall of the city had twelve foundations, and in them the names of the twelve apostles of the Lamb." (Rev. 21:2, 10-14.) Again the symbolism is perfect. As there are twelve tribes of Israel, who are the Lord's chosen people, so they were ruled by twelve princes—"the princes of Israel, heads of the house of their fathers, who were the princes of the tribes, and were over them." (Num. 7:2.) These princes held the equivalent of the apostolic office and position and were called upon to bear witness of Jehovah and his saving power and to lead their people in paths of truth and righteousness unto that same eternal life which we ourselves now seek. They were leaders in the congregation or church as it existed in Israel.

And as it had been among his people in the days of their birth as a nation, so Jehovah ordained that it should ever be. He organized his congregation or church and called his twelve princes in the meridian of time. It was to the saints in that holy organization that Paul said: "Ye are . . . built upon the foundation of the apostles and prophets, Jesus Christ himself being the chief corner stone." (Eph. 2:19-20.) How fitting that the names of the twelve apostles of the Lamb are in the very foundations of the Celestial City! They are the ones who held the keys of salvation for all men in their days. And there are no inhabitants within the sacred walls except those who believed the apostolic witness and obeyed the heaven-sent counsel of those sent to minister in their day. It is, of course, implicit in the whole presentation, for God is no respecter of persons, that there are other names also in the foundations and walls, names in addition to the Twelve of Jesus' day. Surely the names of the prophets and seers and legal administrators of the ages are all there.

There is no way to describe the Celestial City. In our finite state we cannot comprehend the glory and wonder of it all. There are no words in our language that can convey to our earthbound minds the eternal brilliance and shining brightness that prevail where God is. To give us some glimmer of what is involved, the holy account speaks of a city whose length and breadth and height are beyond understanding. The city is a cube that measures twelve thousand furlongs, close to fifteen hundred miles, in length and breadth and height. The inspired account says that "the city was pure gold, like unto clear glass," and "the foundations of the wall of the city were garnished with all manner of precious stones," which are named as being jasper, sapphire, chalcedony, emerald, sardonyx, sardius, chrysolite, beryl, topaz, chrysoprasus, jacinth, and amethyst. Then the account says: "And the twelve gates were twelve pearls; every several gate was of one pearl: and the street of the city was pure gold, as it were transparent glass." As we have heretofore seen, the celestial earth is described as being like a sea of glass and fire, and as a sphere like unto crystal, none of which we can fully comprehend.

"And I saw no temple therein," John continues, "for the Lord God Almighty and the Lamb are the temple of it." Both God and Christ dwell on the celestial earth and in the Celestial City, and the city and the whole earth (and in the ultimate sense of the word, they are one and the same) are, in fact, a temple. The whole earth in that day will be a Holy of Holies—not a Holy of Holies into which the high priest alone will enter once each year on the day of atonement, there to make atonement for the sins of the people and to pronounce the ineffable name, but a Holy of Holies where all the saints will dwell on all days, and where they, having been redeemed by the blood of the Lamb, will shout praises to God and the Lamb, using all their names, including many we do not even yet know.

"And the city had no need of the sun, neither of the moon, to shine in it: for the glory of God did lighten it, and the Lamb is the light thereof." (Rev. 21:15-23.) Of course there is no need for a sun by day and a moon by night, for the earth will have become a sun. It will be its own sun. Hence Paul's statement, "Our God is a consuming fire."

703

(Heb. 12:29.) Hence Isaiah's queries: "Who among us shall dwell with the devouring fire? who among us shall dwell with everlasting burnings?" (Isa. 33:14.) Hence Joseph Smith's statement relative to the saints who gain eternal life: "Although the earthly tabernacle is laid down and dissolved, they shall rise again to dwell in everlasting burnings in immortal glory, not to sorrow, suffer, or die any more; but they shall be heirs of God and joint heirs with Jesus Christ." And also: They must be "able to dwell in everlasting burnings, and to sit in glory, as do those who sit enthroned in everlasting power." (*Teachings*, p. 347.)

"And the nations of them which are saved shall walk in the light of it: and the kings of the earth do bring their glory and honour into it." All those who dwell therein have eternal life. "And the gates of it shall not be shut at all by day: for there shall be no night there. And they shall bring the glory and honour of the nations into it. And there shall in no wise enter into it any thing that defileth, neither whatsoever worketh abomination, or maketh a lie: but they which are written in the Lamb's book of life." (Rev. 21:24-27.)

Our apostolic author continues: "And he [the angelic ministrant] shewed me a pure river of water of life, clear as crystal, proceeding out of the throne of God and of the Lamb." These are the waters of which men shall drink and never thirst more. "In the midst of the street of it, and on either side of the river, was there the tree of life, which bare twelve manner of fruits, and yielded her fruit every month: and the leaves of the tree were for the healing of the nations." Adam in his ancient Eden was denied the privilege of partaking of the fruit of the tree of life, lest doing so he should live forever in his sins. But now, all who are freed from sin through the blood of the Lamb shall partake forever of that fruit of which men eat and never hunger more. "And there shall be no more curse: but the throne of God and of the Lamb shall be in it; and his servants shall serve him." Whereas the earth was cursed so that it brought forth thorns, thistles, briers, and noxious weeds, whereas man was required to eat his bread in the sweat of his face; whereas sorrow and death passed upon all men—all this in the beginning—now the ransom has been paid and all things have become new. The curse is gone and the earth is blessed, and all who dwell thereon enjoy peace and joy and life. "And they shall see his face; and his name shall be in their foreheads." All men shall see God, and on the crowns they wear will be his name—the name of God!—for they have exaltation and are themselves gods. "And there shall be no night there; and they need no candle, neither light of the sun; for the Lord God giveth them light: and they shall reign for ever and ever."

And of all of this John says (and what need he say more?): "Blessed are they that do his commandments, that they may have right to the tree of life, and may enter in through the gates into the city." (Rev. 22:1-5, 14.)

Eternal Life and Godhood

Full salvation is eternal life, and there is no other degree of eternal reward that has any special allurement for us. As Joseph Smith taught: "Salvation consists in the glory, authority, majesty, power and dominion which Jehovah possesses and in nothing else; and no being can possess it but himself or one like him." Let this definition weigh heavily upon us. It is the Lord's way of identifying the greatest of all the gifts of God, which is eternal life. Think of its meaning; it speaks of *glory!*, *authority!*, *majesty!*, *power!*, and *dominion!* In each instance they are to be the same characteristics as those possessed by the Lord Jehovah himself.

We are aware that the Eternal Father ordained and established a system of salvation to enable his spirit children to advance and progress and become like him. It was called the gospel of God. Christ was the chief advocate of this great and eternal plan and was chosen to be the Savior and Redeemer through whose good offices all of its terms and conditions have become operative. Hence, it is now called the gospel of Jesus Christ as a witness to all men that salvation is in Christ and in him alone. In his position as the Father's witness, as the chief proponent of the Father's plan, Christ proposed, as the Prophet taught, "to make" all mankind "like unto himself, and he was like the Father, the great prototype of all saved beings; and for any portion of the human family to be assimilated into their likeness is to be saved; and to be unlike them is to be destroyed; and on this hinge turns the door of salvation." (*Lectures on Faith*, lecture 7, paragraph 16.)

Thus those who gain eternal life, which is exaltation, become like God. They believe what he believes, know what he knows, and exercise the same powers he possesses. Like him they become omnipotent, omniscient, and omnipresent. They have advanced and progressed and become like him. They are the ones who receive an inheritance in the Celestial City.

"Thou art God," Enoch said to the Father, and "thou hast made me, and given unto me a right to thy throne." (Moses 7:59.) Man may sit on God's throne. Jesus said to the Three Nephites: "Ye shall have fulness of joy; and ye shall sit down in the kingdom of my Father; yea, your joy shall be full, even as the Father hath given me fulness of joy; and ye shall be even as I am, and I am even as the Father; and the Father and I are one." (3 Ne. 28:10.) Men may be even as Christ is and be one with him and his Father. And Jesus, announcing a principle of universal application, said: "To him that overcometh will I grant to sit with me in my throne, even as I also overcame, and am set down with my Father in his throne." (Rev. 3:21.) The Father, the Son, and all those who gain eternal life—which is the name of the kind of life that God lives—shall sit on the same throne and be one in all things.

Life both here and hereafter is very personal and real. We know what the associations of life are in this sphere and what they will be for the faithful in the realms ahead. Godly and upright living in both realms centers in the family unit.

There is no more sweet or tender or loving relationship known on earth than that which should exist between a man and his wife. And they twain should have like feelings for their children and descendants and for their parents and progenitors. With this in mind, we quote the inspired word that says: "And that same sociality which exists among us here will exist among us there, only it will be coupled with eternal glory, which glory we do not now enjoy." (D&C 130:2.)

And this brings us to the part celestial marriage plays in gaining eternal life. The revealed word acclaims: "In the celestial glory there are three heavens or degrees; and in order to obtain the highest, a man must enter into this order of the priesthood [meaning the new and everlasting covenant of marriage]; and if he does not, he cannot obtain it. He may enter into the other, but that is the end of his kingdom; he cannot have an increase." (D&C 131:1-4.) Eternal life or exaltation grows out of the continuation of the family unit in eternity. Exalted beings—who shall sit with God on his throne and be as he is—shall go to the highest heaven in the celestial world. Such is the sole and only place where the family unit continues. There they will have eternal increase, meaning spirit children in the resurrection forever and ever. Those who go to all lower kingdoms do not and cannot have such an increase.

In the resurrection all shall come forth from their graves. Every living soul will be resurrected; all will gain immortality. Those who believe and obey the fulness of gospel law, having been raised in immortality, will also be raised unto eternal life. The difference between those who have immortality only and those who have both immortality and eternal life is one thing: the continuation of the family unit in eternity. Those who go to the highest heaven in the celestial world will have eternal life because the family unit continues. Those who go to the lower two heavens in that kingdom, or to the terrestrial kingdom, or to the telestial kingdom, will have immortality only. Of them it is written: "For these angels did not abide my law; therefore, they cannot be enlarged, but remain separately and singly, without exaltation, in their saved condition, to all eternity; and from henceforth are not gods, but are angels of God forever and ever." In the resurrection men are raised to be angels or to be gods. Angels have immortality only; gods have both immortality and eternal life.

Of those who enter the Lord's order of matrimony and who keep their covenants and are true and faithful in all things, the Lord says: "They shall pass by the angels, and the gods, which are set there, to their exaltation and glory in all things, as hath been sealed upon their heads, which glory shall be a fulness and a continuation of the seeds forever and ever." That is to say, eternal life consists of two things: (1) the continuation of the family unit in eternity, which means a continuation of the seeds or the everlasting begetting of children; and (2) the receipt of the fulness of the glory of the Father, which is all power in heaven and on earth.

"Then shall they be gods, because they have no end; therefore shall they be from everlasting to everlasting, because they continue; then shall they be above all, because all things are subject unto them. Then shall they be gods, because they have all power, and the angels are subject unto them." (D&C 132:17, 19-20.) What saith the holy word about such glorious ones as these? It saith: "They are they who are the church of the Firstborn." Their membership is in the eternal church in the eternal heavens; the Church of the Firstborn is the church among exalted beings.

"They are they into whose hands the Father has given all things—they are they who are priests and kings, who have received of his fulness, and of his glory." They are the same kings and priests who lived and reigned with Christ on earth during the thousand years. And now they have received the fulness of the glory of the Father; they have all power in heaven and on earth; there is nothing they do not know and no power they do not possess. They "are priests of the Most High, after the order of Melchizedek, which was after the order of Enoch, which was after the order of the Only Begotten Son." They hold the power and authority of God, the very power by which the worlds were made; indeed, now they are creators in their own right; and in due course worlds will come rolling into existence at their word.

"Wherefore, as it is written, they are gods, even the sons of God." Having such high and glorious status, how could they be anything less than gods? "Wherefore, all things are theirs, whether life or death, or things present, or things to come, all are theirs and they are Christ's, and Christ is God's."

Viewing such a glorious destiny, shall we become high and lifted up in our feelings? Shall we let a holier-than-thou spirit enter our hearts? Let us, rather, remember that "they shall overcome all things," and that unless we so achieve, we shall not be numbered among them. "Wherefore, let no man glory in man, but rather let him glory in God, who shall subdue all enemies under his feet." We are not the ones who created these high rewards; we cannot resurrect ourselves; we cannot raise ourselves unto eternal life and place ourselves on the throne of God. All this is his doing; let us rejoice in him.

"These shall dwell in the presence of God and his Christ forever and ever." Theirs is an inheritance in heaven. "These are they whom he shall bring with him, when he shall come in the clouds of heaven to reign on the earth over his people. These are they who shall have part in the first resurrection. These are they who shall come forth in the resurrection of the just." And it is of them that we have spoken as we have recounted how the heavens would roll together as a scroll; how the saints on earth would be caught up to meet the Lord in the air; and how the dead in Christ would rise first.

"These are they who are come unto Mount Zion, and

unto the city of the living God, the heavenly place, the holiest of all." This is the Celestial City of which we have spoken. "These are they who have come to an innumerable company of angels, to the general assembly and church of Enoch, and of the Firstborn." John saw their number as ten thousand times ten thousand and thousands of thousands.

"These are they whose names are written in heaven, where God and Christ are the judge of all." Is he not telling us here that the names of all the exalted are written in the Lamb's Book of Life, and that their names, as well as those of the Twelve Apostles of the Lamb, shall be inscribed in the foundations and pillars, and on the thrones and royal seats, and in all the places of worship in the true Eternal City? "These are they who are just men made perfect through Jesus the mediator of the new covenant, who wrought out this perfect atonement through the shedding of his own blood. These are they whose bodies are celestial, whose glory is that of the sun, even the glory of God, the highest of all, whose glory the sun of the firmament is written of as being typical." All this glory, and all these wonders, and all this exaltation come because of the atoning sacrifice of the Lord Jesus Christ.

"And he makes them equal in power, and in might, and in dominion." (D&C 76:54-70, 95.) "And then shall the angels be crowned with the glory of his might, and the saints shall be filled with his glory, and receive their inheritance and be made equal with him." (D&C 88:107.)

And thus endeth our witness for the present moment. This work is completed. When more light is available and added revelations have been received, others with greater spiritual endowments will enlarge and perfect it. But for the present, according to our best judgment and understanding, we have testified of the coming of the Lord Jesus Christ to rule and reign on earth in the last days.

Our witness is true, and our doctrine is sound. He came once, and he shall come again. And nearly all that must precede that dread day has already transpired. God grant that "when he shall appear, we," according to the promises, "shall be like him" (1 Jn. 3:2), and that we shall find peace and glory with him, first in the New Jerusalem and then in the Holy Jerusalem.

Behold, and lo, the Bridegroom cometh, and that blessed year—the year of his redeemed—is at hand. The kingdoms of this world are falling, and the Lord God Omnipotent reigneth. Praise ye the Lord!

INDEX

Aaronic Priesthood, restoration
of, 117-18. *See also* Priesthood
Abiding the day of the Lord, 538-41
Abinadi, 631-32
Abomination of desolation, 471-72, 474-75
Abraham, 10; seed of, 182-84, 245; God's
promises to, 244-45, 262-63; many
claim, as father, 260-61; children of,
would do his works, 261; inheritors of
blessings of, 264-65; land of Canaan
given to, 321-22
Adam: fall of, 13; gospel was preached to,
96-97, 234; transgression of, men are
not punished for, 135; held conference
at Adam-ondi-Ahman, 579-80; stands
next to Jesus in priesthood, 581-82; will
gather his righteous posterity, 582-83;
role of, in judgment, 584; will return
keys to Christ, 585-86
Adam-ondi-Ahman: the Lord will appear
first at, 578-79; Adam held council at,
579-80; accounting for stewardships at,
582-83; sacrament to be administered at,
587; location of, 587-88
Adoption of Gentiles into Abrahamic
covenant, 245
Adultery, 82
Age of Restoration, 87, 90
Agency: spirits are endowed with, 12;
active operation of, 234
Ages, seven, of eternity, 11-23
Alexander the Great, 129, 423
Allenby, Edmund, 253
America: preparing of, as land of liberty,
93-94; Lehi and Mulek led people to,
187, 206-7; whole of, is Zion, 295;
darkness in, at Christ's death, 409;
influence of, until Second Coming, 491
Ancient of Days, 582, 584. *See also* Adam
Angels: ministering of, 97; role of, in
restoring gospel, 101, 104; seven,
plagues unleashed by, 382-87, 393-98;

fall of Babylon decreed by, 442-43;
attending Christ's second coming,
566-67; difference between gods and, 708
Animals, enmity of, shall cease, 658
Antichrists, 71-72. *See also* False
Christs; Prophets, false
Apostasy: complete, to precede
Second Coming, 36, 40-41; was
never universal until after Jesus'
ministry, 37-38; is sign of times,
40-41; breeds sin, 42-43; Peter's
denunciation of, 83-84; total,
calls for total restoration, 98; of
Israel caused scattering, 186-87;
of Lamanites, 207-9; promises
concerning, 260; plague of, 395-96
Apostles, twelve: Jesus blessed,
before ascension, 8; role of, in
judgment, 520; Comforter
promised to, 678-79; names of, in
foundations of celestial
Jerusalem, 702
Armageddon: is holy war, 398, 476; will
be universal conflict, 449-50, 479;
slaying of wicked at, 451-53; description
of warfare of, 455-56; hope of
repentant at, 457-58; righteous shall
triumph at, 458-59; is day of judgment,
460; location of battlefield of, 464; the
abomination of desolation, 471;
alliance of nations in, 477, 481;
righteous martyrs of, 478; wicked king at,
478-79; great slaughter at, 483; God's
power manifest at, 484-85; three great
events rising from, 490
Asaph the seer, 511-12
Ascension of Christ, 6-9
Assyria, 362-63
Athanasian Creed, 48
Atomic warfare, 408, 451, 455-56
Atonement: eternal significance of, 9;
age of, 14-17

713

yoke of, to be broken, 608-9

Gifts of Spirit: false prophets deny, 81; restoration of, 88

God the Father: created spirit children, 11-12; work and glory of, 37, 562-63; "without body, parts, or passions," 48, 77; denial of, by false prophets, 77; literal Fatherhood of, 134; remembers all nations, 168; has decreed gathering of Israel, 193-95; is God of Gentiles also, 232; desires to save all his children, 234; seeming harshness of, 498-99; men have robbed, in tithes, 545-46; everything done by, is to bless his children, 660-61; knowledge of, to fill earth, 675-77; becoming like, 706

Godliness, form of, 44, 82

Gods: false, men make unto themselves, 73-74, 197; men may become, 708-10

Gog and Magog, 63, 481, 696; cause of, is evil, 482-83; defeat of, 485-87; two conflicts involving, 488

Gospel: was taught in preexistence, 12; is covenant of salvation, 38-39, 98, 338-39; restoration of, Nephi sees, 53-54; is only true doctrine, 72; restoration of, great significance of, 96; was preached from beginning, 96-97; depends on Holy Ghost and revelation, 97; fulness of, given to various dispensations, 98; to be preached to all earth, 99-100, 132, 134-37, 533; saves obedient and condemns wicked, 108; true church is built upon, 126-27; basic tenets of, 134-35; preaching of, in times of war, 142; fulness of, Book of Mormon contains, 160; gathering of Israel to, 200; among Jews, 222; went first to Jews, then all Israel, then Gentiles, 238; modern message of, 335-36; net of, parable concerning, 345; law of, men are judged by, 518-20; doctrines of, lead to eternal life, 538; seeking refuge in, from the Lord's anger, 542-43; prepares men for Second Coming, 572-73; the Lord will reign by, 590-91; is covenant of peace, 608; shall continue in Millennium, 672; doctrines and ordinances of, are eternal, 673-74; goes forth as warning, 685. *See also* Church of Jesus Christ of Latter-day Saints; Restoration of gospel; Salvation, plan of

Government, Jesus holds rights of, 595, 596-98

Grace, salvation by, 77, 135

Great and abominable church: devil is founder of, 51-52; riches of, 52, 438; widespread influence of, 54, 440-41; includes all systems of evil, 54-55, 63-64, 143-44, 439-40; wrath of God to smite, 56, 144-45, 441; destruction of, 63, 66-67, 312-13; devouring fire to smite, 493; at war with itself, 558-59. *See also* Babylon

Great and dreadful day of the Lord, 495; is day of wrath, 496-500; is time of vengeance, 500-504; the righteous long for, 505, 507-8. *See also* Second coming of Christ

Grecian Empire, 129

Gutenberg Bible, 90

Hail, plagues of, 382, 398

Hananiah, 426-27

Harlots, mother of. *See* Great and abominable church

Harvest of souls, 137

Heaven: new, and new earth, 305-6, 356, 612; departing of, as scroll, 381, 451, 635-36; half-hour silence in, 382, 635-36; signs in, 410; council in, 583; war in, 666-67

Herod Antipas, 18-19

Highway cast up in great deep, 327, 624-25

Holiness, City of, 283

Holy Ghost: identifies true church, 78; always accompanies gospel, 97; will testify of Book of Mormon, 180-81; Jesus is manifested to Gentiles by, 240; apostles were to receive, 310; is first Comforter, 679

kindness of, 507-8; judgment is committed to, 517; was not of world, 532; was prophet like unto Moses, 556-57, 560; none can hide from, 567-68; blessed Adam at Adam-ondi-Ahman, 580; will govern in all things, 596-98; to reign on David's throne, 603, 604-5; as Branch of David, 604-5; the righteous caught up to meet, 636; men will dwell with, during Millennium, 652-53; as Second Comforter, 679-80; warnings given by, as chief watchman, 686-90. *See also* Second coming of Christ

Jews: devout, attitudes of, toward Jesus, 17-18; sufferings of, to bring forth God's words, 167-68; Jesus came to, 220; definition of, 221-22; righteous leaders of, 222-23; blessings and cursings of, 223-25; gathering of, 225, 239; Book of Mormon to go to, 226; Messiah will restore, a second time, 226-27; conversion of some, before Millennium, 228-29; gathering of, to Palestine, 229; shall recognize crucified Christ, 230-31, 269-71; God will remember his covenants with, 249-50; scourging of, 252-53; captivity of, as type of latter days, 424-26; mourning of, for crucified Messiah, 469-71; flight of, to mountain refuge, 472-74. *See also* Israel

Joel, 106

John the Baptist, 102-3, 117-18

John the Revelator: saw great and abominable church, 52; foresaw restoration of gospel, 99, 104-5; as Elias, 105; foresaw plagues of last days, 379-80; foresaw fall of Babylon, 434-35; ministry of, 647; vision of, of celestial Jerusalem, 701-5

Joseph: stick of, 156-57; Lehi was descendant of, 157; fruit of loins of, would write, 158; branch of, to be broken off, 187-88, 211; remnant of, New Jerusalem built for, 305; prophesied of Joseph Smith, 332

Judah, stick of, 156-57

Judge, unjust, parable of, 347-48

Judgment: parables concerning, 344-48; Armageddon is day of, 450, 459-60; psalmic utterances concerning, 511-12; Isaiah's prophecies concerning, 513-15; different days of, 515-16; is committed to the Son, 517; at Second Coming, 517-18; by gospel law, 518-20; role of apostles in, 520; final day of, 520-21; modern revelation concerning, 521-22; day of, is near, 523; of ungodly, 567; of righteous by hierarchy of judges, 584; at Adam-ondi-Ahman, 584-85

Justice, vengeance involved in, 500-501

Keys: restoration of, 101, 116-20, 202; to bind on earth and in heaven, 125; are revealed by Adam's authority, 582. *See also* Authority

Keystone of true religion, Book of Mormon is, 180

Kingdom: of God on earth, 2, 123, 594-95; restoration of, to Israel, 309-11; saints will possess, 586

Kingdoms, earthly: Nebuchadnezzar's dream concerning, 127-30; kingdom of God will subdue all, 130-31; will make war with Lamb, 439-40; involved in Armageddon, 477; political and ecclesiastical, fall of, 493-94

Kings and priests, righteous to become, 640, 708-9

Kirtland Temple, keys restored in, 119-20

Knowledge, outpouring of, 111, 675-77

Kolob, reckoning of time on, 30-31

Korihor, 71-72

Laborers in vineyard, parable of, 348-49

Lamanites: history of, 207-8; apostasy of, 208-9; scattering of, by Gentiles, 209-10; gathering of, 210-13; Israel's gathering will follow pattern of, 214; call to, to return to sheepfold, 218-19

Lame man, Peter healed, 85-86